THE JAPANESE WARTIME EMPIRE, 1931–1945

This book is based on a conference sponsored
by the U.S.-Japan Friendship Commission; the
Joint Committee on Japanese Studies of the
American Council of Learned Societies and the
Social Science Research Council; the Institute
for International Studies at Stanford
University; and the Hoover Institution on
War, Revolution, and Peace.

THE JAPANESE WARTIME EMPIRE, 1931–1945

Edited by
Peter Duus, Ramon H. Myers,
and Mark R. Peattie

CONTRIBUTORS

Wan-yao Chou
Peter Duus
Carter J. Eckert
L. H. Gann
Ken'ichi Gotō
George Hicks
Hideo Kobayashi

Y. Tak Matsusaka
Ramon H. Myers
Takafusa Nakamura
Mark R. Peattie
E. Bruce Reynolds
Louise Young

Princeton University Press / Princeton, New Jersey

Library of Congress Cataloging-in-Publication Data

The Japanese wartime empire, 1931–1945 / edited by Peter Duus, Ramon
H. Myers, and Mark R. Peattie ; contributors Wan-yao Chou . . . [et
al.].
p.   cm.
Includes bibliographical references and index.
ISBN 0-691-04382-5 (cloth : alk. paper)
1. Asia—History—20th century—Congresses.   2. World War,
1939–1945—Asia—Congresses.   3. World War, 1939–1945—Occupied
territories—Congresses.   4. Sino-Japanese Conflict, 1937–1945—
Occupied territories—Congresses.   5. Asia—Military relations—
Japan—Congresses.   6. Japan—Military relations—Asia—Congresses.
7. Japan—History—1926–1945—Congresses.   I. Duus, Peter, 1933–   .
II. Myers, Ramon Hawley, 1929–   .   III. Peattie, Mark R., 1930–   .
IV. Chou, Wan-yao.
DS35.J38   1996
950.4'1—dc20   95-37203
                                                           CIP

This book has been composed in Linotron Bembo

Princeton University Press books are printed on acid-free paper and meet the guidelines
for permanence and durability of the Committee on Production Guidelines for Book
Longevity of the Council on Library Resources

Printed in the United States of America by Princeton Academic Press

10 9 8 7 6 5 4 3 2 1

This book is dedicated to James William Morley, whose teaching, scholarship, and public service have advanced the understanding of East Asian Studies in the United States.

Contents

PART IV: Japan's Wartime Empire in Other
  Perspectives

Preface

The Japanese military takeover in Manchuria between September 18, 1931, and March 9, 1932, was a critical turning point in East Asian history. It marked the first surge of Japanese aggression beyond the boundaries of its older colonial empire, an imperium that had gained the tacit approval of the Western Powers. It set Japan on a collision course with China, leading in five years' time to a war of vast destruction and utter futility for both nations. In turn, that conflict led to a sudden, unprecedented, and unanticipated expansion of Japanese power in Asia: a thrust into Southeast Asia, a confrontation with the Western colonial powers, and a brief Japanese interregnum in that part of the globe. In sum, the Japanese seizure of Manchuria marked the rise of a virulent new Japanese imperialism that, thrusting off the restraints of the old imperial status quo, challenged and ultimately shattered Western imperialism in Asia before it, in turn, was overthrown by the West.

This volume, a companion to our earlier studies, *The Japanese Colonial Empire, 1895–1945* and *The Japanese Informal Empire in China, 1895–1937*, concludes our study of modern Japanese colonialism and imperialism. As such, it does not attempt to provide a comprehensive history of the surge of Japanese imperialism in Asia from 1931 to 1945. Rather it seeks to illuminate, by example, some of the more significant processes and institutions of that imperialism: the creation of a Japanese-dominated East Asian economic bloc centered in northeast Asia, the mobilization of human and physical resources in the older-established areas of Japanese colonial rule, and the penetration and occupation of Southeast Asia.

This study, following the pattern of our two earlier volumes, is the product of a conference held in August 1991 at the Hoover Institution on War, Revolution, and Peace, Stanford University. The editors wish to thank the Hoover Institution, the Institute for International Studies at Stanford University, the U.S.–Japan Friendship Commission, and the Social Science Research Council for their financial support for both the conference and the preparation of this volume. We also wish to express our gratitude to the editorial staff of Princeton University Press, as well as the staff of the East Asian Collection of the Hoover Institution, particularly Tim McGuire, who indexed the finished volume.

We thank the following individuals, institutions, and enterprises for permission to reproduce items in their collections or publications: Professors Peter Duus and Carter J. Eckert; the Hoover Institution East Asia Collection and Archives; Rōdōsha, Tokyo, for illustrations from Shin Gisu, *Eizō ga kataru "Nikkan heigō" shi* [Images that narrate the history of Japan's annexation of Korea] (1987); and Mainichi shimbunsha, Tokyo, for illustrations from *Bessatu ichi oku nin no Shōwa shi, Nihon shokumin shi: Manshū, NichiRō sensō kara kenkoku-metsubō made* (A special history of 100 million people during Shōwa: Japan's colonial history: Manchuria from the Russo-Japanese War and the building of a country to its destruction] (1978).

As in our previous two volumes, we have adhered to the Wade-Giles system of romanization for Chinese names and places; to the Hepburn system, with appropriate macrons, for names and places in Japanese; and to the McCune-Reischauer system for Korean.

Introduction

Japan's Wartime Empire: Problems and Issues

Peter Duus

When John Seeley observed that the British had "conquered and peopled half the world in a fit of absence of mind,"[1] he meant to suggest that the British Empire was not the product of any master plan nor even of a consistent set of goals, but rather grew through a process of accretion stretching across generations, even centuries. A trade treaty was signed here, a border war fought there, a protectorate established elsewhere, and slowly the British metropole brought overseas territories under its web of formal and informal domination. Certainly there is truth in this view. Even British leaders with concrete visions of empire, such as Disraeli, usually improvised, following the path of least resistance rather than a priori goals. British imperialism, in other words, was opportunistic, taking advantage of fortuitous circumstances when it could, and always exploiting the weakness of others.

While Japanese imperialism appears more purposive than British imperialism, it was no less opportunistic, and nowhere was that opportunism more evident than in the final phase of Japanese expansion—the creation of Japan's wartime empire. From 1931 onward Japanese military and political leaders projected Japanese dominion beyond the "turbulent frontiers" of Japan's original empire (the colonies of Taiwan and Korea, the leasehold in Manchuria, and the treaty port enclaves in China) by taking advantage of the continuing debility of central authority in China and the collapse of European colonial regimes in Southeast Asia. Although counterfactual propositions are impossible to prove or disprove, it seems plausible that had neither of these opportunities existed, the Japanese empire might not have expanded as dramatically as it did in the 1930s and early 1940s—or perhaps not have expanded at all. In other words, any explanation of Japan's wartime expansion must take into account the international context. What was going on outside

[1] John Seeley, *The Expansion of England* (Chicago: University of Chicago Press, 1971), p. 12.

Japan was as critical to the dynamic of wartime expansion as what was going on within.

There can be little doubt that the absence of any strong authority in China provided an opportunity—and an inducement—for the Kwantung Army to seize control of the three northeastern provinces in 1931–32 and encouraged further Japanese incursions into north China in the late 1930s. After the fall of the Ch'ing dynasty, a myriad of regional or local powers contested control over the political center, but none was able to establish hegemony. Indeed, many Japanese intelligence officers, journalists, and scholars came to the conclusion in the 1920s and 1930s that China was not an "organized state" at all but a loose and disorganized congeries of regional political units.[2] Even the strongest of these, the Kuomintang government at Nanking, had failed to establish effective control beyond the lower Yangtze Valley and the Kwangtung region. In the minds of the Japanese, this vulnerability licensed their military intrusions into the Chinese mainland.

The outbreak of war in Europe, and the early victories of Nazi Germany, were similarly opportune. When Nazi forces overthrew metropolitan regimes in the Netherlands and France, colonial governments on the periphery were cut adrift, with little guidance from the former metropole and few resources to defend themselves. With startling candor, Japanese politicians, journalists, and intellectuals in 1940 spoke about the need "not to miss the bus," that is, not to fail to capitalize on the Nazi victories in Europe. First through an accommodation with the French colonial authorities in Indochina, and then through a military blitzkrieg after December 8, 1941, Japanese military and naval forces advanced into the region with enormous speed, handily displacing or bypassing the old colonial regimes.

By taking advantage of these opportunities, at the end of 1942 the Japanese had acquired formal or informal dominion over perhaps 340–350 million people populating a vast area stretching from the Solomon Islands in the mid-Pacific to Burma's border with India, and from the rain forests of New Guinea to the icy shores of Attu and Kiska, an empire that quite exceeded the most fevered imaginings of the Meiji leaders. Indeed, its scale was impressive by any standard. The wartime empire embraced five to six times the population of the prewar French and Dutch empires or about three-quarters of the population of the British Empire (table I.1). What makes these figures even more startling is that the European metropoles not only had a head start of several centuries but commanded far greater productive and economic re-

---

[2] For an interesting discussion of this idea, see Miwa Kimitada, *Kyōdōtai ishiki no dochakusei* (Tokyo: San'ichi shobō, 1978), pp. 21–47.

TABLE I.1
Japan's Wartime Empire

	Population	Territory (km^2)
Original colonies		
Korea	22,899,000 (1940)	220,769
Taiwan	5,212,000 (1940)	35,961
Karafuto	332,000 (1940)	36,090
Kwantung Territories	1,134,000 (1940)	3,461
Nanyō	113,000 (1940)	2,149
TOTAL	29,690,000	
Other territories		
Manchukuo	43,234,000 (1940)	1,303,143
Occupied China	200–250,000,000 (est.)	??
TOTAL	243–293,234,000	
Borneo	783,000 (1939)	32,258
Dutch East Indies	69,435,000 (1939)	1,904,346
Burma	16,119,000 (1939)	605,000
Philippines	16,356,000 (1940)	296,295
French Indochina	23,500,000 (1938)	740,400
Timor	461,000	7,330
Thailand	14,464,000 (1937)	513,447
Malaya	5,333,000 (1939)	132,027
TOTAL	146,451,000	
GRAND TOTAL	389–439,685,000	
British colonies	449,100,000	35,094,900
French colonies	55,693,000	11,936,000
Dutch colonies	60,987,000	2,045,200

Sources: For original colonies and other territories: *Asahi nenkan 1943* (Tokyo: Asahi Shimbunsha, 1943). For British, French, and Dutch colonies: *Sekai nenkan 1939* (Tokyo: Jitsugyō no Nihonsha, 1939).

sources. By contrast Japanese wartime expansion proceeded very far and very fast on a comparatively limited material base.

Hegemony over this huge territory, however, was more illusion than reality. As Jack Snyder has recently observed, Japan's wartime empire was a classic case of "overexpansion."[3] It was characterized by *military overcommitment* (a campaign of conquest difficult if not impossible to sustain given the country's human and material resources), by *territorial overextension* (expansion beyond the point where the material costs exceeded the material benefits), and by "self-encirclement" (pursuit of

[3] Jack Snyder, *Myths of Empire: Domestic Politics and International Ambition* (Ithaca, N.Y.: Cornell University Press, 1991), chaps. 1, 2, 4. My definition of "overexpansion" slightly modifies Snyder's.

policies that created an opposing alliance of forces that vastly outnumbered Japan and its allies.) Not only were the Japanese unable to maintain this empire, but in losing it they lost their older territorial possessions as well. Imperial overreach, as Snyder points out, proved so self-destructive that the empire ended up in receivership.

THE DYNAMICS OF WARTIME EXPANSION

What induced the Japanese leaders in the 1930s to take such disastrous advantage of the opportunities produced by changing circumstances in East and Southeast Asia? The answer is necessarily complicated. Changes in leadership were frequent during the 1930s, and different leadership factions favored expansion for quite different reasons. There is general agreement that one cannot explain the wartime empire simply as the work of the Japanese army. It is true that the Japanese military leadership succeeded in commandeering the initiative in foreign policy after the successful takeover of the three northeastern Chinese provinces in 1931–32, but it did so with the full complicity of other elites. There emerged a coalition of pro-expansionist forces, whose conflicting demands were resolved not by mutual concession but by mutual inclusion. Practically no imperialist demand went unanswered. Instead of pursuing a manageable and minimal expansionist agenda as the Meiji oligarchs had, the leaders in the 1930s and 1940s pursued a maximal and unmanageable one, as many of them knew even as they decided to go to war with the United States in 1941.

If one looks at the context of decision making, it becomes apparent that changes in the domestic political economy and in the international trade regime played a crucial role in greasing the slippery slope toward overexpansion. When Japan acquired its first overseas empire at the turn of the century, its industrial revolution was just getting under way. By the 1930s, however, the manufacturing sector accounted for 40 percent of the gainfully employed labor force, and exports had risen to 20 percent of the GNP. The impact of industrialization was felt everywhere in Japanese society, from the remotest farm village to the central ministries in Tokyo. This is not to argue that industrialization *caused* Japan to expand or would have done so even had opportunities not existed. Rather it simply suggests that structural changes accompanying industrialization *predisposed* the Japanese leadership toward overseas expansion rather than some alternative set of foreign policies.

First of all, in the 1920s the uneven development of the economy generated worries about overpopulation. After the rice riots of 1918, many officials, politicians, and journalists were apprehensive that the country was outgrowing its food resource base. While the Meiji government, to the extent it had a population policy, tended to be pronatalist—more babies meant more soldiers—postwar leaders voiced fears that the agrarian sector of the economy had not expanded fast enough to feed the population. To deal with the problem, the government decided to increase food imports from the colonies. During the 1920s the governments-general in both Korea and Taiwan carried out successful programs to expand rice production. In fact, so successful were these programs that colonial rice imports depressed domestic rice prices, contributing to a decade-long recession in the agricultural sector.[4] As a result, the overpopulation problem came to be defined less as a question of food resources—which, in fact, were quite adequate—than of rural poverty, that is, a problem of demand as well as supply.

An alternative solution to the problem of overpopulation was the acquisition of new overseas territory for settlement and agricultural development. The seizure of Manchuria was justified in part on these grounds. During the 1930s civilian and military officials launched a variety of plans for promoting rural migration to Manchuria. None of these were any more successful than earlier efforts to promote agricultural migration to Korea. The expansion of the empire invariably created more employment opportunities for small shopkeepers, company employees, and petty officials than for sturdy farmer-settlers. But the perceived need for *Lebensraum,* reinforced by the importation of German geopolitical ideas, was a significant factor in predisposing certain elements of the elite (mainly in the military, the economic bureaucracy, and the parties of the Left) toward expansion onto the continent.

Second, the changing industrial structure created a new kind of dependence on the outside world. By the 1930s growth in the textile light industry, the leading sector at the turn of the century, had leveled off. Instead, expansion of output had become most visible and dramatic in heavy industry—chemicals, metallurgy, machinery and engineering, and the like—all with an enormous appetite for resources and raw materials not found at home. In 1934, for example, Japan produced only 63 percent of the copper, 69 percent of the pig iron, 9.16 percent of the crude oil, and none of the rubber it consumed. The economy was also almost totally dependent on imports of such critical nonferrous metal resources as tin, nickel, lead, and aluminum.

---

[4] Ramon H. Myers and Yamada Saburō, "Agricultural Development in the Empire," in *The Japanese Colonial Empire, 1895–1945,* ed. Ramon H. Myers and Mark R. Peattie (Princeton, N.J.: Princeton University Press), 1984, pp. 420–54.

This growing dependency on external sources of supply at first was not of concern to industrialists, who were able to obtain what they needed in the world market. But military and civilian bureaucrats charged with national security planning worried that economic dependency meant strategic vulnerability. As early as 1915 Colonel Ugaki Kazunari, chief of the Military Affairs Section of the War Ministry, noted that while Japan was able to produce its own warships and heavy ordnance, it lacked secure access to iron ore and other strategic materials. During the 1920s staff officers in the war ministry, including Koiso Kuniaki and Nagata Tetsuzan, advocated a comprehensive mobilization plan and structure that would enable Japan to maximize its resources in time of war, and officers in the navy began to think about ways of securing adequate supplies of oil. National security goals came to include the achievement of self-sufficiency in key resources.[5]

Self-sufficiency at a level needed for a war emergency could be achieved in several ways: stockpiling through purchases in the world market, direct investment in offshore extraction or production, or direct political control over resource-rich territory. All three methods were tried in the 1920s and 1930s with varying degrees of success. For example, after the outbreak of the war with China in 1937 the Japanese government began vigorously stockpiling key resources imported from the United States and Southeast Asia. But the idea of obtaining resources through territorial expansion became increasingly attractive in the late 1930s. This was not simply because new opportunities emerged in the resource-rich regions of Southeast Asia, but also because the basic nature of the world trade regime seemed to be changing.

Many political, bureaucratic, and intellectual leaders believed that the world economic crisis of 1929 signified the collapse of a liberal international economic order. The rules of the old order were being abandoned, even by the Anglo-American powers that had established them. The gold standard was giving way to managed currencies, free trade was being supplanted by rising tariffs and trade quotas, and open economic borders were being pushed aside by the creation of exclusive regional economic blocs. In 1933 at the Ottawa Conference Great Britain and the Dominions agreed to a system of preferential trade aimed at excluding imports from third countries, and the Roosevelt administration began to talk about the creation of a Pan-American Union that would bind the United States closer economically to its southern neighbors.

Until the late 1920s the Japanese leadership had more or less accepted

---

[5] Michael A. Barnhart, *Japan Prepares for Total War: The Search for Economic Security, 1919–1941* (Ithaca, N.Y.: Cornell University Press), chap. 1.

the notion of a world economic order based on free trade, and had tried to integrate the Japanese economy into it. However, with the onset of the world depression, as economic nationalism and protectionism gathered strength in the Western economies, the Japanese encountered trade barriers in British, Dutch, and American colonial markets. In response Japanese policymakers pondered an alternative to a free-trade regime: why not establish a self-sufficient economic bloc through political means rather than remaining dependent on the world market for key resources? Such a policy seemed to be the only sure guarantee of economic survival in an increasingly fragmented world market. When the United States began to impose embargoes on the export to Japan of key strategic materials in 1939–40, the idea of an economic bloc gained wider support. It was a key factor in persuading certain reluctant elites like the navy leadership to support an ambitious program of expansion to the south.

Not all the concerns outlined above—the growing resource dependency, the need for total mobilization, the problem of "overpopulation," or the breakdown of the free-trade system—were shared equally by all leaders in the 1930s and 1940s. But their convergence created a political context in which all demands for expansion reinforced rather than competed with one another, creating the basis for a broad coalition in favor of expansion. One has only to look at the major government decisions on foreign policy from 1936 onward to trace the ballooning accretion of expansionist goals, based less on an evaluation of what Japan was capable of doing than on what particular elements in the army, navy and bureaucracy wished to do. If there were dissenters in this process of defining ever broader goals, it was those like Yoshida Shigeru or Yamamoto Isoroku, who did not disagree about the problems Japan faced but had a more realistic sense of Japan's limitations and the strengths of its potential opponents.

Indeed, a new self-confidence among Japanese political and bureaucratic elites provided the psychological context for territorial expansion in the 1930s. The Meiji leaders had been much more attentive to the sensibilities of the Western nations during the first phase of Japanese imperialist expansion. In 1894–95, Prime Minister Itō Hirobumi and Foreign Minister Mutsu Munemitsu had constantly fretted about the possibility of foreign intervention in the war with China, and they quickly knuckled under when the Russians, the Germans and the French demanded at the end of the war that the Liaotung Peninsula remain in the hands of the Chinese. Their caution reflected knowledge that Japan was no match for the Western powers, either singly or collectively, in military, economic, and financial strength, and that defiance of the Western powers would invite national disaster.

This sense of limitations had diminished considerably by the 1930s, however. While few Japanese leaders doubted the material superiority of the Americans and the Europeans, they appear to have been emboldened by a perception that the West no longer counted, or at least no longer counted the way it had during the age of "high imperialism." The lack of a Western response to the Manchurian incursion may have encouraged the belief that not only the Kuomintang regime but the Western Powers as well were paper tigers. The Americans and the British appeared reluctant to do much more than wave an unloaded pistol, as Secretary of State Stimson had put it. This made it easy for many Japanese leaders to conclude that the Western powers had withdrawn their interest from East Asia. New fractures in the ranks of the Western powers—between the German and Italian dictatorships and the parliamentary regimes in France and Great Britain—also worked to Japan's advantage. As Nazi armies enjoyed early successes in 1940–41 many Japanese leaders convinced themselves that a Nazi victory in Europe would open the door for a major realignment of the world's powers. The views of Foreign Minister Matsuoka Yōsuke, who envisioned a Eurasian alliance (the Axis powers plus the Soviet Union) to counterbalance the Anglo-American hegemony, were the most extreme but not completely idiosyncratic.

Neither did many Japanese leaders appear intimidated by the enormous disparity in economic strength between Japan and its Western adversaries. When the Japanese leadership decided to go to war in 1941, they had very accurate assessments of the industrial capacity of the United States but gambled that early victories would boost public morale and stimulate productivity.[6] By substituting wishful thinking for realistic strategic assessment, a failure by no means uniquely theirs, they chose to take a calculated risk. Even as the wartime empire began to crumble around them Japanese leaders continued to put on a bold face on their manifest economic inferiority. As Foreign Minister Shigemitsu told the Diet in early 1944:[7] "What American and Britain rely on most is their material strength. The importance of material strength in war cannot be denied. But is it a factor that decides the ultimate outcome of a war? . . . Our assurance of victory is based neither on number nor on volume, nor on geographical advantage. It is born of the exuberant fighting spirit and the complete unity of the nation." What the Japanese lacked in material strength, in other words, they made up for with determination, perseverance, and willingness to sacrifice.

[6] *Japan's Decision for War: Records of the 1941 Policy Conferences, 1941,* trans. Nobutaka Ike (Stanford, Calif.: Stanford University Press, 1967), pp. 219–21.

[7] *Contemporary Japan* 13, no. 2 (February 1944): 308.

These brave words dismissed stark economic realities that became obvious even to the ordinary Japanese as the war drew on. While wartime production expanded in some critical sectors, the metropolitan economy did not grow fast enough to defend or sustain the far-flung empire. In 1944, for example, Japan produced 28,180 aircraft, about 43 percent more than it had the previous year, but this output was dwarfed by the 92,196 planes the Americans produced. In most sectors of the economy production had already begun to decline in 1943, even before Allied air raids began a systematic destruction of the country's industrial base. Under these circumstances there was little chance that an "unconquerable will to fight" would lead Japan to victory, yet the Japanese leaders continued to tell the people—and themselves as well—that it would.

THE IDEOLOGY OF WARTIME EMPIRE

In constructing myths of domination to justify the policies that led to overexpansion, the Japanese leadership faced several problems: The first was how to legitimize imperialist expansion in a world where colonialism was no longer legitimate. By the end of World War I the colonial empires had come under attack not only by indigenous nationalist movements like the Congress party in India and the new revolutionary regime in the Soviet Union but by the leaders of the imperialist states themselves. In his "Fourteen Points" speech Woodrow Wilson had proclaimed that national self-determination was "an imperative principle of action, which statesmen will ignore at their peril." Other Allied statesmen incorporated Wilsonian rhetoric in their own statements of war goals, and by the end of the war the acquisition of dominion over "backward" peoples had to be disguised in new language that made proper obeisance to the Wilsonian construction of nationhood.

Well aware of the anti-imperialist tone of world opinion, the Japanese government hastened to assure the other powers that it was not pursuing a policy of imperialist expansion in the old mode. In September 1931 the Hamaguchi cabinet took care to inform the League Council that Japan had "no territorial designs in Manchuria." Even when military occupation was complete, the three northeastern provinces were not reorganized into a formal Japanese colony but transformed into the new independent state of Manchukuo. As Professor Matsusaka points out in his essay, Kwantung Army staff officers would have preferred simple and direct annexation but worried that such a move would provoke international repercussions. The fiction of an independent state allowed them to circumvent the diplomatic and political constraints of the post-Versailles world order. As one Kwantung Army staff memorandum put it, "While neither the Nine Power Treaty nor the League Covenant permits Japan to resort to direct action to separate Manchuria from China proper, these treaties do not, and should not be allowed to, interfere with China's partition at the Chinese people's own volition."[8] The invention of Manchukuo was presented as an act of national "volition" on the part of its residents, and its state apparatus was staffed from the top downward by "natives" like Henry Pu-yi.

This resolution of the problem was not entirely successful. The Western Powers, viewing Manchukuo as a puppet state, refused to recognize its existence as they had recognized new states constructed at the Paris Peace Conference. The principal reason was the total absence of any evidence that Manchukuo was the product of a local demand for national self-determination. Before the takeover the most vocal advocates of Manchurian "independence" had been found among Japanese residents rather than among the indigenous population. Nor had the creation of the new state been confirmed through any act of popular ratification, such as a plebiscite, that demonstrated that a majority of the inhabitants favored the creation of a new state—as, for example, the German annexation of Austria was confirmed by plebiscite in 1938. Since the new state turned its face against the rhetoric and symbolism of Chinese nationalism, and since it quickly became apparent that the Manchukuo state apparatus was completely under the control of the Japanese authorities, it is not surprising this attempt to accommodate the "right of national self-determination" lacked international credibility.

When the Japanese established the Reorganized National Government at Nanking in the occupied territories of China in 1940, they were more attentive to the symbols of Chinese nationalism. Had they not been, it would have been difficult to secure the collaboration of the former Kuomintang leader, Wang Ching-wei. While the government of Manchukuo had rejected the "Three People's Principles," the new Nanking government, manned by former Kuomintang members who had defected from Chungking, openly embraced them, declaring itself the true guardian and successor of Sun Yat-sen's ideology. Reluctantly the Japanese even agreed to let the Wang regime use the tricolor Kuomintang flag, albeit with a little "pigtail" pennant proclaiming "peace, national reconstruction, and anticommunism." The reality of the regime was not so different from that of Manchukuo, with Japanese advisers serving at almost every level, but the Japanese clearly hoped to give

[8] James William Morley, ed., *Japan Erupts: The London Naval Conference and the Manchurian Incident, 1928–1932* (New York: Columbia University Press, 1984), pp. 332–33.

greater plausibility to the fiction of the regime's national independence by appropriating the accepted symbols of Chinese nationalism.

In both Manchuria and north China the Japanese deployed pan-nationalist rhetoric and symbols to legitimize the establishment of domination. In the case of Manchukuo, the Japanese used neotraditionalist concepts such as "the kingly way" (ōdō) or "harmony of the five races" (kyōwa) to portray Manchukuo as a Pan-Asian polity guided by classical Confucian political principles. By the mid-1930s, however, more cosmopolitan supporters of expansion, such as the Shōwa kenkyūkai intellectuals, called for a "scientific" explanation of Japan's continental policy that would make sense to outsiders. The resulting formulations—the idea of an "East Asian Gemeinschaft" (Tōa kyōdōtai) or "East Asian Federation" (Tōa renmei), and ultimately the notion of a "New Order in East Asia" (Tōa shin chitsujo)—all attempted to reconcile Pan-Asianist rhetoric with the idea of national self-determination.

The New Order in East Asia announced in November 1938 assured that Japan had no designs on Chinese territory, no desire to curb China's independence, nor any hostility toward the Chinese people—themes sounded earlier in Manchuria—but it also proposed the construction of a new regional political order based on mutual aid and cooperation among the "independent" states of Japan, China, and Manchukuo. In this way, the Konoe government tried to define its desired framework of relations among the East Asian nations in terms of the region's common interests (joint defense against communism, close economic cooperation, and the creation of a new "East Asian" culture) rather than in terms of Japan's special interests.[9]

A second ideological problem was how to interpret the expansion of the wartime empire beyond the boundaries of the Sinitic world. In the Meiji empire notions of dōbun (common culture) and dōshu (common race) were plausible justifications for colonial domination, and to speak of helping "younger brothers" in Taiwan or Korea or China made some sense. The Japanese shared with their neighbors in Northeast Asia a common writing system, common religious and philosophical traditions, and common physical features. The New Order in East Asia also assumed a degree of cultural commonality. But the wartime empire encompassed more distant cultural worlds, where dōbun and dōshu fit the cultural realities poorly if at all. The ideological scaffolding erected

[9] A detailed treatment of the origins of the New Order in East Asia and the Greater East Asia Co-Prosperity Sphere may be found in Kimitada Miwa, "Japanese Policies and Concepts for Regional Order in Asia, 1938–1940," in The Ambivalance of Nationalism: Modern Japan between East and West, ed. James W. White, Michio Umegaki, and Thomas R. H. Havens (Lanham, N.Y.: University Press of America, 1990), pp. 133–56.

to legitimate the Meiji empire, and slightly altered to justify expansion on the continent, had to be rebuilt more radically to include the former European colonies in Southeast Asia—French Indochina, the Dutch East Indies, the Philippines, Malaya, Burma, and even Thailand.

On June 29, 1940, Foreign Minister Arita Hachiro adumbrated a new ideological vision in a radio speech:

> In order to realize [the establishment of world peace], it seems to be the most natural step that peoples who are closely related to one another geographically, racially, and economically should first form a sphere of their own for coexistence and co-prosperity and establish peace and order within that sphere, and at the same time secure a relationship of common existence and prosperity with other spheres. . . . The countries of East Asia and the regions of the South Seas are geographically close, historically, racially, and economically very closely related to each other. They are destined to cooperate and minister to one another's needs for their common well-being and prosperity, and to promote peace and progress in their regions. The uniting of all these regions in a single sphere on the basis of common existence and assuring thereby the stability of that sphere is, I think, a natural conclusion.[10]

In early August the new foreign minister, Matsuoka Yōsuke, gave this vision its name: the "Greater East Asia Co-Prosperity Sphere" (*Dai Tōa kyōeiken*).

As Arita's statement makes clear, the concept of a Greater East Asia Co-Prosperity Sphere stretched beyond the boundaries of earlier Pan-Asian visions. Commonalities of geography and economy were set side by side with "common culture" and "common race." As this suggests, the older Pan-Asianist vision was diluted by geopolitical thinking that emphasized mutual economic advantage rather than simple cultural linkages. Only by doing so could the Japanese leadership create plausible ties between populations living in the old Sinitic cultural sphere and the more complex and diverse societies of Southeast Asia.

It is possible to dismiss the formulation of the Greater East Asia Co-Prosperity Sphere as an act of simple diplomatic cynicism since its announcement came precisely at the moment when key Japanese military and naval leaders successfully pushed for a "move south." In this context, the Co-Prosperity Sphere can be read as imperialist opportunism disguised as national mission—as a slogan cynically cobbled up to justify a new phase of expansion, as earlier the notion of a New Order in East Asia was cobbled up to win over collaborators from the ranks of the Chinese nationalists. But the simplest reading of a text, as we are

---

[10] Gaimusho, *Nihon gaikō nenpyō narabi-ni shuyō bunsho,* 2 vols. (Tokyo: Hara shobō, 1965–1966), 2:433–34. (Hereafter *NGKNSB.*)

constantly reminded, is not always the most revealing. What is striking about the concept is how rapidly it acquired the status of a national goal, embraced by Japanese leaders as enthusiastically in private counsels as in public pronouncements. This suggests that the idea fulfilled ideological functions much broader than opportunistic justification for a new and more aggressive expansionist policy in Southeast Asia.

One obvious function was to construct a new vision of national identity. For two generations, the Japanese leadership had lived with a sense of their country's "backwardness." The creation of a Greater East Asian Co-prosperity Sphere offered the possibility of leaping from the baggage train of history into its vanguard. One is struck by how frequently politicians and intellectuals referred to the "world-historical significance" of the Greater East Asia Co-Prosperity Sphere, and how often they associated it with the onset of a new phase of world history. In a speech to the 1942 Diet, Prime Minister Tōjō proclaimed, "It is truly an *unprecedentedly grand undertaking* that our Empire should, by adding [the regions in the GEACPS], establish *everlasting* peace in Greater East Asia *based on a new conception,* which will mark a *new epoch in the annals of mankind,* and proceed to *construct a new world order* along with our allies and friendly powers in Europe."[11] The persistent emphasis on the "new"—a "new conception" of peace in Asia, a "new epoch in the annals of mankind," a "new world order"—signaled a compelling and deeply felt urge to break free from followership.

What made the concept of a *new* order so appealing was that it would supplant an *old* order created by and for the Anglo-American powers. It promised that the Japanese, not the British and the Americans, would lead the world into the future. In the view of many Japanese politicians, bureaucrats, and intellectuals, events had discredited not only laissez-faire capitalism and free trade but Anglo-American political hegemony as well.[12] This was a recurrent theme in the writing and thinking of Prime Minister Konoe, who presided over the promulgation of the Greater East Asia Co-Prosperity Sphere. As early as 1918 he had railed against the victors' peace contrived at Paris to ratify Anglo-American hegemony. In his view the Versailles settlement promoted neither "democracy" nor "humanitarianism" but had created a new international status quo that left the British and the Americans in control of the lion's share of the world's territory and resources.[13] The linkage between the creation of a Greater East Asia Co-Prosperity Sphere and the assault on

[11] Ibid., p. 576 (emphasis added).

[12] Cf. William Miles Fletcher III, *The Search for a New Order: Intellectuals and Fascism in Prewar Japan* (Chapel Hill, N.C.: University of North Carolina Press), 1982, chap. 7.

[13] Konoe Fumimaro, "Ei-Bei hon'i heiwashugi o haisu," *Nippon oyobi Nipponjin* (December 1918); Konoe Fumimaro, *Seidanroku* (Tokyo: Chikura shobō, 1936). pp. 97–115.

Anglo-American hegemony became tighter—and was more shrilly pro-claimed—after 1941.

The new ideological construct allowed the Japanese to portray the war not as a crass contest over power and wealth but as a stage in a momentous historical process that would give birth to a more just international order. As Foreign Minister Tani Masayuki told the nation in a radio address in December 1942, the world was "now at a great turning point":

> [America's] motive is to strengthen its world hegemony. It would place Japan in East Asia and Germany and Italy in Europe under the Versailles structure, or more correctly it would have these countries submit to the pressure of American hegemony, many times heavier than that of the Versailles structure, so that they will have no chance to rise. . . . It goes without saying that the aim of the war of greater East Asia is to free greater East Asia from the yoke of America and Britain . . . and to contribute to the peace of the world by constructing an order in East Asia under which all the races and nations within the area will attain their proper place and exist together and prosper together.[14]

The wartime struggle, in short, was a contest over the reorganization of the international system on new principles, and the "Versailles system" became a metaphor for the predatory, aggressive, and self-interested character of the old order.

The vision of a Greater East Asian Co-Prosperity Sphere also legitimized the dismantling of liberal institutions at home. It is no coincidence that by the time of Foreign Minister Matsuoka's announcement of the Co-Prosperity Sphere in August 1940, the construction of a domestic "New Order" (*shintaisei*), aimed at ending political conflict, was well underway.[15] Both these "new orders" reinforced one another symbolically. The coming of a new historical epoch called for abandoning not only the liberal international order created by the Western nations but also the liberal domestic order—particularly the parliamentary structure and capitalist institutions—that Japan had imported from the West in the Meiji era. If liberalism was to be dethroned abroad, then logical and emotional consistency required that it be dethroned at home as well. The revolt against the West explicit in the vision of the Greater East Co-Prosperity Sphere was implicit in the "New Order Movement."

The New Order Movement was also intended to provide a domestic

---

[14] *Contemporary Japan* 12, no. 1 (December 1943): 151–52.
[15] Gordon Mark Berger, *Parties out of Power in Japan, 1931–1941* (Princeton, N.J.: Princeton University Press, 1977), chap. 6.

political base for the creation of the Co-Prosperity Sphere. Unless the Japanese were able to resolve the "contradictions" and "conflicts" that sprung from the liberal institutional structure and had bedeviled Japanese society since World War I, the country would lack the strength to fulfill its "historic mission." In 1940 Prime Minister Konoe made this connection quite clear in an address to the Preparatory Commission for Establishing a New Political Order: "If [Japan] is to bring the China Incident to a successful conclusion while adjusting itself to the international situation and taking a leading part in the establishment of a new world order, it must concentrate upon the accomplishment of this task the moral and material resources of the nation to the utmost degree so as to be in a position to take independently, swiftly, and resolutely appropriate measures to meet whatever situations may arise. . . . Consequently, there has arisen the pressing demand for the setting up of a new structure in politics, economy, education, culture and in all phases of the life of the State and the people."[16] No doubt any Japanese wartime government, like wartime governments everywhere, would have curbed political dissent and economic competition, but the vision of the GEACPS permitted Konoe to describe this process as "uplifting the political ideals and enhancing the political consciousness of the nation."[17]

Finally, the concept of a Greater East Asia Co-Prosperity Sphere prepared an ideological basis for collaboration with indigenous elites in the areas under Japanese domination. The appeal to a Pan-Asianist vision permitted the Japanese to reconcile local anticolonial aspirations for national independence with their own desire for regional hegemony. In a similar fashion Nazi foreign policy had deployed the slogan of Pan-Germanism to win external support for its expansionist drive. In explaining the takeover of Austria to the Reichstag in 1938, Hitler observed, "The Reich and German Austria belong together, not only because they are inhabited by the same people, but because they share a common history and culture. . . . [The Anschluss is] a way of serving the best interests of our two countries—the interests, rather, of the German people, whose sons we all are, wherever we may have been born."[18] Concealing the quest for domination in a mist of ethnic fraternity, Hitler used pan-nationalist rhetoric to turn an act of national annihilation into an act of national unification.

[16] *Yokusan kokumin undō shi* (Tokyo: Yokusan undō shi kankōkai, 1954), pp. 83–84 (emphasis added).

[17] Ibid., p. 100.

[18] Franz von Papen, *Memoirs*, trans. Brian Connell (London: Andre Deutsch, 1952), p. 422. As early as 1920 the party program asserted the unity of the German folk. "We demand the union of all Germans—on the basis of the rights of self-determination of all peoples—into a greater Germany."

In the case of Japanese pan-nationalism, the vision of a Greater East Asia Co-Prosperity Sphere held out the possibility that European colonial regimes would be supplanted by a benevolently generous Japanese metropole and newly liberated indigenous national regimes—and not by a new Japanese colonialism. According to this vision, for the Anglo-American powers the Great East Asia War was a colonial war to retain their power and influence in Asia, but for the peoples of the region it was something quite different. As Foreign Minister Shigemitsu told the Diet in October 1943: "To East Asia and its peoples, this is a war of racial awakening—a war for the renascence of East Asia. No wonder that all the peoples of East Asia have risen *en masse* to join this supreme and stupendous enterprise. . . . The present war is to us a war of national emancipation, which to our enemy is nothing but a war of aggression. . . . The war of greater East Asia is a war for justice to combat aggression. It is a war of liberation."[19] The construction of a Greater East Asian Sphere promised a postcolonial future for Asia.

As we have already seen, the Japanese vision of regional unity stressed commonalities of economic interest as well as ethnic or cultural similarities. By the late 1930s it was axiomatic for many Japanese that their country was a "have-not" nation in a world economy dominated by "have" nations like Britain and the United States. In this respect the interests of the Japanese could be identified with those of the colonial peoples in Southeast Asia. By liberating the colonial peoples, not only would Japan lay the foundation for their national independence, it would also create a regional economic bloc that would benefit its inhabitants rather than outsiders. The construction of the Greater East Asia Co-Prosperity Sphere would establish a new economic symbiosis between Japan and its neighbors, and its benefits would redound to all.

The Japanese government never announced a definitive master plan for the creation of a regional economic bloc, but official propaganda and public discourse sounded recurrent themes. One was that Japan would enjoy a position of leadership within the Greater East Asia Co-Prosperity Sphere. Despite repeated assurances that decisions on common economic policies—tariffs, currency, prices, distribution, and the like—were to be made collectively and not imposed from above, it was clear that Japan was to have a major coordinating or managerial role since it was the most advanced and sophisticated economy in the region. The boundaries between what was to be decided collectively and what was to be managed unilaterally by Japan, however, were not always well defined. The goal of the economic bloc was also portrayed as being the overall economic development of the region rather than the

---

[19] *Contemporary Japan* 12, no. 11 (December 1943): 1530.

narrow interests of Japan. In contrast to the practices of the prewar colonial regimes, relationship among the members of the sphere were to be nonexploitative. Indeed, much discussion of the sphere stressed the need for overall planning, whether that entailed resource development or the promotion of light or heavy industry where local conditions were suitable. Finally, in contrast to the hegemonic blocs of the Western Powers, the Greater East Asia Co-Prosperity Sphere was not intended to be completely autarkic; autarky, it was often argued, would retard development, not promote it.

The Greater East Asia Declaration promulgated in 1943 echoed many of these ideological themes. Intended as a counterstatement to the Atlantic Charter enunciated by Roosevelt and Churchill in 1941, the document declared that the war was being fought to "liberate Greater East Asia from the thrall of the Anglo-American powers" who had oppressed and exploited the people of the region in pursuit of their own national prosperity. It committed the nations of the region to building a Greater East Asia based on "coexistence and co-prosperity," "mutual respect for sovereign independence," "mutual cooperation and assistance," "the development of each people's creativity," "economic development," and the "elimination of racial prejudice."[20] The language of the declaration, overflowing with references to "mutuality," "solidarity," "cooperation," and "independence," was intended to appeal to the leaders of the indigenous nationalist movements who attended the Greater East Asia Conference. By 1943, however, this high-minded rhetoric was beginning to wear thin as it was tested against the reality of Japanese hegemony.

THE REALITY OF THE WARTIME EMPIRE

Imperial overexpansion ultimately stripped the vision of a Greater East Asian Co-Prosperity Sphere of its promise. The concept never provided a general pattern for policy in the occupied areas. It was much too skimpy a garment to cover the bloated wartime empire. When the tide of battle turned against Japan at the end of 1942, the strains of waging a war eroded all but the most perfunctory commitment to the ideals of "co-prosperity" and "coexistence" in most parts of the empire. While some Japanese officials and civilians took the idea of liberating Asia seriously, most directed their energies toward keeping the war machine functioning; and as Allied air and submarine attacks severed lines of communication with the metropole, political and economic disruptions stirred resentment and resistance against Japanese authority.

[20] *NGKNSB*, 2:594.

Parade in Ta Tung Square, Shinkyō (capital of Manchukuo), to commemorate the Manchukuo emperor's first visit to Japan, May 2, 1937.

Leaders attending the Greater East Asia Conference, November 5, 1943. *Left to right*: Premier Ba Maw of Burma, President Chang Ching-hui of Manchukuo, Premier Wang Ching-wei of the Nanking government, Premier Tōjō of Japan, Premier Wan Waithayakon of Thailand, President José Paciano Laurel of the Philippines, and Premier Subhas Chandra Bose of the Free State of India.

Japan's puppet leader of China, Wang Ching-wei, visiting Manchukuo in 1940 to confirm fraternal relations between his government and Manchukuo.

A factory manufacturing automobile frames and parts in Antung, Manchukuo, August 1942.

Entrance of a brothel in Korea where comfort women worked. The banner on the right reads: "Welcome to Those Heroes Who Are Fighting to Win Our Sacred War." The banner on the left reads: "Sincere, Wholehearted Services Rendered Here."

Korean schoolchildren worshiping at a shrine.

"This is the 'status quo' for the East Asia of America and England!" (Japanese cartoon, 1940).

Commander Homma, head of the Philippines Expeditionary Force, debarking at Santiago, Lingayan Bay, February 20, 1943.

TABLE I.2
Greater East Asia Co-Prosperity Sphere

Region	Political Structure	Economic Relationship	Ideological Construction
The original colonies (Taiwan, Korea)	Direct colonial administration	Economic development (foodstuffs, semimanufactured and manufactured goods)	Assimilation
The new client states (Manchukuo, Reorganized Nationalist Government)	"Independent state"	Economic development (semimanufactured and manufactured goods) Resource extraction	Independence
The former European colonies (Burma, Philippines, Indonesia, Indochina)	Military government leading to "independence"	Resource extraction	Liberation
(Java, Malaya)	Military government		
The allied state (Thailand)	Independent state	Trade	Parity

As the essays in this volume demonstrate, policy and practice varied widely from one part of the wartime empire to another. (The diverse metropole-periphery relations within the wartime empire are shown in schematic form in table I.2.) The Greater East Asia Co-Prosperity Sphere was not the result of careful prewar planning, Professor Gotō suggests, but a series of improvisations shaped by local circumstances. This is not to say that there was no planning. On the contrary, there was a profusion of planning and planners—and a surfeit of plans for developing Manchuria, occupied China, and the newly conquered "Southern Regions," and for the integration of these regions with the metropolitan economy. But planners worked at cross-purposes with different ends in mind. Even the best-laid plans had to be adjusted to rapidly changing wartime conditions, and many were simply abandoned. The talismanic invocation of the vision of a Greater East Asia

Co-Prosperity Sphere was often the only element that gave planning any semblance of coherence. What really drove the development of policy was the differing nature of the opportunities presented the Japanese.

The main dichotomy in policy was between the regions included in the New Order in East Asia (the old colonies of Taiwan and Korea, Manchukuo and the occupied areas in China) and those newly embraced by the Greater East Asia Co-Prosperity Sphere (the "Southern Regions"). The societies of Northeast Asia were treated quite differently from those of the former European colonies in Southeast Asia. In Northeast Asia Japanese economic policy stressed not only the production of foodstuffs and extraction of mineral resources but also the production of semimanufactured and manufactured goods for the metropolitan economy. As Professors Myers and Eckert point out, the encouragement of industrial development in colonial areas was unique to Japanese imperialism. No other modern imperialist power, with the possible exception of the British in India, embarked on such an extensive program of colonial industrialization.

Why did Japan do this? One reason, no doubt, was that Japanese civilian and military planners, who saw the Western industrial economies as their main economic rivals, had no fear of colonial competition. In the older colonies, Taiwan and Korea, the colonial governments began to encourage industrial development with the help of domestic businessmen like Noguchi Jun.[21] In Manchukuo, after attempting to promote the growth of a modern manufacturing sector with the help of the quasi-governmental South Manchurian Railway Company, Japanese officials eventually turned to metropolitan firms, including the *zaibatsu,* for capital and managerial guidance. These policies gave private businessmen a stake in the development of the region and assured them that the development of the dominated economies would complement rather than compete with the domestic economy. But in Northeast Asia the Japanese also found that they did not have to begin industrialization from scratch. For example, the Chang Hsueh-liang regime prepared the way for the industrialization of Manchukuo by developing physical plant (the Mukden arsenal) and human resources (high levels of public education), and in occupied coastal cities of China foreign and Chinese investors had built a burgeoning industrial sector that the Japanese could exploit for their own purposes.[22]

The situation was rather different in the "Southern Regions," where European colonial economies revolved around the exchange of colonial

[21] Barbara Molony, *Technology and Investment: The Prewar Japanese Chemical Industry* (Cambridge, Mass.: Harvard University Press, 1990), chaps. 4–5.

[22] After the fall Tientsin, for example, Japanese firms rather quickly gobbled up cotton spinning mills owned by foreign or Chinese capital.

foodstuffs and mineral resources for Western (and to a certain extent, Japanese) manufactured goods. While the Japanese government uttered pious promises about developing the region economically, Japanese planners projected a continuation of the old colonial policies, with some variation in the mix of output. As Professor Peattie demonstrates, planning for the "southern advance" gave priority to military requirements for raw materials such as oil, tin and other minerals, timber, and rubber. Apart from resource extraction, Japanese planners were concerned only that the local economies remain self-sufficient and not constitute an economic drain on the metropolis. Indeed, planning documents even anticipated that a deterioration of local living standards ("economic hardships imposed on native livelihood") might result from the acquisition of resources vital to the war effort.

While the Japanese invested in infrastructure and enterprise in Northeast Asia, in the "Southern Regions" they took over mines, plantations, oilfields, and factories already built by the Western colonizers. Development policy focused on the production of foodstuffs, oil, minerals, and some new primary products like raw cotton. In contrast to Manchukuo or North China where "national policy companies" like Mangyō and the North China Development Company played a critical role in Japanese plans, existing Western enterprises were simply turned over to private Japanese companies, most of them large metropolitan firms affiliated with the old or the new *zaibatsu* conglomerates. The creators of the Manchurian economy, ideologically committed to a planned economy and state capitalism, may have been visionaries experimenting with new forms of political economy, but in the "Southern Regions," where planners were most interested in immediate returns, development was to be left to the "enthusiasm and creativity of entrepreneurs with economic power." Quite different conceptions of the political economy, and quite different models of development, were clearly at work in Northeast and Southeast Asia parts of the wartime empire.

The ideological construction of relations between Japan and the "Southern Regions" was also subtly different from that in the pre-1941 portions of the wartime empire. In the older colonies of Taiwan and Korea, a policy of cultural assimilation, long touted as a policy goal but never really implemented, underwent rapid acceleration in the late 1930s. The *kōminka* movements described by Professors Eckert and Chou attempted a massive cultural incorporation of the indigenous populations by forcing them to abandon their indigenous languages and even their indigenous names. While nothing so drastic was attempted in either Manchukuo or the occupied areas in China, cultural policy, as we have already seen, stressed older Pan-Asianist conceptions such as racial harmony, fraternal bonds, and the creation of a "common East Asian culture." As Professor Young notes, Manchukuo was referred to as a "brother country" (*kyōdaikoku*) or as a "branch house" (*bunke*) of Japan. The relationship imagined to exist between the Japanese and subject peoples in these regions assumed the existence of long-standing natural bonds of commonality or fictive kinship.

In the "Southern Regions," by contrast, the Japanese proclaimed themselves the "liberators" as well as the "brothers" of the local populations. As Prime Minister Tōjō remarked on a visit to Manila in 1943, "The aim of the present war is to bring to their knees America, Britain and Holland, who have long wielded their baneful influence in East Asia and have been satisfying their greedy ambitions at the sacrifice of the peoples of greater East Asia, and to exterminate their influence, thereby establishing a new order based upon ethical principles in which each people therein will have their proper place."[23] The Japanese made a careful show of sympathy for the cause of national independence throughout Southeast Asia. When Japanese forces marched into Burma in 1942, for example, they were accompanied by the famous "Thirty Comrades," young Burmese nationalists who had been given military training at Hainan and who became the nucleus of the Burma Independence Army. And while the Japanese were busily eradicating the use of indigenous languages in Taiwan and Korea, in Burma they were dethroning English, the colonizers' language, and replacing it as the official language with Burmese.

The most tangible demonstration that the Japanese had come as liberators were their promises of independence to Burma, the Philippines, and Indonesia in 1942–43—and to Indochina in the final days of the war. Gestures of emancipation or liberation met with considerable skepticism in Northeast Asia, where indigenous regimes enjoying international recognition had been displaced by those under Japanese domination, but in Southeast Asia the commitment to liberation served to narrow the political distance between the Japanese and indigenous leaders, allowing them to collaborate with the Japanese without a sense of betraying the nationalist cause. Interestingly enough, as Professor Gotō points out, their postwar fate was rather different from Nazi collaborators like Vidkun Quisling, whose very name has become a synonym for "turncoat" or "traitor." The presumption was that even if they had collaborated with the Japanese they had done so to further the goal of national independence.

These ideological differences paralleled contrasts in political relationships. In the older colonies of Korea and Taiwan, where full assimilation remained the goal, direct colonial rule continued. Governors and

---

[23] *Contemporary Japan* 12, no. 5 (May 1943): 645.

other top-level officials were dispatched from Japan, and the indigenous population could obtain posts only in the lower echelons of the administrative hierarchy, usually serving in routine clerical positions rather than in managerial or decision-making roles. By contrast, in Manchukuo and occupied China, where the fiction of independence was maintained by signing of formal treaties and placing of indigenous leaders in the highest positions of formal authority, political links with metropolitan authority were mediated by Japanese advisers who guided the implementation of policies devised in Japan and who served as the real administrative managers of these regimes. In all of these areas, the Japanese were also able to draw on a body of lower-echelon collaborators, many of whom had been educated in Japan. As Carter Eckert reminds us in his essay, the wartime empire was served not only by civil officials recruited from the Korean population but by Korean military officers trained at the Manchurian academy.

The diverse and scattered "Southern Regions," whose cultural and political ties with Japan were looser, presented a much more complicated political problem. As several essays in this volume suggest, the Japanese moved into the area with caution. Preinvasion plans enjoined Japanese occupying forces to use existing administrative structures and to avoid premature encouragement of indigenous nationalist forces, but no consistent practice was followed. In French Indochina, the Japanese military struck a deal that left colonial authorities in place even at the risk of alienating the anticolonial movement; in the Philippines, Malaya, Burma, and the Dutch East Indies, the Japanese immediately dismantled the old colonial regimes, replacing them initially with Japanese military government while making conciliatory gestures toward local nationalist leaders like José Laurel, Ba Maw, Mohammad Hatta, and Sukarno; and in Thailand they made a formal alliance (a "shotgun marriage," as Professor Reynolds calls it) with the ruling oligarchy, whose leader, Phibun Songkhram, sought aid from Japan and shared with its leaders an admiration for the fascist regimes in Europe.

Apart from the division of the Dutch East Indies into two zones, one under army control and the other under the navy, the Japanese occupiers left most old colonial boundaries intact in Southeast Asia. Neither did they dislodge indigenous civil servants, who, liberated from European management, usually had no qualms about working for the Japanese. Government office, after all, continued to provide high prestige and financial security no matter who was on top. The position of local nationalist politicians was more delicate, and often they remained deeply suspicious of the Japanese authorities. As the papers by Professors Gotō and Reynolds clearly show, leaders like Laurel, Hatta, Sukarno, and Phibun not only distrusted the Japanese "liberators" but did their best not to be tagged as their puppets.

In one respect, however, nearly all parts of the wartime empire resembled one another. Outside of the older colonies of Korea and Taiwan, occupied by the Japanese for a generation, the overlay of Japanese power was extremely thin. Military occupation throughout the territories dominated after 1931 was limited to control by "points and lines." While Japanese police and gendarmerie contained dissent and resistance in Korea and Taiwan, in the rest of the Co-Prosperity Sphere Japanese hegemony remained extremely vulnerable. In Manchukuo, in the occupied areas of China, and in Southeast Asia the Japanese authorities held the cities and the major railway lines but they had only a weak grasp over the countryside.[24] This was perhaps the most significant symptom (and defect) of Japan's overexpansion. Even had the Japanese succeeded in holding off the Allied counteroffensive, one can well imagine that the wartime empire eventually would have been eroded from within under assault by indigenous resistance movements that got their start in the territorial interstices between the "points and lines." In north China, for example, anti-Japanese guerrilla movements, supported by the local populations and backed by both the Nationalist and the Communists, managed to tie down Japanese military forces that might otherwise have been diverted to operations in the Pacific and Southeast Asia.

But it was in Southeast Asia, where the reach of Japanese power most egregiously exceeded its grasp, that the structure of the fragmented and overextended wartime empire was most fragile. Despite all gestures and assurances that Japan was interested only in the liberation of the region, anti-Japanese resistance movements sprang into being everywhere. Even in Burma, where the local welcome perhaps had been the warmest at the beginning of the war, the Burma Independence Army, organized with Japanese approval, became a recruiting ground for the anti-Japanese resistance. In Indochina it was the Vietminh, in the Philippines the Hukbalahaps, and in Malaya the Malayan People's Anti-Japanese Army that mounted armed guerrilla activities against the Japanese forces. Only in the Dutch East Indies was overt armed resistance minimal, but even there scattered underground groups were organized. The Japanese forces made no lasting bonds with the indigenous populations, and nowhere were they remembered with much fondness after 1945.[25]

One reason, no doubt, was the ruthless manner in which the Japanese authorities exploited the local population. As the war effort grew increasingly desperate, and manpower shortages developed, the Japanese

[24] Kobayashi Hideo, *Daitōa kyōeiken no keisei to hōkai* (Tokyo: Ochanomizu shobō, 1975), p. 534.

[25] An interesting case study is presented in Otabe Yuji, "Japanese Occupation Policy in Singapore, 1942–1945," in *Western Interaction with Japan: Expansion, the Armed Forces, and Readjustment, 1859–1956,* ed. Peter Lowe and Herman Moeshart (Sandgate: Japan Library, 1990), pp. 84–90.

imperial authorities began to commandeer labor. In Southeast Asia and Korea, hundreds of thousands of men were either lured or dragooned into labor service battalions as *rōmusha* (essentially forced laborers) to build roads, construct airstrips, or lay railway lines needed for the war effort. Ruthlessly exploited, they worked under brutal supervision in brutalizing conditions, often with barely enough to eat, let alone with adequate medical care or other amenities. For example, it has been estimated that the construction of the Burma-Siam Railway between Moulmein and Bangkok—the notorious "railway of death"—took the lives of one hundred thousand Burmese and Malay Indian laborers. And, as Mr. Hicks's essay tells us, in Korea, Taiwan, the Philippines, and elsewhere the Japanese military also "recruited" tens of thousands, perhaps hundreds of thousands, of women to serve as "comfort women" (*ianfu*)—prostitutes in military brothels. Memories of these exactions in work and flesh are still vivid in Asia today.

Among those untouched by these brutalities, wartime economic changes also engendered bitter memories of the Japanese occupation. Throughout the wartime empire, but particularly in Southeast Asia, Japanese domination was associated with the steady deterioration of living standards and economic conditions. The overextended empire simply did not function as the dreamers of a harmonious regional economic bloc had hoped. To begin with, communication lines, oil fields and refineries, mining facilities, and the like were either destroyed by Japanese air attacks or sabotaged by retreating Allied forces. Reconstruction was hampered by the departure of European technicians, who either fled or were interned in prison camps, and replacement parts and new equipment needed to get production facilities working again were in short supply. In some cases, rather than rebuild the local infrastructure, the Japanese chose instead to strip it or turn it into scrap metal. Second, under a basic policy decision in November 1941, Japanese forces in Southeast Asia were ordered to live off the land, obtaining food and other supplies locally and relying on the metropolitan economy for supplies only in the most urgent cases. The Japanese military commandeered what they needed, requiring forced deliveries at fixed prices. Goods were paid for by military scrip at first, and later by nonconvertible special bank notes whose value steadily dropped. Finally, the Japanese occupation completely disrupted the prewar pattern of trade, in which the Southeast Asian colonies had sent about half their exports to the European metropolitan countries (and in the case of Malaya to the United States). The Japanese domestic economy was too limited and too overburdened to absorb a similar amount. With tight rationing and other constraints on civilian consumption, Japan provided no outlet for the sugar, tea, coffee, or even the rubber that earlier had gone to Europe and North America. Nor could the Japanese provide the region with the manufactured goods that had come from Europe and the United States.

The results, predictably enough, were severe economic disruptions: chronic shortages of all goods, but especially foodstuffs and basic consumer goods like oil, salt, soap, matches, and clothing; rampant inflation that raised the cost of living everywhere; black marketeering, hoarding, and speculation that eroded the social fabric; a decline in customs dues and other public revenues that impoverished indigenous governments and brought the deterioration of public services; endemic official corruption and extortion; and widespread unemployment, both in cities and plantations, as production declined. While these symptoms of economic deterioration varied from country to country, no part of the empire escaped them completely. Even in the metropole, the ordinary population suffered many of the same hardships as the dominated peoples in the Co-Prosperity Sphere

REMEMBERING THE WARTIME EMPIRE

The gap between the vision and the reality of the wartime empire has persisted in the postwar historical memory of the Greater East Asia Co-Prosperity Sphere. Even today, as local communities dispute what kind of exhibits to install in "war memorial museums" (sensōkan), as foreign ministry officials debate what sites the imperial couple should visit on their trips abroad, as prime ministers fumble for soothingly ambiguous words of repentance, and as the Diet debates resolutions apologizing for the war contested memories lurk at every turn. Although most Japanese probably deplore the war, if they think about it at all, there are also intellectuals, academics, journalists, and politicians who refuse to recognize what Ueyama Shumpei has called the central hypocrisy of the wartime ideology: "Domination of Asians by Caucasians was colonization but domination of Asians by Asians was colonial liberation."[26] And these Japanese have not hesitated to express themselves in public, often with unfortunate consequences for Japan's relations with the rest of the world.

The American occupation forces tried to expunge all positive memory of the wartime empire by striking the term "Greater East Asia Co-Prosperity Sphere" from the lexicon of public discourse. The new high-school history text prepared under American supervision in 1946, *Kuni no ayumi,* made no mention of it even as a contemporary term. But it

---

[26] Ueyama Shumpei, *Daitōa sensō no imi: gendaishi bunseki no shiten* (Tokyo: Chūō kōronsha, 1964), p. 53.

was the Tokyo war crimes trials that altered the narrative of the wartime empire even more radically by stripping the war of any "world-
historical significance" or any redeeming historical value at all. The final judgment of the tribunal marked it as a war of aggression aimed at
domination of East Asia, the Pacific Ocean, and the Indian Ocean, a
matter of national shame to be expiated by the reconstruction of Japan
as a peace-loving democracy.

During the 1950s, the Tokyo trials view of the war became orthodox
among the intellectual community, and thus in the media as well. It
buttressed their deep commitment to the antiwar clause in the new constitution and to a pacifist critique of conservative foreign policy. "Progressive" intellectuals hoped that the Tokyo trials reading of the wartime empire would prevent a recurrence of Japanese aggression and
expansion. As Ienaga Saburō wrote, "A careful reconfirmation of the
truth about the Pacific War and making these facts as widely known as
possible are the only ways to avoid another tragedy. It is a solemn
obligation incumbent upon those who survived the conflict, a debt we
owe to the millions who perished in the fires of war."[27] Among those
millions, Ienaga made clear, were the other peoples of Asia, who had
suffered under Japanese domination.

Revaluation of the wartime empire, however, was already beginning
during the post-Occupation "reverse course." With the incorporation of
Japan into the wall of anti-Communist containment in East Asia, sur-
vivors from the prewar political world felt freer to justify the wartime
effort. As Minister of Education Okano Seigo remarked in the Diet in
1953: "I do not wish to pass judgment on the rightness or the wrong-
ness of the Greater East Asia War, but the fact that Japan took on so
many opponents and fought them for four years . . . proves our superiority."[28] In a less ambiguous vein some prewar politicians pointed out
that the war had checked the spread of Bolshevism in East Asia. These
views did not catch on with the public, or within the intellectual community, who remembered the dark side of the war—and were profoundly unsettled by the return to the political world of men like Kishi
Nobusuke, one of the architects of Manchukuo.

It was not until the early 1960s, as the development of the Cold War
tarnished the Tokyo trials version of World War II, that apologists for
the Greater East Asia Co-Prosperity Sphere opened up public debate.
Military intervention by the United States in Korea, France in Indochina and Algeria, and Great Britain in Egypt made it appear that West-

---

[27] Ienaga Saburō, *The Pacific War, 1941–1945: A Critical Perspective on Japan's Role in World War II* (New York: Pantheon Books, 1978), p. 245.

[28] *Tosho shinbun,* Feb. 21, 1953.

ern democracies loved the international status quo more than they loved peace; the suppression of the Hungarian revolution cast doubt on the link between socialism and internationalism by suggesting that the Soviet Union acted more from nationalist impulses than socialist; and the Chinese invasion of Tibet raised similar questions about the "anti-imperialism" of the People's Republic. In short, it seemed that the wartime defenders of democracy were as intent on pursuing their own power interests as they alleged that wartime Japanese leaders had been, making it more difficult for the former Allies to claim the moral high ground. As Ueyama Shumpei pointed out, even though democracy might be demonstrably superior to fascism, that did not guarantee that the democracies would always be peace-loving.

In 1963 Hayashi Fusao launched the heaviest attack on the Tokyo trials view in a series of articles in *Chūō kōron,* later published under the title *Daitōa senso kōtei ron (An Affirmation of the Greater East Asia War).* By his own admission Hayashi was not a historian but a patriotic Japanese who wanted to "disgorge something caught in his chest." By "affirming" the Greater East Asia War, and thus stripping the Japanese of their guilt complex about it, he hoped to rekindle national confidence and pride. His book raised the issue of war responsibility—who started the war and when? His answer was simple: "The Greater East Asia War was the finale of a hundred years' war." It had begun with the arrival of the Westerners, who shattered the peace Japan maintained with its neighbors for more than two centuries, and it had continued down to 1945, as the Japanese attempted to hold back the onslaught of Western imperialism in Asia. The echoes of wartime rhetoric resounded through the book. "America," he wrote, "fought for a 'white Pacific,' Japan fought for a 'yellow Greater East Asia Co-Prosperity Sphere.'" By situating the war in a *longue durée* Hayashi read it not as an act of Japanese aggression nor as a struggle for the redistribution of colonial territories but as a heroic effort by Japan to liberate the oppressed Asian peoples from their Western masters.[29] As he pointed out, the flags of the newly independent Asian nations flying at the Olympics were a reminder that the "hundred years' war" against the West had made its mark on history.[30]

The obvious objections to Hayashi's thesis were raised by Ueyama Shumpei in his *Daitōa senso no imi (The Meaning of the Greater East Asian War):* first, Japan itself became a colonial power by the turn of the cen-

---

[29] Hayashi Fusao, *Shintei: Daitōa senso kōteiron* (Tokyo: Roman, 1974), p. 317.

[30] To be sure, Hayashi admitted that the new nations in postwar Asia were not simply "children of the war." They were the product as well of indigenous nationalism and the anticolonial policies of the Soviet Union. But this was not to deny the contribution of the Japanese. Ibid., p. 311.

tury; second, all the battles in Japan's "hundred years' war" were fought on Asian soil; and third, the colonial peoples "liberated" by the Japanese during the Pacific War were happy to see them leave. Ueyama did not think that Japan bore exclusive responsibility for the war, but he saw the "hundred years' war" simply as a century of Japanese aggression. Since the 1890s, he declared, the Japanese had fought against Asians rather than against Europeans, and they had annexed territory for their own benefit, not for the benefit of the colonial peoples. Under the Greater East Asian Co-Prosperity Sphere this pattern of aggression continued as Japanese colonial domination supplanted European. To judge from the precedents of Korea and Taiwan, it was by no means certain that the liberation of colonial peoples would have been achieved had Japan been victorious. What the war produced was not a liberated Asia but a divided Asia, with socialist regimes like the Chinese arrayed against those aligned with the American bloc like Japan and the SEATO countries.[31]

While Ueyama drew upon Marxist interpretations of the war, his position on the question of war guilt or war responsibility was pacifist. The full burden of war responsibility could not be placed on the Japanese leadership, he argued, since wars require two parties. No matter who fired the first shot, the other side had to fire back before hostilities could begin, and thus war guilt was not to be found in any particular state but in the nation-state itself. Indeed, the "original sin" of the nation-state was its inherently war-loving, aggressive character. "Sovereign states," he concluded, "cannot judge other sovereign states." In effect, he rendered the Tokyo verdict meaningless.

The debates of the 1960s, carried on at a time when many Japanese were coming to see themselves as war victims too, relativized the conflict in the same way that some German historians and intellectuals relativized the Holocaust. As Charles Maier has noted, those reluctant to accept collective guilt for the horrors of the Nazi period handled the problem in two ways: one was to consider Nazism as an aberration from the course of German history that suddenly afflicted the German people, and then disappeared without a trace after defeat; the other was to point out that the horrors committed by the Nazis were matched by those of other nations and that the potential for mass murder lay hidden in the entrails of all modern states.[32] By asking how different the Holocaust was from the Soviet liquidation of the kulaks and the Old Bol-

---

[31] Ueyama, *Daitōa sensō no imi*, pp. 37–58.

[32] "The central issue [in this controversy]," Charles Maier has noted, "has been whether Nazi crimes were unique . . . or whether they are comparable to other national atrocities, especially Stalinist terror." Charles S. Maier, *The Unmasterable Past: History, Holocaust, and German National Identity* (Cambridge, Mass.: Harvard University Press, 1988), p. 1.

sheviks, the fire-bombing of Hamburg, Dresden, and Tokyo, or the atomic attacks on Hiroshima and Nagasaki, these German historians and intellectuals relativized Nazi butchery by questioning its uniqueness. And even if one did not raise this moral question, it was still possible to proclaim that Nazism was not an exclusively German phenomenon but part of a more general mid-twentieth-century trend toward "fascism" or "totalitarianism."

In the early 1980s, "affirmation" of the Greater East Asia Co-Prosperity Sphere led to the so-called "textbook controversy," when the governments in Beijing and Taipei, Pyongyang and Seoul, in an unprecedented show of unanimity, condemned the alleged attempt of the Ministry of Education to erase Japan's history of aggression by insisting on revision of high-school textbooks. Leaving aside for a moment the accuracy of these charges, the episode did raise the legitimate question of whether it is appropriate for one country to protest the content of education in another. The cultural Right, particularly within the Liberal Democratic Party, self-righteously contended that the Asian protests amounted to foreign interference in domestic politics. And since the passages in question—particularly the substitution of the word "advance" for "aggression" in describing Japanese activities in China during the 1930s—involved the question of how one was to read the war, the textbook controversy reignited the feelings stirred by Hayashi Fusao twenty years before.

In his *Daitōa sensō e no michi* (*The Road to the Greater East Asian War*) (originally serialized in the conservative journal *Shokun*) Nakamura Akira railed not so much against the Tokyo trials interpretation of the war as against the attempt of the Chinese and the Koreans to set the historical agenda for Japan. There was no need to kowtow to the Chinese version of the war, he said, nor to anyone else's. The Japanese should not fear foreign opprobrium in writing the history of their own country, nor should they even seek to solicit the "understanding" of others. To do so would be to subordinate Japan to outsiders, and no country in the world did that, unless it was still under colonial control. After all, Nakamura pointed out with some justice, the Japanese had not insisted that either the Chinese or the Koreans revise the errors, distortions, and myths in their own textbooks, and they had no right to do the same to the Japanese. In any case, there could be no "common understanding of history among all nations" since history was invariably linked to national feelings and national interests.[33]

Like Hayashi, Nakamura denied that the war was aimed either at the acquisition of territory or at world domination. The Japanese leaders

---

[33] Nakamura Akira, *Daitōa sensō e no michi* (Tokyo: Tentensha, 1990), pp. 1–3, 18.

had not wanted to start a war, he said, and they had tried to avoid it at all costs until the very end of the U.S.–Japanese negotiations.[34] In a sense, Nakamura described wartime expansion as a "necessary imperialism" impelled by the needs of national defense and national survival. Before the China Incident, he argued, Japan did not seek "territory for territory's sake" but "advanced" into other countries and secured "rights" there in the quest of protecting national "self-existence." The war in China, which Nakamura admitted was mounted to "chastise" the Chinese government, had little to do with either self-defense or survival, and even though the Japanese tried desperately to resolve the incident, it was prolonged by the American support and aid for the Chiang Kai-shek regime. When Japan was overwhelmed by the "ABCD encirclement" in 1941 it had no choice but to break out of it by moving south.

The remarkable durability of the myth of the Greater East Asia Co-Prosperity Sphere owes much to the long postwar effort to recover national self-esteem. The myth has appealed perhaps most strongly to members of the wartime generation who remembered the war's idealistic side. Kobori Keiichi, a Tokyo University literature professor who has leveled frequent attacks at the Tokyo trials view, recalled that as a schoolboy he had clipped the Greater East Asia Declaration from the newspaper to paste in his scrapbook. For him the themes in the declaration—liberation from political and racial discrimination, brotherhood among the peoples of Asia, the commitment to economic and material development, and so forth—were neither hypocritical cant nor mendacious propaganda but an expression of ideals no less genuine than those embodied in Japan's postwar "peace constitution."[35] In a recent essay Kobori has gone so far as to suggest the Greater East Asia Co-Prosperity Sphere is an idea whose time has come again—despite all its bad associations.

The moral relativization of the war by men like Hayashi Fusao and Nakamura Akira also found an audience among members of the post-

---

[34] Nakamura did not take up the theme of the "liberation of Asia" as Hayashi did. For him, the war revolved around two main issues: first, a clash between the United States and Japan over the "Open Door principle," involving a collision between the "realistic needs" of Japan and the "abstract, moralistic demands" of the United States; and second, a struggle against the spread of communism, which began with Siberian expedition, expanded with the Manchurian incident, and continued with the fight against Comintern intrigue before the China Incident. Neither, of course, pitted Japan against Asians. Oddly enough, Nakamura tries to link these two themes directly by suggesting that war broke out with the United States because Japan refused to countenance demands for the withdrawal of Japan's "anticommunist occupation forces" in China. *Ibid.*

[35] Kobori Keiichi, "A Letter of Gratitude to the War Dead," *Japan Echo* 11 (Special Issue, 1984): 38–45.

war generation who were brought up on the Tokyo trials version in their school classes—and were puzzled by it. "We were taught that for inexplicable reasons the entire country had gone mad," reminisced Hasegawa Michiko, a philosophy professor born in 1945, "thinking it could achieve the impossible and convinced that wrong was right."[36] This version of the war demanded that Japan alone was at fault. It required accepting what Nakamura Akira has called a "self-tyrannizing view of history" (*jigyakushikan*) or a "Japan-bashing view of history" (*Nihon danzai shikan*). As Japan recovered its international respectability such self-hatred no longer seemed appropriate. When Hasegawa read other works about the war—memoirs, reminiscences, fiction—she discovered that many Japanese had died horrible deaths in the great incendiary raids against Tokyo in 1945, in the underground tunnels of Iwo Jima, and in the nuclear holocausts that struck Hiroshima and Nagasaki—and that these horrible deaths had been inflicted by an enemy whose face was rarely seen in the school texts. It was this discovery that led her to embrace the consoling message implicit in Hayashi's notion of the "hundred years' war": if you look at the other side, the Japanese were not so bad after all.

Perhaps most important, the affirmative view of the war has received the tacit and sometimes the overt support of the Liberal Democratic Party. No LDP prime minister ever acknowledged war responsibility in any clear-cut fashion, as many postwar German leaders have done. More often than not, their actions reminded the public that the Japanese too were victims of the war. During the 1980s, Prime Minister Nakasone Yasuhiro embarked on a deliberate campaign to revive older symbols of national strength and unity in order to enhance national self-esteem. It is striking that in 1985, a few months after the fortieth anniversary of the German surrender, when President Weizsäcker urged the German people to take responsibility for the war and the horrors it had wrought, Prime Minister Nakasone paid an official visit to the Yasukuni Shrine in Tokyo, where Japan's war dead—including General Tōjō and other wartime leaders convicted as "war criminals" by the Tokyo tribunal—are enshrined. And his minister of education, Fujio Masayuki, who spent most of his brief tenure in office with his foot in his mouth, publicly took the position that General Tōjō was not a war criminal because the Tokyo verdict "cannot be considered correct."

The LDP may not have fully embraced the "affirmative" view of the war expressed by Hayashi and others but its leaders certainly have also been reluctant to embrace the Tokyo trial view. In 1990, Prime Minister Takeshita, a man whose utterances were usually cloaked in ambiguities,

---

[36] Hasegawa Michiko, "A Postwar View of the Greater East Asia War," ibid., p. 29.

remarked, "The question of whether or not [World War II] was a war of aggression is a problem for future historians to decide." In part, this reluctance to admit that Japan was at fault was a matter of conviction, in part a matter of political expedience. No less than other members of the prewar generation, many conservative politicians felt that some war aims were justified and that Japan had been forced to go to war by the inflexible position taken by the United States in 1940–41. But rejecting the Tokyo tribunal view was also a way of building political support, not only among cultural conservatives but also among special interest groups representing Japanese war victims—among them the Japanese Association of War-Bereaved Families. And by refusing to acknowledge publicly full responsibility for the waging of a war of aggression the LDP leaders avoided reopening the costly and embarrassing question of restitution to wartime victims in other countries.

To be sure, the tight link between the political establishment and the "affirmative" view of the war has loosened. The Ministry of Education has begun to approve textbooks that deal with subjects like the Korean, Chinese, and other Asian women pressed into service as "comfort women" during the wartime period. In August 1993, for the first time since the war ended, a Japanese prime minister, Hosokawa Masahiro, announced his personal belief that the Pacific War was a "war of aggression, a war that was wrong." At the annual August 15 ceremony commemorating the end of the war, he told an audience that included the emperor and empress, "I would like to take this opportunity to express deep condolences to victims of the war and their relatives in neighboring countries in Asia and those around the world."[37] While there was widespread editorial support for the prime minister's statement, it was by no means unanimous—and some truculent defensiveness was also to be found. One high LDP official rejected the statement with indignation: "Japan should reflect on its wartime conduct if it deserves remorse, but it is blasphemy against history to define Japan's war acts as aggression with all the responsibility falling on Japan."[38]

Nostalgia for the Great East Asia War and the Greater East Co-Prosperity Sphere has not found direct expression in Japanese foreign policy, but the continuing struggle over how the war is to be remembered has undermined Japan's efforts to emerge as a major regional leader in Asia. The wartime myths lie just beneath the surface of political consciousness, like shells left over from a battle long ended. When one of them detonates, the damage to Japan's relations with its neigh-

---

[37] *Japan Times Weekly,* Aug. 23–29, 1993. A government spokesman also indicated that the Hosokawa government was considering a Diet resolution expressing remorse and apologizing for Japan's "war of aggression."

[38] Ibid.

bors is not inconsiderable. In May 1994 Nagano Shigeto, the newly appointed minister of justice who earlier had served as the Self Defense Force chief of staff, criticized former Prime Minister Hosokawa for referring to World War II as a war of aggression, and insisted that Japan had been trying to liberate Asia from the Western colonial powers. His statement, immediately but grudgingly retracted, wiped away the goodwill generated by Hosokawa's gesture of conciliation. In Seoul, where Nagano's effigy was burned in front of the Japanese embassy, the *Dong-A Ilbo* asked a question still on the minds of many Asians:

> Every time such irresponsible and preposterous remarks prompted international protests and criticisms . . . Japan invariably tried to quell the ensuing uproar by retracting the statements in question or censuring those who made the remarks.
>
> Why do such problems recur so often? We cannot but reason that it is because such perversion of historical facts reflects the subconscious attitude of the Japanese, be they conservative or progressive. In other words, the Nagano remarks have again revealed the deep-seated real thinking of the Japanese. . . .
>
> If Japan does not face historical facts squarely and teach historical truths to its younger generation, how can we build a sense of trust toward Japan as a partner in this Asia-Pacific era?[39]

Unless the Japanese liberate themselves from the spell of false history, it seems, the half-buried myths of the wartime empire still threaten to sap their considerable potential for peaceful economic and political leadership in Asia.[40]

---

[39] *Korea Focus,* May–June 1994, pp. 142–43.

[40] Many Japanese intellectuals and politicians are quite aware of these realities. As Etō Shinkichi has pointed out, in most Asian countries the concept of the GEACPS has only unpleasant, negative and offensive associations, and a revival of the idea is sure to be confused with a revival of the ghost of prewar expansionism. And in a recent round table discussion in *Sekai* Sunobe Ryōzō and Yui Tasaburō urged their countrymen to reexamine recent Japanese history not because outsiders tell them to but because it is important problem for the Japanese themselves. *Asahi shinbun,* Jan. 27, 1993.

PART I

Japan's Wartime Empire and the Formal Colonies

CHAPTER 1

Total War, Industrialization, and Social Change in Late Colonial Korea

Carter J. Eckert

In *White Badge*, Ahn Junghyo's novel of the Korean combat experience in Vietnam, the central character comes to see his life and, by extension, his country's long march toward modernity, as "a succession of wars."[1] It is a discomfiting metaphor, darkly ironic and laden with intimations of violence and death, but its power lies in its resonance with Korean history. War or the threat of war, the growth of industrialization, and social change have all been closely intertwined in Korea during the past one hundred years.

Vietnam was, in fact, only the most recent of the many wars that, in Ahn's words, have "fueled the modernization and development of the country."[2] Between the end of the Korean War and the first dispatch of South Korean troops to Vietnam—indeed, throughout most of the nearly five decades that have elapsed since Korea's liberation from Japanese colonial rule in 1945—it was the Cold War that continued to provide the context and rationale for massive transfusions of capital and technology into the peninsula from abroad, while serving at the same time as a sharp domestic spur to economic development on both sides of the demilitarized zone. Even the Korean War of 1950–53, despite its terrible physical and human devastation, can be said to have advanced the industrialization process by helping to sweep aside the last remnants of an old social order based on landed wealth and by bringing windfall opportunities and profits to a nascent capitalist class.[3]

Like the historical process of industrialization itself, moreover, the link with war reaches far back beyond the 1960s, or even the 1950s. At

[1] Ahn Junghyo, *White Badge: A Novel of Korea* (New York: Soho Press, 1989), p. 8.

[2] Ibid., p. 40.

[3] See Carter J. Eckert, Ki-baik Lee, Young Ick Lew, Michael Robinson, and Edward W. Wagner, *Korea Old and New: A History* (Cambridge, Mass.: Korea Institute, Harvard University, 1990), pp. 394–99, 401–2. See also Yi Taegun, *Han'guk chŏnjaeng kwa 1950-nyŏndae ŭi chabon ch'ukchŏk* [The Korean War and capital accumulation in the 1950s] (Seoul: Tosŏ Ch'ulp'an Kkach'i, 1987); Jung-en Woo, *Race to the Swift: State and Finance in Korean Industrialization* (New York: Columbia University Press, 1991), esp. pp. 43–117.

the turn of the century Japan's confrontation and eventual conflict with Tsarist Russia played a key role in the laying of Korea's first railway lines, one of the premier symbols of industrial civilization at the time. In 1917 the establishment by Japanese investors of the peninsula's first large-scale industrial plant, the Chōsen Spinning and Weaving Company, was a direct result of a boom in the Japanese textile industry stimulated by World War I.[4] Of all the periods of war before 1945, however, none had so direct and momentous an impact on Korean industrialization and social change as the last decade or so of colonial rule that began in the aftermath of the Manchurian Incident of 1931 and culminated in the second Sino-Japanese and Pacific War of 1937–45.

INDUSTRIALIZATION BEFORE 1931

Industrialization in Korea before the 1930s was relatively limited. Dominated by powerful landed aristocratic interests, the late Choson state (1392–1910) had been unable to marshal either the will or the financial resources to carry out a program of industrial development along Meiji Japanese lines, and private Korean wealth tended to remain concentrated in agriculture well into the colonial period. Not surprisingly, the early colonial regimes also saw little point in building up a sophisticated industrial structure on the peninsula that would simply reproduce, or worse, compete with, developing industries in the metropole. To Japanese colonizers in this early period, the primary economic functions of Korea, or Chōsen, as the colony was called, were to serve as an inexpensive export granary for Japanese consumption and as a market for Japanese manufactured goods. Industrialization, such as it was, was thus confined for the most part to the construction of a modern infrastructure (including roads and railways) geared toward the primary sector and trade with Japan. Factories and other business firms established during this period were also generally engaged in activities like rice milling that accommodated these same interests. Indeed, until 1920 a so-called Company Law was in effect that required all businesses to be officially licensed by the Government-General, thus allowing the colonial authorities to keep industrialization within acceptable bounds.[5]

---

[4] Pak Ch'anil, "No-Il chŏnjaeng ijŏn Ilbon ŭi tae-Han kyŏngjejŏk ch'imnyak kwa Han'guk ŭi pyŏnmo" [The economic invasion and transformation of Korea before the Russo-Japanese War], in Kuksa Hakhoe, ed., No-Il chŏnjaeng chŏnhu Ilbon ŭi Han'guk ch'imnyak [Japan's invasion of Korea around the time of the Russo-Japanese war], (Seoul: Ilchogak, 1986), p. 159; Carter J. Eckert, Offspring of Empire: The Koch'ang Kims and the Colonial Origins of Korean Capitalism (Seattle: University of Washington Press, 1991), p. 42.

[5] Ibid., pp. 27–28, 41.

Korea's first real burst of industrialization came during, and to no small extent as a result of World War I. Preoccupied with the fighting in Europe, the Western Powers temporarily abandoned their markets in Asia, and Japanese businessmen were quick to take advantage of the opportunity. Exports of Japanese products, especially textiles, soared during the war, and demand continued to exceed supply, in spite of a rapid proliferation of new facilities. As a result, Japan found itself unable to meet the needs of its own colonies for manufactured products, and the colonies, in turn, began for the first time to consider expanding industry beyond the agricultural sector. As already noted, in Korea this led to the establishment of the Chōsen Spinning and Weaving Company in 1917, an event that was seen at the time as heralding a new industrial future for the peninsula.

The effects of the Great War on Japan and its colonies continued even after the armistice was signed in 1918. In less than five years the war had transformed Japan from a debtor to a creditor nation and created a fund of surplus capital that sought an outlet in the colonies. In Chōsen itself, Japan's seizure of Shantung in 1914 had generated a strong official interest in north and central China, as well as in Manchuria, as potential market areas for the colony's products. Gradually the Government-General came to the conclusion that an enlarged continental market would permit a certain degree of industrialization on the peninsula that would complement rather than compete with the metropole and simultaneously enhance the wealth and value of the colony. Thus in 1920 the Government-General, long under attack from prominent Japanese capitalists like Shibusawa Eiichi for its "militaristic" attitude toward private enterprise, and headed by a new and more moderate governor-general, Saitō Makoto (1920–27; 1929–31), abolished the Company Law and instituted a system of routine legal registration of companies identical to that in effect in Japan itself. Existing tariffs between Japan and Korea were also largely removed within the next few years, thereby allowing a free movement of capital goods for the establishment of modern machine factories.[6]

As a result of such changes, industry in Korea saw an expansion and diversification from about 1916 as both Japanese and Korean capitalists began to establish new factories. Most of the new plants, especially those owned by Koreans, tended to be small in scale, with capitalization hovering around ten thousand yen, but large-scale facilities, capitalized at one million yen or more, also began to appear on the peninsula for the first time during this period. Between 1916 and 1919 alone over twenty new factories were established with capitalization ranging from

---

[6] Ibid., pp. 42–43.

one to thirty million yen. In addition to silk and cotton textiles, their activities encompassed mining and shipbuilding, pig iron and steel, lumber, brewing, medicine, cement, sugar and flour refining, electricity, and brickmaking.[7] As Nakamura Takafusa has noted, "the wave of industrialization and incorporation brought by World War I was also the beginning of industrialization in the hitherto suppressed colonies."[8]

The manufacturing sector (including mining) continued to grow, albeit modestly, in the 1920s, and both production and the number of factories doubled between 1920 and 1930.[9] Of particular importance during this period was the first major development of Korea's extensive hydroelectric resources in the northern part of the peninsula. Surveys conducted by the Government-General shortly after the annexation had originally estimated the maximum electrical potential of Korea's rivers at only about 57,000 kilowatts, but subsequent studies in the 1920s showed that a more accurate estimate was nearly forty times that amount, or about 2.25 million kilowatts. The discovery of this new source of cheap energy led to the establishment in 1927 by Noguchi Jun, president of the Japan Nitrogenous Fertilizer Company (JNFC), of a large subsidiary, the Chōsen Nitrogenous Fertilizer Company (Chōsen Chisso) in South Hamgyong Province. As Barbara Molony has observed, since Noguchi was generally obliged by the Government-General to reserve one-half to two-thirds of his power at each facility for public use, his projects gradually made coal-based thermoelectric plants obsolete and gave Chōsen's industry an enormous source of inexpensive electricity.[10]

All this notwithstanding, one must be careful not to overstate the extent of industrialization that took place in the 1920s. Noguchi's first plants, for example, did not begin operation until 1930, and their full impact was not felt until later in that decade. Throughout the 1920s, moreover, as throughout the colonial period, economic changes and problems in the metropole had a direct, and often profound, influence on Chōsen's economy, as well as on the Government-General's economic policies. Between the end of World War I and the Manchurian Incident of 1931, Japan experienced a series of social and economic

[7] Soon Won Park, "The Emergence of a Factory Labor Force in Colonial Korea: A Case Study of the Onoda Cement Factory" (Ph.D. dissertation, Harvard University, 1985), pp. 19–22.

[8] Takafusa Nakamura, *Economic Growth in Prewar Japan*, trans. Robert A. Feldman (New Haven: Yale University Press, 1983), p. 152.

[9] Park, "Emergence," p. 37.

[10] Barbara Molony, *Technology and Investment: The Prewar Japanese Chemical Industry* (Cambridge, Mass.: Council on East Asian Studies, Harvard University, 1990), pp. 156–73.

crises beginning with the rice riots of 1918 and continuing through the 1920s with a stock-market panic and postwar recession, the great Kantō earthquake of 1923, the financial crisis of 1927, and, finally, the onset of the Depression in 1929. All of these events reverberated deeply in Korea, constraining economic, and especially industrial, growth in the colony.

Of particular importance were the rice riots of 1918, which occurred just as Chōsen's rulers were beginning to take a more liberal view of the colony's industrial development. In response to the riots, the immediate cause of which had been the inflation and spiraling rice prices of the war years, the new Government-General that took office in 1920 announced an ambitious thirty-year program to increase the colony's rice production through a variety of improvements, including higher-quality seeds, extensive use of fertilizers, better methods of cultivation, and enhanced irrigation facilities. While the government never returned to the anti-industrial stance of the Company Law era, the plan to increase rice production was a clear signal that the colony's official priorities and funds would continue to be concentrated on agriculture for the foreseeable future. As it turned out, the plan was abandoned in 1933, only thirteen years later, after Japan began to experience an overproduction of rice and irate Japanese landlords started demanding that the Japanese government protect them against the inundation of cheap rice from Chōsen and Taiwan. Throughout the 1920s, however, the plan remained the centerpiece of the Government-General's economic policy, and it was not until the 1930s that Chōsen's industry began to come into its own.[11] But the industrialization of the 1930s had less to do with rice policies than with the imperial concerns and ambitions of the Japanese army.

THE MANCHURIAN CONNECTION

In Korea's colonial history, as on colonial maps, the main roads often lead to Manchuria. To be sure, the Manchurian connection was not the only factor in the industrialization of the 1930s. The worldwide depression that buffeted Japan at the beginning of the decade led the Japanese government in 1931 to pass the Major Industries Control Law, which instituted industrial cartels controlling production, sales, and pricing. This, together with the passage or strengthening in the 1920s of various pieces of social legislation like the Factory Laws, encouraged a number of large Japanese firms to establish subsidiaries in Korea, where electric

[11] Andrew J. Grajdanzev, *Modern Korea* (New York: International Secretariat, Institute of Pacific Relations, 1944), pp. 92–93.

power and labor were both abundant and cheap, and, more to the point, where neither the Control Law nor the Factory Laws were in effect. From about 1933 the colony thus saw a remarkable growth of modern, large-scale enterprises in such areas as processed food, cement, fertilizer, and above all textiles. It was during this period, for example, that many of the great Japanese spinning mills like Kanebō and Tōyōbō first set up operations on the peninsula, and the region stretching from Seoul (then called Kyŏngsŏng or Keijō) to In'chon, encompassing the suburb of Yŏngdŭngp'o, began to take on the industrial character that it has retained down to the present day.[12] Such changes in the colony's economy were the subject of a detailed report, secret at the time, by the Bank of Chōsen in 1935. The report cataloged the recent rapid prolif-eration of large-scale industrial firms and noted their connections with new business groups like Noguchi's, as well as with old *zaibatsu* like Mitsui and Mitsubishi.[13]

Still, the significance of Manchuria looms large in this period. Chō-sen's business community greeted the Japanese invasion of Manchuria in 1931 with nothing short of euphoria. In May 1932, only two months after the new state of Manchukuo had been proclaimed, the Chōsen Business Club, an elite fraternity of Japanese and Korean entrepreneurs and officials, sponsored a major symposium at the Chōsen Hotel on the promotion of trade with Manchuria. A month later the Keijō Chamber of Commerce and Industry invited Government-General officials from the Bureau of Industry to its general meeting "in order to solicit their opinions on [the question of] export trade with Manchuria—[a subject that is] at present the focus of attention of people in commerce and industry throughout the country."[14] And from 1932 on, each annual commemoration of the Manchurian Incident on September 18 elicited panegyrics from businessmen that were later published in the leading business journals.[15]

Such enthusiasm for Manchuria on the part of Chōsen's businessmen was not misplaced. Between 1929 and 1939 Korea's foreign trade, ex-cluding trade with Japan, increased by nearly eight times, from ¥35 million to ¥269 million. Most of this trade involved exports to Man-

[12] Jerome B. Cohen, *Japan's Economy in War and Reconstruction* (Minneapolis: University of Minnesota Press, 1949), pp. 10–11; Eckert, *Offspring of Empire*, pp. 176, 191–92; Park, "Emergence," pp. 49–57.

[13] Chōsen Ginkō Chōsaka, *Saikin Chōsen ni okeru daikōgyō yakushin to sono shihon keitō* [The recent rapid advance and capital connections of large-scale industry in Chōsen], Research Report no. 16 (March 1935).

[14] "Zaikai henpen" [Business notes], *Chōsen jitsugyō kurabu* 10 (1932) 32.

[15] Eckert, *Offspring of Empire*, p. 169.

churia: 77 percent of the total in 1933, 63 percent in 1937, and 76 percent in 1939. As the Bank of Chōsen's 1935 report indicated, companies like Kanebō and Tōyōbō were, in fact, coming to Korea in the 1930s not only to escape restrictions in the metropole but also to exploit the vast new Manchurian market that had been opened up by Japanese military forces. Within a year after the incident at Mukden, Korea's cotton cloth exports to countries other than Japan surged upward by more than 500 percent. By 1938, when cotton cloth sales to yen bloc countries were restricted to increase the inflow of foreign exchange, the exports had increased again by two-and-a-half times.[16]

The private sector's interest in Manchuria was more than matched by a similar interest on the part of the colonial authorities. Indeed, Chōsen's rulers had long shown a certain orientation toward the north in many of their key economic policies and activities. Spearheading much of this effort in the early years had been the Bank of Chōsen. An imperial ordinance in 1917 had made the bank's notes the sole legal tender in the Kwantung Leased Territory, and by the early 1920s the bank was doing more business in Manchuria than in Korea. As noted above, the Government-General itself, the bank's primary shareholder, was also keenly interested in the Manchurian market, and in 1917 sent a quasi-official fact-finding mission there and to north and central China to explore the possibility of developing economic ties with the region. The mission's report emphasized the importance of Chōsen's unique geographical position as a link between Japan and the Asian continent, a theme that was subsequently taken up by businessmen and bureaucrats at a major conference on Chōsen's economic policy convoked by the Government-General in 1921. From very early on the peninsula's official development policy was thus closely connected with a vision of Japanese economic expansion on the Asian mainland.[17]

After 1931 the Government-General's interest in Manchuria expanded exponentially, and Chōsen's rulers were eager to further ties between the new state and the colony. Indeed, even before the state of Manchukuo had been formally established, the colonial authorities had already sent a mission there to gather information. Soon thereafter the Government-General began to set up official trade agencies in Manchukuo's major centers to expedite "the advance of Chōsen commerce and industry into Manchuria and Mongolia."[18] In February 1933 the

---

[16] Ibid., pp. 171–72. Chōsen Ginkō Chōsaka, *Saikin Chōsen ni okeru daikōgyō yakushin*, p. 1.

[17] Eckert, *Offspring of Empire*, pp. 44–45.

[18] "Zaikai henpen," *Chōsen jitsugyō kurabu* 10 (1932): 40.

quasi-official Chōsen Trade Association was formed with government financial assistance specifically to promote trade between the colony and its northern neighbor. In 1936 the Government-General held another comprehensive conference on colonial economic policy, the first since 1921, in which trade with Manchuria, including transit trade, was a major topic of discussion. Among other things, the report of the conference called for the establishment of free ports in key northern transit cities like Ch'ŏngjin, Najin, Unggi, and Chinnamp'o. The Government-General also pledged itself to work with the Manchurian authorities to restructure and reduce existing tariffs between Chōsen and Manchukuo.[19]

Trade with Manchuria was taking on added significance for Japanese businessmen and officials during the 1930s as a result of an increasingly critical, even hostile, reaction on the part of many foreign countries to Japan's growing ascendancy in international commerce, especially in textiles. In 1936, for example, only about two months before the Government-General's conference on economic policy, the president of the American Cotton Textile Institute had described Japanese imports as a "genuine menace" to American industry. Such views were becoming widespread in the United States and Europe and were contributing to a growing international drift toward protectionism and regional autarky.[20] In Japan as well, by the middle of the decade the idea of coordinating and integrating the three economies of Japan, Chōsen, and Manchukuo within a Japan-Manchukuo Bloc (Nichiman ittai) was becoming a common motif in bureaucratic parlance and policy. It was, in fact, the keynote of the 1936 Government-General conference on economic policy, which proposed in its report that industrial development in Korea be geared toward "a closer integration of the Japanese and Manchurian economies" in order for Japan "to achieve a victorious position in the international economic war."[21]

Trade, however, was not the only concern of the Government-General officials who were promoting regional economic integration in the 1930s. Manchuria had long been regarded by the Japanese army as the first line of defense against a possible attack from the Soviet Union or, secondarily, China, and economic planning and development were generally deemed in army circles to be functions of military aims and strategy. Chōsen's governors-general, all but one of whom between 1910 and 1945 were prominent army officers, tended to share these views,

---

[19] Eckert, Offspring of Empire, p. 168.

[20] Ibid., p. 138.

[21] Chōsen Sōtokufu, Chōsen Sangyō Keizai Chōsakai shimon tōshinsho [The final report of the Commission on the Industry and Economy of Chōsen] (Keijō, October 1936), p. 1.

and economic development and military goals often overlapped in the Korean context long before the second Sino-Japanese War. Even Governor-General Saitō, whose career had been in the navy, was not unsympathetic to the army's perspective. As Kobayashi Hideo has pointed out, Saitō's encouragement of Noguchi in the 1920s to develop Chōsen's hydroelectric resources was closely related to perceived continental military needs at the time.[22]

After the Manchurian Incident the army came to play an ever more powerful role in the Japanese government. Economic policy, in turn, became increasingly tied to military aims and strategy, as evidenced by an approximately 20 percent rise in the military component of the Japanese budget between 1931 and 1936. By 1936 the military accounted for nearly half of the country's total expenditures, and the Japanese were living in what was referred to at the time as a "semi-wartime" economy.[23] In Chōsen, the two governors-general who ruled during this period, Ugaki Kazushige (1931–36) and Minami Jirō (1936–42), were apt symbols of the militarization of policymaking. From the beginning both had supported the Kwantung Army's position during the Manchurian Incident, Ugaki as Chōsen's governor-general, and Minami as minister of war, and both were strong advocates of greater industrialization on the peninsula as part of a larger continental military policy.

Building on Saitō's work in the 1920s but going far beyond it, Ugaki promoted industrialization more than any of his predecessors, and encouraged the large influx of Japanese private capital mentioned above with protective tariffs, subsidies, and other inducements. He became a special patron to Noguchi Jun, whose continuing development of the electrochemical industry in the northern part of the peninsula meshed perfectly with Ugaki's own sense of Chōsen's economic importance to the Kwantung Army.

Minami, like Ugaki, also offered economic incentives to private investors, including low-interest financing, expanded limits on company bond issues, assistance in the expropriation of land for industrial use, and generous tax rates. Having spent two years as commanding general of the Kwantung Army before being appointed governor-general, moreover, Minami was, if anything, even more in sympathy with the army's needs than Ugaki. As in his closing remarks at the Government-

---

[22] Alvin D. Coox, *Nomonhan: Japan Against Russia, 1939* (Stanford: Stanford University Press, 1985), pp. 9–11; Michael A. Barnhart, *Japan Prepares for Total War: The Search for Economic Security, 1919–1941* (Ithaca, N.Y.: Cornell University Press, 1987), pp. 22–49; Eckert, *Offspring of Empire*, p. 116; Kobayashi Hideo, *Daitōa kyōeiken no keisei to hōkai* [The rise and fall of the Greater East Asia Co-Prosperity Sphere] (Tokyo: Ochanomizu shobō, 1975), p. 88.

[23] Cohen, *Japan's Economy in War and Reconstruction*, pp. 5, 9.

General's conference on economic policy in 1936, he repeatedly emphasized the need to coordinate economic planning among Japan, Chōsen, and Manchukuo for the sake of national defense. To make his point he sometimes compared the tripartite relationship to a living body in which Japan was the torso (*dōtai*), Chōsen the arm (*ude*), and Manchukuo the fist (*kobushi*). It was an analogy that epitomized the personality and vision of the man who presided over Chōsen's industrial development in the late 1930s.[24]

INDUSTRIALIZATION FOR WAR

In July 1937, with the incident at the Marco Polo Bridge and the eventual war in China, what had been at first a heuristic metaphor in time took on the character of an urgent mission. When Minami had spoken of Chōsen playing the "arm" to Manchukuo's "fist," he had been envisioning a wartime role for the colony in which Chōsen would serve as an economic provisioner to the Japanese army on the continent, both directly, through the development of its own industries, and indirectly, as a transit station for Japanese goods. The metaphor was translated into policy at a Government-General conference in September 1938, where Chōsen was officially designated as an "advance military supply base" (*zenshin heitan kichi*) and the government laid plans for a rapid development of military-related industries, including light metals (aluminum and magnesium), coal, oil and its substitutes, ammonium sulfate, explosives, machine tools, motor vehicles, railroad rolling stock, ships, leather, mining equipment, and even aircraft. To ensure funding and implementation of its war goals, the Government-General gradually instituted an extensive system of financial and other economic controls, including rationing, that paralleled measures also in effect in Japan itself, and a special economic police force was set up in November 1938 to enforce these.[25]

Perhaps because of a scarcity of paper and the urgencies of war, the official economic statistics after 1938, and especially after 1941, are less systematic and comprehensive than for earlier periods. Nevertheless, the trend after 1930 and through the "semiwar" and war years is clear: war and the preparation for war dramatically changed Chōsen's economic structure, transforming the peninsula into a semi-industrialized

[24] Eckert, *Offspring of Empire*, pp. 72, 115–16. See also Coox, *Nomonhan*, pp. 12–13, 34, 47, 58; and James B. Crowley, *Japan's Quest for Autonomy: National Security and Foreign Policy, 1930–1938* (Princeton, N.J.: Princeton University Press, 1966), pp. 87–90, 123, 126.

[25] Eckert, *Offspring of Empire*, pp. 77, 114–17, 107–8. See also Chōsen Sōtokufu, *Shisei sanjūnen* [Thirty years of administration] (Keijō, 1940), pp. 507–8.

outpost of empire. In 1921 total industrial production amounted to only slightly more than ¥200 million. Nearly a decade later it was still under ¥300 million. By 1937, however, it had shot up to almost ¥1 billion, and by 1943 it had exceeded ¥2 billion. In 1921 industrial production had accounted for only 15 percent of the colony's total economic output. During the war years it climbed to almost 40 percent, and the number of factories increased by a factor of two-and-a-half between 1936 and 1943, from about six thousand to nearly fifteen thousand.[26] By the early 1940s, there were some areas of industry where Chōsen could even rival Japan itself. A yearbook from 1943, for example, described the Chōsen Oil Company in Wonsan, established in 1935 and later expanded during the war, as "not only the king of the peninsula's oil world but . . . in fact a contender for first place in Japan's oil industry."[27]

The nature of industrial production also changed as a result of the war. Before the 1930s, and even as late as 1935, light industries such as textiles, food, ceramics, lumber, and printing predominated. While many of these industries continued to flourish after 1937 by adapting their production to specific war needs, by 1940 it was heavy industries like chemicals, machines and tools, metals, gas, and electrical products that had moved into first place. Of these, chemical plants, so crucial to the war effort, accounted for the bulk (about 37 percent) of production, but the machine and tool industry also saw considerable growth during the war. Although machines and tools still represented only about 6 percent of total industrial production in 1943, that figure nevertheless signified a 300 percent expansion since 1936. The industry's self-sufficiency quotient also more than doubled between 1939 and 1944, climbing from about 25 to 52 percent.[28]

By 1945 the physical landscape of the country had been noticeably altered. Where once there had been only rice fields, there were now also factories and clusters of factories, especially in South Hamgyŏng and Kyŏnggi, the two most industrialized provinces in the country. The bulk of heavy industry was concentrated in South Hamgyŏng, near the port of Wŏnsan and, even more, around Hŭngnam, the site of Chōsen Chisso. When Noguchi had founded the company in the late 1920s, Hŭngnam had been a tiny fishing village of about forty households. By

[26] Chosŏn Ŭnhaeng Chosabu, *Chosŏn kyŏngje yŏnbo, 1948* [Choson economic yearbook, 1948] (Seoul, 1948), p. I-99.

[27] Ogura Masatarō, ed., *Chōsen sangyō nenpō, 1943* [Chōsen industrial yearbook, 1943] (Keijō: Tōyō keizai shinpōsha, 1943), p. 114.

[28] Sang-Chul Suh, *Growth and Structural Changes in the Korean Economy, 1910–1940* (Cambridge, Mass.: Council on East Asian Studies, Harvard University Press, 1978), p. 106; *Chosŏn kyŏngje yŏnbo*, 1948, pp. I-100, I-105.

the end of the war, Chōsen Chisso had spawned twenty-eight subsidiaries, Hŭngnam's population had risen to 180,000, and the surrounding area had become the center of a sprawling electrochemical complex. Other industrialized regions in the north included the areas around the ports of Ch'ŏngjin and Sŏngjin in North Hamgyŏng, and the environs of Chinnamp'o, the port city of P'yŏngyang.[29]

While there was little heavy industry in the south, most of the food, printing, woodwork, and textile companies were located there, and during the war it became the hub of the machine and tool industry as well, accounting for more than 70 percent of the industry's total production in 1940. Of particular importance was the Kyŏngsŏng-Inch'ŏn area of Kyŏnggi province mentioned above. This region underwent further industrialization during the war, and by 1939 its products by themselves represented nearly 30 percent of Chōsen's total industrial output, including about 32 percent of the colony's textiles and over 50 percent of its machines and tools.[30] The war effort also reached outside the capital region to bring significant economic change to other southern cities and provinces as well. The city of Taegu was a case in point. Located on the main railway route between Pusan, Kyŏngsŏng, and Sinŭiju, it had long been an important provincial administrative and commercial city, but it was not until the second Sino-Japanese War that it began to function as an industrial center. Between 1937 and 1941 both its industrial production and the number of its factories increased by more than 600 percent, and its industrial work force more than doubled, from about 4,300 to 10,000.[31]

The Question of Social Change

The purely economic, statistical story of Chōsen's military-oriented industrialization in the 1930s is well documented and generally undisputed. The story of the effects of the war and the industrialization on Korean society is, by contrast, little researched and highly controversial. Many Korean scholars writing in the postcolonial era have tended to discount the socioeconomic significance of the 1930s—indeed, of the entire colonial period—on the grounds that the Korean people, except for a small group of collaborators, neither participated in nor benefited

[29] Himeno Minoru, Chōsen keizai zuhyō [The Chōsen economy in graphs] (Keijō: Chōsen tōkei kyōkai, 1943), p. 278; Chosŏn kyŏngje yŏnbo, 1948, p. I-101; Molony, Technology and Investment, pp. 168–69. Park, "Emergence," pp. 52–54.

[30] Masahisa Kōji, "Sangyō tōshi to shite no Keijō no genzai oyobi shōrai" [The present and future of Seoul as an industrial city], Chōsen, September 1941, pp. 32–33.

[31] Taegu Sisa P'yonch'an Wiwonhoe, Taegu sisa, 3 vols. (Taegu: Taegu Si, 1973), 2:260–64.

from the economic development that took place. On the contrary, the Koreans, according to this view, were largely victims of such development, either as persecuted nationalists fighting the expansion of Japanese power, or simply as unwilling but helpless victims crushed by the juggernaut of militarism and war. Colonial industrialization, in a word, was basically a Japanese phenomenon, something imposed by alien overlords that had little if anything to do with Koreans or Korean history.

Consider, for example, the assessment of the period in the 1948 economic yearbook published by the Bank of Chosŏn, the first such journal to appear in Korea after the Liberation in 1945. After describing in quantitative terms the remarkable "leaps" that industry made in the 1930s, the authors of the yearbook conclude by saying that "although Chōsen's industrialization represented one facet in the development of Japanese capitalism, it did not signify the development of the Korean national economy." Here, in succinct and unequivocal terms, is the leitmotif of most Korean-language scholarship on colonial industrialization written in the past four decades.[32]

In one sense this interpretation can scarcely be questioned. In promoting industrialization the colonial authorities were not primarily concerned with the welfare of the Korean people, and they were certainly not committed to the development of an independent Korean national economy. Their chief concern, especially after 1937, was rather with carrying out what Governor-General Minami referred to as "total war" (sōgō kokuryoku sen). As Mark Peattie and Michael Barnhart have pointed out, this was a concept that emerged from the Japanese army's studies of World War I and gradually came to play a prominent role in the army's strategic planning in the 1930s. It stressed the need in modern warfare not only for well-trained soldiers and effective weapons but also for a complete, coordinated mobilization of the country's economic and human resources. As Minami himself put it in 1938: "With the Great War as a turning point, the essence of modern warfare has consisted in concentrating on the maintenance of national defense by integrating the entire strength of the country. [This] is so-called total war. The main principle of total war is simply to combine these two forces, the spiritual power of the nation and the economic power of the nation. In the end, both the spiritual power of the nation and the integration of materials come down to human factors and material factors. [We] can therefore enhance the effectiveness of general mobilization here by suf-

---

[32] *Chosŏn kyŏngje yŏnbo, 1948*, p. I-99. For a sampling of the Korean-language historiography, see Kang Man'gil, *Han'guk hyŏndae sa* [A history of modern Korea] (Seoul: Ch'angjak kwa Pip'yŏng Sa, 1984), pp. 113-34.

ficiently bringing the power of government to bear on these two factors with proper, strong, and clear authority."[33]

Minami's comments underscored the essentially utilitarian perspective from which the army tended to regard the people over whom it ruled, whether in Chōsen or in Japan itself. In Chōsen, moreover, such arrogance of power was compounded by another element: an ingrained, often unconscious, racism, which lay at the heart of much of the discrimination and exploitation from which Koreans suffered after the annexation in 1910. During the eight, ultimately desperate, years of total war, the attitude of Minami and his successors led to numerous excesses, including the conscription of large numbers of Koreans for virtual slave labor in Japan and other parts of the empire, and the adoption by the Government-General of a policy of coercive assimilation that aimed at the obliteration of Korean cultural consciousness.[34]

That Korean scholars balk at the thought of assigning historical value to a period that encompassed such horrors is understandable. But history is seldom, if ever, uniformly progressive. On the contrary, it is always complex, never sentimental, and more often than not laced with irony. Such ironies abound in the 1930s. To ignore them and attempt to compress the complexity of the period into a simple historiographical paradigm of victimization and nationalist struggle is to do injustice both to the reality and the discipline of history, as well as to the ability and ingenuity of the Koreans themselves.

It is time to consider the possibility of other paradigms, not to contradict so much as to complement the existing historiography. Throughout their long history the Koreans have shown a remarkable,

[33] Chōsen Sōtokufu, *Chōsen sōtokufu jikyoku taisaku chōsakai kaigiroku* [Proceedings of the Chōsen Government-General commission on policy for the current situation] (Keijō, September 1938), pp. 9–10. See also Mark R. Peattie, *Ishiwara Kanji and Japan's Confrontation with the West* (Princeton, N.J.: Princeton University Press, 1975), pp. 49–83, 185–222; Barnhart, *Japan Prepares for Total War,* pp. 22–49; and Crowley, *Japan's Quest for Autonomy,* pp. 87–91.

[34] See Eckert, *Offspring of Empire,* pp. 229, 235–39. See also Chong-Sik Lee, *Japan and Korea: The Political Dimension* (Stanford: Hoover Institution Press, 1985), pp. 13–20. Recently discovered Japanese army reports from China during the war confirm that the army also drafted thousands of young women in the empire and occupied areas, including girls as young as twelve, to serve the sexual needs of Japanese combat troops and officers. About 80 percent of these girls, euphemistically called "comfort women" at the time, came from Korea. See George Hicks, *The Comfort Women: Sex Slaves of the Japanese Imperial Forces* (n.p. [Australia]: Allen and Unwin, 1995); Shim Jae Hoon, "Haunted by the Past," *Far Eastern Economic Review,* February 6, 1992, p. 20; *Korea Newsreview,* January 18, 1992, p. 34 and January 25, 1992, pp. 5–7. See also Saburō Inenaga, *The Pacific War: A Critical Perspective on Japan's Role in World War II* (New York: Pantheon Books, 1978), pp. 158–59, and Meiron and Susie Harries, *Soldiers of the Sun: The Rise and Fall of the Imperial Japanese Army* (New York: Random House, 1991), pp. 235–36, 244–45, 409.

indeed magnificent, capacity to adjust, survive, and often flourish under the influence or domination of larger foreign powers. The late colonial period was no exception. For the great majority of the population, the hope of independence, so compelling at the time of the March 1 movement in 1919, gradually faded with the growth of Japanese military power and was hardly more than a distant memory by the 1930s. Except perhaps for a minority of dedicated and politically active nationalists, few Koreans were able to envision the end of Japanese rule until it was suddenly and unexpectedly upon them in 1945. Colonialism and militarism, on the other hand, were everyday facts of life to which one had to adapt in order to get on with the business of living. Depending on personal background, inclination, and talent, most Koreans naturally seized whatever opportunities for advancement were available in the colonial system. Ironically, it was the 1930s that opened the door of opportunity as never before. War preparation and total war not only brought industrialization to the peninsula, but in doing so, it also propelled, and in some cases initiated, a process of social change in Korea that has continued down to the present.

WORKERS AND TECHNICIANS

In 1933 the Chōsen Industrial Bank reported that the colony's total number of wage workers (rōdōsha) in manufacturing, mining, transport, construction, and other industries was about 214,000. Ten years later, in 1943, the Government-General informed the eighty-fifth session of the Imperial Diet in Tokyo that the number of workers in these same industries was 1.75 million, an increase of more than 800 percent. Most of these workers, nearly 400,000 of whom were in the manufacturing sector, were Korean: even in 1936, before the war, the number of Japanese workers accounted for only slightly more than 11 percent of the total, and by 1943 this figure had dropped to about 7 percent. Case studies of individual companies, moreover, have confirmed this huge expansion of Korean labor in the 1930s and early 1940s. In 1930, when Noguchi Jun opened his first factory in Hŭngnam, his workers numbered only about 3,000. By 1944 his companies were employing over 55,000 people, and the great majority of them, between 63 and 88 percent depending on the individual enterprise, were Korean. War and industrialization had clearly been effective in pulling Koreans out of the rice fields and into the cities and factories.[35]

---

[35] An Pyŏngjik, "Nihon Chisso ni okeru Chōsenjin rōdōsha kaikyū no seichō ni kansuru kenkyū" [A study of the growth of the Korean working class in the Japan Nitrogenous Fertilizer Company], Chōsen shi kenkyūkai ronbunshū [Collected essays of the Chō-

Such growth notwithstanding, most Korean historians have been re-luctant to acknowledge any qualitative advance in labor development during the colonial period. They have argued, instead, that racial preju-dice and discrimination by Japanese employers tended to keep Korean workers at unskilled levels in the workplace, and that the wartime mo-bilization of Korean workers was essentially "spurious," a temporary swelling of numbers that did little to improve the caliber of the work force and left no important legacy for the postcolonial period.[36]

Actual empirical research on individual companies and industries, es-pecially the work of Soon Won Park and a group of Korean and Japa-nese scholars under the guidance of Professor An Pyŏngjik at Seoul National University, casts doubt on this interpretation. The contention, first of all, that the experience of unskilled workers in modern industrial settings contributed little or nothing to the development of a profes-sional work force simply does not stand up to either logic or evidence. Throughout the last fifteen or so years of colonial rule, for example, tens of thousands of Korean construction workers were employed over considerable periods of time by Noguchi Jun and others to build large-scale plants and factories. In the case of the Pujŏn hydroelectric facility alone, Noguchi used over eleven thousand Koreans from South Ham-gyŏng and neighboring provinces. Although they were hired on a con-tractual basis for the project's duration rather than as regular em-ployees, and received no systematic training, their primary work experience nevertheless involved them in the routine and discipline of modern industry, and, as Professor An suggests, they were in that sense at least one step removed from the Korean peasants who performed only seasonal nonagricultural work to supplement their incomes, if they left the agricultural sector at all.[37]

Regular factory workers, however unskilled, were, of course, even

---

sen History Research Society], no. 25 (Tokyo: Ryokuin shobō, 1988), pp. 160–61, 163–64; "Singminji Choson ui koyong kujo e kwanhan yon'gu" [A study of the employment structure in colonial Choson], in *Kŭndae Chosŏn ui kyŏngje kujo* [The economic structure of modern Chosŏn] ed. An Pyŏngjik, Yi Taegŭn, Nakamura Tetsu, and Kajimura Hideki, (Pibong Ch'ulp'an Sa, 1989), p. 397.

[36] See Soon Won Park, "The First Generation of Korean Skilled Workers: The Onoda Cement Sunghori Factory," *Journal of Korean Studies*, 7 (1990): 56. One finds a similar perspective among some Japanese scholars interested in colonial Korea. See, for example, Hashitani Hiroshi, "1930–40 nendai no Chōsen shakai no seikaku o megutte" [Concern-ing the character of Chōsen society in the 1930s and 1940s], *Chōsen shi kenkyūkai ron-bunshō*, no. 27 (March 1990), pp. 132–33. Hashitani's article is actually an attempt to present a more balanced view of the colonial legacy than is generally found in the existing Japanese-language historiography, but he is unwilling to attribute any fundamental "qual-itative" change in Korean society to the wartime industrialization of 1937–45, despite what he describes as an "overwhelming quantitative" change in the industrial structure and, I would add, despite evidence to the contrary in his own article. See below, n. 51.

[37] An, "Nihon Chisso," pp. 165–69.

further removed from the world of the peasant. It appears, moreover, that despite the realities of racial prejudice and discrimination, significant numbers of Korean workers were in fact able to rise to factory positions of skill and responsibility, especially during the latter half of the colonial period. Once again the war was a key factor, but it is also true that before the war—indeed, from the annexation onward—many Japanese employers, at least in the large-scale facilities, seem to have recognized their dependence on an experienced Korean labor force and taken various steps to ensure that they would always have one. In hiring they tended to select those applicants who gave the best promise of developing into skilled workers, and the new recruits were then generally put through a training program in which they progressed from novices to apprentices to full-fledged regular workers (honshokkō). Although they were generally paid at a considerably lower rate than Japanese employees, who were generally more highly skilled, and were paid at the higher rates prevalent in Japan itself, the Korean workers, like the Japanese, were also rewarded and encouraged to remain at the factory through an elaborate incentive system of bonuses and pensions.[38]

It was war, however, that ultimately led to improvement in the quality and status of the Korean workers. As the conflict in China wore on and eventually spread to the Pacific, not only did the need for skilled workers in the factories increase; Japanese employers were also forced to turn to Koreans to fill posts that were being vacated by Japanese workers who were being drafted into the army. This was particularly necessary after November 1941, when a full-scale conscription program was put into effect in Japan, but there is evidence of Koreans gradually replacing Japanese in the workplace even before that date. According to the personnel records of the Onoda Cement Company in Sunghori, for example, the proportion of Japanese regular workers—those who had been through the factory's three-year training program—declined by 4 percentage points between 1935 and 1941, while the proportion of Korean regular workers rose by exactly the same percentage. Even greater and more important was the drop in the proportion of Japanese novices and apprentices at the factory during this period, 19 percent and 6 percent respectively, with again a corresponding increase in the proportion of Koreans in those categories.[39] One sees a similar phenomenon reflected in the JNFC's reports on its various subsidiaries in Hŭngnam. Again the respective increase and decrease in the relative proportion of Koreans and Japanese in the work force was about 10 percent between 1935 and 1938.[40]

---

[38] Park, "First Generation," pp. 62–82.
[39] See chart, ibid., p. 68.
[40] See chart in An, "Nihon Chisso," p. 160.

To be sure, the colonial system imposed unspoken limits, even during the war, on how high a native might climb in the factory organization, and the gains by Korean skilled workers during the war years came mainly at the lower levels of the hierarchy. They were by no means confined to the lower levels, however, and even there the results were noteworthy. In the internal reports of the JNFC, for example, the company's workers in Chōsen were divided into three major groups. At the bottom were the novices and apprentices. Above them were the regular or "ordinary" (*futsū*) workers, who, in turn, were divided into three categories, "second," "first," and "superior," depending on their experience and skills. Finally, at the very top were the shop managers (*yakuzuki kōin*), including the foremen. As one would expect, the majority of the Korean workers in each company fell into the apprenticeship class and the lower two levels of the regular worker group. Nevertheless, in most cases between about 12 and 20 percent of the Koreans were also listed as superior regular workers, and between 1 and 6 percent were included in the *yakuzuki* class. These figures are basically in accord with a general study of Korean skilled workers published in 1943, although slightly higher, and may therefore be seen as representative.[41]

The war also fostered the development of a small class of Korean engineers or technicians (*gijutsusha*). Before the 1930s the colonial authorities had shown little interest in developing Chōsen's technological base beyond a rudimentary level, and even as late as 1936 there was still only one professional industrial school of college rank in the country. In the semiwar atmosphere of the mid-1930s, however, the Government-General launched a program to upgrade the colony's vocational and technical education at all levels, from elementary schools to Keijō Imperial University, and some progress was made in this regard in the next decade. Nevertheless, it was still far from sufficient to meet the growing demand for engineers, and most Koreans wishing to pursue an advanced technical career had to supplement the relatively limited education they could receive in Chōsen with study in Japan.[42]

Because of inconsistencies in the relevant documents, not the least of which is the definition of *gijutsusha*, it is virtually impossible to arrive at a precise assessment of the increase of Korean engineers during the war. That a significant increase did occur, however, is clear. Of the various sources available, the official census data appear to embrace the broadest definition of "engineer," and therefore present the most dramatic picture. According to this information, in the four years between 1940 and

[41] See charts ibid., pp. 176–77. See also An, "Singminji Choson," p. 406.

[42] Eckert, *Offspring of Empire*, pp. 144–46; An, "Singminji Choson," p. 423. See also Chōsen Sōtokufu, *Chōsen Sangyō Keizai Chōsakai shimon toshinsho*, pp. 57–60.

1944, when the last census was taken, the number of Korean engineers multiplied by a factor of three, from a little more than 9,000 to nearly 28,000. Such a figure was all the more extraordinary in that it represented more than twice the number of Japanese engineers recorded for that year. Other official sources tell a more modest, but still impressive, story. One, a 1943 report on Chōsen labor and technology, defined "engineers" as managers in industry, mining, transport, and other areas of business who were involved in a practical application of their technical knowledge; people who were engaged in such things as design, construction estimates and inspection, machine and tool work, medical treatment, hygiene, and research; and, finally, anyone who supervised such work. According to this report, the total number of engineers in the country was about 20,000, over 32 percent of whom were Korean. Similar reports from 1941 and 1942 support this estimate with figures, respectively, of 30 and 32 percent.[43]

The level of sophistication of the Korean engineers is also difficult to determine, although, as Professor An has suggested on the basis of the available educational statistics, it was in general almost certainly lower than that of the Japanese engineers in Chōsen. As in their attitude toward skilled Korean factory workers, Japanese policymakers and employers tended to see the function of Korean engineers primarily as one of assisting a core of highly trained Japanese engineers and as replacing or supplementing Japanese of equivalent education and experience at lower and middle levels of work.

Nevertheless, the general educational level of the Korean engineers should not be disparaged. It was no mean thing for a Korean during the colonial period to obtain a middle-school diploma, which involved five additional years of study beyond the six years of elementary school, and most Korean engineers were middle-school graduates. Between 15 and 30 percent of them also went on to professional school, junior college, or university, and some of them managed to attain very high positions even within the colonial environment. One of Noguchi's chief engineers at the Pujŏn hydroelectric facility, for example, was a Korean who had graduated from Daiichi Higher Common (Middle) School in Keijō and continued his studies in electrical engineering in Tokyo before being hired first by the Tokyo Electric Company and finally by Chōsen Hydroelectric.[44]

[43] An, "Singminji Chosŏn," pp. 423–26. See also Gary Saxonhouse, "Working Koreans in Korea and Japan in the Inter-War Period," (Unpublished paper, Department of Economics, University of Michigan, 1984), pp. 56–61.

[44] An, "Singminji Chosŏn," p. 426. Chōsen Sōtokufu, *Chōsen Sangyō Keizai Chōsakai kaigiroku* [The proceedings of the Chōsen Government-General commission on Chōsen industry and economy] (Keijō, October 1936), p. 666.

ENTREPRENEURS AND OTHER MANAGERS

A common misconception persists that Chōsen was virtually bereft of native entrepreneurial or managerial talent when colonial rule came to an end in 1945. This notion is fed not only by the natural feeling of nationalist resentment that underlies much Korean scholarship on the colonial era, but also by an exclusive scholarly focus on the official statistics of paid-in industrial capital, according to which the Japanese accounted for over 90 percent of the total by the end of the colonial period.[45] Such statistics present several major problems, however, and the almost exclusive focus on essentially large-scale corporate owner-ship and capitalization obscures what was, in fact, a rather diverse and extensive Korean participation in the colonial economy.

It is important here, first of all, to keep in mind that Chōsen was a Japanese colony and that Japanese domination of the economy was therefore to be expected. From a developmental, as opposed to a na-tionalist perspective, what is surprising, even if one accepts the statistics of capitalization at face value, is not that the Korean share was so small, but rather that the Japanese authorities allowed the Koreans to have a share at all, let alone as much as 10 percent. That they did so had as much to do with politics as economics, and reflected a calculated, and ultimately successful, attempt to weaken an extremely volatile national-ist movement by dividing it along class lines.[46] Although the scope of native participation here, as in other areas of endeavor, was inevitably constrained by the circumstances of colonial rule, the Government-General never entirely blocked the rise of Korean entrepreneurs and managers, even during the war. Indeed, once again in certain respects the war proved to be an occasion of opportunity.

The figure of 10 percent does not, in fact, even begin to tell the full story of Korean involvement in the colonial economy. For one thing, the nationality of the industrial capital in the statistics was determined solely on the basis of the nationality of the various company presidents or chief executive officers. It therefore gives no indication of Korean equity participation in Japanese-run companies. It is clear, however, from other sources that such participation existed, even though a sys-tematic study of it has yet to be undertaken. Judging from the case of the textile magnate Kim Yŏnsu, for example, it would appear that the colony's bigger Korean businessmen had considerable interest and little if any difficulty in investing in Japanese companies, including some of the largest firms in both Chōsen and Manchukuo. And such activity

---

[45] See, for example, Sang-Chul Suh, *Growth and Structural Changes*, p. 110. Suh's fig-ures are taken from the *Chōson kyŏngje yŏnbo, 1948*, p. I-318.

[46] See Eckert, *Offspring of Empire*, pp. 45–49.

was not confined to the most prominent entrepreneurs. Before the 1930s, the statistics included a mixed or "joint" capital category in addition to separate categories for Japanese and Korean capital, and in 1929, the last year for which such statistics are available, over 30 percent of the total paid-in capital was listed as "joint." In colonial business directories from the 1930s, moreover, one can find numerous Koreans identified as company officers or major stockholders in Japanese companies, especially in provincial towns and cities, where the Japanese presence was smaller and perhaps less overwhelming than in Keijō.[47]

Even evaluating Korean entrepreneurial and managerial activity solely in terms of total equity share in the colony's paid-in industrial capital, however, actually excludes most of the Koreans who should be considered in any such assessment. Again from a developmental perspective, what is important here is not so much the extent of Korean investment but rather the number of Koreans who invested, many of whom, like Yi Pyŏngch'ŏl and Ku Inhoe—later the founders, respectively, of the Samsung and Lucky groups—were breaking their ties to the land and taking their first steps into the world of industrial enterprise. By this standard the statistics look very different. Over 40 percent of the number of industrial enterprises at the end of 1941 were run by Koreans. In some areas such as beverages, pharmaceuticals, and rice mills, Korean firms represented over 50 percent of the total, and even in key wartime industries like metals (together with machines and tools), chemicals, and textiles, they accounted, respectively, for about 28 percent, 30 percent, and 39 percent of the total. These figures, moreover, are only for corporations, and according to a 1941 study by the Keijō Chamber of Commerce and Industry, over 90 percent of the city's factories were unincorporated. Given their small size, most of them were probably owned and operated by Koreans.[48]

Despite wartime controls and forced amalgamations, it is evident that considerable numbers of Korean entrepreneurs continued to be active in the industrial sector well into the early 1940s if not later. Indeed, the war brought windfall profits to some of the larger firms with close connections to the Government-General like the Kyŏngsŏng Spinning and Weaving Company. But it also gave rise to numerous small companies, many of which might well have been left out of the official statistics. Soon Won Park, for example, notes that the war years saw a proliferation of small Korean-managed glycerin-processing factories to service the dynamite industry, as well as a huge clustering of Korean subcontractors for machine parts in the Kyŏngsŏng-Inch'ŏn area.[49]

---

[47] Ibid., pp. 51–56.

[48] Ibid. See also *Chosŏn kyŏngje yŏnbo, 1948*, p. I-100.

[49] Eckert, *Offspring of Empire*, pp. 122–25; Park, "Emergence," p. 54. See also Saxonhouse, "Working Koreans," pp. 28–61.

Scholars who focus their attention on the statistics of paid-in industrial capital also fail to see many other kinds of rising entrepreneurial and managerial talent in the late colonial period. The figures cited above, for example, are for the industrial sector only. They do not include the large numbers of Korean entrepreneurs who were involved in other types of business, especially commerce and finance. Although the major colonial commercial and financial institutions, especially in Keijō, were owned by Japanese, Koreans had been very active in founding small and medium trading companies and banks since around the turn of the century, and the subsequent expansion of the imperial marketplace into Manchuria and China in the 1930s created a business boom that benefited big and small businessmen alike and drew many more Koreans into these two areas. According to a Bank of Chōsen survey of Korean and joint Korean-Japanese companies throughout the business spectrum in the colony's major cities in 1941, commercial firms alone accounted for over 20 percent of the authorized capital. As in the case of the industrial sector, one also finds in the business directories of the 1930s a substantial number of Koreans listed as officers or major shareholders in trading companies headed by Japanese.[50]

Still other kinds of Korean managers can be found in the white-collar class that burgeoned in the 1930s to serve the needs of the Government-General and various quasi-official institutions like the Chōsen Industrial Bank and the Bank of Chōsen, as well as the larger Japanese companies that dominated the private sector of Chōsen's economy. Regrettably, research in this area, especially on the large Japanese companies, both private and semiprivate, has been severely hampered by the difficulty of finding or getting access to primary documents, and also by the prevailing tendency of scholars to treat such organizations simply as symbols and vehicles of imperialist exploitation.

A small but growing body of substantive empirical work, however, is beginning to make its presence felt, and it is becoming clear that more Koreans were involved in these organizations than has been commonly thought. Contrary to the conventional view, the door here was never completely closed to the native population, even at some of the higher levels, and positions in the Japanese corporate or bureaucratic world, with secure tenure, relatively good pay, and considerable prestige within the imperial milieu, attracted many of the educated Korean elite. In retrospect, these positions were clearly an important training

---

[50] Yi Han'gu, *Ilcheha Han'guk kiŏp sŏllip undong sa* [The history of efforts to establish Korean companies under Japanese imperialism] (Seoul: Ch'ŏngsa, 1989), pp. 200–201. See also Nakamura Sukeyoshi, ed., *Chōsen ginkō kaisha kumiai yōroku* [Digest of Korean banks, companies, and associations] (Keijō: Tōa Keizai Jinhō Sha, 1933), passim.

ground for many of the people who planned and implemented South Korea's industrialization in the 1960s. The bureaucratic posts were certainly no less, and possibly even more, important in this respect than the positions in the private firms, because the industrialization of the 1930s, as later in the 1960s, was led by the government and characterized by a very close interaction between the public and private spheres.[51]

Koreans had been working in these organizations, especially in the Government-General, since the beginning of the colonial period, but as we have seen in other areas, in most cases it was the war that accelerated the process of recruitment and advancement. In the main government offices in Keijō, for example, Koreans consistently occupied between 18 and 25 percent of the high (*chokunin*) ranks and between 30 and 36 percent of the junior (*hannin*) ranks of the Government-General between 1931 and 1942. Although the proportion of Koreans to Japanese officials declined by about 6 percent in this period, the number of Korean officials of both ranks increased, respectively, by 22 and 52 percent By 1942 there were nearly sixteen thousand such Korean officials in the central government.

In the provinces one sees an even more pronounced rise in the numbers of Koreans holding official posts. There, during this same period, the number of Koreans of high rank increased by 400 percent while those of junior rank grew by about 150 percent, with the most dramatic increases coming after the establishment of Manchukuo and later during the war in China. In the provinces, moreover, the proportion of Korean to Japanese officials also rose during this period, especially during the war. For the high officials the proportional change was modest, from about 2 to 4 percent, but the proportion of Korean junior officials jumped from about 18 percent to over 31 percent, with the biggest increases coming after 1939.[52]

---

[51] See Eckert, *Offspring of Empire*, pp. 103–26. Hashitani, in "1930-40 nendai no Chōsen," p. 141, argues that such Koreans cannot be regarded as "carriers of modern commerce and industry" because most of them were involved or associated in one way or another with the agricultural sector. In fact, however, the agricultural sector became highly commercialized during the colonial period, and it is likely that the work experience of Korean agricultural bureaucrats and company employees was more similar to their counterparts in commerce and industry than Hashitani suggests. By his own evidence, moreover, a considerable number of Koreans with higher education were also finding jobs in the nonagricultural sectors. On the commercialization of agriculture during the colonial period, see Eckert, *Offspring of Empire*, chap. 1; see also Im Pyŏngyun (Rimu Byonyūn), *Shokuminchi ni okeru shōgyōteki nōgyō no tenkai* [The development of commercial agriculture in the colonies] (Tokyo: Tōkyō daigaku shuppankai, 1971).

[52] *Chōsen Sōtokufu tōkei nenpō, 1931–1942* [Statistical yearbooks of the Chōsen Government-General, 1931–1942]. The conventional interpretation of these same statistics is, of

Another avenue of bureaucratic advancement for Koreans lay in the financial institutions closely affiliated with and monitored by the Government-General, particularly the Bank of Chōsen and the Chōsen Industrial Bank. Of the two, the Industrial Bank (Chōsen Shokusan Ginkō) was the more liberal in its employment and promotion of Koreans, a reflection of the attitude and policies of its chief executives, especially Aruga Mitsutoyo, who was president of the bank from 1919 to 1937. It was also more deeply and directly involved in the industrialization of the 1930s than the Bank of Chōsen, and through its extensive loans and investments became by 1945, like Noguchi's Chōsen Chisso, a kind of colonial *zaibatsu*.[53]

A detailed study of the Industrial Bank's Korean employees by Karl Moskowitz in 1979 leaves no doubt that the bank was a vital locus for upwardly mobile Korean managers throughout the colonial period. Even before the expansion of its industrial interests in the mid-1930s and the effects of conscription during the war, the bank had prided itself on cultivating its Korean employees, who had consistently comprised about a third of the bank's total managerial staff and were distributed throughout its multifaceted field of operations. Subsequent war-related industrialization and finally war itself forced the bank to broaden its Korean component even further. By 1944 the overall hiring quota for Koreans had risen to between 45 and 50 percent, and even more significantly, the Korean subquota for the higher positions in the bank rose from 20–25 to 40–45 percent. Koreans, who were not drafted until very late in the war, were clearly benefiting from the shortage of Japanese manpower in the bank. As in the case of the bureaucracy, this trend was especially strong in the bank's provincial offices, where the proportion of Koreans had always been relatively high. There, by the end of the war, Koreans came to outnumber their Japanese colleagues and in some branches had even replaced the Japanese staff entirely.[54]

In contrast to the situation in the Government-General and quasi-official institutions like the Industrial Bank, the path to managerial success for Koreans in the large Japanese private companies appears to have

---

course, negative, stressing the barriers to Korean advancement in the bureaucracy. See, for example, Wonmo Dong, "Japanese Colonial Policy and Practice in Korea, 1905–1945: A Study in Assimilation" (Ph.D. dissertation, Georgetown University, 1965), pp. 354–60.

[53] Eckert, *Offspring of Empire*, pp. 87–88, 94–96. See also Cho Kijun, *Han'guk chabonjuŭi sŏngnipsaron* [Discourses on the formative history of Korean capitalism] (Seoul: Taewangsa, [1973] 1981), pp. 444–46.

[54] Karl Moskowitz, "Current Assets: The Employees of Japanese Banks in Colonial Korea" (Ph.D. dissertation, Harvard University, 1979), pp. 270–95.

been much narrower. Whether because of discrimination, intense competition with Japanese applicants for what were clearly highly desirable jobs, or both of these factors, few Koreans seem to have been called and even fewer chosen. Professor An Pyongjik's careful study of the JNFC's employees in Chōsen, for example, shows that even as late as 1940, the number of Korean white-collar workers (*shain*) in the company's various subsidiaries was generally very small—in some cases, like that of Chōsen Chisso, as little as 1.2 percent. Unlike the situation with the Industrial Bank, moreover, in most cases the war did not lead to a higher proportion of Korean white-collar employees. In fact, the proportion declined from about 9 to about 4 percent between 1935 and 1940.

Nevertheless, it is important to note that although the proportion of Koreans to Japanese declined overall in the JNFC complex, the total *number* of Korean white-collar workers rose by 55 percent. The proportion of Koreans, moreover, did not decline in every case. At the Chōsen Mining Development Company and the Sihŭng Railroad, two other JNFC subsidiaries, the proportion of Koreans increased, and in the case of the latter, it went up by as much as 20 percent, thereby making Korean *shain* the majority by 1940.[55]

Such variations were probably due, as Professor An has noted, to differences of technological sophistication among the various subsidiaries,[56] and this, in turn, may also suggest some caution about taking the JNFC complex as representative of all large-scale private Japanese firms in Chōsen. It is possible that a major reason for the great predominance of Japanese personnel even into the war years was the company's need for technically oriented, as opposed to general, managers, whose work in a crucial war industry might well have exempted them from the draft. It is not at all unlikely that other, as yet unstudied, private Japanese companies in less technologically demanding industries like mining, railroads, and textiles, or in nonindustrial areas like commerce, may have had a pattern of Korean managerial representation that was more similar to the Chōsen Mining Development Company and Shihung Railroad, or even to the Chōsen Industrial Bank, than to the JNFC complex as a whole.[57]

[55] An, "Nihon Chisso," p. 163.

[56] Ibid., p. 164.

[57] That the number of Koreans employed by the government-run railroad system showed a remarkable increase during the war at both the general and higher levels seems to support this hypothesis. See Chŏng Chaejŏng, "Chosŏn Ch'ongdokbu Ch'ŏltoguk ŭi goyong kujo" [The employment structure of the Choson Government-General Bureau of Railways], in An Pyŏngjik et al., *Kŭndae Chosŏn ŭi kyŏngje kujo*, pp. 432–71.

SOLDIERS AND OFFICERS

Social change also took other forms in the wartime environment of the 1930s and 1940s. One tends to think of the South Korean army, for example, as a product of post-1945 American influence and the Korean War, which to a great extent it was.[58] Nevertheless, the birth of what later became the nucleus of the South Korean professional officer corps and the beginning of the militarization of South Korean society, which reached its apogee in the 1960s and 1970s under President Park Chung Hee (Pak Chŏnghŭi), can be traced back to the late colonial period.

By the end of the Chosŏn dynasty, Korea had a very long history of civilian rule, and the military, never highly regarded, appears to have fallen into desuetude. State attempts at reform failed, and after the country became a Japanese protectorate in 1905, the old army gradually disappeared. The palace guards were replaced by Japanese policemen in 1906, most of the army units were disbanded in 1907, and the army itself was officially abolished at the end of July 1909, about one year before the annexation.[59] During the first half of the colonial period an officer's career in the Japanese army seems to have been more or less beyond the realm of possibility for the average Korean. Although small numbers of Koreans had been graduating from the Japanese Military Academy in Tokyo since 1883, after 1915 the only Koreans to attend the academy were, with one exception, members of the royal family or aristocracy, including Yi Kang, the fifth son of King (later Emperor) Kojong, and Kojong's seventh son, the crown prince Yi Un.[60]

Like so much else, however, the situation here too changed in the 1930s in the wake of the Manchurian Incident. In September 1934 the Government-General for the first time instituted military training courses in all of Chōsen's higher common (middle) schools,[61] thus initiating a process of militarization that led in 1938 to the promulgation

[58] See Robert W. Sawyer, *Military Advisors in Korea: KMAG in Peace and War* (Washington: Office of the Department of Military History, Department of the Army, 1962). See also Bruce Cumings, *Origins of the Korea War, vol. 1: Liberation and the Emergence of Separate Regimes* (Princeton, N.J.: Princeton University Press, 1981), pp. 173, 175–76; Gregory Henderson, *Korea: The Politics of the Vortex* (Cambridge, Mass.: Harvard University Press, 1968), pp. 334–60.

[59] See Martina Deuchler, *Confucian Gentlemen and Barbarian Envoys: The Opening of Korea, 1875–1885* (Seattle: University of Washington Press, 1977), pp. 103–4; C. I. Eugene Kim and Kim Han-Kyo, *Korea and the Politics of Imperialism, 1876–1910* (Berkeley: University of California Press, 1967), pp. 140, 151.

[60] Yi Kidong, *Pich'am ui kunindul: Ilbon yuksa ch'ulsin ui yoksa* [Soldiers of tragedy: the history of the graduates of the Japanese Military Academy] (Seoul: Ilchogak, 1982), p. 251.

[61] Ibid.

of a voluntary system of Korean participation in the regular army and five years later to a general conscription. By the end of the Pacific War, there were nearly two hundred thousand Koreans in the Japanese army and another twenty thousand in the navy.[62]

In 1932, moreover, even before the establishment of military training courses in the schools, Japanese military officers from the Chōsen army who were attached to the schools began to urge Korean students to apply to the military academy in Japan, a recommendation that continued to be made throughout the decade and, indeed, until the end of the war. By 1945 a total of 141 Koreans had received diplomas from the academy since the late nineteenth century, and no less than half of them had graduated after 1933. As one scholar, Yi Kidong, has put it, "the number of Korean students who attended the academy in the last twelve years of Japanese imperialism was equivalent to the total number of Korean students who had attended the academy during the previous fifty years."[63]

Gaining admission to the academy was no easy matter even for Japanese, and it was particularly difficult for Koreans. In addition to having to pass comprehensive physical and written examinations, prospective Korean cadets had the added burden of having to compete with Japanese applicants, for whom Japanese was, of course, a native language, and whose education in the regular Japanese school system was generally superior to the preparation most Koreans could obtain in Chōsen. Depending on their background and resources, therefore, Koreans wishing to enter the academy in the 1930s and 1940s tended to follow one of two paths. Most, about 60 percent, applied directly to the academy in Tokyo (moved to Zama during the war) for the four-year program, which consisted of a two-year preparatory course (*yoka*) followed by a two-year regular course (*honka*).

Others with less chance of passing the exam in Japan took a more indirect route, through Manchuria.[64] The Japanese authorities in Manchukuo had planned from the beginning to set up their own military academy in the country to train officers for the Manchukuo army, but it was not until 1937 that a short-term officer candidate school, the

---

[62] Eckert, *Offspring of Empire*, pp. 244–45; Chong-Sik Lee, *Japan and Korea*, p. 13. See also Miyata Setsuko, *Chōsen minshū to "kōminka" seisaku* [Policy of making the Korean people into imperial citizens] (Tokyo: Miraisha, 1985), pp. 50–147.

[63] Yi Kidong, *Pich'am ŭi kunindŭl*, pp. 2, 42, 251. See also Suzuki Hajime, "Nihon rikugun shikan gakkō ni ryūgaku shita Dai Kan Teikoku gakusei: sono zaikō no shijitsu" [The students of the Great Han Empire who studied at the Japanese Military Academy: the historical facts regarding their attendance] *Kan* 8, no. 8 (August 1979): 3–44.

[64] Yi Kidong, *Pich'am ŭi kunindŭl*, p. 252; Suzuki Hajime, "Nihon rikugun," pp. 40–42.

Central Army Training Institute (Chūo Rikugun Kunrensho) was founded in Mukden. In 1939 this was superseded by the establishment in Hsinking of the Manchukuo Military Academy (Manshūkoku Rikugun Gunkan Gakkō), more informally known as the Dōtokudai, a regular four-year school under the supervision of the Kwantung Army with two-year *yoka* and *honka* courses modeled on the academy in Japan. Cadets were divided into two groups, a Manchukuo (*Mankei*) group, which included Koreans as well as Chinese and Mongolians, and a Japanese (*Nikkei*) group; each year the entire *Nikkei* and the top ten or so *Mankei* cadets in the *yoka* were sent to Zama to complete their final two years of *honka* as "foreign students" (*ryūgakusei*) at the Japanese Military Academy in Zama. After graduation all the cadets from the Dōtokudai, both *Nikkei* and *Mankei*, returned to the continent to serve as second lieutenants in the Manchukuo army.

The Manchukuo Military Academy and its predecessor, the Central Army Training Institute, which also sent its best students to Japan for the *honka* course, provided a doorway by which poor but bright Koreans could gain entrance to the Japanese military elite. Although after admission the Korean cadets were held to the same academic standards as their Japanese counterparts, the entrance examinations for *Mankei* and *Nikkei* were administered separately, and Korean applicants had to compete for entry to the academy only with Chinese or Mongolians, whose Japanese education was certainly no greater, and often considerably less, than their own.[65]

Of all the Korean military figures with Manchurian roots, including Paek Sŏnyŏp and Chŏng Ilgwŏn, both of whom later served as South Korea's Army Chief of Staff in the 1950s, the one who became most famous was, of course, Park Chung Hee. Park is interesting, however, not only because of his subsequent political career, but also as an example of how even an indigent peasant boy, though one of exceptional intelligence, could take advantage of the systemic opportunities available to Koreans in the late colonial period to rise to the ranks of the Japanese officer corps.

Park was born in 1917, the youngest of seven children, in a small

[65] General (ret.) Yi Hallim, taped interview, Seoul, July 12, 1990. General, later Ambassador, Yi was Pak's classmate both in Manchukuo and later in Zama. See also the following works: Manshūkoku Gun Kankō Iinkai, ed., *Manshūkoku gun* [The army of Manchukuo] (Tokyo: Ranseikai, 1970), pp. 615–22; Yamazaki Masao, ed., *Rikugun shikan gakkō* [The Military Academy] (Tokyo: Shūgen shobō, 1984), pp. 25–26, 68; Kiyoizumi Nobuo, ed., *Sakufu banri: Manshūkoku gunkan gakkō nikisei no kiroku* [The north wind of ten thousand leagues: the record of the second class of the Manchukuo Military Institute] (Hadano: Dōtokudai nikisei kai, 1981), pp. 28–29; Suzuki Hajime, "Nihon rikugun," pp. 40–42.

village near the North Kyŏngsang provincial town of Kumi. His family was among the poorest of the ninety or so households in the village— so poor, in fact, that decades later, even after he had become president of South Korea, whenever he spoke publicly or privately of his childhood, his thoughts invariably turned to the poverty of his early years, which he blamed for stunting his growth.[66]

Although poor, Park studied hard and was an excellent student. After graduating at the top of his elementary school class in Kumi, he was admitted to the prestigious, government-run normal school in Taegu, which waived tuition expenses for students and obliged them in return to teach in the primary-school system after graduation.[67] Such a career offered a good salary, security, and status by colonial standards and would have been the envy of many Koreans. But even during his five years as a student in Taegu, Park seems to have had his mind on other things. Since childhood he had aspired to be a soldier and been fascinated by famous Japanese, Korean, and Western military figures, including Yi Sunsin and Napoleon.[68] At Taegu Normal, even as his general academic record worsened with each year,[69] his interest in the army

[66] See Yi Sang'u, *Pak chŏnggwŏn 18-lyŏn: kŭ kwŏllok ŭi naemak* [The Park regime of 18 years: the inside story of its power] (Seoul: Tonga Ilbo Sa, 1986), p. 15. See also Yi Nakson, "Pak Chŏnghŭi Changgun—kŭ ka kŏrŏ on palchach'wi" [General Park Chung Hee—the path of his life], in *Pak Chŏnghŭi Changgun tamhwa munjip 1961–1963* [The collected speeches of Park Chung Hee], ed. Sin Pŏmsik (Seoul: Taeto'ng-nyong Pisosil, 1965), pp. 593–94; Paek Namju, ed., *Hyongmyong chidoja Pak Chonghŭi* [The revolutionary leader Park Chung Hee] (Seoul: Inmulgye Sa, 1961), pp. 42–50. The most reliable biography of Park Chung Hee to date is a recent work by Cho Kapche, editor of *Wolgan Chosŏn*: Cho Kapche, *Pak Chŏnghŭi*, vol. 1: *pulman kwa purun ŭi sewol, 1917–1960* [Park Chung Hee vol. 1: the years of discontent and misfortune, 1917–1960] (Seoul: Tosŏ Ch'ulp'an Kkach'i, 1992). While Cho's study is not, and does not aspire to be, a definitive scholarly biography, it is nevertheless a superb piece of investigative journalism, based on extensive interviews with Park's family members, classmates, teachers, and associates, as well as on numerous new primary materials obtained by the author. Cho's work was first published in Japan as *Paku Chōnhi: Kankoku kindai kakumeika no jitsoroku* [Park Chung Hee: the true story of Korea's modern revolutionary], trans. Nakamori Yoshitaka (Tokyo: Aki shobō, 1991). The Korean edition is a revision, and in some cases an expansion, of the Japanese version.

[67] Cho Kapche, *Pak Chŏnghŭi*, pp. 60–61; Yi Sang'u, *Pak chŏnggwŏn*, p. 15.

[68] Pak Chŏnghŭi, "Na ŭi sonyŏn sijŏl" [My childhood], *Wolgan Chosŏn*, May 1984, p. 95. This brief account of Park's childhood was drafted by Park himself in April 1970 as part of an autobiography that was never completed. Kim Chongsin, Park's public relations secretary at the time, subsequently used it as a reference to write a children's biography of Park, published that same year, and Park's original handwritten manuscript remains in Kim's possession today. See "In'gan Pak Chonghui che p'yongga" [A reappraisal of Park Chung Hee the person], *Wolgan opsobo* (October 1991), pp. 172–96.

[69] See Cho Kapche, *Pak Chŏnghŭi*, pp. 65–66. Park's academic record for Taegu Normal, a copy of which was discovered by Cho Kapche among Yi Nakson's personal papers after his death, seems to reflect a decreasing interest in his course of study. Park ranked

found a natural outlet in the military training program that had been added to the school's curriculum. Even today his former classmates still remember his uncommon enthusiasm for such training, and the zest with which he played the bugle during military exercises.[70] Park in fact became a favorite of the Japanese army officer who supervised the school's military courses and was frequently held up as a model for the other students.[71] By 1937, when he was posted to Mun'gyŏng Elementary School (Mun'gyŏng Sŏbu Kongnip Simsang Sohakkyo) in the northern part of his home province, Park seems already to have been well on his way toward deciding to become a professional soldier—a natural inclination that was apparently reinforced by subsequent friction with Mun'gyŏng's principal, as well as by an unhappy arranged marriage.[72]

Yu Chungsŏn, who lived with Park for a time in Mun'gyŏng, recalls that he decorated his room with a popular portrait of Napoleon on a white horse.[73] He also recollects Park's determination to become an army officer and his feeling that his best chance for success lay in Manchuria. According to Yu, Park slit his finger and wrote a "blood letter" (hyŏlsŏ) directly to the Manchurian Military Academy pledging "to die for the sake of the country" (isshi hokoku). This letter, which subsequently appeared in one of the Manchukuo newspapers, caught the eye of a Korean captain, Kang Chaeho, who was one of the examiners for the academy.[74] Under Kang's guidance, Park subsequently took the examination in Mutanchiang in October 1939, placed fifteenth on a list of 236 successful candidates, and entered the academy in the spring of 1940.[75] Two years later he completed the yoka and was one of five ca-

---

sixtieth out of ninety-seven students in his first year, forty-seventh out of eighty-three in his second year, sixty-seventh out of seventy-four in his third year, seventy-third out of seventy-three in his fourth year, and sixty-ninth out of seventy in his final year. Yi Nakson was Park's personal secretary from July 1961 to December 1963.

[70] Yun Ch'idu, Hwangbo Kyun, taped interviews, Taegu, August 2, 1990. Both Yun and Hwangbo are alumni of the fourth class (sagisaeng) of Taegu Normal School, as was Park himself. See also Cho Kapche, Pak Chŏnghŭi, p. 67.

[71] Ibid., pp. 67, 70.

[72] Ibid., pp. 71–85.

[73] Yu Chungsŏn, taped interview, Seoul, August 13, 1990. Yu was also a teacher at Mun'gyŏng Elementary School at the time. In a 1962 letter to Yi Naksŏn, Chŏng Sunok, one of Park's former students, also recalled seeing the picture of Napoleon. See Cho Kapche, Pak Chŏnghŭi, p. 76.

[74] Yu Chungsŏn interview; see also Cho Kapche, Pak Chŏnghŭi, pp. 76, 87. Such "blood letters" (kessho in Japanese) were a not uncommon phenomenon during this period in both Chōsen and Taiwan. See the article in this volume by Wan-yao Chou; also Miyata Setsuko, Chōsen minshū to "kōminka" seisaku, p. 79.

[75] "Lu-chun Chun-kwan Hsueh-hsiao tierh-ch'i yui-k'e sheng-t'u ts'ai-yung k'ao-shih chi-ke-che kung-kao" [Report of those passing of the entrance examination for cadets in

dets, two *Nikkei* and three *Mankei*, who were honored at the academy's commencement ceremony with imperial prize money (*onshi shōkin*) awarded on behalf of Emperor P'u-i by his personal aide-de-camp. After completing his military education in Zama, Park graduated in the fifty-seventh class of the Japanese Military Academy in 1944 and was commissioned a second lieutenant in the Manchukuo army. By the end of the colonial period he had been promoted to the rank of first lieutenant.[76]

SUBJECTS OF THE EMPIRE

Park Chung Hee's Manchurian route to a professional career in the Japanese army points up yet another path of social change in this period: that of Koreans who took advantage of the opportunities afforded by the expansion of the Japanese empire.

In late February 1932, about three weeks before the official inauguration of Manchukuo, the well-known Christian reformist Yun Ch'iho wrote in his diary that "as a Korean patriot I would like to see Japan succeed in its Manchurian policy, for . . . having secured that great treasure house the Japanese nation may feel so relieved of its economic fears that it may be inclined to be somewhat more generous in its political and economic treatment of the Koreans in Korea." "A Japan-controlled Manchuria," he added, "will have room for employment of a large number of educated Koreans."[77]

Although arrogance and racism, as well as fear and suspicion, continued to leave many Japanese officials and businessmen feeling at best ambivalent about enlarging the scope of Korean duties and responsibilities, there is also no question that the expansion of the imperium after 1931 did to some extent fulfill Yun's hopes and expectations. By the early 1940s Koreans were living in a vast imperial domain that stretched from Tokyo across the Asian continent and down into Southeast Asia and the Pacific. Koreans were no longer on the geographical

---

the second class of the preparatory course of the Military Academy], *Cheng-fu kung-pao* [The government gazette], no. 1,716 (Hsinking, January 6, 1940). See also Cho Kapche, *Pak Chonghui*, pp. 86–87.

[76] *Manshū nichi nichi shinbun*, March 24, 1942. See also Suzuki Hajime, "Nihon rikugun," pp. 40–42; Yi Naksŏn, "Pak Chŏnghŭi Changgun," p. 594. According to Cho Kapche (who is here following Yi Nakson's personal notes), Park received a watch directly from Emperor P'u-i and responded with a formal speech, but there is no indication in the newspaper account cited above that such an exchange took place or that P'u-i even attended the ceremony. See Cho Kapche, *Pak Chŏnghŭi*, p. 94. Park's Japanese name during this period was Takagi Masao.

[77] Kuksa P'yŏnch'an Wiwŏnhoe, *Yun Ch'iho ilgi* [The diary of Yun Ch'iho], 11 vols. (Seoul: Kuksa P'yŏnch'an Wiwŏnhoe, 1973–88), 10:16 (entry for February 22, 1932).

periphery but now close to the center of the new empire. More than any other of the subject peoples, with the possible exception of the Taiwanese, they were adept in the imperial language and accustomed to the imperial culture. When they went to Manchukuo, or beyond Manchukuo to even more distant parts of the empire, they could now also to some extent leave behind the psychological burden of colonialism and feel the empowerment of an insider, a feeling that the Japanese authorities did their best to encourage during the war with constant propaganda celebrating the "oneness" of Chōsen and Japan.[78] In short, many Koreans were in an ideal position to take advantage of whatever opportunities might arise in the newly conquered territories, where the work to be done was immense and the Japanese were in great need of assistants who spoke their language and who, if not entirely to be trusted, were at least more trustworthy than the natives.

Research in this area, unfortunately, has scarcely begun, and any exposition at this point must necessarily be brief and tentative. There is, however, certainly enough evidence to suggest that further work is warranted. We know, for example, that Korean businessmen joined their Japanese counterparts in welcoming the expansion of the empire into Manchuria and China, and it is likely that Kim Yonsu's establishment of a huge ten-million-yen textile subsidiary near Mukden in 1939 was only the largest and most conspicuous example of what was in fact a range of Korean entrepreneurial activities in Manchukuo. Again, although precise figures and dimensions have yet to be determined, we also know that Koreans were involved not only in the Manchukuo army, as noted above, but in the Manchukuo police force and bureaucracy as well, and could be found in the offices of the Kwantung government as well.[79] Teaching in the Manchukuo educational system also

[78] See Eckert, *Offspring of Empire*, pp. 169–71, 235–39.

[79] Ibid., 169–71, 177–79; F. C. Jones, *Manchuria since 1931* (London: Royal Institute of International Affairs, 1949), pp. 70–71; Yi Kidong, "Ilbon chegukkun ŭi Han'gugin changgyodŭl" [Korean officers in the Japanese imperial army], *Sindonga* August 1984, p. 491. One of the best sources of information here is the *Cheng-fu kung-pao,* the official bilingual (Chinese and Japanese) gazette of the Manchukuo government. From the gazette's assorted notices and reports, including property and business registrations, lists of people awarded professional licenses and certificates, and rosters of successful academic and civil service examinees, one begins to get a sense of some of the opportunities that Manchukuo held out to Koreans, not only to those in the largely agricultural immigrant Manchurian-Korean population, but also to Koreans from Chōsen with more urban, middle-class aspirations. See, for example, *Cheng-fu kung-pao*, nos. 1,185 (March 21, 1938), pp. 567–68, and 1,470 (March 10, 1939) on Korean entrepreneurship in the mining industry; nos. 1,739 (February 2, 1940), pp. 57–59, and 1,847 (June 22, 1940), pp. 580–83, on bureaucratic recruitment through examinations. Because of the difficulty of distinguishing Koreans from Chinese or, after 1940, Koreans from Japanese, simply on the basis of name, it is very likely that the actual number of Koreans in the *Cheng-fu kung-pao*

supported a good number of Koreans from Chōsen, including, for example, middle-school level instructors specializing in a variety of subjects: English, commerce, mathematics, pedagogy, horticulture, physical education, home economics, history, geography, forestry, physics, chemistry, agriculture, and drawing, as well as Japanese language and "national ethics" (*kokumin dōtoku*). Numerous Koreans from Chōsen also seem to have have found professional niches in Manchukuo as technicians, veterinarians, dentists, and, above all, medical doctors.[80]

is much greater than the number of those who are clearly identifiable as Koreans in the gazette by some kind of ethnic or geographical notation. Information about those passing examinations, for example, is often limited at best to the name of the examinee, examination number (and occasionally ranking), and the place where the examination was taken, more often than not in Manchukuo. A good illustration of this problem can be seen in the case of Park Chung Hee and Yi Hallim, both from Chōsen, who were identified on the Manchukuo Military Academy's January 1940 list of successful entrance examinees not as Koreans but as applicants who took the examination in Mutanchiang and Mukden, respectively; see n. 75 above. One encounters a similar problem of ethnic identification in other sources as well. See Gaimushō Jōhōbu, *Gendai Chūka Minkoku Manshū Teikoku jinmeikan* [Modern biographical dictionary of the Chinese Republic and Manchu Empire] (Tokyo: Tōa dōbunkai, 1937), and Kimura Takemori, *Zai Man Nichi-Man jinmeiroku* (Dairen: Manshū nichi nichi shinbun sha, 1937).

[80] See *Cheng-fu kung-pao*, nos. 1,364 (October 24, 1938), pp. 447–86, and 1,427 (January 12, 1939), pp. 237–42, on middle school teachers; no. 1,189 (March 25, 1938), pp. 713–14, on Korean technicians; no. 1,425 (January 10, 1939), pp. 178–79, on Korean veterinarians; no. 1,373 (November 4, 1938), pp, 46–55, on Korean dentists; nos. 1,369 (October 29, 1938), pp. 581–90, 1,371 (November 1, 1938), pp. 7–11, and 1,433 (January 19, 1939), pp. 421–26, on Korean doctors.

It is possible that Koreans deemed loyal to the empire, as well as Japanese, were replacing politically questionable Chinese natives in some professional positions. Though hardly conclusive, a November 1938 listing of newly registered medical doctors (cited above) is striking in that regard, especially when one considers the enormous pool of Chinese in Manchukuo (about 36 million people, including about 2 million Manchus, together amounting to 96 percent of the total population at the end of 1937). Koreans from Chōsen in the January 1938 listing accounted for about 48 percent of the 323 individuals named, thus exceeding even the number of Japanese (about 37 percent) and clearly dwarfing the number of Chinese, including some from Kwantung and Taiwan, who altogether made up only about 15 percent of the total.

Contemporary Chinese denunciations of Japanese (and Korean) behavior in North China and Manchukuo also lend some support to this view. In 1936, for example, one Chinese man in North China wrote: "In the so-called East Hebei Autonomous Government, as in the illegitimate Manzhouguo . . . the village normal school and the county middle school have been forced to hire people from the 'friendly power' as Japanese language teachers and school physicians. Besides carrying out the policy of cultural invasion and paralyzing the population, their most important responsibility is the surveillance of anti-Japanese and anti-Manzhouguo dangerous elements." Sherman Cochran, Andrew C. K. Hsieh, and Janis Cochran, trans. and ed., *One Day in China: May 21, 1936* (New Haven, Conn.: Yale University Press, 1983), pp. 212–13; see also pp. 219, 222, 243. My thanks to Prof. Vipan Chandra for bringing this book to my attention. See also Eckert, *Offspring of Empire*, pp. 170–71; South Manchuria Railway Company, *Sixth Report on*

Significant numbers of Koreans from Chōsen also lived and worked in other parts of Japanese-occupied Asia during the 1930s and 1940s. Directories from the early 1940s of the Korean population in China list thousands of Koreans residing in virtually all the major occupied cities in the northern, central, and southern parts of the country, and even in Mengchiang, the Inner Mongolian state established by the Kwantung Army in 1937.[81]

Two features of this extensive Korean diaspora are particularly arresting. One is the wide range of employment opportunities that China appears to have offered. If there were numerous Korean petty restaurateurs, shopowners, and innkeepers, as well as a number of Koreans engaged in nefarious activities like smuggling and narcotics trafficking, there were also many Koreans who were pursuing more ambitious and prestigious entrepreneurial and professional careers. In Shanghai alone, which contributed more than two thousand names to the 1944 directory, the Korean occupational spectrum encompassed not only factory guards, manual workers, barbers, and taxi drivers, but also small and medium entrepreneurs, factory foremen, military personnel, technicians, students, professors, doctors, white-collar workers (in banks, business firms, research institutes, and newspaper companies), and even officials of the Chōsen Government-General and the Shanghai municipal government. Most of the Koreans in Shanghai, in fact, identified themselves as white-collar workers (shain), which included people working in Japanese (and, presumably, Chinese) banks and companies such as the Bank of Shanghai, the Bank of Taiwan, Mitsui Bussan, and Mitsubishi Shōsha, as well as Koreans in both Shanghai-based and Chōsen-based Korean companies.[82]

Such dispersion and diversity seem to bespeak a remarkable eye for the main chance, wherever in the burgeoning empire it could be found. And this, in turn, brings us to a second observation about the Korean population in China: the bulk of the Koreans there in the 1940s were

---

Progress in Manchuria to 1939 (Dairen: South Manchuria Railway Company, May 1939), p. 146; Kagayaku Manshū [Flourishing Manchukuo] (n.p.: Manchuria Daily News, n.d.), p. 4.

[81] See Shirakawa Hideo, ed., Zai Shi Hantōjin meiroku [Directory of Koreans in China], vols. 2–4 (Shanghai: Shirakawa yōkō, 1941–44). See also Jones, Manchuria since 1931, p. 66.

[82] Ibid. For the 1944 section on Shanghai, see Zai Shi Hantōjin meiroku, 4:1–97. On Korean involvement in smuggling and the narcotics trade, see T. A. Bisson, Japan in China (New York: Macmillan, 1938), pp. 129, 131, 144–45, 151, 383; Cochran et al., One Day in China, pp. 213–14, 219, 243. From 1938 on Koreans were also recruited by examination into the Japanese consular police in China. See Lincoln Li, The Japanese Army in North China, 1937–1941 (Tokyo: Oxford University Press, 1975), pp. 32, 39n39.

relative newcomers. The directory for 1941 (though not for 1944) notes not only the home city or county in Chōsen of the Koreans listed but also the date on which each took up residence in Shanghai. By far the great majority arrived after the city's fall to the Japanese in November 1937. A comparison of the two directories also reveals that the Korean population of Shanghai nearly quadrupled in the three years between 1941 and 1944.[83] Once again, as in Manchukuo and even Chōsen itself, the war had disrupted the status quo and enlarged the arena for Korean advancement. One is struck here in retrospect by the prophetic quality of an article by Kim Yehyŏn, a consultant to the Chōsen Fire and Marine Insurance Company, who at the beginning of the war in 1938 wrote: "Once the war thus comes to an end [with a Japanese victory], it is not difficult to imagine that we Koreans as well, openly advancing into northern or central or southern China, can reap various benefits as the third party."[84]

CONCLUSION

War preparation and finally the China and Pacific War reshaped Korea's economy and society in the 1930s and early 1940s, activating or accelerating a process of industrialization and social change that is still going on today in the southern half of the peninsula. Although much of the actual physical plant was later either lost to political division, or damaged or destroyed in the civil war that ravaged the country only five years later, the essential industrial infrastructure remained and became the basis for postwar economic reconstruction in the 1950s and a great new spurt of industrialization in the 1960s. Nowhere is this more evident than in the textile industry, which dominated the export sector of South Korea's export-led economy in the 1960s and early 1970s. The textile industry of the 1960s was not something that suddenly sprang into existence as a result of the Park regime's much celebrated five-year development plans. On the contrary, it represented the culmination of a process of development that had begun during World War I and blossomed in the 1930s after the Manchurian Incident. The postcolonial contribution of American aid to this process was essentially to provide the capital and technology with which to reconstruct and expand the colonial base built by Chōbō, Tōyōbō, Kanebō, Dai Nippon, and other Japanese companies, as well by the Korean-run Kyŏngsŏng Spinning

[83] *Zai Shi Hantoōjin meiroku*, 2:52–82.
[84] Kim Yehyon, "Shina Jihen go ni shosubeki Hantōjin no yōi" [Korean strategies in the aftermath of the China Incident], *Chōsen jitsugyō kurabu* 16 (1938): 64–65.

and Weaving Company. That the industry was already poised for export by 1958, only five years after the end of the Korean War, was a clear sign of the depth of the colonial legacy.[85]

The social legacy of the last fifteen years of colonial rule was also important. Obviously much more empirical work, both on the late colonial period itself and on the links between the colonial and postcolonial eras, needs to be done before any kind of authoritative assessment can be made, and we must also be careful not to exaggerate the extent of social change that actually took place: most of the Korean population in 1945 were still poor peasants living in the countryside. Nevertheless, by 1945 many others, certainly hundreds of thousands, and perhaps as many as two million or more, had left the land to become something new: factory workers, technicians, businessmen, bureaucrats and other white-collar workers, military officers, and other professionals. Indeed, most of the major social forces in South Korea that together produced the rapid development of the 1960s and early 1970s, including Park Chung Hee and the South Korean military, had their origins in the late colonial period.

To suggest such connections between the past and the present is not to put forward any kind of apology for Japanese imperialism. It is not to say, for example, that colonialism was Korea's only possible route to industrialization and social change, that Koreans themselves would not have been able to carry it out on their own. Nor is it to forget or excuse the terrible physical and psychological suffering that colonialism, and particularly the last decade of wartime mobilization, inflicted on the general population. As already noted, the main purpose of Japanese policies during the 1930s and 1940s was not to increase Korean opportunities for a better life but to enhance imperial power and serve the war effort. That numerous Koreans were able to improve their lot during this period was an irony of the exigency of war and a testimony not to Japanese generosity but to Korean capability and determination.

We must also not be so blinded by a developmental outlook that we lose sight of the negative elements of the colonial legacy. This essay has deliberately focused quite narrowly on some of the opportunities for Korean advancement in wartime Chōsen, a historically important aspect of colonialism in Korea that has been largely neglected in the existing literature. It need hardly be said, however, that this was only one facet of a complex colonial history whose darker aspects have been more extensively documented elsewhere. And even Korean success in the colonial system had its price. More often that not it meant some form of collaboration with Japanese officials and policies. Such collab-

---

[85] See Eckert et al., *Korea Old and New*, p. 396.

oration became a particularly explosive issue during the second Sino-Japanese and Pacific wars and immediately after liberation, contributing to the division of the country and subsequent civil conflict, and it is an issue that still has not been laid to rest, or even fully acknowledged, in South Korea today.[86] It should also be noted that the authoritarianism that for decades epitomized South Korean politics owed much to the political character of the various Korean elites generated during the late colonial period, not least of all to the military.[87] And who, finally, can adequately measure the traumatic impact of the colonial experience on the Korean psyche, only one effect of which has been to create a historiography of the pre-1945 period that is often driven by emotion and is virtually Manichean in its stark depictions of Japanese oppression and Korean opposition?

When all is said and done, however, the historical significance of the late colonial period stands on its own, quite apart from whatever positive or negative attributes one may choose to assign to it. The purpose of the historian, after all, is not to praise or blame, but rather to explain, in this case to illuminate the origins of modern Korea. From that perspective, as we look back over what Braudel might call the *longue durée* of Korean industrialization since the late nineteenth century, the wrenching years of total war that defined the last phase of Japanese colonial rule stand out in bold relief.[88]

[86] See Eckert, *Offspring of Empire*, pp. 239–52. It is only in the last several years that South Koreans have begun openly to examine and discuss both the issue and the extent of Korean collaboration during the late colonial period. In July 1991, for example, Yi T'aeho, a professor in the fine arts department at Chŏnnam National University in Kwangju, startled the public by revealing in an article, complete with photographs, that a number of the country's most famous artists had produced paintings in support of Japanese imperialism and the war effort in the 1930s and 1940s. At about same time, another professor, Yi Hangnyong, who had himself been a county magistrate in South Kyongsang during the late colonial period, made a formal public apology to the people of that county for working with the Japanese authorities to extract forced donations for the war effort. See, respectively, *Sisa chŏ'nŏl*, no. 92 (August 1, 1991), pp. 68–70, and *Han'guk ilbo*, July 12, 1991.

[87] See Eckert, *Offspring of Empire*, pp. 257–59.

[88] See Fernand Braudel, *On History*, trans. Sarah Matthews (Chicago: University of Chicago Press, 1980), pp. 25–54.

CHAPTER 2

The *Kōminka* Movement in Taiwan and Korea: Comparisons and Interpretations

Wan-yao Chou

For most of the period from 1937 to 1945, when Japan was at war, first with China and then with the Allies, the Japanese empire expanded with enormous speed. The expansion was neither modest in scope nor restrained in method. By the summer of 1942, Japan's perimeter encompassed, in addition to Japanese-occupied regions of China, the Kuriles, Attu, Kiska, Kiribati, the Solomon Islands, Western New Guinea, the Sunda Islands, and Burma, and thus enclosed an immense area—so large, in fact, as to stretch the empire well beyond its capabilities.[1] Military campaigns and geographical expansion, needless to say, require human resources, and wartime Japan felt this need increasingly acutely as the war progressed.

Before 1937, when the second Sino-Japanese War began the phase of rapid expansion of the Japanese empire, Japan had already acquired several colonies. The two major ones were Taiwan, annexed in 1895, and Korea, which was formally incorporated into the empire in 1910. Given the large population of these two colonies, a combined total of some 27 million human beings,[2] it was natural that Japan would involve them in its war effort.

How did Japan mobilize its colonial populations in wartime? What methods did the colonizer adopt to assure and enhance the loyalty of its colonial peoples? To answer these questions, this chapter presents a

I wish to thank Stanford University, the Chiang Ching-kuo Foundation (USA), and Professors Ramon H. Myers and Mark R. Peattie of the Hoover Institution for supporting my study of the *kōminka* movement.

[1] Alvin D. Coox, "The Pacific War," in *The Cambridge History of Japan*, vol. 6, *The Twentieth Century*, ed. Peter Duus (Cambridge: Cambridge University Press, 1988), pp. 345–61.

[2] In 1937, excluding Japanese residents, Taiwan had a population of 5,261,404, and Korea had a population of 21,682,855. See T'ai-wan-sheng wen-hsien wei-yüan-hui, *T'ai-wan-sheng t'ung-chih-kao* (Taipei, 1960) (hereafter *TWSTCK*), chüan 2, "Jen-ming chih: Jen-k'ou p'ien," table XIV:1; Chōsen Sōtokufu, *Chōsen sōtokufu shisei nempō (1939)* (Seoul, 1941), p. 18.

comparative study of the *kōminka* movement in Taiwan and Korea.[3] Setting aside the processes by which the Japanese colonial authorities launched the *kōminka* movement, my emphases will be on the Taiwanese and Korean responses toward the movements' programs, in the hope that this inquiry can shed some preliminary light on this hitherto obscure but important aspect of the wartime Japanese empire in general, and the wartime histories of Taiwan and Korea in particular.

THE DESIGNATION AND BEGINNING OF THE *KŌMINKA* MOVEMENT

The *kōminka* movement can be viewed from two perspectives, as an intensification of an ongoing process of assimilation and as an integral part of the wartime mobilization of the Japanese empire as a whole. The term *kōminka* in Japanese literally means "to transform [the colonial peoples] into imperial subjects." In other words, the *kōminka* movement was a movement aimed at shaping the colonized in the image and likeness of the colonizer. In this sense, it can be regarded as an "assimilation" movement, but in an extreme form. Japanese colonizers in Taiwan and Korea were guided by a vaguely defined policy of assimilation from the very outset of their rule in the two colonies. Yet, this policy was realized essentially in an administrative sense, and was never intended to extend constitutional rights to the colonized.[4] During the wartime period, the ultranationalist fervor in the Japanese homeland was reflected in the colonies by the excessive, even fanatical character of the *kōminka* movement.[5] The primary and ultimate aim of *kōminka* was to make the colonial peoples "true Japanese," not only in deed but in

[3] The Taiwan part is mainly based on my Ph.D. dissertation, "The *Kōminka* Movement: Taiwan under Wartime Japan, 1937–1945" (Yale University, 1991). My understanding of the Korean *kōminka* movement comes from a reading of Japanese and English primary and secondary sources.

[4] Japanese colonialism was self-contradictory, if not self-defeating, in the sense that the realization of its proclaimed goal of assimilation would have annihilated the very relationship between the colonizer and the colonized that defined colonialism. The historian Mark R. Peattie has offered important interpretations of the unique and inherently contradictory nature of Japanese colonialism in his various works. For example, see Mark R. Peattie, "Introduction" and "Japanese Attitudes toward Colonialism, 1895–1945," in *The Japanese Colonial Empire, 1894–1945*, ed. Ramon H. Myers and Mark R. Peattie (Princeton, N.J.: Princeton University Press, 1984), pp. 13–15, 96–99, 123–24; "The Japanese Colonial Empire, 1895–1945," in *The Cambridge History of Japan*, ed. Peter Duus, vol. 6: The Twentieth Century, pp. 237–44; *Nan'yō: The Rise and Fall of the Japanese in Micronesia, 1885–1945* (Honolulu: University of Hawaii Press, 1988), pp. 103–5.

[5] The late Gregory Henderson coined the term "colonial totalitarianism" to describe Japan's rule in Korea, and identified a "totalitarian climax" in Korea during the wartime period. See Gregory Henderson, *Korea: The Politics of the Vortex* (Cambridge, Mass.: Harvard University Press, 1968), p. 104.

"spirit." For anyone familiar with the Japanese wartime diction, in which the term *seishin* (spirit), as in "the spirit of the military nation" (*gunkoku seishin*) and the "imperial nation's spirit" (*kōkoku seishin*), was endlessly repeated, it is not surprising that "spirit" would be the touchstone of the wartime Japanization movement in the colonies. But why was there such a need to remake the colonial peoples in Japan's image at this juncture of Japan's imperial history? The reason lies in the fact that the ever-expanding conflict proved to be one that Japan proper could not fight alone; wartime pressures demanded the mobilization of all colonial resources and manpower. Yet, without the colonial subjects' wholehearted loyalty toward the mother country such mobilization would be incomplete. The *kōminka* movement was, therefore, essential to Japan's war effort. As a result, Japanization and war mobilization were interwoven and mutually supporting.

Technically speaking, the Japanization movements in Taiwan and Korea had different names. In Taiwan, this movement was invariably referred to as *kōminka undō* (imperialization movement), whereas the colonial government in Korea called its efforts to Japanize Koreans *kōkoku shinmin ka*, literally meaning "to transform [Koreans] into the imperial nation's subjects."[6] However, the term *kōminka* was also used informally in Korea,[7] as *kōkoku shinmin* can be abbreviated as *kōmin*. Present-day scholars also have a tendency to refer simply to the *kōminka* movement, whether in Taiwan or Korea, a usage that I shall follow throughout this chaper.[8] There was, however, a difference in nuance in the way the word was used in Taiwan and Korea because of the circumstances in which the Japanization campaigns were launched in each colony. Since the difference has a definite historical significance, it deserves some elaboration.

The formal designation of the Japanization movement in Korea as "*kōkoku shinmin ka*" was not arbitrary. On October 2, 1937, the so-called "Oath as Subjects of the Imperial Nation" (*kōkoku shinmin no*

[6] For example, see *Chōsen jijō (1940)* (Seoul: Chōsen Sōtokufu, 1939), pp. 96, 97. The principal slogan of the movement was "*naisei ittai*" ("Japan and Korea Are One Entity," or "Japanese-Korean Unity"). See Ki-baik Lee, *A New History of Korea*, trans. Edward W. Wagner with Edward J. Shultz (Cambridge, Mass.: Harvard University Press, 1984), pp. 352–53. See also Carter Eckert, *Offspring of Empire: The Koch'ang Kims and the Colonial Origins of Korean Capitalism, 1876–1945* (Seattle: University of Washington Press, 1991), p. 236.

[7] For example, see Mitarai Tatsuo, *Minami sōtoku no Chōsen tōchi* (Seoul: Keijō Nippōsha, 1942), pp. 7–11; *Keijō Nippō*, October 2, 1942 (morning edition), p. 3.

[8] See Kang Chae-on, *Nihon ni yoru Chōsen shihai no yonjūnen* (Osaka: Osaka shoseki, 1983), pp. 139, 141; Miyata Setsuko, *Chōsen minshū to "kōminka" seisaku* (Tokyo: Mirai sha, 1985); Sani Michio, "Kōminka kyōiku to 'hantō' no kodomotachi," in *Chōsen no kindaishi to Nihon*, ed. Hatada Takashi (Tokyo: Yamata shobō, 1987), pp. 158–72.

seishi) was introduced by the Korean Government-General during the period when Minami Jirō was governor-general (1936–42).[9] This proclamation clearly marked the beginning of the *kōminka* movement in Korea, since the recitation of the oath by Koreans was made compulsory at all public gatherings. There were two sets of oaths, one for the adult population and a linguistically simpler version for children and teenagers, each having three articles. The oath for adults reads:

1. We are the subjects of the imperial nation; we will repay His Majesty as well as the country with loyalty and sincerity.
2. We the subjects of the imperial nation shall trust, love, and help one another so that we can strengthen our unity.
3. We the subjects of the imperial nation shall endure hardship, train ourselves, and cultivate strength so that we can exalt the imperial way.[10]

The significance of the Korean recitation of the oath can be better appreciated when it is understood that in Taiwan no parallel ceremony existed. This contrast reminds us that, whereas Taiwan was merely a newly designated province of the Ch'ing dynasty when it was annexed by Japan, Korea, before its demotion to the status of a colony, had been an independent nation. Perhaps due to this difference in the historical circumstances under which Taiwan and Korea became Japan's colonies, securing the loyalty of the population in each colony posed a different problem for the colonizer.[11] The fact that Koreans were obliged to take an oath and Taiwanese were not was thus symbolic of the degree of difficulty faced by Japan in obtaining the loyalty of the peoples of these two colonial territories.

In the case of Korea, the concept of "the nation" was clearly emphasized in the oath. It goes without saying that "the nation" here meant Japan. This seems to suggest that the colonial government in Korea had to compete, in its endeavour to transform Koreans into Japanese, with the historical fact that Korea had once been an independent nation. The required recitation of the oath on each and every public occasion represented, on the one hand, a spiritual undermining of Korean nationalism—be it in the dynastic or in the modern sense—and, on the other, a daily ritual of indoctrination of Koreans in Japanese state ideology. In contrast, the colonial authorities in Taiwan do not seem to have found it

[9] Chōsen Sōtokufu, *Shisei sanjūnin shi* (Seoul, 1940), p. 790.

[10] *Chōsen jijō (1940)*, p. 102; for the oath for children and teenagers, see p. 101.

[11] For an overall comparison of Japanese colonial rule in Korea and Taiwan, see Edward I-te Chen, "Japan: Oppressor or Modernizer?" in *Korea under Japanese Colonial Rule: Studies of the Policy and Techniques of Japanese Colonialism*, ed. Andrew T. Nahm (Kalamazoo, Mich.: Center for Korean Studies, Western Michigan University, 1973), pp. 251–58.

necessary to impose a ceremony of the same nature upon the Taiwanese. Taiwan, because it was a frontier province on the periphery of China, was incorporated into the Japanese empire through a process that involved little dismantling of the authority of imperial symbols or even of the authority of the provincial government.[12] Moreover, the colonial government in Taiwan gave the Taiwanese a two-year grace period to choose either to stay or to leave.[13] Psychologically, this policy must have created a sense of resignation in those Taiwanese who could have left but chose to stay, and those who had left but decided to return. Notwithstanding the weaker nationalist resistance of the Taiwanese, colonial authorities in Taiwan had to deal with a different but analogous problem, that of Han Chinese cultural identity, which I will discuss below.

Because there was no event in Taiwan as drastic and unprecedented as the introduction of the oath in Korea, the beginning of the *kōminka* movement in Taiwan was not as clearly marked, though it appears that the term appeared sometime in late 1936.[14] The inauguration of the movement was one of the three principal policies adopted by the seventeenth governor-general of Taiwan, Kobayashi Seizō (1936–40), who took office in the fall of 1936, the two others being those of industrializing Taiwan and the realization of a "southward advance."[15] On April 1, 1937, the use of Chinese in newspapers was abolished as a result of pressure from the colonial government,[16] marking the first implementation of measures to carry out Kobayashi's *kōminka* policy. To Japan's colonial populations, the Marco Polo Bridge Incident on July 7, 1937,[17]

[12] Shortly before the Japanese troops marched ashore on the island of Taiwan in the summer of 1895, the provincial government was dissolved after its officials left for the Chinese mainland, thus creating a political and institutional vacuum wherein the minimal imperial presence ceased to exist.

[13] A fair number of Taiwanese, mostly gentry members and merchants, did move back to mainland China, but many finally, perhaps painfully, decided to return to Taiwan where their families had taken root too deeply to relocate elsewhere. See Wu Wen-hsing, *Jih-chü shih-ch'i T'ai-wan she-hui ling-tao chieh-ts'eng chih yen-chiu* (Taipei: Cheng-chung shu-chü, 1992), pp. 24–31.

[14] Shirai Asakichi, "Taiwan kōminka no shō mondai," *Taiwan jijō*, January 1940, p. 32.

[15] See Taiwan Sōtokufu Jōhōbu, *Jikyokuka Taiwan no genzai to sono shōrai* (Taipei, 1940), p. 7.

[16] All but one newspaper complied with this "Japanese only" policy and discontinued their Chinese columns on April 1, 1937. The only Taiwanese-managed and -owned newspaper, *Taiwan shinminpō*, was allowed to gradually decrease its Chinese columns until their total disappearance by the end of June of that year. See I-lan-hsien wen-hsien wei-yüan-hui, *I-lan-hsien chih* (repr. I-lan, 1969), "ta-shih-chi," p. 52.

[17] In Taiwan and Korea the Marco Polo Bridge Incident was often referred to as the "Recent Incident" (*konji jihen*) or simply "the Incident" (*jihen*). It was commonplace for people in the *kōminka* era to say that "since the 'Recent Incident' . . . " or "since 'the

marked the coming of a new era. The two *kōminka* movements were initiated shortly before and after it. Thus in both Taiwan and Korea, the eight years from 1937 to 1945 were unmistakably the *kōminka* era.

As a transformative policy, the *kōminka* movement naturally touched almost every aspect of life in the colonies. Theoretically, whatever was deemed Japanese was to be imposed upon the colonial peoples, while whatever was considered Korean or Taiwanese (or Chinese) was to be expunged in both colonies. In general, the movement had four major definable programs, namely "religious reform," the "national language" movement (*kokugo undō*), the name-changing campaign (*kaiseimei* in Taiwan; *sōshi kaimei* in Korea), and the recruitment of military volunteers (*shiganhei seido*). Although it may appear that both governments-general in the two colonies adopted similar programs for their respective Japanization movements, they actually addressed different issues, and consequently their approaches to the *kōminka* movement were not identical. Let us turn to each of the four.

Shintoism versus Indigenous Religions

"Religious reform" was high on the agenda of the *kōminka* movement. Both in Taiwan and in Korea, and perhaps to a lesser degree in Micronesia,[18] the colonial governments promoted the Japanese state religion, Shintoism, at the expense of indigenous religions. During the *kōminka* era, the number of Japanese shrines (*jinja*) in Taiwan increased significantly. Thirty-eight out of the total sixty-eight *jinja* in Taiwan were built between 1937 and 1943.[19] The authorities encouraged the general public to pay visits to *jinja*, especially to the Taiwan Grand Shrine located in present-day Yüan-shan, Taipei. The colonial government was able to boast a record figure of approximately 150,000 visitors to the shrine in two days on October 28 and 29, 1942, on the occasion of its most important festival of the year.[20] Apart from their public observance of Shinto ceremonies, Taiwanese were also advised to maintain a domestic altar (*kamidana*) in each household, and were expected to wor-

---

Incident' . . . " For the usage "Recent Incident," see *Kōnan shimbun* (hereafter *KNSB*), July 3, 1941 (evening ed.), p. 2; *Goen*, 34, no. 7 (July 1941): 45; Tsuda Katashi, *Naisen ittai ron no kihon rinen* (Seoul: Ryokki remmei, 1940), p. 85. For "the Incident," see Shirai Asakichi and Ema Tsunekichi, *Kōminka undō* (Taipei, 1939), pp. 156–57; *Chōsen jijō (1939)* (Seoul: Chōsen Sōtokufu, 1938), p. 374.

[18] For Japan's attempt to assimilate Micronesians into Japanese religion, see Peattie, *Nan'yō*, pp. 106–8. 225–29.

[19] Ts'ai Chin-t'ang, "Tai-wan ni okeru shūkyō seisaku no kenkyū, 1895–1945" (Ph.D. dissertation, Tsukuba University, 1990), p. 149.

[20] "Hontō jiji nisshi," *Taiwan keisatsu jihō* (hereafter, *TWKSJH*), no. 325 (December 1942) (pages are unnumbered).

ship every morning the *taima* (paper amulets) distributed from the Ise Shrine, the holiest of Shinto sites in the Japanese homeland.[21] According to official figures, in 1941 about seven out of ten households in Taiwan received Ise Shrine paper amulets, though one doubts that such religious charms were actually venerated by Taiwanese.[22]

In the name of *kōminka* Japanese colonial administrators not only promoted Shinto but also attempted to stamp out the traditional indigenous religion, a hybrid of Buddhism, Taoism, and folk beliefs. One Japanese local official under the governorship of Kobayashi Seizō even went as far as to demolish native temples. The extremity of such a "religious reform" provoked strong protests from the Taiwanese as well as harsh criticism from the Diet in Japan proper. The temple demolition operation was halted when Hasegawa Kiyoshi (1940–44) replaced Kobayashi Seizō as the governor-general of Taiwan in late 1940.[23] Nevertheless, the number of native temples had by then decreased by one-third.[24]

In Korea, on the other hand, the colonial government concentrated its efforts on the subjugation of Christianity, Korea's most active and influential religion.[25] During the *kōminka* movement, the colonial authorities adopted harsh measures against Korean Christian communities. Unlike the situation in Taiwan, the number of *jinja* in Korea did not increase significantly, notwithstanding the near doubling of minor shrines (*jinshi*). Korea had 60 shrines in 1939 and 73 when the war ended, while the number of minor shrines increased from 470 to 828 during the period 1939–42.[26]

---

[21] The Ise Shrine was the principal center of worship for Amaterasu, the goddess and first ancestress of Japan's imperial house. The Ise Shrine was made the highest shrine in the early Meiji period and thereafter distributed talismans nationwide and later to the colonies. See Helen Hardacre, *Shintō and the State, 1868–1988* (Princeton, N.J.: Princeton University Press, 1989), pp. 84, 86–87.

[22] See Yokomori Kumi, "Taiwan ni okeru jinja: kōminka seisaku to no kanren ni oite," *Taiwan kingendaishi kenkyū*, no. 4 (October 1982), p. 200. Wu Cho-liu (1900–1976), the famous Taiwanese (Hakka) writer, revealed in his memoir that he never worshipped the Ise paper amulets kept in his house. See Wu Cho-liu, *T'ai-wan lien-ch'iao*, trans. Chung Chao-cheng (Taipei: Nan-fang ts'ung-shu ch'u-pan she, 1987), p. 109.

[23] Yokomori, "Taiwan ni okeru jinja," pp. 202–6.

[24] See Ch'en Ling-jung, *Jih-chü shih-ch'i shen-tao t'ung-chih hsia ti T'ai-wan tsung-chiao cheng-ts'e* (Taipei: Tzu-li wan-pao wen-hua ch'u-pan she, 1992), p. 254.

[25] The Korean indigenous religion, Ch'ondogyo (the Religion of the Heavenly Way), played a leading role in the March First Independence Movement of 1919. However, its anti-Japanese influence declined after 1920 because of internal strife and repression by the colonial authorities. See John Kie-chiang Oh, "Ch'ondogyo and Independence Movements," in *Korea's Response to Japan: The Colonial Period, 1910–1945*, ed. C. I. Eugene Kim and Doretha E. Mortimore (Kalamazoo, Mich.: Center for Korean Studies, Western Michigan University, 1977), pp. 123–26.

[26] "Sankō tōkeihyō," *Chōsen jijō (1940)* (Seoul, 1939), p. 10; "Sankō tōkeihyō," *Chōsen jijō (1944)* (Seoul, 1943), p. 9. Chen Ling-jung, *T'ai-wan tsung-chiao cheng-ts'e*, p. 53.

In Korea, the Shinto shrine issue emerged as early as 1935 and stemmed from the new policy that obliged Koreans to worship at Shinto shrines. Unlike most Taiwanese Christians who seemingly acquiesced in this matter,[27] those in Korea often refused to visit the shrines. In September 1937, for example, the students of seven schools refused to do so. The authorities did not take the confrontation lightly; they subsequently closed down these schools.[28] For Korean Christians, the question of whether or not to visit a Shinto shrine was a serious one,[29] for the performance of rituals there directly conflicted with the Christian tenet that God is the one true deity; worship at the site of another religion amounted to idolatry. As the *kōminka* movement intensified, the colonial government's pressure on Korean Christians to observe Shinto rites increased. In May 1938 the Presbyterian Church decided to close its schools throughout Korea to show its defiance of the observance of Shinto ceremonies.[30] However, in September of that year the Korean Presbyterian General Assembly was forced to pass a resolution supporting the government view that to participate in ceremonies at Shinto shrines was a patriotic rather than a religious act.[31] Meanwhile, a vigorous anti–shrine worship movement came into being. Many Christian organizations were disbanded as a result of their refusal to comply with the authorities on the Shinto shrine issue. From June 1940 onward, more than two hundred churches were closed down; seventy ministers and two thousand or so Christians were arrested; more than fifty ministers died in jail.[32]

The statement of disbandment issued in early 1944 by the religious association for Korean Adventist churches provides us with a glimpse of how difficult the situation had become for Korean Christians at the height of the *kōminka* movement. Part of the statement reads:

---

[27] Taiwanese Christians, mostly Presbyterians, complied with official pressures concerning Shinto ceremonies, although occasionally some of them did refuse to pay visits to the Shinto shrine. See Huang Wu-tung, *Huang Wu-tung hui-i lu* (Irvine, Calif.: Taiwan Publishing Co., 1986), p. 117; T'ai-wan chi-tu chang-lao chiao-hui tsung-hui li-shih wei-yüan-hui, *T'ai-wan chi-tu chang-lao chiao-hui pai-nien-shih* (Taipei: Centenary Publication Committee, Presbyterian Church of Formosa, 1965), pp. 257, 390.

[28] Mun Kuk-chu, *Chōsen shakai undōshi jiten* (Tokyo: Shakai hyōron kai, 1981), p. 62.

[29] Kondō Kenichi, ed., *Taiheiyō senka no Chōsen oyobi Taiwan* (Chigasaki: Chōsen shiryō kenkyū kai, 1961), p. 12.

[30] See Spencer J. Palmer, "Korean Christians and the Shinto Shrine Issue," in Kim and Mortimore, *Korea's Response to Japan*, pp. 144–45.

[31] Chong-Sik Lee, *Japan and Korea: The Political Dimension* (Stanford, Calif.: Hoover Institution, 1985), p. 11.

[32] Kang, *Chōsen shihai no yonjūnen*, p. 149; Palmer, "Korean Christians," p. 150. In post-colonial Korea, the Shinto shrine issue created a wide gap between those who had complied and those who had not.

This church was established by American missionaries and has existed for more than forty years. . . . As a result, we unknowingly were influenced by the thought of our enemies, America and England alike, and we worshipped their Western customs and habits so that our oriental indigenous good customs were gradually destroyed. . . . Furthermore, we should dissociate ourselves from the position of being members of religious organizations and return to that of natural human beings (shizenjin). Thus, as the children of His Imperial Majesty, we should serve our country, and as the subjects of the imperial nation (kōkoku shinmin toshite), we, of course, pledge that we will repay our country's benevolence with all our will and might, acting in accordance with the demands of the present situation in the Greater East Asian War. . . .[33]

These agonizingly constructed phrases attest to the immensity of official pressure on the Korean Christian community and demonstrate that, for Korean Christians, compliance with the government's pressure was often a matter of lip service.[34]

It is proof of the barren ground for Shinto in Taiwan and Korea that, despite the most intense efforts of the colonial authorities to promote it, in each territory Shinto disappeared with hardly a trace once Japan's colonial rule came to an end.[35] Upon Japan's defeat, one of the matters that the colonial authorities in Taiwan and Korea regarded as most urgent was to protect the sacred objects in the Shinto shrines from being desecrated by the local population.[36] This showed prescience, especially in Korea, since the first thing that the people there did to vent their hatred toward the Japanese was to set fire to Shinto shrines.[37] In Taiwan there was less violence against Shinto shrines, but there, too, Shintoism was completely eradicated in a very short time.

THE "NATIONAL LANGUAGE" MOVEMENT

The kōminka movement strongly promoted use of the "national"—Japanese—language. When officials of the colonial government first ar-

[33] Keijō nippō, January 7, 1944 (morning ed.), p. 3.

[34] Chong-Sik Lee, The Politics of Korean Nationalism (Berkeley: University of California Press, 1963), pp. 269–70.

[35] This also holds true in the case of Micronesia. See Peattie, Nan'yō, p. 108. The outright failure of Shintoism to take root in Japan's colonies in spite of all missionary efforts may have much to do with Shintoism's lack of transcendental qualities, essential to if not requisite for any vital religion, as Mark Peattie insightfully suggests.

[36] Morita Yoshio, Chōsen shūsen no kiroku: Bei So ryōgun no shinchū to Nihonjin no hikiage (Tokyo: Gannandō shoten, 1986), pp. 107–13.

[37] Wi Ji Kang, "Religion and Politics Under Japanese Rule," in Kim and Mortimore, Korea's Response to Japan, p. 118; Richard E. Kim, Lost Names: Scenes from a Korean Boyhood (New York: Praeger, 1970), p. 164.

rived at Taiwan in mid-July 1895, they referred to their own language as *Nihongo* (Japanese), but within a year it was officially known as *kokugo* (the national language), and so it remained until the end of the colonial era.[38] In Korea, the designation of the Japanese language changed over time, as follows:

1891	*Nichigo* (Japanese), in the name of the Institute for Japanese Language
1895	*gaikokugo* (foreign language), as in the text of the law on primary schools
1909	*Nihongo* (Japanese), as in the text of regulations for common schools (futsū gakkō)
1910–45	*kokugo* (national language)[39]

The designation of Japanese as the national language foreshadowed its critical role in the *kōminka* movement. Although at the outset of Japanese rule education in both colonies did not exclude the indigenous languages in the elementary-school curricula, it eventually did so during the *kōminka* movement. In Taiwan, classical Chinese, read in Taiwanese dialects, was taught in elementary schools, but class time spent on this subject was diminished gradually during the prewar period. Finally, in April 1937, classical Chinese completely disappeared from the curriculum.[40] In Korea, the same misfortune befell the Korean language, or *Chōsengo*. From 1911 to 1938, Korean was a required subject in elementary schools; during this period, however, class time spent on Korean was much shorter than that spent on Japanese, which was also a required subject.[41] In 1938, Korean was further degraded to the status of an optional subject. Worse still, in 1941 it was completely removed from the curriculum, although still listed as optional.[42]

[38] See the written suggestions submitted to Kabayama Sukenori, the first governor-general of Taiwan (1895–96), by Izawa Shūji, who then headed the Education Bureau of the colonial government, in Taiwan kyōiku kai, *Taiwan kyōiku enkakushi* (repr. Tokyo: Seishi sha, 1982), pp. 6–10. In the spring of 1896, the Government-General of Taiwan changed the name for the Japanese language training institutes from *nihongo denshūsho* to *kokugo denshūsho*. See *Taiwan kyōiku enkakushi*, pp. 17–18.

[39] Yi Suk-cha, "Nihon tōchika Chōsen ni okeru Nihongo kyōiku: Chōsen kyōiku rei to no kanren ni oite," *Chōsen gakuhō*, no. 75 (April 1975), p. 101.

[40] *TWSTCH*, chüan 5, "Chiao-yü chih: chiao-yü she-shih p'ien," p. 53.

[41] Yi Suk-cha adroitly compares the percentage of class time spent on the Japanese language to the percentage of class time spent on the Korean language in her article "Nihongo kyōiku," pp. 105–12. For example, in 1894, 12.3 percent of class time was spent on Japanese and 22.2 percent on Korean. In 1922, the Japanese proportion had increased to 37.6 percent, while that of Korean had declined to 11.7 percent; and in 1938, the proportions were 33.1 percent and 8.3 percent respectively. In 1941, 29.3 percent of class time was taken by Japanese, and Korean was no longer taught.

[42] Yi Suk-cha, "Nihongo kyōiku," pp. 102, 112. According to Richard E. Kim, Korean

Needless to say, the colonizers felt that speaking the "national language" was a prerequisite for being a true Japanese.[43] As an educator and promoter of the Japanese language in Taiwan put it, "the national language is the womb that nurtures patriotism."[44] This view was widely shared by his fellow colonizers, and spreading the use of Japanese among the general public became an important task for them. In order to provide Japanese-language schooling for those who did not attend or could not afford formal schooling, Taiwan's colonial authorities started setting up outreach programs called "national language study programs" (kokugo kōshōjo) island-wide in 1929. A similar program offering a shorter study period also came into existence and was called the "basic national language study program" (kan'i kokugo kōshōjo).[45] By April 1937, there were 2,812 "national language study programs" with a total enrollment of 185,590 students, and 1,555 "basic national language study programs" with a total enrollment of 77,781 students.[46]

These widespread outreach programs were closely tied to the official campaign to increase the number of colonial subjects who understood the "national language" (kokugo kaisha, or "national language speakers"). In 1937, when the kōminka movement commenced, "national language speakers" made up 37.38 percent of the entire population in Taiwan, and were expected to increase to 50 percent by 1943.[47] In the event, the percentages grew faster than anticipated and, no doubt to the great delight of the colonial government, in 1940 the number of "national language speakers" had already reached 51 percent, and in 1943, no less than 80 percent.[48] Nonetheless, one should be aware of how these numbers were derived. According to official criteria, Taiwanese counted as "national language speakers" basically fell into the following four categories: children presently studying at an elementary school or its equivalent; graduates of an elementary school or its equiv-

---

language and history were taught to Korean children only in the first and second grades, and from the third grade up all schoolchildren were required to speak Japanese at school and expected to speak Japanese at home as well. But from 1940 onward, even first- and second-graders were no longer taught Korean language and history. See Kim, Lost Names, pp. 71–72, 77–78.

[43] Chōsen Sōtokufu Jōhōka, Atarashiki Chōsen (Seoul, 1944; repr. Tokyo: Fūtō sha, 1982), p. 62.

[44] Yamazaki Mutsuo, Kokugo mondai no kaiketsu (privately published: Taipei, 1939), p. 53.

[45] Sung Teng-ts'ai, Kokugo kōshūjo kyōiku no jissai (privately published: Taipei: 1936), p. 37.

[46] Taiwan kyōiku enkakushi, p. 1054.

[47] Ibid.

[48] Taiwan jijō (1942), p. 132; KNSB, October 12, 1943 (evening ed.), p. 1.

alent; students presently studying at a Japanese language outreach program; and graduates of a language outreach program.[49]

Given the rigor with which Japanese educators performed their duties, there is little doubt that an average elementary-school graduate could converse in Japanese with satisfactory fluency. But how fluent in Japanese were those who only attended classes in an outreach program? As a matter of fact, the outreach programs required much shorter schooling time—sixty to one hundred school days a year for two to three hours each day—and one could complete the program in a one- to four-year period.[50] Furthermore, the official statistics are potentially misleading in that one was counted as a "national language speaker" even if one dropped out of the program immediately after the survey was done. My review of primary sources has led me to believe that the real numbers of Taiwanese capable of speaking Japanese were significantly less than the official percentages of "national language speakers."[51]

After the commencement of the "national language" movement, the population was discouraged from speaking Southern Fukienese (a language spoken by about 80 percent of the population) as well as other indigenous languages.[52] During the *kōminka* era, although the government never systematically banned local languages, some institutions did proscribe Southern Fukienese, perhaps only on a temporary basis. Occasionally, Taiwanese might find that they were forbidden to speak in their mother tongue aboard a bus or when visiting a city hall.[53]

Among programs promoting the national language in Taiwan, one stood out: the program to recognize so-called "National Language Families" (*kokugo katei*). This program began in Taihoku (Taipei) prefecture in 1937, and was later duplicated by other prefectures islandwide.[54] In general, a family wishing to be granted the "National Language Family" designation had to apply for it and prove that all family members spoke only Japanese at home.[55] After an application was ac-

[49] Sung, *Kokugo kōshūjō kyōiku no jissai*, p. 37.

[50] Ibid.; *Taiwan kyōiku enkakushi*, p. 1051.

[51] A youth wrote to an official saying that one year of study in an outreach program had not helped his mother; she still could not speak a word of Japanese. See *Taiwan nichi nichi shimpō* (hereafter *TWNNSP*), April 10, 1940 (evening ed.), p. 2.

[52] Taiwan's population comprised mainly Fukienese, Hakka, and aborigines. In general, Fukienese spoke Southern Fukienese (commonly known as Taiwanese), Hakka spoke Hakka, and the aborigines spoke about a dozen languages among themselves.

[53] For example, *TWNNSP*, January 31, 1941, p. 4; October 20, 1940, p. 5.

[54] Ibid., February 14, 1940, p. 5; April 20, 1941 (evening ed.), p. 2; *Takao shimpō*, June 17, 1940, p. 7; *Tō Taiwan shimpō* (hereafter *TTWSP*), March 23, 1941, p. 3; March 27, 1941, p. 2.

[55] Taichū prefecture held to a lower standard by which only active family members

cepted, the family would receive, among other things, a tablet bearing the inscription "*kokugo no ie*," or "*kokugo katei*," in a special ceremony, to be hung by the front door of its residence as a symbol of honor.[56]

Because of the lack of sources, we do not know the total number of families that were so designated before the war ended. But one source reveals that from 1937 to 1943, 3,448 households in Taihoku, or about 1.3 percent of the city's total, received the title.[57] Given the fact that Taihoku was the capital and cultural center of the colony, it would be logical to assume that the average island-wide figure would have been lower than 1.3 percent.

The "National Language Family" program targeted well-educated Taiwanese and was intended to make them examples for the rest of the society. It was presumably an honor, but there were also material rewards that came with the designation, such as better chances for children of such families to enter supposedly good schools, or priority for employment in government or public organizations.[58] Because rewards were involved, it is difficult to determine how sincerely the Taiwanese elite endorsed this program in the context of the *kōminka* movement. It is, however, clear that quite a number of Taiwanese from "National Language Families" did not follow the "Japanese only" rule at home or in public as strictly as the title demanded.[59]

Compared to the program in Taiwan, the "national language" movement in Korea had a good deal of ground to make up. In contrast to the 37.8 percent of the Taiwanese population claimed as "national language speakers" in 1937, in Korea, even as late as 1938, the percentage was only 12.38.[60] In the years that followed the number of "national language speakers" grew steadily but not spectacularly as shown in table 2.1.

The percentages of "national language speakers" in Taiwan and in Korea differed greatly. The Korean figures were arrived at by adding up two groups of people: one was "those who understand a little [Japanese]" (*sōkaishi eru mono*) and the other was "those who could carry on an ordinary conversation [in Japanese]" (*futsū kaiwa ni sashinaki mono*).[61]

---

were required to speak Japanese. See Nagata Jōdai, *Minfu sakkō no gutaisaku* (privately published: Taipei, 1938), pp. 84–85.

[56] Some prefectures gave money for the conferees to have their tablets custom-made. See Taiwan Sōtokufu, *Taiwan no shakai kyōiku* (Taipei, 1941), pp. 199, 209.

[57] *KNSB*, November 2, 1943 (evening ed.), p. 2.

[58] *TTWSP*, March 27, 1941, p. 2.

[59] Wu Wen-hsing, "Jih-chü shih-ch'i T'ai-wan tsung-tu-fu t'ui-kuang jih-yü yün-tung ch'u-t'an" (part 2), *T'ai-wan feng-wu*, 37, no. 4 (December 1987): 74; *TWNNSP*, February 4, 1941 (evening ed.), p. 2.

[60] "Sankō tōkeihyō," *Chōsen jijō (1940)*, p. 10.

[61] Ibid.

TABLE 2.1
Proportion of Korean Population Educated to Speak Japanese, 1938–1943

Year	Population	"National Language Speakers"	Percentage
1938	21,950,716	2,717,807	12.38
1939	22,098,310	3,069,032	13.89
1940	22,954,563	3,573,338	15.57
1941	23,913,063	3,972,094	16.61
1942	25,525,409	5,089,214	19.94
1943	25,827,308	5,722,448	22.15

Source: Kondo Ken'ichi, ed., *Taiheiyō senka shumatsuki Chōsen no chisei* (Tokyo: Chōsen shiryō hensan kai, 1961), p. 200.

According to official criteria, those who spoke Japanese as fluently as fourth graders in elementary school were considered to belong to the former group, while the latter category included those who spoke Japanese as fluently as elementary-school graduates.[62] Given the vagueness of these criteria, it is difficult to decide whether Korea's standard of who qualified as a "national language speaker" was equivalent to Taiwan's.

There were a number of reasons for the much lower percentage of "national language speakers" in the Korean population. First, Korea formally became a Japanese colony fifteen years later than Taiwan did, if we do not count the five-year period from 1906 to 1910 when it was under Japan's tutelage. This shorter period of colonization could explain to some extent Korea's lag in "national language" acquisition. Second, Korea was more than four times larger than Taiwan in terms of population and 6.5 times larger in land area. Given Korea's sizable territory and large number of people, the Korean colonial government's task of propagating the Japanese language was definitely more difficult than its counterpart's in Taiwan. Third, the illiteracy rate in Korea was very high to start with. According to a census taken in 1930, 77.7 percent of Koreans read neither Korean nor Japanese, and only about 15 percent of school-age Koreans were enrolled in elementary schools.[63] In contrast, the percentage of Taiwanese children who were enrolled in elementary schools in 1930 was twice as high—30.6 percent—and the government in Taiwan was able to increase the percentage to an impressive 71.1

[62] Kondō Kenichi, ed., *Taiheiyō senka shūmatsuki Chōsen no chisei* (Tokyo: Chōsen shiryō hensan kai, 1961), pp. 194–95.
[63] Ko Chun-sŏk, *Kōnichi genron tōsōshi* (Tokyo: Shinsen sha, 1976), pp. 278–79.

percent in 1944.[64] Finally, the government in Korea started language outreach programs only in 1938, nine years later than in Taiwan. Although these programs boasted a yearly average enrollment of three hundred thousand students from 1938 to 1941,[65] this figure could only add a meagre 1 percent or so to the percentage of "national language speakers." Like the colonial government in Taiwan, Korea's colonial authorities also conferred the designation "National Language Family" on Koreans who could prove that they spoke only Japanese in public and at home.[66] All the same, it is difficult to determine the number of such families.

Notwithstanding the striking similarities between the "national language" movements in Taiwan and Korea, the respective colonial governments did show crucial differences in their attitudes toward indigenous languages. In Taiwan, as mentioned earlier, Taiwanese might occasionally find that they were forbidden to speak the language of their birth when aboard a bus or when visiting a government office. Despite sporadic prohibitions, speaking indigenous languages did not seem to constitute a threat to colonial rule. In contrast, because the colonial authorities in Korea drew connections between Korean nationalism and the Korean language, Koreans might open themselves to serious punishment if they tried to preserve their mother tongue.[67] The harsh measures the colonial government of Korean adopted against those who continued to promote the Korean language are exemplified in the infamous October 1942 Korean Language Society incident, which resulted in the arrest and imprisonment of 33 leading figures of the society, some of whom were subjected to torture.[68]

After the number of "national language speakers" in Taiwan reached 51 percent of the population in 1940, some optimistic colonizers hoped that Taiwan would eventually become *kokugo Taiwan,*[69] or "national language Taiwan," meaning that everyone in Taiwan would speak Japanese, an unrealized goal by the time the war ended in 1945. Still, if the

[64] E. Patricia Tsurumi, *Japanese Colonial Education in Taiwan, 1895–1945* (Cambridge, Mass.: Harvard University Press, 1977), Appendix B, pp. 244–45.

[65] Chōsen Sōtokufu, *Chōsen sōtokufu shisei nenpō: Shōwa jūroku nendō* (Seoul, 1943), p. 158.

[66] See Chun Kwang-yong, "Kapitan Lee," trans. Marshall R. Pihl, in *Listening to Korea: A Korean Anthology*, ed. Marshall R. Pihl (New York: Praeger, 1973), p. 95.

[67] Mark R. Peattie, "The Japanese Colonial Empire in the China and Pacific Wars," paper presented at the conference on "Fifty Years After—The Pacific War Reexamined," held at Lake Yamanaka, Tokyo, November 13–17, 1991, p. 7, note 14. Cited with the permission of Professor Peattie.

[68] For a personal account, see Lee Hi-seung, "Recollections of the Korean Language Society Incident," in Pihl, *Listening to Korea*, pp. 19–42.

[69] *Taiwan nippō*, March 6, 1943, p. 2.

Korean colonial government had ever similarly hoped to build a *kokugo Chōsen*, it would have had a much longer way to go. In either case one suspects that it would have taken a good deal of statistical juggling by Japanese colonial authorities to manufacture a *kokugo Taiwan* or *Chōsen*. In sum, we may say that the "national language" movement in Taiwan was significantly more successful than that in Korea. Again, under the surface of apparently similar Japanization programs, one can discern differences in the ways each colonial government carried out its program.

THE NAME-CHANGING CAMPAIGN

On February 11, 1940, the Governments-General in Taiwan and Korea simultaneously proclaimed a set of newly revised regulations concerning household registration that made it legally possible for colonial subjects to replace their original names with Japanese ones. Thus began the name-changing (*kaiseimei*) campaign, which accorded with the transformative principles of the *kōminka* movement. Theoretically, a Taiwanese or a Korean who became a true Japanese should be essentially the same as an ethnic Japanese, in form and substance (in Japanese, *jisshitsu keishiki tomoni naichijin to gōmo kotonaru tokoro no nai*, or, to put it more concisely, *keishinittai*).[70] One of the "forms" that had hitherto distinguished Japanese from the colonial people was the use of names.

Although both colonial governments wanted to make their subjects adopt Japanese names, their reasoning and approaches differed. In Taiwan, the official reason for the name-changing program was twofold. On the one hand, the colonial government declared that assimilating Taiwanese into Japanese culture had always been the ultimate goal of Japanese rule. (I should note here that Japanese colonizers took great pride in the self-perception that while Japan supposedly aimed to assimilate the colonized, western colonization was supposedly characterized by mere economic exploitation.) On the other hand, the government claimed that the Taiwanese had demonstrated the "spirit" of imperial subjects during Japan's war in China and that, in testimony to this loyalty, many of them wished to bear names similar to those of ethnic Japanese.[71] The first of these assertions implied that the name-changing policy was an inevitable outcome of Japanese colonial rule, while the second suggested that such a policy was a reasonable response to Taiwanese wishes. In fact, there was more propaganda than truth in both claims.

[70] *TWNNSP*, February 11, 1940, p. 3; Mitarai, *Minami sōtoku*, p. 24.
[71] *TWNNSP*, February 11, 1940, p. 3.

In Taiwan, according to the new regulations, the name-changing program was a matter for the household rather than the individual; only the head of a household could apply for a name change on behalf of the members of the entire family. One should note that not every Taiwanese family that wished to have the names of its members officially changed to Japanese ones was eligible for this program. There were qualifications to meet. A prospective family must be first recognized as a family in which all its active members spoke Japanese at home. The second qualification was rather abstract; that is, the members of a prospective family must endeavor to cultivate a disposition appropriate for imperial subjects and be full of "public spirit."[72] Given the fact that applicants for name changing had to meet these two qualifications, the *kaiseimei* program in Taiwan was not mandatory.

Interestingly, the choice of new names was restricted. A prohibition against the use of improper names was made public when the *kaiseimei* program commenced. As proclaimed by the authorities, improper names fell into the following four categories: (1) names of Japan's emperors, (2) names of famous historical personalities, (3) surnames indicating the geographical origins of Chinese names previously held by the applicants, (4) other improper names such as names of contemporary important figures and eccentric names.[73]

Among these four prohibitions, the third is most relevant to the subject of this essay and needs some elaboration. In Chinese culture, to change one's surname—let alone to a foreign one—is one of the most humiliating things a person can do. If it became inevitable, therefore, people preferred to choose the least demeaning possible name. Because Chinese geographical names usually consist of two characters, as most Japanese surnames also do, they may pass for Japanese surnames. Thus, by adopting a geographical name as his new Japanese surname, a name changer would have been able to establish an obvious and recognizable link between his old and new names. For instance, Ying-ch'uan, in present-day Honan, is supposedly the place from which the ancestors of people named "Ch'en" came. As a result, it was a time-honored tradition for a Ch'en to be referred to, on some occasions, as a "Ying-ch'uan Ch'en." The same characters that make up "Ying-ch'uan" are pronounced "Eigawa" in Japanese, which happens to be a normal Japanese surname. Thus, it would make an ideal name change for a Taiwanese surnamed "Ch'en" to adopt "Eigawa" as his new Japanese surname,

---

[72] Mamiya Sadakichi, *Taiwan kaiseimei sōdan (kaiseimei ni tomonau: meigi kakukae shoshiki)* (privately published: Tainan, 1941), pp. 7–9.

[73] *TWNNSP*, February 11, 1940, p. 3; Taketa Hisao, *Ronsetsu bunrei kaiseimei tokuhon zenshū* (Taipei: Taiwan kaiseimei suishin kair, 1943), pp. 60–61.

thereby keeping his given name name intact in the written form, although now pronounced in Japanese. Apparently the colonial authorities foresaw that, should such a practice be allowed, there would have been a strong tendency for Taiwanese to use place names indicating their geographical or ancestral origins as their new surnames. The prohibition against geographical names demonstrated some cultural discernment on the part of the authorities, for the effect was to prevent Taiwanese from expressing their Han Chinese identity through their name choices.

The Taiwanese response to the name-changing program was tardy at the outset. In April 1940 only twelve households were granted name changes in the first round (name-changing permits were granted monthly in the first year), and by the end of the year the total was 1,357.[74] The following year, however, witnessed a rapid increase. In January 1941, 2,014 Taiwanese households officially adopted new names, and by the end of the year name changers made up about 1 percent of the total population.[75] By the end of 1943, a total of 17,526 households comprising 126,211 individuals had adopted new names; that is, slightly more than 2 percent of the total population.[76] On January 24, 1944, the Government-General relaxed the requirements, and this led to a surge in name changes.[77] From then on the figures grow sparse, and it is difficult to estimate the final number of Taiwanese who officially adopted Japanese names. But from one source, at least, we may infer that perhaps about 7 percent of the population had adopted Japanese names when the war came to an end in August 1945.[78]

Reviewing the rare lists of name changers, one finds that there were hardly any violations of the four guidelines regarding improper names. Nonetheless, it is easy to detect some conspicuous patterns in new name choices. The new surnames were quite often related to the original family names in one way or another. Just to give a few examples, a person surnamed Huang would prefer a new Japanese surname like Tomota, for Tomota is no more than the single character *huang* dissected

[74] Mamiya, *Kaiseimei sōdan*, p. 160. For the list of name changers, see pp. 161–252.

[75] *TWNNSP*, February 11, 1941 (evening ed.), p. 2; Suzuki Takashi, "Senjika no shokuminchi," in *Iwanami kōza Nihon rekishi* 21, no. 8 (1977): 243.

[76] *KNSB*, January 24, 1944 (evening ed.), p. 2.

[77] For instance, Japanese proficiency requirement was lifted for children and the elderly. Also, families whose member(s) served in the military, government, or public organizations were automatically eligible for name changes. See *KNSB*, January 24, 1944 (evening ed.), p. 2.

[78] A local gazetteer compiled by Taipei County records that among its population of 519,498, 37,742, or over 7 percent, had their Chinese names restored after the war. My inference is based on the assumption that Taipei's percentage was representative. See *T'aipei hsien-chih* (repr. Taipei: Ch'eng-wen ch'u-pan she, 1972), *chüan* 4, p. 1663.

into two characters, *kung* and *t'ien*.[79] Another preferred pattern was to choose a Japanese surname whose characters made up the old surname or part of it, such as Lin-Kobayashi/Nagabayashi, Lü-Miyagawa, and Chang-Hasegawa.[80] The connections are visually detectable. Other patterns show a more subtle link between old names and new ones.[81]

As pointed out previously, the name-changing program in Taiwan was not compulsory, but evidence shows that some public figures were subject to pressure to endorse it by adopting Japanese names.[82] The postwar official historical view that Taiwanese were "forced" to have their Chinese names changed to Japanese ones is an overstatement, though not entirely incorrect.[83]

In Korea, the name-changing program was by nature mandatory. The Korean program was called *sōshi kaimei*, which betrays its basic difference from the *kaiseimei* program in Taiwan. *Kaiseimei* literally means to "*change one's surname* and given name." *Sōshi kaimei*, on the other hand, means to "*create family names* and change one's given name." Here lies the ostensible reason why the colonial government in Korea imposed the name-changing program upon Koreans. As is widely known, Koreans have relatively few surnames—a total of 250 in 1930 for a population of more than twenty million.[84] In order to justify their demand that Koreans change their names, the Japanese colonizers were at pains to argue that the 250 Korean surnames were *sei* (clan names) rather than *shi* (family names). This, the authorities reasoned, was because Koreans had not yet developed a "modern family system":[85] and hence, family names had to be created. In terms of etymology, the distinction between *sei* and *shi* is not completely incorrect. Yet to say that because Koreans did not have family names in the strict sense, they must therefore adopt Japanese ones, was conspicuously manipulative in this particular historical situation.

To illustrate their arguments, the Japanese colonizers presented to Koreans an analysis of Japanese naming customs in terms of the *sei-shi*

[79] In the first round of *kaiseimei*, a Taiwanese named Huang Ch'i-shih adopted a new Japanese name, Tomota Shigeyoshi. See *TWNNSP*, April 14, 1940, p. 2.

[80] Ibid., January 25, 1941, p. 3; Mamiya, *Kaiseimei sōdan*, p. 170; Chung I-jen, *Hsin-suan liu-shih-nien* (Taipei: Tzu-yu shih-tai ch'u-pan she, 1988), pp. 236–37.

[81] Common name-change patterns include what I would call the "anagram pattern," the "component pattern," the "enclosure pattern" and the "synonym pattern." See Chou, "The *Kōminka* Movement," pp. 135–37.

[82] For example, see Yeh Jung-chung, *Lin Hsien-t'ang hsien-sheng chi-nien-chi* (Taichung: Lin Hsien-t'ang hsien-sheng chi-nien-chi pien-chi wei-yüan-hui, 1960), p. 69.

[83] *TWSTCK, chûan* 1b, vol. 2, p. 38.

[84] See Chōsen Sōtokufu, *Chōsen no sei* (Seoul, 1934), p. 1. Kim, Yi, Pak and Ch'oe, in that order, were the most common surnames.

[85] Mitarai, *Minami sōtoku*, p. 22.

distinction. In Japan, Minamoto, Taira, Fuji, and Tachibana are *sei* or clan names, while Konoe, Kokura, Minami, etc., are *shi* or family names. Konoe Fumimaro, then prime minister, who came from an illustrious family, was brought in as an elucidative example. Fujiwara was Konoe Fumimaro's *sei*, emblematic of his clan, while Konoe was his *shi*, representing his family. In other words, adopting new, though Japanese-style, family names did not mean that Koreans were to discard their clan names. On the contrary, name changing was meant to help "modernize" the Korean family system.[86]

The name-changing program began in Korea on February 11, 1940, and allowed the population six months to change their Korean *sei* to Japanese *shi*. According to the new laws, those who failed to register new surnames when the registration period ended would find that their former *sei* automatically become their new *shi*. In his autobiographical work *Lost Names*, Richard E. Kim vividly recounts how ruthlessly the local authorities carried out the name-changing program in his home town. As a fourth-grader, on the morning of February 11 he braved a bitter snow storm on his way to school, only to have his teacher tell him to go home and not report back until he had acquired a Japanese name. Left with little choice, Kim's father, a highly respected anti-Japanese intellectual, went to the police station to register a new name; so did many other parents. Kim's father and some of his friends dressed in traditional Korean attire and wore black armbands. After they registered their new names, they all went to the village cemetery to mourn over the loss of their old names with their ancestors. "By twelve o'clock," writes Kim, "all the children in our class have new names."[87] We should note that similar measures of compulsion did not occur in Taiwan.

Governor General Minami Jirō once said, "It goes without saying that the revision of these [household registration] laws is not one that of its nature forces the general public on the peninsula [i.e., Koreans] to adopt Japanese *shi*."[88] The laws indeed did not specify that the new names should be Japanese ones. Thus, theoretically, a Korean could just adopt his clan name as his new family name. Nonetheless, in reality, a Japanese new name was almost unavoidable. Richard Kim's description of how the Koreans reacted to the name-changing program also tells us that no matter how hard the colonial government tried to make Koreans believe that the program only "created" new family names and did not do away with their clan names, for Koreans it was unmistak-

---

[86] Ibid., p. 23.
[87] Kim, *Lost Names*, pp. 99–106.
[88] Zenshō Eisuke, *Chōsen no seishi to dōzoku buraku* (Tokyo: Tōkyō shoin, 1943), p. 32.

ably a program that aimed at making them give up their Korean names and adopt Japanese ones. Despite official rhetoric, they simply "lost their names."

The Korean name-changing program was very much of a coercive nature. According to official estimates, by August 11, 1940, more than 3.17 million households had new family names; this number was 75 percent or so of the total households. Late registrants were said to be continuing to pour in.[89] Those Koreans who refused to change their names, or failed to do so on time, were discriminated against in various ways. For instance, their children were denied entrance to school and advancement in higher education, and they themselves were deprived of job opportunities or demoted to less important positions.[90] Korean school faculty and staff members who did not adopt Japanese names are said to have been dismissed from their positions.[91] However, how consistent was this punitive policy remains to be examined.

In contrast to the policy in Taiwan, however, the Korean Government-General did not prohibit Koreans from adopting new surnames that indicated their geographical or ancestral origins. On the contrary, many Koreans adopted new names in the Japanese fashion that bore easily discernible connections with their ancestral places. For instance, Koreans surnamed "Pak" had a predilection for adopting "Takamura" as their new surname for the good reason that the two Chinese characters that make up "Takamura" can be an abbreviation of the three that stand for Kŏ Hŏ Ch'on, the place from which their supposed ancestor, Hyŏkkŏse, originated. Similarly, Koreans surnamed Yun favored Sakahira, Suzuhira, Suzuhara, or Hiranuma as their new Japanese surnames, because the ancestors of the Yuns supposedly came from Lake Yong Tŏk at the foot of P'a Pyŏng Mountain (Sakahira in Japanese) in P'a Chu, formerly known as Yŏng pyŏng Mountain and Yŏng wŏn (Suzuhira and Suzuhara, respectively). The characters making "Hiranuma" mean "flat marshes," reminiscent of P'a Pyŏng ("flat hills"), making the surname a good one for Yuns. Apart from making obvious connections with ancestral places, the Koreans, like their Taiwanese counterparts, showed a marked preference for new names that bore visually recognizable associations with their former names. Such a preference is exemplified in name-changing patterns such as Pak-Kiboku, Ch'oe-Yamayoshi, and Hwang-Tomota: in these cases, the character of a Korean surname is di-

---

[89] *Chōsen jijō (1941)*, p. 214. By the end of 1941, the percentage went up to 8.15. See *Atarashiki Chōsen*, p. 78.

[90] See Chōsen Minshushugi jinmin kyōwakoku shakai kagakuin rekishi kenkyūsho kindaishi kenkyūshitsu, *Nippon teikokushugi tōchika no Chōsen*, trans. Kim Yu-hyon (Tokyo: Chōsen seinen sha, 1978), p. 218.

[91] Ko, *Kōnichi genron tōsōshi*, p. 281.

vided into two characters, which are then given their Japanese pronunciation. Phonetic similarity was also popular, as reflected in the patterns of Ch'oe-Sai, Yu-Umori, Kwak-Kaku, Han-Kanda, etc.[92]

In many cases, the precise meaning of a new name was perhaps only clear to the name changer; indeed, a name-changer might use his new name to make a hidden protest. For instance, Richard Kim's father adopted the name Iwamoto, a choice that the authorities regarded as suitable because the Kims were living by a rocky mountain, and *iwamoto* means "foundation of rock." However, the real reason Kim, a Presbyterian, chose this surname was that it echoed the words of Jesus: "On this rock I will build my church."[93] A solemn expression of resistance! Some Koreans, however, unequivocally expressed their protest in their new names. For instance, a Korean named Chŏn Pyŏng-ha adopted a new name pronounced "*tennō heika*," exactly in the way Japanese address their supposedly divinely descended and hence inviolable emperor. Laughable though the name seems, it was a choice that could not have been more blasphemous in the eyes of the Japanese colonizers. There were also cases where Koreans sacrificed their lives to keep their names.[94]

Despite the fact that the name-changing programs in Taiwan and in Korea both served the same goal of transforming the colonial peoples into "true Japanese," the respective colonial governments adopted very different methods in carrying out this program. In general, the name-changing program in Taiwan was more incentive-based and less coercive than that in Korea. The difference between the Taiwanese and the Korean name-changing programs tends to substantiate the commonly held view that Japanese rule in Korea was harsher, whereas in Taiwan it was more benign. Moreover, the Taiwanese and Korean responses to the name-changing program also attest to the essential differences in their respective relationships with the colonial ruler: the Taiwanese relationship with the colonizers was more conciliatory, while the Korean one was more confrontational.

THE MILITARY VOLUNTEER PROGRAM

Before the war Taiwanese and Koreans were not liable to military service. Nonetheless, with a population of about 24 million, Korea had long been regarded as a major reserve of human resources. Ever since 1932, one year after the Manchurian Incident took place, the Chōsen

[92] Shini Hiroshi, "Sōshi mondō," pt. 2, *Keijō nippō*, August 20, 1941 (evening ed.), p. 3.

[93] Kim, *Lost Names*, pp. 105–6.

[94] Suzuki, "Senjika no shokuminchi," p. 241.

Army (Japanese troops stationed in Korea) had been seriously considering the possibility of involving Koreans in the military. In June 1937, one month before the Marco Polo Bridge Incident, the Army Ministry asked the Chōsen Army to offer its suggestions concerning the recruitment of Koreans for military service. In response, the Chōsen Army submitted on July 2 a document entitled "Opinions Concerning the Korean Volunteer System," which suggested that an experimental volunteer system be set up for young Koreans.[95]

On February 22, 1938, the "Laws concerning Army Special Volunteers" were promulgated, which established what was commonly known as the Volunteer System (shiganhei seido). According to these regulations, young Koreans of age seventeen or older could apply to be army volunteers, provided that they met certain requirements. To be qualified for the volunteer program, one needed to be 160 cm in height, receive an A classification in an army physical examination, have an elementary school education or its equivalent, have no criminal or prison record, and also satisfy other requirements.[96] An aspirant had to submit application forms, a physical examination, and other required documents to the police station in the area in which his household was registered. After careful screening at several administrative levels, those who were chosen for further consideration were asked to take both oral and written tests. The written test topics consisted of the "national language," "national history," and arithmetic; the oral test focused on aspirants' "thought, attitudes, and language" with special attention to their proficiency in Japanese.[97] Koreans who were put on the final list entered "the Army volunteers training camp" for six months of military training, and then joined the Army.[98]

Applications for the volunteer program were reported to have poured in in overwhelming numbers, enabling the Government General of Korea to boast of the great enthusiasm among young Koreans for this program. Table 2.2 compares the total numbers of applicants to those of successful applicants for each year between 1938 and 1943. The first group of volunteers was sent to the front in northern China as early as the summer of 1939.

In August 1943, the Government-General took a further step, and implemented the "Navy Special Volunteer System." It was reported that within a month or so after recruitment began, about ninety thousand Koreans applied for the new program.[99] Both the army and the

[95] Miyata, "Kōminka" seisaku, pp. 51–52.
[96] Ibid., p. 58.
[97] Ibid., pp. 59–60.
[98] Chōsen Sōtokufu shisei nempō (1941), p. 158.
[99] Kondō, Chōsen oyobi Taiwan, pp. 34–35.

TABLE 2.2
Number of Korean Military Volunteer Applicants and Those Chosen

Year	Applicants	Successful Applicants
1938	2,946	406
1939	12,348	613
1940	84,443	3,060
1941	44,743	3,208
1942	254,273	4,077
1943	303,294	6,300

Source: Kondō Ken'ichi, ed., *Taiheiyō senka no Chōsen oyobi Taiwan* (Chigasaki: Chōsen shiryō kenkyū kai, 1961), p. 33.

navy volunteer programs were abolished in 1944 when general conscription was introduced. Back in 1937 when the volunteer program was only under consideration, general conscription had been considered something only achievable in future decades.[100] But the practical and urgent need to mobilize Korean human resources for the war effort meant that the conscription system had to be implemented much earlier than anticipated.

In Taiwan, a similar army volunteer program was introduced in 1942. Actually, as early as the fall of 1937, the colonial authorities had already begun recruiting Taiwanese as supply carriers for the military.[101] As Japan's invasion of China intensified and expanded, Taiwanese were also recruited as interpreters of Fukienese, Cantonese, and Mandarin.[102] During the war, the number of Taiwanese supply troops and interpreters was kept secret from the general public, and therefore it is hard to know the total number of recruits.

What I have called the "blood plea" (*kessho*) mania during the volunteer recruitment campaign is worthy of mention. Early in the recruitment of military porters, it was reported that some young men had sent in their application forms each with an attachment written in their own blood pleading for the honor of serving in the military.[103] The first documented "blood plea," dated December 14, 1937, reads: "Long live the Emperor. I am a man of Japan. I possess the spirit of Great Japan. No matter how difficult the task might be, if it is for the sake of His Imperial Majesty as well as for that of our nation, I will not regard it to be

[100] Miyata, *"Kōminka" seisaku*, pp. 52–53.

[101] See Cheng Ch'un-ho, "Wasurerareta Nipponhei," in *Tsuisō* (Newsletter of the Taiwan Southern Star Reunion Association; Taipei, 1988), p. 50.

[102] Shirai Asakichi and Ema Tsunekichi, *Kōminka undō* (Taipei: Tō Taiwan shimbō sha, 1939), p. 167.

[103] Ibid., pp. 157, 166, 335.

difficult. Please take me as a supply carrier."[104] Accompanying this "blood plea" was a rising-sun flag drawn in blood. (Since the national flag simply features a red sun on a white square field, it was comparatively easy to draw on a white handkerchief with blood from a finger.) Written on both sides of the red sun were the slogans: "Long live His Imperial Majesty!" and "Long live the Imperial Military!"[105] The rising sun drawn in blood and accompanied by short slogans became the typical pattern of later "blood pleas."

This act of writing a "blood plea" was to be repeated on a much larger scale in 1941 when Taiwanese were informed that the "Army Volunteer System" would be implemented in the following year. From this time onward it became the fashion for Taiwanese youth to demonstrate their patriotism—a fashion that lasted perhaps until the very end of colonial rule. Evidence is insufficient for us to determine whether the first Taiwanese youth who submitted a "blood plea" did so on his own initiative, or whether the act was suggested by the authorities. I believe the latter alternative is more likely in view of the fact that the same phenomenon was also prevalent in Korea.[106] The former president of South Korea, Park Chung Hee, was said to have written a "blood plea" in his youth. Also, we must not lose sight to the fact that the "blood plea" practice was widespread in Japan proper during wartime. War mobilization in the two colonies was in many aspects an extension of that in the mother country.

The Taiwanese response to the army volunteer program appears to have been more impressive than the Korean response in terms of the ratio of applicants to the population. In 1942, 425,921 Taiwanese, or 14 percent of the male population, turned in applications for one thousand or so volunteer slots.[107] The second round of the army volunteer program had even more applications—601,147 applicants for the same number of slots.[108] Certainly, there were "fake applicants" who applied with the full knowledge that they could not possibly be accepted as volunteers because of old age or poor health. A certain degree of cynicism seems to have lurked in this seemingly genuine patriotic movement.

---

[104] Ibid., pp. 334–35. In Japanese, the "blood plea" reads: "*Tennō heika banzai. Watashi wa Nippon no otoko desu. Yamato damashi ga arimasu, donna kurushi koto demo, Tennō heika no tame, kuni no tame nara, kurushi to wa omoimasen. Gunpu ni shite kudasai.*"

[105] Takeuchi Kiyoshi, *Jihen to Taiwanjin* (Tokyo: Nichiman shinkō bunka kyōkai, 1940), picture pages, unnumbered.

[106] Miyata, *"Kōminka" seisaku*, p. 79.

[107] *KNSB*, June 10, 1942, p. 2. The male population at that time in Taiwan was about 3 million. See *Taiwan tōsei yōran* (Taipei, 1945), p. 23.

[108] *KNSB*, February 13, 1943 (evening ed.), p. 2.

In 1943, navy volunteer systems were simultaneously implemented in Taiwan and in Korea. In Taiwan's first round of applications, 316,097 men applied for roughly three thousand training slots.[109] As general conscription was expected soon to be put into effect in Taiwan, the "Navy Volunteer System" was abolished in late 1944, as was the "Army Volunteer System" in 1945. Up to this point, about 16,500 Taiwanese youth had gone to war—5,500 or so as army volunteers, and 11,000 or so as navy volunteers.[110] General conscription was implemented in April 1945. When the war finally ended in August 1945, the number of Taiwanese who had been recruited into the military totalled 207,183, including soldiers and civilian employees. Of these, 30,304 died in service.[111]

One may ask why so many young Taiwanese and Koreans responded to the call for military service. A commonly held view asserts that young people were forced to apply; such a view is to some extent valid. Nevertheless, to categorically deny the existence of genuine volunteers will prevent us from probing the psychological effects of the *kōminka* movement on Taiwanese and Korean youth. Aside from coercion, there are several factors that might have contributed to young men's apparent enthusiasm. First, the colonial authorities blatantly promoted these programs in highly moral tones. In news media, military service was depicted as the highest honor bestowed upon colonial subjects. Along with compulsory education and taxpaying, it was one of the citizens' "three great obligations" (*sandai gimu*), and the one that colonial subjects had not yet been called on to fulfill.[112] The colonizer even drew an analogy between taxpaying and military service, calling the latter the "blood tax."[113] The implementation of the "Army Volunteer System" in Taiwan was hailed as "the islanders' highest honor" (*tōmin no saikō eiyo*), or "the supreme glory" (*mujō no kōei*).[114] The same high-sounding language was echoed in Korea.[115]

Second, local authorities used various channels to mobilize young men for these programs. One source reveals that in a district meeting in Keijō (Seoul), it was decided that for the purpose of promoting the

[109] Ibid., July 23, 1943 (evening ed.), p. 2; September 22, 1943, p. 2; Taiwan Sōtokufu, *Shōwa nijūnen Taiwan tōchi gaiyō* (Taipei, 1945), p. 73.

[110] Ibid., p. 72.

[111] See Yang Pi-ch'uan, ed., *T'ai-wan li-shih nien-piao* (Taipei: Tzu-li wan-pao ch'u-pan bu, 1983), p. 187.

[112] *Goen*, 34, no. 7 (July 1942), p. 43; *TWKSJH*, no. 317 (April 1942), p. 12.

[113] Miyata, *"Kōminka" seisaku*, p. 107.

[114] *KNSB*, July 8, 1941, p. 4; July 9, 1941 (evening ed.), p. 2; July 3, 1941, p. 2; July 9, 1941 (evening ed.), p. 2.

[115] Miyata, *"Kōminka" seisaku*, p. 107.

volunteer program, town representatives were to visit the family of every elementary-school graduate in the area under their charge. Principals of elementary schools were to appeal to the Youth Corps—organizations set up in 1920s with the function of a continuing education program and the purpose of cultivating in elementary-school graduates the qualities of loyal and good subjects[116]—attached to their schools. High-school principals were to persuade their graduates to apply for the volunteer program.[117] In the case of Taiwan, although I have not come across direct sources detailing how the authorities mobilized young Taiwanese for the volunteer program, circumstantial evidence shows that the Youth Corps were the main organizations through which the authorities mobilized young Taiwanese. During the *kōminka* era the Youth Corps for men and women alike seem to have been readily at the disposal of the authorities for the *kōminka* programs.

In addition, peer pressure seems to have played an important role in young people's "volunteer fever," for example in the writing of "blood pleas." But writing a "blood plea" seems also to have assumed a life of its own, signifying a heroic and romantic act of patriotism among young people, including young girls. Women were not recruited into the fighting forces, but they could be directly involved in the war effort by becoming nurses. Many young women responded to official recruitment campaigns for wartime nursing assistants in more or less the same fashion as their male counterparts did to the volunteer program. A young girl in Taiwan likened wartime nursing assistants to "female military volunteers."[118] It was also not uncommon for young girls to send in "blood pleas" expressing their deep desire to go to the front as nurses.[119] The impact of these officially praised "heroic young people" upon their peers is, of course, difficult to measure in precise terms, but the influence appears to be rather significant.

Finally, to some young men pride was at stake in the colonial subjects' response to the volunteer program. The military was an arena where one could truly compete with ethnic Japanese and prove the high qualities of one's race, or even its superiority to that of the Japanese. This explains why some proud Koreans were determined to be "more Japanese than a Japanese" (*Nipponjin ijō Nipponjin*).[120] Nor is it surprising that Taiwanese veterans took great pride in remembering that their perfor-

[116] Taiwan Sōtokufu, *Taiwan jijō (1936)*, pp. 203–4.

[117] *Keijō nippō*, November 6, 1941, p. 4.

[118] *KNSB*, March 20, 1942 (evening ed.), p. 2.

[119] *TWKSJH*, no. 310 (September 1941), "Hontō jiji nisshi"; *TTWSP*, February 7, 1942, p. 2.

[120] Miyata, *"Kōminka" seisaku*, p. 79.

mance had equaled, if not exceeded, that of Japanese servicemen.[121] Thus, ironically and paradoxically, even if the colonial governments could make a young person act as a Japanese, that youth's earnest wishes to behave like a "true Japanese" might still come from a deep sense of pride in his or her ethnic origins as well as the will to compete with the ruling race.

Conclusion

From the comparisons presented in the previous sections, one might easily get the impression that the measures adopted by the colonial government in Taiwan in carrying out the *kōminka* movement were more benign than those in Korea. In terms of response, the way Taiwanese responded to each *kōminka* program varied. In general, religious reforms met the coldest reception; the name-changing program was also unpopular among Taiwanese, at least in the beginning. With regard to the "national language" movement, the rapid growth of the population of "national language speakers" during the *kōminka* era seems to suggest a certain degree of success. Finally, the volunteer program, targeted at young people, seems to have aroused enthusiasm among them.

Korean response to each of the *kōminka* programs largely followed the same pattern, but the Koreans often showed more resistance and less compliance than the Taiwanese in each case. Scholars in the field of Japanese colonial history have long noticed that the colonial experiences of Taiwan and Korea differed in that the interactions between the ruler and the ruled in Korea were much more violent and stormy than those in Taiwan. The study of the *kōminka* movement helps substantiate this impression.

The study of the *kōminka* movement also leads us to ponder its impact upon historical developments in postcolonial Taiwan and Korea. There is no doubt that the *kōminka* movement was imposed by the Japanese colonizers upon their colonial subjects and that most colonial subjects passively complied with it. Nonetheless, Japan's attempts to instill loyalties among its colonial subjects were not without their successes, and this wartime Japanization movement had a particularly strong influence on the Taiwanese and the Koreans who spent their formative years in the *kōminka* era. As is often true of many political campaigns in modern times, youth is perhaps more receptive to political indoctrination than other age groups. Miyata Setsuko points out in the

---

[121] For example, see Ch'en Yung-tai, "Fukuin shite yonjūni shūnen . . . no kaikō," *Tsuisō*, p. 21; Ch'en Fen-hsiang, "Kako no tsuisō," Ibid., p. 40.

preface to her book on the Korean *kōminka* policy that some of her Korean friends of the *kōminka* generation, when drunk, sing nothing but Japanese military songs, and on suitable occasions they can still recite the "Imperial Rescript on Education," "Admonitions on the Battlefield," the names of Japanese emperors, and similar fragments of remembered propaganda.[122] It is no surprise that a Taiwanese veteran would still consider that he was once a Japanese and would be more than ready to sing Japanese military songs for an interviewer.[123] One should note that Miyata's friends are Korean expatriates who continued to live in Japan after the war ended, and it is understandable that the influence of the *kōminka* movement upon them should remain intact. Conversely, Koreans in Korea proper, having finally regained independence, seem to have long eradicated a great part, if not all, of the imprint the *kōminka* movement left on their lives.

The impact of the *kōminka* movement upon Taiwanese, however, took a different turn. I suspect that the *kōminka* movement, though it failed to convert Taiwanese into true Japanese, did cause some confusion of national identity among Taiwanese, particularly the younger generation. In other words, the *kōminka* movement may not have succeeded in turning Taiwanese into Japanese, but it may have succeeded in making them less Chinese, more easily alienated from a Chinese government that not only failed to live up to their expectations but also disheartened them by various acts of misconduct and bloody repression.[124]

In summary, the *kōminka* movements in Taiwan and in Korea seem to have shared very similar features, but if the movements are examined closely, the similarities are only surface-deep. Not only did the two colonial governments adopt very different approaches to their respective *kōminka* movements, but also the responses of Taiwanese and Koreans differed significantly. In the postcolonial era, the impact of these movements also precipitated very divergent historical developments in Taiwan and Korea; their respective histories can only be properly understood if the influence of the *kōminka* movement is appreciated—an area that, of course, awaits more research.

[122] Miyata, *"Kōminka" seisaku*, p. 2.

[123] See Usui Kazumitsu, *Shōson* (Osaka: Kōbō U, 1987), pp. 4–5. Furthermore, in an interview I conducted with Chang Tzu-ching, a Taiwanese World War II veteran, Chang offered to sing Japanese military songs for me.

[124] Certainly, the best-known and most serious conflict between Taiwanese and the Nationalist government in the postwar period was the February 28 Incident of 1947. For a recent study, see Lai Tse-han, Ramon H. Myers, and Wei Wou, *A Tragic Beginning: The Taiwan Uprising of February 28, 1947* (Stanford, Calif.: Stanford University Press, 1991).

PART II

Japan's Wartime Empire and Northeast Asia

CHAPTER 3

Imagined Empire: The Cultural Construction of Manchukuo

Louise Young

For most Japanese today "Manchukuo" has receded into the recesses of history books, a dusty relic of a rather sordid past. Yet for their countrymen and women of half a century ago, the name of the Japanese puppet state in Northeast China evoked associations more positive and immediate: the efficiency and martial spirit of the Japanese army in Manchuria, the splendor of the new colonial cities built by Japanese capital and know-how, the utopian promise of planned Japanese agricultural colonies. It was in 1905, following its victory in the war against Russia, that Japan first acquired a sphere of influence in the provinces of Northeast China and entered the ranks of the imperialist powers. Over the course of the next forty years, this foothold on the continent grew into an empire of striking proportions. The Japanese built the former Russian rail network into the mighty South Manchurian Railway, a company that ranked among the five most profitable Japanese enterprises for much of the imperial period.[1] The forces created to protect the new possessions evolved into the Kwantung Army, the most celebrated of Japan's colonial garrison forces. Hundreds of thousands of Japanese farm emigrants moved to Northeast China, and by 1945 over a thousand Japanese villages dotted the rural landscape.

Much of this activity took place during the wartime phase of empire in Manchuria. Between the Manchurian Incident of 1931 and the defeat in 1945, Japan engaged in empire building on a grand scale, transforming Manchuria from a sphere of influence into the puppet state of Manchukuo. The new face of empire showed itself in three arenas of activity—military conquest, economic development, and population settlement. First, under the guidance of the Kwantung Army, thousands spilled their blood in a series of military campaigns collectively known as the Manchurian Incident, which aimed to extend military

---

[1] The SMR was ranked first in 1929 and fourth in 1943. Nakamura Seishi, "Hyakusha rankingu no hensen," *Chūō kōron keiei mondai* (special issue, Fall 1977); *Kigyō tōkei sōran* (Tōyō keizai shinpō-sha, 1943).

control over the whole of Northeast China. Second, elaborate plans were undertaken to make Manchuria an extension of the Japanese economy, tying its development in an intimate new relationship to domestic production goals. Finally, a grandiose plan to send a million Japanese to settle their families in the Manchurian hinterland was designed to rear a new generation of "continental Japanese" who would secure a more thorough domination of colonial society. In the service of these three endeavors more than a million Japanese soldiers, entrepreneurs, and agricultural emigrants did in fact cross the sea. While these groups invested their future and sometimes their lives in the making of Manchukuo, at home many times their number labored to build the empire in indirect, though no less essential, ways. During the military campaigns of 1931–33 a wave of war hysteria swept Japanese society, generating the domestic political and social support that gave the Kwantung Army freedom of action. Businessmen and intellectuals, fired by utopian visions of economic opportunity, used their social standing to sell the idea of staking Japan's future on Manchukuo's development. Local elites led rural communities to endorse plans for the transportation of as many as half their villagers to the new land. Although they never set foot in Manchuria, these people were empire builders nonetheless. What they constructed became the metropolitan infrastructure of imperialism. For all the changes wrought on the Manchurian landscape, imperialism exacted a corresponding transformation at home.

This metropolitan structure was built both as a social movement and as a cultural construction. Domestic society mobilized itself in a wide range of ways to support military, economic, and social expansion into Manchuria. Whether it was army propaganda campaigns, chamber of commerce committees, youth group observation trips, housewives' collection drives, or emigration aid societies, a variety of social movements played a part in the ongoing process of mobilization for empire. Mobilization, in turn, involved the formation of an ideological consensus to support the imperial projects. This consensus building generated a set of images of the empire, a cultural edifice constructed in stages as the impulse of imperialism moved from military, to economic, to settlement. The Japanese first knew Manchukuo as a battlefield, then it became associated with various schemes for economic development, and finally it was linked with the vision of hardy Japanese pioneers in an expansive social frontier. For the vast majority of Japanese, this imagined empire was more real than its physical embodiment across the sea.

Imperialism wove an increasingly intricate web of connections between empire and metropolis. Military occupation set in place one network of ties; economic development engendered another. Both of these were intertwined with the associations generated by Japanese settlement. Each soldier who fought to defend the "Manchurian lifeline," each shipment of cement used for the development of Manchukuo, and each tenant farmer who settled in the "new heaven on earth" added to the whole. This tapestry of imperial experiences depicted the story of Japan's domination over another people, but through the eyes of the imperialist. Chinese and Korean inhabitants of Northeast China had their own versions of this history, which plays only a small part in this story. For the subject of this essay is not Japan in Manchuria, but Manchuria in Japan.

WAR FEVER: 1931–1933

The Manchurian Incident was a historical watershed for Japan. Between September 1931 and the Tangku truce of May 1933, Japan's Kwantung Army carried out a series of campaigns to overthrow the political administration of warlord Chang Hsüeh-liang and expel his army from the four provinces of Northeast China known as Manchuria. Japan's new military imperialism had two distinctive characteristics. First, in the initial phases of the conflict, the Kwantung Army deliberately subverted the authority of the central government in Tokyo and expanded the theater of war on its own initiative. The government consequently split into two opposing factions, one pushing for and the other trying to hold back military expansion. Second, after militarily occupying Manchuria, the Kwantung Army set itself up as the new political authority in the region, ruling through the puppet government of Manchukuo. Thus, the first phase in the construction of Manchukuo represented an aggressive army bid for political power at home and in the empire.

The success of this endeavor owed much to the outbreak of war fever in 1931. The latest action on the China continent provided the lead news story for almost two years. War songs set the fashion in popular music while battlefield dramas filled the stage and screen. National and local elections were dominated by the burning foreign policy issue and candidates held to account for "weak knees" on the Manchuria question. School children collected money to buy planes and steel helmets. Crowds thronged to railway stations to send off and welcome home their local regiments. For the twenty-one months of war with China, Manchuria obsessed the nation.

The Manchurian war fever began with a news war. Japan's largest newspaper chains, the *Asahi shimbun* and the *Mainichi shimbun*, fought with the fledgling NHK radio network to capture the growing consumer market for news. Spurring a rise in popular demand for news from the front, the Manchurian campaigns put a premium on the scoop, and gave special advantage to radio. With its unique ability to put news on the air the minute it came in on the wire, NHK was able to expand rapidly during the Manchurian Incident. Radio competed with the press by increasing its regular news programming from four to six times a day, as well as through *rinji nyūzu*—unscheduled news flashes. This device was first employed, appropriately, to scoop the big dailies on the events of September 18. In a special report that interrupted the early morning calisthenics program, a six-minute news broadcast broke the story of the "clash between our Railway Defense Corps . . . and the Chinese First Brigade."[2]

The newspapers fought back as best they could, pouring money into shuttling special correspondents and teams of photographers in unprecedented numbers back and forth across the Sea of Japan. By November 15, the Asahi had sent at least thirty-three special correspondents to Manchuria, and the Mainichi chain fifty by January 1.[3] To counter radio's *rinji nyūzu*, the newspapers employed the longstanding practice of *gogai* or extras, sometimes putting out two separate multipage, photo-filled extras between the morning and evening editions.[4]

Starting in the news media, the Manchurian war boom quickly spread to other areas of mass culture. Just as the press and radio sensationalized the war to compete for a share of the news market, other culture industries promoted the consumption of war theme products to buoy up sluggish earnings during a period of economic depression. In the process, books, magazines, movies, records, and other forms of popular entertainment took the mood of national crisis primed by the news media and infused it with the boisterousness of a carnival. But the significance of the media's warmongering went beyond mere sensationalism. While the government was still divided over whether to encourage the Kwantung Army's occupation of Manchuria or try to restrain it, the mass media endorsed the occupation, turning itself into an unofficial propaganda wing of the army.

After a decade-long policy of championing disarmament and a soft-line toward China, this position was a dramatic volte-face on the part of the Asahi and Mainichi papers.[5] In the Asahi's case, editorial decisions made close on the heels of September 18 stated that "though the newspaper remains in favor of disarmament," in the interests of "unifying public opinion behind the army," the paper would not "criticize or op-

---

[2] Ikei Masaru, "1930 nendai no masu media—Manshū jihen e no taiō o chūshin toshite," in Miwa Kimitada, ed., *Saikō taiheiyō sensō zen'ya—Nihon no 1930 nendairon toshite,* (Tokyo: Sōseiki, 1980), p. 146.

[3] Abe Shingo, "Manshū jihen o mawaru shinbungai," *Kaizō,* November 1931, pp. 36–39; Eguchi Keiichi, "Manshū jihen to daishimbun," *Shisō,* no. 583 (January 1973), p. 100.

[4] Ibid., pp. 36–37.

[5] Eguchi Keiichi, *Jūgonen sensō no kaimaku* (Tokyo: Shōgakkan, 1988), pp. 99–105; William Morton, *Tanaka Giichi and Japan's China Policy* (Folkstone, Kent: Dawson Publishing, 1980), pp. 70–74, 86–95, 100–101, 118–20, 138–39, and passim.

pose in any way military action or the military itself." Mainichi executives decided that their paper would treat China "as an enemy country" and therefore refrain from using "titles and honorifics for Chinese nationals."[6] In practice, reports wired in by special correspondents in the field came straight from the lips of Kwantung Army spokesmen. As one contemporary described the situation, "not only did virtually all the coverage from the front take a hard-line slant," but reports from Tokyo journalists "gave preferential treatment to army information" and journalists in the rest of the country were "following suit."[7]

The popular impact of such policies was dramatic. On the first anniversary of the Manchurian Incident, the chief of staff of the Third Division, Colonel Inuzuka Hiroshi, observed how much things had changed since the beginning of the war. "At first there were quite a few Japanese who judged the army as if it were on trial. Consciousness of Manchuria was nil."[8] Yet within six months it had become all-consuming. Manchuria was turned into a "lifeline" which required the sacrifice of lives and treasure: to hold it Japanese were willing to fly in the face of concerted Western opposition and relinquish their place among the great powers in the League of Nations.

The path from indifference and ignorance to national obsession was trod, for many ordinary Japanese, by skimming the daily news, listening to popular songs, or reading their favorite magazines. The self-appointed educators in the mass media took to their task with enthusiasm, setting forth a popular catechism on "why we fight."

The first response to this question became the battlecry of the Manchurian Incident: *Mamore Manmō seimeisen!*—defend the Manchurian-Mongolian lifeline! The slogan's popular appeal underscored a new sense of connectedness between the ordinary citizen and this faraway place known only from maps. In popular magazines the nature of the connection was drawn in terms both personal and immediate, resurrecting memories of the Russo-Japanese War, fought on Manchurian soil, and tapping the anxieties of a society in severe economic distress.

Memories of a conflict that had cost ¥1.8 billion and mobilized over a million soldiers confused the war's aims with the subsequent peace settlement. The much-repeated phrase, the "payment of a hundred

---

[6] Toyama Bunzō (Kempei shireikan), "Osaka Asahi Osaka Mainichi no jikyoku ni taisuru taidō kettei ni kansuru ken hōkoku," October 19, 1931; *Manshū jihen to kokumin dōin* ed. Fujiwara Akira et al. (Tokyo: Ōtsuki shoten, 1983), p. 96.

[7] Abe, "Manshu jihen o mawaru shinbungai," p. 36.

[8] *Nagoya shinbun*, September 18, 1932, cited in Eguchi Keiichi, "Manshū jihen to minshū dōin—Nagoya shi o chūshin toshite," in *Nitchū senso shi kenkyū*, ed. Furuya Tetsuo (Tokyo: Yoshikawa kōbunkan, 1984), p. 127.

thousand lives and a billion yen in blood and treasure for Manchuria,"[9] implied that, as most people believed, Japan had fought Russia in 1904 over Manchuria. Forgetting that it was, in fact, the struggle for control over Korea that had precipitated the war, and that Japan had gained its Korean colony as a result of the victory, Japanese in the 1930s somehow felt that Manchuria comprised the single benefit and the sole compensation for a tremendous sacrifice. The renewed popularity of Russo-Japanese war songs, especially elegies like *Sen'yū* (Comrade), revived the tragic associations of Manchuria, and projected the memories of the human cost of the war into the meaning of "lifeline."

> Here, many hundreds of leagues from home,
> The red setting sun of distant Manchuria shines down
> On a stone at the edge of a field
> Beneath which my friend lies.

> It grieves me to think of the brave hero
> Who only yesterday headed the charge,
> Ruthlessly setting upon the enemy—
> I wonder will he sleep well here

> At the height of the battle
> I raced blindly to the friend
> Who had been at my side,
> As he fell suddenly, the flag with him.

The popularity of *Sen'yū* had made phrases such as given phrases like "red setting sun" (*akai yūhi*) and "hundreds of leagues from home" (*koko wa okuni o nanbyaku ri*) evocative associations with Manchuria.[10] Reentering popular currency after 1931, their association with death and sacrifice reinforced a sense of "blood debt" to the Russo-Japanese War generation. Employing a familiar Confucian vocabulary of familial obligation, appeals to "defend the lifeline" in 1931–33 suggested that the young owed it to their parents to protect the Manchurian empire. A reader's poem (*senryū*) published in the popular magazine *Kingu* depicted service on the Manchurian battlefront as forging a special bond between father and son.

> Remembering Manchuria with a full heart,
> He leaves the warmth of the fire,
> To see his firstborn off to Manchuria.[11]

[9] See for example, "Ie no hikari shimbun," *Ie no hikari*, January 1932, p. 166.

[10] *Sen'yū*, lyrics reprinted in Hamano Kenzaburō, ed., *Aa Manshū* (Tokyo: Jūgen shobō, 1970), p. 119.

[11] Asō Jirō, "Senryū," *Kingu*, April 1932, p. 245.

In addition to popular images of a line of blood and spirit that indebted the living to the dead, the "lifeline" came to symbolize an economic umbilical chord. For a society mired in depression, the image of an economic lifeline reflected the hope of recovery and fears of even worse collapse. Articles in best-selling magazines like *Kingu* (King) and *Ie no hikari* (Light of the Home) called Manchuria a "bottomless treasurehouse," "unlimited land," "inexhaustible resources"—in short the "key to the national economy." An illustrated map in *Kingu* depicted Manchuria as a cornucopia of resources. From the ground emerged heaps of iron ore, glinting mountains of gold, and smokey piles of coal. The endless plain teemed with livestock: galloping horses, lowing cows, roaming camels, and grazing sheep. The rich earth yielded soybeans, cotton, wheat, sorghum, barley, and countless other grains. When Japan unlocked the treasurehouse, these articles optimistically predicted, abundance would wash over Japan's shores.

The images of Manchuria as abundance and economic plenty combined with an argument that Manchuria represented a strategic economic connection, a vital safeguard of Japan's independence. Japan's poverty of resources, for both military and civilian production, dictated the need to hold on to Manchuria: with Manchuria in tow Japan could not be subjected to economic blackmail.[12] In this way, the culturally constructed "lifeline" that tied Japan to Manchuria drew on emotional baggage of the past as well as economic insecurities of the present.

The catechism on "why we are fighting" went beyond the connection between Manchuria and Japan, between empire and metropolis. It spoke as well to the relations between Japan and the world. Japanese imperial ideology had from the start been highly sensitive to international standing, taking pride in a perceived superiority over other Asian countries and obsessively concerned with the attitudes of the Western powers. As Japanese imperialism entered a new phase in the 1930s, the imperial discourse on Self and Other became more overtly chauvinistic, expressing race hates and race fears forcefully and vociferously. While their troops were overrunning Manchuria, the Japanese told themselves: we are fighting because we are better than the Chinese and because we are not afraid of the West.

Resentment that Chinese dared to snatch from Japanese hands the precious "Manchurian lifeline" was quickly transformed into victory euphoria as news of the fall of city after city came in over the wires. These seemingly effortless victories unleashed a wave of self-congratulatory articles about the drubbing Japan was giving China and of the

---

[12] "Dare ni mo wakaru Manshū jijō omoshiroi ebanashi," ibid., pp. 33–56; "Manshū wa Nihon no seimeisen," *Ie no hikari*, January 1932, p. 166.

ineptitude of the Chinese soldiery. Incessant boasting about the "two hundred thousand Chinese against ten thousand Japanese" took no notice of China's widely advertised nonresistance policy. Transforming this statistic into an index of China's martial deficiency, popular magazines gave rise to a sense that each Japanese soldier was worth twenty of the enemy's. As major military targets such as Mukden and Kirin were occupied virtually without bloodshed, in magazines like *Shonen kurabu* (*Boys' Club*) voluntary withdrawal, voluntary disarmament, and other forms of nonresistance were transformed into a cowardly and disorganized retreat. Resurrecting old Sino-Japanese War images, stories on the Incident invariably showed Chinese soldiers in the act of "bolting," "escaping," "running off," "hiding"—or as the favorite phrase had it, "fleeing pell-mell like scattering spider babies" (*kumo no ko o chirasu yō ni nigemadotte imasu*).[13] Ultimate proof for this judgment was provided, according to popular wisdom, by China's appeal for League of Nations mediation in the dispute. As a schoolboy summed it up: "Japan is good at war. China didn't win so they brought the issue to the League of Nations."[14]

While tall tales of Chinese cowardice circulated and Japanese congratulated themselves on their legendary military prowess, strong criticism from the West invoked shrill denunciations of "outside pressure" and assertions of the *seigi*, or righteousness, of Japan's actions. The thinly veiled fear behind the bluster manifested itself in a contradictory tendency first to inflate the extent of the threat and then to minimize its significance. Scores of articles in such unlikely places as the household magazine for farmers *Ie no hikari* gave blow-by-blow accounts of the Sino-Japanese controversy in the League, raising the specter of worldwide economic sanctions and war. Though sanctions had never been on the table at the League, it was widely reported in Japan that Council resolutions censuring Japan's actions threatened Japan with an "international economic blockade if it did not withdraw its troops."[15] A boom in war-scare literature with titles like "If Japan Should Fight" warned that it was "only a matter of time" before the "unavoidable clash between America and Japan."[16]

Exaggerating the Western threat on the one hand, these same popular magazines turned rhetorical somersaults to quell public fear of reprisals.

[13] Imamura Kakichi, "Manshū no Shinahei," *Shonen kurabu*, February 1932, p. 75; Suzuki Gyōsui, "Teki no shōkō ressha o kōgeki suru waga hikōki," ibid.

[14] Hirata Minoru, "Hayaku nakayoshi ni," in "Bokura wa me no mae ni Manshū jihen o mita," ibid., p. 68.

[15] "Seppaku shite kita Manshūkoku no shōnin," *Ie no hikari*, August 1932, p. 182.

[16] Hirata Shinsaku, "Nihon moshi tatakawaba," *Shōnen kurabu*, May 1932, pp. 81–92; "Manshūkoku shōnin ni taisuru kakkoku no ikō," *Ie no hikari*, November 1932, p. 56.

A *Kingu* article explained that since America was dependent on Japanese imports it would never apply sanctions. But even if it should, ventured the author, with a few substitutions and "national will," overcoming trade dependence on food, oil, cotton, and so forth "would not be difficult." The war bogey was similarly dismissed. "I cannot imagine sanctions leading to war," an army officer was quoted as saying. Neither anti-Western bluster nor derision of the Chinese were new to imperial rhetoric, but the explosive force and all-inclusiveness of antiforeign ideas circulated in the early thirties was. Xenophobia in the mass media helped mobilize public support for the unprecedented step of withdrawal from the League, the first time since the Meiji Restoration that the Japanese government had taken action to isolate the nation from the Western diplomatic community.

The military imperialism initiated on September 18, 1931, brought images of Japan-Manchurian connections and national antipathies to the forefront of public consciousness, making the military project in Manchuria part of the active vocabulary of empire-building. Although sporadic military operations in Manchuria continued even after the ceasefire of May 1933, home-front mobilization and cultural production never again achieved the intensity of those early years. The associations and images of the Manchurian battlefield circulated during this high-growth phase became the first building blocks of the cultural edifice of Manchukuo, in which people at home learned to live and breath their empire.

The Manchuria Boom: 1933–1937

As the military situation was brought under control and the Tangku Truce of 1933 signaled a formal end to hostilities, the nature of the imperial project in Manchuria began to change. With the creation of the puppet state of Manchukuo in 1932, the extension of Japanese political control over the four provinces of Northeast China opened up a new frontier for economic expansion. The warlord regime of Chang Hsüeh-liang was driven out and a pro-Japanese faction enlisted to help the Kwantung Army administer the new state. The new puppet government acted quickly to sweep away the network of legal barriers used by Chang to obstruct Japanese economic penetration.

Before 1932 Japan's geographic scope of activity had been confined to the Kwantung Leased Territory and the railway zone in South Manchuria. The instrument of penetration, the enormous public-private colonial railway concern Mantetsu (South Manchurian Railway), had been mainly active in the transport of soybeans. In the first five years of Manchukuo's existence, however, the existing structures of economic imperialism were radically transformed, altering economic policy in Manchuria and Japan, as well as the relationship between the two economies.

First, under a new regime of imperial management known as the "controlled economy," the Manchukuo government carried out a bold experiment in planned economic development and state capitalism. Second, economic expansion in Manchukuo became a critical tool in Japanese domestic economic policy, helping to reflate a stagnant economy. A large-scale industrial and infrastructural development financed by a rush of public and private funds soaked up idle capital, while the accompanying leap in exports to Manchuria helped put Japan's factories back to work. Finally, the integration of the two economies, called the "Japan-Manchuria bloc economy," committed both empire and metropolis to a strategy of mutual dependence from which neither could readily withdraw. In investment alone Japan committed over ¥1.4 billion between 1932 and 1937, a sum nearly equaling its total overseas investments before 1930.[17] This sum did not readily permit a pulling back or radical shift in strategy. Together these three changes defined the new face of economic imperialism.

Domestically this transformation was attended by the emergence of an economic boom, generating a new wave of popular enthusiasm for empire building even as the military campaigns were receding from the front pages. Still feeling the flush of victory and consumed with the domestic and international economic crisis, people turned eagerly to the paths opened up before them in Manchuria. The mass media rang with watchwords of economic imperialism, as "Economic construction" and "Japan-Manchuria bloc" replaced "Manchurian lifeline" in the headlines. Politicians of Left and Right pinned their hopes on a new economic order in Manchukuo, free of what both called "the excesses of capitalism." Bureaucratic power struggles over the authority to oversee Manchuria's development rocked the government. The business world looked to a "Manchurian prosperity" to swing the economy around and offer an avenue for sustained growth.

The Manchukuo government, dominated by the Kwantung Army, and the executives of Japan's leading business firms were key players in the new economic imperialism. Both had specific agendas for Manchukuo, and each needed the cooperation of the other to pursue these. From the first policy statements on the controlled economy that emerged from the Manchukuo government, it became clear to big business leaders that they did not see eye to eye with the Kwantung Army

[17] Yamazaki Hiroaki, Shibagaki Kazuo, and Hayashi Takehisa, *Nihon shihonshugi*, vol. 6, *Kōza teikokushugi no kenkyū* (Tokyo: Aoki shoten, 1973, p. 250.

on the goals of the game. This conflict of interest led businessmen to a strategy of cooperating in name with Manchukuo government aims, while in practice carrying out their own informal economic policy.

In the early phases of policy formation, the Manchukuo government sent mixed signals to the private sector about its role in Manchuria's new economic regime. On one hand, the Kwantung Army made sporadic efforts to court the goodwill of businessmen, inviting the Japan Chamber of Commerce to send delegates to a conference on economic policy in January 1932, and making army representatives available to meet with businessmen and discuss their concerns.[18] On this occasion spokesmen professed the army's desire to cooperate with private industry. Businessmen came away feeling sanguine about working with the army, announcing their intention "to give as much financial support as possible to the construction of the new Manchuria."[19]

Yet this show of welcome was compromised by information appearing in the press about army hostility to capital. At a meeting in December 1931 with business leader Yamamoto Jōtarō, Army Minister Araki Sadao reportedly declared the army's intention to "exclude monopoly profits of capitalists" from Manchuria. Even while Kwantung Army Commander Honjō Shigeru was toasting the fortunes of his corporate guests, he was being quoted as saying: "We want to use Manchuria as the means to renovate (kaizō) Japan . . . and intend to absolutely exclude finance capital and the influence of political parties from Manchuria." Such opinions were summarized in what became known as the Kwantung Army's unofficial slogan for Manchurian development: "zaibatsu wa Manshū ni hairu bekarazu"—"big business must not come into Manchuria."[20]

To many business executives, proof of army antagonism to their interests came with the announcement of the Manchukuo government's "Economic Construction Program" in March 1933. Tokyo and Osaka business leaders felt that state planning and economic controls should be used only for the purpose of discouraging the growth of industries that would compete with existing domestic production—opinions that were clearly communicated to the army. As the businessmen stressed most

---

[18] William Miles Fletcher III, *The Japanese Business Community and National Trade Policy, 1920–1942* (Chapel Hill: University of North Carolina Press, 1989), p. 78.

[19] *Tokyo Asahi*, April 2, 1932, cited in Suzuki Tōzaburō, "Man-Mō shinkokka to Nihon no kinyū shihon," *Kaizō*, May 1932, p. 66.

[20] Suzuki Takashi, "Manshū keizai kaihatsu to Manshū jūkogyō no seiritsu," *Tokushima Daigaku gakugei kiyō (shakai kagaku)* 13, special issue (1963): 99. For typical media treatments see Suzuki Takeo, "Nichi-Man burokku keizai-ron no sai-kentō," *Kaizō*, January 1933, pp. 53–67, and Suzuki Tōzaburō, "Man-Mō shinkokka to Nihon no kinyū shihon," ibid., May 1932, pp. 64–71.

vociferously, the controlled economy should not be employed to restrict the freedom of action of capital in the development of Manchuria, interfere in the management of industry, or limit the rate and use of profits.[21] The Economic Construction Program ignored this advice, serving notice to big business that "national control" would be "exerted on important economic activities" to protect "the interests of the people as a whole" and to prevent economic development being "monopolized" by an "exclusive class of people."[22]

Within Japanese business circles this program was viewed with unabashed scorn. In what represented a typical opinion, an Osaka industrialist ridiculed the army for its shortsighted hostility to capital. "If the policy of complete economic control is applied to Manchukuo industrialization, it will act as a check on the flow of urgently necessary capital from Japan. Such an arbitrary order cannot possibly have any appeal for capital in a capitalist system. Moreover, widely publicizing the fact that certain parties in Manchuria want to exclude capitalists has created an even greater impediment to capital investment. . . . There is no other way for Manchukuo to get the capital it needs except from Japanese capitalists. Capital in the current meaning of the term will not invest on the basis of patriotism."[23]

Although information emanating from Manchukuo and the anticapitalist thrust of the Economic Construction Program may have dampened business ardor for participating in state-controlled industrial development, private enterprise had no intention of backing away from Manchukuo. Yet unlike the Manchukuo government, profits stood at the top of its agenda. This did not mean that it opposed government policy outright, but rather tried to turn the situation to its own advantage. Thus business executives adopted a wait-and-see attitude toward the more radical elements of the Economic Construction Program, such as state ventures in resource development, and moved forward boldly in areas that had proved profitable in the past, like consumer exports. Despite their reservations about the direction of Manchukuo government policy, business leaders judged that the best advantage lay in a show of cooperation rather than public antagonism. Calculating that

[21] Business views were expressed in the various discussions on economic policy held in Manchuria and Japan throughout 1932 and 1933. For a summary of the positions of Tokyo zaibatsu and Osaka industrialists, see *Nichi-Man tōsei keizai seisaku-ron no yōshi* (1933), Tōkyō shōkō kaigisho, microreel no. 107, pp. 608–17. See also Nihon shōkō kaigisho shusai, *Manmō keizai shisatsudan hōkoku narabi ikenshō* (Tokyo, 1932) and Mantetsu keizai chōsakai, *Tai Man keizai seisaku ni kansuru kakushū iken* (Dairen: Mantetsu, 1932).

[22] South Manchurian Railway Company, *Fifth Report on Progress in Manchuria to 1936* (Dairen, 1936), p. 98.

[23] Mantetsu, *Tai man keizai seisaku*, pp. 15–16.

there was room within the Economic Construction Program for businessmen to pursue their own agendas, they lent support to the imperialist experiment in state capitalism and Japan-Manchuria economic integration.

As private enterprise and the Manchukuo state operated their independent initiatives to bring about the "Japan-Manchuria partnership," conflicting visions of that partnership emerged in the public debate over Manchurian development. In the daily press, government and business pamphlets, leading economic journals, and highbrow magazines like *Chūō kōron* (*The Central Review*), a tangle of buzzwords and theories jostled one another. Known variously as the "Japan-Manchurian controlled economy," the "Japan-Manchuria bloc," the "Japan-Manchuria partnership," or an "inseparable relationship"; "economic construction" or "economic development"; "coexistence and coprosperity," "autarky," or "self-sufficiency," the variety of policies that collided under these rubrics were so multifaceted, self-contradictory, and confusing, that one observer jokingly referred to it as a problem of "excess knowledge." "This rampant production is leaving people lost in confusion, not because of "inadequate knowledge" (*ninshiki busoku*), but because of "excess knowledge" (*ninshiki kajō*) of Manchurian economic conditions. Isn't it time to subject the "uncontrolled" and excess production of Japan-Manchuria controlled economy theories itself to some "control" and consolidation?"[24]

The Manchurian paradise depicted by Manchukuo government planners was the model of state capitalism, industrialization proceeding in steps according to a well-ordered plan. Influenced by the example of the Soviet Five-Year Plans, architects of the Manchukuo government's *Outline of Economic Construction in Manchuria* claimed to be practicing "Kingly Way economics," a term invented to disassociate Manchukuo from Marxist ideology. Promising to build "the only economic structure of its kind in the world," Kwantung Army planners envisioned that a radical program of state control over "important economic activities" would permit "coordinated development" between "every branch of the economy." In the *Outline of Economic Construction*, Kwantung Army planners used terms like "rationalize," "coordinate," and "control" to announce the fundamental reform of capitalism under state auspices. The Manchukuo experiment promised to usher in a new era of statist harmony.[25]

---

[24] Suzuki Takeo, "Nichi-Man burokku keizai-ron no sai-kentō," *Kaizō*, January 1933, pp. 53–54.

[25] Tanaka Kuichi, "Manshūkoku no keizai 10-kanen keikaku—sono keizai kensetsu

The private sector had its own visions of Manchukuo's future. Rather than looking to a utopia of reformed capitalism, the business community dreamt of a panacea to economic depression. *Tōyō keizai shimpō* (the *Far Eastern Economic Review*) and other economic journals spoke confidently of the curative power of "Manchuria prosperity."[26] They noted that trade was expanding and had given the economy a healthy inflationary boost. The investment world had "turned its attention to Manchuria." Because of the unshackling of Japanese rights and interests under the new regime, the rise in demand for Japanese goods due to the economic construction program, and the establishment of the "Japan-Manchuria bloc" economy, "hopes were running very high" for the new Manchuria.[27]

Economist Takahashi Kamekichi explained the popular perception that Manchuria had provided the solution to Japan's economic "deadlock" in terms of the complementary needs of metropolis and empire.

> In the current era of global overproduction of commodities, much labor and productive capacity lies idle in Japan as well. By simply mobilizing this excess capacity, we can easily supply all the goods urgently required as a result of the Manchurian problem. In the past Japan would have had to pay for the construction of Manchukuo with gold, but now she can pay in goods. . . . Killing two birds with one stone, as it were, the economic construction of Manchukuo is simultaneously furnishing the expenditure for necessary programs of "industrial relief" and "unemployment relief." . . . The League of Nations predicted that the independence of Manchuria would destroy the Japanese economy, but far from it, it has been the saving and strengthening of Japanese capitalism.[28]

The mood of self-congratulation and confidence reflected in Takahashi's commentary was characteristic of public discourse on the "Japan-Manchuria partnership." It was a heady moment: the battles had been won, economic construction was changing the face of Manchuria, and while the rest of the world was still mired in depression, the Japanese economy had turned itself around.

These visions of "development" and "construction" shared a common framework. But under the grand slogans, concrete proposals emerged that fundamentally contradicted one another. For the Manchukuo government, the "bloc economy" envisioned in its Economic Construction Program meant creating an autarkic trading sphere that would provide for self-sufficiency in wartime. As Takahashi pointed

---

yōkō," *Chūō kōron*, April 1933, pp. 64–70; South Manchurian Railway, *Fifth Report on Progress*, p. 98.

[26] "Junchō ni kōjō suru Manshū zaikai," *Tōyō keizai shimpō*, August 9, 1934, p. 19.

[27] "Manshū kankei kaisha no tōshi kachi," ibid., September 9, 1933, p. 23.

[28] Takahashi Kamekichi, "Manshūkoku shisatsu hōkoku ki," *Chūō kōron*, October 1934, p. 252.

out, this argument was based on observations of mobilization during the Great War. "From the perspective of the wartime economy, the purpose of the Japan-Manchuria economic bloc is to guarantee resources. . . . Because of the shortage of goods during and immediately after the war in Europe, all countries made it a priority to guarantee the supply of resources. Certain parties advocate Manchurian development on this basis."[29] The Kwantung Army wanted Northeast China as a particular kind of resource base, that is, a source of materials necessary for military industries. Hence, its interest in "resource development" extended little beyond the progress of mining—coal, iron, magnesite, and other materials necessary to heavy industry and light metals production. Agricultural products, even the famed soybeans, were low on the Kwantung Army's priority list.

The Manchukuo Economic Construction Program envisioned not only securing strategic resources in Manchuria, but actually refining and manufacturng them on site. Thus, its picture of the new Manchuria featured "special companies" that linked industrialization with national defense, and efficiently managed the development and conservation of strategic resources. Manchukuo government publications showcased vaunted "industrial successes" such as the Manchuria Arsenal Corporation, the Showa Steelworks, the Manchuria Chemical Industry Company, the Manchuria Petroleum Company, and the Dowa Automobile Manufacturing Company.[30]

But what domestic businessmen envisioned gaining from the "Japan-Manchuria partnership" was something altogether different. As one Osaka businessman averred:

Manchuria has recently become an incredible boom area as a consumer market for Japanese goods. This year's exports have approached ¥300 million, more than ten times what they were only a few years ago, and far surpassing exports to China. . . . Because Osaka products make up between 60 and 70 percent of these exports, we have great hopes for the future of Manchukuo and want to strive to develop Manchukuo and raise domestic purchasing power. Japan's foreign trade is beginning to face great obstacles, the foremost due to economic pressure from England. Now more than ever Manchuria is an absolutely vital lifeline for domestic commerce and industry—the single free place where we may increase our trade.[31]

[29] Takahashi Kamekichi, "Manshū keizai no genjō to zentō," Kaizō, October 1934, p. 35.

[30] Rikugunshō shimbunhan, Manshū jihen boppatsu man 4 nen Manshūkoku gaikan (Tokyo: Rikugunshō, 1935), pp. 9–15; Tanaka, "Manshūkoku no keizai 10-kanen keikaku"; South Manchuria Railway, Fifth Report on Progress, pp. 79–111.

[31] Manshū dai hakuran kai kyōsan kai, Nichi-Man jitsugyō kyōkai kiyō (Dairen, 1933); Tōkyō shōkō kaigisho, microreel no. 139:2248, p. 441.

Amidst all the talk of bold new solutions to the historic crisis and following the world trend toward the segmentation of the globe into trading blocs, business hopes pinned on Manchuria harked back to the fabled China market.

In contrast to the Kwantung Army's concern for wartime exigencies, business leaders imagined the Japan-Manchuria bloc economy as a peacetime trading sphere. While the army's point of reference was economic mobilization during World War I, businessmen had in their minds the more recent experience of worldwide depression. With the global economy suffering from an excess of production, went the argument, the key was not to guarantee resources (as in the army's view) but to guarantee markets.[32]

Unlike the Kwantung Army, domestic business leaders were strongly opposed to the industrialization of Manchuria. In the words of the influential Japan Industrial Club: "As much as possible Manchuria should be made into a supplier of materials. It is a mistake to encourage new industrial production that will compete with Japanese domestic industry. . . . Manchurian tariffs should be kept as low as possible to encourage the import of Japanese products. Industrial goods should be produced within Japan and exported to Manchuria."[33] In other words, business leaders were not looking for fundamental change in the economic relationship between Japan and Manchuria, which was based on imports of primary agricultural products and export of consumer goods. Opposed to the growth of a manufacturing industry in Manchuria that would compete with domestic production, they defined "development" differently than the Kwantung Army. In their terms, "development" signified expansion of the agricultural sector, which would mean more money in the pockets of Chinese peasants and a larger market for Japanese goods.

As much as businessmen might welcome the idea of a secure market, many of them had mixed feelings about the message a "Japan-Manchuria bloc" might convey to the rest of the world. In the words of an Osaka industrialist: "this term can be so easily misunderstood. . . . I think the slogan 'Japan-Manchurian partnership and cooperation' (*Nichi-Man teikei kyōchō*) conveys a much more appropriate image."[34] The concern here was not to give any encouragement to the rise of global protectionism, for business leaders were well aware of their dependence on European and American markets. In this sense, the busi-

[32] Takahashi, "Manshū keizai no genjō to zentō," p. 35.
[33] Mantetsu, *Tai Man keizai seisaku*, p. 14.
[34] Manshū dai hakuran kai, *Nichi-Man jitsugyō kyōkai kiyō*; Tōkyō shōkō kaigisho microreel, no. 139:2257, p. 450.

ness view of a "Japan-Manchuria partnership" was premised on continuation of a trade relationship with the West, in contrast to the Manchukuo government vision which was premised on a rupture of that relationship.

The contradictions in the two blueprints meant that despite the public veneer of cooperation, public and private sectors pursued development plans at cross-purposes. By 1935 it was widely reported that progress in Manchukuo development had come to an impasse. The government's Economic Construction Program was about to run aground due to lack of capital. The South Manchurian Railway, which had financed most of the new ventures, was badly overextended, Manchukuo Government finances "were shaky," and the small amount of direct private investment was in "deep trouble." The basic unprofitability of most of the government ventures did not hold out hope that capital would be forthcoming, either.[35]

The situation for private industry's market development plan was equally grim. Exports had risen, but these were limited to machines, metal, wood, and cement—materials used for "economic construction" and dependent on the continued flow of Japanese capital into Manchuria to finance their purchase. Not only had the fabled consumer market failed to materialize, but exports of textiles and other consumer goods had stagnated. As economists pointed out, this was due to Manchuria's agricultural depression and the catastrophic drop in exports of soybeans, the country's main cash crop. Japan's import policy was only aggravating the problem; to protect its own depressed agricultural sector tariffs were raised against Manchurian exports such as soybeans, barley, and sorghum.[36]

Despite the often lucid and penetrating analyses of the causes of the impasse in Manchurian development, these same analysts suddenly found new reservoirs of optimism when a "Five-Year Development Plan" was announced in 1936, and after the Kwantung Army negotiated a deal at the end of 1935 that opened North China to Japanese economic penetration. Reviews heaped praise on the Five-Year Plan, and congratulated both parties in the partnership of the corporate giant Nissan and the Manchukuo government. Blithe advocates of a "Japan-

[35] "Mantetsu no kokkateki shimei to sono jitai," *Ekonomisto*, September 11, 1935, pp. 24–25; Ōkura Kinmochi, "Manshū keizai no tokushūsei o saguru," ibid., July 11, 1935, p. 12; "Shinsetsu kaisha no genkyō ni miru Manshū keizai kōsaku no shinten jōkyō (I)," ibid., November 21, 1935, p. 35.

[36] "Nichi-Man bōeki no bunseki," ibid., October 11, 1935, pp. 114–17; "Manshūkoku no bōeki to Nihon shōhin no yushutsu jōtai," *Tōyō keizai shimpō*, October 20, 1934, pp. 16–17; Ōkura Kinmochi, "Manshūkoku keizai kensetsu no zentō," *Ekonomisto*, July 11, 1935, p. 13; "Nichi-Man bōeki mondai no kentō," ibid., June 1, 1935, pp. 12–13.

Manchuria-China bloc" optimistically predicted that what had failed in Manchuria would work in China. It would be much easier, economists blithely asserted, to develop that consumer market in densely populated North China.[37]

As it took shape in the mid thirties, this utopian vision of Manchukuo was both seductive and tenacious. Having once captured people's imagination, it proved remarkably difficult to dislodge. There was of course, all the blood and treasure spilt in the acquisition, and all the resources committed to the building of the new state. But more than this, Japanese had invested tremendous hope in Manchukuo. Perhaps it was their dreams that they found most difficult to turn their backs on.

THE EMIGRATION BANDWAGON, 1937–1941

The Japanese government's announcement in 1936 of its intent to carry out mass Japanese emigration to Manchuria signaled a radical new departure for the imperialist project. Fantastic in the scope of its ambition, the plan aimed to send a million farmers and their families to Manchuria in the space of twenty years, a figure equivalent to a fifth of the 1936 farm population.[38] Linking social policy in the metropolis and empire, the home government sought to make the Manchurian population 10 percent Japanese through the export of the impoverished tenant farmers who were the most visible manifestation of Japan's own rural crisis. Manchurian colonization represented integration of home and empire on a wholly new scale. Immigration became a tool for the Japanizing of Manchuria, the first step in a process of incorporation that in the past had transformed *gaichi* or outside territories such as Hokkaidō and the Ryūkyū Islands into what Japanese referred to as the *naichi*—the home islands.

The emigration policy was the product of a nationwide movement. Well before its announcement in 1936, schemes for mass migration were circulated in the universities and the mass media, argued over by prefectural and national bureaucrats, and promoted by a host of colonization societies in the countryside. After 1936 these rumblings burst forth in an emigration fever, as organizations and individuals through-

[37] "Tairiku seisaku no hatten to waga zaikai," ibid., May 11, 1936, pp. 9–22; Naitō Kumaki, "Hokushi keizai shinshutsu ni kansuru shiken," *Tōyō keizai shimpō*, November 27, 1937, pp. 30–36; "Tōkaku sōsai Yasukawa Yūnosuke shi ni Hokushi keizai kōsaku o kiku," ibid., November 13, 1937, pp. 29–35; "Manshū sangyō 5-kanen keikaku no zenbō," ibid., May 11, 1937, pp. 31–33; "Chō-Man-Shi tōshi no zentō," ibid., December 21, 1936, pp. 25–28.

[38] Manshū iminshi kenkyūkai, *Nihon teikokushugika no Manshū imin* (Tokyo: Ryūkei shoten, 1976), p. 45.

out the nation leapt onto the emigration bandwagon. The so-called "rural literature" movement (*nōmin bungaku*) spawned a new genre of "colonization literature," supported by literary prizes and tours of the Manchurian settlements.[39] *Tairiku kaitaku (Continental Colonization)* (*Manshū ijū geppō) (Manchurian Emigration Monthly)*, and other journals on the topic proliferated, while academic groups like the Japanese Association for the Advancement of Science (*Nihon gakujutsu shinkō*) devoted a committee to research and publication on the subject. Like the war fever and the economic boom before it, the emigration fever swept the worlds of print and politics.

Although over three hundred thousand people[40] emigrated under the program, emigrants were conspicuous in their absence from the movement itself. The idea of mass migration was always more appealing to those who wanted others to leave than to those who were expected to go, and people needed to be enticed, cajoled, exhorted, bribed, and bullied into moving to this strange place they knew nothing about. Why so many were ultimately convinced to migrate had less to do with the attractions of Manchukuo than with the sheer magnitude of pressures placed on them to leave.

These pressures were coordinated by what was, in effect, a huge emigration machine. A well-organized movement tied to an elaborate bureaucratic apparatus performed the various tasks of planning, recruitment, financing, transportation, settling, supply, and support involved in the emigration project. This machine operated at three critical levels—the national, the prefectural, and the community (village and county). Cooperation between all three levels was necessary for the movement to be a success. The national machine, run through the central government in Tokyo, provided policy guidelines, funding, prepackaged recruitment materials, and liaison with the colonial administration in Manchukuo. The prefectural machine coordinated recruitment drives and channeled government funds and other resources to local communities. The village and county machines did the legwork of the emigration movement, recruiting the settlers and mobilizing their communities to facilitate the migration. All three were vital; none could function without the other two.

The significance of this emigration promotion machine went beyond the settlers themselves. Its elaborateness and size reflected the extent to which Japanese society as a whole had been drawn into the process of settlement imperialism. Thus in addition to its ostensible raison d'être,

---

[39] Hashikawa Bunzō, ed., *Senka Manshū ni agaru* (Tokyo: Shūeisha, 1964), p. 495.

[40] Nagano ken Manshū kaitaku kankōkai, *Nagano ken Manshū kaitakushi sōhen* (Nagano, 1984), p. 309.

the emigration movement served a second, unacknowledged purpose. By involving, for every individual sent over, countless others at all stages in the mobilization process, the movement enabled a widespread vicarious participation in the Japanizing of Manchuria. The over-organized character of the movement, the duplication and overlapping of effort, the endless make-work tasks, all served to get as many people as possible thinking, talking, working for, and believing in the emigration project, thus building a consensus behind the empire.

Most Japanese adults emigrated through the so-called "village colonization" program.[41] Under this system, an *imindan* or settlement of between two hundred and three hundred households was recruited either by subdividing a village and sending a third of its population (*bunson imin*), or by mobilizing volunteers from a number of villages in a particular district (*bunkyō imin*). In effect this system involved the participating village or district as an entire community. Everybody, from the mayor down to the third sons of tenant farmers, got drawn into a collective effort to remake the social, political, and economic structure of the village.

At the village level the mobilization began with the decision to develop countermeasures to alleviate the economic crisis. Sometimes this decision came after pressure from a local emigration movement, sometimes after lobbying from prefectural authorities. In either case, such a decision reflected consensus among the village elite. Next, an office was set up within the town hall with direct links to the mayor and vice mayor. This office administered several departments that linked up with local voluntary organizations like the reservists, youth groups, and farm cooperatives.

After a survey calculating the optimum farmer-to-land ratio in the village furnished emigration leaders with a depopulation target, recruiting began in earnest. A rally was held and a fact-finding mission dispatched to gather firsthand information on the site of colonization. On the mission's return, a welcome-back celebration took place, speeches were made, and an exhibit of materials brought back from the continent opened with pomp and circumstance. The prefectural bureaucracy, Manchurian Emigration Council, Colonial Ministry, Agriculture and Forestries Ministry, prefectural leadership of the women's groups, youth groups, and farm cooperatives all sent experts to lecture and persuade. Movies were shown and pamphlets distributed. Roundtable discussions were organized on a neighborhood basis to convince people to go.

---

[41] 422 *imindan* of between two hundred and three hundred people were sent to Manchuria. 319 of these were were recruited as a town or village unit. Manshū kaitakushi kankōkai, *Manshū kaitakushi* (Tokyo, 1966), p. 332.

The colony embarked in waves—every six months over a period of three years. Even after the last colonists went over, the village continued support activities: sending "relief packages" (*imon bukuro*) and "encouragement packages" (*shōrei bukuro*), making visits, and sometimes sending new recruits. Thus, for most of the villages involved, the frenetic pace of emigration promotion kept residents in a buzz of activity for the duration of the war.[42]

Pontificating about the glories of the "new heaven on earth" (*shin-tenchi*) in Manchuria, ministers, bureaucrats, mayors, and youth group leaders added yet another dimension to the cultural edifice of Manchukuo. In magazines like the Manchuria Emigration Council's *Opening Manchuria-Mongolia* and *New Manchuria-Mongolia*, and Sangyō Kumiai's widely circulated *Ie no hikari* (*The Light of the Home*), images of hardy Japanese settlers filling up the vast open spaces of the Manchurian frontier gave new meaning to an empire understood in terms of a defensive "lifeline" and "economic partnership." In the process, the imagined Manchuria became more than a vital military outpost and a buttress for the domestic economy. Bound literally and figuratively by ties of kinship, it was turning Japanese, and being remade in the image of the mother country.

This transformation was articulated in self-consciously racial terms that borrowed from mytho-historical accounts tracing the origin of the Japanese people back to the divinely descended Emperor Jimmu, founder of the Japanese state in 660 B.C. and mythic progenitor of what was called the "Yamato race." Speeches by ministers of colonization urged "soldiers of the hoe" to "Go! Go and colonize the continent! For the development of the Yamato race, build the new order in Asia!"[43] Koiso Kuniaki, head of the ministry in late 1939, titled one tribute to the "pioneers who battled with the soil of North Manchuria," "The strength of one hoe." He urged the public to express its gratitude and support for this "holy endeavor of the race."[44] The grandiose rhetoric made of immigration something much more than a mere economic prospect for impoverished and land-hungry farmers; they were seeding the empire with the "racial spirit" of the Yamato people.

The racial expressions that filled the new lexicon of empire were prominent in the slogans chosen to represent the emigration project. Manchuria was frequently referred to as a "brother country to which Japan had given birth" (*Nihon ga unda kyōdai-koku*).[45] As one article

---

[42] Nōrinshō keizai kōseibu, *Shin nōson no kensetsu* (Tokyo: Asahi shimbunsha, 1939), pp. 533–50.

[43] Hatta Yoshiaki, "Tairiku no yokudo wa maneku," *Ie no hikari*, April 1939, p. 35.

[44] Koiso Kuniaki, "Ichi kuwa no chikara," ibid., October 1939, p. 31.

[45] Hatta, "Tairiku no yokudo wa maneku," p. 35; Koiso, "Ichi kuwa no chikara," p. 31.

explained, Manchukuo was not just a colony of Japan, but blood kin. The imperial relationship became a metaphorical representation of Japan's extended family system where "Japan is the stem family and Manchuria is the branch family." Observing the hierarchical relations maintained between stem and branch, Japan acted as "parent" to the infant nation of Manchukuo, rearing it to become a "splendid nation just like Japan."[46]

The policy of recruiting second and third sons to set up branch families in Manchuria reinforced this idea of kinship. Recruitment literature stressed that "the rich soil of the continent beckoned" especially to second and third sons whose "bleak expressions registered their despair at making a life for themselves on the family farm."[47] In similar fashion the language of the village colonization program literally signified the creation of a "branch village" (bunson). As Ie no hikari urged: "Set up a branch family in Manchuria through village colonization" (bunson imin de Manshū e bunke).[48] In this way the metaphors of reproduction and family were invoked to suggest a connection of race and blood between the two nations.

As it was envisioned, Manchurian settlement would plant the seeds of a new racial order on the continent. One of the key goals, it was frequently asserted, was to build what Japanese called a "harmony of the five races" (gozoku kyōwa).

> The harmony of the five races is made up of Chinese, Mongolians, Manchurians, Koreans, and Japanese. . . . But Japanese make up only eight hundred thousand of the Manchurian population of over thirty million. With this small number, it is difficult to stand at the head of the five races and lead them forward. Moreover, most of these eight hundred thousand are bureaucrats and businessmen, few of whom plan to stay permanently on the soil of Manchuria. This situation will never produce the harmony of the five races. If Japanese do not settle in Manchuria for posterity—build their stronghold there, live out their life on its shores, and bury their remains in its soil—the great task of harmony of the five races cannot be carried out.[49]

Thus, Japanese immigration became a vital task in the building of a new racially harmonized imperial society.

Discussions of gozoku kyōwa never omitted to underscore the crucial point that harmony did not in any way imply equality. The frequency with which propagandists felt compelled to assert "the superiority of the Japanese race" was as noteworthy as their ingenuity in varying the

---

[46] "Tokugo—tairiku wa maneku Manshū kaitakusha montō," Ie no hikari, April 1939, p. 141.

[47] Hatta, "Tairiku no yokudo wa maneku," p. 35.

[48] "Tokugo—tairiku wa maneku Manshū kaitakusha montō," p. 145.

[49] Ibid., pp. 141–42.

iteration of this concept. The position of the "Yamato people" was expressed variously as "heart" (*kakushin*), "pivot" (*chūjiku*), and "axis" (*chūsū*) of the five races. Assuming the "position of leadership" (*shidōteki chii*) and the "guiding role" (*shidōteki yakuwari*), Japan was to become the "leader of the Asian continent" (*Ajia tairiku no meishu*), the "head of the five races" (*gozoku kyōwa no sentō*), the "driving force of racial harmony" (*gozoku kyōwa no suishinryoku*), or all of these at once. Their role was to "lead and enlighten" (*shidō keihatsu*) the other races of Manchukuo, and to undertake their "moral reform (*tokka*) and "guidance" (*yūeki*).[50] Just as homilies of harmony in Japan's factories, villages, and marketplaces enjoined capitalists and workers, landlords and tenants, large and small enterprises to assume their proper place in the ladder of wealth and power, in Manchukuo, *gozoku kyōwa* envisioned a hierarchy of race and power in the empire.

Women figured prominently in this imagined Manchukuo, in contrast to the military and economic imperiums. "Continental mothers" and "continental brides" were the target of frequent appeals to the patriotic spirit of Japanese women. *Ie no hikari* was filled with *bidan*, or inspirational tales, about these female pioneers, which highlighted the unique contribution that a woman's strength and a woman's endurance made to the building of colonial society.

One such story, entitled "The New Brides Who Protected the Village," explained how the men in a settlement of recruits from the Tokyo area had, after a bad harvest, given up and decided to disband the settlement. Several young brides, who "had come to the continent burning with hope," then "bravely stood up and argued with their husbands" to put a stop to the defeatism, delivering the following speech.

> At our wedding ceremony in Tokyo under the blessing of the governor, did we not pledge our tears to build Tokyo Village Colony in the Manchurian heaven and to become the cornerstone of peace in the East? . . . At home, too, crops are sometimes a success and sometimes a failure. To declare the soil no good and abandon the settlement after a single crop failure without really knowing the truth—how will this look to those at home who are counting on us? And what about the Manchurians watching us Japanese settlers do this—what will they say? We have pledged our future, and promised to build Tokyo Village permanently on this spot. Now more than ever you men need to rouse yourselves to be brave and redouble your efforts for us.[51]

[50] Miura Etsurō, ed., *Manshū ijū dokuhon* (Tokyo: Kaizōsha, 1939), pp. 31–35; "Tokugo—tairiku wa maneku Manshū kaitakusha montō," pp. 141–42; Ishiwara Jirō, *Manshū imin to seinendan* (Tokyo: Dai Nippon rengō seinendan, 1937), p. 40.

[51] "Kaitaku bidan—tairiku ni saku Yamato Nadeshiko," *Ie no hikari*, October 1940, pp. 15–17.

In such stories it was the women who could be counted on to understand and endure hardship, and who thereby provided the moral fortitude and the stick-to-it-iveness necessary to make the "holy mission" a reality.

In its magazine version, the "new heaven on earth" was populated exclusively by such paragons of traditional "feminine virtue." In addition to giving pious speeches, women of the Manchurian frontier were expected to be breeders of a new generation of "Manchurian Japanese." Drawings and photographs of settler women seemed always to catch them with a baby at the breast. The caption for a drawing entitled "The Joy of the Harvest" explained that it was portraying "immigrant soldiers of the hoe at the close of a day of busy harvesting. The glow of the sunset is reflected in the face of the young father. The Manchurian Japanese baby suckles at the ample breast of his mother. . . . Does this not symbolize the blessings of Japanese youth?"[52] A photograph of a settler's wife with her family, titled "The Joy of Breeding," referred both to the women's family and to the herd of sheep grazing in the yard behind her. "Looking out onto a spectacular view, the young mother, the continental dog, and the plump and healthy second generation born in Manchuria play happily together on the second story of the shepherd's house," read the caption.[53]

The presence of women in the imagined imperial landscape reflected the new sense of intimacy with which Japanese regarded Manchukuo. The empire had been domesticated: the battlefield was transformed into a vegetable garden, the commodity market supplanted by a Japanese farm community. Yet another expression of the Japanizing of the empire, the projection of images of motherhood and connubial life made Manchukuo seem more like home every day.

The Manchurian colonization movement of the late 1930s made up the third and final phase in the Japanese construction of Manchukuo. Much had changed since 1931, and this was reflected in the character of the mobilization effort at the close of the decade. The emigration bandwagon was driven more by pressures from above than was the war fever or the economic boom. Hence, in contrast to the raucous popular jingoism of the "lifeline," or the ambitious utopianism of the "partnership," the preachy self-righteousness of the settlement project spoke down to people in the voice of authority. Empire had become the patriotic duty of citizen to the state.

CONCLUSION

Within the relatively short space of fifteen years, expansionism rapidly evolved through three phases. The building of Manchukuo saw a burst of military conquest between 1931 and 1933, economic integration be-

---

[52] "Shūtaku no yorokobi," ibid., November 1939.
[53] "Manshū kaitaku tokugo," ibid., October 1939, p. 1.

tween 1933 and 1937, and agrarian colonization between 1937 and 1941. These were stages of imperial construction. At home an infrastructure of support emerged to complement a new superstructure of domination in the empire. In the early 1930s, the war fever at home and military campaigns in Manchuria established army rule over Manchukuo. In the middle of the decade, the domestic Manchuria boom and the Manchukuo government's Economic Construction program extended state control over the economy and effected the integration of the domestic and imperial markets. In the late 1930s, the emigration bandwagon and the settlement program created in Manchuria a racially segmented society that was dominated by Japanese.

While these changes were taking place in the empire, at home Japan became a thriving marketplace for imperial ideology. The mass media packaged the "defense of the lifeline" as popular entertainment. The business world promoted the "yen bloc" as a path out of economic depression. Village leaders pushed "the new paradise" as a grand patriotic experiment in social engineering. In their zeal to sell empire to the home population, these imperial propagandists were not wholly motivated by patriotism and belief in the imperial idea. Indeed, most had other agendas in mind—raising profits, cutting political deals, eliminating social problems—that were a far cry from the grand rhetoric. And the Japanese people were by and large enthusiastic consumers of imperial ideology. Buying a Manchukuo fantasy offered escape from a domestic society that held little to hope for and much to fear.

We often think of wartime Japan as an era of rampaging militarism brought on by the state. Its most extreme depiction sees the army wrenching government out of the hands of feeble politicians and grinding a defenseless citizenry under its boots. Yet if one looks closely at the patterns of public-private interaction during the 1930s, a rather different picture emerges. Although the decade showed a clear trend toward the increasingly intrusive presence of the state in private life, this was not caused by a unilateral and unrelenting power play by government.

In the early part of the decade, before the wartime censorship and the thought control apparatuses were in place, the mass media voluntarily turned themselves into a propaganda machine for the army. Although business leaders had privately opposed much of the Kwantung Army's program for Manchukuo, they put up a show of support and kept their disagreements behind closed doors. Calculating that they could adapt the framework of the program to their own purposes, business leaders relinquished a central role in setting the terms of policy. In the late 1930s, the village elite assumed leadership roles in the emigration movement. Standing at the head of the networks of organizations that dominated local society, these individuals were in a unique position to exert power on grass-roots Japan. Their enthusiastic cooperation with the national and prefectural emigration campaigns placed at the disposal of bureaucrats a local machinery of mobilization. In all three cases, the power of government grew, in no small part, because Japanese society gave it that power.

Manchukuo was the first acquisition of the wartime empire, and it remained the centerpiece of the Greater East Asian Co-Prosperity Sphere. The grandiosity and vaulting ambition that imbued Japan's vision of Manchukuo was typical of the wartime empire in its entirety. The plan to overcome militarily the whole of China and Southeast Asia, not to mention the harnessing of their vast resources, was a leap into the realm of fantasy. Like the visions of Manchukuo, the hubris of Japan's wartime empire was not the isolated expression of a few individuals, but the collective consciousness of an age.

CHAPTER 4

Managing Occupied Manchuria, 1931–1934

Y. Tak Matsusaka

The occupation of Northeast China in 1931 and the subsequent establishment of the puppet state of Manchukuo presented the Japanese with a host of problems in the management of imperial policy for which there were few meaningful precedents. In theory, the strategy for territorial rule was fairly simple. A nominally independent government headed by the former Ch'ing emperor P'u Yi was to be established over the provinces of Fengt'ien, Kirin, Heilungkiang, and Jehol.[1] Formal relations between Japan and the new state were to be governed by the norms of international diplomacy. Japan would lay no official claim to authority over Manchurian affairs beyond rights and interests protected by bilateral treaties. The founders of Manchukuo, however, never intended independence to be anything more than a fictional construct designed to mask the reality of Japanese control. For all intents and purposes, the territory would be managed as a Japanese possession and would enjoy no more sovereignty than the colonies of Taiwan or Korea.

This scheme, however, proved to be far more complex in practice than expected. The Japanese were accomplished imperialists and were thoroughly familiar with the management of colonies, protectorates, and spheres of influence as well as territories under wartime occupation. The administration of a puppet state, however, was a matter beyond their direct experience. Policymakers had little choice but to improvise. During the first half of the 1930s they experimented with a variety of institutional arrangements, many of which proved to be unworkable.

Difficulties inherent in this process of devising a new form of imperial rule were compounded by political rivalry among ministries of the Japanese government. The conquest of Manchuria in 1931 presented the army, the Foreign and Colonial ministries, and their subordinate agencies in the territory with new opportunities as well as challenges. Each group sought to establish its jurisdictional claims in Manchukuo and to push the process of institutional experimentation in a direction favor-

---

[1] Although claimed from the outset, Jehol was not subjugated and incorporated into the Manchurian state until 1933.

able to its own sectional interests. More often than not, the rationality of administrative design took second place to the dictates of interagency politics. The management of the puppet state thus suffered not only from the trial-and-error process of organizational development, but from a plethora of aspiring puppeteers.

By the middle of the 1930s, the army had managed to reorganize territorial administration under its control. This new system, directed by a cabinet agency known as the Manchurian Affairs Bureau, proved to be effective, enduring with relatively little change until the end of the Second World War. Moreover, the experience of political experimentation in Manchuria offered army leaders important lessons for imperial administration elsewhere. The management strategies and institutional structures devised in Manchuria during the first half of the 1930s would find useful applications in Japan's vast wartime empire in China after 1937.

Background: Japan's Sphere of Influence in Northeast China, 1905–1931

Japanese imperialism had sunk deep roots in Northeast China long before the conquest of 1931. For more than a quarter-century following the Russo-Japanese War (1904–5), Japan maintained a sphere of influence in Manchuria where it exercised a substantial degree of political, economic, and military control. The Japanese achieved greater success than any of their Western rivals in encroaching on Chinese territory under the system of informal empire.[2] The institutions developed in the course of expansion were sophisticated and effective in their time. They also constituted the basic building blocks from which the Japanese assembled Manchukuo and the administrative system of the 1930s. A brief consideration of the structures and strategies of informal imperialism in Manchuria, therefore, is in order.

Japanese practices in Northeast China between 1905 and 1931 represented a variant of what one group of scholars has described as "railway imperialism." This technique exploited the far-reaching military, economic, and administrative ramifications of controlling a regional transportation monopoly as a strategy for territorial domination.[3] The South Manchuria Railway Company (SMR), a quasi-official joint-stock cor-

---

[2] The concept of informal empire in China is discussed in Peter Duss, "Japan's Informal Empire in China, 1895–1937: An Overview," in *The Japanese Informal Empire in China, 1895–1937*, ed. Peter Duus, Ramon H. Myers, and Mark R. Peattie (Princeton, N.J.: Princeton University Press, 1989), pp. xi–xxix.

[3] Clarence B. Davis and Kenneth E. Wilburn, Jr., with Ronald E. Robinson, eds., *Railway Imperialism* (Westfield, Conn.: Greenwood Press, 1991), p. 3.

poration established in 1906 in order to manage the railway concession granted Japan in the Treaty of Portsmouth, was the single most important Japanese institution in the territory.[4] By the 1920s it had diversified into a wide range of subsidiary ventures in mining, manufacturing, and trade. In both the scope and scale of its operations, the SMR was comparable to the largest of the *zaibatsu*, Japan's big business combines. At the same time, this extraordinary company was considerably more than a successful economic enterprise. The SMR was an agency of the Japanese government, its top officers appointed by Tokyo and its operations subject to state supervision. The development of military railroads and other strategic facilities was an important part of its mission, and in this respect the SMR may be regarded as a covert army installation. The company's charter also provided for the exercise of administrative powers in the Railway Zone, a special territorial concession comprised of station towns and mining districts along the four-hundred-mile route between Talien and Ch'angch'un. The SMR, then, was in effect an organ of colonial administration.[5]

In addition to the railway and associated rights, the Japanese controlled a small area on the tip of the Liaotung Peninsula known as the Kwantung Leased Territory.[6] Although amounting to no more than thirteen hundred square miles, the Leased Territory was an important enclave of Japanese colonial power in the region, providing a secure site for the army and navy bases at Port Arthur and the commercial metropolis of Talien, Manchuria's principal seaport. Until the 1930s, Kwantung also represented home to more than half of the Japanese resident population in Manchuria.[7] The government of the Leased Territory was a civilian agency responsible to the Colonial Ministry in Tokyo, which not only administered territorial affairs, but exercised police and

[4] For general background on the SMR, see Andō Hikotarō, ed., *Mantetsu: Nihon teikokushugi to Chūgoku* (Tokyo: Ochanomizu shobō, 1969); Kaneko Fumio, "Sōgyōki no Minami Manshū tetsudō: 1907–1916," *Shakai kagaku kenkyū* 31 no. 4 (January 1980): 171–201; Harada Katsumasa, *Mantetsu* (Tokyo: Iwanami shoten, 1981); in English, see Ramon H. Myers, "Japanese Imperialism in Manchuria: The South Manchuria Railway Company, 1906–1933," in Duus, Myers, and Peattie, *The Japanese Informal Empire in China*, pp. 101–32.

[5] Police and judicial powers in the Railway Zone were exercised by the government of the Kwantung Leased Territory, described below.

[6] There are few studies of the Leased Territory as a subject in its own right. It is generally treated in conjunction with the South Manchuria Railway Company. On the structure of the Kwantung Government and its jurisdiction, see Kurihara Ken, "Kantō totokufu mondai teiyō," in *Tai Man-Mō seisaku no ichimen*, ed. Kurihara Ken (Tokyo: Hara shobō, 1966), pp. 37–60.

[7] Minami Manshū tetsudō kabushiki kaisha shomubu chōsaka, *Waga kuni jinkō mondai to Man-Mō* (Dairen: SMR, 1928), pp. 68–69.

judicial powers in the Railway Zone. The governor of Kwantung also supervised, on behalf of the Colonial Ministry, the operations of the SMR and another quasi-official corporation known as the Manchurian Telephone and Telegraph Company.[8]

While Japanese strategy in Manchuria included formal colonial elements, the overall approach remained within the framework of the unequal treaty system in China. Accordingly, the diplomatic apparatus of the Foreign Ministry played a major role in the management of Manchuria. As elsewhere in China, Japan maintained an extensive network of consulates in the region. Under the terms of extraterritoriality, these diplomatic offices exercised police and judicial powers in the so-called treaty ports, cities open to foreign residence and business activity. Consuls also supervised self-governing associations of Japanese residents within their areas of jurisdiction.[9] The consul general in Mukden was the Foreign Ministry's principal representative in the territory. He not only coordinated consular activity, but also served as a special envoy to Chinese authorities in Manchuria whose ties to the central government were unstable and often no more than nominal. This mission assumed particular importance during the 1920s when the three northeastern provinces (Fengt'ien, Kirin, Heilungkiang) were governed as an autonomous political unit by the warlord Chang Tso-lin. Although Chang was never the faithful client, let alone puppet, that some Japanese hoped he would be, he looked to Japan for financial and military assistance. The consul general sought to use Chang's needs as leverage to influence the administration of Manchuria.[10]

Finally, as might be expected, the Imperial Japanese Army figured prominently in Manchurian affairs. The army regarded the protection of Japanese interests on the continent as one of its primary responsibilities. It also saw itself as an instrument of imperial expansion and armed diplomacy, thus competing with the Foreign Ministry for lead-

[8] The Colonial Affairs Ministry was created in 1929. Prior to that time, a Cabinet agency known as the Colonial Bureau held essentially the same responsibilities.

[9] See Mark R. Peattie, "Japanese Treaty Port Settlements in China, 1895–1937," Duus, Myers, and Peattie, in *The Japanese Informal Empire in China, 1895–1945*, chap. 6.

[10] On the relationship between the Mukden consul general and Chang Tso-lin, see John W. Dower, *Empire and Aftermath: Yoshida Shigeru and the Japanese Experience, 1878–1954* (Cambridge, Mass.: Harvard University Press, 1979), chap. 3. In practice, the influence of the consul general was undermined by the competing influence of Japanese military advisers assigned to Chang, of the Kwantung Army, and of army intelligence. Chang was also never quite as compliant as the Japanese optimistically believed him to be. See Gavan McCormack, *Chang Tso-lin in Northeast China, 1911–1928: China, Japan, and the Manchurian Idea* (Stanford, Calif.: Stanford University Press, 1977), pp. 13–14. For a series of studies on the role of the Foreign Ministry in Manchuria, see the articles in the compilation *Tai Man-Mō seisaku no ichimen*, cited above.

ership in continental affairs, particularly in Manchuria. The most important consideration defining the army's interest in the territory, however, was the fact that national defense policy after 1907 formally incorporated Northeast China into Japan's strategic perimeter. Under this policy, Japanese military authorities unilaterally assumed responsibility for the external security of the territory without regard to Chinese consent or cooperation. Defense planners not only saw Manchuria as a staging area for operations against Russia (subsequently, the Soviet Union) and China south of the Wall, but by the 1920s as a source of strategic economic resources to be exploited in the event of a blockade or embargo against Japan.[11] In order to ensure maximum military readiness as well as remind Chinese regional authorities of the risks of incurring Japanese displeasure, the army maintained a division-strength garrison in Port Arthur and an additional six battalions of special guard troops stationed within the Railway Zone. Following administrative reforms in 1919, this garrison was renamed the Kwantung Army.[12]

Four major agencies were thus responsible for the conduct of various aspects of Japanese policy in Manchuria. Not unexpectedly, this arrangement, sometimes described as "four-headed" management, did not always function smoothly. Compartmentalized decision making and the lack of strong central coordination encouraged frequent interagency disputes. Contemporary observers often cited this system as a major source of difficulty in the conduct of territorial affairs. Japanese officials in Manchuria were among the most vocal critics and persistently called for reforms. In practice, however, the problem does not appear to have been as serious as critics claimed. Interagency bickering was politically noisy, but before the late 1920s there were few cases where policy failures could be blamed on the compartmentalized structure as such. A tendency to exaggerate the evils of divided authority in Manchuria was characteristic of the rhetoric of interagency competition.[13]

[11] On Manchuria in Japanese defense policy, see Tsunoda Jun, *Manshū mondai to kokubō hōshin* (Tokyo: Hara shobō, 1967); Bōeicho bōei kenshūsho senshishitsu, *Daihon'ei rikugunbu* [Imperial General Headquarters: Army Section], 10 vols. (Tokyo: Asagumo Shinbuasya, 1967–75), vol. 1, chap. 2; Kitaoka Shin'ichi, *Nihon rikugun to tairiku seisaku* (Tokyo: Tokyo daigaku shuppankai), 1978; Michael Barnhart, *Japan Prepares for Total War: The Search for Economic Security, 1919–1941* (Ithaca, N.Y.: Cornell University Press, 1987), chap. 1.

[12] See Alvin Coox, "The Kwantung Army Dimension," in Duus, Myers, and Peattie, *The Japanese Informal Empire in China*, pp. 396–438.

[13] Banno Junji suggests that much of the debate during this period about "dual" and even "triple diplomacy" centered on structural issues and did not necessarily reflect differences in policy content. Banno Junji, *Kindai Nihon no gaikō to seiji* (Tokyo: Kenbun shuppan, 1985), pp. 77–78.

Indeed, while the existence of some substantive differences cannot be denied, a broad consensus as to general programmatic direction was a characteristic feature of Japanese policy in Manchuria until 1928. The actual degree of divergence between the courses of action advocated by so-called "hard-liners" and "moderates" were not great. All factions agreed that military, economic, and geopolitical considerations demanded the preservation of Japan's sphere of influence in Northeast China. Consensus also extended to railway imperialism as a general strategy. Agreement on these matters, in turn, provided the basis for a rational division of labor among agencies active in Manchuria. Underneath a fractious exterior, there was a considerable degree of practical cooperation and mutual respect, albeit grudgingly extended, among soldiers, diplomats, colonial administrators, and railway men.[14]

For a number of reasons this consensus began to erode during the late 1920s. Some were external, such as disagreements over how to assess the threat of Chinese nationalism to Japanese interests.[15] Other causes were largely internal to Japanese politics. Of particular significance was a growing restiveness within the army's officer corps: opposition to the arms reduction policies of the government, deep resentment over what was perceived as the antimilitary orientation of civilian leaders, factional conflict over the distribution of command and staff leadership posts.[16] In the thinking of many middle-echelon officers, these issues were intimately linked to what they regarded as the government's weak foreign and defense policies. They expressed particular dissatisfaction with the situation in Manchuria where, in their view, the government had adopted a policy of passivity when bold action was demanded, of peaceful negotiation when the application of force offered the only effective solution. A growing number were convinced that the old system of informal empire in China was no longer viable and that radical alternatives were required.[17]

[14] This conclusion is based on my study of the pre-Incident history of the SMR. Y. Tak Matsusaka, "Japanese Imperialism and the South Manchuria Railway Company, 1904–1914," (Ph.D. dissertation, Harvard University, 1993).

[15] See Ogata Yōichi, "Tōhoku kōtsū iinkai to iwayuru 'Mantetsu hōi tetsudō mō keikaku,'" Shigaku zasshi 86, no. 8 (August 1977): 39–72; by the same author, "Dai 2 ji 'Shidehara gaikō' to 'Man-Mō' tetsudō kōshō," Tōyō shigaku 57, nos. 3–4 (March 1976): 178–212; Yoshii Ken'ichi, "Man-Mō tetsudo⁻ mondai no tenkai to Tanaka naikaku," Niigata daigaku jinbun kagaku kenkyū, no. 69 (July 1986): 1–46. These studies strongly suggest that most Japanese policy makers did not consider the Chinese nationalist challenge in Manchuria to be as serious a threat as their public rhetoric indicated.

[16] See Leonard A. Humphreys, "Crisis and Reaction: The Japanese Army in the "Liberal" Twenties," Armed Forces and Society 5, no.1 (fall 1978): 73–92.

[17] For a general analysis of these developments, see Sadako N. Ogata, Defiance In Manchuria: The Making of Japanese Foreign Policy, 1931–1932 (Berkeley: University of California Press, 1964).

Many of the staff officers assigned to the Kwantung Army during the late 1920s were associated with this dissident trend. They were, moreover, particularly well positioned to engage in direct action in order to advance their views. The first move of this kind came in 1928 when senior staff officer Komoto Daisaku engineered the assassination of Chang Tso-lin. While the anticipated military crisis failed to materialize, the action succeeded in aggravating Sino-Japanese tensions over Manchuria, creating a climate increasingly favorable to advocates of a military solution. A second and better-planned attempt to seize the territory three years later, masterminded by Lieutenant Colonel Ishiwara Kanji and Colonel Itagaki Seishirō, succeeded. On September 18, 1931, the Kwantung Army, acting without the sanction of home authorities, launched the first of a series of operations against Chinese regional forces that would place the larger part of Manchuria under Japanese military control by the end of the year.

The Origins of the Puppet State, September 1931–March 1932

Lieutenant Colonel Ishiwara and his associates had originally planned to install a "simple, straightforward and dictatorial" form of administration in Manchuria operating under the conventions governing the wartime administration of occupied territories.[18] The Manchurian Incident was an act of war resulting in the conquest of Northeast China. The Kwantung Army was an army of occupation. Ideological embellishments notwithstanding, garrison leaders intended to govern Manchuria in a manner consistent with these basic realities. A Provisional Government-General under the direct control of the Kwantung Army was to be superimposed upon the existing Chinese provincial and district administration. Local Chinese officials would be granted a considerable degree of autonomy in exchange for their cooperation and their renunciation of allegiance to either the former Manchurian regime or the nationalist government in Nanking. The primary functions of the Government-General were to provide for external defense, to maintain

---

[18] The Japanese army had acquired considerable experience in managing occupied territories prior to 1931: Manchuria and North China during the Sino-Japanese War (1894–95), Tientsin during the Boxer Rebellion (1900), Manchuria during and after the Russo-Japanese War (occupation between 1904 and 1907), Shantung during the First World War, and Siberia (1918–1922, North Sakhalin until 1925). General procedures and regulations had been routinized after the Russo-Japanese War. One of the principal functions of the Kwantung garrison and the government of the Leased Territory until 1919 was, in fact, to establish a zone of occupation in southern Manchuria to serve as a rear base area in the event of a conflict with Russia. There are some striking similarities between the Japanese army's occupation administration in 1904–7 and the Kwantung Army's plans in 1931. For a study of occupation policy during the Russo-Japanese War, see Oyama Azusa, *Nichi-Ro sensō no gunsei shiroku* (Tokyo: Fuyō shobō, 1973).

internal peace and civil order, and to generate sufficient revenues to cover its own expenses. It would also direct territorial economic development, but the actual task of implementing economic policy would be turned over to the South Manchuria Railway Company. A large and complex administrative apparatus was to be avoided since these arrangements would only be temporary. Once the situation in Manchuria had been stabilized and the diplomatic issues precipitated by the Incident resolved, garrison leaders anticipated formal partition, annexation, and the establishment of a permanent colonial administration.[19]

Much to the Kwantung Army's disappointment, however, Tokyo refused to sanction this scheme. While the home authorities were not unwilling to taking advantage of developments in Manchuria to press new demands on the Chinese, they found any settlement involving partition and annexation unacceptable. Central army authorities were more sympathetic to the general goals of garrison leaders than their civilian counterparts, but the possibility of adverse international reaction, particularly from the Soviet Union, led them to argue for restraint. The need to enforce discipline within the army was also a consideration.[20] During the early months of the Incident, authorities in Tokyo were thus united in their opposition to the Kwantung Army's actions. They instructed garrison leaders to desist from any further expansion of hostilities and to refrain from interference in local government. The settlement of the Incident, they insisted, should be left to duly constituted authorities.

It was in an effort to circumvent these instructions that garrison leaders resorted to the subterfuge of Manchurian independence. By orchestrating an ostensibly indigenous movement calling for the separation of the territory from China proper, Ishiwara and his associates sought to remove the political outcome of events in the territory from the reach of Tokyo. A "Manchurian Free State" was to be a front behind which they could act without constraint while formally denying responsibility. Presenting the home government with a series of faits accomplis, garrison leaders hoped they could, in time, persuade their superiors of the wisdom of their more radical course of action.[21]

[19] Among the studies of the Manchurian Incident providing background for this essay are Ogata, *Defiance In Manchuria*; James Crowley, *Japan's Quest for Autonomy: National Security and Foreign Policy, 1930–1938* (Princeton, N.J.: Princeton University Press, 1969); Mark R. Peattie, *Ishiwara Kanji and Japan's Confrontation with the West* (Princeton, N.J.: Princeton University Press, 1975); James William Morley, ed., *Japan Erupts: The London Naval Conference and the Manchurian Incident, 1928–1932* (New York: Columbia University Press, 1984).

[20] Kitaoka Shin'ichi, "Rikugun habatsu tairitsu (1931–35) no saikentō: taigai, kokubō seisaku o chūshin to shite," *Nenpō kindai Nihon kenkyū Shōwa ki no gunbu*, 1979, no. 1, pp. 57–58.

[21] Garrison leaders had committed themselves to a strategy of independence on Septem-

There were undoubtedly some among the Japanese settler community in Manchuria who were genuinely committed to territorial self-rule.[22] Organizations such as the Manchurian Youth League called for the creation of a state based on pan-Asian cooperation and Confucian principles of government. While such ideas strongly influenced the development of official ideology in Manchukuo, they had little impact on the actual design of the administrative apparatus.[23] A document issued by garrison headquarters in January 1932 frankly defined the central principle of Manchurian politics: the new territorial state was to adopt "the external form of a constitutional, republican government . . . but maintain the internal reality of a centralized dictatorship imbued with the political authority of our empire."[24] Kwantung Army leaders thus regarded the creation of a new state in Northeast China as no more than an expedient vehicle through which they could exercise power. From a functional perspective, the government of independent Manchuria was to serve as a substitute for a more conventional occupation regime.

To be sure, the plans drafted by garrison leaders during the first two months of 1932 called for the creation of what appeared to be a substantial edifice of government, modeled in part on the imperial Chinese state. It was divided into judicial, control (inspection and audit), legisla-

---

ber 22, but there was considerable ambiguity among staff officers as to what this meant. A variety of plans and programs were discussed between late September and December. As late as the beginning of December, an ambiguous scheme for establishing a Japanese Government-General in Manchuria in addition to a nominally independent Manchurian government was under consideration. See for example, Kwantung Army Staff, "Man-Mō mondai kaiketsu sakuan," (esp. qualifying note written by Ishiwara Kanji) in Tsunoda Jun, ed., *Ishiwara Kanji Shiryō*, 2 vols. (Tokyo: Hara shobō, 1967), 2:85 (hereafter as *IKS* 2). Also see Ishiwara Kanji, "Man-Mō tōji hōan," October 1, 1931, ibid., pp. 86–87; "Man-Mō jiyūkoku setsuritsu an taikō" (prepared by Kwantung Army legal adviser Matsuki Tamotsu), November 1931, *Manshū jihen kimitsu seiryaku nikki* (hereafter Katakura Diary) 11/7/31 in *Gendai shi shiryō*, vol. 7, *Manshū jihen*, ed. Kobayashi Tatsuo and Shimada Toshihiko (Tokyo: Misuzu shobō, 1964 (hereafter *GSS* 7), pp.248–56; "Manshū totokufu kansei sankō an" (Matsuki Tamotsu), December 5, 1931, Katakura Diary 12/5/31, pp. 287–90.

[22] See for example, Yamaguchi Jūji, *Kieta teikoku Manshū* (Tokyo: Asahi shinbunsha, 1967). Yamaguchi was an employee of the SMR railroad division who enthusiastically embraced the Kwantung Army's program at first. A sense of disappointment if not betrayal is evident in his account.

[23] By the summer of 1932, Ishiwara himself had come to favor such views: Manchukuo would provide the outlines of a more broadly applicable political model for Japanese rule in East Asia where national independence, international cooperation, and Japanese imperial hegemony could be reconciled. However, as Mark Peattie has pointed out, Ishiwara was unable to persuade his colleagues to embrace this broader vision. Toward the end of his tenure on the Kwantung Army staff, which expired in August 1932, he became increasingly isolated. See Peattie, *Ishiwara Kanji*, chap. 5.

[24] Kwantung Army Headquarters, "Man-Mō mondai zango shori yōkō," January 27, 1932, Katakura Diary 1/28/32, pp. 361–62.

tive, and executive branches, the latter consisting of a Council of State and seven Cabinet departments: civil affairs, foreign affairs, defense, finance, industry, transportation, and justice. Supreme authority was vested in P'u Yi, who was to be elevated to the status of emperor at an appropriate time. The capital was to be established at Ch'angch'un, subsequently renamed Hsinking, in central Manchuria. Ethnic harmony was to be a guiding principle of Manchurian administration. All citizens of the new state, regardless of national or ethnic origin, including Japanese, were to be eligible for government service.

Behind this grand facade, however, stood a nearly vacant lot. Few government offices, at least during the first half of the 1930s, were intended to do any serious work. The purpose behind elaborating such an ostentatious edifice of state was largely symbolic, to impress the subject people with the strength and permanence of the new order. The top posts, reserved exclusively for Chinese, were ceremonial for the most part. Appointments were made with the aim of coopting former regional officials, and had little relationship to the actual exercise of power in Manchukuo. The functional centers of authority directing general administration, military affairs, and economic policy were located outside the formal organization of government, operating with minimal reference to the elaborate structure of councils and ministries.[25]

General administrative affairs, for example, were managed under the direction of a detachment of Kwantung Army Headquarters known as the Special Affairs Unit [*tokumubu*]. This body, reporting to the garri-

---

[25] This assessment of the nature of government in Manchukuo is admittedly somewhat oversimplified and demands considerable qualification: 1) Many among the local Chinese elite were prepared to support any stable regime that would preserve order, guarantee local autonomy, and minimize taxes and other imposts. Some played an active part in setting up provisional self-governing organs preliminary to Manchuria's declaration of independence. Their cooperation after the founding of the state was essential to the structure of power designed by the Kwantung Army. (For a study of the evolution of relations between the Japanese and the local Chinese elite, see Hirano Kenichiro, "The Japanese in Manchuria, 1906–1931: A Study of the Historical Background of Manchukuo" [Ph.D. dissertation, Harvard University, 1983].) Whether the cooperation of local elites can be construed as evidence supporting the claim that Manchukuo was a genuine national state, however, is dubious. Almost all colonial regimes during the late nineteenth and early twentieth centuries accommodated or coopted to some degree the precolonial power structure. 2) There were also significant differences of opinion among garrison leaders as to the exent to which the state apparatus was to be developed. Ishiwara, for example, increasingly favored the establishment of a fully functional government. 3) The establishment of a mass political organization known as the Concordia Association was another important element in the Kwantung Army's scheme for territorial government. Its purpose was to provide a vehicle for popular participation in the political order. 4) Some organs of the Manchurian government would be expanded subsequently, particularly those dealing with economic matters.

son's chief of staff, was composed of a mixed group of staff officers and civilian advisers, many of whom had served in the headquarters unit (Section 3) originally set up to handle occupation affairs.[26] The directives of the Special Affairs Unit were implemented through a relatively obscure agency within the Manchurian government known as the General Affairs Board of the Council of State. This agency, one of the few functioning organs within the state apparatus, was officially responsible for the setting of national policy, the formulation of the budget, and the appointment of all personnel. The presidency of the board was reserved for a Japanese, who was to report covertly but nonetheless directly to the Kwantung Army Chief of Staff.[27] Indicative of the degree to which the General Affairs Board was a creature of the Kwantung Army was the fact that the first appointee to this post was Komai Tokuzo, the former civilian chief of the Special Affairs Unit. Garrison leaders described this system of covert political dictatorship as the "internal guidance [naimen shidō]" of Manchukuo. While justified as a form of political tutelage, it was, in fact, little more than a way to conceal the real source of power.

This system of internal guidance, however, was only part of the overall scheme for territorial management. In fact, puppet government in a narrow sense was limited to matters of central administration. In other areas, garrison leaders dispensed with even the pretense of working through the structure of the Manchurian state.

---

[26] Designed at the time of its establishment in December 1931 to serve as an organ of provisional government in its own right, the Special Affairs Unit (described until February 1932 as the Government Affairs Unit [tōjibu]) was originally organized into five functional departments: administration, finance, industry, transportation, and external relations. With the establishment of Manchukuo, this detachment withdrew itself from an overt role in territorial government, working behind the scenes to formulate policy and oversee its execution. Kwantung Army Headquarters, "Genkō katōteki seido (shin seiken juritsu made)," December 5, 1931, Katakura Diary 12/5/31, pp. 286–87.

[27] Manshūkokushi hensan kankōkai, Manshūkoku shi sōron (Tokyo: Manshū dōhai engokai, 1970), pp. 217–18. It is significant that the Manchoukuo Yearbook, designed for foreign consumption and thus geared for public relations, contains the following description: "The General Affairs Board is called the central organ of the Council of State Affairs as it handles not only budgets but national policies. In Manchoukuo, the Department of Finance takes charge only of the National Treasury and the financial administration; the basic principles in forming the state budget and its assessment are controlled by the Prime Minister who has the authority of making administrative decisions in the General Affairs Board, the organ for establishing national policies." Manchoukuo Yearbook 1934, p. 79. On the accountability of the board president, see Kwantung Army Chief of Staff Hashimoto Toranosuke to Army Vice Minister Koiso Kuniaki, "Manshūkoku ni taisuru Nihonjin shuyō shokuin ni kansuru ken tsūchō," May 24, 1932, in Gendai shi shiryō, vol. 11, Zoku Manshū jihen, ed. Inaba Masao, Kobayashi Tatsuo, and Shimada Toshihiko (Tokyo: Misuzu shobō, 1965) (hereafter cited as GSS 11), pp. 836–37.

In the vital field of national defense, for example, they employed the fiction that the government of P'u Yi had prevailed upon Japan for military assistance. Apart from provisions for the establishment of some "native" auxiliary units, external security as well as domestic peacekeeping functions were to be entrusted entirely to the Japanese army. The new state would, of course, pay for this service out of its own revenues.[28] The role of the Kwantung Army as the protector of Manchukuo would be eventually sanctioned in a bilateral defense pact after normal relations were established between Tokyo and Hsinking. Such an agreement would serve, in effect, to legitimize the permanent stay of a Japanese army of occupation in Manchuria.

The preference for such an arrangement, rather than using the military equivalent of "internal guidance," is hardly surprising. Direct responsibility for the defense of the territory, without even the fiction of a request for protection from the Chinese, had been an axiomatic element in the army's strategic planning since the end of the Russo-Japanese War. Moreover, armed force provided the foundations of Japanese power in Manchukuo. Placing real guns in the hands of puppet troops presented a far greater risk than granting illusory political authority to puppet officials. The Kwantung Army had no intention of taking such chances.[29]

Economic policy, another vital area of concern, was likewise to be managed under the fiction of a contractual agreement with Japan. While the constitution of Manchukuo included provisions for departments of Industry and Transportation, most of the actual work was to be farmed out to a Japanese agency: in this case, the South Manchuria Railway Company. This arrangement was not only central to the Kwantung

---

[28] Kwantung Army Headquarters, "Man-Mō mondai zango shori yōkō," January 27, 1932, Katakura Diary 1/28/32, p. 361.

[29] The constitution of Manchukuo included provisions for a department of defense as well as land and sea forces, and a "national" army was eventually organized. Earlier during the planning process, Ishiwara and his colleagues had explicitly ruled out the possibility of providing Manchukuo with even a nominal military establishment. Existing Chinese provincial units as well as the forces of the old regime were to be disarmed and disbanded. They had, however, modified their position by March. The apparent reason for this change was the need to use Chinese auxiliaries in pacification operations and as a means as well to absorb demobilized soldiers who might otherwise resort to banditry. As of January 1932, for example, Chinese provincial armies had been assigned to maintain order in Kirin and Heilungkiang; the Kwantung Army was directly responsible for Fengt'ien alone. These forces, however, were to be held under strict Japanese control, their size kept to a minimum, and their mission restricted to supporting the Kwantung Army in peacekeeping efforts. For a discussion of the Manchukuo Army, see Coox, "The Kwantung Army Dimension," pp. 412–14. A formal policy governing the army of Manchukuo was formulated in 1933. Army Ministry, "Manshūkoku rikugun shidō yōkō," September 1933, GSS 7:590–91.

Army's schemes for managing Manchuria, but was also a key element in subsequent rivalry between Japanese agencies with jurisdictional claims in the territory. For these reasons, it deserves special consideration here.

The promotion of rapid economic development was second only to the pacification of the territory among the priorities of the Kwantung Army's postconquest agenda. Garrison leaders understood that the stability of the new state would depend far more on restoring prosperity than on refining the political structures of government. The implementation of aggressive policies to accelerate recovery from the worldwide depression and the aftereffects of war was an urgent task of government in Manchuria. Territorial development, moreover, was central to the long-term program formulated by Ishiwara and his colleagues. In their view, the importance of Manchuria to Japan's economic security had been sufficient to justify committing the nation to a perilous course of armed expansion.[30]

All things being equal, Kwantung Army leaders would have preferred to assume direct control of development policy rather than rely on an outside civilian organization like the SMR. At same time they were acutely aware that, unlike territorial defense which was the chief function of the garrison, or general administration which could be orchestrated by headquarters personnel trained in occupation affairs, managing territorial development on a long-term basis was a task beyond the capabilities of existing staff and organization. The SMR, on the other hand, was an established development agency with a proven record, involved in a broad range of commercial and industrial enterprises. Key sectors of the territorial economy of interest to the army were already being developed under the company's direct or indirect control. Moreover, the SMR enjoyed a long-standing reputation as a sound investment and would thus provide a major conduit for capital from the home islands.[31]

There was, however, one major obstacle to this scheme. Apart from the power to mobilize SMR facilities in a military emergency, the

[30] On Ishiwara's view of economic development in Manchuria, see Peattie, *Ishiwara Kanji*, pp. 96–101. For general background on military economic policy and continental expansion, see Barnhart, *Japan Prepares for Total War*, chap. 1. An example of the Kwantung Army's early economic plans can be found in Kwantung Army Headquarters, Section 3, "Man-Mō kaihatsu hōsaku an," December 8, 1931, Katakura Diary 12/9/31, pp. 291–92.

[31] Some company officials had actively cooperated with Ishiwara in helping to develop the economic aspects of the Kwantung Army's occupation plans in early 1931. Hara Akira, "1930 nendai no Manshū keizai tōsei seisaku," in Manshūshi kenkyūkai, *Nihon teikokushugika no Manshū*, (Tokyo: Ochanomizu shobō, 1972), pp. 8–17.

Kwantung Army had no direct authority over company operations. Under normal circumstances, the managers of the SMR reported to the governor of the Kwantung Leased Territory who, in turn, received his instructions from the minister of colonial affairs. The garrison's plans would therefore require the cooperation of these authorities. Given the relationship between Tokyo and the Kwantung Army in late 1931 in early 1932, such cooperation was unlikely. Moreover, having circumvented Tokyo in the military and political aspects of their program, Ishiwara and his associates were unwilling to give the home government the leverage that a request for economic cooperation would entail.

Garrison leaders sought to sidestep this problem by establishing an informal local agreement with company managers. Over a long history of institutional evolution, the SMR had acquired considerable decision-making autonomy, and in practice, the supervisory authority of the Kwantung governor and the Colonial Ministry had never been strong.[32] The SMR thus enjoyed a great deal of latitude in formulating its economic program so long as its activities did not run afoul of the general framework of policy set in Tokyo. Considering the situation in the territory after September 1931 and the paralysis of central authority, it was not beyond the discretionary power of the company to enter such an informal agreement.

Indeed, there were a number of reasons why it was advantageous for the company to cooperate with the army. In a preliminary overture made in October 1931, garrison leaders offered the SMR a monopoly on railroad and air transportation, a central role in banking and currency regulation, control over the distribution of Manchuria's principal cash crops, and broad responsibility for the development of strategic raw materials. While this prospect was daunting, it was also seductive. The company was to be granted sweeping powers over the territorial economy and exclusive rights to exploit the opportunities opened by new circumstances in Manchuria.[33]

At the same time, Ishiwara and his colleagues applied the stick as well as the carrot in their efforts to persuade company officials to cooperate. They implied that, in the absence of a voluntary agreement, they would be forced to consider alternatives that might prove to be less favorable to the SMR. Some of the preliminary plans drafted by garrison staff made ominous mention of the possibility of nationalizing the SMR, dissolving the company into its component enterprises, and expropriat-

---

[32] In practice, both the army and the Foreign ministry had played a much more important part in giving direction to the SMR during the 1920s than the company's officially designated supervisors.

[33] Kwantung Army Headquarters, "Mantetsu kaisha ni taisuru yōbō jikō," Katakura Diary, 10/5/31, pp. 203–4.

ing railroad earnings to underwrite the expenses of the Kwantung Army as well as the new government.[34] In theory, the company's political and legal status would make such action nearly impossible, but in view of Tokyo's inability to control events in Manchuria, exclusive reliance on lines of authority that required enforcement by the home government was not advisable. The creation of the new state, moreover, would upset the entire system of imperial rights and concessions upon which the company's status rested. Given the army's control of the legal apparatus of the puppet state, nationalization was not an idle threat. The outlook for the SMR was therefore uncertain at best. Even setting aside possible gains, circumstances recommended a policy of what might be described as preemptive cooperation.[35]

An agreement was reached during the first week of January 1932. Under its terms, the SMR would establish a special detachment of economic experts drawn from its vast research apparatus to serve as a counterpart to the Kwantung Army's Special Affairs Unit. This new organ, known as the Economic Research Group [Keizai chōsakai], would function unofficially as Manchuria's central economic planning bureau, taking broad policy direction from the Special Affairs Unit and producing detailed plans. The SMR itself would be responsible for implementing most of these plans. According to company officials, the SMR was to serve as a "substitute for the state" in economic policy.[36] Work on a comprehensive economic plan began in February and a preliminary draft was completed by May.[37]

The role to be played by the SMR in postconquest Manchuria illustrates the extent to which the Kwantung Army's schemes minimized the scope and scale of the territorial state. The key fields of economic policy and national defense were to be placed under direct Japanese control. Even the pretense of self-rule was thus limited to general administration. Appearances notwithstanding, the Manchurian state was a minimal construct. Ishiwara himself nearly admitted as much in response to subsequent criticism about the structure and function of the new gov-

---

[34] Matsuki Tamotsu, "Manshū totokufu kansei sankō an," GSS 7:288.

[35] Kusayanagi Daizō, Jitsuroku Mantetsu chōsabu, vol. 2 (Tokyo: Asahi shinbunsha, 1979), p. 222.

[36] Hara, "1930 nendai no Manshū keizai tōsei seisaku," pp. 8–17; Yamada Gōichi, "Manshū tōsei keizai to san'i ittai sei no hossoku," in Kindai Nihon to Chūgoku (Tokyo: Kyūko shoin, 1989), pp. 252–55; Noma Kiyoshi et al., 15 nen sensō to Mantetsu chōsabu (Tokyo: Hara shobō, 1986), p. 21. The phrase "substituting for the state" is found in Minami Manshū tetsudō kabushiki kaisha keizai chōsakai iinkai, "Manshū keizai tōsei saku yōshi," June 20, 1932, in Minami Manshū tetsudō kabushiki kaisha keizai chōsakai, Manshū kankei ritsuan chōsa shorui, vol. 1 (Dairen: SMR, 1935), part 1 (hereafter MRCS 1.1), pp. 48–50.

[37] "Manshū keizai tōsei saku (kōhen, seisaku hen)," May 1932, ibid., pp. 51–88.

ernment, when he remarked, "this so-called Ch'angch'un government is not quite as important as people commonly believe it to be."[38]

The Kwantung Army's designs clearly had a makeshift quality about them, but they were not without an elegance of their own. Territorial government was to be based on simple and pragmatic arrangements, making use of accessible resources and organizations. The army established a system of rule that, apart from the window dressing of independence, did not depart greatly from its original plans for an occupation regime. Indeed, considering the field conditions and the pressing timetable under which Ishiwara and his colleagues worked, their achievements in laying the foundations of a new form of Japanese control in the territory were quite impressive. In the space of six months, they had conquered Manchuria, severed its political ties with China proper, established a functional military dictatorship, and instituted a working economic policy apparatus. By the spring of 1932, Kwantung Army leaders appeared well on the way to achieving most of their objectives. What remained was to force Tokyo to acknowledge these realities and revise its policies accordingly.

THE DEBATE OVER PROTECTORATE STATUS FOR MANCHUKUO AND THE THREE-IN-ONE COMPROMISE, MARCH–AUGUST 1932

The reaction in Tokyo to the founding of Manchukuo, formally announced on March 1, 1932, was mixed. On the one hand, this development marked the final defeat of efforts to contain the Incident. Throughout the closing months of 1931, moderates among military as well as civilian leadership had held out hope of regaining control of the situation in the territory and restoring, insofar as possible, the status quo ante. By the beginning of the new year, however, prospects for such an outcome had become dim at best. In January, Acting Consul General Morishima Morindo reported from his post in Mukden that not only was the Kwantung Army adamant about proceeding with the establishment of a Manchurian state, but considerable progress in this direction had already been made. Public opinion in the territory, he noted, was accepting independence as an accomplished fact. "Given that such circumstances already prevail at this point, it may be too late for the government to attempt to carry out an entirely different policy line," he warned. Morishima recommended that Tokyo consider accepting the "new state as an established reality."[39] Even before March, then, a sense of resignation had begun to take hold in leadership circles.

---

[38] Ishiwara Kanji, "Isōgai taisa no tame," June 1932, in *IKS* 2:100.

[39] Morishima to Inukai, 1/12/32, in *Nihon gaikō bunsho—Manshū jihen*, vol. 2, part 1 (Tokyo: Japan Ministry of Foreign Affairs, 1979) (hereafter as *NGB—Manshū jihen* with volume and part numbers), pp. 344–45.

On the other hand, there was also a growing tendency in some official quarters to see developments in Manchuria in a more positive light, not as a crisis to be contained, but as an opportunity to be exploited to Japan's overall advantage. Central army authorities began to reconsider their attitude when it became clear that the Soviet Union was not planning any aggressive countermeasures to the Kwantung Army's actions.[40] Moreover, Araki Sadao, the new army minister appointed in December, was more openly in favor of a radical shift in Japan's Manchuria policy than his predecessor.[41]

Incipient optimism about developments in Manchuria was not limited to the army but emerged among civilian leaders as well. For example, in the memorandum cited above, Consul General Morishima argued that the Kwantung Army's scheme for establishing an independent state had definite merits from a diplomatic perspective. The same fiction that allowed the garrison to circumvent Tokyo's instructions could also be used to deflect international criticism directed against Japan. He noted that while the powers had issued harsh verbal condemnations of Japanese aggression against China, they were not anxious to embroil themselves directly in the Manchurian crisis, let alone intervene on China's behalf. Under these circumstances, suggested Morishima, the international community might be willing to accept the pretense that Manchukuo was the outcome of an indigenous separatist movement as an expedient way to avoid confrontation. "In discussing the construction of a new state, our external explanation should be based on the principles of national self-determination," he wrote. He added, "even though we may not be able to fully conceal [*impei*] Japanese manipulation behind the scenes, we must conduct ourselves in such a way as to be able to formally disclaim any such activity, thereby denying a third party any pretext to intervene."[42]

Whether rooted in resignation or fresh optimism, official thinking in Tokyo began moving during the early months of 1932 toward an acknowledgment of conquest, partition, and the establishment of a new regime as faits accomplis. Less than two weeks after the formal an-

[40] *Daihon'ei rikugunbu*, 1:338–39. The Soviet Union had made overtures for a nonaggression treaty by the end of 1931. By the beginning of the new year, Soviet representatives were hinting at the possibility of relinquishing control of the Chinese Eastern Railway in north Manchuria, a clear sign that they were prepared to acknowledge Japanese hegemony in the territory as a whole.

[41] Kitaoka, "Rikugun habatsu no tairitsu," pp. 60–63.

[42] Morishima to Inukai, 1/12/32, *NGB—Manshū jihen*, vol. 2, part 1, pp. 344–45. Morishima is clearly arguing in favor of using the *pretense* of independence as a diplomatic ploy. He is not suggesting that Japan actually treat Manchukuo as an sovereign state. The Foreign Ministry's subsequent use of this pretense as a means to justify its own claims to leadership in Manchuria policy would muddle the issue, but it is important to note that diplomats never had any illusions about the nature of the state.

nouncement of the birth of the new state, the cabinet of Prime Minister Inukai resolved in principle to extend formal recognition to P'u Yi's government.[43] Full commitment to this new course in Manchuria, however, was contingent on the settlement of a number of issues concerning administrative structure and policy leadership. Three major points of contention emerged in the course of discussions during the spring and summer of 1932 involving responsible ministries in Tokyo as well as the Kwantung Army.[44]

First and foremost was the question of accountability. To whom would Japanese leaders involved in "guiding" Manchukuo answer? Neither military nor civilian authorities in Tokyo were satisfied with the existing situation in which the Kwantung Army, using the Manchurian state as a cover, operated without responsibility to the home government. In purely military matters, the solution involved a straightforward restoration of normal discipline: garrison leaders would be required answer to their superiors in the army chain of command. The Kwantung Army's role in directing political and economic affairs, however, was a different matter. Given that Manchuria was not under formal wartime occupation, these areas of activity were outside normal military jurisdiction. Some civilian leaders argued that the Kwantung Army should withdraw from involvement in all nonmilitary affairs in Manchuria and turn over the management of political and economic policies to a new civilian agency, but neither the garrison nor the central army leadership were willing to consider such a measure.[45] The alternative under consideration was to officially sanction the Kwantung Army's activities while demanding, in return, formal accountability to Tokyo. The Special Affairs Unit, for example, would continue to engage in the "internal guidance" of general administration, but it would be required to report to designated agencies in the home government.

[43] Cabinet resolution, "Man-Mō mondai shori hōshin yōkō," March 12, 1932, NGB—Manshū jihen, vol. 3, part 1, pp. 442–43.

[44] Much of the following discussion is based on Shimizu Hideko, "Tai-Man kikō no hensen," Kokusai seiji—Nihon gaikōshi no shomondai 3, no. 2 (1967): 138; Baba Akira, Nitchū kankei to gaisei kikō no kenkyū (Tokyo: Hara shobō, 1983), pp. 248–49; Yamada, "Manshū tōsei keizai to san'i ittai sei no hossoku," pp. 280–83.

[45] The idea of enforcing a strict division between military and civil affairs in Manchuria was first recommended by Mukden Consul General Hayashi Kyūjirō in a proposal to establish a high commission for Manchurian affairs during the early part of the Incident. Hayashi hoped to prevent the Kwantung Army from engineering its own political settlement. Hayashi to Shidehara, "Zai Man-Mō gyōsei kikan setchi ni kansuru iken jōshin ni tsuite," October 25, 1931, NGB—Manshū jihen, vol.1, part 2, pp. 183–84. General Koiso Kuniaki, at the time chief of the Army Ministry's Military Affairs Bureau, vigorously opposed such a separation. In his view, the army would play an overall role in any settlement of the Manchurian Incident. Hayashi Kyūjirō, Manshū jihen to Hōten sōryōji, ed. Baba Akira (Tokyo: Hara shobō, 1978), p. 142.

Second, authorities in Tokyo, military and civilian alike, had grave concerns about the effectiveness of the system of covert government as designed by Ishiwara and his associates. By May, considerable evidence had emerged that garrison leaders were not able to maintain discipline among Japanese officials serving in the new government. Contrary to the original intention of keeping the state apparatus simple, large numbers of Japanese, many of whom had dubious qualifications, had been appointed to office. Factionalism among these officials, reflecting in part growing division within the garrison leadership, had caused serious problems in some instances. The General Affairs Board appeared unable to assert its authority. Officials in Tokyo believed that the system of "internal guidance" alone was an inadequate guarantee of control. They saw an urgent need for some sort of formal, external supervision to be imposed on the Manchurian government.[46]

Third, Tokyo called for a redefinition of the functions performed by established Japanese civilian institutions in Manchuria. No less important was a clarification of their working relationship to the Kwantung Army and their official status with respect to the government in Hsinking. The old division of labor between the four agencies was no longer relevant. The mission of the consular apparatus in postconquest Manchuria, for example, required serious reconsideration. What would be the role for diplomats in a territory that was independent in name but a colony in reality? The future of the Kwantung Government was likewise uncertain. What need had Japan for an enclave on the Liaotung Peninsula with the whole of Manchuria under its control?[47] Perhaps most problematic of all was the status of South Manchuria Railway Company. While there was no question of a continued role for the SMR in the new Manchuria, jurisdiction and responsibility presented a serious problem. The ad hoc economic policy apparatus established in January by a local agreement between the company and garrison leaders had no official standing and was in conflict with established chains of command. Serious economic planning would not be possible until this situation was resolved.

The concerned ministries in Tokyo generally agreed on the urgency of these problems but held substantially different opinions as to their solutions. Some of the differences were rooted in divergent administrative philosophies. Conflicting sectional interests, however, also contributed to the debate. How to manage Manchuria policy was inseparably

---

[46] Yamada, "Manshū tōsei keizai to san'i ittai sei no hossoku," p. 281; Alvin Coox, *Nomonhan: Japan Against Russia, 1939,* 2 vols. (Stanford, Calif.: Stanford University Press, 1985), 1:65.

[47] The future of extraterritoriality and old treaty provisions governing the status of the Railway Zone and the Leased Territory were an important part of the overall debate over Japan–Manchuria relations.

linked to the question of who would do the managing. The Army, Foreign, and Colonial ministries were each no less determined to secure institutional advantage than to promote their points of view.

The Army Ministry, for example, favored the establishment of what essentially amounted to a protectorate over Manchukuo.[48] Deputy Minister Koiso Kuniaki prepared a proposal in June that called for the creation of a new agency to oversee the management of political and economic affairs in the territory. Described as an Intendancy-General (sō-kanfu), it would exert on-site supervisory control over the operations of all civilian agencies in Manchuria as well the nonmilitary functions of the garrison staff. The new agency would also have a substantial staff of its own, organized into functional departments for administrative, consular, legal, colonial, and economic affairs. Koiso's plan imposed external supervision on the Manchurian government with a rather heavy hand. He also envisioned the Intendancy-General as a quasi-military agency reporting directly to the Cabinet but under effective army control. Civilian officials were to play an unmistakably subordinate role in Manchuria. Candidates for the office of Intendant-General would be drawn exclusively from among general officers of the army.

Foreign Ministry officials agreed with General Koiso as to the need for a new agency to oversee Manchurian affairs, but they were concerned that the establishment of a structure with such a frankly colonial coloring as contained in his proposal would defeat the purpose of maintaining the fiction of independence. The Foreign Ministry favored the creation of an agency that would adopt the form of a special embassy. This nominally diplomatic organ would provide most of the supervisory and coordinating functions of Koiso's structure while strictly adhering to the pretense of Manchurian sovereignty. Under the embassy proposal, the ambassador would officially "advise" the Manchurian government.[49] At same time, he would supervise the internal guidance work of the Special Affairs Unit. The embassy would also assume on-the-spot control over the SMR and the administration of the Leased Territory. Consular officials would assist the ambassador at the local level and would head up major subdivisions in embassy staff. Ministry officials also had other reasons for favoring this form, grounded in sec-

---

[48] Baba, *Nitchū kankei to gaisei kikō no kenkyū*, pp. 252–53; Shimizu, "Tai-Man kikō no hensen," pp. 138–39.

[49] Deputy Foreign Minister Arita, who prepared his agency's version of the proposal for a supervisory organ in Manchuria, carefully avoided use of title "ambassador," referring to the office instead by the generic term "head official." Earlier proposals had used the term "high commissioner." An analysis of other Foreign Ministry plans and memoranda at this time, however, suggests that its officials were clearly thinking in terms of an embassy. Ibid.; Baba, *Nitchū kankei to gaisei kikō no kenkyū*, pp. 250–52.

tional interests. The same fiction designed to deflect international criticism also provided the foundations for the Foreign Ministry's claims to a continued role in territorial policy. Diplomacy, after all, would have no meaning in a colonial Manchuria.

Although the Colonial Ministry had an important stake in this debate, its influence in government was not in the same league as the Army and Foreign ministries. As a second-string agency, it was not in position to take the initiative in formulating an overall solution. On the other hand, its formal authority over the SMR provided some measure of leverage in the discussions. Its minimum goal was to preserve channels of control through the Kwantung governor. Beyond this, ministry officials hoped to parlay their jurisdiction over the SMR into broader authority over economic affairs in Manchuria.[50]

The question of creating a supervisory agency, of course, could not be settled through discussion in Tokyo alone. The Kwantung Army firmly opposed both the Army and the Foreign ministry proposals, arguing instead for preserving the status quo for the time being.[51] Although Koiso's proposal was close to what the Kwantung Army had originally envisioned before shifting to a strategy based on territorial independence, garrison leaders, having committed themselves to an alternative course, no longer saw heavy-handed external control as a viable option. They argued that the situation in Manchuria was delicate and that it would be politically unwise to compromise the pretense of independence with such an intrusive structure as an Intendancy-General. In form, the Foreign Ministry's scheme of establishing an embassy was preferable, but the idea of civilian dominance in leadership was not acceptable to the garrison any more than it was to central army leaders. Ishiwara and his associates acknowledged that existing arrangements might not be ideal but suggested that some of the problems as perceived in Tokyo had been overstated. The system they had designed was adequate and should be given time to work before considering any major reform.[52]

Discussion continued through the early summer. By the beginning of July, however, it was clear that none of the major parties to the debate were willing to concede their positions.[53] This deadlock was resolved by

[50] On the Colonial Ministry's economic plans, see Yamada, "Manshū tōsei keizai to san'i ittai sei no hossoku," p. 259; also see "Nichi-Man keizai kondakai tokubetsu iinkai dai 1 kai kaigi gaiyō," November 1932, in *MRCS* 1.1:587–92.

[51] Kwantung Army Headquarters, "Tai-Man-Mō saku," May 21, 1932, *GSS* 11, pp. 636–39; Hashimoto Toranosuke (Kwantung Army Chief of Staff), "Manshūkoku shidō yōryō," June 1932, ibid., pp. 640–41.

[52] Ishiwara, "Isōgai taisa no tame," pp. 100–102.

[53] Yamada, "Manshū tōsei keizai to san'i ittai sei no hossoku," pp. 280–83. Envoys dispatched to Manchuria by the Army Ministry were unable to persuade garrison leaders.

a timely compromise plan offered by Tani Masayuki, chief of the Foreign Ministry's East Asia Bureau, who had recently returned from talks with the Kwantung Army.[54] The key to Tani's proposed compromise was the appointment of a single official to fill concurrently three key posts in Manchuria: garrison commander, Kwantung governor, and a newly created office of "ambassador extraordinary and plenipotentiary." Because of the military role, candidates for this triple post would be limited to active-duty general officers of the army. As garrison commander, the occupant of this post would be responsible for all military affairs in Manchuria, including external defense and internal security. In this capacity, he would report to his superiors in Tokyo through the normal chain of command. As Kwantung governor, he would administer the Leased Territory, exercise police and judicial powers in the Railway Zone, and most importantly, supervise the operations of the South Manchuria Railway Company. In this role he would receive instructions from the minister of colonial affairs. As Japan's ambassador to Manchukuo, he would oversee all political affairs of the territory, supervising internal guidance as well as the new state's foreign relations. Members of the garrison's Special Affairs Unit would receive concurrent appointments as staff officials of the embassy. The ambassador would be advised by a civilian counselor, a responsibility Tani himself would later assume. In his capacity as a diplomat, the holder of this triple office would report to the Foreign Minister.

Tani's plan, dubbed the "three-in-one" system, was well received and quickly gained broad endorsement. It was acceptable to the Kwantung Army because it preserved the garrison's established role with a minimum of modifications. At the same time, it satisfied Tokyo's concern for accountability, supervision, and interagency coordination. The plan established fairly clear lines of responsibility for political and economic as well as military affairs. It also provided, through the triple office, a mechanism for interagency coordination. Provisions for the external supervision of Manchurian government affairs were perhaps somewhat weaker than authorities in Tokyo would have desired, but with a veteran foreign ministry official like Tani in the position of counselor, the plan at least offered a framework through which greater order and discipline could be imposed on the process of "internal guidance."

The Tani plan also managed to satisfy, at least in some measure, the sectional concerns of rival ministries in Tokyo. While Kwantung Army personnel, rather than professional diplomats (with the exception of the

---

[54] Shimizu, "Tai-Man kikō no hensen," pp. 139–40; Baba, *Nitchū kankei to gaisei kikō no kenkyū*, pp.254–57; Yamada, "Manshū tōsei keizai to san'i ittai sei no hossoku," pp. 284–86.

counselor), would staff the embassy, the Foreign Ministry's acquisition of supervisory power over the office of ambassador represented a significant gain. The plan also left the Colonial Ministry's jurisdiction intact, a outcome that, given the weak position of the agency, was something of a victory. Both the Army and Foreign ministry proposals would have reduced the role of Colonial Affairs substantially.

The three-in-one plan, however, seems to have incorporated relatively little of the Army Ministry's position beyond a common concern shared by all agencies in Tokyo for accountability, supervision, and coordination. The arrangement was close in form to what the Foreign Ministry had proposed and in substance to the status quo favored by the Kwantung Army. It bore little resemblance, however, to the powerful Intendancy-General outlined in the Army Ministry's scheme.

At the same time it is important not to lose sight of the fact that the Kwantung Army, despite its earlier record of insubordination, was after all part of the Japanese army's institutional family. The three-in-one system granted the army's personnel and organization a paramount position in managing Manchuria policy, and in this respect gave Koiso and other Army Ministry officials little reason to complain. Moreover, the prospects for unity within the army had been improving during the preceding months. The growing rapprochement between garrison leaders and their superiors in Tokyo since the beginning of year has been noted. No less important was the fact that routine personnel transfers beginning during the summer had significantly altered the makeup of the Kwantung Army itself.

Japan's Manchurian garrison was not a military organization of fixed composition. Command personnel and administrative staff, as well as combat and support units, were subject to regular rotation. The men who engineered the Manchurian Incident and designed the apparatus for territorial government were on temporary assignment, and when their tour of duty was over, they would be replaced by new appointees selected by army authorities in Tokyo. Thus while it is convenient to speak of a "Kwantung Army perspective" in discussing the events of late 1931 and early 1932, it is more accurate to refer to the views of those officers who happened to be on watch in Manchuria at the time: Commander Honjō Shigeru, Chief of Staff Hashimoto Toranosuke, staff officers Ishiwara and Itagaki, and junior members of the garrison's brain trust like Captain Katakura Tadashi. Insubordination, likewise, was characteristic of the actions of the officers of this particular watch and not something institutionally inherent in the Kwantung Army.[55]

---

[55] James Weland offers a different view in his dissertation on the Kwantung Army. He suggests that the nature of its mission as a vangard force in Manchuria predisposed garri-

Attitudes and perspectives would change with the replacement of these officers, and there was no reason to believe that their successors would continue in their footsteps.

Underscoring the prospective changes in the relationship between central army authorities and the Manchurian garrison was the fact that General Koiso himself was in line to replace Hashimoto as Kwantung Army chief of staff in August. At the same time, Ishiwara Kanji, who, more than any other officer on the garrison staff, had been responsible for shaping events in Manchuria during the past year, was also scheduled for reassignment. By the end of the summer, a new Kwantung Army would be in place, and it would be possible to carry out a unified army policy without debilitating squabbles between garrison and center.

It is not clear whether these considerations influenced the Army Ministry's position on the Tani plan. In any event, central army leaders gave their endorsement, and the cabinet adopted the three-in-one system as a provisional measure at the end of July. Less than two months later, Tokyo officially extended recognition to the Manchurian government. General Mutō Nobuyoshi, the first to fill the triple post, concluded with chief executive P'u Yi a series of military and commercial treaties defining the formal basis of the relationship between Tokyo and Hsinking.

THE PROBLEM OF THE SOUTH MANCHURIA RAILWAY COMPANY, SEPTEMBER 1932–DECEMBER 1933

By the autumn of 1932, one year after the outbreak of the Incident, Japan was firmly committed to a new course in Manchuria. However, the consensus forged in late summer, which had laid the groundwork for this commitment, proved to be short-lived. The army, its position in Manchuria substantially strengthened by the restoration of normal discipline within its chain of command, began planning in September to expand its authority beyond the terms defined by the three-in-one system. The first steps in this effort were initiated by General Koiso shortly after his arrival in Manchuria, and his principal target was the South Manchuria Railway Company.

Control over the resources and facilities of this quasi-official corporation was essential to the management of a comprehensive territorial policy. Ishiwara and his associates had addressed this need through informal, bilateral cooperation. Ideally, however, they would have preferred more direct and formal authority over company operations.

---

son leaders to autonomous and even insubordinate action. James Weland, "The Japanese Army in Manchuria: Covert Operations and the Roots of Kwantung Army Insubordination" (Ph.D. dissertation, University of Arizona, 1977).

Tani's plan attempted to strike a compromise between the army's wishes and the existing system of supervision in providing for the concurrent appointment of the garrison commander as governor of the Leased Territory.

For Chief of Staff Koiso, however, this arrangement remained inadequate. While the army could in effect issue direct orders to company officials through the triple post, any instructions were subject to the approval of the minister of colonial affairs in Tokyo. Moreover, this chain of command left open an avenue of appeal for the traditionally autonomous SMR, weakening the garrison commander's authority. The army, in short, still required cooperation from civilian officials above as well as below in order to make use of the SMR in economic planning.

Koiso's interest in revising this system, however, was motivated by more than general administrative principle. The new chief of staff was one of Japan's foremost experts on industrial mobilization policy. In 1917 he had written a pioneering tract on the economics of national defense, emphasizing the importance of Manchuria's strategic resources.[56] Not surprisingly, he ranked economic planning in Manchuria high among the priorities of his new office. Koiso, like many Japanese economists at this time, believed that the most effective and efficient arrangement for managing a planned economy centered on the creation of state-sponsored cartels that would control production throughout a particular sector of industry.[57] The establishment of such organizations in Manchuria would also provide a mechanism for coordinating economic policy with the home islands, instituting a scheme similar to the "imperial cartels" being discussed in contemporary Britain.[58] For example, a single horizontal trust could be created to control iron and steel production in Japan as well as Manchuria.

Koiso's outlined his views in a memorandum issued in September. The SMR's existing organization, through which corporate management exerted integrated control over a wide range of enterprises in transportation, mining, manufacturing, and trade, posed a major obstacle to the implementation of his program. Ideally, the conglomerate structure would be broken up into its component enterprises, which

[56] On Koiso's contributions to the development of the industrial mobilization policy in Japan, see Boeichō bōeikenshūsho senshishitsu, *Rikugun gunju dōin (1) keikakuhen* (Tokyo: Asagumo shinbunsha, 1967), pp. 37–50.

[57] For example, see Kojima Seiichi, "Kensetsuteki tenkan no daibō," *Keizai ōrai: Dai Manshū kaihatsu gō*, April 1932, pp. 37–44; by the same author, *Mantetsu kontsuerun tokuhon* (Tokyo: Shunjūsha, 1937).

[58] Raymond F. Betts, *Uncertain Dimensions: Western Overseas Empires in the Twentieth Century* (Minneapolis: University of Minnesota Press, 1985), p. 99.

would be reorganized as independent companies. These companies would form the nuclei for Manchuria's control cartels. The SMR itself would specialize exclusively in the management of railroads.[59]

This scheme had far-reaching ramifications. The establishment of full army authority over the company was a precondition for it; and this, in turn, demanded a major revision of the recently implemented three-in-one system. Although Koiso's ideas had the full endorsement of the Army Ministry, a major political fight with civilian authorities was inevitable, and careful planning was essential. At the same time, the Colonial Ministry, the main source of anticipated resistance, was a vulnerable target and under concerted pressure could be forced to relinquish its claims.

Indirect evidence that such pressure was being orchestrated by the army at this time may be found in a paperback reader on Manchukuo published in September under the name of Army Minister Araki Sadao. This book, designed for popular consumption, contained the following passage:

> That the SMR is a political plum for the men of the parties, that the company considers only the interests of its stockholders, is an impression deeply etched in the hearts and minds of the people. . . . The SMR has become too much the capitalist. It has forgotten its history and the purpose behind its creation. It has become too fond of profit and has lost sight of the fact that it owes its existence to the state and its citizens. . . . Ultimately, our ideal would be for the SMR to be freed from the clutches of the stockholders who constitute only a small segment our nation and people as a whole. However, this must wait. We must first free the SMR from the clutches of the political parties.[60]

"Political parties" in this context was a fairly transparent reference to the Colonial Ministry, a portfolio granted to the Minseitō's Nagai Ryūtarō as part of the bargain creating the "National Unity Cabinet" of Admiral Saitō Makoto in May 1932.

This turn of events alarmed SMR officials who had hoped that the bargain struck with Ishiwara and his colleagues would be honored by the new leadership. Koiso's proposal, however, did not take them en-

[59] Kwantung Army Headquarters, "Nichi-Man keizai tōsei jikkōjō no kiso yōken ni kansuru iken," September 1, 1932, in *MCRS* 1.1:24–26. There is some ambiguity in Koiso's plan about whether an institution known as the South Manchuria Railway Company would continue to exist after the proposed reform. The plan also makes mention of a holding company that would own stock in former SMR subsidiaries. Some later proposals equated this holding company with a reformed SMR. In others, the SMR was to be the name of the specialized railroad management company. For the purposes of this discussion, such nuances are not important.

[60] *Shin Manshūkokui tokuhon*, authorized by Araki Sadao (Tokyo: Jitsugyō no Nihon sha, 1932), pp. 358–59.

tirely by surprise. Aware that the cartel argument was quite popular among economists as well as military planners, the Economic Research Group had included a lengthy critique of this method of industrial control in draft economic plans prepared in earlier during the year.[61] Between September and December, the company's research staff redoubled their efforts to dissuade their counterparts in the Special Affairs Unit against any structural reform of the SMR. In a planning document written in December, they argued:

> The advantages of multi-unit management have provided the basis of the path of development that has led to the SMR as it is today. Ventures that would have likely been impossible to undertake as independent enterprises have been successfully nurtured through the supportive mechanisms of combined management. Achievements to date in the economic development of Manchuria may be regarded as the product of such a program. Under the prevailing international situation, much of the future of Manchurian industry lies in the creation of defense industries and other ventures that must be undertaken regardless of profitability. The possibility of managing such operations as independent enterprises is nonexistent. Moreover, given the lack of staying power of independent enterprises in the midst of the world depression today, the economic construction of Manchuria would become as fraught with risk as a pile of eggs.

The authors also responded directly to public attacks being launched against the South Manchuria Railway Company by army spokesmen. They answered the radical rhetoric in its own terms by suggesting that the cartel plan would only benefit the *zaibatsu*:

> The SMR is a national monument to the Russo-Japanese War, acquired at the risk of the nation's fate. While it is in name nothing more than a railway company, there is no question in anyone's mind that the SMR has served as an extension of the [Japanese] state, carrying out the empire's Manchurian policy, fostering the continental expansion of the Japanese nation. Only the most ignorant can believe that the SMR is no more than a profit-seeking company. . . . Considering the extent to which capitalistic business management has hurt the interests of the masses of people at home, it is clear that the combined management of Manchuria's key industries under the SMR, given the company's special characteristics, is the most rational and equitable approach. If these key industries were to be released to the management of the *zaibatsu*, Manchuria would be transformed into nothing more than a colony of Japanese monopoly capitalism, and the management of Manchuria would be perverted. Such an eventuality would betray the high ideals with which

---

[61] Minami Manshū tetsudō kabushiki kaisha keizai chōsakai, "Manshū keizai tōseisaku (kōhen, seisakuhen)," May 1932, MRCS 1.1:84–88.

the Imperial Army undertook to challenge the evil and exploitative policies of the old militarist cliques, to create a just Manchurian state that would rescue the masses from their misery. Would this not be tantamount to "driving the tiger from the front door while inviting the wolf in from the back?"[62]

These arguments failed to persuade Koiso and the new leadership of the Kwantung Army. On the contrary, by the beginning of the new year, they began drafting specific plans in consultation with the Army Ministry for the reorganization of the South Manchuria Railway Company. Top company officials were secretly ordered to prepare a feasibility assessment during the spring. They stalled as much as possible, citing the need for more study and asking for an opportunity to prepare a comprehensive counterproposal. Negotiations with army representatives continued throughout the summer. For the most part, the Colonial Ministry appears to have been kept in the dark during this process.[63]

Koiso and Army Ministry officials pressed forward with preparatory steps during the first half of 1933, but they remained cautious about bringing a formal proposal before the government. While reorganization of the SMR was the principal objective, it could not be accomplished without simultaneously eliminating the Colonial Ministry's influence over the company. Further groundwork would be required before the army was ready to launch a full-fledged campaign to reform the three-in-one system.

However, an indiscreet interview given to a reporter for the *Manshū nippō* (*Manchuria Daily News*) by Colonel Numata Takazō, a senior staff officer of the Kwantung Army, derailed this strategy. Numata revealed the outlines of reorganization plans under discussion between the company and army representatives. Published on October 23, the contents of the interview were almost immediately picked up by the press in the

[62] Minami Manshū tetsudō kabushiki kaisha keizai chōsakai, "Manshū keizai kensetsu dai 1 ki sōgō keikaku an, riyū oyobi setsumei," December 1932, ibid., pp. 527–28.

[63] Takahashi Yasutaka, "Minami Manshū tetsudō kabushiki kaisha kaiso keikaku ni tsuite," *Shakai kagaku tōkyū* 27, no. 2 (April 1982): 67–77; Okabe Makio, "Nihon teikokushugi to Mantetsu—15 nen sensōki o chūshi ni," *Nihonshi kenkyū*, no. 197 (November 1978): 76–77. The Colonial Ministry publicly claimed that it was not informed until October when the proposal was leaked to the press. Later, in response to questions in the Diet, ministry officials admitted that they had been consulted in July. The ministry's official position was that direct discussions between the Kwantung Army and the SMR were unauthorized and in violation of lawful procedures. Ministry of Colonial Affairs, "Kaiso mondai kankei tōben shiryō sō an (miteikō)," date uncertain, probably early 1934, in Ministry of Colonial Affairs, *Mantetsu kaiso mondai kankei shorui*, 1934 (Carbon and mimeograph copies, University of Tokyo Social Science Research Institute Library), document 1, pp. 1–16.

home islands, triggering a heated public debate that lasted for more than two months.[64] These circumstances forced the army's hand prematurely.

The SMR Employees' Association, an organization representing the company's permanent staff, had heard disturbing rumors about the army's proposal since the spring and had been quietly discussing its implications for quite some time. The emergence of the plan as a public issue provided the association with an opportunity to organize an opposition movement. Members of the Economic Research Group were among the ringleaders of this movement. On October 28, the Employees' Association issued a statement that declared: "The South Manchuria Railway Company is the legacy of the great Meiji Emperor, a crystallization of the flesh and blood of the Japanese people. . . . It is only proper that the reorganization of the SMR be discussed throughout the nation in the full light of day."[65] In the spirit of promoting such discussion, members began writing articles for publication and organizing propaganda teams. They also made plans to attend the annual stockholders' meeting in December where they would not only speak against the proposal but attempt to rally a negative vote.[66] Such an action, of course, would only be symbolic. The government owned 50 percent of the company's stock, making it impossible for a stockholders' meeting to challenge official policy. A symbolic vote could nonetheless cause the government serious political embarrassment.[67]

The Colonial Ministry also took advantage of the public debate to attack the army proposal. In an interview on October 31, a spokesman told the *Asahi* newspaper that ministry officials had only received word of the reorganization plan from SMR officials the day before and that there had been no formal contact on this matter from the Army Ministry. He also remarked pointedly that the issue of company organization had been discussed and settled in March when a bill calling for an expansion of the SMR's authorized capital had been submitted to the Diet. An increase from ¥440 to ¥800 million had been approved with

[64] Events following the public disclosure of the reorganization plan have been covered in a number of studies. In addition to Takahashi cited above, see, for example, Makita Kensuke, "1930 nen dai ni okeru Mantetsu kaiso mondai," *Rekishi hyōron*, no. 289 (April 1974): 36–50; Hara Akira, "'Manshu' ni okeru keizai tōsei seisaku no tenkai: Mantetsu kaiso to Mangyō setsuritsu o megutte," in *Nihon keizai sieshu shiron*, ed. Andō Yoshiō, 2 vols. (Tokyo: Tokyo daigaku shuppankai, 1976), 2:209–96.

[65] *Manshū kaihatsu 40 nen shi*, 3 vols. (Tokyo: Manshikai, 1964), 1:252.

[66] *Tokyo Asahi shinbun*, December 7, 1933.

[67] Hōjō, *Sogō Shinji to tairiku*, pp. 111–13. Also see Joshua A. Fogel, trans., *Life Along the South Manchurian Railway: The Memoirs of Itō Takeo* (Armonk, N.Y.: M. E. Sharpe, 1988), pp. 128–31.

the understanding that no major changes in the status of the company were under consideration. He suggested that the timing of the army proposal was "extremely troubling."[68]

As the debate continued with growing acrimony, this line of criticism was further developed in an article by Kaji Ryūichi, a member of the Economic Research Group, published in the influential monthly *Chūō kōron* in November. Kaji implied that the army had acted in bad faith by waiting until October to release news of its plans. Investors had been lured into purchasing company stock with an increase in dividend payments and a special 3 percent premium offered on new shares. Colonel Numata's disclosure was made just one day after the final deadline for new subscriptions, noted Kaji. Even more disturbing was the fact that the army itself had promoted the sale of single fifty-yen shares throughout the countryside, and people of modest means had scraped together the money in order to demonstrate their patriotism. Kaji implied that the army was betraying the trust of the "little people" it purportedly championed.

Expressions of concern about the impact and fairness of the reform were not restricted to SMR employees and Colonial Ministry officials. Financial markets in Tokyo had reacted negatively to Numata's press leak. Not only did SMR stock prices fall markedly, but a recent bond issue proved to be extremely unpopular even though the company's bonds had long been considered among the more secure investments available. Rumors were circulating that another bond issue, originally scheduled for November, had been postponed. Financial confidence in the SMR, historically solid, had been severely shaken despite the company's healthy business performance during the past year. Even the Japan Chamber of Commerce adopted a resolution at its November meeting opposing the reorganization plan.[69] This vote of no confidence on the part of the business and financial community was not a development that the army, anxious to proceed with its economic program in Manchuria, could ignore.

Prime Minister Saitō expressed strong displeasure about the handling of this policy initiative. The Army Ministry, pushed into a defensive position, recognized that its plans for the SMR were in serious jeopardy. Koiso and his associates in the Kwantung Army were determined at first to ride out the storm of criticism. Pressure from the Army Ministry and stiffened resistance from the SMR finally forced them to back down. The prime minister put an end to debate in a speech before the

[68] *Tokyo Asahi shinbun*, October 31.
[69] Ibid., November 16, 23.

Diet on December 24, rejecting any major reorganization initiatives for the time being.[70]

THE MANCHURIAN AFFAIRS BUREAU AND THE CONSOLIDATION OF ARMY POWER, 1934

Army leaders emerged chastened from the political fiasco of late 1933. While the experience forced them to reconsider tactics, however, their commitment to the general line of reform initiated by General Koiso remained unchanged. If anything, the extraordinary difficulty encountered in an attempt to carry out what was essentially a relatively simple plan for corporate reorganization underscored the need to revise the existing system of jurisdiction and leadership in Manchuria policy. The fact that the Colonial Ministry, encouraged by its recent political victory, was not only planning to tighten its control over the SMR but seeking a broader role in the management of economic policy in Manchuria only strengthened the army's resolve.[71] A renewed attempt at reform, however, would not target the SMR alone or even directly. Indeed, it had never been the intention of army leaders to address the question of reorganizing the company in isolation from the larger issue of overhauling the three-in-one system. Only Colonel Numata's press leak had forced them into this disadvantageous position. The mistake would not be repeated. Given an appropriate opportunity, Army Ministry officials planned to restructure the decision-making process in Manchurian affairs from top to bottom.

The fall of the Saitō Cabinet and its replacement by a government headed by Admiral Okada Teisuke in July 1934 presented just such an opportunity. As a condition for supplying a minister to the new Cabinet, army leaders demanded that serious consideration be given to a basic reform of the three-in-one system. The Army Ministry prepared a formal proposal in August. Their plan called for the following measures:[72]

1. All areas of Colonial Ministry jurisdiction in Manchuria were to be transferred to a new Cabinet agency known as the Manchurian Affairs Bureau. This agency would be staffed by representatives of the Army, Foreign,

[70] Takahashi, "Minami Manshū tetsudō kabushiki kaisha kaiso keikaku ni tsuite," pp. 98–99; Makita, "1930 nen dai ni okeru Mantetsu kaiso mondai," p. 47; Hara, "Manshū ni okeru keizai tōsei seisaku no tenkai," pp. 219–23.

[71] Ministry of Colonial Affairs, "Kaiso mondai kankei tōben shiryō sō an (miteikō)" pp. 10–16; Baba, *Nitchū kankei to gaisei kikō no kenkyū*, p. 260.

[72] Shimizu, "Tai-Man kikō no hensen," pp. 140–42; Baba, *Nitchū kankei to gaisei kikō no kenkyū*, pp. 266–69.

and Finance ministries and headed by an active-duty army officer. In practice, the post of bureau chief was to be filled concurrently by the army minister and that of deputy chief, by an official of the Finance Ministry. The Colonial Ministry was pointedly denied a seat on this body.

2. All powers exercised by the Kwantung governor as the front-line representative of the Colonial Ministry were to be transferred to the Japanese embassy in Manchukuo. The embassy, in turn, would be substantially expanded. The administration of the Leased Territory would be managed by an office subordinate to the ambassador, and the colonial gendarmerie integrated with consular police under an embassy department headed by the chief of the Kwantung Army's military police. Supervision of the SMR was to be the responsibility of yet another department of the embassy headed by the Kwantung Army's chief of transportation policy.

3. The status of the ambassador plenipotentiary was to be redefined as that of a special official under direct supervision of the prime minister. In practice, the Manchurian Affairs Bureau would exercise a supervisory role on behalf of the prime minister. The Foreign Ministry would continue to oversee the ambassador's duties with regard to Manchukuo's foreign relations and the supervision of consular officials,[73] but the primary line of accountability would be shifted out of the ordinary diplomatic chain of command. The practice of concurrently appointing the Kwantung Army commander to the post of ambassador would be continued.

4. An official economic planning agency, known as the Japan-Manchuria Economic Council, was to replace entirely the provisional apparatus maintained by the Kwantung Army's Special Affairs Unit and the SMR's Economic Research Group. One of priorities of this body would be to facilitate tie-ups between Manchurian and Japanese industry along the lines favored by Koiso.

Army Ministry officials described the new arrangements as a "two-in-one" system based on the fact that the proposal completely eliminated the Colonial Ministry's voice in Manchurian affairs and demoted the Kwantung governor to a subordinate official of the embassy. The new supreme official in Manchuria would wear only two hats: those of Kwantung Army commander and ambassador to Manchukuo. In reality, however, given the reduced authority of Foreign Ministry over the office of ambassador, the scheme granted the army nearly unified control of territorial affairs.

Both the Foreign and Colonial ministries vigorously protested this plan, and a bitter debate ensued, lasting almost five months. They charged that the system proposed by the army amounted to the installa-

---

[73] Consuls continued to play an active role in supervising the affairs of Japanese nationals in Manchuria.

tion of military rule [*gunsei*] in Manchuria. Following the example set by the SMR Employees' Association, the staff of the Kwantung Government organized a protest movement that was highlighted in September by the threatened mass resignation of colonial gendarmes. The SMR Employees' Association endorsed the movement.[74] The company's Economic Research Group criticized the plan for an Economic Council as an attempt to introduce traditional relations of colonial exploitation in Manchuria. Wrote one member of the group, "Japan's claim that Manchuria is an independent country is no more than camouflage."[75]

Despite vocal opposition, however, the army refused to yield on the key points of its plan and implicitly threatened to bring down the Okada government if its wishes were not fulfilled. The Cabinet and its subcommittees discussed various counterproposals between August and December. Negotiations produced some minor concessions. The Colonial Ministry was granted a seat on the Manchurian Affairs Bureau, but its voice was to be limited to matters pertaining to Japanese immigration. The Foreign Ministry won a slight modification of army's plan to remove the ambassador's office from the diplomatic chain of command. Technically, the ambassador would be both a special official accountable to the prime minister and a diplomat reporting to the foreign minister. In practice, however, the concession meant little beyond its face-saving value. The compromise did not give the Foreign Ministry any more authority over the ambassador than the army plan had conceded in the first place. In the end, the measures passed by the Cabinet in December were quite close to the original plan submitted in August.[76]

The army's sweeping victory in this reform initiative stands in sharp contrast to the political disaster of 1933. A number of factors account for this change in fortunes. The most simple was the fact that Army Ministry officials were able to pursue a coherent strategy without the kind of blunder that had frustrated earlier efforts. More important, perhaps, was a general shift in national politics favorable to the army, marked by the formation of the Okada cabinet.[77] The army's political ascendancy had begun with outbreak of the Manchurian Incident. The state of quasi-emergency in effect since late 1931, coupled with the judi-

[74] Shimizu, "Tai-Man kikō no hensen," pp. 143–48; Baba, *Nitchū kankei to gaisei kikō no kenkyū*, pp. 270–94.

[75] Tanaka Morie, "Nichi-Man keizai iinkai ni kansuru shomondai," August 1934, in *MRCS* 1.1:552.

[76] Imperial ordinance, "Tai-Man jimukyoku kansei," December 26, 1934, *GSS* 7:600–601.

[77] See Gordon Berger, *Parties Out of Power in Japan, 1931–41* (Princeton, N.J.: Princeton University Press, 1977), chap. 3.

cious political exploitation of the terrorist activities of junior officers, gave the army powerful leverage to expand its authority in a broad range of affairs. Given the simultaneous decline in the prestige of traditional civilian leadership, the army gradually emerged as the new center of gravity in Japanese politics. A growing number of civilian bureaucrats began consciously allying themselves with military leadership, actively supporting the army's agenda. This trend, however, took some time to gather momentum, even after the assassination of Prime Minister Inukai and the fall of the last party cabinet in May 1932. Tactical mistakes aside, the failure of the SMR reorganization plan was testimony to the fact that the dynamics of national politics had not changed sufficiently by 1933 to allow the army to dictate terms in Manchuria. By 1934, cumulative developments appear to have tipped the political equilibrium. The corruption scandal that contributed to the fall of the Saitō cabinet further damaged the reputation of traditional civilian leadership.[78] Reports in June of a massive buildup of Soviet forces in eastern Siberia reinforced the general sense of crisis, inevitably strengthening the hand of military authorities.[79] The debate over the plan for a Manchurian Affairs Bureau may be regarded in this context as one of the first major tests of the army's newfound political power.

There was, however, more to the success of the army's initiative in 1934 than political competence and favorable changes in the balance of power. It is important not to overlook the fact that the Army Ministry's proposal had considerable merit from an administrative point of view. It addressed a number of legitimate concerns about the shortcomings of the three-in-one system, which in any case had never been meant to be a permanent arrangement, and had been adopted more for reasons of political expediency than administrative rationality. Sentiment in favor of overhauling the existing arrangements in Manchuria had grown substantially by the summer of 1934. Indeed, the failure of the army's efforts in 1933 was due more to the manner in which the issue was broached than to any widespread opposition to the idea of reform itself.[80]

[78] On this scandal (the Teijin affair), see Arthur E. Tiedemann, "Big Business and Politics in Prewar Japan," in *Dilemmas of Growth in Prewar Japan*, ed. James W. Morley (Princeton, N.J.: Princeton University Press, 1971), pp. 294–95.

[79] *Daihon'ei rikugunbu*, 1:352.

[80] A commentary published in the economic journal *Daiyamondo* in November 1933 is revealing: "The reorganization of an enterprise such as the SMR into a holding company is only natural. The current reorganization plan [as revealed by Numata] restores what has been a rather irregular and irrational structure to the mainstream of business management practice. From this perspective, the proposal is entirely appropriate. . . . This plan probably reflects the aims of the central military authorities. If so, and if one might excuse the discourtesy, it is extremely well done considering it is an army draft. To be frank, this reporter cannot agree with everything the army has been doing and saying. Most people

Significantly, Tani Masayuki, the architect of this structure, was himself among the more vocal proponents of reform. Based on his experience as counselor to the embassy in Manchukuo, he had come to the conclusion by the middle of 1934 that "the three-in-one system has regrettably failed to function as intended."[81] The main problem with the system was its failure to go far enough in unifying authority. While it provided for coordination and unified supervision at an intermediate level of policy management, decision-making bodies, both superior and subordinate, remained compartmentalized. Tokyo's supervisory powers continued to be divided among three ministries with no mechanism to harmonize their directives. The bureaucracies of the Kwantung Government, the SMR, and the consular network had been essentially unaffected by the measures adopted in 1932. While all subordinate officials in Manchuria were to report to the Kwantung Army commander in one or the other of his official roles, the expectation that this single official would be able to ensure the cooperation and accountability of a traditionally fractious group of agencies was not realistic.

The army's plan dealt effectively with these shortcomings. The Manchurian Affairs Bureau solved the problem of coordination at the top, providing a special mechanism, for the first time in the long history of Japanese expansion in Manchuria, to unify policy in Tokyo. The placement of all Japanese civilian agencies under the aegis of the embassy addressed the need for integration at the bottom, strengthening accountability as well as facilitating coordination. The establishment of an Economic Council supplemented these arrangements in the increasingly important sphere of development policy.

The elimination of the Colonial Ministry's role in Manchuria was also a measure that had considerable support outside the army. The mainstream economic bureaucracy in Japan regarded the pretensions of this agency to leadership in Manchurian development as an obstacle to serious planning. The Finance Ministry, in particular, had become active in territorial affairs, dispatching officials to serve in the Manchurian government.[82] The structure of the Manchurian Affairs Bureau may be interpreted as an effort to replace the role of Colonial Affairs with Finance. The Foreign Ministry frankly welcomed the exclusion of Colo-

---

probably feel the same way. But from a purely economic point of view, and limiting consideration to the question of reorganizing the SMR, I do not hesitate in stating my full agreement with the plan." Excerpt from *Daiyamondo*, November 11, 1933, in *Mantetsu kaiso mondai kankei shorui*, document 1. The declaration of the Japan Chamber of Commerce cited above reflects similar ambivalence, supporting the general idea of reorganization, but calling for more cautious deliberation and study.

[81] Baba, *Nitchū kankei to gaisei kikō no kenkyū*, p. 260.

[82] On the activities of these new economic experts, see Hoshino Naoki, *Mihatenu yume: Manshūkoku gaishi* (Tokyo: Daiyamondosha, 1963).

nial Affairs. Diplomats had never been happy with the role of colonial bureaucrats in Manchuria, regarding them as upstarts who had usurped authority properly belonging to the Foreign Ministry.[83] More importantly, Tani's assessment of the failings of the three-in-one system laid much of the blame on the obstructive role played by both the bureaucracy of Kwantung Government and its superiors in Tokyo.

In fact, Foreign Ministry officials had supported most of the general provisions of army plan and had even contributed to its formulation earlier during the summer.[84] Their only real objection to the proposal lay in the revision of the ambassador's status and the consequent reduction of the Foreign Ministry's influence in territorial affairs. The army justified this measure by arguing that the expansion of the ambassador's responsibilities, particularly his absorption of the powers of the Kwantung governor, had fundamentally changed the nature of the office. While it was useful for the purposes of international diplomacy to retain the title of ambassador, the official was in fact no longer a diplomat by any stretch of the definition.

The army's argument was by no means specious. On the contrary, ever since the establishment of Manchukuo, the Foreign Ministry's claims to a major role in territory had rested on shaky ground. State-to-state diplomacy, given the nature of the Manchurian government, was nothing more than a charade played before the international audience. In reality, the Japanese governed the territory, and under these circumstances, the traditional functions served by diplomatic officials were no longer meaningful. Morishima Morindo, the perceptive consul general quoted earlier, foresaw this problem from the outset and had recommended a redefinition of consular roles. He suggested that Japanese consuls in a Manchurian puppet state would serve as regional "intendants [tandai]" or "prefects [chiji]," officials who would function as the principal representatives of Japanese authority in outlying areas of Manchuria.[85] Morishima's scheme would have had consular officials assuming responsibilities more appropriate for a colonial administrator than a diplomat.

Indeed, between the spring of 1932 and the reforms of 1934, the Foreign Ministry had been gradually drifting into colonial administration

[83] See for example, Acting Consul General Morishima Morindo to Foreign Minister Shidehara, "Manshū ni okeru gyōsei kikan no tōitsu ni kansuru shi an sōfu no ken," November 30, 1929. Japanese Foreign Ministry Archives, S15301, U.S. Library of Congress microfilm, ff. 111–40. This proposal is a good example of a pre-Incident effort on the part of the Foreign Ministry to eliminate the authority of the then newly created Colonial Ministry. The SMR was to be placed under the direct supervision of the consul general in Mukden.

[84] Shimizu, "Tai-Man kikō no hensen," p. 141; Baba, Nitchū kankei to gaisei kikō no kenkyū, p. 265.

[85] Morishima to Foreign Minister Yoshizawa Ken'ichi, 1/22/32, NGB—Manshū jihen, vol. 2, part 1, pp. 352–53.

in its efforts to carve out a place in the new Manchuria. In terms of function, its concept of the embassy differed little from the Army Ministry's Intendancy-General. The office of ambassador plenipotentiary had been, from the beginning, more suited to oversee the affairs of a protectorate than to serve a purely diplomatic mission. The reforms of 1934 would have further strengthened this aspect of the ambassador's office. Insofar as colonial administration was not within the purview of the Foreign Ministry, the army's call to redefine the status of this office was far from unreasonable.

It would be wrong, therefore, to interpret the army's initiative in 1934 as a simple grab for power. Given the premises of Japanese policy in Manchuria, the army's proposal for reform was a rational attempt to create administrative structures consistent with the realities of territorial management. Manchukuo had been conceived by Ishiwara and his colleagues as an alternative to straightforward dictatorial rule by the Japanese army. For all the subsequent structural embellishments and elaboration of the program, the essential nature of the Manchurian state remained unchanged. In fact, what is perhaps most noteworthy about the process of administrative reform in Manchuria between 1932 and 1934 is not that the army eventually succeeded in consolidating control over the territory, but that the process took so long.

Civilian agencies persisted in asserting an active role in territorial policy well after changing conditions had rendered their original purposes obsolete. The consular network and the government of Kwantung were agencies established to carry out an imperial strategy that no longer had any real relevance in postconquest Manchuria. While the resources and facilities of the SMR remained of great value to policymakers, the institution itself, as an agent of railway imperialism, had outlived its usefulness. The tenacity of these organizations in resisting reform after the founding of Manchukuo created a problematic system of "dual imperialism" where the apparatus of informal empire existed side by side with an entirely new form of territorial control. The army was not politically strong enough in 1931 and 1932 to exclude civilian authority entirely, and its position had been weakened by disunity between the garrison and the military leadership in Tokyo. On the other hand, civilian agencies were not strong enough themselves to assert an alternative direction, to change the fundamental nature of Manchukuo, or even to modify the army's agenda to any significant degree. The three-in-one compromise conceded control of the situation on the ground to the army's Manchurian garrison. In the final analysis, these arrangements did little more than allow civilian agencies to supervise the garrison commander. Through the reforms of 1934, the army finally managed to throw off what it regarded as unwanted civilian interference and eliminate the redundancy of dual imperialism.

Over the next three years, the army used its newly consolidated authority to accelerate its program in Manchuria. Plans emphasized economic development as a priority. Discussion of a second phase of economic construction began in 1935 and culminated in the formulation of an ambitious five-year military-industrial plan to be implemented beginning in 1937. Reorganization of the SMR was carried out piecemeal. The company was gradually forced to divest its industrial holdings and concentrate on railway management. The army, supported by bureaucrats from the ministries of Finance, Commerce, and Industry, began building an economic apparatus centered on a new group of Manchurian corporations and joint ventures.[86]

The Foreign Ministry played no more than a marginal role in the territory after the creation of the Manchurian Affairs Bureau. The abolition of extraterritoriality in 1937 further diminished the importance of the consular apparatus. In any event, new developments resulting from the army's north China operations increasingly came to occupy its energies. The SMR likewise began turning what attention it could spare to events south of the Wall. The company was in fact actively encouraged by the army to set up subsidiaries in north and central China, regions where the strategy of railway imperialism still found useful applications. These efforts laid the groundwork for the establishment of the North China Development Corporation in 1938.[87] This redirection of institutional energies by the Foreign Ministry and the SMR represented an acceleration of a new cycle of aggressive Japanese expansion in China. The founding of Manchukuo had rendered the mission of these agencies of informal empire in Northeast China obsolete. The reforms of 1934, suggests one scholar, served to restore them to their original functions at the cutting edge of Japanese imperialism.[88]

The establishment of the Manchurian Affairs Bureau also represents a milestone in the developing strategy of puppet government. Manchukuo originated as an ad hoc solution to circumvent the political obstacles to installing a conventional occupation regime. Yet once the ini-

[86] Hara, "'Manshū' ni okeru keizai tōsei seisaku no tenkai," pp. 216–39. The Nissan combine, relocated and reorganized as the Manchurian Industrial Corporation in 1938, absorbed most of the subsidiaries divested by the SMR.

[87] See Takafusa Nakamura, "Japan's Economic Thrust into North China, 1933–1938: The Formation of the North China Development Corporation," trans. Robert Angel in *The Chinese and the Japanese: Essays in Political and Cultural Interactions*, ed. Akira Iriye (Princeton, N.J.: Princeton University Press, 1980, pp. 220–51. Also see Katsumi Usui, "The Politics of War," trans. David Lu, in *The China Quagmire*, ed. James William Morley (New York: Columbia University Press, 1983).

[88] Hamaguchi Hiroko, "1930 nen dai nakaba no tai-Man seisaku ritsuan ni kansuru 1 kōsatsu—Man-Mō kenkyūkai o chūshin ni," in *Kindai Nihon seiji no shosō*, ed. Nakamura Katsunori (Tokyo: Keiō tsūshin, 1988), pp. 382–84.

tial flaws in the scheme were corrected and channels for civilian interference sufficiently restricted, army leaders began to see in the concept of the puppet state a generic alternative to occupation government. Even before 1937, this trend in army thinking was evident in the establishment of autonomous regimes south of the Wall. After 1937, the model would be applied to China as a whole. An agency patterned after the Manchurian Affairs Bureau, known as the Asia Development Board [*Kō-A in*] was established in 1938 to manage affairs in occupied China. In 1942, this line of institutional development was taken to its logical conclusion in the creation of the Ministry for Greater East Asian Affairs.[89]

CONCLUSION

Between 1931 and 1934, the Japanese devised and gradually perfected in occupied Northeast China a new strategy for managing empire. The arrangements they created to rule Manchukuo defy classification in conventional terms of "formal" and "informal empire." Informal imperialism is, almost by definition, a means of compromising the sovereignty of an independent nation. Inasmuch as the independence of Manchukuo was a fiction to begin with, the "informal" qualities of Japanese control in the territory were no more than extensions of the same pretense. The category of formal empire is likewise inapplicable. Renouncing any colonial claims in Manchuria was an essential part of the Japanese strategy.

In terms of the quality and degree of control exercised by Japan over territorial affairs, however, the system established in postconquest Manchuria was equivalent to colonial rule. Managed from within through the mechanism of internal guidance and from without under the authority of a residency-general disguised as an embassy, Manchukuo enjoyed no more sovereignty than Korea. It is doubtful if formal annexation would have led to any significant expansion of real Japanese authority in the territory. Moreover, controls imposed by the Japanese tightened and grew increasingly heavy-handed over time, as evidenced in the sequence of development from the Kwantung Army's early plans, to the three-in-one system, to the reforms of 1934. The abolition of extraterritoriality in 1937 may be regarded, indeed, as an indication of Japanese confidence in the security of their hegemony. This quintessential element of the old system of unequal treaties had been designed to protect foreign nationals from Chinese authority. In Manchukuo, extraterritoriality had become superfluous since there was no longer any power in the land that was not Japanese.

[89] See Baba, *Nitchū kankei to gaisei kikō no kenkyū,* chap. 9.

CHAPTER 5

Creating a Modern Enclave Economy: The Economic Integration of Japan, Manchuria, and North China, 1932–1945

Ramon H. Myers

Previous scholarship has described the thinking and activities of military officers like Ishiwara Kanji and others to transform Manchukuo and Japan into a national defense state—particularly in the planning of Manchukuo's industrialization and the mobilization of its physical and human resources.[1] Other research has focused on how the Japanese army between 1937 and 1941 tried to increase its economic control over north China to integrate that region with Manchukuo and Japan so as to form a new regional economic bloc and thereby strengthen Japan's capability to wage war.[2] These accounts have described the economic planning that characterized Japan's new economic mobilization and industrialization efforts. Building on these studies, this chapter introduces a new concept that I call the "modern enclave economy" to describe the unusual pattern of modern economic development that took place in northeast and east China in the age of twentieth-century imperialism.

Between 1931 and 1945 the Japanese military created the independent state of Manchukuo and various Chinese puppet regimes in north China. By using Chinese leaders and elite to govern their subjects, the Japanese military, along with a reluctant Japanese government, tried to create a regional economic bloc that would not only make imperial Japan self-sufficient in raw materials but increase that nation's industrial strength and ability to wage war against its enemies. This new economic pattern of development by one state imposing its special style of economic domination on another represented a break with the pattern of economic control by a state over its colony.

I am particularly grateful for the helpful suggestions and criticisms by Mark R. Peattie regarding early drafts of this chapter. All the caveats for appropriate responsibility apply.

[1] Mark R. Peatie, *Ishiwara Kanji and Japan's Confrontation with the West* (Princeton, N.J.: Princeton University Press, 1975), chap. 6.

[2] Lincoln Li, *The Japanese Army in North China, 1937–1941* (New York: Oxford University Press, 1975), chap. 6.

The Western powers never undertook any significant industrialization of their colonies before World War II; nor did Japan, until it radically changed its colonial and imperial policies after 1931. Even in India the British made no striking attempt to transfer advanced technology and industry to that country and deliberately try to integrate the new industries of India with those at home. The typical pattern of Western–style colonial development had been the evolution of a small modern economic-social sector alongside a traditional sector based on primary economic activities like agriculture, which served as a source of supply of raw materials as well as a market for the colonizing regime.[3] That same pattern also had characterized Japan's economic activity in pre-1931 China.

Japan's economic interests in China had originally consisted of commercial spheres of influence centered around certain Chinese coastal cities and the few Japanese-managed railways. These spheres of influence had been developed from the privileges wrested from the Ch'ing monarchy and the Republican governments through treaties imposed by Japan. By operating at lower costs in these spheres of influence, Japanese trading companies and merchants had sold finished products produced in Japan through their outlets in China and assembled and processed Chinese raw materials through their organizations for export to Japan and elsewhere. Since Japan had only a small sphere of interest in China, the Japanese did little manufacturing there, but because Japan's economic control was greater in Manchuria, Japanese mining and industry flourished in the territory. Even so, by 1931 Japanese economic activities in China, as measured in value of assets, investment, and trade, still far exceeded those of the other foreign powers.[4] But these activities were still very small in size and confined to the treaty ports and only a few Japanese settlements in the interior. Most important of all, only the product markets between China and Japan were integrated, or, to put it another way, only goods and services were exchanged between the two sovereign states.

Between 1931 and 1945 this pattern of trade and economic activity between Japan and northeast and north China radically changed. Japan's military and government began creating a modern enclave economy in that region, comprising mines, industries, transportation and communication networks, and services—hospitals, schools, research institutes, and the like.[5] These new facilities constituted networks of electrical

[3] Donald Winch, "Colonies," in The New Palgrave Economic Development, ed. John Eatwell, Murray Milgate, and Peter Newman (New York: Norton, 1989), p. 69.

[4] Peter Duus, Ramon H. Myers, Mark Peattie, eds., The Japanese Informal Empire in China, 1895–1937 (Princeton, N.J.: Princeton University Press, 1984), introduction.

[5] Tung-pei wu-tzu t'iao-chieh wei-yuan-hui yen-chiu tsu, Tzu-yuan chi ch'an-yeh [Re-

power, mining, iron and steel manufacturing, weapons and ammunition production, chemicals and ore processing, cement, vehicles and machine tools, and other goods and services using modern technology. Organization and management were undertaken only by Japanese, although they employed Chinese unskilled and skilled workers. More important, the new facilities represented the integration of the factor market economies of Japan, Manchukuo, and north China as well as the product markets in these same areas. The new economic activities, however, were insulated from all other markets in Manchukuo and north China, because the relative price changes in those markets did not affect the structure of prices in the modern enclave economy. The new markets representing the modern enclave sector, however, profoundly influenced all other markets in the region because of their size and methods of financing, as will be discussed below.

This new arena of modern economic activity was not small. In fact, its combined capital assets were valued at many times those of Japanese assets in China before 1931, but more significantly, they far exceeded the size and value of mining and manufacturing owned by the Chinese south of Manchukuo. Before 1937 the Chinese industrial heartland was located in the east-central and southeast provinces, with Shanghai and Canton serving as the largest cities for industry and commerce. Chinese industry, of course, still was very labor-intensive and depended on small factories and upgraded handicraft establishments, with mines scattered in different provinces under Chinese and foreign ownership. By late 1943, however, the center of gravity of industry and mining in China had shifted northward because of the expanded modern enclave economy.

North and northeast China now produced 89 percent of the country's coal output, 53 percent of its iron ore output, 94 and 97 percent of its iron and steel, 85 percent of electrical power, 79 percent of cement, 86 percent of salt, 69 percent of ammonium sulfate, 99 percent of soda ash, 66 percent of caustic soda, and 95 percent of machine tools (table 5.1).

What were the specific characteristics of this modern enclave economy of Northeast Asia between 1931 and 1945? A national-cultural unit, Japan, owned and managed an integrated economy in a foreign territory, northeast and north China, for the purpose of producing and distributing raw materials, intermediate products, and final goods for industrialization and war. Very little, if anything, produced in this modern enclave economy benefited ordinary consumers. Ownership in this integrated market system consisted of special property rights for

---

sources and industries] (Shenyang: Chung-kuo wen-hua fu-wu-she Shen-yang yin-shua-ch'ang, 1947), vol. 1, part 2, pp. 130–31. This twenty-volume set, published 1947–48, is cited as *TPTC,* with appropriate volume and page numbers.

TABLE 5.1

Major Commodity Output in Manchuria and North China as a Percentage of China's Total Output, 1943 (thousands of tons unless otherwise noted)

Commodity	Manchuria	Percentage	North China	Percentage	Combined Output	Percentage
Coal	25,220	48.8	22,229	40.6	47,885	89.4
Iron	1,702	88.5	116	6.6	1,826	94.5
Steel	495	91.0	34[a]	6.4	520	97.4
Electrical power[b]	2,098	66.5	487	19.3	2,158	85.8
Cement	1,503	66.0	301	13.2	1,804	79.2
Salt	883	26.1	2,035	60.4	2,918	86.5
Ammonium sulfate	92	69.0	—	—	102	69.0
Soda ash	59	60.0	37	39.4	94	99.4
Caustic soda	6	33.3	6	33.3	12	66.6
Machine tools[c]	547	95.0	??	??	547	95.0
Iron ore	5,498	43.5	1,307	10.3	6,805	53.8

Source: Tung-pei wu-tzu t'iao-chieh wei-yuan-wei yen-chiu tsu, *Tzu-yuan chi ch'an-yeh* [Resources and industries] (Shenyang: Chung-kuo wen-hua fu-wu-she Shen-yang yin-shua-ch'ang, 1947), vol. 1, part 2, pp. 130–31.

[a]Planned.

[b]Thousands of kwh.

[c]Millions of yuan.

Japanese authorized by laws established within the foreign territory. Japanese management of the modern enclave economy consisted of publicly owned, capitalist–type corporate entities empowered to raise funds and operate on behalf of their Japanese owners to coordinate production and distribution.

The Japanese and Manchukuo states owned the majority of stock shares in these new capitalist corporations. Special laws empowered the corporate managers and their teams to operate the enclave enterprises according to certain rules. Industrial output targets were set by Japanese military planners but only served as guidelines, not like the mandated quotas established in a centrally planned economy. Japanese corporate managers could contract with firms other than those assigned to establish a new industry or economic activity. In other words, Japanese enterprises had considerable freedom to function like private enterprises in a free market, but they also operated in a corporation holding company structure that possessed the power to set price, exchange certain outputs, transfer and acquire modern technology, and so forth.

We now turn to a brief discussion of how this modern enclave economy evolved after 1931 as Japanese military planners imposed their domination on northeast and north China as well as Japan.

THE JAPANESE MILITARY'S VISION OF A NEW ECONOMIC ORDER

As early as mid-1933, Ishiwara Kanji on the staff of the Kwantung Army had proposed to General Imada Shintarō of the Army General Staff a new strategy for imperial Japan.[6] Flushed with his recent victory of masterminding the Japanese takeover of Manchuria, Ishiwara predicted that Japan would ultimately be involved in a great war with the Anglo-Saxon nation-states. Therefore, Japan must immediately prepare for that expected worldwide conflict and to that end establish a new East Asian Alliance (*Tōa Remmei*). This new confederation of Asian states would combine their military and economic strengths under Japan's leadership. According to Ishiwara, that would be done by Japan taking "quick steps to create, as the nucleus of this East Asian Alliance, a new Manchukuo state. That state would take the lead in establishing an Asian Federation based on the cooperation and friendship of China and Japan."[7]

Ignoring Nationalist China's reaction and world opinion of the time, Ishiwara offered some concrete suggestions as to what must be done to realize these goals.[8] New troops should be posted in Manchukuo to maintain regional security. The old laws regulating the South Manchuria Railway Company (SMR) and the Kwantung Leased Zone must be abrogated, and those two bodies governed by the state of Manchukuo. The Kwantung Army Headquarters should create the Special Affairs Department (*Tokumubu*) to guide Manchukuo state policymaking and to guarantee the passage and enforcement of new laws. Every effort should be undertaken to encourage huge numbers of Japanese to emigrate to Manchuria, particularly in the north, to develop its rich resources. Meanwhile, the Manchukuoan and Japanese economies should be integrated by making their currencies equivalent in value to ensure that Japanese living and working in Manchukuo enjoyed living standards comparable to those in Japan. Moreover, Japan should not engage in intrigue and play one Chinese clique off against another when negotiating with Nationalist China. Some consideration also should be given to developing certain resources in north China to facilitate Manchukuo's economic development. Japan's top military priority, however, must still be the containment of the Soviet Union in Asia; Japan should not become embroiled in China.

[6] Inada Masao, Kobayashi Tatsuo, Shimada Toshihiko, and Tsunoda Jun eds., *Taiheiyō senso e no michi* [The road to the Pacific War], 8 vols. (Tokyo, Ōsaka, Kyushū, and Nagoya: Asahi shimbunsha, 1962–63), supplement vol., p. 214.

[7] Ibid.

[8] Ibid.

While we may never know the nature of the closed-door discussions held by the Japanese military on these issues or of the information contained in secret memoranda circulated among army officers and studied inside the War Ministry in Tokyo, it is clear that the general thrust of the Ishiwara strategy was agreed upon by Japan's military leaders in Tokyo and in Shinkyō (Hsinking), the new capital of Manchukuo.[9] They particularly concurred with Ishiwara's concept of an East Asia Alliance based on the union of Japan, Manchukuo, and north China.[10] They did not agree, however, on the form it should take. The military factions held differing opinions: some wanted to annex Mongolia outright and rapidly move to sever north China from the Nanking regime; others like Ishiwara preferred to concentrate on the development of Manchukuo and to integrate that new state closely with Japan. While military objectives and means were continuously debated, the Kwantung Army leaders did agree that the development of Manchukuo into an economic powerhouse should immediately commence. To that end, they made sure that they were the real power holders in Manchukuo. In form, the territory had an independent government, manned by Chinese officials under the rule of the newly enthroned Emperor P'u Yi. In fact, it became a puppet state controlled by the Kwantung military (see the chapter by Y. Tak Matsusaka in this volume).[11]

Although the Japanese military high command in Tokyo agreed that the new state of Manchukuo should play an important role in the new East Asia Alliance, they resisted the ambitious development plans demanded by the Kwantung Army. At the outset, none of the top leaders in Shinkyō had any clear, long-term vision of how they intended to develop this new East Asia Alliance. In hindsight we can observe that military and political crises were the driving force shaping the evolution of the alliance. For example, it was only after Japanese troops crossed the Great Wall into Hopei province of north China in 1933 that the Japanese military perceived new opportunities to exploit north China's resources more effectively than ever before.[12]

Despite the cleavages within the ranks of Japanese army officers,

[9] Ibid., p. 215, for another Ishiwara proposal, drafted in August 1935, advancing the same argument.

[10] Ibid., pp. 216, 231–55.

[11] Katsuji Nakagane, "Manchukuo and Economic Development," in Duus, Myers, and Peattie, *The Japanese Informal Empire in China.*

[12] Takafusa Nakamura, "Japan's Economic Thrust into North China, 1933–1938: Formation of the North Development Corporation," in *The Chinese and the Japanese: Essays in Political and Cultural Interactions,* ed. Akira Iriye (Princeton, N.J.: Princeton University Press, 1980), pp. 221– 26.

there was agreement among them to develop a new economic strategy to give substance and form to their concept of an East Asia Alliance. That new strategy consisted of the creation of a modern economic enclave in Manchukuo, later in north China, that represented the integration of resources and factor markets in Japan and northeast and north China. American policymakers of the day like Stanley Hornbeck, chief of the U.S. State Department's Far Eastern division, and Ambassador Joseph Grew in Tokyo, had little inkling of the commitment by military leaders in Manchukuo and north China to develop an enclave economy that would integrate the markets of those territories with that of Japan for the purpose of building a vast military-industrial complex capable of supporting Japan's military and imperial ambitions. Both Hornbeck and Grew were convinced that "sooner or later, the army would find the development of Manchuria prohibitively expensive. Then Japan would have to disgorge its conquest, the army would be disgraced, and the moderate civilians who favored close ties with the West would return to power."[13] Their completely mistaken assessment stemmed from the fact that they completely underestimated the capabilities and will of the Japanese military to organize a new kind of economy.

CREATING THE MODERN ENCLAVE ECONOMY IN MANCHUKUO

In 1931, Manchuria's three provinces supported only around thirty million people but contained rich mineral reserves, especially fossil fuels like petroleum and coal. A small railway grid radiated from the Liaotung Peninsula, developed by the SMR, to connect with a Chinese trunk line traversing north China in the south and running to the Soviet border in the north. Some ¥2.3 billion, (around US$1.1 billion) worth of foreign investment had flowed into the region; 76 percent of it was Japanese, with transportation, mining, and commerce absorbing most of that amount.[14] Since the turn of the century, Manchuria's value of coal, soybean, and food grain exports had far exceeded its imports. This resource-rich, labor-scarce region had been the object of Chinese immigration ever since the late nineteenth century, but especially in the 1920s, when civil war throughout China and harvest disasters forced young people to migrate to support their struggling families in north China villages.

---

[13] Michael A. Barnhard, *Japan Prepares for Total War: The Search for Economic Security, 1919–1941* (Ithaca, N.Y.: Cornell University Press, 1987), p. 115.

[14] Ramon H. Myers, *The Japanese Economic Development of Manchuria, 1929–1945* (New York: Garland, 1982), chap. 1, table 3, p. 20. In 1931, one hundred Japanese yen equaled almost US$50.

The First Phase: 1932–1936

The Kwantung army officers were well aware of these favorable economic conditions when they masterminded their takeover of the region in 1931. They reasoned that "because Japan lacked raw materials, its domestic market was limited, and population pressure extremely great, Japan's policy toward the Asian mainland should be based on managing Manchuria as a key link."[15] The Kwantung Army officers had no intention of turning the Chinese and other ethnic groups in Manchuria into loyal Japanese, as Japan's officials began doing in 1937 in their colonies of Korea and Taiwan (see Wan-yao Chou's chapter in this volume). Instead, they wanted the world to believe that Manchukuo was a sovereign Chinese state yet allied with its neighbor, Japan. Beyond that facade, the army officers intended to build a new kind of economic system integrated with Japan's economy in the event that Japan had to go to war. This new economic system, the modern enclave economy, would be directed and manned by Japanese who lived in the region on a permanent basis.

By March 1, 1932, Japanese army officers had drafted such a plan for Manchukuo. Ambitious in scope but lacking specifics, this plan called for improving the region's transport and communications infrastructure; expanding the supply of raw materials from agriculture, forestry, and aquatic resources; constructing new industry and mines; upgrading commerce and finance; and encouraging the region's private sector to develop its resources for improving public welfare and revitalizing local communities and their private organizations.[16]

A number of concrete steps were taken by the Kwantung Army to implement this broad plan. First, the Japanese yen was made convertible with the new Manchukuo monetary unit, the yuan, on a one-to-one basis, an easy administrative reform that overvalued the local currency and helped to ignite an import boom from Japan. As a result, between 1932 and 1936 the region ran a trade deficit, with intermediate products and capital goods dominating imports. Second, the nationalized SMR was to supervise and expand the region's railway and communication system. Finally, the Manchukuoan state would create 266 new business enterprises in the region between 1932 and 1935 with an investment of ¥987,233,000, of which nearly 59 percent was to be supplied by the Manchukuoan government, the SMR, and the Japanese

---

[15] Minami Manshū tetsudō kabushiki kaisha, chōsabu, *Manshū einen keikaku shiryō* [Materials for long-term Planning for Manchuria] (Tokyo: Ryūkei Shosha, 1980) (Hereafter *MEKS*), part 1, vol. 2, supplementary chart no. 15.

[16] Ibid.

government, with the remaining 41 percent representing private capital from the private sector.[17] Of this nearly one-billion-yen investment, 36 percent was earmarked for manufacturing, 22 percent for new energy, 12 percent for mining, and 30 percent for activities such as commerce, finance, and agriculture (table 5.2).

Most important, the plan called for building twenty-four modern industries by combining old firms and mines, along with new ones, with similar enterprises in Japan proper to produce ferrous and nonferrous metals, cement, petroleum, coal, chemicals, textiles, leather, vegetable oils, flour, tobacco, and the like. The Kwantung military wanted to organize each industry under the management of a single large company funded mainly by public investment, supplemented by private capital. These new state-owned companies were to be managed by government officials and private businessmen charged with the task of building new factories and mines and upgrading existing ones. The Japanese military officers believed this system would avoid "the evils of an uncontrolled [market] system by having the necessary state controls to plan a healthy, vigorous national people's economic system."[18]

Let us examine how this modern enclave economy worked. The Kwantung Army first established the General Affairs Office (Sōmucho) to manage this new enclave as well as Manchukuo's economy. That office coordinated special departments and bureaus to develop "a system of plan and regulation to control and develop the economy of northeast China."[19] It designated a single enterprise or joint-stock company as the agent to coordinate an entire industry on a vertical and horizontal production and distribution basis. This system was called "one enterprise managing one industry" (ichi gyō ichi sha chūi).[20] Each special company had a director and vice-director appointed by the General Affairs Office, with the necessary business experience and administrative skills. When such a company was formed, the state immediately passed a special law outlining that company's rules of governance, regarding its objectives and the procedures necessary to acquire capital, purchase assets and materials, hire labor and managers, dispose of earnings, set wages and other incentives, and so forth. It was to function as a private business enterprise by contracting freely with other firms to expand production capacity, meet output targets, and distribute output. It paid low taxes to the state, set its own wages and prices, sold an assigned output to designated firms, and paid high fixed dividends to

[17] Ibid., supplement 19. See also ibid., shiryō, part 4, statistical materials, table 2, pp. 461–76, listing new companies established by end of 1935.

[18] Ibid., supplement 15.

[19] Ibid., supplement 17.

[20] Ibid.

TABLE 5.2

Special Companies Created during 1932–1935 and Their Capital Investment, According to Economic Sector (thousands of yen)

	1932			1933			1934			1935			Total			
	Number	Public Capital	Private Capital	Number	Public Capital	Private Capital	Number	Public Capital	Private Capital	Number	Public Capital	Private Capital	Number	Public Capital	Private Capital	Percentage of Total Output
Banking	1	30,000	15,000	1	1,000	1,000	14	8,750	6,850	4	1,000	800	20	40,750	23,650	6
Exchange trusts	3	1,100	275	1	2,000	1,200	1	500	125	1	600	600	6	4,200	2,200	1
Miscellaneous financial institutions	1	500	375	2	6,080	6,020	2	120	43	2	160	65	7	6,860	6,503	2
Commerce	7	2,050	1,515	9	2,235	1,048	16	15,285	5,335	35	9,465	7,270	67	29,035	15,167	4
Shipping, transport	2	4,000	4,000	3	400	190	8	1,230	920	7	2,010	1,755	20	7,640	6,865	2
Communications	—	—	—	1	50,000	29,375	3	1,600	400	—	—	—	4	51,600	29,775	7
Electrical generation	—	—	—	4	1,500	773	6	91,230	90,730	5	490	490	15	93,220	91,943	22
Manufacturing																
Cotton textiles	—	—	—	2	1,150	1,150	2	3,500	2,000	2	200	150	6	4,850	3,300	} 36
Chemicals	—	—	—	3	26,550	14,025	4	7,550	3,200	4	1,050	975	11	35,150	18,200	
Paper	—	—	—	1	50	50	—	—	—	1	1,500	1,500	2	1,550	1,550	
Machine tools	—	—	—	—	—	—	4	9,200	4,325	1	3,000	750	5	12,200	5,075	
Metals	1	2,000	2,000	2	101,000	82,250	3	18,000	6,750	1	5,000	1,250	7	126,000	92,250	
Ceramics	—	—	—	1	3,000	3,000	5	6,150	4,050	5	11,620	5,825	11	20,770	12,875	
Brewing	—	—	—	4	2,470	2,470	4	14,000	5,200	—	—	—	8	16,470	7,770	
Food processing	1	200	50	4	550	163	5	2,650	2,538	2	8,000	3,250	12	11,400	6,000	
Materials	—	—	—	—	—	—	1	100	40	2	600	175	3	700	215	
Miscellaneous	—	—	—	—	—	—	2	3,100	850	—	—	—	2	3,100	850	
Mining	—	—	—	2	2,600	2,525	5	33,450	25,938	7	21,500	19,250	14	57,550	42,713	12
Fishing	—	—	—	—	—	—	2	3,000	1,020	—	—	—	2	3,000	1,020	—
Agriculture, forestry	2	2,100	2,025	1	250	62	3	3,200	1,550	3	21,500	11,875	9	27,050	15,512	4
Building, construction	1	1,000	1,000	2	1,000	300	8	5,510	3,690	4	5,810	5,660	15	13,320	10,650	2
Other	4	358	1,985	3	700	326	4	565	215	9	13,825	5,550	20	15,448	6,289	2
TOTAL	23	43,308	36,439	46	202,535	145,925	102	238,690	165,867	95	107,330	67,140	266	581,863	404,371	100

Source: Manshū tetsudō kabushiki kaisha, chōsabu, Manshū einen keikaku shiryō (Tokyo: Ryūkei shosha, 1980), part 1, vol. 2 (1980), table 1, suppl. 19.

shareholders. Each company's management had to consider these incentives and constraints and yet devise the most efficient means of production and distribution to meet payroll, pay shareholders, and supply a designated quota to other firms and the Japanese army.

Consider the following examples. In the case of steel manufacturing, a new company called the Iron-Steel Refining Company was made responsible for managing and coordinating the activities of the Showa Steel Works and the Penhsihu Ore Mining Company in Manchukuo and the Japan Steel Corporation in Japan.[21] The Iron-Steel Refining Company then contracted with other firms and integrated their operations to meet the steel production targets set by military planners. This same company also was charged with contracting with gold, copper, and lead mines and their refining plants in Manchukuo to expand their production of those metals. This type of agency-contracting arrangement applied to all other industries in the military complex.

Likewise, the Dōwa Automobile Joint-Stock Company was established by the Manchukuo government in 1936 with the target of producing within five years 5,000 vehicles, repairing 9,600 more, and supplying necessary parts for another 9,000.[22] Dōwa contracted with four companies in Japan to supply the necessary financial capital and equipment: Tokyo Gas-Electrical Company, Mitsui Heavy Industry, Toyota Automobile Company, and Kangami Automobile Company. The assembly plants built in Manchukuo used the Toyota's engineering design. The new plants built in Shenyang (Shinkyō), Feng-t'ien (Mukden), Harbin, Mou-tan-chiang, and other cities imported equipment from all four companies. In the first three years these plants assembled basic frames and constructed parts; the plan called for these plants and shops to employ 5,860 workers and pay over ¥3 million in wages.[23] The company established distribution and service outlets in all of Manchukuo's large cities. It is not known how many plants and shops actually were constructed, but in 1946–47 a Chinese inspection team visiting the region reported that only slightly more than 3,000 vehicles were ever assembled by this particular company.

Our last example is the Tenhōsan Mining Joint Stock Company, established by the Manchukuo government in 1937. Its task was to mine and refine lead, copper, silver, and aluminum near the T'ien-pao mountain range, located not far from Anshan in central Manchuria. Two Manchukuo companies supplied this new enterprise with capital: the

[21] Ibid.

[22] Minami Manshū tetsudō kabushiki kaisha, chōsabu, *Jidōsha kōgyō kankei shiryū* [Materials on the automobile industry] (Tokyo: Ryōkei Shosha, 1980), part. 2, vol. 7, p. 4.

[23] Ibid., p. 41.

SMR provided around ¥8 million, and the South Manchuria Daikō Gyōmei Company another ¥1 million.[24] Tenhōsan used these funds to build a road and single track to the lead mine, establish a mine to produce 75,000 tons of ore, and annually refine 5,000 tons of lead, 6,380 tons of copper, and 750 tons of aluminum. The company's staff of 68 managers and technicians were mainly Japanese.

Each joint-stock company had the right to negotiate with other companies to develop its new industry using advanced technology. It contracted with the other firms assigned by military planners to supply capital and materials. Japanese executives, managers, and technicians operated these new companies and negotiated with counterparts in Manchukuo and Japan. Paying low taxes, they retained their profits for future expansion. Their principal obligations, however, were to pay the assigned earnings for capital shares held by the public sector and private holders and to meet targets set by military planners. Their capital funds came from the Manchukuo government, the SMR, and companies in Japan and Manchukuo. Each company could also contract with agents outside the network of enterprises it supervised, as long as it fulfilled its other obligations. All companies were closely monitored by departments of the General Affairs Office, and they reported their annual progress to that office.

Between 1932 and 1936, Japanese bureaucrats, engineers, accountants, clerks, technicians, businessmen, skilled workers, and farmers poured into Manchukuo. They constructed new factories and initiated an economic boom. The SMR spent heavily to expand the region's railway system and communications. But just as this new enclave economy began to take shape, new crises confronted the Kwantung Army's planners.

The December 1936 Sian Incident had produced an unexpected coalition between the Nationalist government, led by Chiang Kai-shek and the Kuomintang party, and the Communists and their guerrilla armies, that tried to block Japan's penetration of north China. In 1937, the United States began imposing trade sanctions on Japan, even initiating an embargo on strategic materials that Japan desperately needed to expand its military complex. Manchukuo's Kwantung military leaders now felt compelled to accelerate the pace of regional economic development, in part because of the satisfactory economic gains already achieved, and in part because of the new threats. Fearing that war was more likely than ever, these officers redoubled their efforts to expand Manchukuo's productive capacity for national defense. A new phase of

---

[24] Minami Manshū tetsudō kabushiki kaisha, chōsabu, *Enkō kankei shiryō* [Materials on lead mines] (Tokyo: Ryōkei Shobō, 1980), part. 2, vol. 6, pp. 21–22.

economic mobilization commenced, for the purpose of expanding the embryonic enclave economy and reorganizing its structure.

The Second Phase, 1936–1937

In 1935 Ishiwara Kanji, now head of the Operations Section [*Sakusenka*] of the Army General Staff, urged a survey of Manchuria's development in order to prepare the empire for the possibility of war.[25] On June 20, 1936, the General Staff drafted a proposal, pushed by military officers in Manchukuo, arguing that Manchukuo must accelerate resource development, among other things by quickly expanding the Manchurian military-industrial complex to counter an attack from the Soviet Union. One month later, on July 23, the General Staff prepared still another draft report, titled "The Requirements for Developing Industries to Prepare for War." This draft stipulated that Manchuria, Japan, and north China (northern Hopei and southern Chahar) should be integrated and their resources developed as quickly as possible for a possible war with the Soviet Union.[26] These proposals reflected the new sense of urgency within the Army Ministry in Tokyo to carry out a full-scale review of Manchuria's first phase of development and to prepare new long-term development plans for mobilizing that region's resources.

Other groups in Tokyo also focused on Manchukuo's industrialization. In the fall of 1935 Ishiwara and Miyazaki Masayoshi, head of the Tokyo branch office of the Economic Research Association (*Keizai Chōsakai*), established the Japan-Manchukuo Finance-Economic Research Association (*Nichi-Man Zeisei Keizai Kenkyūkai*).[27] Their first project, to prepare a financial proposal for Manchukuo's new five-year industrial development plan, called for a ¥3 billion investment to produce 7.5 million tons of steel and 45 million tons of coal. This association began cooperating with the SMR's Economic Research Association (*Mantetsu Keizai Chōsakai*) to improve this draft plan; a report was eventually sent to the Army Ministry on September 3, 1936. Thus, in 1935–36 several studies already focused on how to expand Manchukuo's modern economic enclave to make the East Asia Alliance a reality.

[25] Shimada Toshihiko and Inaba Masao, eds., *Gendaishi shiryō: Nitchū sensō* [Contemporary historical materials: The Sino-Japanese War], vol. 1 (Tokyo: Misuzu shobō, 1964) (hereafter *NCS*), p. 703.

[26] Minami manshū tetsudō kabushiki kaisha, chōsabu, *Manshū gokanen keikaku ritsuan shorui* [A series of planning documents on the Manchurian five-year plan] (Tokyo: Ryōkei, 1980), part. 1, vol. 1, introduction, p. 2. (Hereafter *MKR*, with appropriate part, volume, and page numbers.)

[27] *NCS* 1:704–7.

Well aware of these studies, the Army Ministry willingly supported them. In August 1936 the ministry proposed its own "Draft Outline for Policies to Develop Manchuria."[28] This proposal called for a five-year industrial development plan managed by the Manchukuo government in close cooperation with Japan. This new plan, together with the draft plan for the five-year development of Manchuria's resources prepared by the two agencies just mentioned, became the basis for reviewing, coordinating, and preparing a new five-year Manchurian industrial plan. After drafting this new plan, the Army Ministry sent it to Manchukuo for further study. In October 1936, staff personnel of the Kwantung Army, the Manchukuo government, and the SMR met at T'ang-kang-tzu city's famous hot springs to complete yet another draft.[29] After expanding the capital financing component of the plan, they returned it to the Army Ministry in November 1936.

On November 25, 1936 the Army Ministry decided to send the plan to government ministries, departments, and sections for further evaluation.[30] The ministries of Commerce and Industry, Agriculture and Forestry, and Finance reviewed the plan as instructed in a series of conferences held in early January 1937, and returned it to the Army Ministry after making further revisions. The Army Ministry then asked the Kwantung Army to reexamine the plan, and in January 1937 the Kwantung Army issued a new version. In April 1937, the Kwantung Army's General Staff returned the plan to the Army Ministry, and it was again reviewed within the Japanese government and finally approved. On June 10, 1937, the Army Ministry published the plan, which cited the enormous financial contributions to be forthcoming from the Japanese and Manchukuo governments and the private sector.[31] The plan also listed the high targets for goods to be exchanged between Manchukuo and Japan, the skilled technicians and engineers required, and the output goals for industrial sectors.

Japan's system of intragovernmental communication (*ringi seido*) at long last had produced a consensus among the military authorities, bureaucrats, and technocrat managers and planners in both Manchukuo and Japan. As early as April 11, 1936, however, the Manchukuo government had already moved ahead to establish the Manchukuo Industrial Development Long-Term Planning Commission under the chairmanship of Oshikawa Ichirō.[32] Born in 1899 in Kagoshima prefecture, Oshikawa had graduated from the Department of Economics of Tokyo

[28] *MKR*, part 1, vol. 1, introduction, p. 4.
[29] *NCS*, 1:717–18.
[30] *MKR*, part 1, vol. 1, introduction, pp. 5–6.
[31] *MEKS*, pp. 2–5.
[32] Ibid.

Imperial University and had studied at Oxford. In 1927, he joined the SMR and became section chief of its General Affairs Office in Harbin. He quickly advanced to become head of the company's Department of Industry (*Sangyōbu*) which was responsible for the SMR's economic planning and development.

Oshikawa's commission had four sections: one for planning long-term enterprise growth and financing, another for agriculture, a third for Japanese migration to Manchuria, and the last for financing these three activities. The commission first met at the Yamato Hotel in Dairen, with ninety-one persons attending, to discuss its tasks.[33] For the next six months, these four sections held conferences and drew up plans for creating a new fiscal and banking system, streamlining those organizations assigned to build the necessary infrastructure for agriculture and animal husbandry, and reforming the legal system to facilitate the establishment of modern corporate enterprises.[34] These plans were extensive and ambitious. In design and content their main purpose was to create the new foundations for enlarging the modern economic enclave that had already formed. They also provided the basis for the ambitious five-year heavy industry plan that the Army Ministry had finally negotiated between the Japanese and Manchukuo governments. In other words, these two broad planning efforts complemented each other to initiate the second phase of Manchuria's modern enclave development, which covered the period 1937–41.

The Kwantung Army hoped that by 1941 Manchukuo's infrastructure, factories, mines, and energy output would enable Japan's military to be self-sufficient and fully prepared for large-scale war. It also wanted at least 10 percent of Manchukuo's population to be Japanese, and estimated that by 1956 at least one million Japanese households, or five million individuals, would live in the region.[35] The Kwantung Army also hoped that Manchukuo could produce enough coal, iron ore, petroleum, and other raw materials to meet the demands of East Asia's military-related industries. Moreover, the military leaders wanted to have all railroad lines and communications thoroughly integrated as one efficient system and linked with waterways and ports. Finally, Manchukuo must supply enough food grains and livestock products to satisfy the needs of the East Asian economic bloc. These grand goals depended not only entirely on how successfully Manchukuo carried out the first five-year plan between 1937 and 1941, but

[33] Ibid., pp. 6–7.
[34] Ibid. See description of the second period of Manchukuo's economic construction, August 5, 1936 (pp. 187–91) and sec. 3 (pp. 193–448).
[35] *TPTC,* 1.2:57.

also on the Japanese government financing Manchukuo with slightly more than ¥1 billion yen and its private sector contributing another ¥8.5 billion.[36]

Manchukuo's First Five-Year Industrial Plans

Manchukuo now manufactured its own weapons, munitions, aircraft, vehicles and so forth. Its industries, such as steel, chemicals, energy, and machine tools, were being further expanded.[37] The new plan called for Japan to supply Manchukuo between 1937 and 1940 with machines, construction materials, technicians, and other industrial necessities in exchange for materials such as iron, steel plate, coal, oil, lead, salt, caustic soda, paper, etc.[38] These new arrangements might have succeeded if Japan's military had not become embroiled in war with China in 1937, the very first year of the Five-Year Plan. Once war broke out, Japan's industries found it impossible to fulfill their commitments to Manchukuo. To make matters worse, when the European conflict erupted in 1939, Japan no longer received strategic goods and materials from abroad.[39] By late 1940, Japan no longer supplied Manchukuo with the necessary intermediate products, capital, and technology to sustain the expansion momentum achieved in Manchukuo between 1937 and 1939.

In the first two years of the first Five-Year Plan, production sometimes matched the output targets (see table 5.3). After 1939, except in rare instances, production fell far short of the targets. In some industries, such as coal mining, the Japanese police mobilized more Chinese workers, and kept production increasing until 1941. The Manchukuo government also began constructing several dams and hydroelectric works on the Yalu and Sungari rivers. The new factories constructed in Shenyang also produced additional output. A new automobile plant, based on the Detroit design of Henry Ford, even manufactured a few vehicles. A new aircraft plant in Shenyang was modeled on the technology of the Junker aircraft plant in Germany, but it never built an operational plane. By 1940–41, shortages of strategic materials were so severe that the productive capacity in military-related industries could not be efficiently used. The textile, shoe, tobacco, and food-processing industries were particularly hard hit by raw materials shortages, and their output declined.

Still adhering to the framework of a "single company managing one

[36] Ibid., p. 61.
[37] Ibid., p. 62.
[38] Ibid., pp. 69–71.
[39] Ibid., p. 71.

TABLE 5.3

Industrial Output Targets and Actual Performance under Manchukuo's First Five-Year Plan, 1937–1941 (metric tons unless otherwise noted)

	1936	1937		1938		1939		1940		1941		Index (1936 = 100)
		Target	Actual	Target	Actual	Target	Actual	Target	Actual	Target	Actual	
Iron[a]	369	850	811	910	857	1,760	1,023	2,350	1,062	3,325	1,388	376
Steel ingots[a]	364	580	516	620	585	655	525	1,039	532	2,027	561	157
Steel plate[a]	328	500	456	543	534	570	459	760	467	1,642	522	146
Steel materials[a]	167	400	246	535	349	395	353	557	386	1,038	410	246
Coal[a]	13,672	15,328	14,387	17,390	15,988	20,730	19,401	24,000	21,120	27,510	24,190	177
Oil	—	66,000	75,000	75,000	80,449	75,000	73,503	170,400	79,077	170,400	113,243	—
Zinc	—	1,900	2,175	2,577	2,150	14,319	2,261	31,850	4,815	50,525	3,800	200
Lead	—	2,200	1,585	2,993	2,573	12,395	2,854	27,487	8,788	46,152	9,540	434
Copper	—	—	—	390	104	1,365	186	3,160	500	266	538	
Asbestos	—	150	100	350	150	2,000	5,148	3,500	5,486	5,000	4,828	
Gold[b]	—	4,230	3,709	5,141	3,147	4,924	2,488	6,267	2,222	8,469	2,361	
Electrical power[c]	1,350,506		1,623,970		2,133,386		2,534,481		2,988,711		3,519,790	261
Caustic soda	—		11,122		44,903		54,407		64,811		61,520	553
Ammonium sulfate	182		214		193		153		219		—	190
Aluminum	—		—	1,500	967	4,500	3,257	8,500	5,026	1,500	8,030	
Magnesium	—		—		—	500	—	400	—	1,000	89	—
Vehicles[d]	—		—		—		—		—	85	—	—
Large vehicles[d]	—		—		—		—		—	2,150	3,880	—

Source: TPTC, vol. 1, part 2, table 11, pp. 62–63.
[a] Thousands of metric tons.
[b] Kilograms.
[c] Thousands of kwh.
[d] Units.

industry," the Kwantung Army managed to establish a new holding company in 1937 and 1938, through a leading bureaucrat in Japan, Kishi Nobusuke, who worked closely with Kwantung Army officers like Itagaki Seishirō.[40] Kishi had close ties with Ayukawa Gisuke, the head of Nissan Corporation, which he had built up rapidly since World War I, largely thanks to close ties with the military and their lucrative contracts. Kishi invited Ayukawa to set up still another new conglomerate in Manchukuo that would take the lead in expanding the small heavy-industrial base that had taken shape before 1936. In 1937 Ayukawa became president of the newly formed Manchurian Heavy Industry Corporation (*Manshū Jukōgyō Kabushiki Kaisha*), or Mangyō, as it was known in Manchukuo.

In 1937 alone, the Manchukuo government created seventy-nine new corporate enterprises to expand the region's industrial-military complex (table 5.4). The largest thirty-eight enterprises of these received 15.9 billion yuan worth of capital, of which only 25 percent came from Japan. Of the remainder, almost half (47 percent) represented borrowed funds, with the largest share being supplied by banks. Mangyō was the largest conglomerate of all, having 3.7 billion yuan worth of capital and receiving 32 percent of all capital provided to the top 38 enterprises from within Manchukuo.

On May 1, 1937, the Manchukuo government issued Imperial Ordinance No. 66, which listed the rules for controlling and regulating these enterprises; it became law nine days later.[41] Government ministries and their respective ministers now managed even more enterprises. Instead of a Japanese businessman being selected to direct a new corporation as before, a Japanese bureaucrat or minister was put in charge. This minister, possessing power to intervene in company management policies and procedures, alone had the authority to approve or deny any requests by these special enterprises. He monitored their reports of stoppages or slowdowns, and replacement of top company personnel. He also imposed fines when company executives violated the heavy-industrial law.[42]

By 1941 these new companies were using the funds created by the

---

[40] Chalmers Johnson, *MITI and the Japanese Miracle: The Growth of Industrial Policy, 1925–1975* (Stanford, Calif.: Stanford University Press, 1982), p. 131.

[41] Takahashi Teizō, *Manshū keizai toseihō* [Laws for the control of the Manchurian economy] (Mukden: Manshū Shūbunkan, 1943), p. 106. In 1931, Imperial Ordinance No. 40 was issued by the Japanese government. It listed the large-scale industries to be brought under direct government supervision. These rules, revised in 1937, were influenced by the administrative regulations for Manchukuo heavy industry in laws promulgated in May 1937 (see ibid., p. 108).

[42] Ibid., pp. 112–38.

TABLE 5.4
Capital Shares of Private and Public Sectors in New Joint-Stock Companies Created in Manchukuo in 1937 (thousands of yen)

SPECIAL JOINT-STOCK COMPANIES
(38 enterprises)

Capital Investment from Japan

Paid-in Capital			Company Debentures	Borrowed Capital			Total Capital from Japan		
Government	Private	Total		Banks	Companies	Total	Government	Private	Total
11,952	1,065,106	1,177,058	2,041,870	636,072	241,262	877,334	111,952	3,984,310	4,096,262

Capital Investment from Manchuria

Paid-in Capital					Borrowed Capital				Total Capital		
Government	Mangyō	SMR	Other	Total	Banks	Companies	Mangyō	Total	Government	Private	Total
1,346,565	867,710	108,084	352,257	2,674,616	3,933,964	3,643,145	1,455,614	5,513,175	1,346,565	10,484,371	11,830,936

REGULATED SPECIAL JOINT-STOCK COMPANIES
(41 enterprises)

Capital Investment from Japan

Paid-in Capital	Borrowed Capital			Grand Total
	Banks	Companies	Total	
274,046	16,450	500	16,950	290,996

Capital Investment from Manchuria

Paid-in Capital					Borrowed Capital				Grand Total		
Government	Mangyō	SMR	Other	Total	Banks	Mangyō	SMR	Total	Government	Private	Total
92,619	993,891	67,200	171,135	1,324,845	374,525	780,079	950	1,155,554	92,619	2,381,780	2,480,399

Source: TPTC, vol. 1, part 2, tables 6 and 7, pp. 40–41.

Manchukuo government to purchase materials for expanding plant capacity and production. This inflationary policy increased investment by roughly sevenfold compared to the 50 percent increase in output between 1937 and 1940.[43] As more money circulated and chased fewer goods, the prices of intermediate and finished products skyrocketed. The massive inflation initiated within the modern economic enclave spilled into the local economy of the cities and extended into the rural heartland. Farmers and other suppliers withheld their products as their purchasing power declined.

The hyperinflation generated by the modern enclave economy greatly alarmed the Japanese, and in late 1941 they took steps to control the scarcity of goods, production stoppages, and declining morale that inflation had produced. On January 25, 1942, the Manchukuo government passed Ordinance 228 with 38 regulations that governed the operation of special Control Associations (*Tosei Kumiai*).[44] These were to supervise companies supplying the scarce raw materials and intermediate and consumer goods that the modern economic enclave desperately needed. Each Control Association was responsible for guaranteeing the supply of certain goods, fixing their prices, and distributing these to the companies that controlled the twenty-four key industries in the modern economic enclave.

Manchukuo's Second Five-Year Industrial Plan

In mid-1941, the Manchukuo military authorities began drafting a second five-year manufacturing plan for the period 1942–46. In November 1941, the China-Manchukuo-Japan Economic Cooperation Association further revised this plan, which included targets for material inputs and skilled labor, and for the first time, included the military-manufacturing complex in Japan's colonies.[45] It called for slightly higher output targets than those actually reached in Manchukuo in 1941. Planners seemed to believe that China, Manchukuo, Japan, and its formal colonies could achieve the targets, based on the actual output produced in the fourth and fifth years of the first Manchukuo development plan. (See table 5.5, showing the second Five-Year Plan to include the Japanese empire's military-manufacturing complex.)

The new plan also assumed that Japan would not supply the neces-

[43] Minami Manshū telsudō kabushiki kaisha, chōsabu, *Manshū infureeshun chōsa hōkoku* [A survey report on inflation in Manchuria], *Mantetsu chōsabu: sōgō chōsa hōkokusho* [The Research Bureau of the South Manchurian Railway Company: A Collection of Survey Reports], ed. Nomo Kiyoshi and Miwa Takeshi (Tokyo: Akishobō, 1982), p. 472.

[44] Takahashi Teizo, *Manshū heizai toseihō,* pp. 139–54.

[45] *TPTC,* vol. 1, part. 2, p. 72.

TABLE 5.5

Production Targets under the Second Five-Year Plan for the Wartime Japanese Empire, 1942–1946 (thousands of metric tons unless otherwise noted)

		1942	1943	1944	1945	1946
Steel plates, materials	Japan	4,930	5,430	5,930	6,430	7,130
	Korea	70	70	70	70	70
	Total	5,000	5,500	6,000	6,500	7,200
	Manchukuo	517	589	606	726	952
Steel ingots	Japan	5,775	6,269	6,834	7,510	8,387
	Korea	87	87	87	87	87
	Total	5,862	6,356	6,921	7,597	8,474
	Manchukuo	884	1,184	1,263	1,275	1,576
Iron	Japan	4,739	5,049	5,629	6,272	6,975
	Korea	367	500	500	540	710
	Total	5,106	5,549	6,129	6,812	7,685
	Manchukuo	1,390	1,660	1,760	1,960	2,290
Iron ore	Japan	2,287	2,809	3,110	3,180	3,250
	Korea	3,340	4,090	4,400	4,800	5,000
	Total	5,627	6,899	7,510	7,980	8,250
	Manchukuo	6,570	9,000	10,700	12,700	14,900
Coal	Japan	61,000	63,500	65,000	67,000	69,000
	Korea	7,000	7,700	8,550	9,490	10,630
	Sakhalin	6,500	7,300	8,580	10,100	11,500
	Taiwan	3,000	3,200	3,400	3,700	4,200
	Total	77,500	81,700	85,530	99,290	95,330
	Manchukuo	27,500	31,450	35,780	40,230	44,930
	North China	27,000	31,000	35,600	39,600	44,300
Electrical power[a]	Japan[b]	261	341	178	642	395
	Korea[b]	200	217	339	323	749
	Taiwan[b]	69	—	160	22	98
	Total	530	558	677	987	1,242
	Manchukuo[c]	321	237	345	296	395
	North China[c]	55	55	45	85	44
Copper	Japan	68.0	70.5	74.1	75.0	75.0
	Korea	8.5	8.8	8.8	9.0	9.4
	Total	76.5	79.3	82.9	84.0	84.4
	Manchukuo	1.1	1.2	1.3	5.0	5.2

TABLE 5.5 *Continued*

		1942	1943	1944	1945	1946
Lead	Japan	16.0	18.0	20.8	23.2	23.9
	Korea	9.0	9.0	9.0	10.4	13.3
	Total	25.0	27.0	29.8	33.6	37.2
	Manchukuo	9.1	11.0	12.2	12.2	12.2
Zinc	Japan	60.0	65.5	70.0	78.0	80.0
	Korea	5.0	6.0	6.0	11.8	19.7
	Total	65.0	71.5	76.0	89.8	99.7
	Manchukuo	3.8	4.2	6.8	8.9	8.9
Aluminum	Japan	60.0	65.0	75.0	80.0	90.0
	Korea	7.2	23.6	42.4	63.2	70.0
	Taiwan	13.8	20.0	20.0	20.0	20.0
	Total	81.0	108.6	137.4	163.2	188.0
	Manchukuo	10.0	15.0	15.0	15.0	15.0
Ammonium sulfate	Japan	1,387	1,610	1,720	1,840	1,920
	Korea	486	580	580	580	580
	Taiwan	—	—	—	80	80
	Total	1,873	2,190	2,300	2,500	2,580
	Manchukuo	246	250	273	295	301
	North China	24	24	24	104	224

Source: TPTC, vol. 1, part 2, table 2, pp. 70–71.
Note: Items like synthetic oil, machine tools, and vehicles are excluded because data did not indicate area of production or only cited output from Japan proper.
ᵃThousands of kwh.
ᵇAnnual increment of electrical energy.
ᶜBy adding equipment each year.

sary equipment, machinery, and capital to north China, Manchukuo, and elsewhere but that new capacity already being built would be coming on line to augment that supply. Tokyo's planners now limited Manchukuo's economic role in the East Asian bloc, thus making its second Five-Year Plan less ambitious than the first.[46] Japan's military leaders in Tokyo understood that Manchukuo's modern economic enclave was still underdeveloped. The war's expansion in 1942 meant that Tokyo had seized the economic planning initiative from Manchukuo's army officers.

[46] Ibid., pp. 72–73.

In 1942, then, Manchukuo and Japan's military leaders drafted the "Outline of Basic National Policy for Manchukuo" that included planning for the next decade of economic, political development, and people's welfare.[47] This plan had two major goals: to build a new national defense system and to continue long-term industrial development. But as the Pacific War broadened, Japan and its East Asian bloc partners had to devote their productive capacity and output to the larger war effort.

After late 1943 Japan began to be ground down under the crushing weight of American military and industrial power. As early as 1942 Japan could no longer protect its vital sea lanes, and consequently, the production of basic metals, chemicals, and fuels rapidly declined in the East Asian bloc. By 1943 Japan began to lose control of its airspace. In July, September, and December of that year, B-29 bombers attacked Anshan and Shenyang and caused considerable damage.[48] In October, Manchukuo authorities began dispersing key military factories, even moving some underground, an action that severely reduced the region's productive capabilities.[49] Meanwhile, the Manchukuo military and police desperately mobilized raw materials, especially food grains from local markets, to ship to Japan and to supply Japanese troops in China. Manchukuo's modern economic enclave was disintegrating.

In early 1945, the end was definitely in sight, but the Manchukuo military was not ready to surrender. Before June, many troops of the Kwantung Army were sent to defend Japan; in March the Manchukuo government drew up a plan to increase the production of explosives because their supply had become acutely short.[50] In these same months, army officers made plans for producing German-style rockets that carried special explosives and could be placed on aircraft and small submarines.[51] In June, they planned to mobilize and distribute more food grain and essential consumer goods, but that never happened because of Japan's surrender on August 15.[52]

In sum, Manchukuo's two ambitious five-year plans to expand its modern economic enclave represented the creation of much productive capacity that was never efficiently used; most of the output of raw materials and intermediate products produced by this new capacity were never processed to become final products and therefore wasted, often as

---

[47] Ibid., p. 73.

[48] Ibid.

[49] Ibid., p. 74. None of these plans were ever implemented.

[50] Ibid., pp. 74–75.

[51] Ibid., p. 14.

[52] Ibid., pp. 19–23. Also Manshū jijō annaijo, *Manshū kokusaku kaisha sōgō yōran* [A comprehensive survey of Manchukuo's policy for companies] (Shinkyō: Manshu jijō annaijo, 1939).

inventory; and the scarce capital allocated to this bold industrialization effort represented a very high opportunity cost for the Japanese people. Had Japan's leaders found the courage to achieve a political reconciliation with China in 1938–39 and avoided war with the United States in 1941, Manchukuo's ambitious modern economic enclave might have become the motor force for Manchukuo's industrialization.[53] But war intervened, and the region's industrialization was aborted.

DEVELOPING A JAPANESE ECONOMIC ENCLAVE IN NORTH CHINA

As early as the teens and twenties, the Japanese had been surveying resources in north China. After the Japanese military occupied German concessions in Shantung in World War I, they quickly sent their investigation teams into that large province to survey mining and agricultural resources as well as to examine social and political conditions. The SMR also established research units in Peking and Tientsin to study the region. The Japanese soon became aware of north China's resource potential, and while their assessments were mixed, they tilted toward an optimistic view that resources were abundant and could be cheaply developed. But anyone who read Japanese intelligence and survey reports had to realize that the countryside was dirt poor and barely could support its huge population, of whom the vast majority lived at near subsistence level.[54] This evaluation, however, was tempered by another view that argued that the Chinese in these provinces wanted self-government and relief from the violence and burdens imposed on them by bandits, Communist guerrillas, and local officials. The Japanese believed they were well positioned to help the region's populace, especially their elite, to develop their resources to achieve a better life while obtaining special advantages for themselves.

This was certainly the rosy viewpoint promoted by right-wing extrem-

[53] Elizabeth B. Schumpeter opined in 1939 that politics would determine Japan's fate to be free "to build up her industries and her trade." According to her, everything depended on Japan reaching a political solution with China, and on the United States "retreating to some extent from a position in which she seems to be extending the Monroe Doctrine to such Asiatic regions as the Netherlands East Indies and French Indo-China." See E. B. Schumpeter, ed., *The Industrialization of Japan and Manchukuo, 1930–1940* (New York: Macmillan, 1940), pp. 860–61. This classic work described Japanese and Manchukuo industrialization, but it could not describe the powerful role of military-strategic thinking in plans for the industrialization of East Asia under Japanese leadership, given the secrecy in which Japan's military planned and promoted Manchukuo's industrial-military complex after 1931.

[54] For the rural investigations carried out by the SMR in the 1930s and early 1940s, see Ramon H. Myers, *The Chinese Peasant Economy: Agricultural Development in Hopei and Shantung, 1890–1949* (Cambridge, Mass.: Harvard University Press, 1970).

ists like Kurihara Hikokurō in 1936. Born in 1879 in the poor prefecture of Tochigi, Kurihara studied at Nihon and Aichi universities and then managed a journal. He later became a member of the Tokyo Council and in 1927 was elected to the Diet. He also became head of the Japan Sword Society, a right-wing organization, and a member of the National Alliance (*Kokumin Dōmei*), another ultranationalist political party, formed in December 1932 by Adachi Kenzo and Nakano Seigo. Their party advocated government control of strategic industries and financial institutions, as well as the creation of a Japan-Manchukuo economic bloc. In 1935 Kurihara wrote a tract called *Discussing the Truth about North China*.[55]

Although his account of north China's potential resource development lacked analytical rigor, it was representative of many Japanese surveys, which drew upon the standard Chinese provincial statistics. Kurihara correctly noted that the region depended primarily upon farming, so that food grains were basic to its economy. He also accurately underscored the underdevelopment of manufacturing, in which only food processing, the cotton textile industry, and the service sector offered any nonfarm employment. North China's large foreign trade imbalance made it an importer of consumer and capital goods, and equilibrium was only achieved through large inflows of remittances from Chinese workers in Manchuria and Southeast Asia and the capital supplied by foreign and Chinese businessmen. Such economic underdevelopment did not deter Kurihara from describing an optimistic scenario in which he saw cotton and food grain yields trebled by applying more fertilizer, livestock flourish by improving the soil and water management, and coal mining greatly expanded by modern transport. For these reasons, Kurihara believed that "the economic value of north China not only is enormous, but it provides a stable market for Japanese manufactured products."[56]

None of Kurihara's assessments considered the financial requirement necessary to build a modern infrastructure and launch a "green revolution." Nor did he recognize the fragility of the farming system, in which output could dramatically decline because of poor harvests or a modest reduction of the work force. Nor did the Japanese realize the difficulties they might encounter in developing this region if they also had to wage war elsewhere at the same time. Just as Kurihara was not daunted by the high costs for building a modern Japanese economic

---

[55] Kurihara Hikokuro, *Hoku-Shi no shinsō o danzuru* [Discussing the truth about north China] (n.p., 1935), p. 126.

[56] Ibid.

enclave in north China, neither were the Kwantung Army and the SMR worried about similar obstacles.

Although the T'ang-ku Agreement of 1933 brought an uneasy peace to north China, the Kwantung Army, in conjunction with the Japanese military garrison in Tientsin and the SMR, considered ways of establishing new organizations to develop mineral and agricultural resources in the region. The Kwantung Army decided to set up public-private companies with special rights to construct railroads, develop mines, and build factories, the strategy it had adopted in Manchukuo. In January 1935 the Japanese military had successfully established a Chinese puppet regime in T'uangzhou, just south of the border separating Manchukuo and north China, the Chi Tung Anti-Communist Autonomous Government. This regime was led by a Chinese civilian, Yin Juh-keng, and had jurisdiction over twenty-two counties in northeastern Hopei just north of Peking and T'ientsin, with a combined population of around seven million. Then, on January 13, 1936, the Japanese Army, Navy, and Foreign ministries in Tokyo agreed on a new plan to make north China's five provinces completely autonomous under a Chinese form of governance like the Chi Tung puppet regime and Manchukuo.[57] In this way, the Japanese hoped to establish puppet Chinese regimes throughout north China, and eventually in central China, under rulers who took their instructions from Japanese military authorities and merely served as client states for Japan in a new East Asian Alliance. The Japanese military then would apply the formula used in Manchukuo for developing a modern economic enclave in these new regimes.

Japanese Military Plans to Develop North China

On July 20, 1937, the Second Section of the Army General Staff's First Department argued that all disturbances in north China must be quickly terminated to improve relations between Japan and the foreign powers.[58] It also called for taking steps to limit the flight of capital from the region, especially silver and gold, and to unify the currency system. The Japanese military wanted to restore normalcy as soon as possible. These considerations still did not deter Japan's military machine from attacking Shanghai in the hope of engaging the Nationalist government's elite divisions and knocking them out of the war.

[57] Nakamura, "Japan's Economic Thrust into North China," p. 230.

[58] Nihon Kindai Shiryō Kenkyūkai, *Nichi-Man zaisei keizai kenkyūkai shiryō: Izumiyama Sanroku kyūzō* [Materials on the Japan-Manchukuo Finance and Economic Research Association: The former records of Mr. Izumiyama Sanroku], 4 vols. (Tokyo: Nihon kindai shiryō kenkyūkai, 1970) (henceforth *NMZK*), 2:23.

Meanwhile, in August 1937 the SMR's president, Matsuoka Yōsuke, taking his cue from the Kwantung Army, proposed a scheme for governing north China.[59] His plan called for creating a new puppet regime in north China similar to the Chi Tung government.

Matsuoka's plan for Chinese governance of the five northern provinces depended on retaining traditional Chinese organizations and customs. The new government would control Hopei, Shantung, Shansi, Suiyuan, and Chahar provinces. A small team of top-level Japanese advisers would help the Chinese establish their new regime. Manchukuo would quickly recognize this new state; Japan would help the new government with an economic development plan; the military would facilitate the creation of a new central bank to unify the currency and peg it to the Japanese yen; and the SMR stood ready to build an economic enclave in the new entity.

One month before Matsuoka's plan was circulated, the SMR's new Department of Industry (*Sangyōbu*) already had drafted an "Outline of a Plan to Develop the Industry of North China," based on three important assumptions: Japan and Manchukuo must cooperate to oppose the advance of communism; Japan must have a comprehensive plan, which it still lacked, to develop East Asia's resources; and, north China was a good market for Japan, and its rich resources should be developed. Therefore, the Japanese should build a modern economic enclave to extract and process raw materials for Japan's economy and industrialize north China.

The plan called for the building of a new steel plant in Tientsin having the capacity to produce 500,000 tons of steel and 100,000 tons of steel plate, ingots, and other products. North China could then export 450,000 tons of steel to Japan each year. Another project was to construct a coal liquefaction plant in Tientsin and another in Shansi province's P'ing-ting prefecture, to export 320,000 tons of fuel to Japan each year. This enclave of modern plants and mines would increase coal production in Hopei, salt in Tsingtao, and ammonium sulfate, cotton, gold, pulp, and electrical energy in other areas.

The new enclave would be served by an integrated railroad system embracing the five provinces and having 1,419 additional kilometers of railroad track. Roads were to be more than doubled, and navigable rivers greatly improved. The three major harbors at Tsingtao, T'ang-ku, and Ch'in-huang-tao were to be enlarged and modernized.[60] A new

[59] Ibid.

[60] Minami manshū tetsudō kabushiki kaisha, chōsabu, "Kita Shina sangyō kaihatsu keikaku shiryō" [Materials on the industrial development plan for north China], in Ni-Tchū sensō shiryō henshū iinkai, *Ni-Tchū sensōshi shiryō: senryo shihai* [Historical materials on the Sino-Japanese War: The management of occupied territories], 4 vols. (Tokyo: Kawade shobō shinsha, 1975), vol. 4 (hereafter *NTSS* 4), pp. 283–86.

central bank must issue a standard currency and peg it to the yen. Finally, a large capital fund had to be created to develop this modern economic enclave.

Organizing the Modern Economic Enclave in North China

Between 1936 and 1938, Japanese investment in China increased from ¥1.1 billion to ¥1.8 billion. In 1938, around 38 percent of that investment went to mining and industry, 27 percent to finance, 19 percent to commerce, and the remainder to transport and communications, real estate, public utilities, agriculture and fisheries, and other activities.[61] The Japanese had invested 60 percent, or ¥1.0 billion, in north China alone, with 37 percent going to central China and only 1.0 and 1.3 percent, respectively, to south China and Mongolia and Sinkiang.[62] Thus, although Sino-Japanese relations had worsened in these three years, Japanese investment in China had increased by over 60 percent, with around three-fifths of the increase flowing into north China.

Between January 1938 and March 1939, the Special Affairs Bureau of the Japanese military instructed the North China General Affairs Research Office to draft a comprehensive nine-year plan to increase the output of iron and steel, coal, alumina, fuel, and electricity.[63] Throughout 1938, the North China General Affairs Research Office held numerous conferences to plan the increase of raw and processed materials exports to Japan.[64] The nine-year plan contained some ambitious goals: coal production to be boosted from 12.8 million tons in 1938 to 56 million tons in 1945; the 3 million tons of coal exported to Japan in 1938 to be increased to 23 million tons in 1945, or about twice the total coal produced in north China in 1938; iron ore production to be raised from 483,000 tons in 1938 to 2.7 million tons; and iron ore exports to rise from 83,000 tons in 1938 to 1.3 million tons.[65] Similar ambitious targets were set for steel, salt, cotton, and other products. These industries were to be developed by a large-scale, quasi-public holding company, called the North China Development Joint-Stock Company, which ultimately supervised and coordinated more than two dozen private companies.

[61] On the development of Tientsin and Ts'ingtao harbors, see Matsuzaki Yūjirō, *Hoku-Shi keizai kaihatsuron* [Essays on the economic development of north China] (Tokyo: Daiyamondosha, 1940), pp. 6–14.

[62] NTSS 4:284–85.

[63] Ibid., pp. 288–99.

[64] Ibid., p. 371. See also Kita Shina kaihatsu kabushiki kaisha, jikakubu, *Kita Shina kaihatsu jigyō no gaiken* [An Outline of north China developmental tasks] (n.p., 1941).

[65] Ibid., p. 319.

The company's head office, comprising a general affairs department and a management department, was in Tokyo. Its Peking branch office had a general affairs department and a development office with six sections: transportation, industry, resources, soil survey, physical and chemical experimentation, and northwest China affairs. The allowable capital fund was ¥350 million, with half coming from the Japanese government and half from the private sector. The actual paid-in capital came to ¥99.3 million yen, of which almost half (¥43.7 million) came from the private sector and the remainder from the government. This total was realized by the sale of seven million shares, priced at fifty yen per share. The new company's president was Ōtani Son'yu, a person of high social standing in Japan and a member of the famous Nishi Honganji sect.[66] By December 1940 the company had already employed 669 Japanese as managers, and by late December 1938, it already controlled nineteen companies employing 39,080 Japanese and 163,000 Chinese throughout north China. By the end of 1940, the number had increased to thirty companies (see table 5.6 for a breakdown of projects, workers hired, capital invested, and return on capital stock).

In late 1940 another eight companies were operating in the region, especially in Shansi, to mine coal and iron ore for the Japanese military and export to Japan. The SMR, the North China Development Joint-Stock Company, and Japanese financial conglomerates invested capital and supplied technical manpower and equipment to these companies. The Kō-Chū Company was a Japanese financial conglomerate that operated as many as thirteen coal mines in north China; in 1939, it exported 4.1 million tons of coal to Japan.

The Japanese Economic Enclave in North China after 1937

The Japanese military machine that rolled into Shansi province soon after the Lukouchiao Incident on July 7, 1937, occupied T'aiyuan, Yangch'uan, and other key cities by November 9 and controlled the key railroad lines like the T'aiyuan-Shihchiachuang trunk line. The Shansi provincial warlord Yen Hsi-shan fled to southern Shansi, and the Communists were building their base areas in remote parts of the province, thereby leaving the Japanese free to control the railroads, roads, and mines formerly built by Yen Hsi-shan's administration. Within a year or so, the Japanese controlled nine coal mines, five iron and steel manu-

[66] Ibid., p. 373. Ōtani Son'yu was born in Kyoto in 1886, educated at Shinshū Daigaku (after 1922, Ōtani Daigaku), affiliated with Honganji Temple in Kyoto, and graduated as a priest. During the Russo-Japanese War he was the section chief in charge of the Liaotung Peninsula. He later traveled to China, America, and Europe. He was elected to the House of Peers and served until 1937, when he joined the Konoye cabinet for one year.

TABLE 5.6
Subsidiary Private Companies of the North China Development Joint-Stock Company
(capitalization figures expressed as in thousands of yen)

	Date Created	Primary Functions	Japanese Labor Force	Total Allowed Capital	Paid-in Capital	Dividend Rate (percentage)
Kō-Chū	5/5/39	Trade with Japan	2,200	10,000	10,000	6
North China Transport	4/17/39	Railroad management	29,495 (73,389 Chinese)	300,000	239,700	0
T'angku Transport	2/24/37	Manage port of T'angku and repair ships	101 (2,435 Chinese)	6,000	6,000	6
Tsingtao Harbor	9/23/38	Storage	420 (488 Chinese)	2,000	2,000	6
Ka-hoku Wireless and Telephone	7/31/38	Wireless and telephone communication	2,430 (4,033 Chinese)	35,000	20,500	6
North China Electrical, Ltd.	2/1/40	Generating and transmitting electricity	512 (2,723 Chinese)	100,000	49,750	5
Tientsin Electrical, Ltd.	8/10/37	"	—	8,000	4,000	?
Chi-tung Electrical, Ltd.	12/8/37	"	—	3,000	750	?
Chefoo Electrical, Ltd.	6/15/38	"	15 (117 Chinese)	2,000	1,200	6
Chinan Electrical, Ltd.	1/1/40	Electricity and electrical machinery and parts	44 (348 Chinese)	4,000	2,000	8
Mongolia-Sinkiang Electrical, Ltd.	5/27/38	Electricity and electrical machinery	402 (348 Chinese)	18,000	18,000	4
Chiao-ao Electrical, Ltd.	12/40	"	103 (531 Chinese)	8,000	8,000	12
Ta-t'ung Coal	1/10/40	Coal extraction and marketing	606 (6,822 Chinese)	40,000	30,000	12
Ching-hsing Coal, Ltd.	7/22/40	"	151 (246 Chinese)	30,000	20,100	—

TABLE 5.6 Continued

	Date Created	Primary Functions	Japanese Labor Force	Total Allowed Capital	Paid-in Capital	Dividend Rate (percentage)
North China Coal Distribution, Ltd.	10/30/40	Sale and export of coal	482	20,000	10,000	—
Meng-ching Ore Production and Distribution, Ltd.	12/20/40	Purchase and distribution of coal	—	2,000	500	—
Shantung Mining	5/12/23	Coal mining and distribution	23	5,000	2,250	—
Lung-yen Iron Ore	7/26/39	Mining and sale of iron ore	249 (3,199 Chinese)	20,000	13,945	0
North China Alumina Mining	12/9/39	Mining and sale of alumina	99 (163 Chinese)	5,000	3,800	6
North China Gold Mining	4/9/38	Gold mining	6	4,000	4,000	0
North China Salt, Ltd.	8/20/39	Salt production and distribution	316 (198 Chinese)	25,000	16,250	5
Far East Chemical Industry	3/5/38	Chemical processing of salt and brine	27 (22 Chinese)	3,000	3,000	—
North China Cotton	3/19/38	Storage and sale of cotton; sale of other agricultural products	38 (152 Chinese)	3,000	1,500	5
Shantung Electrical	2/14/41	Mining and sale of coal	—	8,000	5,000	—
Chung-hsing Coal Mining	11/27/40	Supplying coal to military	—	2,240	—	—
Liu-ch'uan Coal Mining	"	"	—	600	—	20
Ta-wen Coal Mining	"	"	—	490	—	20
Tzu-hsien Coal Mining	"	"	—	1,080	—	20
Chiao-tso Coal Mining	"	"	—	1,050	—	20
Shansi Coal Mining	"	"	—	2,460	—	20
Shih-ching-shan Iron Ore and Steel Mfg.	11/29/40	Supplying iron and steel to military	—	8,645	—	—
Shansi Iron and Steel Mfg.	11/27/40	"	—	5,799	—	—

Source: Ni-tchū sensōshi shiryō: senryō shihai, vol. 4, pp. 371–543, and statistical table insert.

facturing companies, five cotton spinning factories, five flour mills, eight electrical generating companies, eight chemical processing plants, two paper mills, and eight other factories.[67] All of these factories were controlled by affiliates of the North China Development Joint-Stock Company.[68]

The Okura and Kō-Chū companies owned and operated most of the coal mines and iron and steel works in Shansi. Okura was a major investor in the Shansi Coal Mining Company and continued to operate that company even after it became part of the North China Development Joint-Stock Company. On December 20, 1938, representatives of the Okura and Kō-Chū companies signed an agreement to operate the coal mines of Yangch'uang.[69] Okura greatly increased its investments in Shansi province projects, from ¥1.6 million in 1939 to ¥3.8 million in 1943.[70] Its expenditures for operating all its Shansi enterprises rose from ¥1.6 million in 1939 to ¥11.1 million in 1941, which still allowed it a modest surplus of around ¥1 million.[71] By the war's end, the Japanese enclave in Shansi had increased coal and iron ore production far above prewar levels.

Developments in Shansi were replicated elsewhere in north China as the Japanese companies increased the production of basic raw materials. But after 1941, shortages of labor, machinery, and other inputs worsened.[72] In spite of these scarcities, however, Japanese companies redoubled their efforts to increase the output of coking coal, salt, soda ash, caustic soda, and iron ore (see table 5.7). The Japanese military placed high priority on production of these items and made every effort to keep the railway system operating. They posted guards and mobilized gangs of coolie workers to repair tracks and bridges when guerrillas damaged or destroyed them. Not only was the railway well maintained until 1945, but freight and passenger traffic on the system even increased. Roughly 60 percent of all railroad cars continuously operated during this period. The Japanese worked particularly hard to keep traffic moving and not let it pile up in the yards. When a team of thirty-five Japanese experts visited north China in April 1944 to survey mines, factories, railroads, and the like in the Japanese economic enclave, they reported that labor had become scarce, machines and parts were deteri-

---

[67] Okura zaibatsu kenkyūkai, *Okura zaibatsu no kenkyū: Okura to tairiku* [Studies of the Okura financial conglomerate: Okura and mainland China] (Tokyo: Chikafuji Shuppansha, 1982), pp. 240–41.

[68] Ibid., pp. 242–43.

[69] Ibid., p. 245.

[70] Ibid., pp. 250–51.

[71] Ibid., p. 255.

[72] Ibid., p. 257.

TABLE 5.7
Resource and Commodity Production and Railway Traffic in Japan's North China Economic Enclave (tons unless otherwise noted)

	Soda Ash	Caustic Soda	Salt	Salt Supplied to Japan	Coking Coal	Iron Ore	Iron Ore Supplied to Japan
1938	12,731	—	—	—	—	—	—
1939	24,945	1,976	1,067,600	393,300	10,925	—	—
1940	36,074	3,299	857,900	659,100	12,658	120,000	24,000
1941	39,212	4,085	1,498,600	736,400	14,692	136,000	72,000
1942	39,664	4,208	1,432,700	934,300	14,738	171,000	70,000
1943	30,902	3,286	1,698,000	956,800	13,643	489,000	63,000
1944	—	—	2,024,200[a]	1,110,000[a]	16,620[a]	1,138,000[a]	200,000[a]

	Railway Freight Traffic	Railway Passenger Traffic (persons)	Railway Personnel (persons)	Japanese Railway Personnel (percentage)
1938	—	—	81,183	24
1939	6,837,000	29,615	101,560	27
1940	8,393,000	40,231	112,022	27
1941	9,655,000	38,904	129,202	28
1942	10,920,000	56,500	140,004	27
1943	12,089,000	85,187	144,823	27
1944	14,511,000[b]	—	145,000[c]	25

Source: Hoku-Shi Mōkyō sangyō shisatsudan hōkokusho: for cols. 1 and 2, p. 303; for cols. 3 and 4, p. 309; for col. 5, pp. 227–29; for cols. 6 and 7, pp. 159–60; for col. 8, p. 80; for col. 9, p. 83; for cols. 10 and 11, p. 86.
[a]Planned.
[b]Incomplete.
[c]Estimate.

orating and in scarce supply, railway and other transport services were running down, and more efficient use of electrical energy was needed if planned targets were to be achieved.[73] But this same report stated that the economic enclave continued to perform fairly well and was not about to collapse soon.[74]

Unlike the modern enclave economy of Manchukuo—built around manufacturing, transport, and energy production—north China's modern enclave economy consisted mainly of extractive industries and remained viable until almost the end of the war. These industries depended mainly on a large, unskilled Chinese labor force and the maintenance of railway transport. The Japanese companies managing the industries were able to sustain their activities in much the same way as in Manchukuo at the same time.

CONCLUSION

In Manchukuo and north China between 1931 and 1945, the Japanese created a modern economic enclave organized by holding companies that supervised many private companies. Using the formula of "one enterprise for one industry," the Japanese military used state regulation and supervision to guide these private enterprises to build a new military-industrial complex in isolation from the traditional and treaty-port economies of northeast and north China. The Japanese military protected this modern economic enclave through special laws that endowed Japanese enterprises with the right to contract with other enterprises in Japan, Manchukuo, and north China.

The Japanese military, assisted by the SMR and the Japanese government, drew up two five-year economic plans for Manchukuo after 1937, and a nine-year economic plan for north China, stipulating the output of goods to be sent to Japan and used within the region. After 1941, severe inflation, shortage of skilled workers, scarcity of machinery and parts, continual breakdowns in the transportation system, and other difficulties made it impossible for Manchukuo to achieve its goals. Even so, this remarkable Japanese economic mobilization effort in northeast and north China shifted the center of gravity of industry on the Chinese mainland from the east-central provinces to the north. Within only a decade, Japanese planners and publicly sponsored private companies had greatly increased modern production capabilities in coal, iron ore, steel, chemicals, machine tools, and the other products. In

[73] Dai Tōashō, *Hoku-Shi Mōkyō sangyō shisatsudan hōkokusho* [An observation team's report on industries in north China and the Mongolian border region] (n.p., May 1944), table 7. This report was listed as top secret.

[74] Ibid., pp. 10–14.

north China this modern enclave even maintained high utilization rates and increased output until 1943–44 when inflation and wartime influence took their toll.

Japan's modern enclave economy in northeast and north China represented a new pattern of state-initiated economic development in the twentieth century that had some similarities with the planned economies of the Soviet Union and Eastern European nations but also significant differences. Northeast and north China resembled the Soviet-style economies in that state organs designed and implemented periodic input and output plans for the economy, and a bureaucracy regulated modern industries and their enterprises. But there were three fundamental differences: the state empowered large-scale modern corporations or joint stock companies to manage one or more industries; this new type of organization represented a mixture of public and private property rights that enabled state resources to be merged with private enterpreneurship, modern technology, and financial capital; and finally, these large-scale companies had considerable authority over their allocation of resources and pricing.

The modern enclave economy created by the Japanese military and bureaucracy was a new phenomenon created by a powerful authoritarian regime in the age of twentieth-century imperialism. It seems to have been a special type of economic organization especially suited to those twentieth-century states that exercised enormous power over their citizens and imposed their will on their client states or puppet regimes. It was not a logical economic development stage beyond the great power–colony relationship of the late nineteenth and early twentieth centuries, to which Japanese colonialism originally conformed. Instead, the modern enclave economy was a type of economic organization uniquely suited for regimes ruled by a single party or by militarists who greatly valued modern technology for building an advanced military complex.

CHAPTER 6

The Yen Bloc, 1931–1941

Takafusa Nakamura

When the world economy fragmented into different monetary blocs in the 1930s, Japan responded by establishing a monetary bloc of its own. This economic institution facilitated the expansion of Japanese imperialism into northeast and north China, to integrate those regional economies with Japan's economy. After 1931, the Japanese yen and Chinese yuan currencies used in Manchukuo and north China were convertible on a one-to-one basis. After 1937, however, Japanese military expansion into central and south China did not include extending the yen bloc to those vast areas. This chapter describes how and why Japan was able to impose the yen bloc only on northeast and north China but nowhere else.

The formation of this yen bloc must be placed in the context of the international monetary environment of the early 1930s. By the mid-1930s, the gold standard for the world economy had collapsed. Beginning in the summer of 1931, the gold reserves of many countries had become depleted because of the Austrian and German financial panics. On September 21, 1931, the Bank of England suspended convertibility of the pound to gold, a decision quickly extended to all British territories and dominions except South Africa. After an eighty-day struggle to uphold the gold standard, in early December 1931 Tokyo abandoned it. The United States, under Roosevelt's New Deal policies, suspended the convertibility of the dollar to gold in April 1933 (although convertibility was reinstated at depreciated parity in early 1934). In 1935, Belgium, France, the Netherlands, and other gold bloc countries were compelled to abandon convertibility. Thus, the gold-standard system, the basis of a stable international monetary regime for over a century, had collapsed.

The countries and colonies of the British Empire, along with Argentina, the Scandinavian countries, and three Baltic countries signed the Ottawa Agreement, which contained a clause allowing countries to establish bilateral tariffs. Capital transactions in the markets connected to London were already effectively denominated in sterling. The United States had intended to erect trade barriers, and its capital transactions were, in practice, also restricted to the Western Hemisphere. Meanwhile, Germany tried to expand commodity trade in the 1930s by establishing trade agreements with the Central European countries.

Japan's leaders now feared the international economy would fragment into a sterling bloc (including Scandinavia and part of South America) and a dollar bloc (North and South America, except Canada and Argentina). Therefore, they drew up plans as early as March 1932 to incorporate the newly established state of Manchukuo into a monetary bloc dominated by the yen. Before describing how that development occurred, it is useful to review Japanese monetary policy in Northeast China in an historical perspective.

Ever since the First Sino-Japanese War, many of Japan's leaders had cherished the ambition of extending Japan's empire to include the Asian continent. Japan's victory in the Russo-Japanese War had secured that country's right to control Kwantung province (Dalian and Lushun) on a leasehold basis, as well as the 495-square-kilometer zone to operate the South Manchuria Railway (SMR) line between Lushun and Changchun. The Japanese government insisted that the yen be made the official currency in these regions, authorizing the Ying-k'ou branch of the Yokohama Specie Bank to issue banknotes backed by silver yen in exchange for military scrip issued during the Russo-Japanese War.[1] The government also allowed Bank of Japan and Bank of Chōsen (Korea) notes to circulate in this area.[2] In this way, the Japanese government tried to expand its economic influence in South Manchuria, but severe fluctuations in the price of silver relative to gold made it difficult for Japanese businesses to expand their transactions. Another problem was that the Chinese preferred to use silver in their daily transactions, and the Bank of Chōsen's notes did not find great acceptance in Manchuria. For the next quarter-century, then, Japanese business had to adapt to a complex currency exchange environment in Manchuria, and the yen was one of many currencies that circulated.

ESTABLISHING THE YEN BLOC

Two important events occurred in September 1931. The Kwantung Army began occupying Manchuria on September 18 and established the Manchukuo puppet state on March 1, 1932. Then on September 21, came Britain's suspension of the convertibility of the pound as well as of gold exports. These developments did not seem to adversely affect

---

[1] Manshū chūō ginkō shi kenkyūkai, *Manshū chūō ginkō shi* [History of the Manchuria Central Bank] (Tokyo: Tōyō keizai shimpōsha, 1988), p. 34.

[2] Ibid., p. 36.

Japan's economy. Japanese cotton textile exports rapidly expanded in the early 1930s, stimulated greatly by favorable yen exchange rates, which made their prices in other currencies very cheap. But this sudden export expansion quickly caused serious trade frictions with India, the United States, and particularly Britain, whose governments soon reacted by levying tariffs aimed at reducing the purchase of Japanese goods. Frustrated by not being able to expand exports because of rising foreign trade barriers, Japan's officials and traders looked elsewhere for an export market that Japan could control and that could be integrated with Japan's colonial empire of Taiwan, Korea, South Sakhalin, Kwangtung province, and the mandated islands in Micronesia. Manchukuo was such an area; moreover, that area could supply Japan with abundant coal and iron reserves to build heavy and military industries in both Japan and Manchuria.

The first step to establish the Manchukuo monetary system was to create the Manchuria Central Bank (MCB) in Changchun on June 11, 1932. Vice Governor Kyoroku Yamanari, the former director of the Bank of Taiwan, became that bank's manager. Yamanari had acquired considerable experience handling silver money in Shanghai, and under his leadership the MCB quickly adopted a traditionalist monetary attitude in which silver served as the standard unit of account.

When the world depression began in 1929, Chinese commodity prices had not declined as was the case in the advanced countries suffering deflation, because China's market economy was on the silver standard and silver prices in the world economy were on the decline. In 1933 and after, however, the rise in the price of silver encouraged a great outflow of silver from China to world currency exchange markets like New York and London, and, as a consequence, commodity and services prices in China began to decline.

Meanwhile, Manchukuo's currency, the yuan, followed the same trend as the currencies of gold-standard nations but still appreciated relative to the yen, which had depreciated more seriously against the U.S. dollar throughout 1932. Thus, Manchukuo's yuan rose from ¥93.19 per 100 in July 1932 to ¥110 per 100 yuan in 1933. This exchange-rate fluctuation worried the officers of the Kwantung Army, who feared that Manchukuo's exports might further decline and depress the economy even more. They now proposed that the yuan be pegged to the yen at parity, hoping to reverse the region's export decline. But the Japanese government and the Bank of Japan refused to take their proposal seriously because they feared trade retaliation from Japan's major world buyers in the West.

Meanwhile, the U.S. government's implementation of a silver purchasing policy in June 1934 further raised silver prices, and the Manchukuo yuan rose even higher to ¥120 per 100 yuan. Fearful that rising silver prices would further deflate the Manchukuo economy and eager to stabilize the yuan, the Manchukuo monetary authorities made the currency inconvertible. That action finally produced a new policy when, in April 1935, the Japanese government decreed the yen and the yuan unconditionally interconvertible at parity.[3] At the same time, the yen was fixed at 1s. 2d. sterling. This new currency policy marked the incorporation of Manchukuo into the Japanese monetary empire.

These policies to form a yen bloc were formulated by the Army Ministry and the Ministry of Finance in Tokyo, but the Kwantung Army and the Japanese officials of the Manchukuo puppet regime had the responsibility of implementing them. The MCB's position to manage this new currency system received support when the Bank of Chōsen withdrew from Manchukuo and two other banks, the Shoryu Bank and the Manchuria Bank, closed their doors in December 1935, leaving the MCB totally in charge of monetary affairs in Manchukuo. But soon powerful pressures were at work to expand this yen bloc to include north China.

EXPANDING THE YEN BLOC TO NORTH CHINA

The T'ang-ku Agreement, finalized in June 1933, established a demilitarized zone, known as the War Zone, that was bounded by the Great Wall, Po-hai (the Gulf of Po-hai), and Pai-he (the Pai River). This War Zone was intended to serve as a buffer between Manchukuo and the Chinese mainland and also provide a base for the Kwantung Army to prepare its invasion of north China. When the Chinese government erected tariff barriers to protect such domestic industries as rayon, sugar, and paper, Japanese merchants in Dairen shipped their goods by sea to the War Zone's coast with the tacit approval of the Kwantung Army, and these products were then smuggled into the markets of north China.[4]

In June 1935, the Tientsin Garrison, the permanent Japanese military force located in Tientsin (north China), took advantage of an assassination in the Tientsin concession to penetrate into Hopei province. Among other things, the Tientsin Garrison demanded that the Chinese central government's Kuomintang (KMT) representatives and army personnel leave the province. After intense negotiations, the Nationalist

---

[3] It was published in November 1935.

[4] Minami Manshū tetsudō kabushiki kaisha, Tenshin shitsu, chōsabu (the author is Tamaki Nobuo), *Kito chiku no bōeki gaikyō to kanzei jijō* [A survey on foreign trade and tariffs in the Chi Tung region], February 1936; and *Kito tokushu bōeki no jitsujō* [The real state of Chi Tung special trade), June 1936.

government's General Ho Ying-ch'in accepted those terms with General Umezu Yoshijirō to conclude the Umezu-Ho Agreement. In June, Kwantung Army officers used a clash between Sung Che-yuan's army and Japanese soldiers and diplomats as a new justification to demand the withdrawal of Sung's army from Ch'a-ha-erh province. That demand, too, was accommodated in an agreement between Doihara Kenji and Ch'in Te-ch'un.

These two acts of aggression were part of a larger joint effort by the Tientsin Garrison and the Kwantung Army to create another Manchukuo in north China. Both field forces, particularly the Tientsin Garrison, tried to develop the region's resources. The Kwantung Army, for example, asked the SMR to set up a new investment company, the Hsing-chung Corporation, and, to that end, helped the SMR to finance its activities. Again, in November 1935, a new puppet government, the Chi Tung Anti-Communist Autonomy Committee, or Chi Tung government, was established in the War Zone with the assistance of both army groups. In December 1935, they helped establish another puppet regime, the Chi Ch'a Autonomy Committee, headed by Sung Chu-yuan, a north China warlord who was linked to the Nanking government. Sung survived by declaring his willingness to cooperate with Japan, but he transferred his allegiance to Nanking when Sino-Japanese relations worsened in late 1936 after the Suiyuan incident, another plot fomented by the Kwantung Army.

In Tokyo in August 1936, the Five Ministers (Prime Minister and ministers of the army, navy, foreign affairs, and finance) of the Hirota Kōki cabinet announced the "Standard for National Defense Policy." As part of this new national policy, the Army, Navy, and Foreign ministries had drafted a document called "Policies for Practices in China."[5] These policies called for the following: (1) to make north China a "special region" that would be anti-Comintern, pro-Japanese, and pro-Manchukuo; (2) to obtain resources for Japan's national defense and to expand transportation facilities accordingly; and finally, (3) at some future time to make all of China anti-Soviet and pro-Japanese. This "special region" would ultimately encompass the five provinces of north China (Hopei, Ch'a-ha-erh, Shantung, Shansi, and Honan). At the present, however, Japan was to limit its divide-and-conquer efforts to Hopei and Ch'a-ha-erh provinces. Rather than claim official sovereignty over those two provinces and thus encounter resistance from the Nanking government, Japan would control them through puppet re-

[5] Shimada Toshihiko and Inaba Masao, eds., *Gendai shi shiryō: Nitchū sensō* [Contemporary historical materials: The Sino-Japanese War], vol. 1 (Tokyo: Misuzu shobō, 1964), pp. 359–71.

gimes that also controlled finance, industry, and transportation. The Chi Ch'a and Chi Tung regimes would be active primarily in economic affairs. For example, customs tariffs should be officially attributed to the Chi Ch'a government, but a local financial institution like the Bank of Hopei would serve as a central bank to regulate monetary policy for the two territories.

This plan also recognized the need to improve the railway, harbor, and other transport infrastructures that would give the Japanese cheap access to iron ore, coking coal, salt, cotton, liquid fuel, wool, and other resources to satisfy Japan's military requirements. These many economic programs, originally drafted by the army in 1935, became Japanese national policies in the summer of 1936. But, by March 1937, the Nanking government and the Chi Ch'a government had strongly resisted Japanese expansionist aims, and Sino-Japanese relations were greatly damaged, making efforts to reach a peaceful accord impossible.

It was under these circumstances that the Bank of Chosen first began to operate in north China.[6] In May 1936, it supported the establishment of a new central bank for the Chi Tung government. The Chi Tung Bank, with a total capital of five million yen, was authorized to issue banknotes for the Chi Tung regime that would be unconditionally interconvertible with those notes issued by the Bank of Chōsen. The Bank of Chi Tung issued notes amounting to some five million yen but suspended its operations after its building was destroyed at the beginning of the Second Sino-Japanese War in July 1937.

In the Tientsin concession, the Yokohama Specie Bank and four other foreign houses issued silver-backed notes totalling around 786,000 yuan. Extensive smuggling in the Chi Tung area had increased the demand for Japanese yen, so the Bank of Chōsen resumed yen-denominated transactions in 1935 and recommended the same course to other Japanese banks.

The Nanking government, meanwhile, introduced sweeping monetary reforms of its own in November 1935, hoping to stabilize an economy that was plagued by a torrential outflow of silver coinage and massive price deflation.[7] The Nanking government decided to abandon the silver standard and adopt a managed currency system in which three major banks—the Bank of China, the Central Bank, and the Communication Bank—issued banknotes denominated in *fapi*, the new official

[6] For information on the Bank of Chōsen, see Chōsen ginkō shi kenkyūkai, *Chōsen ginkō shi* [History of the Bank of Chōsen] (Tokyo: Tōyō keizai shimpōsha, 1987), pp. 506–10.

[7] For further information, see Nozawa Yutaka, ed., *Chūgoku no heisei kaikaku to kokusai kankei* [Currency reform in China and China's international relations] (Tokyo: Tōkyō Daigaku Shuppankai, 1981).

currency. The Central Bank, which had long assisted the central government, was already on close terms with the Nanking government, but the Bank of China and the Communication Bank operated very independently. In April 1935, the Nanking government issued bonds totalling 100 million yuan to raise additional capital for all three banks to become government agencies. These banks immediately called for the withdrawal of all silver from circulation.

The British government took a keen interest in the Nanking government's monetary reforms. It sent a special mission, headed by Leith Ross, which successfully argued in favor of fixing the fapi at 1s. 2½d. That decision was significant in two ways: first, the Chinese yuan was no longer backed by silver; and second, its fixed relation to the British pound implied that Britain would recognize the new Chinese currency. Stopping in Tokyo on his way to China, Leith Ross suggested Anglo-Japanese assistance for the Chinese monetary reform, but the Japanese government, having no great sympathy for the Nanking government, rejected his proposal.[8] The Japanese military viewed the Nanking government's policy to unify the Chinese monetary system as an attempt to frustrate its plan to penetrate north China. The Tientsin Garrison then issued a statement, couched in the form of an informal interview with its chief of staff, expressing criticism of this new monetary policy, and prohibited the shipment of silver coinage to Shanghai and Nanking. Despite such interference, by the end of 1936, the Nationalist government's monetary reform had succeeded in helping to stabilize the Chinese economy and arousing nationalist fervor to oppose Japan's economic invasion in the north. As a consequence, Japan's penetration of north China encountered new resistance.

As Manchukuo increasingly became an extension of Japan proper (see the chapter by Ramon H. Myers in this volume), Japan's military activities in that region had also progressed satisfactorily. Kwantung military officers, however, still wanted to integrate Manchukuo with north China and thereby bring greater glory to themselves. They argued that Manchukuo's natural resources were insufficient to meet all of the military's requirements, especially in light of the Five-Year Plan to expand armaments and key industries that Colonel Ishiwara Kanji, chief of the Operations Division of the Japanese army's General Staff, had proposed in 1936. Ishiwara's plan had called for setting up weapons and other heavy industries in Japan and Manchukuo to expand the military's capability to resist the Soviet army. His plan envisioned very ambitious targets: automobile and steel production to be increased 2.7 times, aluminum production 4.8 times, armaments production 2.1 times, and air-

---

[8] Ibid., p. 277.

craft and military vehicle production 10 times. These ambitious targets, according to the Japanese military, could not be achieved without access to the coal, iron ore, salt, and fiber resources of north China.[9]

Military and even civilian officials also argued that north China was a region that could supply Japan with a dependable source of materials independent of the U.S. and Britain and that need not be acquired through foreign trade in a world market that was steadily contracting. The needs of Japan's military had so greatly increased Japan's imports that, by 1936, they had created an enormous balance-of-payments deficit. To resolve this crisis, the Japanese government now began to regulate imports. Expanding the yen bloc to north China in order to develop that region's natural resources could enable Japan to acquire those resources without being dependent on the acquisition of foreign exchange to buy those same resources.

China under Japanese Occupation

After the Marco Polo Bridge Incident of July 7, 1937, the Second Sino-Japanese war rapidly spread across China from Mongolia to Shanghai by August of that year. The Tientsin Garrison became part of the North China Area Army, whose intelligence bureau began to govern the areas occupied by the Japanese military.

To sever the Nanking government's control over north China, the North China Area Army organized the creation of a Chinese "Temporary Government" headed by Wang K'o-min in December 1937, which served as the puppet government over north China's three provinces of Shansi, Shantung, and Hopei. Meanwhile, the Kwantung Army had advanced into Ch'a-ha-erh and Mongolia in August and set up its own puppet "Mongolian Government" in October 1937. Then, in March 1938, the Central China Area Army occupied Shanghai and Nanking to create its own puppet government for central China, headed by Liang Hung-chih. In this way, three Japanese armies controlled separate huge territories through their individual puppet regimes.[10] Prime Minister Konoe Fumimaro announced that Japan would no longer negotiate with the Nanking government, and he expected a new Chinese central government to be established in January 1938, an idea conceived by the North China Area Army.

Each of these three Japanese-occupied territories had its own monetary system. The territories occupied by the North China Area and

[9] For these plans, see Takafusa Nakamura, *Economic Growth in Prewar Japan* (New Haven, Conn.: Yale University Press, 1983), pp. 276–85.

[10] For details of the three puppet governments, see Nakamura Takafusa, *Senji Nihon no Kakoku keizai shihai* [Japan's dominance of the Chinese economy at war] (Tokyo: Yamakawa Shuppansha, 1983), pp. 106–10.

Mongolia armies were immediately absorbed into the yen bloc. The Chinese United Reserve Bank (*Rengo Junbi Ginkō*) was established as the central bank for the north China area (Hopei, Shantung, Shansi, and northern Honan). That organization's nominal head was Wang Shih-ching, but actual control lay with a Japanese adviser group headed by Sakatani Kiichi. In the Mongolia region (including Ch'a-ha-erh and Suiyuan provinces), the Mongolia Bank was inaugurated in November 1937 under the guidance of the Manchuria Central Bank. Despite occasional difficulties, these two different monetary systems both belonged to the yen bloc, and both currencies were set at parity with the yen.[11]

In Shanghai, however, the Central China Area Army did not attempt to set up its own bank or currency but continued to employ the fapi. Thus, those areas of China north of the Chiao-Chi railway line between Lien-yun-kang and Chengchou belonged to the yen bloc, while those areas south of that line were left to the fapi, because the Shanghai banks connected with the Nanking government and the sterling bloc were considered too powerful to confront. By now, Japan had decided to regard north China as an extension of the Japanese homeland but to treat central and southern China as a foreign territory like Hongkong.

The reasons for the existence of separate monetary spheres is as follows. When the war broke out, of the two major banknotes then circulating in north China, almost 80 percent were fapi, issued by three Shanghai banks and their north China branches; another 19 percent were notes of the Bank of Hopei. Immediately, the Japanese army's Bank of Chōsen began to issue its own notes in Japanese-occupied areas: the currency in circulation soon totaled some fifty million yen. As hostilities spread, the Chinese government declared a bank holiday in order to prevent financial panic. That policy led to a severe tight-money situation, and the Bank of Chōsen's yen depreciated sharply against the fapi. The fapi, which had traded at 103 yuan per ¥100 yen before the war, rose to 88 yuan per ¥100 by the end of August 1937. The Japanese army decided to withdraw the notes of the Bank of Chōsen and to extend the circulation of the United Bank's notes. Another countermeasure Japan took to defend the yen was to designate the United Bank as the sole central bank authorized to issue banknotes. Thus, there began a long monetary battle between the yen (or United Bank note) and the fapi.

When the United Bank opened its doors, its policy to exchange its

---

[11] For establishment of the two central banks, see ibid., pp. 147–57. For more detailed analysis of these monetary struggles see Kuwano Hitoshi, *Senji tsūka kosai shiron* [On the history of wartime monetary operations] (Tokyo: Hōsei Daigaku Shuppankyoku, 1965), especially chaps. 3 and 4.

currency for other notes was as follows. The bank's notes would be exchanged with the yen at parity. Fapi issued by banks in southern China would not be honored after the first three months, but that deadline would be extended to twelve months for notes of the northern region, including those of the branches of the three central banks. During that transition period, the "northern fapi" would be exchanged at parity with the United Bank's own currency. The Japanese army considered that the Nanking government's economic power depended on the strength of the fapi, which also was supported by Britain and the United States. If depreciation of the fapi exchange rate occurred, then inflation would ensue; but if the United Bank's currency appreciated, that would weaken the fapi and perhaps weaken or even destroy the Nanking government.

The Japanese expectations of an improved yen-fapi exchange rate were not fulfilled, and Chinese in the occupied areas continued to hoard fapi instead of holding the United Bank's notes and yen. When the fapi declined to ninepence sterling in June 1938, the Union Bank's notes declined as well in response to new Nanking government exchange regulations. This development occurred because the latter's notes were convertible only with the fapi and the yen, and foreign remittances to hinterland China had to be converted from the Union Bank's notes into fapi. In fact, at this time there was no way to exchange Union Bank notes for fapi except through the foreign banks in the Tientsin Concession, because foreign-exchange transactions vis-à-vis the yen were strictly regulated. These conditions created an exchange-rate arbitrage opportunity between Shanghai and Tientsin, and speculators made windfall profits from this spread of exchange rates by trading Bank of Chōsen notes in Shanghai for fapi in Tianjin. For example, ¥1 = 1 United Bank yuan = 1 fapi, but 1 traded at 1s. 2d., whereas 1 fapi traded at 8d.–9d.[12]

This curious exchange rate system had come about as a result of Japan's consistent trade imbalances in the mid-1930s. Japan had always enjoyed a surplus with the yen bloc but experienced deficits with other trade partners. For example, Japan ran a ¥263 million surplus with the yen bloc in 1936 but a ¥534 million deficit with its other trade partners; in 1937, that relationship was ¥353 million versus ¥962 million; and in 1938, ¥601 million versus ¥574 million. In 1937, as deficits began to expand because of increased imports of industrial raw materials and munitions, the Japanese government instituted more rigid restrictions on foreign trade and currency exchange. Thus, although the yen appreciated against the fapi, it was impossible to exchange the United Bank's notes into foreign currencies via the Japanese yen.

[12] Ibid., pp. 39–42.

There were other reasons for the weakness of the United Bank's currency. The bank's notes circulated only in Japanese-occupied cities and in limited areas along Japanese-controlled railway lines. In the areas held by the Nanking government and the Communists, however, other currencies prevailed, including the fapi and notes from old northern banks and the Communist army. The cool reception of United Bank's notes was due partly to its parity with the depreciated fapi and partly because of the expanding issue of United Bank notes. Under the terms of the special "Azuke-ai Keiyaku" contract, the Bank of Chōsen had agreed to provide large sums of money to the United Bank for military needs. The contract stipulated that the two banks would simultaneously deposit equivalent sums in each other's accounts. In practice, however, the United Bank's deposit in the Bank of Chōsen was not drawn upon, while the funds the Bank of Chōsen deposited with the United Bank were immediately withdrawn and spent by the Japanese army.[13] This mechanism inevitably increased the supply of the United Bank's notes, which expanded by 450 percent between 1938 and 1941. All these developments helped to generate severe inflation in north China in 1938 and 1939.

The parity of the United Bank's note with the fapi remained in effect until mid-1940, as a means of controlling trade between northern and central China.

JAPANESE EXPORTS TO THE YEN BLOC

In the 1930s, the Chinese government rapidly increased its tariff rates in order to reclaim tariff autonomy, protect China's infant industries, and exclude Japanese goods. These new tariff barriers also hindered trade between the Japanese enclaves and the Chinese mainland. Japan's exports to China fell precipitously, and Japanese businessmen, already squeezed by the world economic crisis, began to complain to their home government.

The Kwantung Army had always wanted to destabilize north China's polity by first destabilizing its economy. To that end, the Kwantung Army encouraged smuggling by Japanese, Manchurian, and Chinese merchants from Kwangtung into the Chi Tung area on the coast of the War Zone, and that smuggling activity greatly increased after mid-1933.

After the Marco Polo Bridge Incident, Japan's Ministry of Finance and Ministry of Commerce and Industries imposed regulations to protect Japan's balance of payments and to expand war production at home. Those regulations directly controlled the manufacture, consumption, stocking, and exchange of imported goods for private use. The government wanted to acquire surplus dollars and pounds to pay

[13] On the "Asuke-ai keiyaku" contract, see ibid., pp. 26–27.

for the imports of strategic materials, including iron ore, oil, rubber, and rare metals, that came almost exclusively from the United States and the British Commonwealth.

Japanese exporters, however, preferred to maintain a favorable trade balance with the yen bloc, where constantly rising prices, spurred by rampant inflation, made their business exceedingly profitable. The yen-yuan parity allowed Japanese merchants to transfer their gains to Japan.

Economic regulation of the yen bloc increased after Japan's Ministry of Commerce and Industry issued the "Act for Export Regulation to Manchukuo, Kwantung Province, and China," which it had been possible to pass because of the new National Mobilization Law. This act required that exports to the yen bloc areas be approved by government-established associations to control the total value and volume of various exports and allocate them among their constituents. Increasingly, it proved impossible for the Japanese government to control the profit-oriented activities of exporters to the yen bloc, and Japanese exports to those areas continued to grow.[14]

In 1940–41, Japan's export regulations also served to increase north China's imports from the United States and the British Empire. The region's total exports also grew from ¥803 million in 1939, to ¥1,271 million in 1940, to ¥1,429 million in 1941. Of that total, the United States and Britain shared 25 percent, 31 percent, and 41 percent in those years, respectively; the yen bloc, however, received only 62 percent, 51 percent, and 45 percent. The difference can, in part, be explained as a result of the exchange mechanism in the Tientsin market between the United Bank's yuan and the fapi. Because the rigorous controls over north China's economy had boosted the yuan against the fapi after 1940, imports valued in fapi were more profitable. Moreover, the fapi was convertible into dollars and pounds. Therefore, imports from the United States and the British Empire areas continued until the outbreak of the Pacific War. During the Pacific War, however, many consumer goods were also secretly imported into Shanghai, although it is not clear how that occurred. Yet the people who visited Shanghai in those war years remember abundant goods circulating in markets.

JAPANESE IMPORTS FROM THE YEN BLOC

In August 1936, as already noted, Japan had expected Manchuria and north China to become major suppliers of strategic natural resources, but Manchuria's riches never matched the expectations of Japanese planners. For example, all efforts to find oil ended in failure, and the iron ore deposits of Anshan and Kung-chang-ling, while abundant, were

[14] For details, see Nakamura, *Senji Nihon,* pp. 222–25.

of low grade. But Japan still wanted to establish industrial and weapons factories on the broad Manchurian plain. Therefore, an SMR subsidiary, the Shōwa Steel Company, developed a process to extract pig iron and, secondarily, steel products from low-grade ore; some surplus pig iron was then exported to Japan, while the steel produced was used almost exclusively for construction projects in Manchukuo. But expanding Manchurian industrialization also prevented the export of Fushun coal to Japan. To deal with such problems, the military prepared the 1936 Five-Year Plan, calling for Manchuria's heavy industry to account for 30 percent of total Japanese production, with the other 70 percent coming from Japan proper. In this plan, the production of synthetic oil was an important strategic target, because the yen bloc's petroleum was almost nil. One factory was eventually constructed to recover petroleum from the oil shales of Fushun. But all of these efforts were expensive and wasteful of Japan's scarce resources of capital and skilled labor.

Japanese hopes to extract resources—coal (both as a fuelstock and for liquefaction), iron ore, salt, cotton, and wool—from north China also proved unrealistic. For instance, the Japanese Army had expected the Lung Yan iron ore mine in Mongolia to contain considerable ore, but in reality its deposits were poor.

Even so, beginning in autumn 1937, Japanese business firms competed to expand their activities into the newly occupied territory. Enterprises whose workers had left for the war were operated by the North China Area Army, which planned to organize a national company to run five primary industries: cotton spinning, grain milling, wool weaving, brewing, and sugar production. That plan received official sanction from the Japanese Cabinet as the North China Development Corporation (NCDC), and, in November 1938, the Diet authorized its formation as a holding company for numerous railway, telephone and telegraph, coal, electric power, salt, and iron enterprises (see also the chapter by Ramon H. Myers in this volume).[15]

Although northern China's iron ore resources were rather meager, coal and salt were abundant. Coal deposits of the Ta T'ung mine in Shansi and the British-run K'ai Luan mine in Hopei were indispensable sources of coking coal for Japan. Hopei and Shantung had other promising coal deposits as well. Six NCDC subsidiaries were created to manage the six largest coal mines, except for the K'ai Luan mine and the Ta T'ung mine in Mongolia, which the SMR operated under the direction of the Kwantung Army.[16]

Coal production in north China declined radically when the war

---

[15] For establishment and activities of the NCDC, see ibid., pp. 135–46.
[16] Ibid., pp. 181–83.

broke out, because of the departure of workers and managers, the stoppage of railway traffic, and the war itself. To deal with these difficulties, the North China Area Army took over the mining of coal for export to Japan. Although wartime coal shipments from Manchuria to Japan declined, total coal exports from China increased. North China's coal production quickly rose from 13.9 million tons in 1939 to 25.1 million tons in 1942, and coal exports to Japan rose from 1.7 million tons in 1938 to 2.9 million tons in 1939 and 4.5 million tons in 1942.[17] As part of its effort to accomplish this doubling of prewar coal production levels, between October 1939 and February 1940 the North China Area Army commandeered 60 percent of the railway capacity that had carried wheat and other foods to Peking and Tientsin. Meanwhile, the army also allocated a portion of its supplies to keep food prices in large cities from skyrocketing. Most of Japan's coal supply came from the K'ai Luan mine, which escaped war damage and continued to produce as usual. The Kai-Luan mine, from which Japan imported over 600,000 tons per year between 1939 and 1944, remained Japan's preeminent supplier, but because its resources were insufficient for all of Japan's needs, a program was initiated to expand transport infrastructure, including the construction of new railway lines and harbor improvements at T'ang-ku.

Salt had been produced along the Hopei and Shantung coasts since antiquity, but the Chinese government forbade its export. When the war interrupted Japan's importation of salt from Africa by soda industries, the Japanese turned to north China's salt. This and other efforts by Japan to obtain more resources from the yen bloc naturally meant reducing the Chinese people's standard of living.

Forming the Quasi-Yen Bloc

Japan continued to expand the yen bloc until the outbreak of the Pacific War. Inspired by Germany's conquest of France in May–June 1940, the Japanese military was eager to advance into Southeast Asia, where the navy coveted the oilfields of the Netherlands East Indies and the army wanted a base at Hanoi in French Indochina. The military chose to act swiftly, lest Axis victories in Europe induce Germany to claim Southeast Asia as well. Convinced that the continued flow of U.S. and British materiel and economic aid would enable the Nanking government to continue its struggle against Japan, the Japanese military determined to interdict the supply routes connecting southwest China with French Indochina and Burma. Japanese control of Hanoi quickly blocked the route from Southeast Asia. Japan's advance into French Indochina, how-

[17] Ibid., p. 313.

ever, represented both a decisive step toward the Pacific War and an extension of the yen bloc into Southeast Asia. Therefore, in the summer of 1940, Britain agreed to open the Burma Road for three months, hoping that such military pressure from South Asia would provide some relief to Nationalist China.

In the early 1940s, Southeast Asia also replaced Korea and Taiwan as Japan's main rice supplier. Rice shortages in Japan's major cities had caused serious unrest in late 1939, because available stocks in Tokyo were sufficient for only a few days' demand. Poor harvests in the colonies, especially in Korea, where increased domestic consumption also contributed to the supply shortage, had produced these low reserves. Japan's own domestic consumption had been outpacing its production since the 1920s. In previous years, the imports of Indica-variety rice from Southeast Asia had declined because of Japanese dietary preferences for rice produced in their colonies, but when Korean and Taiwanese supplies proved inadequate, imports from French Indochina, Thailand, and Burma again increased.

With almost all of its foreign-exchange reserves used for urgently needed strategic imports from the U.S. and Britain, Japan found it more difficult to pay for its rice imports. In late 1940 an agreement was reached between the Yokohama Specie Bank and the Bank of Java that would enable rice payments to be made in yen. The agreement stipulated the following: (1) The Specie Bank would open a guilder account with the Bank of Java, and vice versa; (2) each bank would provide the required funds to the other according to existing deposits; and (3) when necessary, account balances would be offset against each other. In effect, this agreement allowed Japan's trade with the Netherlands East Indies to be settled in yen, which benefited the East Indies, then running a trade deficit with Japan.[18] This pact, however, also had the effect of partially incorporating the East Indies into the yen bloc.

In July 1941 the Specie Bank concluded a similar agreement with the Bank of Indochina, with the crucial difference that Japan ran a consistent, unilateral deficit with French Indochina. Under the agreement, Japanese rice imports were to be paid for in Indochinese currency, the piastre, to be issued by the Bank of Indochina.[19] The latter's yen ac-

---

[18] "Shokin ran-in ginkō kan kyōtei yōryō (Fu Okura jikan dan)" [Summary of the contract between Yokohama Specie Bank and the Dutch Indochina Bank, with an address by the vice minister of finance], December 24, 1940, in Nihon Ginkō, Chōsashitsu, *Nihon Kin-yū kinyūshi shiryō Shōwa hen* [Collection of materials on the history of Japanese finance, Shōwa period) 34 (1973): 335–36.

[19] "Nihon futsuin ginkō kan kyōtei yōkō seiritsu ni kanshi okura jikan dan" (Address by the vice minister of finance on the conclusion of the outline of a contract between Japan and French Indochina), 4 July 1941, ibid., pp. 336–37.

count at the Yokohama Specie Bank, however, was never drawn upon. French Indochina signed this unfavorable agreement only because of Japanese military pressure. Japanese imports of Thai rice were paid in credits to the Specie Bank from a sydicate of Thai banks.[20] By these money exchange arrangements, imperial Japan guaranteed a stable source of rice for its people.

SOME TENTATIVE CONCLUSIONS

The yen bloc, first created in Manchuria and north China, was partly extended into French Indochina and the Netherlands East Indies. This monetary empire, however, was still fragile and reflected Japan's economic vulnerability. A patchwork of institutional agreements only enabled Japan to acquire the resources it needed.

Although occupied by the Japanese military, central and southern China managed to resist Japanese military and economic control because of popular support for the Nationalist government's fapi currency, issued between 1937 and 1941. Backed by the dollar and the pound, the fapi remained strong even after the Pacific War broke out.

By 1942, the Japanese military had rapidly occupied an extensive area stretching from Burma to the Solomon Islands, but those territories were never really integrated into the yen bloc, and they retained their own currencies. The Japanese military scrip issued in those areas after the outbreak of hostilities never gained wide currency, as no provision had been made for direct exchange or for convertibility with the yen. Finally, because Japanese financial policymakers were unable to deal with the serious inflation that their military scrip introduced into newly occupied areas, the yen bloc remained confined to the areas that Japan had brought under its control before the Pacific War began in late 1941.

[20] "Yokohama Shōkin Ginkō no taikoku ginkō dan yori no shakkan seiritsu ni kanshi Tōkyoku dan" (Address by the authority on the conclusion of the credit contract between the Bank Group of Thailand and the Yokohama Specie Bank), 1 August 1941, ibid., p. 337.

PART III

Japan's Wartime Empire and Southeast Asia

CHAPTER 7

Nanshin: The "Southward Advance," 1931–1941, as a Prelude to the Japanese Occupation of Southeast Asia

Mark R. Peattie

Historians have now generally come to identify the entry of Japanese military power into Southeast Asia in 1940 and 1941 as one of the most immediate causes of the Pacific War, a conflict which, in turn, led to the brief Japanese interregnum in the region between the prewar Western colonial order and the postwar emergence of independent Southeast Asian states.[1] The study of the complexities—diplomatic, political, economic, and military—of the emerging confrontation between Japan and the West over Southeast Asia in the two years before the Pacific War has been the focus of a considerable monographic literature. One of its central problems has been the question of causation and motivation. Some scholars have been content to see the apparently sudden Japanese interest in Southeast Asia in the summer of 1940 as completely opportunistic, viewing it as the result of a swift and cataclysmic change in the pattern of global power brought about by the German blitzkrieg in Europe: by drastically weakening the authority of the European colonial powers over their Southeast Asian colonial possessions, it left those territories vulnerable to the play of Japanese ambition and pressure. Yet, in the past several decades, others have begun to push back the chronological threshold of Japanese ambitions in Southeast Asia and, while eschewing any Japanese "plot" or long-range plan for hegemony there, have begun to trace the Japanese interest in Southeast Asia as far back as the Meiji period.

Early in this century, the Japanese themselves had given a name to this interest—the *nanshin* or "southward advance"—a vague and polemical term in prewar Japan. For the advocates of the prewar *nanshin*

I should like to acknowledge the assistance of the Joint Committee on Japanese Studies of the American Council of Learned Socities, the Social Science Research Council, and the University of Massachusetts at Boston in the research for this paper.

[1] Harry Benda, *The Japanese Interregnum in Southeast Asia* (New Haven, Conn.: Yale University Press, 1968).

ron (the "southward advance concept") it embodied the idea that, by virtue of historical ties dating back to the sixteenth century, of economic necessity, and of its place as the moral exemplar of Asia, Japan had a destiny to advance its influence toward the *Nan'yō*—the "South Seas"—an equally nebulous term which, after World War I, came to be thought of as including all of what is now Southeast Asia, Melanesia, and Micronesia.[2] Utterly discredited after the collapse of Japanese ambitions in World War II, both the term *nanshin* and the study of Japan's prewar role in Southeast Asia lay essentially discarded for a quarter of a century. Then, in the mid-1970s, seeking to understand the historical background to the current difficulties of Japan in its relations with Southeast Asian peoples, the Japanese political scientist Yano Tōru took up the *nanshin ron* in several popular but seminal works, not as an ideological prescription, but as a context within which to identify policies, pressures, institutions, and personalities—mostly private but to an extent governmental—that marked an evolving Japanese interest in Southeast Asia.[3] Over the past decade and a half a growing number of scholars, Japanese and Western, have taken up the topic. Some have critiqued and refined Yano's somewhat hasty treatment, while others have struck out on their own to assay what the southward advance meant in concrete terms, to test the influence it had as a concept in Japanese business and foreign policy, to trace its historical evolution, to periodize it, and to dissect the motivations and ideas of its prewar advocates. Not surprisingly, a good deal of this scholarship has focused on the prewar decade closest to the outbreak of the Pacific War, seeking in the particularities of the Japanese *nanshin* indications of attitudes, interest, and intent that were to influence official policies during Japan's wartime occupation of Southeast Asia.

This chapter brings much of this specialized scholarship together in

---

[2] A further word of explanation is necessary concerning Japanese geographic terms relevant to the subject of this paper. While the "South Seas" eventually came to include all the regions I have mentioned here, it could at times have a more restrictive meaning, centering largely on the former German islands of Micronesia which Japan was awarded as a League of Nations mandate in 1922. I have myself used that definition in my own treatment of the Japanese rule in Micronesia, *Nan'yō: The Rise and Fall of the Japanese in Micronesia, 1885–1945* (Honolulu: University of Hawaii Press, 1988). In the 1920s the Japanese began to make a distinction between the "Inner South Seas" (*uchi nan'yō*) which comprised their mandate in Micronesia and the "Outer South Seas" (*soto nan'yō*) conceived as occupying all of Southeast Asia, Melanesia, and even Australia and New Zealand. Finally, in the 1930s, official Japanese documents and public pronouncements began to use the term "Southern Regions" (*Nampō*).

[3] See Yano Tōru, *"Nanshin" no keifu* [The genealogy of the "southward advance"] (Tokyo: Chūkō Shinsho, 1975), and *Nihon no Nan'yō shikan* [Japan's historical perspective of the "South Seas"] (Tokyo: Chūkō Shinsho, 1979).

order to present a survey of Japan's involvement in the region from the renewal of Japanese expansion in Asia in the early 1930s to the eve of the Pacific War. In doing so, I have adopted a generally thematic approach and have consciously avoided detailed discussion of the complex weave of international and domestic events involved in Japan's sudden thrust into Southeast Asia in 1940–41, which has been dealt with extensively elsewhere. As I shall argue at the conclusion of this essay, this penultimate phase of Japanese imperialism was the consequence of a complex interplay of circumstance and motivation, of ideology and hard interest; but it took place within a context of the formal authority of Western colonialism, an experience that was unique in the history of Japanese imperial expansion.

BACKGROUND TO 1931

The wraith-like interest of late Meiji Japan in Southeast Asia was simply part of the general Japanese expansionist perspective of the era and was manifested largely by the few adventurers who entered the region, as well as by a number of romantic polemicists who saw the *Nan'yō* as an outlet for Japanese talents and ambitions. The patterns of the miniscule Japanese migration to Southeast Asia had paralleled the larger Japanese emigration to China during the same period. Initially, they had reflected the movement of marginal elements of society from the poorer regions of southern Japan, beginning with a tiny number of adventurers and itinerant peddlers, and followed by a second wave of shopkeepers and a large number of prostitutes brought in by the more opportunistic and ruffian elements who had entered the region.[4] Up to World War I, therefore, the Japanese economic presence in Southeast Asia had been largely that of small-scale commercial ventures catering mainly to local indigenous populations. It had involved no appreciable Japanese exports nor investment of Japanese capital.

Two developments in the last years of the Meiji era had appreciably raised the level of Japanese interest in Southeast Asia. The first of these was the vaguely expressed and not always logical *nanshin* stance taken by elements in the Japanese navy seeking to strengthen the navy's position in its bureaucratic competition with the army and the latter's *hokushin* (northward or continent-oriented) strategy. The other was the increasing volume of popular works that dealt with Southeast Asia and its importance to Japan. Without doubt, the most most widely read of

---

[4] These patterns have been traced in a series of articles, collectively entitled "Senzen-ki hōjin Ajia shinshutsu" [The prewar Japanese advance into Southeast Asia], comprising a special issue of *Ajia Keizai*, 26, no. 3 (March 1985).

these treatments was *Nangokki* (*A Record of Southern Countries*), published in 1910 by the well-connected journalist, historian, and Diet member Takekoshi Yosaburō (1865–1950), who had traveled through Southeast Asia two years before. The book's powerful stylistic appeal and arresting dicta on the importance of the region to Japan gained for it a wide audience and helped to diffuse *nanshin* ideas among the Japanese public in the years before World War I.

Yet in terms of actual Japanese involvement in Southeast Asia, the first significant step took place during World War I. First, by fortuitous events, the nation was able to gain a territorial foothold in the tropical Pacific. The arrangements of the Anglo-Japanese Alliance which permitted Japan to clamber onto the Allied side at the outset of the war (and then to retire to the sidelines for most of the rest of it) provided the pretext for the naval expedition that brought all of German-held Micronesia north of the equator under Japanese control. De facto Japanese control assured that Japan was named as a mandatory power over the islands by the League of Nations at the outset of the 1920s. With the occupation of Micronesia, Japan's *nanshin ron* in fact became a *nanshin*, and the flurry of media attention in Japan given to the nation's newest territorial acquisition and to its economic and strategic importance, introduced the Japanese reading public to the riches of the *Nan'yō*. Thus the acquisition of Micronesia, Shimizu Hajime has noted, made it possible to consider the "South Seas," including Southeast Asia, more clearly within the horizons of Japanese interest.[5]

In an even more important way World War I was fortuitous for an expanded Japanese economic role in Southeast Asia. Just at a time when the growth of the modern Japanese industrial economy made it possible to produce manufactured goods across a wide range of items and to accumulate at least a modest pool of industrial capital for investment overseas, the war sharply reduced European exports to and capital investment in Southeast Asia. This opened up attractive possibilities for the expansion of Japanese trade and capital into the region. Both smaller Japanese ventures and branches of the large Japanese-based firms like Mitsui Bussan and Mitsubishi Shōji began to sell not only textiles, but also a wide assortment of Japanese light manufactured goods in Southeast Asia. Japanese capital, though still small in comparison to the scale of Western capital, began its entry into the region, particularly to support rubber cultivation. The worldwide shipping shortage after the out-

[5] Gabe Masaakira, "Nihon no Mikuroneshia senryō to 'nanshin'" [Japan's occupation of Micronesia and the 'southward advance'], *Keio Daigaku Hōgaku Kenkyū* 55, no. 8 (August 1982): 85; and Shimizu Hajime, "Taishō shoki ni okeru 'nanshin ron' no ichi kōsatsu" [One observation on the "southward advance concept" in the early Taishō period], *Ajia Kenkyū* 21 (April 1983): 6–7.

break of World War I also affected Southeast Asia and gave an opening to Japanese shipping. As a result, the three major companies plying the lucrative route between Japan and the Netherlands East Indies came to enjoy handsome profits. This development of comprehensive Japanese shipping services to Southeast Asia, combined with the increased opportunities there for private Japanese entrepreneurs, soon led to a small but significant growth in Japanese emigration to the region. Finally, all these developments contributed to the increased attention to Southeast Asia by elements of the Japanese government and by Japanese trade associations and banking institutions.[6]

In these ways the expansion of a Japanese economic presence in Southeast Asia during World War I established important connections— in commerce, industry, banking, and transportation—between Japan and Southeast Asia. These were to become essential base points for a second and more concerted surge of Japanese activity in the 1930s. Just how these Japanese economic activities in the Taishō period influenced Japanese views of Southeast Asia and how they shaped the *nanshin ron* during the 1930s are complicated questions and have been the subject of several extended essays by Japanese specialists in recent years.[7] While such studies have presented a number of differing perspectives, one can draw from them a number of generalizations summarizing the Japanese relationship with Southeast Asia during World War I and in the immediate postwar years.

To begin with, the spate of Japanese commentary on Southeast Asia in those years differed in character from both the late Meiji literature on the subject and the later pronouncements on a "southward advance" in the early Shōwa years. Most of the small volume of late Meiji writing had been undertaken by a few colorful individuals: journalists and politicians whose contact with Southeast Asia was limited and tran-

---

[6] Shōda Ken'ichirō, "Senzen-ki: Nihon shihonshugi to Tōnan Ajia" [The prewar period: Japanese capitalism and Southeast Asia] in *Kindai Nihon to Tōnan Ajia kan* [Modern Japan and the view of Southeast Asia] ed. Shōda Ken'ichirō (Ajia Keizai Kenkyūjo, 1986), pp. 151–202; and Shimizu Hajime, "*Nanshin ron*: Its Turning Point in World War I," *Developing Economies* 25, no. 4 (December 1987): 389–91.

[7] For rather differing perspectives see Shimizu, "Taishō shoki ni okeru 'nanshin ron' no ichi kōsatsu"; Yano Tōru, "Taishō-ki 'nanshin ron' no tokushitshu" [Special characteristics of the Taishō period "southward advance concept"], *Tōnan Ajia Kenkyū* 16 (1978): 5–31; Ōbata Tokushirō, " 'Nanshin' no shiso to seisaku no keifu" [The genealogy of the "southward advance" thought and policies] in Shōda, *Kindai Nihon no Tōnan Ajia kan*, pp. 10– 18; and Shimizu Hajime, "1920 nendai ni okeru 'nanshin ron' no kishu to Nan'yō Bōeki Kaigi no shisō" [The conclusion of the "southward advance concept" during the 1920s and the idea behind the South Seas trade conference] in *Ryō-taisen kanki Nihon-Tōnan Ajia kankei no shosō* [Various aspects of Japan-Southeast Asia relations between the world wars], ed. Shimizu Hajime (Ajia Keizai Kenkyūjo, 1986), pp. 3–46.

sient. The great flood of books, pamphlets, and articles that appeared during the Taishō period was largely the product either of active economic participants on the spot (such as rubber planters and traders) who wrote from extensive experience in Southeast Asia, or of faceless trade missions, associations, and groups seeking to promote Japanese economic activity there. Hence, while Meiji writing on Southeast Asia tended to purvey a romantic and mystical expansionist message, Taishō commentary, while not entirely devoid of rhetoric, tended to be more practical in nature, introducing the economy, trade, and industries of the region and relaying information on how enterprising individuals could turn a quick profit there. These publications were hortatory only to the extent that they viewed exploitation of the economic resources and opportunities in Southeast Asia as a solution to the economic problems that beset Japan at the end of World War I.[8] But at this stage, the Japanese view of Southeast Asia scarcely perceived it as essential to the nation's security, nor did it include any discussion of the strategic importance of the region in a military sense. Pan-Asian and anticolonial (anti-Western) arguments appeared in some of these publications, but generally their approach was reflected in a Japanese expression at the time—"southern resources, northern people," *nambutsu hokujin*—which aptly summed up the businesslike concern with the practical exploitation of the material resources of Southeast Asia for personal profit and national gain.[9]

Yet Taishō pronouncements on Southeast Asia raised questions that lay behind all Japanese commentary on the region prior to World War II. Since, with the exception of Thailand, all of Southeast Asia was under the political control and economic domination of Western colonial powers, how was a "southward advance" of Japanese influence to be achieved? What moral justification existed to persist in such an attempt? What practical expectation existed for displacing Western power in the region? Eventually, stridently ideological answers and more militant solutions would be provided to these questions. But in the Taishō era, Japanese government policy and private ambition had no thought (and no choice) but to pursue purely economic interests in the region and to advance them almost entirely within the Western colonial context. Yet, among many who wrote on the subject during these years, there was a common assumption that Southeast Asia was essentially virgin territory, its resources untapped and its potential unfulfilled through the neglect, mismanagement, and incompetence of its nominal

---

[8] Yano, "Taishō-ki ni okeru 'nanshin ron,'" pp. 17–20, 31; Shimizu, "1920 nendai ni okeru 'nanshin ron'," pp. 5–7.

[9] Shimizu, "Taishō shoki ni okeru 'nanshin ron'," pp. 42–43.

Western colonial rulers. In this view, fortune had temporarily put in other hands one of the great resource areas of the globe, but the Japanese, by virtue of their skill, industry, and adaptability had a right to attempt its exploitation and development.[10]

The 1920s, however, witnessed a temporary dimming of such hopes and an unexpected contraction of the Japanese economic presence in Southeast Asia. The economic depression of 1920 slowed, and in some cases halted, Japanese investment in the region. One reason was the postwar collapse of the rubber industry, which had been a magnet for a good number of Japanese coming to Southeast Asia during the war years. There was, as well, the fact that once the war was over, Western goods and capital (often in greater volume than anything Japan could raise for overseas ventures) began to flow back again into Southeast Asia, while Japanese enterprises were confronted with renewed competition from Western colonial ventures. With the drying up of Japanese investment capital a good number of weaker Japanese businesses in Southeast Asia went under. Given these disappointments and the reduced expectations for quick profit, much of the bullish *nanshin* literature of earlier years disappeared during the latter half of the 1920s and the first half of the 1930s. Yet the economic difficulties that shook out the weaker elements of the Japanese economic presence served to strengthen the position of those that remained. Indeed, this process, combined with steps to strengthen Japanese currency and to rationalize Japanese industry at home, enabled Japanese commerce in Southeast Asia not only to withstand the tidal wave of depression at the end of the 1920s, but to be part of a resurgent trade drive that was to push Western colonial competition to the wall in the next decade.

THE JAPANESE ECONOMIC EXPANSION INTO SOUTHEAST ASIA IN THE 1930s

The Japanese economic thrust into Southeast Asia at the outset of the 1930s was undertaken as part of the nation's effort to deal with economic problems at home and abroad. Among these, there were two critical challenges. The first was the need for new export markets for Japan's light industrial manufactures in order to reduce the severe balance-of-payments problems brought on by the Great Depression and by the boycott of Japanese goods by the Chinese. The second was the necessity for accessible and reliable sources of raw materials, partic-

---

[10] For examples of this sort of thinking, see Satō Shirō and Ono Kyōhei, *Nangoku* [Southern countries] (Tokyo: Maruzen, 1914), pp. 35–38, and Yamada Kiichi, *Nanshin-saku to Ogasawara guntō* [The southward advance policy and the Bonin Island] (Tokyo: Minyusha, 1916), pp. 32–57.

ularly ores, in order to feed the increasing demands of Japan's military-
related industries in the tense international environment after 1931. For
both of these purposes Southeast Asia seemed ideal: it was not too distant, its colonial territories had as yet no competing light industries of
their own, and as both business and government had begun to recognize, the region was a treasure house of those raw materials sought by
Japan.

Yet it bears repeating that in the early years of the decade, the motivation for Japan's penetration of Southeast Asia was still basically economic and not strategic. By and large, Japanese entrepreneurs were still
willing to work through existing Western colonial institutions. For this
reason their enterprises were often viewed favorably by the colonial
authorities, if they appeared to contribute to Western colonial economic
development. Only later, when the Japanese economic drive appeared
to be both injurious to the colonial economies and a political threat to
the colonial order, did Western colonial regimes respond with hostile
countermeasures.

Before assaying the impact of Japan's burgeoning economic presence
in Southeast Asia in the first half of the 1930s, it is important to limn its
contours in the broadest strokes. To begin with, it represented an activity of relatively modest scale in comparison to Japan's economic relations with the rest of the world at the time, particularly as compared to
Japan's trade with China.[11] It was, moreover, concentrated almost entirely in the insular territories of Southeast Asia—the Straits Settlements
(Malaya), the Philippines, and the Netherlands East Indies. Of these, it
was the East Indies, with their great size, vast potential market, and
huge reservoir of resources that were the focus of Japanese attention.

In considering the success of Japan's economic drive into Southeast
Asia in the first half of the decade one must keep in mind that the
Japanese operated there with little political leverage. The Western imperial powers had the advantage of political as well as economic control
over their colonial territories, being able to call upon import quotas to
maintain their favored economic position and on gunboats and garri-
sons to enforce their authority. The Japanese, as Howard Dick reminds
us, were obliged to conduct their business without the privileges of
treaty port status, extraterritoriality, and spheres of interest of the sort
that they shared with other imperialist powers in China, and without

[11] As measured in ¥1,000 units, for example, the total value of Japan's trade with
Southeast Asia from 1932 through 1936 was 660,283; with China it was 1,070,627; with
other Asian countries it was 1,611,246; with North America 1,200,296; and with Europe
388,356. Hua-sing Lim, "The Value, Composition, and Significance of Japanese Trade
with Southeast Asia, 1914–1941" (D. Phil. dissertation, University of London), 1981, p.
94.

the almost entirely free hand that they enjoyed in their client state, Manchukuo.[12]

Yet, in mounting an export drive in Southeast Asia at the outset of the 1930s, Japanese firms were able to count upon some formidable advantages: lower labor costs relative to Europe and the United States, lower shipping costs, in part due to the closer proximity of Japan to Southeast Asia, and most importantly, the decision by the Japanese government, in 1931, to devalue the yen, which made made Japanese manufactured goods considerably cheaper than those of Japan's Western colonial competitors. Japanese exporters and investors could also count on an effective weave of governmental, institutional, and financial support that could provide investment capital, assist them in gathering information about Southeast Asian markets, publicize Japanese goods in Southeast Asia, make representations to Western colonial governments on behalf of Japanese trade and investment, and undertake the necessary foreign currency exchange.

Elements of the Japanese government had been involved in facilitating Japanese trade with Southeast Asia since the beginning of the century, of course. The Ministry of Agriculture and Commerce had long been active in sounding out opportunities for Japan trade and investment. Japanese consulates at key centers of Japanese immigration and economic activity in Southeast Asia, like Surabaya in the East Indies and Davao in the Philippines, and Japanese consulates general, particularly those at Singapore and Manila, were unusually assiduous, not only in protecting the interests of local Japanese communities, but in reacting quickly to any colonial law or Western activity that appeared to discriminate against Japanese trade and investment. Finally, since late Meiji, the Taiwan Government-General had promoted Japanese economic activity in Southeast Asia through a variety of informational, cultural, and financial means.[13]

In the private sector the branch networks of the great Japanese trading firms like Mitsui Bussan and Mitsubishi Shōji, with their offices, godowns, and docks, located in all the main entrepots of Southeast Asia, along with those of the leading Japanese shipping companies, were themselves major assets in the competition for trade. In addition, specialized Japanese banks that were particularly positioned to facilitate Japanese trade and investment in the region had established firm con-

---

[12] Howard Dick, "Japan's Economic Expansion in the Netherlands Indies Between the First and Second World Wars," *Journal of Southeast Asian Studies* 20, no. 2 (September 1989): 267.

[13] For a detailed discussion of the activities of the Taiwan Government-General in this regard see Nakamura Takashi, "Taishō 'nanshin-ki' to Taiwan" [The Taishō "southward advance era" and Taiwan], *Nampō Bunka* 8 (1981): 209–27.

nections with Southeast Asia within the first two decades of the century. Of these the two most powerful were the Bank of Taiwan and the Yokohama Specie Bank (the latter having some seventy-six branches in Southeast Asia by the end of World War II), both of which not only financed a good deal of the Japanese export trade to Southeast Asia, but handled most of the foreign currency exchange involved in the trade.[14]

A range of commercial associations were also of great assistance to Japanese trade and investment in Southeast Asia. Prominent among them were the Japanese trade associations and chambers of commerce in the larger cities of the region, in addition to the various hyphenated, colony-specific trade associations that linked Japanese economic interests with those of the various Southeast Asian territories. But no private institution played a more comprehensive or more influential role in the Japanese penetration of Southeast Asia than the *Nan'yō Kyōkai*—the South Seas Association. Established in 1914 in Tokyo by a galaxy of prominent Japanese, including four barons (Shibusawa Eiichi among them), an array of business tycoons, and a sprinkling of entrepreneurs with successful experience in Southeast Asia like Inoue Masaji,[15] the association, from its outset, had major backing from the Foreign Ministry, the Ministry of Agriculture and Commerce, and the Taiwan Government General. From the provisions of its charter it would seem that its founders intended it to play a role in Southeast Asia not unlike that which the *Tōa Dōbunkai* exercised in China,[16] one that would include a

---

[14] A discussion of the currency exchange functions of both banks in facilitating the Japanese textile trade with Southeast Asia can be found in Yoshihara Tatsuno, "Senkan-ki Nihon no tai 'Nampō' bōeki kin'yū no kōzō, Yokohama Shōkin Ginko, Taiwan Ginko o chūshin ni" [The structure of currency circulation involved in Japan's interwar trade with "the southern area" centering on the Yokohama Specie Bank and the bank of Taiwan] in Shimizu, *Ryō-taisen*, pp. 155–206.

[15] Businessman, writer, and ardent nationalist, Inoue Masaji (1877–1947) was a major figure in the Japanese economic penetration of Southeast Asia. In his youth a chance acquaintance with China expansionist Arao Sei fired in Inoue a Pan-Asianist vision that was to lead to a lifetime spent in travel and business in Asia and to the authorship of a vast number of books on Japan's role there. One of the founding members of the *Tōa Dōbun Shoin*, Inoue traveled into the interior of China during the Boxer Rebellion, gathering intelligence. He served in various capacities as adviser to the Korean government and royal court, 1905–1909, and in that capacity may have helped to strengthen the Japanese grip on the peninsula. A trip to Southeast Asia in 1910 sensitized him to the great potential for Japanese exploitation of the region. He soon became director of a company established for this purpose and subsequently became one of the founders and directors of the *Nan'yō Kyōkai*. During the interwar years Inoue travelled throughout Southeast Asia, both as an entrepreneur with private interests in the region and as an adviser to the Japanese government concerning its resources and problems.

[16] See Douglas R. Reynolds, "Training Young China hands: Tōa Dōbun Shoin and Its Precursors, 1886–1945" in *The Japanese Informal Empire in China, 1895–1937*, ed. Peter Duus, Ramon H. Myers, and Mark R. Peattie (Princeton, N.J.: Princeton University Press, 1989), pp. 210–71.

systematic effort not only to gather information, but also to train young Japanese to become fluent in the local languages and familiar with local customs in order to be the vanguard of an expanding Japanese presence in the "South Seas." Beyond this, the association was to undertake a range of activities, commercial, cultural, educational, and informational, that would bring Japan and the countries of Southeast Asia into closer contact. In carrying out this mandate, the association, beginning in 1918, opened permanent trade exhibitions in various parts of Southeast Asia that dispensed information about Japanese products, and, from 1928, provided systematic training of personnel for Japanese enterprises in the *Nan'yō*, including language instruction in Dutch and Malay. The association annually sent scores of young Japanese to serve in Japanese-managed firms in Southeast Asia, Melanesia, and Micronesia. Branches of the association were established throughout Southeast Asia, but the most important overseas office of the association was the *Taiwan Nan'yō Kyōkai* which sponsored the same range of activities as its parent organization, not only in Taiwan, but throughout the region. By the 1930s, the monthly journal of the association, the *Nan'yō Kyokai Zasshi* (later simply called *Nan'yō*), was respected as the most authoritative source of information on Southeast Asia. Eventually, the association grew beyond its function as a facilitator of Japanese trade and investment in Southeast Asia and came to assume a major intelligence role in the various territories of the region.[17]

Finally, in enumerating the assets available to assist Japanese firms seeking to trade or invest in Southeast Asia, one should mention the development, over time, of two informal structures in the region. The first of these relates to the prewar Japanese settlement communities in Malaya, the Philippines, and the Netherlands East Indies. William Swan has argued that it was these clusters of on-the-spot, small-scale Japanese entrepreneurs—generally immigrants engaged in plantation agriculture—who provided the experience, the knowledge, and the local contacts that made it possible for later and larger Japanese investors to succeed in Southeast Asia. Conversely, Swan asserts, it was the absence of a significant Japanese immigrant presence and thus the absence of local entrepreneurship that kept Thailand and French Indochina (and, presumably, Burma after 1937) from becoming areas of significant Japanese investment until the eve of the Pacific War.[18]

The other structure of major importance to the Japanese economic penetration of Southeast Asia in the early 1930s, which again existed

---

[17] Yano, *Nanshin no keifu*, pp 76–77; Yano, "Taishō-ki 'nanshin ron'," pp. 25–26; and Obata, "Nanshin no shisō," pp. 12–13.

[18] William Swan, "Aspects of Japan's Pre-war Economic Relations with Thailand," in *Thai–Japanese Relations in Historical Perspective*, ed. Chaiwat Khamchoo and E. Bruce Reynolds (Bangkok: Innomedia, 1988), pp. 91–92.

mainly in the insular colonial territories, was a vertically integrated and Japanese controlled distribution system for Japanese exports. At the top, it linked together the large Japanese trading houses, shipping firms, and warehouse companies and at the bottom it used the numerous small Japanese shops and bazaars located in the countryside as well as in the large cities. It was the existence of this distribution system that was to stand Japanese business in good stead in all but the fiercest and most organized of Chinese boycotts against Japanese goods in Southeast Asia in the decade prior to the Pacific War.[19] Only in Singapore, where a sufficiently large portion of Japanese goods passed through a complex of Chinese wholesalers, importers, and retailers to a large population of Chinese consumers, was Japanese trade always vulnerable to Chinese economic pressure.

While a comprehensive discussion of Japanese economic expansion in Southeast Asia is beyond the scope of this chapter, it may be useful to touch briefly and selectively upon its effect in the three colonial areas where it had the greatest impact: Malaya, the Philippines, and the Netherlands East Indies. In all three territories, obviously, the target of the Japanese trade offensive was the large, economically depressed indigenous populations whose tastes, daily needs, and pocketbooks would shape their receptivity as consumers. In reaching this indigenous market it was inexpensive textiles, historically Japan's most advantageous light industry, that provided the cutting edge of the Japanese economic advance. While Japanese-manufactured cloth, particularly cotton goods, was attractive to these indigenous consumers in terms of price (as compared to the same categories of Dutch, British, and American cotton goods), it was apparently also the high quality of Japanese cotton goods that soon earned them a dominant place in the textile markets of Southeast Asia.[20]

The impact of this textile offensive was soon apparent. Whereas in 1933 the Japanese had been the second largest supplier of textiles in the Philippines (after the United States), for example, within a few years

[19] Dick, "Japan's Economic Expansion," pp. 250–51, and Denis Soo Jin Koh and Kyoko Tanaka, "Japanese Competition in the Trade of Malaya in the 1930s," *Tōnan Ajia Kenkyū* 21, no. 4 (March 1984): 389.

[20] Masuda and Gotō have shown, for example, that in the East Indies the boom in Japanese textiles came when higher-grade cotton fabric (bleached and starched cotton material used in the manufacture of Javanese batik) was introduced into the colony in 1931 and among Indonesians soon became the textile of choice for everyday clothing. Masuda Ato and Gotō Ken'ichi, "Nihon-Indoneshia keizai kankeishi kenkyū no jōsetsu ni mukete; dai ichiji Nichi-Ran'in kaishō zengo no Ranryō higashi indo shijō ni okeru Nihon nempu shiron" [An introduction to research on the history of Japanese-Indonesian economic relations: the effort of the Japanese cotton industry to enter the Indonesian market before and after the first Japan–Netherlands East Indies negotiations], *Waseda Daigaku Shakai Kagaku Tokyū* 12, no. 3 (May 1977): 131–35.

Japanese advantages of cost, speed of delivery, and the ability to produce designs of high quality (often copied, it must be said, from American prints) threatened to overwhelm that indigenous market. In Malaya, Japanese competition with Chinese traders in cotton piece goods became cut-throat, and it so damaged the British textile trade to Malaya (as it did elsewhere in Asia) that by mid-decade the British government turned to quotas to limit these items. In the East Indies, the effect of the Japanese textile drive was the most dramatic of all. Howard Dick has shown that not only did Japanese domination in this single trade category drive the Netherlands from its position as chief trading partner with its own colony by 1932, but the doubling of Japanese textile exports to the Indies, 1931–34, almost compensated for the loss during those years of domestic Japanese cotton exports to China caused by Chinese boycotts and the establishment of Japanese mills in China. Masuda Ato and Gotō Ken'ichi have demonstrated that Japan's overall favorable balance of trade with Southeast Asia, which it achieved by mid-decade, was almost entirely due to its trade with the East Indies, which was largely dependent on the influx of Japanese textiles in the early years of the decade.[21]

From textiles, the Japanese export drive went on to dominate, or at least make significant inroads into, the markets for a wide range of manufactured goods: ceramics, iron goods, automotive equipment, glass, bicycles, beer, and cement, to name just a few. In all three insular colonial territories Japanese competition in light industrial manufactures began to cause a serious shrinking of export markets for Britain, the Netherlands East Indies, and the United States and, in the case of Malaya and the Netherlands, began to erode colonial distribution systems.[22]

Fishing was an activity to which Japanese investors turned after the decline of the rubber industry in the 1920s. With their highly scientific methods, well-equipped vessels, and well-organized fleets, the Japanese soon gained a dominant position in the principal territories of Southeast Asia. They supplied, for example, 40 percent of the fish consumed in Malaya and about half the catch for Singapore, and came to hold a virtual monopoly on all aspects of the fishing industry in the region, from canning to marketing.[23]

Finally, in their aggressive trade drive in the 1930s, the Japanese reac-

[21] M. C. Guerrero, "A Survey of Japanese Trade and Investments in the Philippines, with Special References to Philippine-American Reactions, 1940–1941," *Philippine Social Sciences and Humanities Review* 31 (March 1966): 23–27; Koh and Tanaka, "Japanese Competition," pp. 377–79, and Masuda and Gotō, "Nikon-Indoneshia Keizoi Kankeishi Kenkyū," pp. 91 and 97.

[22] Guerrero, "Japanese Trade and Investments," pp. 36–42; Koh and Tanaka, "Japanese Competition," p. 381; and Dick, "Japan's Economic Expansion," p. 253.

[23] Ibid., p. 259; Guerrero, "Japanese Trade and Investments," pp. 59–60.

tivated a shipping war in Southeast Asia. It was begun by Ishihara Hiroichirō (1890–1970), the single most prominent Japanese business figure in Southeast Asia before the Pacific War. With luck, shrewd dealing, and ruthless determination Ishihara had built an industrial empire in iron mining in Malaya in the 1920s.[24] In 1931, with the encouragement of the Japanese government, he had opened a shipping line sailing between Java and Japan. By offering freight charges at 20 percent less than the current rate, the new line competed not only with Dutch and British concerns, but also with established Japanese shipping companies. The Dutch were so seriously hurt by Ishihara's aggressive entry into the lucrative Japan–East Indies route that the Netherlands entered into a series of protracted negotiations with Japan to solve the problem before it became ruinous. For its part, the Japanese government, wishing to avoid an internecine freight war among Japanese companies, intervened to compel all Japanese shipping interests in the Japan–East Indies shipping trade to consolidate their resources into a single company. In 1936, the Netherlands and Japan agreed to a 60 percent Japanese and a 40 percent Dutch share of the Japan–East Indies freight route.[25]

By the mid-1930s, Western colonial governments in Southeast Asia were beginning to react to this Japanese trade onslaught with hostility and alarm. In seeking to halt the inrush of Japanese textiles, British authorities in Malaya enacted stiff currency control regulations and es-

[24] Businessman and nationalist, Ishihara went on to extend his operations to bauxite and other ores and to broaden the scope of his enterprises to the Philippines. During the late 1920s he developed close associations with the military and the right wing in Japan and is known to have given money both to ultranationalists like Ōkawa Shumei and to the plotters behind the Young Officers' Rebellion of February 1936. For these reasons he was arrested after the rebellion, but quickly released for lack of evidence. In the latter 1930s, he became involved in various Pan-Asian and anticolonial activities, including covert support for Indonesian nationalists. Imprisoned after World War II as a Class A war criminal, he was released in 1948 and reentered the industrial world and economic activity in Southeast Asia. For an extended discussion of Ishihara's general ventures in Malaya, see Tessa Morris-Suzuki, "The South Seas Empire of Ishihara Hiroichiro: A Case Study in Japan's Economic Relations with Southeast Asia, 1914–1941" in *Japan's Impact on the World*, ed. A. Rix and M. Mourer (Nathan, Australia: Japan Studies Association of Australia, Griffith University, 1984). Ishihara's mining ventures in Malaya, specifically, are discussed in Yasukichi Yasuba, "Hiroichiro Ishihara and the Stable Supply of Iron Ore," in ed. Saya Shiraishi and Takashi Shiraishi, *The Japanese in Colonial Southeast Asia*, Translation of Contemporary Japanese Scholarship on Southeast Asia, vol. 3 (Ithaca, N.Y.: Southeast Asia Program, Cornell University, 1993), pp. 139–54. For a survey of the Japanese iron investments in Malaya in general, see Yuen Choy Leng, "Japanese Rubber and Iron Investments in Malaya, 1900–1941," *Journal of Southeast Asian Studies* 5, no. 1 (March 1974): 26–33.

[25] Dick, "Japan's Ecnomic Expansion," pp. 255–57. For a detailed discussion of these matters see Shimizu Hiroshi, "Dutch-Japanese Competition in the Shipping Trade on the Java-Japan Route in the Interwar period," *Tōnan Ajia Kenkyū* 26, no. 1 (June 1988): 13–22.

tablished textile import quotas. Earlier in the decade, the Netherlands East Indies government had passed the Crisis Import Ordnance designed to impose quotas on a whole range of Japanese goods, and, in the Philippines, Japan was forced by the United States to come to a gentleman's agreement limiting its cotton exports to that colony.[26] Parallel measures were undertaken in all the insular colonies restricting foreign investment, export of strategic materials, immigration, and landownership, all of which were clearly aimed at the Japanese economic advance. During the second half of the decade these restrictions had indeed begun to blunt the Japanese trade drive.

The Japanese economic offensive in Southeast Asia in the 1930s and the Western colonial reaction to it deserve comment. First, while there were definitely cases of Japanese fraud, evasion of import quotas, and underhanded trade practices,[27] recent scholarship argues that, by and large, the advance of Japanese exports was due less to Japanese commercial dishonesty, a charge that Western colonial competitors were all too quick to make, than to Japanese entrepreneurial abilities. Japanese manufactured goods, produced by a highly rationalized and efficient domestic industry, were welcomed by indigenous consumers because of their price and quality, a fact that caused a good deal of resentment among the Western colonial powers in Southeast Asia. At the time, Western colonial regimes were loud in their suspicions that the Japanese economic advance was the harbinger of political and military designs on the region. That charge is probably valid for the last years of the decade, but almost certainly not true for its early years. Much of the Western condemnation of the means and objectives of the Japanese export drive in the 1930s was, in fact, a smokescreen to conceal the fact that Western industrial economies proved themselves incapable of competing with Japan in the large indigenous markets of Southeast Asia.[28] In any event, it is obvious that Western colonial authorities were not consistent about the undesirability of an expanded Japanese presence in the region. The encouragement given to Japanese iron mining in Malaya by British colonial authorities and the support given to Japanese hemp production in the Philippines by the American cordage industry right up to the Pacific War, are more than isolated cases of Western encouragement for Japanese investment in Southeast Asia when it served Western purposes.[29]

---

[26] Dick, "Japan's Economic Expansion," p. 254; Koh and Tanaka, "Japanese Competition," p. 398; Guerrero, "Japanese Trade and Investments," pp. 26–27.

[27] See Koh and Tanaka, "Japanese Competition," pp. 383–88.

[28] Dick, "Japan's Economic Expansion," p. 266. For an example of special pleading of this sort see Amry Vandenbosch, *The Dutch East Indies: Its Government, Problems, and Politics* (Berkeley: University of California Press, 1941), pp. 236–37.

[29] Leng, "Japanese Rubber and Iron Investments," p. 3, and Hayase Shinzo, "American

What really alarmed colonial authorities, Tessa Morris-Suzuki and Howard Dick have argued, was not the loss of colonial trade per se, but rather the fact that Japan's successful competition in manufactured goods eroded the economic links between the colonial powers and their colonial peoples in Southeast Asia and thus weakened Western colonial authority. Thus, in evaluating the decline in Japanese exports to Southeast Asia in the second half of the decade, it is important to keep in mind that it was almost entirely due to political decisions made by Western colonial governments, rather than to any lessening in the Japanese ability to compete. The popularity of Japanese commodity goods among the indigenous peoples of Southeast Asia had demonstrated that there was an alternative to Western colonial economies, and in this sense, the Japanese economic penetration of the East Indies was a first step in its decolonization, taken even before the invasion by Japanese forces in 1942.[30]

At all events, the Japanese economic drive in Southeast Asia was seriously slowed in the latter half of the decade. This decline and the Western colonial policies that caused it appear to have had three important consequences. The first of these was a fundamental restructuring, by 1940, of the long-standing pattern of Japanese trade with Southeast Asia. Whereas Japan's Southeast Asian trade—particularly its import trade—had been almost entirely confined to the insular territories of the region, the nation's increased requirements for raw materials after the outbreak of the China War and the sanctions applied by Britain, the Netherlands, and the United States against Japan's trade with their Southeast Asian colonies, forced a reorientation of that trade. Japan's reliance on Thailand after 1937 and on French Indochina after 1940 for imports of certain critical materials (among them, rice, rubber, and coal) essentially accounted for this restructuring.[31] That did not, of course, reduce Japan's hunger for the strategic resources of insular Southeast Asia. To the contrary, that appetite led to a gathering determination to acquire those resources by force.

The second result of the Western restrictions on the entry of Japanese exports, capital, and migration into Southeast Asia was more ideological in character. The Western attempt to freeze Japan out of the region served to heighten anti-Western and anticolonial sentiments among Japanese who dealt with Southeast Asia and even, belatedly, among the

---

Colonial Policy and the Japanese Abaca Industry in Davao, 1898–1941," *Philippine Studies* 33 (1985): 515–17.

[30] Morris-Suzuki, "Ishihara Hiroichiro," pp. 158–59, and Dick, "Japan's Economic Expansion," p. 253.

[31] Swan, "Japan's Pre-war Economic Relations with Thailand," pp. 88–89.

Japanese who were resident there.[32] It is probably no coincidence that the emergence of renewed *nanshin* and Pan-Asian rhetoric in Japanese public discourse appeared about the time that restrictive Western measures began to take effect on Japanese trade.

Finally, the worsening environment for Japanese trade in Southeast Asia by the mid-1930s undoubtedly contributed to the increased merger of government policy and private enterprise in the aggressive pursuit of Japanese economic and strategic interests in the region. A concrete manifestation of this trend was the appearance, at mid-decade, of "national policy companies" (*kokusaku kaisha*). These were semigovernmental corporations, financed by both public and private capital, directed by both public- and private-sector managers, and usually established, at the initiative of the Japanese government, to exploit particular economic opportunities overseas. Their appearance in the 1930s signified the Japanese effort to coordinate more effectively the resources, energies and talents of government and business in strengthening the nation's economic position at a time of increasing isolation in the international community. A model for this kind of corporation already existed in the *Tōyō Takushoku, K.K.* (Oriental Colonization Company) established in 1908 for the economic development and exploitation of Korea. During World War I, the company had diversified its interests by extending its operations into south China and after the war, through a subsidiary firm, had invested in rubber and timber in the East Indies. In 1936, the government established the *Nan'yō Takushoku, K.K.* (South Seas Colonization Company) for the development of Japanese Micronesia and the *Taiwan Takushoku, K.K.* (Taiwan Colonization Company) to do the same in Taiwan. Both of these corporations soon extended the range of their interests to Southeast Asia and carried out investigations for the government concerning investment opportunities there.[33]

But the corporation most heavily actively involved in the aggressive pursuit of Japanese economic interests in Southeast Asia in cooperation of the government was the *Nan'yō Kōhatsu, K.K.* (South Seas Development Company). The *Nan'yō Kōhatsu*, or *Nankō* as it was known colloquially, was established in 1921 by Matsue Haruji, the "Sugar King of Micronesia," for the development of the Japanese mandated islands. By the late 1920s it had become the dominant economic enterprise in Micronesia and the basis for the development of the mandate as a whole.[34] Not exactly a national policy company (in that its management was

[32] This point is made by Morris-Suzuki, "Ishihara Hiroichiro," pp. 159–60.

[33] Dick, "Japan's Economic Expansion," p. 262, and Nihon Keizai Kenkyukai, *Nanshin Nihon shōnin* [Japanese southward advance entrepreneurs] (Ito Shoten, 1941), pp. 180–83.

[34] Peattie, *Nan'yō*, pp. 126–32.

entirely private and its funds mostly so), it nevertheless became closely identified with Japanese government policy. Early in the 1930s, Matsue had begun to invest in plantation enterprises in Dutch New Guinea, by mid-decade it operated copra plantations, trading, and coastal shipping in the Celebes, and by 1941 it is said to have established ten subsidiary firms throughout Southeast Asia.[35] By then the company clearly had begun to move beyond its commercial and investment activities to co-operate with the Japanese government in the development of a strategic interest in the "South Seas." There is strong evidence that the *Nan'yō Kōhatsu* worked closely with the Japanese navy in the construction of airfields in the mandated islands, and Matsue Haruji is known to have been in fairly close contact with the navy in developing strategies for the penetration of the East Indies in the face of stiffening Dutch suspicion and resistance.[36] Of all Matsue's schemes perhaps the boldest was his plan, clandestinely but firmly supported by the Navy General Staff, for the expansion of his company's activities to Portuguese Timor, where, through bribery and political intimidation, Matsue intended to pressure the local colonial government into granting his company a concession to develop the oil fields there.[37] Though this maneuver ultimately failed, it serves as an indication of the degree to which private capital and government policy were cooperating in the aggressive southward advance of Japanese economic and strategic interests in the latter half of the 1930s.

REEMERGENCE OF THE *NANSHIN* IDEOLOGY IN THE 1930s

From the end of the Taishō period to about 1935 there was little public discussion in Japan of the "southward advance" concept, largely due to the temporary dimming of the kind of economic prospects in Southeast Asia that had lured Japanese to the region during World War I. To the extent that there was any discussion at all of the "South Seas" during these years it was largely kept alive by private enterprises with interests in Southeast Asia, such as the Bank of Taiwan, the Yokohama Specie Bank, and the Taiwan branch of the *Nan'yō Kyokai*, as well as by government agencies like the Research Section of the Taiwan Government General, the Commercial Bureau of the Ministry of Commerce and Industry, the Commercial Bureau of the Ministry of Foreign Affairs, and the Colonial Affairs Bureau of the Colonial Ministry, all of which

---

[35] Dick, "Japan's Economic Expansion," p. 262.

[36] Ibid., p. 248, and Gotō Ken'ichi, "Kaigun nanshin ron to 'Indoneshia mondai'" [The navy's southward advance concept and the "Indonesia problem"], *Ajia Kenkyū* 21, no. 2 (July 1984): 18.

[37] Henry P. Frei, *Japan's Southward Advance and Australia: From the Sixteenth Century to World War II* (Honolulu : University of Hawaii Press, 1991), pp. 151–53.

produced a small but steady stream of reports on the "South Seas."[38] There were, as well, the commentaries of a few major entrepreneurs like Ishihara Hiroichirō, Inoue Masaji, Matsue Haruji, and Fujiyama Raita, who spoke of the continuing opportunities for Japanese economic expansion into the region.

The sudden change in the political climate at home and abroad in the first half of the 1930s, however, opened the way to a renewed Japanese interest in the "South Seas." The economic instabilities around the globe in the aftermath of the Great Depression; the militant reorientation of Japan's foreign policy; the nation's sense of international isolation after its Manchurian adventure; the quest for economic autonomy after 1931; and, most of all, the national anxieties directed toward the impending "crisis of 1936," marked by the termination of the Washington Treaty order and the end of Japan's dependence on the principles of collective security; all led to a national search for new ways to enhance Japanese security. In this context it is not surprising that there was renewed interest in Southeast Asia as a source of strategic raw materials needed for Japan's new military buildup. One should be careful, of course, not to view this interest in isolation, since it was part of a general surge in expansionist opinion following Japan's advance upon the Asian continent in 1931. Nevertheless, beginning in 1935 there was a small but significant increase in Japanese popular literature—books, magazines, newspapers—on the desirability of a "southward advance." The general tone of this literature was moderate and vague, stressing the necessity of further advances into the region by economic enterprise, though some of this commentary also spoke—in vague terms, admittedly—of the conjunction of Japan's economic interests in the region with the strengthening of Japanese naval power.[39]

Then, in 1936, a work appeared that, more than any other, brought the idea of a "southward advance" back into public discourse. This was *Nanshin ron* (*On the Southward Advance*) by the journalist Murobuse Koshin.[40] To most readers in the 1990s much of this work would probably now seem gaseous, but it met with tremendous public acclaim in the

---

[38] Yano, *Nihon no Nan'yō shikan*, pp. 168–70.

[39] A good example of this perspective was a reference by the respected scholar Yanaihara Tadao to "our southward advance which has been achieved not by warlike means, but, according to our tradition, by peaceful economic progress, even though it has been under the protection of our naval power." Yanaihara Tadao, "Nan'yō seisaku o ronzu" [Advocating a South Seas policy], *Kaizō*, June 1936, p. 39.

[40] Murobuse Koshin (1892–1970), journalist and prolific right-wing writer across a range of social, cultural, and political topics who began to turn to wider Asian subjects in the 1930s. He was the author of some sixty books and pamphlets. Murobuse's views became increasingly ultranationalist by the mid-1930s, though immediately after World War II he completely changed political direction and became a vociferous critic of the emperor system.

1930s. In part, this was because it shared with Takekoshi Yosaburo's earlier *Nangokki* the same overheated rhetoric that gave it an apparent sense of urgency. Its popularity was also due to the apparent panacea it provided for the nation's ills, foreign and domestic, at a time when the Japanese public hungered for simple and emotional solutions to complicated political and economic problems. Sounding all the obligatory expansionist themes of the day, including the supposed needs of Japan's surplus population, energies, talents, and capital, Murobuse argued not only that a "southward advance" was Japan's inevitable destiny, but also that it was the only rational course for Japan in confronting the looming struggle between expanding economic blocs. Spooning out a mixture of fact and fiction about Southeast Asia, its resources, and its peoples, Murobuse passed on to his readers assertions about Japanese relations with the region that were spurious, exaggerated, or unproven, but which provoked an enthusiastic response.

Nanshin ron seems to have inspired a minor spate of other popular works on the subject which grew in volume as Japan's involvement with the region intensified toward the end of the decade. Beginning about 1940, according to Yano Tōru, this literature led to a good deal of pseudo-intellectualism in Japan about the nation's "southward advance" and, after the outbreak of the war, degenerated still further into a flood of unscholarly works by *nanshin* "boosters" (Yano calls them *nampō-ya*)—writers, artists, and commentators who knew nothing about Southeast Asia, but who were mobilized by the government to propagate the idea.[41]

Given the fact that we tend to think of Japan's penetration of Southeast Asia in connection with Japanese propaganda concerning East Asian "coprosperity" and "Asia for the Asiatics," one curious aspect of Murobuse's book and the *nanshin* works that followed it between 1936 and 1940 was the absence of any pronounced emphasis on Pan-Asianism. In general, their approach to Southeast Asia was the *nambutsu-hokujin* attitude of which I have spoken earlier, one that saw Japanese policy toward the region in terms of pressuring the colonial powers to open the territories, resources and markets of their Southeast Asian colonies to Japanese trade and immigration without restriction, but also without much regard to the future of the colonial peoples there. This is not to say that there was no precedent for Pan-Asian anticolonialism in *nanshin* thought. Traces of it can be found in some of the Taishō period *nanshin* literature. Yet, generally speaking, there was little connection publicly established between the two concepts until 1940. The reason is simple. Pan-Asianism was essentially a concept that had been developed

---

[41] Yano, *Nanshin no keifu*, pp. 166–68.

in the context of Japan's expansion into Northeast Asia, specifically in terms of its relations with China and Korea, and later in terms of its relations with Manchukuo. Without a major reorientation of Japanese foreign policy toward Southeast Asia there was little likelihood that a Pan-Asian ideology would officially embrace that portion of the globe.

As we know, such a reorientation of Japan's foreign policy did indeed occur during the summer of 1940, accompanied, as I shall shortly discuss, with a fusion of Japan's *nanshin* and Pan-Asian concerns. Yet even before that, certain institutions and individuals had begun the process. In his study of the *Dai Ajia Kyōkai* (Great Asia Society) Gotō Ken'ichi has illuminated one of the most active organizations in this regard.[42] Established on March 1, 1933, by a group of leading politicians and military figures including Konoe Fumimarō, Hirota Kōki, Admiral Suetsugu Nobumasa, and navy commander Ishikawa Shingo, the society was designed to undertake an aggressive (and, as it turned out, often shrill) effort to propagate Pan-Asianism as symbolized by Japan's new puppet state of Manchukuo, which had been created on the same day. Initially, the focus of the society's efforts was entirely on the Asian continent, and it viewed Southeast Asia merely as an area that might provide economic support for a Northeast Asian bloc, while remaining an essentially subordinate concern. Within a year after its establishment, however, the society began to take a more holistic approach to Japanese expansion, and with this new perspective it began to set up branch offices overseas. Symbolic of the increased importance of Taiwan as a base for Japanese economic, propaganda, and intelligence activities in Southeast Asia, a Taiwan branch was established in 1936 at Taihoku, with the sponsorship of the colonial government and garrison. Two years before that, with the strong backing of the Taiwan Government General, the society had set up offices in Manila. In his study of the Philippine branch, Grant Goodman has demonstrated how the more blatant Pan-Asianist propaganda efforts like those of the Great Asia Society often worked at cross purposes with the more moderate course of Japanese foreign policy. In the case of the society's Philippine branch, Goodman argues, its overzealous activism and heavy-handed anti-colonial propaganda worked to undermine the efforts of the Japanese Foreign Ministry to cement good relations with the Philippines and to tranquilize American fears concerning Japanese ambitions in the islands.[43]

[42] This paragraph is based largely on Gotō Ken'ichi, "Dai Ajia Kyōkai to 'nampō mondai'" [The Great Asia Society and the "southern area question"] in Gotō Ken'ichi, *Shōwa-ki Nihon to Indoneshia: 1930 nendai "nanshin" no ronri, Nihon kan no keifu* [Japan and Indonesia in the Shōwa Period: the logic of the "southward advance" and the genealogy of the Indonesian view of Japan] (Tokyo: Keiso shobō, 1986), pp. 154–72.

[43] Grant Goodman, "Japanese Pan-Asianism in the Philippines: The Hirippin Dai-Ajia

Over the years, the society's journal, *Dai-Ajiashugi* (*Great Asianism*), increasingly came to give as much space to Japan's material interest in Southeast Asia as it did to the idea of Asian liberation, and it began to accentuate the former after the outbreak of the China War. By September of 1940, the merger of the Society's *nanshin* and Pan-Asian concerns was starkly illuminated by an editorial in *Dai-Ajiashugi* that urged Japan's entry into French Indochina not only as the consolidation of a base for further Japanese military operations in Southeast Asia, but also as an act of Asian liberation and salvation.[44]

Individual Japanese had also begun to draw connections between the material wealth of Southeast Asia and the issue of liberation of the region from Western colonialism. Of these there was no more influential figure than Ishihara Hiroichirō, the mining and shipping magnate I have mentioned earlier. Both Shimizu Hajime and Tessa Morris-Suzuki have shown how the parallel development of Ishihara's *nanshin* ideas and his anticolonial statements stemmed from his personal experience and observations as a businessman in Southeast Asia. As an entrepreneur he had travelled widely in the region and had undertaken the overseas production and shipment to Japan of one of its strategic resources. It is not surprising, therefore, that Ishihara came to see the tropics as the storehouse of the world's natural riches and Japan's control, direct or indirect, over the Southeast Asian portion of the tropics as adding immeasurably to the nation's strength. As Shimizu Hajime has pointed out, this view echoed Takekoshi Yosaburo's dictum, "he who controls the tropics controls the world," and places Ishihara's view within the material or national self-interest tradition of *nanshin* thought.[45]

Yet, at the same time, these scholars tell us, Ishihara's experience as a leading Japanese business figure attempting to operate within the increasingly hostile environment of Western colonialism also helped to fuel his mounting Pan-Asian and anticolonial sentiments. In part, these sentiments stemmed from his growing frustration at the restrictions that the Dutch, British, and American colonial governments undertook to block or hamper his plans for business expansion in Southeast Asia. In part, they also seem to have arisen from a genuine idealism toward what he regarded as the economic and political oppression of colonial peoples of Southeast Asia (though, like most other Japanese expansionists of the time, he seems to have been blind to the even more extreme oppression within Japan's own colonial empire). For either or both of

Kyōkai" in *Studies on Asia*, ed. Robert Sakai (Lincoln, Nebraska : University of Nebraska Press, 1966), pp. 133–42.

[44] Gotō, "Dai Ajia Kyōkai to 'nampō mondai,'" pp. 172–73.

[45] Shimizu, "Ishihara Hiroichirō," pp. 98–99.

these reasons, Ishihara began to take a Pan-Asian and anticolonial stance as early as 1934, and for the years remaining before the Pacific War, he not only wrote frequently and heatedly about the imperatives of liberation for Southeast Asian peoples, but began to undertake a range of activities directed to that goal. He appears to have allowed the facilities of his companies to be used for espionage purposes, to have nurtured relationships between students and intellectuals in Japan and Southeast Asia, and most importantly, to have encouraged Southeast Asian nationalist movements, particularly in the East Indies, through covert but hazardous support for underground Indonesian groups and newspapers.[46]

Because Ishihara reflected the growing nationalist mood of his time in Japan, one that found a variety of ideological justifications for doing what was in Japan's material self-interest, it was easy for him to greet with enthusiasm the concept of "East Asian Co-Prosperity," which was, of course, an amalgam of rock-hard self-interest and vaporous idealism. But as Shimizu and Morris-Suzuki remind us, this seems to have been due not to a simple parroting of the ideas of powerful friends like Konoe Fumimaro, but rather to personal experience and conviction acquired during the prewar Japanese economic intrusion into Southeast Asia. Indeed, in this sense, as the single most influential Japanese in the region, Ishihara may have helped prepare the way for the concept of "East Asian Co-Prosperity."[47]

I leave to others the task of tracing the origins, course, and consequences of Japan's failed attempt, as represented by the Greater East Asia Co-prosperity Sphere, to match naked self-interest and Pan-Asian idealism. Suffice it to say that its definitional extension to include Southeast Asia was the result of a sudden turn in international events and of Japan's opportunism in seizing upon this turn, rather than the consequence of a long-considered or widely held interest in the coprosperity of Southeast Asian peoples. Indeed, Konoe Fumimaro's announcement in November 1938 of a "New Order in East Asia," generally considered to be the precursor of the coprosperity idea, made no mention whatever of the "Southern Regions" (as the "South Seas" were now called). As late as early July 1940, when the "New Order in East Asia" became the "Greater East Asian Order" in official documents, nothing about Southeast Asia was implied. But that month, with the leading elements in the Japanese government and military moving toward a decision to exploit the sudden vulnerability of the French and

[46] Morris-Suzuki, "Ishihara Hiroichiro," pp. 160–63, and Shimizu, "Ishihara Hiroichirō," pp. 88–91.

[47] Ibid., p. 91; Morris-Suzuki, "Ishihara Hiroichiro," p. 163.

Dutch colonies in Southeast Asia, the "southward advance" was rapidly drawing to a convergence with Pan-Asianism. In late July, a Cabinet memorandum on the Netherlands East Indies had referred to the "Greater East Asia Co-Prosperity Sphere," and on August 1 Foreign Minister Matusoka Yosuke made his announcement which gave official sanction to the concept, declaring in the process that the sphere was to include "Southern regions such as the Netherlands East Indies and French Indochina."[48] After that, the term rapidly burst into the public media and in September, in an interministerial meeting, it was given a geographical definition that reflected Japan's now rocketing ambitions: Japan and its formal colonies, Manchukuo, China, French Indochina, Malaya and British Borneo, the Netherlands East Indies, Burma, Thailand, Australia, and New Zealand. Only the Philippines were omitted, out of a desire to avoid arousing the active antagonism of the United States, the one power in a position to thwart Japanese designs.

Shimizu Hajime has written that the incorporation of the "Southern Regions" into the Greater East Asian Co-Prosperity Sphere had profound implications for the *nanshin* concept. First, in one sense, it marked a terminal point in *nanshin* thought. One tends to think of the Sphere as enlarging the importance of Southeast Asia on Japan's imperial horizons. Yet, seen from another perspective, Shimizu has argued, it brought to an end the concept of the "Southern Regions" as distinct and separate, and placed it instead in a subordinate position within a system centered on continental Asia. This transformation harkened back to the vaguely expressed visions of some of the first military proconsuls in Taiwan in late Meiji, generals Kodama and Katsura, who had seen the "South Seas" as an extension of southern China. At the same time, the merger of the *nanshin* and Pan-Asianism marked in a very real sense the triumph of the *nanshin* idea in its most material—now territorial—form. Shimizu points out that whatever slogans of "Asian liberation" may have been flaunted during the Pacific War, most of Japan's pronouncements on the Greater East Asian Sphere in 1940–41 were far more concerned with matters of Japanese economic self-sufficiency than they were with colonial liberation.[49]

NANSHIN AS OFFICIAL POLICY, 1936–1940

Up to the mid-1930s it is possible to view the "southward advance" as a concept developed largely by individuals or as a trend in Japanese trade

[48] Joyce Lebra, *Japan's Greater East Asia Co-Prosperity Sphere* in World War II (Kuala Lumpur: Oxford University Press, 1975), pp. 71–72.

[49] Shimizu, "Ishihara Hiroichirō," pp. 84–85.

and emigration, encouraged in varying degrees and at various times by the Japanese government, but not as a matter of settled policy. In the latter half of the decade, however, the *nanshin* assumed an ever widening place in the priorities of the Japanese government. That it did so was initially due to the obsessions of a nucleus of middle-echelon officers in the Imperial Japanese Navy.

There had been reasons for a general and vaguely expressed interest by the navy concerning Southeast Asia, of course. As mentioned earlier, the "southward advance" concept had been an argument that the navy had used to blunt the army's claims for the priority of a "northward advance" in the interservice tug of war for public esteem and fiscal appropriations. This rivalry had grown keener early in the 1930s due to the navy's plans for a major expansion (and thus for increased demands on funds and resources) in anticipation of the "Crisis of 1936," as well as to the navy's restlessness in the face of the public acclaim for the army after the latter's conquest of Manchuria in 1932. Indeed, the belief by some in the navy that it should not fall behind the army in aggressive moves overseas had been a motive behind the navy's provocation of bloody fighting with Chinese Nationalist forces in Shanghai in February 1932. Yet this oppositional stance by the navy, though it continued up to the eve of the Pacific War, hardly represented either a fundamental or a concrete interest in Southeast Asia per se.

But there was a concern that did bring the region into sharper focus for the navy: fuel for the fleet. By 1929, the entire Japanese navy had been converted to oil, most of which had to be imported from overseas, principally from the United States and the British Empire (including oil from British North Borneo). Some petroleum supplies also came from the Netherlands East Indies, which was by this time a major oil producer, and some thought had been given in the navy to increasing this amount. But while petroleum and its abundant presence in Southeast Asia were long-range strategic considerations for the navy, the fact that, at the beginning of the decade, it was still readily available to Japan on the international market meant that an interest in Southeast Asia and its resources had not yet taken on a sense of urgency for the navy as a whole.[50]

The surge in the navy's interest in Southeast Asia in the mid-1930s was due to the convergence of a number of developments. Two of

---

[50] Yet there were a number of naval personnel, mostly retired officers, like admirals Mukoda Kaneichi and Sōsa Taneji, who came away from visits to the Netherlands East Indies in the early 1930s with profound impressions of the richness of its resources and the necessity for Japan to take more active steps to exploit these. Gotō Ken'ichi, "Kaigun nanshin ron to 'Indoneshia mondai'" [The navy's southward advance concept and the "Indonesian problem"], in Gotō, *Shōwa-ki Nihon to Indoneshia*, pp. 46–47.

these, according to Gotō Ken'ichi, were the termination of Japanese cooperation with the Anglo-American naval powers and the uncertainty of the long-range prospects for Japanese access to oil on the international market.[51] A third was the emerging domination of the hard-line "Fleet Faction," largely located in the Navy General Staff, over those officers, generally in the Navy Ministry, who sought to avoid a confrontation with Britain and the United States. And finally, there was the increasing power in both the army and the navy of ad hoc research and decision-making committees formed outside the normal bureaucratic lines in order to deal with strategic problems that would face the navy in the dangerous period after the naval limitations treaties had lapsed. Staffed primarily by middle-echelon officers (but occasionally assisted by civilian bureaucrats, businessmen, and even scholars), these committees often shaped the basis of later official government policy.

In the navy, one of the first of these groups was the "Research Committee on Plans Concerning the South Seas" (*Tai-Nan'yō Hōsaku Kenkyūkai Iinkai—Tainanken*, for short) established in 1935 after discussions between a small number of *nanshin* enthusiasts—all members of the General Staff and all aligned with the "Fleet Faction"—who believed that a vigorous expansion of Japanese interests into Southeast Asia must be based on solid information. Eventually numbering twenty-one officers, headed by the vice chief of the General Staff, and composed of section chiefs from the General Staff, the Navy Ministry, and the ministry's Naval Aviation Bureau, the committee was the first institutional and systematized effort by the navy to prepare for a "southward advance." It was charged not only with research into the geography, history, resources, trade, industry, communications, and transportation of Southeast Asia and Melanesia, but also with the shaping of the navy's policy toward those regions. An inner working group of the committee worked out a concrete plan for an accelerated economic penetration of the region directed toward an aggressive but peaceful acquisition of its strategic resources and a stepped-up program of Japanese immigration. Two principles were to guide this plan. First, the lead was to be taken by private enterprise and by the Colonial Ministry, with the navy lending only covert assistance (an arrangement behind the navy's abortive Timor scheme mentioned earlier). Second, both Taiwan and Japanese

---

[51] Ibid., pp. 83–84. According to one prewar Japanese source, in 1936, 90 percent of Japan's oil needs had to be imported, with the United States supplying 66 percent of those imports. Under these conditions, the East Indies, with their nearly eight-million-ton annual production in 1939, appeared increasingly valuable as an alternative source. Jerome Cohen, *Japan's Economy in War and Reconstruction* (Minneapolis: University of Minnesota Press, 1949), p. 46.

Micronesia were to be strengthened as bases for separate approaches for this economic advance by centralizing (and militarizing) their administrative structures and by improving their transportation and communications links with Southeast Asia and Melanesia.[52]

Assembled by the *Tainanken*, these ideas soon found their way into a more important document, "Outline of National Policy" (*Kokusaku yōkō*), drawn up in April 1936 by the larger and even more influential First Committee (which included all the members of the *Tainanken*) and intended to reflect the views of the navy as a whole. While making the obligatory acknowledgement of the nation's interests in Manchuria and China, and while taking care to stress the importance of moderation in shaping Japan's foreign policies so as to avoid alarming either the Soviet Union or the Anglo-American powers, the "Outline" emphasized that the "southern countries are the areas we should regard as most important for strengthening our national defense, solving the the population problem and [promoting] economic development." It then went on to speak vaguely of creating the "necessary agencies" and "unified means" for the peaceful economic penetration of the region, as well as for strengthening Taiwan and the Japanese islands of Micronesia for this purpose.[53]

It is perhaps more accurate to view the "Outline" as the navy's claim to a strategic position as a counterweight to the army's self-proclaimed mission on the Asian continent than to see it as the first stage of considered navy plans for the actual conquest of Southeast Asia. Yet there is no doubt that it does mark the beginning of a more insistent, if still peaceful, assertion of the "southward advance" as a national priority. To this extent, it confronted designs for the domination of Northeast Asia by the Japanese Army General Staff which, inevitably, drew up its own "General Principles of National Defense Policy," mentioning the "southward advance" not at all. Despite the army's opposition, however, the navy was able to get a modified version of its document, one that compromised the ambitions of the two general staffs and balanced the two strategic polarities, approved by an interministerial conference on August 11, 1936, as the "Fundamental Principles of National Policy" (*Kokusaku kijun*). As Gotō Ken'ichi sees it, this statement, too, was

---

[52] Ibid., pp. 34–35, and Hatano Sumio, "Shōwa kaigun no nanshin ron" [The southward advance concept of the navy in the Showa era] in *Hishi Taiheiyō sensō* [Secret history of the Pacific War], special issue of *Rekishi to Jimbutsu*, December 1984, p. 278.

[53] The entire document is reproduced in the *Gendai-shi shiryō* [Documents on modern history, hereafter *GSS*], vol. 8, *Nitchū sensō* [The Sino-Japanese War], part 1 (Tokyo: Misuzu shobō, 1964), pp. 354–55, and an English translation (entitled "General Principles of National Policy") is available in Lebra, *Japan's Greater East Asia Co-Prosperity Sphere*, pp. 58–60.

largely a tactical device by the navy to justify its own plans for massive expansion. Yet, at the same time, he notes, it marked the first time that the "southward advance" had been raised to a state policy level.[54] Moreover, it is clear that over the next few years the navy's interest in Southeast Asia became more than tactical; it became a central priority in its intensifying search for strategic resources, particularly oil. More than any other territory in Southeast Asia, it was the Netherlands East Indies—largest in size, richest in resources, and, as the colony of a small power, the most vulnerable to Japanese pressure—that became the magnet for the navy's ambitions.

Though the joint policy statement of August 11 had been drawn up to balance the opposing *hokushin* and *nanshin* priorities of the two services, it is clear from the actions of both over the next year that the issue had not been resolved at all. While the army was busy with its plots and provocations on the continent in 1936, the navy, pushed by its *nanshin* activists in the middle echelon, seized upon every opportunity to advance its own priorities. That year, as Japan was now unfettered by even the pretense of reporting to the League of Nations that it was abiding by the terms of its original mandate in Micronesia, the navy began to push ahead cautiously and covertly with the preliminary militarization of its island territories there.[55] In September, as part of its consolidation of authority in Taiwan to improve it as a base for activities in Southeast Asia, the navy succeeded in having the position of governor-general shifted from a civilian to a military appointment and then went on to maneuver an admiral into the post. That same month, the navy was quick to attempt to exploit an incident in the South China port of Pakhoi in the hope that the affair would give it a foothold on the South China coast.[56]

---

[54] Gotō, "Kaigun nanshin ron," pp. 53–56. The document is reproduced in *GSS* 7.1: 361–62, and an English translation is provided in Lebra, *Japan's Greater East Asia Co-Prosperity Sphere*, pp. 62–64.

[55] See Peattie, *Nan'yō*, pp. 230–56, for a discussion of the actual timing and character of the militarization of Micronesia before the Pacific War.

[56] The incident, September 3, 1936, involved the murder of a Japanese store owner by a Chinese mob in the Kwangsi coastal town of Pakhoi. The navy sent warships to "investigate" the affair, and Captain Nakahara Yoshimasa, a passionate *nanshin* enthusiast and a member of the Operations Division of the General Staff, drafted a memo for his superiors calling for the occupation of Hainan, supposedly as an act of retaliation, but actually as an attempt to establish a sphere of influence in South China. The crisis passed with the withdrawal of Chinese troops from the area and the reluctance of the army to support the navy's hawkish position. For a discussion of the affair, see Akagi Kanji, "Nihon kaigun to Hokkai jiken" [The Japanese navy and the Pakhoi Incident], Keio Gijuku Daigaku Daigakuin Hōgaku Kenkyū Ka, *Shōwa gojūnendo rombunshū* [Thesis collection for 1977] (1978), pp. 133–45.

With the outbreak of the China War in the summer of 1937, the nation's preoccupation with the military crisis, first in north and then in central China, caused the navy to curb its denunciations of the army's *hokushin* priorities and to support army operations in those theaters to the extent that it was logistically and tactically able to do so. At the same time, the navy saw no reason to abandon its *nanshin* ambitions, which it saw as quite separate from the China War. As a matter of practical policy, moreover, the navy was loath to let the army monopolize the government funds and public support generated by the conflict. For these reasons, the navy, in 1938, took advantage of the war to establish control of the South China coast and to seize a number of small islands in the South China Sea. Then, in February 1939, in the largest naval operation of the China War, the navy occupied Hainan and the next month occupied the Spratly Islands. The occupation of Hainan, a major island territory coveted for some years by the navy, was billed as an operation to secure the coast of south China, but in fact it was regarded as the first step in an extension of Japanese naval influence southward toward the Western colonial preserves of Southeast Asia. After the island was firmly in its hands, the navy established on it one of its Special Service Offices (*Tokumusho*), a sure sign of the navy's interest in Hainan as a major center for intelligence operations.[57]

Up to now I have spoken of the navy's "southward advance" ideas in the vaguest terms, because the navy phraseology concerning the concept was itself highly nebulous. In part this was due to the fact that it had initially been viewed more as a bureaucratic tactic than a serious course for navy policy, but also, one supposes, because the navy had not as yet acquired sufficient information about Southeast Asia to know what it wanted to do there. By the late 1930s, due largely to the work of *nanshin*-oriented special committees, like the *Tainanken*, these conditions had changed. From the "Summary Draft of a Policy for the South" drawn up by the navy's National Policy Research Committee in April 1939 we can get a fairly clear picture of what was meant by "southward advance" just short of actual military occupation.[58]

The draft begins with an enumeration of Japanese objectives in the

[57] Hatano, "Shōwa kaigun no nanshin ron," pp. 283–84. The seizure of Hainan was strongly criticized by such moderate navy figures as Yonai Mitsumasa and Yamamoto Isoroku as being unduly provocative of the Western powers. See Aizawa Jun, "Kaigun ryōshiki to nanshin—Hainan-tō shinshutsu mondai o chūshin shite" [The rational faction in the navy and the southward advance, centering on the occupation of Hainan] in Gunji-shi Gakkai, *Dai niji sekai taisen—hassei to kakudai* [World War II—origins and escalation] (Kinsei Sha, 1990), pp. 179–88.

[58] The document is reproduced in full in Lebra, *Japan's Greater East Asia Co-Prosperity Sphere*, pp. 63–67.

region: the acquisition of vital raw materials as a first priority, stimulation of Japanese exports and control of all trade, and promotion of friendly relations with each country there. Concretely, the document recommended that the advance be carried out by specific measures applied to the region: an informed determination as to the strengths and weaknesses of Western colonial control; continuing attempts to pressure Western colonial regimes into abolishing or modifying every restriction on Japanese activities; promotion of further Japanese emigration and the immediate extension of Japanese air routes to the area; ongoing efforts to secure an arrangement of Japanese commercial rights so as to displace the influence of overseas Chinese; promotion of national consciousness among the indigenes (in other words, subversion) and demonstrations to them of Japanese power; inauguration of a range of cultural exchange, and public relations programs designed to enhance the image of Japan among colonial peoples; specialized propaganda efforts tailored to win the support of specific minorities in Southeast Asia—Muslims, overseas Chinese, Catholics, and even Japanese civilian communities; centralizing control of all Japanese cultural and friendship organizations; upgrading and expanding Japan's consular representation; and stepping up the involvement of other Japanese government agencies, particularly the Government-General of Taiwan and the South Seas Government in Micronesia. A perusal of the document leaves no doubt that it was drafted with two objectives in mind : the weakening of all Western colonial authority in the "Southern Regions" particularly that of the Netherlands East Indies, and Japanese domination of all economic activity there. In this sense, the "Summary Draft" reflected the essential nature of Japanese policy toward colonial Southeast Asia in 1936–40, which, as Howard Dick has pointed out, had as its object, not the immediate military conquest of the region, but its "decolonization," a process that would leave it within the Japanese sphere of influence.[59]

By 1939, in any event, the "southward advance" was no longer just a bureaucratic device for the navy, but an increasingly important element in the navy's consideration of the resources needed for the expansion of the fleet, of which oil was only the most important. That year, with the American government's abrogation of the United States-Japan Treaty of Commerce, Japanese naval leaders began serious consideration of alternative sources of petroleum supplies. Since the Netherlands East Indies, by virtue of its proximity and because of existing distribution systems, was the most accessible of the available three major oil-producing areas outside the United States—South America, the Middle East, and

---

[59] Dick, "*Japan's Economic Expansion*," p. 269.

the Indies—the navy was increasingly determined that pressure be put on the colonial government there to increase its oil exports to Japan. By 1939, therefore, the "southward advance" and the expansion of the Japanese fleet (and the resources needed for that expansion) had attained an almost symbiotic relationship in the minds of the navy's aggressive middle echelon, as Michael Barnhart has explained in his excellent study of the economic road to the Pacific War.[60] For these officers, the *nanshin* also provided the navy with a mission that, combined with material supremacy in the West Pacific, would give the navy its long-sought position as the senior service and the true arbiter of the nation's destiny. Yet, for the time being, the navy's cautious leadership made it unlikely that there would be a sudden or massive reorientation of Japan's foreign and military policies in favor of the "southward advance."

The army's interest in Southeast Asia developed in two stages during the 1930s. As early as the first half of the decade, Gotō Ken'ichi informs us, there had been a small number of middle-echelon officers in the Army Ministry's Mobilization Section who had been keenly concerned about the problem of strategic fuels, particularly aviation gasoline. Inevitably, this concern led to a consideration of the oil reserves in the Netherlands East Indies, and ultimately, on the eve of the Pacific War, the army's aggressive interest in a "southward advance," like that of the navy, would indeed be generated by the prospect of acquiring vital raw materials. Yet for most of the 1930s, while it was pouring its energies into military adventures in Northeast Asia, the army high command had viewed Southeast Asia with but slight interest, concluding that the "Southern Regions Question" was best left to the navy. By the end of the first year of the China War, however, Southeast Asia began to impinge on the army's consciousness. In large part this had to do with the existence of an outside supply route to Nationalist China through French Indochina. As the China War dragged on and the Japanese military became frustrated in its efforts to end the war through secret negotiations with the Chungking regime, this army concern with French Indochina increased, though there was little the army could do to halt the flow of materials that passed through it. Thus, when the opportunity did come in 1940–41 to undertake a "southward advance," specifically through Indochina, the army's initial view of that action linked it directly to the China War, whereas the navy continued to see southward expansion as a distinct and separate activity.[61]

[60] Michael A. Barnhart, *Japan Prepares for Total War: The Search for Economic Security, 1919–1941* (Ithaca, N.Y.: Cornell University Press, 1987), pp. 140–141, 147.

[61] Gotō Ken'ichi, "Rikugun nanshin ron no keisei katei" [The formation process of the

THE "SOUTHWARD ADVANCE" AS ARMED INTERVENTION, 1940–1941

A detailed discussion of the complex weave of turbulent international events, international relations, and national decision making involved in the forcible entry of Japan into Southeast Asia, 1940–41, is beyond the scope of this chapter and has, in any event, been provided elsewhere.[62] For these reasons, I shall offer here only the briefest summary, which must suffice as background to any discussion of Japanese preparations and plans for the occupation of the entire region.

The starting point is the radical reorientation of army policy to take advantage of the sudden vulnerability of French Indochina and the Netherlands East Indies in the wake of the conquest of their home governments by the German blitzkrieg in late spring of 1940. On July 3, after a six-week review of the meaning of the drastically changed global situation, the Army General Staff and the Army Ministry approved a new policy document, "Outline of Measures for Dealing with Changes in the World Situation" (*Sekai jōsei no suii ni tomonau jikyoku shōri yōkō*). The "Outline" was a document of momentous proportions, for not only did it reverse Japan's neutral stance in the European war, it formally committed the army to a *nanshin* strategy for the first time in its history. While it called for the occupation of northern French Indochina as the first step in cutting China off from all outside material assistance, it went beyond that to urge that a diplomatic mission be sent to the Netherlands East Indies to pressure its colonial administration into opening to Japan its treasure house of strategic resources, and even contemplated the complete ejection of Britain from Hong Kong and its Southeast Asian territories. Finally, the document was infused with the vision of Japanese hegemony in Southeast Asia as the solution to the twin dilemmas that confronted the nation: the China War and the increasingly critical situation in strategic resources due to the tightening noose of Western restrictions on the export of these items.[63]

---

army's southward advance concept] in Gotō, *Shōwa-ki Nihon to Indoneshia*, pp. 107–10 and 142–43.

[62] See, for example, Sumio Hatano and Sadao Asada, "The Japanese Decision to Move South (1939–1941)," in *Paths to War: New Essays on the Origins of the Second World War*, ed. Robert Boyce and Esmond Robertson (New York: St. Martin's Press, 1989), pp. 383–407, and James William Morley, ed., *The Fateful Choice: Japan's Advance into Southeast Asia, 1939–1941* (New York: Columbia University Press, 1980).

[63] Frei, *Japan's Southward Advance*, pp. 145–46; Barnhart, *Japan Prepares*, pp. 158–59; and Hatano and Asada, "The Japanese Decision," p. 287. The most detailed treatment of this decisive shift in army policy is provided by Hatano Sumio, "'Nanshin' e no senkai: 1940-nen—'jikyoku shōri yōkō' to rikugun" [Toward a turning point in the "southward advance"—the army and the 1940 policy statement "Outline of measures dealing with the situation"], *Ajia Keizai* 26, no. 5 (May 1985): 25–48.

Newly converted to the *nanshin* concept in the summer of 1940[64] and heedless of the possibility and consequences of an antagonistic American response, the army contemplated the possibility of a lightning offensive that would sweep up the French and Dutch colonies in Southeast Asia, should it be unable to obtain from them the concessions it sought. While preparations were being made in the late summer for the negotiations in Batavia, the Japanese army undertook to establish the first Japanese military foothold in Southeast Asia. Following Japanese demands in June, the Vichy-directed French colonial government in Indochina had tentatively agreed to Japanese use of certain airfields in Tonkin as well as to the passage there of Japanese troops to seal off the supply routes to Nationalist China. While the details of these arrangements were to be worked out in discussions in Hanoi, the designated Japanese field force (the South China Area Army), impatient to get on with the occupation of northern French Indochina and unwilling to await until a final agreement was reached, crossed the Sino–Indochinese border on September 22 and four days later made amphibious landings at Haiphong. The *nanshin* had at last been transformed from theory to military reality.[65]

But if the army's occupation of northern French Indochina constituted the first step in a road that would eventually lead all the way to Singapore and Batavia, the army's headlong approach to this operation had once again opened up a major gap between the two services as to the proper nature of the "southward advance." The navy, which for so many years had advocated a forward policy in Southeast Asia, was now alarmed at the army's bull-in-a-china-shop version of the *nanshin*, and

[64] Not just circumstance, but forceful personalities seem to have had much to do with this shift in grand strategy. As in the navy, an aggressive middle echelon played a major role, but in the view of several historians (Yano, *Nanshin no keifu*, pp. 152–54, and Gotō, "Nanshin to zai-Indoneshia hōjin shakai," p. 284), one senior and retired military figure, General Koiso Kuniaki, did much to energize the army in its new appreciation of the strategic importance of Southeast Asia. As colonial minister during the summer of 1940, Koiso drafted a number of memoranda that detailed the expansion of the East Asian Co-Prosperity Sphere concept to include Southeast Asia, and in one notable statement proposed that the Japan-dominated sphere include all of Asia east of Dacca! These memoranda are reproduced in *GSS* 10.3: 466–83.

[65] For a detailed discussion of the first round of negotiations between the Japanese and French colonial authorities concerning the Japanese occupation of northern French Indochina, see Minami Yoshizawa, "The Nishihara Mission in Hanoi, July 1940," in *Indochina in the 1940s and 1950s*, ed. Takashi Shiraishi and Motoo Furuta, Translation of Contemporary Japanese Scholarship on Southeast Asia, vol. 2 (Ithaca, N.Y.: Southeast Asia Program, Cornell University, 1992), pp. 9–54. For an overview of the Japanese army's activities in French Indochina in the late summer and early fall of 1940, see Hata Ikuhiko, "The Army's Move into French Indochina," in Morley, *The Fateful Choice*, pp. 155–208.

after the amphibious landings at Haiphong, refused to cooperate further in military operations in French Indochina. Yet, if army ambitions in Southeast Asia seemed heedless, navy plans, historians have long noted, betrayed a bewildering circularity. Exemplified by one of its own policy papers, "A Study of Policy toward French Indochina" (*Tai-Futsuin hosaku ni kansuru kenkyū*), drawn up on August 1 by the Operations Section of the Navy General Staff, the navy 's approach called for the eventual complete takeover of Indochina, but assumed that such a demarche would would indeed lead to a total embargo of resources, specifically of petroleum, by the United States. In turn, such an embargo would make it necessary to invade the East Indies in order to secure the oil fields there. Unlike the army, the navy assumed that this final step would inevitably lead to war with the United States. The prospect of such a conflict made it imperative, in the navy view, to follow a cautious policy in order to give it time to expand the fleet and stockpile its resources.[66] Thus, the navy, as it had for decades past, invoked the United States as the inevitable enemy whose existence justified its fleet expansion and resource allocations. Yet it refused to consider a further belligerent move into Southeast Asia that might provoke that enemy except under "unavoidable circumstances," by which it meant a crisis situation such as the total embargo of strategic resources by the United States, Britain, and the Netherlands.[67]

In the meantime, both services stayed their hands while they gave the government an opportunity to apply diplomatic pressure on Batavia concerning the trading and political relations between Japan and the Indies.[68] The major issue, of course, was oil. Japan wanted a guarantee of 3.75 million tons annually for five years, but the Dutch, stiffened by the counsel of Britain and the United States, were willing to supply only 2 million tons on a six-month contract, less than half of Japan's needs. Forced to accept that level of supply for the time being, the Japanese delegation pressed ahead with other demands for fixed annual

---

[66] The document is reproduced in full in *GSS* 10.3: 169–71. A year later, with some 58 million barrels of petroleum on hand, Japan was fast drawing down its reserves, and still depended on foreign imports for 90 percent of its needs. Domestic production of crude and synthetic petroleum accounted for 10 percent of the nation's needs, the East Indies supplied another 10 percent, and imports from the United States made up most of the balance. H. P. Willmott, *Empires in the Balance: Japanese and Allied Pacific Strategies to April 1942* (Annapolis, Md.: Naval Institute Press, 1982), p. 68.

[67] Frei, *Japan's Southward Advance*, p. 147; Barnhart, *Japan Prepares*, pp. 164–65, 174–75.

[68] Initially, Prime Minister Konoe had favored Koiso Kuniaki to head the delegation to Batavia, but Koiso's belligerent public pronouncements and his extravagant demands (including his insistence on transportation of the delegation by warship, accompanied by a thousand-man naval landing party) derailed his appointment. He was replaced by Kobayashi Ichizō, minister of commerce and industry.

quantities of bauxite, nickel, rubber, and manganese. It made little progress, however, as the rest of the year slipped by. Early in 1941, the Japanese delegation, under a new head, presented a new set of demands centering on a complete restructuring of the political framework of Japan—East Indies relations, so as to end all ties with the Netherlands, give the Indonesians their independence, and bring about incorporation of the new state into the Co-Prosperity Sphere and into a mutual defense agreement with Japan. These proposals were rejected by the Dutch authorities as tantamount to reduction of the East Indies to the status of a Japanese protectorate. By June it was clear that the mission had failed, and it was withdrawn.[69]

To the Japanese political and military leadership it now appeared that only military force could guarantee access to the riches of the East Indies. Even before the collapse of the negotiations in Batavia, the issue of a forceful *nanshin* had reemerged. The army, stymied by the circular logic of the navy and faced with the results of an internal study that appeared to refute the basic assumptions of its earlier aggressive strategy, agreed to limit the "southward advance" to the occupation of bases in Thailand and southern French Indochina, operations that could be arranged through diplomacy. As both services were now in agreement that war with the United States and Britain was probable at some point, however, the decision was made to undertake covert and overt military preparations for the conquest of Malaya and the East Indies, including establishment of a planning and logistical center on Taiwan, initiation of joint amphibious landing exercises on the beaches of Kyushu, and the occupation of Thailand and southern French Indochina. This last initiative did indeed summon forth a Western reaction of the sort that the navy had feared all along: the total embargo of all trade with Japan—most critically in oil—and the freezing of its assets abroad. In turn, this stranglehold on Japan's resource lifelines did indeed create the "unavoidable situation" that the navy had seen as necessitating the conquest of all of Southeast Asia. Fatally compounding its already heavy commitments in China, Japan decided to strike south, a decision that, predicated as it was on an assault on Hawaii, plunged Japan into the Pacific War.[70]

---

[69] For a detailed discussion of the Japanese mission to the East Indies, 1940–41, see Nagaoka Shinjiro, "Economic Demands on the Dutch East Indies," in Morley, *The Fateful Choice*, pp. 125–53.

[70] Barnhart, *Japan Prepares*, pp. 198–245, and Frei, *Japan's Southward Advance*, pp. 148–49. To break the Allied stranglehold, Japanese authorities estimated that Japan would need to acquire nearly 38 million tons from September 1941 to September 1942. Since the East Indies produced 65 million tons annually (60 percent of that coming from the oilfields on Sumatra), from the navy's perspective, a decision to strike south was indeed unavoidable. Wilmott, *Empires in the Balance*, p. 68.

JAPANESE ESPIONAGE AND SUBVERSION IN SOUTHEAST ASIA, 1931–1941

This last and violent stage of the "southward advance" had been prepared, if only hastily, by the infiltration of a covert Japanese presence into Southeast Asia. Because of the inherent secrecy surrounding Japanese intelligence operations at the time and the fragmentary nature of the records since, it is difficult to trace Japanese espionage and subversion in prewar Southeast Asia in any great detail. It is for that reason, undoubtedly, that there exists no comprehensive Japanese-language study on the subject. There are two generalized English-language accounts of Japanese intelligence in Southeast Asia, one relating to the East Indies and the other to Malaya, but both of these works rely entirely on Western consular and police sources, (though both are undocumented) and both represent, essentially, the perspectives of former colonial powers, particularly in their tendency to exaggerate the scale, depth, and pervasiveness of Japanese espionage and subversion.[71] Yet combining their more reasonable assertions with scattered references to Japanese covert operations drawn from a range of more recent Japanese books and articles, it is possible to discuss these activities in rough outline.

Occasional Western (particularly Dutch and British) suspicions concerning Japanese espionage surfaced as early as World War I and the initial Japanese economic drive into Southeast Asia, but these assertions dealt largely in rumors and unproven reports and are nowhere supported by any evidence on the Japanese side.[72] By the mid-1930s, however, allegations of Japanese spying abounded throughout Malaya, the Philippines, and the Netherlands East Indies. For the most part, they tended to be wildly exaggerated, retailing the view that every Japanese store owner and fisherman was a Japanese government agent. In particular, it was a common charge by Western commentators at the time

[71] Netherlands Information Bureau, *Ten Years of Japanese Burrowing in the Netherlands East Indies: The Official report of the Netherlands East Indies Government on Japanese Subversive Activities in the Archipelago During the Last Decade* (New York, 1942), and Eric Robertson, *The Japanese File: Pre-war Japanese Penetration in Southeast Asia* (Kuala Lumpur: Heinemann Asia, 1979).

[72] Dick, "Japan's Economic Expansion," p. 264, and Shimizu, "Kindai Nihon ni okeru 'Tonan Ajia,'" part 2, p. 31. Two recent studies are relevant to the question of Dutch suspicions concerning Japanese intentions toward the Netherlands East Indies: Elsbeth Lochner-Scholten, "Changing Perceptions of Japan in the Netherlands and Netherlands East Indies before 1942," in *Papers of the Dutch-Japanese Symposium on the History of Dutch and Japanese Expansion, In Memory of the Late Nagazumi Akira*, ed. W. J. G. Remmelink, *Journal of the Japan-Netherlands Institute* 2 (1990): 43–66; and Tsuchiya Kenji, "The Colonial State as a 'Glass House': Some Observations on Confidential Documents concerning Japanese Activities in the Dutch East Indies," ibid., pp. 67–76.

(and in the decades since) that the Japanese navy used the relatively large Japanese commercial fishing fleet in Southeast Asian waters to conduct espionage. Given the ubiquitous presence of Japanese commercial fishing and its proximity to both crowded harbors and lonely coastlines, some Japanese fishing boats were undoubtedly used in such operations, but logic mocks the idea that thousands of ordinary Japanese fishermen were entrusted with Japanese naval codes or with Japanese naval intelligence objectives.[73]

There is evidence that, early in the decade and on a modest scale, the Japanese navy led the way in gathering intelligence in Southeast Asia, largely using commercial contacts to do so. (I exclude here the activities of naval attachés assigned to Japanese consular posts in the region, since their inherent function, like that of service attachés of every nation everywhere, was intelligence.) By and large, the navy's espionage efforts in Southeast Asia seem to have been undertaken, particularly after 1936, in cooperation with the larger Japanese commercial and industrial firms operating in the region, such as the *Nan'yō Kōhatsu* and the *Ishihara Sangyō*, which were among the most militantly expansionist Japanese firms in the tropical Pacific. As the *Nan'yō Kōhatsu* began to extend its activities into New Guinea, the Celebes, the east coast of Borneo, and Portuguese Timor, it willingly became a source of Japanese navy intelligence. There is also clear evidence that the *Ishihara Sangyō* was involved in a case of attempted espionage by the navy in Singapore 1934, and an Ishihara subsidiary, the South Seas Warehousing Company (*Nan'yō Sōkō K.K.*) seems to have served as a cover for Japanese naval spying in the East Indies on a number of occasions in the mid-1930s.[74] Lacking a clear picture of Japanese intelligence objectives in Southeast Asia in these years, it is difficult to say what these espionage operations accomplished or what the navy hoped to accomplish by them, given the modest scale of Western military and naval forces in the region, though they may have largely been directed toward topographical and meteorological matters.

In addition to the intelligence-gathering functions of other elements

---

[73] For references to Western mania about Japanese espionage see, for example, Guerrero, "Japanese Trade and Investments," pp. 42, 68; Gotō, "Nanshin to zai-Indoneshia hojin shakai," p. 282; Dick, "Japan's Economic Expansion," pp. 269–70.

[74] Gotō, "Kaigun nanshin ron," pp. 19–20; Robertson, *The Japanese File*, pp. 137–41; Netherlands Information Bureau, *Ten Years of Japanese Burrowing*, pp. 46–47. Tessa Morris-Suzuki, asserts that Japanese firms with global reach, such as Mitsui Bussan and Mitsubishi Shōji, tended to be a good deal more cautious concerning participation in covert activity in colonial Southeast Asia, given their substantial economic stakes elsewhere in the world. Morris-Suzuki, "Ishihara Shioichiro," p. 163. Nevertheless, by the end of the 1930s, these firms, too, were drawn into the Japanese intelligence net.

of the Japanese government, specifically including the Taiwan Government-General and the Foreign Ministry, a number of civilian and semi-governmental agencies became active in the collection of intelligence in Southeast Asia in the latter half of the 1930s. The *Nan'yō Kyōkai*, with its decades-old contacts throughout the region, was, of course, of great help in this regard and various accounts of Japanese military planning for the conquest of Southeast Asia speak of the assistance rendered by the society before the war.[75] Of even greater importance was the East Asia Economic Research Bureau (*Tōa Keizai Chōsakyoku—Tōa Keichō* for short), an element of the South Manchuria Railway known throughout East Asia for the scale and detail of its information gathering. In 1938, after SMR President Matsuoka Yōsuke directed it to expand its research activities, the bureau undertook a number of steps that eventually made it the premier source of intelligence on Southeast Asia. It began by hiring many specialists from Taiwan (from Taihoku University and the Taiwan Government-General) and by establishing a data office there, after which it set up branches throughout the region and created linkages with major elements in the Japanese government, including the military services and, supposedly, the Cabinet Planning Board. From 1939 to 1941, its activities were generally determined by its own agenda, but in the last year before the Pacific War, commissioned research by the army and navy dominated its work.

Eric Robertson, a former British police official responsible for tracking Japan's covert activities in prewar Malaya, has seen the Japanese resident populations in Southeast Asia as a key element in Japanese espionage and subversion. In his words, they formed "the advance guard of the Japanese army and the fixed point of the Japanese espionage net."[76] While it is clear that in Malaya and the East Indies, particularly, there were indeed individuals in the Japanese communities who worked with Japanese intelligence agencies in spying on and subverting the Western colonial order, the generally commercial orientation (and thus the politically moderate stance) of most of the Japanese community in Southeast Asia, and the improbability of large numbers of ordinary Japanese being entrusted with intelligence functions, tend to make one suspicious of this rather dramatic claim. A more likely and undoubtedly more active espionage element identified by Robertson was the parade of Japanese officials, businessmen, service officers, and traders who passed through Southeast Asia in the last years before the war, many of whom were undoubtedly involved in intelligence work either as observers or couriers.[77]

---

[75] Yano, *Nihon no Nan'yō shikan*, pp. 173–174.
[76] Robertson, *The Japanese File*, p. 7.
[77] Ibid., pp. 142–43.

While the Japanese army did not become generally involved in espionage in Southeast Asia until its sudden policy shift in the summer of 1940, its decision to do so was linked with a more sharply defined objective—the planning for military operations to conquer the area—than had been the case with Southeast Asian intelligence operations of the navy in the mid-1930s. It is for that reason that the army in 1940 undertook a number of major steps in strengthening its intelligence facilities relating Southeast Asia. The first of these was the creation of the *Nakano Gakkō* (Nakano School), an intelligence academy that trained hundreds of commissioned and noncommissioned officers in espionage and subversion operations and which by 1941 sent many of its graduates to Southeast Asia disguised as diplomats, journalists, and businessmen. Having infiltrated the country, these operatives were assigned to clandestine *tokumu kikan*—"special service organizations"—working, initially at least, through the military attachés assigned to the consulates general in the region. In order to collate intelligence on Southeast Asia coming into the Army General Staff, the Intelligence Division of the staff established a "Southern Regions Office" (*Nampō han*) to collect and analyze specialized intelligence on Southeast Asia on an ongoing basis. It also created a research bureau for research of an ad hoc, team-project nature relating broadly to countries in Southeast Asia that the army planned eventually to occupy.[78]

Yet perhaps the most important and certainly the most successful step taken by the army in intelligence collection for the eventual takeover of Southeast Asia was the creation in early 1941 of a Research Department in the Taiwan Army (Japan's field army in Taiwan). As such it reflected the culmination of Taiwan's enormous importance as the springboard for the Japanese penetration of Southeast Asia in the prewar decade. Known to its members as the "Doro Nawa Unit" (literally, a rope made from mud; figuratively, "the unit put together at the last minute"), the Taiwan Army Research Department had as its main task the amassing of data for the military invasion of Southeast Asia, an effort that required research across a range of topics: the preparation of tactical principles and field service regulations for operations in the tropics, recommendations concerning the appropriate weapons and equipment, the collection of information on health and sanitation problems, topography of the countries in which operations would take place, and guidelines for the military administration of countries to be occupied. In carrying out its mission the research unit drew upon a host of informants—employees of the Ishihara Mining Company, the Bank of Taiwan, the *Nan'yō Kyōkai*, and faculty members at Taihoku University, to name a few. Within six months, under the driving leadership of the famous

---

[78] Gotō Ken'ichi, "Rikugun nanshin ron," pp. 118, 130–35.

(some would say infamous) Colonel Tsuji Masanobu, the unit not only became the army's supreme authority on tropical warfare, but worked out the essential outlines for the brilliant Malayan campaign of late 1941 and early 1942.[79]

Throughout 1940 and 1941, the Japanese army, often in collaboration with the Japanese Foreign Ministry, used every opportunity to step up the infiltration of its agents into Southeast Asia, in a race against time to perfect its plans for the invasion of the region. In a well-publicized case in which British police authorities were able to unmask such a clandestine operation, it was revealed that the press attaché at the Japanese consulate general had been able to guide two general staff officers around Singapore, Johore, and as far north as Malacca in order to gauge the strength of British defenses. Their reports, Colonel Tsuji recorded in his memoirs, had much to do with the Japanese decision to attack Singapore from its landward side. Other army agents were despatched to Japanese consulates in the East Indies to assume cover as consular staff or were infiltrated into the archipelago as agents of the Dōmei News Agency in order to make a reconnaissance of the great oilfields at Palembang on Sumatra which Japanese planners were afraid the Dutch would destroy in the event of hostilities.[80]

By this time, too, the Japanese navy had reinvigorated its espionage program in Southeast Asia as part of its accelerated planning for operations to seize the major oil fields there. Indeed, one of the reasons for the long stay in Batavia of the second Japanese mission to the economic negotiations in Batavia in the spring of 1941 was to let the navy members of the mission have sufficient opportunity to collect strategic and military information on the East Indies as well as to lay the groundwork for a Japanese-supported nationalist insurrection in anticipation of a clash between Japan and the colonial government. This intelligence objective was well known to the Japanese Foreign Ministry when it dispatched the mission.[81]

It is difficult if not impossible to assign relative values to the various Japanese intelligence elements operating there between 1931 and 1941. But one has the sense that the intelligence effort as a whole was considerably less systematic and of shorter duration than Western commentators have judged it to be. Certainly the scramble by the Taiwan Army Research Bureau to amass information on Southeast Asia in 1941 im-

[79] Ibid., pp. 129, 134–35; Tsuji Masanobu, *Singapore, the Japanese Version* (Sydney : Ure Smith, 1960), pp. 3–7.

[80] Brian Bridges, "Britain and Japanese Espionage in Pre-war Malaya: The Shinozaki Case," *Journal of Contemporary History* 21, no. 1 (January 1986): 23–25; Gotō, "Rikugun nanshin ron," p. 117.

[81] Hatano, "Shōwa Kaigun no nanshin ron," p. 285.

plied the absence of such a systematically organized pool of information on the region up to that point. Nevertheless, it is clear that the Japanese intelligence penetration of Southeast Asia was massive in the last years before the war and the intelligence it gleaned contributed substantially to the swift conquest of the region in 1942.[82]

Japanese efforts to manipulate the attitudes of the subject peoples of Southeast Asia and, in certain cases, to stir up the fires of latent nationalism were also central elements in the attempt to undermine the Western colonial order. These endeavors differed in character from colony to colony and constituted a range of schemes, from cultural exchanges to outright conspiracies to provoke national insurrection.

Toward the Philippines in the 1930s the Japanese moved with considerable caution, not wishing, by a display of blatantly subversive conduct, to give the United States any pretext to delay the independence that had been promised the Philippines within a decade after the establishment of the Commonwealth. Thus, as Grant Goodman has demonstrated, the official Japanese approach was generally low-key. It involved a cultural effort undertaken largely by Japanese diplomats and businessmen to win the friendship and trust of their Philippine counterparts with an eye toward the day when the Philippines would be independent, when all American forces were withdrawn, and when Japan would be the dominant power in East Asia. The consequent Japanese propaganda in the Philippines in the 1930s emphasized cultural programs, student exchanges, press and radio programs, and personal contacts, all directed to developing a friendly image of Japan among Filipinos, particularly among the Filipino elite. This effort, as I have noted earlier, was to pay dividends during the Japanese occupation of the Philippines during World War II when many of these same Filipino elite found it possible to collaborate with the Japanese occupation regime.[83]

In the case of the Netherlands East Indies, the Japanese purpose was more directly political and subversive, in part because the East Indies were the prime target of Japan's strategic ambitions in Southeast Asia,

---

[82] For example, the two naval representatives attached to the Japanese delegation during the long and futile economic negotiations at Batavia were able to file extensive information concerning the Dutch oilfields at Palembang along with operational recommendations for their capture. These reports were the basis for the plans for the Japanese paratroop assault on Palembang in February 1942.

[83] See Goodman, "The Japanese Cultural Offensive in the Philippines," pp. 39–41. Goodman has also demonstrated that at least a few Filipino political radicals in the 1930s were influenced by the more virulently anti-American and anticolonial propaganda of Japanese Pan-Asian extremists. See his chapter on "Japan and Philippine Radicalism: The Case of Benigno Ramos" in Grant Goodman, *Four Aspects of Philippine-Japanese Relations, 1930–1940*, Yale University Southeast Asia Studies Monograph Series, no. 9 (New Haven, Conn.: Yale University Press, 1967), pp. 133–94.

and in part because there was no sign that the Netherlands had any intention of relinquishing its control over the region in the near future. The Japanese approach, beginning about 1934, was therefore essentially directed toward the manipulation of Indonesian political opinion to inflame it against Dutch colonial rule and to project a sympathetic view of Japan, so that Indonesians would view their liberation and the Japanese *nanshin* as having the same goals.[84] Initially, the means for accomplishing these objectives were the identification of the leadership of the nascent political parties (that is, political leadership of the colonial opposition) and support for influential Indonesian newspapers, which were usually connected with a particular political party. This effort was undertaken by a small core of Japanese journalists in Java, initially devoted to serving the Japanese community there. Becoming sufficiently politicized by the late 1930s, they were induced to fall in with a plan to create a major clandestine Japanese presence within the Indonesian press. Concocted in Tokyo and backed logistically by the Foreign Ministry and financially by powerful right-wing advocates of the "southward advance," the scheme called for the publication of an Indonesian-language newspaper, ostensibly representing a major Indonesian political party, but which, in actual fact, would become the mouthpiece for Japanese interests. The plot was discovered by the Dutch police, its Japanese participants all deported, and its Indonesian co-conspirators jailed, but not before the colonial authorities had been shocked by the extent of Japanese penetration of the Indonesian media.

An important concern of Japanese propaganda in Southeast Asia during the 1930s was the manipulation of religious majorities and ethnic minorities, or more specifically, an effort to shape the views of Muslims and overseas Chinese. The former were the object of a concerted but not very convincing public relations program, which included construction of mosques in Japan, invitations to visit Japan extended to leading Muslim princes, and the dispatch to Southeast Asia of some Japanese specialists and students of Islam, all of which were designed to project an image of Japan as a potent defender of the faith, but which, in fact, achieved few results.[85]

Neutralizing the hostility of the Chinese communities in Southeast Asia was a far more difficult problem for Japanese intelligence. It became an urgent matter after the outbreak of the China War in 1937, not only because of the anti-Japanese boycotts organized by the Chinese,

---

[84] This paragraph is based entirely on Gotō Ken'ichi, "Zai-Indoneshia Nihonjin kisha to 'bunka kosaku,'" pp. 319–34.

[85] Netherlands Information Bureau, *Ten Years of Japanese Burrowing*, pp. 25–26; Robertson, *The Japanese File*, pp. 99–100.

but also because the Chinese in Southeast Asia raised considerable sums for the war of resistance against Japan in the home country, and because Chinese agitation against Japanese aggression damaged the image of Japan as Asian liberator. For these reasons, the Japanese Foreign Ministry made various efforts to influence overseas Chinese opinion, initially, it is said, from its consulate general in Singapore and, after 1939, from its consulate general in Bangkok. It sought to do so through specially subsidized Chinese language newspapers and through attempts to contact and influence important leaders in the Chinese communities, through either bribery or intimidation. Yet none of these initiatives enjoyed any success. After 1940, army intelligence tried to lend a hand, but in spite of its use of graduates of the *Nakano Gakkō* specifically trained for the purpose, its efforts proved fruitless. Chinese populations in Southeast Asia, particularly in Singapore, remained united in their hatred of Japan.[86] The best that Japanese intelligence operatives could do was to mark down those leaders most active in inciting their Chinese compatriots against Japan, an accounting that was to bear the most terrible consequences for the Chinese community in Singapore at the outset of the Japanese occupation of that city in 1942.

On the eve of the Pacific War Japanese intelligence agencies were also involved in endeavors to foment outright rebellion among Southeast Asian indigenous peoples against Western colonial regimes. Joyce Lebra and Louis Allen have separately chronicled the most dramatic and, in some ways, the most successful of these: the efforts to create national independence armies to assist Japanese invasion forces in overthrowing the Western colonial order.[87] These operations were undertaken by army field intelligence organizations—*kikan*—headed by field-grade General Staff officers who were graduates of the *Nakano Gakkō*. The two most famous of these officers, Major Fujiwara Iwaichi and Colonel Suzuki Keiji, were initially sent to Southeast Asia on intelligence tasks whose priorities were not those of national liberation, but they were nevertheless quick to take up that cause.

In October 1941, Major Fujiwara was sent to Bangkok to make con-

---

[86] Ibid., pp. 85, 141–42; Gotō, "Zai-Indoneshia Nihonjin kisha," p. 322; Akashi Yoji, "Japanese Policy Toward the Malayan Chinese," *Journal of Southeast Asian Studies* 1, no. 2 (September 1970): 62.

[87] Joyce Lebra, *Japanese-Trained Armies in Southeast Asia: Independence and Volunteer Forces in World War II* (New York: Columbia University Press, 1977); Louis Allen, "Fujiwara and Suzuki: Patterns of Asian Liberation" in *Japan in Asia, 1942–1945*, ed. William H. Jewell (Singapore: Singapore University Press, 1981), pp. 83–103; and Louis Allen, "Fujiwara and Suzuki: The Lawrence of Arabia Syndrome" in *Themes and Theories in Modern Japanese History: Essays in Memory of Richard Storry*, ed. Sue Henny and Jean-Pierre Lehman (London: Athlone Press, 1968), pp. 230–42.

tact with Indians connected with the Indian national movement, as well as to establish friendly liaison with overseas Chinese and Malay sultans in Malaya and the East Indies. Within a few months his *Fujiwara Kikan*—or *F Kikan*—of five commissioned officers and two Hindi-speaking interpreters had worked out arrangements for suborning Indian troops of the British army in Southeast Asia. By December 1941, this scheme had led to the creation of the Indian National Army, the only major Japanese-sponsored force in Southeast Asia that was to fight alongside Japanese troops.[88]

Colonel Suzuki was dispatched to Burma by the Army General Staff in May 1940, disguised as a correspondent of the *Yomiuri Shimbun* and secretary of the Japan-Burma Association. His assignment was primarily to investigate the possibility of disrupting the Burma Road, but also to make contact with Burmese nationalists. In this second purpose his activities were initially paralleled by an operation being conducted by the Japanese navy.[89] The two efforts were combined in January 1941, however, to form the *Minami Kikan*. Under Suzuki, the *Kikan* was eventually able to smuggle some thirty Burmese ("The Thirty Comrades") out of the colony and to send them to Hainan for combat, intelligence, and political training. Suzuki's organization then infiltrated them back again in the autumn of 1941 through *Kikan* bases established along the Thai-Burmese border. From this nucleus of Burmese volunteers, which included Aung San, the future national leader of Burma, arose the Burma Independence Army which was to be an important and complicating factor in the Allied loss of Burma in 1942.[90]

These operations are of interest for a number of reasons. First, they took place in regions—Burma and Thailand—where Japanese interests had been slim right up to the eve of the Pacific War.[91] The romantic

[88] For the details of the operation see the English translation of Fujiwara's own account, *F Kikan: Japanese Intelligence Operations in Southeast Asia During World War II*, trans. Akashi Yōji (Hong Kong: Heinemann Asia, 1983).

[89] The navy's interest in Burma stemmed from the activities of a former naval officer, a long-time resident in Burma, who was able to elicit the interest of former Naval Academy classmates who had risen to positions of power in the navy and were willing to encourage and even fund the organization of private research on Burma. Lebra, *Japanese-Trained Armies*, pp. 39–40.

[90] See Won Z. Yoon, *Japan's Scheme for the Liberation of Burma: The Role of the Minami Kikan and the "Thirty Comrades,"* Southeast Asia Series no. 27 (Athens, Ohio: Ohio University Press, 1973).

[91] It is curious that there was no Japanese attempt to form an independence army in the East Indies as the Pacific War approached. Joyce Lebra asserts that this was because there was no "lobby" nor any "political officers" in either service committed to the independence of Indonesia as there was in Burma. She implies that the resultant absence of adequate information or expertise on Indonesian nationalism thus precluded the formation of such an organization. (Lebra, *Japanese-Trained Armies*, pp. 78–79). Yet this is incredible when one considers the near decade-long interest of the navy in the East Indies.

idealism displayed by Fujiwara and Suzuki—the "Lawrence of Arabia syndrome" as Louis Allen called it—also provides an arresting contrast with the material and rather cynical outlook of most of the Japanese military in Southeast Asia during the war. But most of all, the initial stages of these operations provided a rare harmony between the motives of the Japanese army (or, at least, of these rather unusual staff officers) and the idealism of Southeast Asian nationalists. It was never again to flourish during the years of actual Japanese occupation. This was in large part due the genuine commitment of these two officers to the independence of Southeast Asian peoples, something that was never a priority of the military commands to which they reported and which was therefore soon given short shrift by Japan's armies of occupation.[92]

The Japanese armed services were not the only government agencies involved in working with underground Southeast Asian nationalist movements on the eve of the war, of course. In the autumn of 1941, the Japanese consulate general in Singapore, with support and direction of Colonel Fujiwara in Bangkok, put together a fifth-column organization code-named *Kame* (The Tortoise), composed of certain Japanese residents in Malaya and members of an anticolonial Malay political association that openly advocated the union of an independent Malaya and Indonesia. The purpose of *Kame* was to use this association to diffuse anticolonial and pro-Japanese propaganda throughout the peninsula and to prepare the groundwork for a joint rising in Malaya and the East Indies as soon as Japan should open hostilities against the Dutch and British. Discovery of the *Kame* organization literally on the eve of the Pacific War and the arrest of its top leadership blunted these schemes, but many of the *Kame* agents soon went free due to the rapid advance of Japanese invading forces.[93]

There were also a number of other organizations and individuals who, with varying degrees of success, undertook a range of minor intelligence activities in Southeast Asia in the several years before the Pacific war. This fact reflected the appearance of literally dozens of "associations" and "societies" purporting to have an interest in the "South Seas" following the government's pronouncement of East Asian Co-Prosperity. Gotō Ken'ichi has illuminated a number of these, including the *Kōa Kyōkai* (Asia Development Society), established in 1940 by the influential right-wing nationalist Iwata Ainosuke who had developed an interest in Southeast Asia through his contacts with *nanshin* advocates in the Japanese navy.[94] Through them, Iwata came to sponsor the activities

[92] Ibid., pp. 7–8.

[93] Cheah Boon Kheng, "The Japanese Occupation of Malaya, 1941–45: Ibrahim Yaacob and the Struggle for Indonesia Raya," *Indonesia*, no. 28 (October 1979): 85–120.

[94] Iwata Ainosuke (1890–1950) spent much of his youth in China where he was involved in a good deal of subversive activity both before and after the fall of the Ch'ing

of a number of "*Nan'yō rōnin*" (Gotō Ken'ichi's term)—younger Japanese who had moved around the East Indies in various occupations and who were imbued, in varying degrees, with anticolonial idealism. In this way, Iwata came to be the patron of a loosely organized intelligence net in Southeast Asia. Seeking to give shape to his expansionist concerns and to give practical training to these potential young activists, Iwata, with the backing of a number of prominent right-wing businessmen, retired service officers, and members of the House of Peers, founded the *Kōa Kyōkai*, whose purpose was to train a cadre of *nampō yōin*—young Japanese who would work to realize Japan's "New Order" in Southeast Asia. A more concrete manifestation of this scheme was Iwata's creation of a private academy in Tokyo, supported in part by the Intelligence Division of the Navy General Staff, for the training of *nampō yōin* (a number of them long-time residents of the East Indies who had been deported by the Dutch authorities) to carry out various intelligence functions in conjunction with the entry of Japanese military forces into Southeast Asia.[95]

One of the more shadowy figures of the Japanese intelligence efforts in Southeast Asia was Ōtani Kōzui.[96] Quondam Buddhist priest, count, archaeologist, wealthy businessman, voluminous writer on Southeast Asia, and possibly intelligence agent, Ōtani had lived off and on in the

---

dynasty. Returning to Japan in 1928, he founded the *Aikokusha*, an ultranationalist and expansionist organization in the tradition of Toyama Mitsuru, and staked out a position as a *hokushin* advocate. As an extreme right-wing nationalist, however, he became a virulent critic of the interwar naval limitations system, particularly of the London Naval Treaty of 1930. His contacts with the antitreaty "Fleet Faction" in the navy brought him in touch with *nanshin* advocates in that service like retired admirals Takeshita Isamu and Sōsa Taneji, and through them he came to know of the circle of Japanese journalists in the East Indies who, in the late 1930s had become devoted to the causes of anticolonialism and Indonesian nationalism. Gotō Ken'ichi, "Iwata Ainousuke to Kōa Kyōkai" [Iwata Ainousuke and the Asia Development Society] in Gotō, *Showa-ki Nihon to Indoneshia*, pp. 237–50.

[95] Ibid., pp. 241, 247–48, 250–52, 254–58.

[96] Ōtani Kōzui (1876–1948), son of the chief abbot of Nishi Honganji in Kyoto, was educated at the Peers School and later studied Chinese and Buddhist classics. An extensive traveler in Asia, he led three expeditions to Central Asia between 1902 and 1909, ostensibly to collect relics from long-lost holy sites of Buddhism, though some have alleged that this was a cover for Japanese military reconnaissance in the region. He became chief abbot of Nishi Honganji upon the death of his father in 1903, but resigned some years later after a financial scandal at the temple. Beginning in 1917, he was engaged in a number of commercial enterprises in the Netherlands East Indies, including a coffee plantation in the Celebes and a spice plantation in Java. He built several villas on Java, where he lived on and off until 1934. Returning to Japan in the late 1930s, he served as adviser to the Cabinet during the war. His voluminous writings on the possibilities for economic development in the East Indies constitute a veritable encyclopedia on the region. Yano, *Nanshin no keifu*, pp. 123–24, and Peter Hopkirk, *Foreign Devils on the Silk Road* (London: Murray, 1980), pp. 26, 190–97.

East Indies since World War I, managing plantations in Java and the Celebes and luxuriating in several villas in Java. His name has been linked to alleged Japanese espionage efforts in Central Asia before World War I, and in the 1930s, his *nanshin* leanings, his supposedly close relations with the Army General Staff, and his active proselytizing for Buddhism within the context of Pan-Asianism, may have been elements in a Japanese propaganda campaign to exploit Buddhism as a tool for extending Japanese influence in Southeast Asia. The veracity or falsehood of these allegations aside, as an important informant and adviser for Japanese military intelligence services, including Tsuji Masanobu's *Doro Nawa* Unit in Taiwan, Ōtani's name does appear in a number of accounts of Japanese intelligence activities in the region just prior to the Pacific War. He also seems to have been involved in an espionage and subversion scheme in Java in 1940 that was designed to collect information on Dutch military defenses around Bandung and to stir up political agitation among the Japanese in central Java.[97]

JAPANESE PREWAR PLANNING FOR THE OCCUPATION OF SOUTHEAST ASIA

In this review of the Japanese prewar penetration of Southeast Asia it remains only to examine the extent, objectives and character of Japanese planning for the occupation of the region. I set aside, of course, the question of Japanese operational planning for the conquest of Southeast Asia which, thanks in part to the intelligence Japan had amassed about the region, was brilliant in its conception and triumphant in its outcome. Rather I turn to planning for the military administration of Southeast Asia which was, on the whole, far less coherent and far less successful in meeting the challenges faced by the various occupation regimes throughout the area.

In pondering the projected occupation of Southeast Asia during 1940–41 Japanese planners had two opportunities within their range of vision: first, the considerable material strengthening of the Japanese war effort that would be achieved by gaining access to the rich resources of the region; and second, the chance to galvanize widespread and long-lasting popular support among the subject peoples of Southeast Asia by making a reality of the Japanese rhetoric of coprosperity. In the long run, the first opportunity came to nought because of the navy's negligence in providing secure means to bring Southeast Asian material resources back to Japan, and the second opportunity was doomed by the obsessive concentration of the Japanese military on the first.

From the outset of Japanese planning for the administration of South-

---

[97] Robertson, *The Japanese File*, pp. 109–10; Gotō, "Nanshin to zai-Indoneshia hōjin shakai," pp. 291–92; and Gotō, "Iwata Ainosuke," p. 236.

east Asia, it was clear that priority was to be given to military (that is, materiel) considerations over those of national independence. The Cabinet Planning Board's statement of August 6, 1940, "Outline of Economic Measures for the Southern Regions" (*Nampō keizai shisaku yōkō*), set the tone. In the creation of a Southeast Asian bloc Japan's military requirements for raw materials were to be given priority and were to be assured by the unlimited export to Japan of certain strategic commodities; Japanese "advisers" would be sent to supervise trade, transportation, and communications within the bloc; Japanese enterprises within the bloc were to be strengthened, but capital was to be raised within the bloc itself.[98]

Despite the longer duration of its interest in Southeast Asia, the navy's fixation on the material aspects of Japanese expansion into Southeast Asia made it unlikely that it would be greatly concerned about the problems of a possible occupation of the region. Thus, it was the army that undertook the first serious research of that sort when the Research Office of the Operations Bureau of the General Staff produced a draft study, "Principles for the Administration and Security of Occupied Southern Regions" (*Nampō senryōchi tōchi chian yōkō*) in March 1941. In this draft, the General Staff planners set forth the three main principles—restoration of public order, the acquisition of strategic materials, and the economic self-sufficiency of Japan's occupation forces— that were formally adopted by the Japanese government as a whole later that year and that were to become a guide for Japanese policy in the initial phase of the Japanese occupation of Southeast Asia.[99]

It is not clear how much thought the General Staff Research Office, or indeed any element of the Japanese government, gave to these matters between March and November of 1941. What is certain is that it was not until the last few weeks before the Pacific War that an Imperial liaison conference, bringing together representatives from the Imperial General Headquarters and the civilian government, met on November 20th to give formal approval to the basic policy document for Japanese military administration in Southeast Asia: "The Essentials for Carrying Out the Administration of Occupied Southern Regions" (*Nampō senryōchi gyōsei jisshi yōryō*).[100]

---

[98] William G. Beasley, *Japanese Imperialism, 1894–1945* (Oxford: Clarendon Press, 1987), p. 228. The full text of the statement is available in GSS 43, *Kokka sōdōin* [National mobilization], Part 1 (Tokyo: Misuzu shobō, 1970), pp. 177–178.

[99] Gotō, "Rikugun nanshin ron," pp. 131–32.

[100] An English translation of this document is provided in Harry Benda, James Irikura, and Koichi Kishi, eds., *Japanese Military Administration in Indonesia: Selected Documents*, Translations Series no. 6, Southeast Asia Studies (New Haven, Conn.: Yale University Press, 1965), pp. 1–3.

Brief and to the point, the November 20 policy statement was bald in its insistence on the priority of Japanese needs over Southeast Asian hopes. It called for the the temporary administration of all occupied territories[101] until political stability had been restored (presumably in the aftermath of combat and the overthrow of former colonial governments). Priority was to be given to Japan's seizure of the strategic resources of the region and to making sure that local economies could make the Japanese occupation forces self-sufficient. The few oblique references to indigenous institutions and national aspirations were dismissive. While it paid lip service to "past organizational structures and native practices," it left the future status of the occupied territories to be determined by Japan, and it cautioned that "premature encouragement of native independence movements shall be avoided."[102] More than this, the welfare of the indigenous populations was to be sacrificed to Japanese military requirements, if need be: "Economic hardships imposed on native livelihood as a result of the acquisition of resources vital to the national defense for the self-sufficiency of troops must be endured."

By omitting any allusions to Pan-Asianism and to the racial affinities between the Japanese and Southeast Asian peoples, the November 20 policy statement clearly abandoned the ideology of coprosperity and the rhetoric of support for national independence in Southeast Asia. Akashi Yōji believes that this readiness to jettison Southeast Asian national aspirations stemmed from the military's recent experience in China, where the army had come to believe that even half-measures toward local autonomy ultimately obstructed military priorities.[103] Be that as it may, the future military occupationnaires of Southeast Asia shared little of the idealism of officers like Fujiwara Iwaichi or Suzuki Keiji, who undertook to stir its peoples into open rebellion. For example, Colonel Watanabe Wataru, assistant chief of staff of the Twenty-fifth Army and architect of the army's harsh policies in Malaya, recalled in later years his contemptuous view of Malay peoples on the eve of the war and his belief that the military occupation there would have to dispense with

[101] Except in Thailand and Indonesia, where separate administrative arrangements had already been made.

[102] While this would seem to mean that Japanese military rule would continue for an indefinite period, the authors of a recent Japanese study of Japan's military administration in Southeast Asia argue that the November 20 policy statement viewed military administration as an interim measure, not as a long-term interregnum, and that with the progress of Japanese policy in the occupied territories, the institutions of military administration would be transformed to new civilian governments created by Japan. Bōeicho Bōei Kenshūjō, Senshibu, *Nampō gunsei* [Military administration of southern areas] (Tokyo: Asagumo Shimbun Sha, 1985), p. 17.

[103] Akashi Yōji, "The Formation of the Malay Military Administration and Its Policies, November, 1941–July, 1942," *Asian Forum* 3, no. 3 (July–September 1971): 140.

"the claptrap policy [of] giving them rosy promises and sympathy. That they had been subjugated so long under British rule was God's punishment. They must be made to examine themselves and show their penitence."[104]

In passing, it is important to mention two other documents, drafted in the last days before the war, that framed Japanese planning for a takeover of Southeast Asia prior to the actual military occupation of the region. The first of these was a joint army-navy agreement on November 26 that allotted the specific geographic areas of administrative responsibility between the two services. By the agreement, the army was to take control of all of Southeast Asia except for the major portions of the East Indies—Borneo, the Celebes, the Moluccas, and the lesser Sunda Islands—which were to be be administered by the navy. This arrangement was made largely to divide the material spoils of Southeast Asia between the two services, but failed, nevertheless, to prevent interservice friction over access to strategic resources during the war.[105] The second policy statement was approved at an Imperial Liaison Conference five days after commencement of hostilities and spelled out in greater detail the plans for Japan's economic exploitation of the territories to be occupied. Utterly devoid of any consideration of the economic well-being of the subject peoples of Southeast Asia, the document, in the words of its drafters, was concerned only with "the rapid aggrandizement and strengthening of the self-sufficient economic power of the Imperial government."[106]

While discussion of the outcome of this planning during Japan's actual occupation of Southeast Asia in 1942–45, lies outside the scope of this chapter, a few comments are in order about its implications for that occupation. To begin with, despite the Japan's prewar rhetoric of coprosperity and its denunciations of colonialism, Japanese plans for the economic exploitation of Southeast Asia represented an imperialism far more rapacious than that of the Western colonial powers it intended to overthrow. The latter had been compelled by their own economic self-interest to provide at least a minimum of public services and economic

[104] Akashi Yōji, "Japanese Military Administration in Malaya—Its Formation and Evolution in Reference to Sultans, the Islamic Religion, the Moslem Malays, 1941–1945," *Asian Studies* (Quezon City) 7 (1969): 84.

[105] Under this agreement the navy acquired smaller oilfields in Borneo that produced high-quality petroleum, but the largest fields in the East Indies, those at Palembang on Sumatra, were left in army hands, a source of bitter regret and recrimination by navy personnel during and after the war. Gotō, "Kaigun nanshin ron," pp. 80–81.

[106] From the English translation of "General Plan of Economic Policies for the Southern Area" (*Nampō keizai taisaku yōkō*) cited in Frank Trager, ed., *Burma: Japanese Military Administration, Selected Documents, 1941–1945* (Philadelphia : University of Pennsylvania Press, 1971), p. 38.

infrastructure for the welfare of their subject peoples. Like all the imperial powers that had exploited China, Japan apparently felt no need to
consider such undertakings. Indeed, William Beasley has noted that the
privileges that the Japanese planned for themselves in Southeast Asia—
close control of trade, mining concessions, domination of transportation and communication systems, supervisory authority over regional
financial structures, and the political arrangements to ensure these privileges—bore ominous similarity to the Japanese informal empire in
China, except that in Southeast Asia, Japan had no intention of sharing
its gains with anyone else.[107]

Second, Japanese planning was insufficiently buttressed by an ideological approach to the peoples of Southeast Asia that could have maintained for long their support for an expanded and extended Japanese
presence there. In his comparative analysis of Japan's occupation regimes in Java and Luzon, Theodore Friend has explored the vacuity of
concepts like *hakkō-ichiu* ("all the world under one roof") whose hierarchical assumptions hardly squared with Japanese protestations of
Asian brotherhood, and has taken note of the fact that Japanese planners
hardly gave thought to the absence of cultural commonalities between
Japan and the peoples of Southeast Asia it proposed to guide.[108]

Third, Japanese planning suffered from an absence of what would
today be called area expertise, being largely left in the hands of military
men who had little knowledge of Southeast Asia and who were absorbed almost entirely in strategic and operational concerns. Thus,
while a great mass of intelligence was collected about Southeast Asia
before the war by military, consular, and private sources, there were
few in the government, and in the military specifically, with sufficient
background to analyze this information for the purposes of putting together a coherent plan for Japan's wartime relationship with Southeast
Asian peoples. Moreover, as Akashi Yōji has noted, prewar misconceptions and prejudices often distorted the Japanese occupation policies toward Southeast Asia. Japanese policy toward the overseas Chinese in
Southeast Asia exemplifies these problems. Few among the army's top
brass or in the military intelligence services had any command of Chinese and no one had any facility in the language in the Twenty-fifth
Army, the force that was scheduled to occupy Malaya and Singapore
where the greatest numbers of overseas Chinese were concentrated.
Moreover, despite the generally moderate policy toward the Chinese
envisioned by the army high command in its November 20, 1941, pol-

---

[107] Beasley, *Japanese Imperialism*, p. 228.

[108] Theodore Friend, *The Blue-Eyed Enemy: Japan Against the West in Java and Luzon,
1942–1945* (Princeton, N.J.: Princeton University Press, 1988), pp, 54–74.

icy statement (in order to gain Chinese commercial experience and capital), virulent anti-Chinese attitudes within the Twenty-fifth Army staff, particularly among those who had fought in China, contributed to the rapid abandonment of any attempt to win the hearts and minds of Chinese in Southeast Asia and, in the case of Chinese in Singapore, led to the massacres of February 1942.[109]

Fourth, the most salient point about Japanese planning for the occupation of Southeast Asia is that there was too little of it. Grant Goodman has written of the "spontaneity . . . the confusion, which characterized the policies of Japan in Southeast Asia, the varieties of patterns of rule, the disparities and divergences within and among agencies of Japanese government . . . the naiveté, as well as the arbitrariness of Japanese actions."[110] Peter Duus has said that the Japanese wartime empire was very much a "bicycle empire," likely to topple immediately unless furiously pedaled forward. This observation particularly applies to the southern wing of the empire and stems in part from a failure in Japanese planning which, in turn, derives from the imbalance between the sudden rush of Japanese ambitions in Southeast Asia in 1940–41 and the time available to plan for their realization. While operational planning for the conquest of Southeast Asia could be and was, brilliantly improvised, the myriad political, economic, and cultural problems that Japan was to confront once it occupied the region required more time than the waning months of 1941 to assay and to solve. The result was a lack of direction and coherence that permeated Japan's occupation from its outset.

Fifth and finally, Goodman's judgment on Japan's unstable wartime interregnum in Southeast Asia points to the absence, prior to 1940, of a concerted Japanese plan to dominate the region. Yet, as I have tried to demonstrate in this paper, the various elements of Japanese involvement in Southeast Asia during the 1930s had provided Japanese leaders with an image of its enormous strategic value, an image that the fortuitous circumstances of 1940–41 made irresistible.

Reflections on the Southward Advance, 1931–1941

In this overview of Japan's involvement in Southeast Asia at the beginning of the 1930s and its aggressive penetration of it by the end of the decade, I have tried to demonstrate that Japanese activities in the region were due to a complex interplay of circumstance and motivation. A

---

[109] Akashi, "Japanese Policy Toward Malayan Chinese," pp. 61–62.

[110] Grant Goodman, "Japan and Southeast Asia in the Pacific War: A Case of Cultural Ambiguity," in *Studies on Japanese Culture* (Tokyo: The Japan P.E.N. Club, 1973), p. 235.

region far over the horizons of the Japanese in earlier decades, remote from Japanese influence or even ambition, Southeast Asia had appeared to hold no pressing strategic relevance for Japan's insular security as had Korea or Manchuria at the close of the nineteenth century, nor, for most Japanese, had it seemed to offer a commercial bonanza, as had China at the beginning of the twentieth. Moreover, those few Japanese who had taken note of its riches had been confronted with the fact that its wealth appeared already spoken for.

Chance had much to do with the shift in these perspectives, first in 1914–18 in terms of unanticipated economic advantage and again, in 1940–41, in terms of unplanned strategic opportunity. It is important to note, moreover, that Japan's ability to take advantage of each of these windfalls represented as much a weakening of Western institutions in Southeast Asia as it did the growth of Japanese power and influence. Circumstance served to strengthen motivation, of course. The way was paved for the aggressive advance of Japanese commerce into Southeast Asia in the early 1930s by the success of Japanese commercial ventures there during World War I. More importantly, the congruence of a rapidly developing military technology, the need for specific strategic resources to keep it running, and the recognition that those resources existed in abundance in Southeast Asia provided the impetus for the sudden surge in Japan's imperial ambitions in the mid-1930s. Without the development of pneumatic tires for military vehicles, aircraft engines using high-octane gasoline, or oil-fired propulsion systems for naval vessels, one might argue that the Japanese political penetration of Southeast Asia would have come much later, if at all.

Yet one may also reasonably argue that Japan's interest in Southeast Asia was the end product of strategic assumptions set down as early as the late nineteenth century. One thinks here of Yamagata Aritomo's famous dicta on the compass of the nation's strategic concerns which he set forth in the 1890s. Manifested in concentric circles of national interest radiating outward from the home islands, Yamagata's strategic doctrine committed the nation to ever-expanding and ever-receding security goals, and involved the Japanese empire in a series of seemingly endless strategic "problems" that troubled its entire history. Each presented the nation with a set of opportunities that balanced the difficulties each posed and Japan's solution to each "problem" seemed to open the door to further opportunites and frustrations. Thus, the "Korean problem" of the Meiji period had laid the groundwork for the "Manchurian problem" of the Taishō; that in turn, ushered in the "China problem" of the first years of Shōwa, which led logically, if not inevitably, to the "Southern Regions problem" of the late 1930s.

It is not necessary to see a long-range plan in this chain of issues or to place upon it a conspiratorial construction. Chance played too great a part in it. Yet a set of attitudes and concerns relating to Japanese security and economic advantage provided a common link among its parts. Certainly, it is reasonable to perceive that *nanshin* exponents like Ishihara Hiroichiro and the officers of the navy's *Tainanken* in the late 1930s wished, at the very least, to establish an informal imperialism in Southeast Asia of the sort that Japan already enjoyed in China.

In this pattern of Japanese ambition in Southeast Asia ideology played a secondary if significant part. The idea of the "southward advance"—a southward destiny for the Japanese people—had never been as important in drawing Japan into Southeast Asia as had been the specific opportunities and hard interests there. As for Pan-Asianism and the idea of Asian liberation, these were latecomers to the ideology of Japanese imperialism in general and to that of the *nanshin* in particular. For those who made policy in Tokyo such notions were useful as pretexts and as incendiary rhetoric to ignite the tinder of Southeast Asian nationalism. But even the most ideological among them never lost sight of Japan's material advantage as the nation's iron-hard purpose in Southeast Asia. Inevitably, such prejudices and priorities poisoned Japanese relations with Southeast Asian peoples and helped to assure the brevity of the Japanese wartime interregnum in the region.

CHAPTER 8

Anomaly or Model?
Independent Thailand's Role in
Japan's Asian Strategy, 1941–1943

E. Bruce Reynolds

Defenders of Imperial Japan are quick to cite the fact that the Greater East Asian War (1941–45) led to the collapse of the prewar colonial regimes in Southeast Asia and to the emergence of independent states throughout the region. Some have gone on to suggest that because the Japanese had aimed at precisely this outcome from the beginning, Japan nobly sacrificed itself to liberate Asia from the yoke of Western colonialism.[1] But are such arguments based on historical fact? What degree of independence did the Japanese envision for states within their Greater East Asia Co-Prosperity Sphere?

This chapter examines Japanese intentions by focusing on their policies toward Thailand, a nation that occupied a unique position within the wartime empire. As an independent Asian state and a formal ally, Thailand's situation differed greatly from that of the former Western colonies—Burma, Malaya, the East Indies, and the Philippines—where Japanese military forces assumed direct control. As its internationally recognized government remained in place after the arrival of the Japanese army, Thailand's status was not analogous to the puppet regimes created by the Japanese in Manchukuo or occupied China, either. Moreover, while both Thailand and Indochina were garrisoned by Japanese troops under treaties with the existing administrations, for reasons of diplomacy and expediency the French colonial regime continued to rule Indochina until 1945. Thus, an examination of the evolution of Japan's policies toward independent Thailand is the best means of gaug-

---

[1] The most famous of such revisionist works is Hayashi Fusao's *Daitōasensō kōteiron* [An Affirmation of the Greater East Asian War] (Tokyo: Banchō shobō, 1974). His thesis is discussed by James W. Morley in *Dilemmas of Growth in Prewar Japan* (Princeton, N.J.: Princeton University Press, 1971), p. 15, and his ideas are affirmed and expanded upon by Hasegawa Michiko in "A Postwar View of the Greater East Asian War," *Japan Echo* 11, Special Issue (1984): 29–37. A recent book portraying the Greater East Asian War as a war of liberation is ASEAN Sentaa, ed., *Ajia ni ikiru Daitōasensō* [The Greater East Asia War which enlivened Asia] (Tokyo: Tentensha, 1988).

ing the extent to which the Japanese intended to promote, or even to tolerate, autonomy within their sphere.

THE GENESIS OF THE JAPANESE-THAI ALLIANCE

The alliance between Imperial Japan and Thailand might be described as a shotgun marriage, since its signing was preceded by the arrival of the Japanese army on Thai soil, but in a sense it was the culmination of a courtship between the two sides that began in 1933. Although Japan had maintained formal diplomatic relations with Siam (as Thailand was called prior to 1939) since 1898, Southeast Asia's lone independent state first became a major object of Japanese attention when it abstained from the League of Nations' otherwise unanimous vote approving the Lytton Report, a document critical of the Japanese seizure of Manchuria. While Siam had refused to take a stand simply to avoid antagonizing either Japan or China, the isolated Japanese chose to interpret the abstention as a display of solidarity and praised it extravagantly.[2]

In the wake of this unprecedented show of Japanese interest in Siam, representatives of a cabal of Thai military officers sought Japanese support for a plot to overthrow the Bangkok government. A coup d'état on June 24, 1932, had ended the absolute monarchy, but traditionalist conservatives had reasserted control. The plotters wanted material support, but particularly hoped that the Japanese might deter a feared intervention by the British or French. Although they got nothing more than verbal encouragement from Japanese Minister Yatabe Yasukichi, and there is no evidence that the Western powers ever seriously considered intervening, the success of the June 20, 1933, coup led to a convergence of interests that greatly intensified relations between Siam and Japan over the next eight years.[3]

While the young military men and civilian bureaucrats who dominated the new regime in Bangkok had rebelled against a reigning monarch rather than seizing power in his name—as had been the case in Japan in 1868—their goals of strengthening and modernizing their country were similar to those of the leaders of Japan's Meiji Restoration. Accordingly, they appreciated the magnitude of Japan's achievements over the previous six decades, and they had a natural interest in learning from the Japanese experience. Also, as their 1933 appeal for Japanese assistance suggests, they recognized that Japan could serve as a

[2] See Ishii Itarō, *Gaikōkan no isshō* [The life of a diplomat], repr. (Tokyo: Chūōkōronsha, 1986) p. 270. Ishii headed the Japanese Legation in Bangkok in 1936–37.

[3] E. Thadeus Flood, "Japan's Relations with Thailand: 1928–1941" (Ph.D. dissertation, University of Washington, 1967), pp. 58–60.

useful diplomatic counterweight to Britain and France, whose colonial territories surrounded Siam.

On the other side, the Japanese desire to strengthen relations with Siam increased in step with an ever-growing sense of isolation throughout the 1930s. Not only had the Manchurian Incident marked the end of Japan's strategy of seeking cooperation with the West, but the other powers had responded to the Great Depression by erecting barriers against the entry of Japanese goods, even into their Asian colonies. Under these circumstances the Japanese viewed Siam as a welcome outlet for their manufactured goods, as well as a source for rice, rubber, and tin. Friendship with Siam also fit neatly into Japan's new look-to-Asia program.[4] Additionally, as an attack on the British Empire became an increasingly real possibility, Japanese military strategists recognized Siam's potential as a launching platform for operations against Malaya and Burma.[5]

The Japanese, who had made special efforts to promote ties between the military services of the two countries, had reason to be pleased when Phibun Songkhram moved up from minister of defense to the premiership at the end of 1938. Phibun had spoken favorably of Japan and had maintained friendly personal relations with the Japanese military and naval attachés in Bangkok. A handsome and charismatic forty-one-year-old artillery officer, Phibun had been a key player in the successful coups of 1932 and 1933. Like China's Chiang Kai-shek and many Japanese officers, he was much impressed by the Fascist and Nazi regimes in Europe, and saw himself as a man of destiny like Napoleon, his personal hero. His decision to change his country's name to Thailand in 1939 is generally interpreted as signaling an ambition to expand the national borders to encompass the ethnically related peoples in neighboring colonial areas.

Although Phibun has often been labelled "pro-Japanese," it is more accurate to say that he and his advisers were thoroughly opportunistic and sought to derive maximum political and diplomatic advantage from shifts in the balance of power. For example, in the summer of 1939,

---

[4] On Japan's economic strategies, see William L. Swan, "Aspects of Japan's Prewar Economic Relations with Thailand" in *Thai-Japanese Relations in Historical Perspective*, ed. Chaiwat Khamchoo and E. Bruce Reynolds (Bangkok: Chulalongkorn University Institute of Asian Studies, 1988), pp. 59–123.

[5] Siam's importance in Japanese plans for the invasion of Malaya was even suggested publicly in a war scenario written by a Japanese naval officer, which was translated and published in the West. See Ishimaru Tōta, *Japan Must Fight Britain* (New York: Telegraph Press, 1936), pp. 255–56. Thai Premier Phibun Songkhram spoke publicly of Japan's strategic designs on Thailand on March 31, 1937, sparking a flurry of diplomatic protests. The incident is described in Ishii, *Gaikōkan no isshō*, pp. 279–81.

when a full German-Italian-Japanese alliance seemed likely and the British appeared weak and vacillating, Phibun steered toward the Japanese camp. He quickly veered back to the middle of the road after the Japanese were embarrassed by the German-Soviet pact and the British and French went to war over Germany's invasion of Poland. Then he again trimmed toward the Axis side when the Germans swept through Western Europe in the spring of 1940, leaving Britain isolated and on the verge of defeat.

In the latter instance, Phibun took advantage of the fall of France in June 1940 to lay claim to Lao and Cambodian regions that had been under Thai suzerainty before being incorporated into French Indochina. He tried various approaches to achieve his territorial goals, but the Japanese move into northern Indochina and the signing of the Tripartite Pact in late September convinced him that he could succeed only with strong Japanese support. To gain this, he secretly promised to allow the Japanese army free passage through southern Thailand if Japan launched an assault on Singapore. In return, the Japanese imposed a truce, at Phibun's request, to halt a subsequent Thai-French border war in January 1941, and helped the Thai extract a portion of the desired land from the French.[6]

But while Phibun had made a secret commitment to the Japanese, he was playing a double game by simultaneously urging the British and Americans to deter any further Japanese advance. He and his advisers recognized that Thailand's independence could best be protected, and the nation's bargaining power maximized, by a great-power standoff. They were by no means oblivious to the dangers of Japanese domination.[7]

Phibun's diplomatic tightrope walk became untenable after July 1941, though, as the Western powers responded to the move of Japanese troops into southern French Indochina with an asset freeze that cut off Japan's oil supply. Phibun publicly declared that Thailand would defend its neutrality against any invader. However, as Japanese-American negotiations headed toward a dead end and hopes for effective Anglo-American deterrence faded, he knew that war was imminent and he sought to minimize the negative impact of the anticipated Japanese advance. From October 1941 Phibun carried on secret discussions with

[6] The most detailed description of the negotiations following the Thai-French border war appears in Flood, "Japan's Relations with Thailand," pp. 415–594.

[7] Thai maneuvers during this period are treated more fully in the author's "Kōhatsu naru shōkoku gaikō: Tai to Nihon nanshin" [Crafty small-nation diplomacy: Thailand and Japan's southern advance], trans. Takahashi Hisashi, in Gunji Shigakkai, *Dainiji sekai taisen: hassei to kakudai* [The Second World War: Outbreak and Expansion] (Tokyo: Kinsei, 1990), pp. 149–63.

Japanese Military Attaché Col. Tamura Hiroshi, an intelligence officer who had responsibility for laying the groundwork for the assaults on Malaya and Burma. Phibun asked that the Japanese spare him the embarrassment of a foreign military presence in the Bangkok area, telling Tamura that he would keep his promise to allow unimpeded passage if the Japanese army limited itself to using remote southern Thailand as a landing area and staging ground.[8]

The sympathetic Tamura tried to convince his superiors at least to delay an advance into central Thailand, but while Japanese at all levels did not wish their country to be seen as having invaded a friendly, neutral, Asian state, military considerations limited Tokyo's flexibility. Army strategists insisted on the early advance of troops from Cambodia to Bangkok because they wished to utilize the Thai railway system as a supply artery for the Malayan campaign. They also wanted to lay the groundwork for an early attack from central Thailand into Burma. The army did agree that Phibun could be offered a multiple choice ultimatum on the eve of the Japanese advance, but to maintain secrecy General (later Field Marshal) Terauchi Hisa'ichi's Southern Army Headquarters (SAHQ) ruled that this could be presented only two hours before landing operations were to begin in southern Thailand. While the minimum demand was free passage and full material support for Japanese troops, if the Thai wished to commit themselves further they could choose a defensive alliance, an offensive-defensive alliance, or membership in the Axis Pact.[9]

Despite the effort to maintain secrecy, however, Phibun had sufficient evidence to anticipate the Japanese offensive. In light of his strong pledges that Thailand would fight any invader, he did not wish to be present when the Japanese came to request the promised free passage, so he left Bangkok on December 6 for the ostensible purpose of inspecting the eastern border region. By the time he reappeared, shortly after dawn on the morning of December 8, Thai soldiers in the southern provinces had already obeyed standing orders and engaged the Japanese invasion force. Although Phibun called a halt to the fighting before key army units in central Thailand became involved, and hastened to accept the minimum Japanese demands, his absence had provided the

---

[8] Bōeichō bōei kenshūjo senshishitsu (hereafter "Senshishitsu"), *Maree shinkō sakusen* [The Advance in Malaya] (Tokyo: Asagumo shimbunsha, 1966), pp. 150–52.

[9] Ibid., pp. 151–52; Senshishitsu, *Daihon'ei rikugunbu* [Imperial General Headquarters Army Section], 8 vols. (Tokyo: Asagumo shimbunsha, 1968–74) 3:135; and Kushida Masao, "Daitōasensō kaishi tōsho ni okeru Nihongun no Taikoku heiwa shinchū" [The Japanese army's peaceful advance into Thailand at the beginning of the Greater East Asian War], pp. 8–15, an unpublished manuscript held by the National Institute for Defense Studies (hereafter, NIDS), Tokyo.

scope for a face-saving show of resistance. In case the Japanese offensive ultimately failed, the Thai could tell the British and Americans that they had attempted to defend their neutrality, but had been forced to bow to overwhelming force. For their part, the Japanese sought to gloss over matters by suppressing news of the clashes with the Thai army and propagating a false story that their forces had entered Thailand in response to a prior incursion by British troops.[10]

At first, Phibun hoped that the Japanese forces might pass through quickly and leave the Thai to their own devices, but it soon became apparent that they had no such intention. The Japanese also pressed for a deeper Thai commitment to the war in hopes of ensuring full cooperation. Having Thailand as an ally would offer obvious propaganda advantages, too. Faced with Japanese pressure and influenced by the magnitude of their initial victories—particularly the sinking of the British warships *Prince of Wales* and *Repulse*—Phibun moved quickly into the Japanese camp. Entering a full-fledged alliance seemed the best way to assuage the Japanese and thereby preserve as much Thai autonomy as possible. In particular, Phibun wanted to ensure that the Thai army, his main base of support, would not be disarmed. The alliance treaty, formally signed on December 21, 1941, also offered a potential dividend in the event of ultimate Japanese victory, as a secret clause promised unspecified assistance in the return of additional "lost territory" to Thailand.[11]

Although Phibun has been criticized for going too far to accommodate the Japanese, especially because of his subsequent decision to declare war on Britain and the United States, it must be conceded that he faced a very difficult situation. The alliance did serve the purposes of preserving the Thai army and allowing the Thai government to maintain control over domestic affairs. For example, because of the alliance, the Japanese military forces, even the dreaded *Kempeitai* (military police), acted with more restraint in Thailand than in the occupied areas, and the Thai were able to resist Japanese efforts to place advisers in government ministries. But this relative autonomy did not meet Phibun's expectations. In return for his strong public commitment to Japan he had hoped that Thailand would be accorded a high degree of respect and special favor as an independent Asia ally. Here, as we shall see, he would be sorely disappointed.

[10] On the events at the beginning of the war, see E. Bruce Reynolds, *Thailand and Japan's Southern Advance, 1940–1945* (New York: St. Martin's Press, 1994), pp. 81–111. The claim of a prior British invasion appears in the evening edition of the *Japan Times and Advertiser*, December 8, 1941. It is refuted in the London *Times* of December 10, 1941.

[11] The full text of the alliance treaty appears in Ota Ichirō, ed., *Nihon gaikōshi: Daitōa sensō senji gaikō* [Japanese diplomatic history: Diplomacy during the Greater East Asian War] (Tokyo: Kajima kenkyūjo shuppankai, 1971), pp. 163–64.

THE GREATER EAST ASIA CO-PROSPERITY SPHERE

Professor Yano Tōru has aptly likened the Greater East Asian Co-Prosperity Sphere into which Thailand entered in December 1941 to a *furoshiki,* the versatile piece of cloth that Japanese use for wrapping and carrying.[12] Just as a *furoshiki* can be unfolded to increase its capacity, the Greater East Asia Co-Prosperity Sphere construct, originally developed in response to the opportunities presented by the defeat of the Netherlands and France in mid-1940,[13] had sufficient flexibility to accommodate an expanding vision of empire. Moreover, just as an attractive *furoshiki* can mask unsightly contents, euphonious words like "co-prosperity" and "cooperation" were employed to disguise less happy realities in Japan's wartime empire.

Genuine Pan-Asian, anti-imperialist sentiments had, of course, moved many Japanese since the Meiji period, but the idealists who urged that Japan's primary mission should be to assist and uplift fellow Asians had seldom exerted much influence on government policy. Instead, Japan had emulated the Western model in building its own colonial empire in Asia, and its leaders had generally attempted to promote national interests through cooperation with the Western powers. While the other powers' refusal to acquiesce in Tokyo's efforts to establish a broader, more self-sufficient empire in the 1930s gave new currency to Pan-Asian rhetoric, Japan's 1937 plunge into a full-scale war against China made a mockery of the claim that in establishing an "Asian Monroe Doctrine" Japan was acting in the interests of Asia as a whole. Although Japanese propagandists claimed that Japan was fighting Chiang Kai-shek only because he was under the sway of the Western powers, it was not a very persuasive argument.

The subsequent war against the Western colonial powers was much easier to reconcile with Pan-Asian and anti-imperialist rhetoric, but many contradictions remained.[14] While Japanese propaganda emphasized the intention to expunge "evil" Western colonial influences from the region, the Japanese occupation forces were instructed to utilize ex-

[12] Yano Tōru, *Nanshin no keifu* [The lineage of the southward advance] (Tokyo: Chūō-kōronsha, 1975), p. 157.

[13] For a discussion of the origins of and the rationale behind the Greater East Asia Co-Prosperity Sphere concept, see Gordon M. Berger, "The Three-Dimensional Empire: Japanese Attitudes and the New Order in Asia, 1937–1945," *Japan Interpreter* 12, nos. 3–4 (Summer 1979): 371–75; and Miwa Kimitada, "Japanese Concepts and Policies for a Regional Order in Asia, 1938–1940," in *The Ambivalence of Nationalism*, ed. James W. White, Michiko Umegaki, and Thomas R. H. Havens (New York: University Press of America, 1990), pp. 133–56.

[14] See the description of the reaction of Japanese intellectuals to the outbreak of the war in Masataka Kosaka's "The Showa Era," in *Showa*, ed. Carol Gluck and Stephen R. Graubard (New York: W. W. Norton, 1992), p. 37.

isting administrative structures and to avoid "premature" encouragement of nationalist groups. Moreover, the Imperial rescript announcing the war made no mention of promoting the independence of Asian states—instead it stressed the restoration of "stability" and "peace"—and the Japanese were laying plans to make strategically located Singapore and the resource-rich areas of Malaya and the East Indies into colonies. Prime Minister Tōjō Hideki did speak of future independence for the Philippines and Burma in an important Diet speech on January 21, 1942, but these were special cases because the Americans had already promised the Filipinos independence and Burmese nationalists were actively assisting the Japanese army.[15]

Even in the case of the Philippines and Burma, though, Tōjō made clear that he did not envision them dealing with Japan on a basis of equality. He indicated that relationships between nations within the sphere would be based on a Confucian-style hierarchy, with each assuming its "proper place."[16] In this new order, the Japanese believed that they had earned an inalienable right to leadership because of their military and economic successes, the glory of their "unbroken" imperial line, and their unique success in synthesizing Eastern and Western cultures.[17] The Military Affairs Bureau's April 1942 public explanation of

[15] John M. Maki, ed., *Conflict and Tension in the Far East* (Seattle: University of Washington Press, 1961), pp. 104–5; Nobutaka Ike, ed., *Japan's Decision for War* (Stanford, Calif.: Stanford University Press, 1967), pp. 251–53; Joyce C. Lebra, ed., *Japan's Greater East Asia Co-Prosperity Sphere in World War II* (Kuala Lumpur: Oxford University Press, 1975), pp. 78–81; and Francis C. Jones, *Japan's New Order in East Asia* (London: Oxford University Press, 1954), p. 331.

[16] The concept of each race finding its "proper," albeit inherently inferior, place is discussed at length in John W. Dower, *War Without Mercy* (New York: Pantheon, 1986), pp. 203–33, 265–66. Mark R. Peattie notes in "Japanese Attitudes toward Colonialism, 1895–1945" in *The Japanese Colonial Empire*, ed. Ramon H. Myers and Mark R. Peattie (Princeton, N.J.: Princeton University Press, 1984), pp. 109–13, that the concept was first promoted in writings of Tōgō Minoru. In "The Three-Dimensional Empire: Japanese Attitudes and the New Order in Asia," p. 372, Berger notes that Foreign Minister Arita Hachirō used the phrase publicly as early as June 1940.

[17] Dower examines the Japanese rationale for leadership over three chapters of *War without Mercy*, pp. 203–90. The cultural theme particularly caught the fancy of Japanese pundits during the heady days of early 1942. They called for the development of a "new Asian culture" that would blend the best characteristics of all the constituent societies, but since they believed that Japan had already synthesized the best that world civilizations had to offer, this amounted to little more than a new slant on the "Japanization" policy long favored as a means of controlling the inhabitants of the Japanese colonies. For examples, see writings by Okawa Shūmei in Lebra, *Japan's Greater East Asia Co-Prosperity Sphere*, pp. 38–40; by Kamei Kan'ichirō in his *Daitōa minzoku no michi* [The path for the peoples of Greater East Asia] (Tokyo: Shōki shobō, 1941), pp. 213–26; and by Ishii Fumio, Count Kuroda Kiyoshi, and Minowa Saburō, respectively, in the *Japan Times and Advertiser*, December 15, 1941, January 6, 1942, and March 29, 1942. The cultural theorists drew

administrative policy in the southern region reflected this master-race mentality. It stressed that since Japan's interests came first: "It is therefore imperative that all measures necessary for Japan's own existence be carried out resolutely. Too much consideration for the inhabitants might engender in their minds a tendency to presume on Japan's kindness with pernicious effect to Japanese rule. Japan is, so to speak, their elder brother, and they are Japan's younger brothers. There must be close unity between these brothers in their efforts to reconstruct New East Asia in which they can live happily together. The fact must not be lost sight of that Japan is the leader, and this fact must be brought home to the inhabitants of the occupied territories."[18]

Theoretically, such policies for "occupied territories" under direct military rule did not apply to Thailand, an allied country whose "independence, sovereignty, and honor" Japan had promised from the beginning to ensure,[19] but a "victory disease"–induced sense of superiority had its impact on Tokyo's policies there, too. Rather than placing Thailand on a pedestal as a model for other Asian peoples aspiring to national self-determination—a policy one diplomat publicly advocated[20]—many Japanese bureaucrats viewed independent Thailand as a troublesome anomaly. Nowhere is this more apparent than in the tendency in 1942 policy papers to categorize Thailand together with the ultimate misfit in Greater East Asia, French Indochina. The common denominator between Asian ally and European colony was the fact that in both Thailand and Indochina treaty relationships made it difficult for the Japanese to operate in the arbitrary, untrammeled fashion to which they had become accustomed.

THE JAPANESE ARMY'S ATTITUDE TOWARD THAILAND

In analyzing the Japanese policy toward Thailand, the role of the army, especially the regional command, SAHQ, deserves special attention be-

---

heavily on the works of Okakura Tenshin, analyzed in F. G. Notehelfer's "On Idealism and Realism in the Thought of Okakura Tenshin," *Journal of Japanese Studies* 16, no. 2 (Summer 1990): 309–55. On "Japanization" in the colonies, see Peattie, "Japanese Attitudes toward Colonialism, 1895–1945," pp. 96–104.

[18] *Japan Times and Advertiser*, 12 April 1942. The tone of this is reminiscent of Nitobe Inazō's injunction: "Merely being kind to [colonial subjects] is insufficient. Primitive peoples are motivated by awe," quoted in Peattie, "Japanese Attitudes toward Colonialism, 1895–1945," p. 88. Also, see the "Plan for Leadership of the Nationalities" in Lebra, *Japan's Greater East Asia Co-Prosperity Sphere*, pp. 118–21.

[19] This pledge was contained in the troop passage agreement of December 8, 1941, the text of which appears in Ōta, *Nihon gaikōshi: Daitōasensō senji gaikō*, p. 161.

[20] See the article by Yanagisawa Ken in the *Japan Times and Advertiser* of April 24, 1942. Yanagisawa had just been appointed to head the Japanese cultural program in Thailand.

cause, particularly in the early phases of the war, military authorities had much leeway to determine its parameters. While the alliance with Japan protected Thai sovereignty in principle, in practice, Thai officials had to cope with Japanese military officers who viewed Thailand as a convenient staging area and cared little about diplomatic niceties.

The Southern Army, then headquartered in Saigon, consistently took a harder line toward Thailand than either Tokyo's Imperial General Headquarters (hereafter, IGHQ), or the military representatives in Bangkok. In large part this is attributable simply to a knee-jerk opposition to any policy that had the slightest potential to interfere with military operations. This attitude is evident, for example, in SAHQ's hostility toward Gen. Imamura Hitoshi's "soft" occupation policies on Java, where the local people had warmly welcomed Japanese forces.[21] In the case of Thailand, however, another factor was a stubborn unwillingness to forgive and forget Phibun's disappearance on the eve of the war and his army's temerity in opposing the Japanese forces.[22] While suspicions about Phibun's absence at the critical moment were well founded, SAHQ's failure to let bygones be bygones can only be considered counterproductive in light of his subsequent willingness to cooperate.

SAHQ's harsh attitude toward Thailand first manifested itself when the Japanese service attachés, staff officers of the Japanese 15th Division, and Thai military authorities agreed to divide up military responsibilities for the assault on Burma. Their plan, hammered out in Bangkok shortly after the initialing of the bilateral alliance on December 11, 1941, provided for active Thai involvement in the invasion and called for Japanese army and air force operations to the south of the planned invasion corridor (the Tak–Mae Sot road), while the Thai forces were to operate to the north. SAHQ had not been consulted, however, and

[21] See Imamura's memoir in Anthony Reid and Oki Akira, eds., *The Japanese Experience in Indonesia: Selected Memoirs of 1942–1945* (Athens: Ohio University Center for International Studies, 1986), pp. 31–77. Also note Burmese leader Ba Maw's comments on SAHQ's attitude in *Breakthrough in Burma* (New Haven, Conn.: Yale University Press, 1968), pp. 205, 308.

[22] In Jōhō Hayao, ed., *Gensui Terauchi Hisa'ichi* [Field Marshal Terauchi Hisa'ichi] (Tokyo: Fuyō shobō, 1978), pp. 336–37, a staff officer recalls that Phibun's absence forced Terauchi to order a land advance into Thailand without knowing whether the Thai would resist or not. He described this as the most "anguished" decision he had seen his commander make. The SAHQ vice chief of staff notes Terauchi's dislike of Phibun on p. 77 of the same volume. It is notable that Terauchi made various inspection tours of the southern region during his more than three and half years as Southern Army commander, but avoided Thailand. Also, see the comments of Hattori Takushirō, quoted in Senshishitsu, *Daihon'ei rikugunbu*, 3:257, on the difference in attitude of IGHQ and SAHQ regarding Thailand.

immediately objected to these arrangements. Its staff officers, who considered their colleagues in Bangkok overly indulgent of the Thai, complained that the pact not only revealed too much about Japanese intentions, but failed to provide an adequate degree of control. Seizing upon a December 15 IGHQ directive that made clear that despite lip service to joint operations "for the sake of upholding Thai prestige," Japan would take "real leadership according to need," they elected to ignore the initial accord and demanded more favorable terms.[23]

On December 30, SAHQ unveiled a sweeping proposal that called for full Japanese access to all manner of Thai facilities, including railways, roads, airfields, naval bases, warehouses, communications systems, and barracks. Moreover, it required the Thai, upon Japanese demand, to improve such facilities. SAHQ even claimed the right to commandeer the limited Thai stocks of fuel and ammunition. The Thai had little choice but to accept these terms, and did so on January 3, 1942.[24]

Although in the wake of this agreement IGHQ found it necessary to warn the regional command to take an "exceedingly indulgent attitude and to be discreet" in handling relations with Thailand,[25] the problems regarding military operations had just begun. Under the joint plan the Thai expected to undertake a campaign toward Kengtung in the Shan States, and three Thai divisions were soon poised on the frontier. Eager to improve his bargaining position by joining in the Japanese rout of Allied forces, Phibun wanted to seize the territories east of the Salween River. SAHQ, however, lacked faith in the Thai army's fighting capacity and wished to avoid military and political complications, so it refused to permit a Thai advance, ignoring complaints from Phibun about his army's declining morale.[26]

When Tokyo finally ordered the unleashing of the Thai army with the fall of Mandalay at the beginning of May 1942, the SAHQ staff complied most grudgingly. Their instructions made clear that the Thai would receive no material assistance in their offensive, but that they would have to accept Japanese direction. If the attack succeeded, Thai-

[23] Ibid., pp. 255–57.

[24] The most complete published version of the agreement appears in Senshishitsu, *Biruma kōryaku sakusen* [The attack on Burma] (Tokyo: Asagumo shimbunsha, 1967), pp. 65–66.

[25] Senshishitsu, *Daihon'ei rikugunbu*, 3:258.

[26] MAGIC Diplomatic Summary, May 18, 1942. These summaries of intercepted Japanese diplomatic messages are held by the U.S. National Archives (hereafter, USNA), but are available in a fourteen-reel microfilm version entitled: "The MAGIC Documents: Summaries and Transcripts of the Top Secret Diplomatic Communications of Japan, 1938–1945" (Washington, D.C.: University Publications, 1980).

land would take administrative responsibility for the area east of the
Salween River (excepting the Karenni State), but was not promised permanent possession. Since the only Allied forces left in the region were
retreating elements of the expeditionary force Chiang Kai-shek had sent
to aid the British, SAHQ declared that Thailand should consider itself
at war with Nationalist China, a state of affairs not desired in the least
by a government wary of a large and economically powerful overseas
Chinese community. Adding insult to injury, SAHQ added a requirement that "Thailand at an appropriate time, shall offer respectful apology through SAHQ for the Japanese officers and men who died at the
hands of the Thai army in southern Thailand in December last year."[27]

Again the Thai swallowed their pride, but although their army succeeded in capturing Kengtung before the end of May, this did not end
the problems between the two allies. The Japanese complained bitterly
when the Thai Publicity Department announced the victory without
prior Japanese approval. Then, when the Thai offensive bogged down
because of logistical difficulties and sickness among the troops with the
onset of the rainy season, SAHQ flatly refused to approve a withdrawal
from forward positions.[28]

Japanese-Thai military frictions were by no means limited to operational matters, though, as the management of enemy assets generated
disagreement throughout 1942. The Japanese had detained British and
American citizens and seized their properties at the outset of the war,
but while they promptly relieved themselves of the burden of caring for
enemy citizens by handing them over to the Thai government, they
showed little inclination to move out of occupied enemy facilities, or to
turn over enemy assets. The Japanese Foreign Ministry had to admit
that under existing treaties the local governments in Thailand and Indochina should, in principle, manage enemy property, but in deference
to military demands it ruled that since the two areas were now strategic
bases, "ensuring public peace and order has become a joint responsibility"
and "when there is direct military necessity, the Japanese army will manage required enemy assets." Moreover, even if no direct military necessity
existed, the Japanese would have the option of declaring an economic necessity and could turn enemy property over to Japanese citizens.[29]

[27] Senshishitsu, *Biruma kōryaku sakusen,* pp. 326–28.

[28] Phairot Chayanam, "Kromkhotsanakon" [The Publicity Department] in *50 pi Krom-
prachasamphan* [50 years of the Public Relations Department] (Bangkok: Krompra-
chasamphan, 1986), p. 52; and a military message of June 29, 1942, contained in the file
"Nanpōgun sakusen kankei shiryō" [Materials related to the Southern Army's operations]
Nansei zenpan 17-2-31, NIDS.

[29] "Futsuin oyobi Tai ni okeru tekisan kanri yōkō" [The essential points for managing
enemy assets in French Indochina and Thailand] January 21, 1942, file A700 9-17, vol. 1,
Japanese Foreign Ministry Archives (hereafter JFMA), Tokyo. This policy was essentially

The Thai, who had strengthened their legal claim to the enemy assets by declaring war on Britain and the United States on January 25, 1942, spelled out their dissatisfaction with Japanese actions in a document that Ambassador Tsubokami Teiji forwarded to Tokyo on February 1. The Thai claimed that only seven of twenty-four enemy commercial properties had been turned over by the Japanese, and in those cases almost all items of value had been removed from the premises. Over the next several months Tsubokami would try without success to reach an understanding that would give the Thai control over enemy properties in principle, but allow the Japanese army free use of them according to the Foreign Ministry's guidelines.[30]

Military issues were negotiated between the two sides through a liaison committee system that had been established from the first days of the war. These committees did a great deal of good work in defusing quarrels, but matters did not always proceed smoothly. For example, the Japanese interpreter for the subcommittee on railroad matters recalled increasingly sour relations between the two sides and "strained and unpleasant" faces on the Thai side. At one session a Japanese lieutenant exploded in a fit of anger at a Thai counterpart and began shouting "baka!" (fool!).[31]

Surely it was just this type of overbearing, undiplomatic behavior that inspired a Thai official, described as a former advocate of cooperation with Japan, to vent his frustration in a June 1942 talk with an interned American acquaintance. The American Office of Strategic Services (OSS), which interviewed the internee after her repatriation, reported: "He told her how all the Thai officials resented being pushed around by the tactless Japs. They had been treated well and with dignity by the people of the United States, Britain, [and] France; by the Danes and other Westerners. But the Japanese were insufferably arrogant and treated them as inferiors. 'We'd rather rule ourselves,' the Thai official told the subject, 'but if we must have outsiders, let us have the Americans or British, not the Japanese.' "[32]

---

affirmed by the Liaison Conference on September 29, 1942. Recorded in Senshishitsu, *Daihon'ei rikugunbu*, vol. 5 (1973), p. 125, the policy stated in part: "Important enemy assets in the Imperial Army's operational areas will be handled in drastic fashion in order to advance the Empire's war power and hinder a postwar enemy comeback. These will be placed under the the the jurisdiction of the Empire and managed in a suitable way." It did note that "special political consideration" was necessary in Thailand, French Indochina, and occupied China.

[30] "Tekisan sesshū ni kansuru ken" [Points in regard to the requisitioning of enemy assets], Tsubokami to Tokyo, February 1, 1942, file A700 9-17, vol. 1, JFMA; and MAGIC Diplomatic Summary, December 7, 1942.

[31] Byodō Tsūshō and Byōdō Shōshin, *Waga ya no Nittai tsūshin* [Our family correspondence between Japan and Thailand] (Tokyo: Indogaku Kenkyūjo, 1979), p. 241.

[32] OSS document XL 2676, Record Group 226, USNA. The Thai official was not identified, but the description fits Prayun Phamonmontri, then minister of education.

The Economic Consequences of Joining the Co-Prosperity Sphere

The war severely disrupted Thailand's government finances and economy. The bulk of Thailand's assets were frozen in British and American banks, and customs duties, an important source of revenue, were reduced because of a general diminution of trade and Japanese abuse of the right to transport military items duty-free. While military supply requirements did ensure a demand for Thai goods, the Japanese paid all expenses of their troops in Thailand with money borrowed from the Thai government.[33] This system enabled the Thai to maintain their own distinct currency—in contrast to the military scrip used in occupied areas—and theoretically provided ample credits for the purchase of needed manufactured goods from Japan. However, such goods were in short supply due to wartime constraints, and an ever-worsening shortage of ships made transport difficult. Consequently, the Thai government piled up unusable yen credits. As the supply of goods shrank and the Thai government had more banknotes printed to satisfy the escalating demands of the Japanese army, inflation spiraled upward.[34]

The Thai had foreseen these negative economic consequences and had appealed for special Japanese assistance from the early days of the war.[35] These pleas, at times sympathetically endorsed by Ambassador Tsubokami, evoked little response from Tokyo. Japan was strapped after nearly five years of war, and many Japanese believed that all Asian peoples should, in the words of the Military Affairs Bureau, "be ready to suffer in the same way as the Japanese in the process of cooperation for the accomplishment of the work of building up New East Asia."[36]

Despite the fact that the Tokyo authorities were neither much inclined, nor even able, to offer substantial economic assistance, they were most eager to integrate Thailand into the new financial order they

---

[33] Hata Ikuhiko comments on such Japanese army practices in *The Cambridge History of Japan* vol. 6, ed. Peter Duus (New York: Cambridge University Press, 1988), p. 302: "In modern history there have been no other instances of a foreign expeditionary army force's adopting a policy of self-sufficiency from the very outset. . . . It was only natural that the Japanese army alienated the inhabitants of the occupied areas, who joked that the 'Imperial Army' (*kōgun*) was an 'army of locusts' (*kōgun*)." At least in Thailand the army did borrow in the local currency rather than printing unbacked military scrip. See Margaret Landon, "Thailand Under the Japanese," *Asia and the Americas* 44, no. 9 (September 1944): 390, and William L. Swan, "Thai-Japan Monetary Relations at the Start of the Pacific War," *Modern Asian Studies* 23, no. 2 (1989): 313–23.

[34] Paul B. Trescott, *Thailand's Monetary Experience* (New York: Praeger, 1971), p. 10; and James C. Ingram, *Economic Change in Thailand* (Stanford, Calif.: Stanford University Press, 1971), pp. 162–64, 185. Total Japanese indebtedness to Thailand for military expenditures would reach approximately 1.5 billion baht by the end of the war.

[35] Tsubokami to Tokyo, December 14, 1941, file A700 9-63, vol. 3, JFMA.

[36] *Japan Times and Advertiser*, April 12, 1942.

envisioned for Greater East Asia. The exchange rate was a matter of particular concern, as the Thai baht had been pegged to the British pound sterling and equalled 1.55 yen before the outbreak of war. As Finance Ministry bureaucrats had established parity between the yen and other currencies within the sphere, they were not satisfied by the Thai government's move on February 1, 1942, to tie the baht to gold at a rate that devalued it only to 1.25 yen. They still viewed the baht as a protruding nail in need of vigorous hammering.[37]

Accordingly, on February 23, 1942, the Liaison Conference, the committee of key Cabinet members and top military officials that functioned as the highest-level decision-making body in wartime Japan, approved a plan to establish parity between the yen and the baht, as well as to halt the practice of repaying loans from Thailand in gold. Instead, Japan would repay them in "special yen," currency that could be converted to gold or foreign currency more freely than regular yen, but only with Japanese government permission. In return for such concessions, the Japanese would offer to stabilize the Thai currency by setting aside "earmarked" gold—bullion that would remain in Tokyo vaults—as a substitute for the reserves frozen in Allied banks.[38]

Further devaluation of the baht and an end to repayment of debts in gold naturally were sensitive issues in Thai political circles. The Thai gave in on the exchange-rate issue in April, but resisted on the matter of debt repayment. On May 2 the sides did announce a compromise under which the Thai accepted "special yen" in repayment for commercial loans and the Japanese agreed that the Thai could periodically request conversion of "special yen" into gold, but it was late June 1942 before a ¥200 million currency stabilization loan to Thailand was finalized and a mechanism established for "special yen" loan settlement. It took another long round of negotiations before the Thai finally agreed on November 24 to accept "special yen" in payment for military expenditure loans, and then only after the Japanese promised that the Thai could obtain repayment in gold of approximately half of the amount loaned.[39]

Although the Thai had driven as hard a bargain as they could, the results of these negotiations were poorly received in Thailand, where prices had skyrocketed, many commodities were in short supply, and the government's attempts to control prices had, in the view of an

---

[37] Ibid., February 5, 9, and 11, 1942.

[38] Sambō Hombu [Army General Staff], *Sugiyama memo*, 2 vols. (Tokyo: Hara shobō, 1967), 2:34. For a fuller explanation of "special yen," see Swan, "Thai-Japan Monetary Relations at the Start of the Pacific War," p. 334.

[39] Ōta, *Nihon gaikōshi: Daitōasensō senji gaikō*, pp. 165–66; Swan, "Thai-Japan Monetary Relations at the Start of the Pacific War," pp. 328–46; and "Shinchū gunpi mondai" [The problem of garrison military funding], file A700 9-32, JFMA.

American resident in Bangkok, "accomplished nothing except to make the black market blacker and to make illegal what might just as well have been done in the open."[40] The Tokyo agreements symbolized the nation's new subservience to Japan and served to focus attention on the fact that multiplying economic problems were the direct result of the war and the Japanese presence.

THAILAND AS A COG IN THE IMPERIAL MACHINE

The effort to achieve parity in exchange rates represented just one aspect of a Japanese push for fuller coordination in organizing their expanded empire and exploiting its resources, an effort that culminated in the creation of a new Greater East Asia Ministry to oversee all aspects of Japanese policy in East Asia. As part of this program Tokyo also developed formal policy guidelines that delineated Thailand's "proper place" as a cog in the imperial machine, a status that impinged on the nation's sovereignty in various ways.

The main opposition to the proposal came from the Foreign Ministry, which was to be stripped of all its functions in East Asia excepting such "purely diplomatic" duties as handling matters of protocol and negotiating treaties. Foreign Minister Tōgō Shigenori charged that the new ministry's proponents were attempting to enlarge the scope of the Asian Development Board, the coordinating body for Japanese activities in occupied China, which he assailed as an utter failure. He also argued that establishment of the new ministry would create a two-headed monster in the foreign relations sphere. Moreover, he pointed out that the peoples of East Asia would not be fooled by what amounted to a thinly disguised colonial ministry, and that this would merely deepen distrust of Japan.[41]

The issue came to a head at the 1 September 1942 cabinet meeting. Tōgō resolutely opposed the plan, but Prime Minister Tōjō, who was constantly struggling to achieve efficient coordination at the top levels

[40] Genevieve Caulfield, *The Kingdom Within* (New York: Harper, 1960), pp. 196–97. Caulfield, a blind American who had previously resided in Japan, was not interned, but was permitted to remain in her home. On the economic problems in mid-1942 and Thai resentment of them, also see the report of the repatriated American Minister Willys Peck: "Internment and Repatriation of the American Legation in Bangkok, Thailand," 892.00/233, RG 59, USNA; and the comments of the Italian Minister in the MAGIC Diplomatic Summary of August 17, 1942.

[41] Gaimushō, *Gaimushō no hyakunen* [One hundred years of the Foreign Ministry], 2 vols. (Tokyo: Hara shobō, 1969), 2:700–705; Tōgō Shigenori, *The Cause of Japan* (New York: Simon and Schuster, 1956), pp. 242–45, 247–49. For a strong defense of the Greater East Asia Ministry concept by one of its key supporters, the chief of the Military Affairs Bureau, see Satō Kenryō, *Satō Kenryō shōgen* [The testimony of Satō Kenryō] (Tokyo: Fuyō shobō, 1976), pp. 377–80.

of the various competing government agencies, was equally determined that it be accepted. Although Tōjō had made plans to dissolve the cabinet, if necessary, to accomplish this end, he ultimately managed to pressure Tōgō into submitting his resignation.[42]

Just as Tōgō had predicted, the Thai government, as well as the Japanese-sponsored Chinese regime in Nanking, responded negatively to the creation of the new ministry. Thai Ambassador Direk Chayanam complained that Thailand had been lumped together with the former European colonies and suggested that the Allies would make effective propaganda use of this situation. But when he expressed Thai dissatisfaction directly to the prime minister, Tōjō brushed off the complaint with assurances that the new setup would benefit Thailand because bilateral relations would be conducted in a less formal and more "brotherly" fashion.[43]

Less than a month after the cabinet's acceptance of the Greater East Asia Ministry, the Liaison Conference approved an outline of policy toward Thailand. While it pointed out the importance of operating within the context of existing agreements and paying heed to Thailand's independence, the economic section of the document claimed Japanese privileges even more sweeping than those extracted in the earlier military agreement. It stated that Japan would "guide or take control of those aspects of the Thai economy that are essential to the prosecution of the Greater East Asian War and those related to the fundamental economy of Greater East Asia." It indicated that Japan should not only direct every aspect of Thailand's financial affairs but also control the nation's transportation system, industrial development, and trade. Despite such concessions as allowing Thailand to manage its internal economic system and promising to interfere as little as possible with "local enterprises and handicraft industries in regard to production of articles for use in daily life, to the extent that they do not interfere with the industrial plan of the Co-Prosperity Sphere," the document made plain Japan's intent to turn Thailand into a handmaiden of Japanese interests.[44]

Simultaneously, the Japanese were pushing a new and expanded cultural program for Thailand, an effort that led to the conclusion of a

[42] Gaimushō, Gaimushō no hyakunen, 2:706–18; Itō Takashi, Hirohashi Tadamitsu, and Katashima Norio, eds., Tōjō naikaku sōridaijin kimitsu kiroku [The secret record of the prime minister of the Tōjō Cabinet] (Tokyo: Tokyo daigaku shuppankai, 1990), pp. 81–87; and Tōgō, The Cause of Japan, pp. 249–53. On Tōjō's frustration with the divided governmental structure, see Shigemitsu Mamoru, Japan and Her Destiny (New York: E. P. Dutton, 1958), pp. 312–13; and Robert J. C. Butow, Tojo and the Coming of the War (Princeton, N.J.: Princeton University Press, 1961), pp. 421–23.

[43] Direk Jayanama [Chayanam] Siam and World War II, trans, Jane G. Keyes (Bangkok: Social Science Association of Thailand, 1978), pp. 84–88; and MAGIC Diplomatic Summaries of September 11, 13, and 17, 1942 on the Chinese reaction.

[44] The text appears in Ōta, Nihon gaikōshi: Daitōasensō senji gaikō, pp. 166–72.

Japanese-drafted bilateral cultural treaty on October 28, 1942. This committed both countries to facilitating "institutions contributing to the promotion of cultural relations" and providing "every possible facility for such purposes."[45] The Thai naturally viewed the expanded cultural program as one more aspect of a Japanese push for domination, leading Premier Phibun to set a backfire against such incursions by establishing a National Culture Institute to promote his own version of Thai culture.[46]

When Ambassador Tsubokami attempted to explain his government's intrusive policies in a November 1942 press interview he predictably cited wartime exigencies, but he went on to argue that regional blocs were the wave of future and that old ideas of sovereignty needed to be revised. In Greater East Asia, independence had taken on a new meaning, Tsubokami declared, and could not be "unbridled." Speaking as a past participant in the Manchukuo experiment, Tsubokami flatly suggested that the Japanese puppet state should serve as the proper model for independent Asian states.[47]

The Thai, who even before the war had made known their fears of "Manchukuo-ization" at the hands of Japanese, might have been surprised by the bluntness of Tsubokami's assertion, but Japanese actions to date had given them every reason to believe that it reflected Japanese thinking at the highest level. Certainly the Japanese definition of "independence" did seem to have a special meaning.

THE BAN PONG INCIDENT

The ill effects of Japanese attitudes and policies had become quite apparent in Thailand by the second half of 1942. Although the government continued to maintain a front of cooperative solidarity with Japan, Thai

[45] Direk, *Siam and World War II*, p. 83. The text of the treaty appears in the *Japan Times and Advertiser*, December 22, 1942.

[46] For more on the Japanese cultural effort, see the author's "Imperial Japan's Cultural Program in Thailand," in *Japanese Cultural Policies in Southeast Asia During World War II*, ed. Grant K. Goodman (New York: St. Martin's Press, 1991), pp. 93–116.

[47] *Japan Times and Advertiser*, November 20, 1942. Tsubokami was repeating a commonly held Japanese view in citing Manchukuo as a model, as Dower notes in *War Without Mercy*, p. 293. The Ministry of Health and Welfare scheme for Greater East Asia described by Dower (pp. 263–90) reflects the spirit of the policies pursued by the Japanese in the fall of 1942. While Dower notes (p. 263) that the document is valuable in understanding the Japanese vision for the Co-Prosperity Sphere, he cites the lack of influence of the ministry that produced it and its mind-numbing length (almost forty-thousand pages) as reasons why that it probably had little influence. He might have added another reason, that by the time it was issued (July 1, 1943), the declining military fortunes of the Axis powers had already made its vision of expanded empire obsolete.

irritation over the continued presence of foreign troops on their soil, economic hardships, and arrogant behavior by individual Japanese— both military and civilian—could not be disguised. In August 1942 the Italian minister reported that minor Thai-Japanese incidents were "almost daily occurrences," and a Japanese message at the beginning of September spoke of "frequent skirmishes" and an increase in thefts and robberies.[48] When, during discussion at the Liaison Committee meeting of September 19, Navy Minister Shimada Shigetarō suggested that more control was needed over Japanese companies and organizations because of their quarreling among themselves and with the Thai, Military Affairs Bureau Chief Satō Kenryō agreed, but complained about "frequent insulting acts" against Japanese soldiers.[49]

Although SAHQ had previously reduced troops levels in Thailand in accordance with IGHQ's instructions to avoid unnecessary provocations, it responded to the growing disorder by ordering the transfer of a combat infantry battalion to Bangkok. Also, Lieutenant Colonel Tominaga Kametarō, a staff officer with a background in public information work, was sent from Hanoi to assist Major General Moriya Seiji, the military attaché responsible for liaison with the Thai authorities. Tominaga quickly recognized how dangerous the situation in Thailand had become. In Bangkok, military discipline was lax, and the troops, who were stationed in the heart of the city, often quarreled with the Thai in the local nightspots. The attaché's office had received many complaints, but Moriya had no authority to discipline the troops and little action had been taken.[50]

As Tominaga had feared, a serious incident erupted in mid-December—not in Bangkok, but near the small town of Ban Pong to the west of the capital. Here, the Japanese had begun construction of the Thailand-Burma railroad, a project that ultimately would claim the lives of tens of thousands of Asian laborers and Allied prisoners of war. In late 1942 Thai workers were employed in the laying of the first fifty kilometers of track between the existing line and Kanchanaburi. The existence of ill-will between the Japanese soldiers supervising the railroad project and the local residents is reflected in memoirs from both sides.[51]

---

[48] MAGIC Diplomatic Summaries, August 17, 1942, and September 4, 1942.

[49] Senshishitsu, *Daihon'ei rikugunbu*, 5:122.

[50] Tominaga Kametarō, *Chototsu hachijūnen* [Eighty reckless years] (Tokyo: Aato kō-pansha, 1987), pp. 169–71.

[51] Iwai Ken, *C56 Nampō senjō o iku* [The C56 (locomotive) goes to the southern battlefields] (Tokyo: Jiji tsūshinsha, 1978), p. 123; and Khomsan (pseud.), "Kiat tamruat Thai thi yuthaphum Ban Pong" [The honor of the Thai police on the Ban Pong battlefield], *Tamruat Samphan* [Police relations] 5, no. 55 (November 1982), p. 10. I am grateful to William Swan for providing me a copy of the latter article.

This mutual hostility flared into open conflict on December 18, 1942. It began when a Buddhist monk clashed with a Japanese guard and was slapped in the face, a serious insult to an ordinary Thai and a grievous affront to a monk. When he complained to a group of Thai laborers, they were incensed, formed a mob, and, under the cover of darkness, attacked a Japanese sentry with bamboo spears and knives. Other Japanese soldiers heard the commotion and rushed to the scene, touching off a melee. By the time peacemakers from both sides were able to separate the combatants, at least two Japanese were dead and a number of participants on both sides injured. Later, Japanese reinforcements from Kanchanaburi were met by a volley of fire from officers at the Ban Pong police station. At least four more Japanese soldiers were killed, including a military doctor, and several sustained wounds. Fortunately, officials from the two sides were able to stop the shooting before more blood was shed.[52]

A series of anti-Japanese incidents followed, including the destruction of about a mile of railroad track, at least two attacks on Japanese soldiers by armed Thai citizens, and stone-throwing by Thai women. A show of force succeeded in restoring a surface calm, but in the view of a Japanese officer, the atmosphere remained "oppressive" and "disagreeable."[53]

Outraged by the incidents, SAHQ lodged demands for the execution of the monk as the instigator, a formal apology and guarantees for the future, and the payment of an eighty-thousand yen indemnity. Phibun sought to restore peace and reach a compromise settlement, but he strongly resisted imposing the death sentence on the priest, arguing that Thai law did not permit such punishment. This led to prolonged and difficult negotiations between the two sides.[54]

The Ban Pong affair capped a year during which, despite the propaganda of cooperation and goodwill poured out by both sides, beneath the surface, relations between the two countries were characterized by disharmony and acrimony. As it was inevitable that the proudly independent Thai would resent the Japanese army's intrusion into their country and the economic disruption this produced, the circumstances

---

[52] On the details of Ban Pong incident, see Iwai, *C56 Nanpō senjō o iku*, p. 134; Khomsan, "Kiat tamruat Thai thi yuthaphum Ban Pong," pp. 10–13; Zenkoku kenyūkai renaikai [The Nationwide Alliance of Kempei Associations], *Nihon kempei seishi* [The true history of Japan's Kempei] (Tokyo: Zenkoku kenyūkai renaikai, 1976), p. 947; Tominaga, *Chototsu hachijūnen*, pp. 172–74; and MAGIC Diplomatic Summary 827, January 4, 1943.

[53] Iwai, *C56 Nanpō senjō o iku*, pp. 135–36; and MAGIC Diplomatic Summary, January 15, 1943.

[54] Nakamura Aketo, *Hotoke no shireikan* [The Buddha's commander] (Tokyo: Shūhōsha, 1958), p. 50; and MAGIC Diplomatic Summary, January 15, 1943.

demanded that the Japanese behave tactfully, display a generous spirit, and adopt policies designed to allay Thai fears about Japanese domination. They failed on all three counts. Instead they had attempted to use the leverage created by their military successes to shoehorn Thailand into a neocolonial niche in an expanded Japanese empire.

FACING UP TO NEW REALITIES

Before news of the Ban Pong incident resounded in Tokyo like the proverbial "firebell in the night," and even before the Greater East Asia Ministry officially opened its doors on November 1, 1942, doubts that the newly occupied territories could successfully be enveloped in an expanded empire had begun to surface. Initially, such concerns had been voiced mainly by diplomats, but by the fall of 1942 confidence in Japanese invincibility had begun to evaporate, even within military ranks.

Diplomats in China, headed by Ambassador Shigemitsu Mamoru, had been among the first to urge that Japan seize the political opportunity presented by the early string of victories in the early months of 1942. The time was ripe, they argued, for Japan to display a magnanimous attitude toward China and thereby encourage Chiang Kai-shek to cease his war of resistance.[55] Also, Shigemitsu wanted to create a coherent and viable political strategy around which military and diplomatic efforts could be coordinated. Foreign Minister Tōgō agreed, but Prime Mister Tōjō and the army then believed that Japan had sufficient strength to consolidate control over the captured territories and dig in for a long war. They also felt that wartime strategy should be dictated by events on the battlefield, with the diplomats playing a purely supporting role.[56]

Although Tōgō's resignation and the Cabinet decision to establish the Greater East Asia Ministry seemed to signal the triumph of the army's point of view, this did not prove to be the case. In the Privy Council—which had responsibility for reviewing major foreign policy initiatives on behalf of the throne—such strong opposition developed that in ten meetings its members failed to reach agreement on the new ministry plan. When Tōjō adamantly refused requests to modify it, the councillors finally approved it to avoid forcing a general resignation of the

[55] Gaimushō, *Gaimushō no hyakunen*, 2:626–27.

[56] An interesting perspective on Shigemitsu's ideas from an army supporter is contained in Matsutani Sei's *Daitōasensō shūshū no shinsō* [The truth about controlling the Greater East Asian War] (Tokyo: Fuyō shobō, 1984), p. 239. Tōjō's views on diplomacy, as expressed at the October 29, 1942, Liaison Conference, are recorded in Senshishitsu, *Daihon'ei rikugunbu*, 5:165. Also, see Tōgō, *The Cause of Japan*, pp. 240–46.

Cabinet, but the usual consensus could not be achieved.[57] An IGHQ diarist characterized the grilling Tōjō received from the "old-style diplomats" at the eleventh and final Privy Council session on the matter as a severe personal attack. Also, the emperor cautioned Tōjō during an October 30 audience that the new policies should be pursued cautiously, and complained that a portion of the military was wrongly attempting to implement the *hakkō-ichiu* (eight corners of the world under one roof) policy through the use of force.[58]

More importantly, however, events on the war fronts were forcing a reevaluation of strategy at IGHQ. In the wake of the navy's disastrous defeat at Midway in June, the Americans had landed on Guadalcanal in early August and had rebuffed repeated attempts to dislodge them. These battlefield failures made it increasingly clear that—as Army Chief of Staff Sugiyama Hajime would later acknowledge—Japan could no longer count on commanding obedience from the East Asian peoples. Accordingly, the army had decided in September to defer the planned direct annexation of strategic territories in Malaya and Sumatra to avoid alienating the local population.[59] Shortly afterward it also dropped its opposition to a declaration of war on Britain and the United States by the Nanking government, and showed a new willingness to consider other measures to enhance the prestige of the Wang Ching-wei regime.[60]

Under such circumstances Tōjō became increasingly open to the ideas of Shigemitsu, whom he had convinced to remain at his post with assurances that the head of the new Greater East Asia Ministry, Aoki Kazuo, also favored a fundamental change of strategy in China. Subsequently, an Imperial Conference of December 21, 1942, approved a new policy that not only permitted a declaration of war by the Nanking regime, but also provided for the handing over of various foreign con-

---

[57] Gaimushō, *Gaimushō no hyakunen*, 2:636, 743–52; and Tōgō, *The Cause of Japan*, pp. 254–55.

[58] Senshishitsu, *Daihon'ei rikugunbu*, 5:165, 434–35. This source, which suggests that the emperor's warning had an important impact in initiating significant policy changes, states that it was delivered at the Privy Council meeting of October 28, but Itō, Hirohashi, and Katashima, *Tōjō naikaku sōridaijin kimitsu kiroku*, p. 110, indicates that it was two days later at a private audience.

[59] Senshishitsu, *Daihon'ei rikugunbu*, 5:156, 490–91, where Sugiyama's extremely frank comments at the December 18, 1942, Liaison Conference are recorded.

[60] This change of heart came in October 1942 after Wang Ching-wei had reemphasized his government's eagerness to enter the war to Baron Hiranuma Kiichirō during the latter's September visit to Nanking. Wang's deputy, Chou Fo-hai, had first raised the issue during a visit to Tokyo in July 1942. See Senshishitsu, *Daihon'ei rikugunbu*, 4:472, 5:165. Like the Thai before them, the Chinese hoped that a declaration of war would provide leverage in dealing with the Japanese army, strengthen their claim to enemy properties, and enhance their position at the peace table in the event of a Japanese victory.

cessions to that government.[61] This would be merely the first step in the general modification of Japanese political strategy, as plans were laid to grant the promised limited independence to Burma and the Philippines. Tokyo also began to look for ways to improve relations with Thailand. Appropriately, given the ill effects of SAHQ's high-handed approach, the new Japanese attitude would first manifest itself through a new military command that would adopt a different strategy.

The possibility of establishing a separate military headquarters in Thailand had come under study in October 1942, when IGHQ decided to create a garrison army command to help stabilize the situation in neighboring French Indochina. The Ban Pong Incident seems to have hastened its creation. Although subordinate to SAHQ, the new headquarters assumed direct control over all troops within Thailand, excepting those engaged in constructing the Thailand-Burma railroad. As a nonoperational support unit, the new garrison army's mandate, like that of its counterpart in Indochina, focused on the maintenance of stability. IGHQ considered this increasingly essential because an Allied counterattack was anticipated in Burma, a theater for which Thailand and Indochina would serve as vital staging grounds and sources of supply.[62]

Tokyo chose the new commander wisely, selecting Lieutenant General Nakamura Aketo, a fifty-two-year-old infantry officer with diplomatic and public relations skills that would stand him in good stead. At the time Nakamura headed the *Kempeitai,* but he had previously served briefly as director of the army's political office, the Military Affairs Bureau, and had spent a longer stint as head of the Soldiers Affairs Bureau, an office that, among other things, set disciplinary standards. Nakamura arrived in Bangkok on January 21, and officially inaugurated the new command on February 1, 1943.[63]

The Thai were extremely apprehensive about the creation of the army headquarters, viewing it as yet another means to effect Japanese control, but Nakamura's assurances that he intended fully to abide by the terms of the alliance and respect Thai sovereignty, coupled with his efforts to cultivate friendly personal relations with the Thai leaders, gradually allayed their fears. Nakamura studied the Thai language, fre-

---

[61] Shigemitsu, *Japan and Her Destiny,* p. 283, and on the debate on the change in China policy at the Liaison Conferences of October 29, November 27, and December 18, see Senshishitsu, *Daihon'ei Rikugunbu,* 5;170, 430–35, 487–91. The same volume, pp. 496–507, covers the Imperial Conference of December 21, 1942.

[62] Ibid., 5:415–17, 6:100–102; and Nakamura, *Hotoke no shireikan,* pp. 21–22.

[63] For more on Nakamura and his career, see the author's "General Nakamura Aketo—A Khaki-clad Diplomat in Wartime Thailand" in Khamchoo and Reynolds, *Thai-Japanese Relations,* pp. 161–202.

quently attended and hosted social functions, and toured various regions of the country. He even took up golf, Phibun's favorite sport.[64]

Even more important were concrete steps taken by Nakamura to reduce the sources of friction between Japanese soldiers and the Thai, including the festering dispute over the Ban Pong Incident. Nakamura convinced his superiors to drop the demand for the execution of the monk who was accused as the instigator. Also, he arranged that the eighty-thousand baht in compensation payments by Thailand be returned to create an aid fund for the families of Thai soldiers who died fighting the Japanese army on December 8, 1941, a truly remarkable gesture given that less than a year earlier SAHQ had demanded an apology from the Thai army for having defended its own territory. As face-slapping by Japanese soldiers had been the source of much ill-will, Nakamura sought to eliminate this and other Japanese actions that offended Thai sensibilities. He had his staff prepare a booklet explaining Thai customs and taboos, a copy of which was distributed to each soldier entering Thailand. Military discipline was strictly enforced, and to make the new emphasis visible, soldiers were required to render military courtesies with great flourish. Also, Nakamura made a serious effort to settle long-standing disputes over enemy property and unpaid bills.[65]

These were important steps in defusing tension between the two sides, and an anti-Phibun Thai politician who escaped to China in mid-1943 attested to the fact that the changes were real and had made an impression. He informed the OSS that the Japanese had "abandoned the use of pressure, ceased making 'requests' that were thinly veiled demands," and had begun "sedulously courting the good will of the Thai people."[66]

THAILAND AND JAPAN'S NEW DEAL FOR ASIA

Winning the hearts and minds of the Asian masses had become all the more urgent after Axis fortunes sank to a new low with the pivotal defeat sustained by German forces on the Soviet front in January 1943. Tokyo advanced plans for Burmese and Philippine independence and

[64] Tominaga Kametarō manuscript (a copy of which is held by the author), p. 373; interviews with Tominaga (April 30, 1987) and Konishi Takeo (May 7, 1987); and Yoshimura Kōzaburō, Ano hito, kono hito [That person, this person] (Tokyo: Kyōdō shuppanbu, 1967), p. 158.

[65] Nakamura, Hotoke no shireikan, pp. 49–50, 53; Tominaga, Chototsu hachijūnen, pp. 175–80; and Fukino Kenshō, Wasureenu Chenmai [Unforgettable Chiangmai] (Tokyo: Kyōdō shuppansha, 1983), p. 60.

[66] Landon, "Thailand under the Japanese," pp. 389–90. Landon uses a pseudonym, but her informant clearly was Sanguan Tularak.

sought to invigorate the Indian Independence Movement by transporting the charismatic Subhas Chandra Bose out from Germany by submarine. Also, Prime Minister Tōjō began a series of goodwill visits, going to Nanking in March, Manchukuo in April, and the Philippines in early May. In late April he had made Shigemitsu foreign minister.

While Tōjō and other army officers saw Japan's "New Deal" for Asia simply as a means to muster support for the war effort, Shigemitsu had a more complex agenda. He hoped to lay the groundwork for a negotiated settlement with the Allies by establishing less selfish war goals that would have more resonance outside Japan. He planned to incorporate such themes as Asian liberation, reciprocal cooperation, independence, and racial equality into a Greater East Asian Declaration—a Japanese equivalent to the Allied Atlantic Charter—which would be unveiled at a grand meeting of Asian leaders. Shigemitsu underscored his desire to address an international audience by directing the drafting of the declaration in English and eschewing the Confucian, hierarchical language of past pronouncements that had made clear the status inequality within the Japanese sphere. Shigemitsu foresaw that even if his hopes for a negotiated peace were not realized, establishing a moral basis for the war effort would permit the Japanese to rationalize it as a noble one, even if it ultimately failed. As his aide Kase Toshikazu put it, "even if we lost—and Shigemitsu and I were certain that we would lose—a fine moral basis would remain for a later comeback."[67]

While China policy had been the centerpiece of the new scheme from the beginning, Thailand clearly required special attention, too. In fact, in May 1943 an IGHQ diarist would describe policies toward China and Thailand and the plans for an Asian conference as the very heart of the new strategy; in late July Tōjō would tell a meeting of Japan's senior statesmen that "Thailand has become the greatest worry with respect to Greater East Asian unity"; and, ultimately, in the fall of 1943, the German minister in Bangkok would advise Berlin that "Japan is interested in developing Thailand as the model for the Greater East Asia Co-Prosperity Sphere."[68]

But how could Thai hearts be captured? Nakamura's policies had reduced tensions, but the Japanese needed to demonstrate their new attitude in some dramatic way. While they could accomplish this in Burma and the Philippines by granting independence, and in China by re-

---

[67] Kase Toshikazu, *Nihon gaikō no shuyakutachi* [Important figures in Japanese diplomacy] (Tokyo: Bungei shunjū, 1974), pp. 182–83; and Akira Iriye, *Power and Culture* (Cambridge, Mass.: Harvard University Press, 1981), pp. 112–21. It was from Prof. Iriye's book that the change in Japanese strategy originally came to my attention. The text of the Greater East Asia Declaration is found in Lebra, *Japan's Greater East Asia Co-Prosperity Sphere in World War II*, p. 93.

[68] Senshishitsu, *Daihon'ei rikugunbu*, 6:534; Itō, Hirohashi, and Katashima, *Tōjō naikaku sōridaijin kimitsu kiroku*, p. 208; and MAGIC Diplomatic Summary, September 23, 1943.

nouncing extraterritorial rights, these measures had no utility in Thailand. Nor could Japan, which was borrowing ever greater sums from the Thai government to support its military forces within the country, offer any financial relief. Ambassador Tsubokami opposed Shigemitsu's proposal to renegotiate bilateral treaties to bring them into line with the new treaties with China, warning that this would only generate "useless fears" on the part of the "deeply suspicious" Thai.[69] This left fulfillment of the Japanese pledge to assist in the restoration of Thailand's "lost territories" as the only practical alternative.

A year earlier, when Tokyo had granted permission for the Thai army's invasion of the Shan States, it had been decided confidentially that Thailand ultimately should receive the states of Kengtung and Mongpan. The Shans were ethnically related to the Thai, and it was popularly believed that the ancestors of the people of Thailand proper had once inhabited the Shan area during their historical migration southward. The Japanese judged that since the British had governed this region separately from the rest of Burma, the cession of the two states would not unduly provoke the Burmese.[70] But as Kengtung and Mongpan were poor, backward areas which the Thai army had already occupied, the Japanese realized that permitting their annexation would not be viewed as a splendid gesture. Something more was required, but no further territory to Thailand's west could be ceded without arousing strong Burmese opposition. The Thai wanted more territory in Indochina, but any move in that direction would upset relations with the French. So the Japanese turned their attention to Malaya, which Tokyo had planned to keep under direct rule. Japan decided to hand over four states—Kedah, Perlis, Kelantan, and Trengganu—that the Thai had ceded to the British by treaty in 1909. These states were largely populated by Malay Muslims with no ethnic or racial link to the Thai, but they had sufficient natural resources to make them an attractive gift.

An Imperial Conference on May 31, 1943, approved the cession of the four Malay and two Shan states to Thailand as part of a broader outline of the new Asian strategy. The Liaison Conference approved detailed plans for the transfer on June 26. As Prime Minister Tōjō had scheduled a tour of the "Southern Region" for early July, it was thought that he could maximize the impact of Japan's territorial gift by delivering it personally in Bangkok.[71]

[69] "Marei oyobi Shan chihō ni okeru Taikoku no ryōdo ni kansuru Nihonkoku-Taikoku aida jōyaku" [The treaty between Japan and Thailand regarding Thailand's territories in the Malay and Shan regions], August 20, 1943, file A700 9-33, JFMA.

[70] Senshishitsu, Biruma kōryaku sakusen, pp. 328–29.

[71] Senshishitsu, Daihon'ei rikugunbu, 6:537; Ōta, Nihon gaikōshi: Daitōa sensō senji gaikō, pp. 174–75, which contains the text of the plan.

The Thai, uncertain of the purpose of Tōjō's visit, were wary, but Phibun and his cabinet turned out at Don Muang Airport on the morning of July 3 to greet him. At a formal conference the next morning Tōjō read a prepared statement, which was simultaneously translated into Thai. Nakamura watched Phibun intently as Tōjō announced the territorial cession. He later recalled that Phibun "displayed a joyful countenance, but not quite a broad smile," and he sensed disappointment on Tōjō's part. Military Affairs Bureau Chief Satō Kenryō later described Phibun's response as "coolness itself."[72]

The Japanese carefully monitored the Thai public reaction to the transfer, and the initial response from the government-controlled press gave some grounds for optimism. Tokyo soon realized, though, that the territorial cession would not have the desired effect.[73] Even on the Japanese side the legality of the transfer had been questioned, and everyone knew that it would have no lasting significance unless the Japanese won the war, an outcome the Thai regarded as increasingly unlikely, particularly after the fall of Italy's Benito Mussolini in late July.[74] Moreover, at a time when Phibun—by now a favored whipping boy in Allied propaganda broadcasts—had begun to worry about his future, the Japanese had added to his problems by making him the receiver of stolen British property.[75]

PHIBUN AND THE GREATER EAST ASIA CONFERENCE

The restoration of "lost territory" to Thailand was, of course, only one element in the Japanese "New Deal" program which unfolded through the summer and fall of 1943. The Burmese formally proclaimed their

[72] Nakamura, *Hotoke no shireikan*, pp. 74–75, 80; Satō, *Satō Kenryō shōgen*, p. 428.

[73] MAGIC Diplomatic Summary, August 18, 1943; and "Tōjō shushō nanpō ryokō oyobi Tai ryōdo mondai no kakkoku ni taisuru hankyō gaiyō [Outline of the impact of Prime Minister Tōjō's southern trip and the Thai territorial issue on various countries], July 22, 1943, file A700 9-33, JFMA.

[74] Yamada Kunitarō, *Meiji shonen no ayumi* [Steps of a Meiji youth] (Nagoya: Yamada Kunitarō Sensei kaisōroku o shuppan suru kai, 1979), p. 226. The Privy Council considered the treaty providing for the territorial transfer on August 18, 1943 ("Marei oyobi Shan chihō ni okeru Taikoku no ryōdo ni kansuru Nihon-Taikoku aida jōyaku," file A 700 9-33, JFMA), and when the question of legality came up, Tōjō brushed it aside, declaring: "I don't know anything about international law, but an occupying army takes measures to possess territory for our side. In regard to the treaty, if it is advantageous to our side, it is adequate. No matter how good the [legal] interpretation is, all depends on winning the war. If we lose, it doesn't matter." Nakamura (*Hotoke no shireikan*, p. 91) believed that a high-level Thai military mission that visited Japan in September and October 1943 returned with a pessimistic assessment of Japan's war prospects.

[75] OSS document 50415, November 24, 1943, RG 226, USNA; Nakamura, *Hotoke no shireikan*, pp. 88–89.

limited independence at the beginning of August, and the Philippines did the same on October 14. The Javanese were permitted to begin participating in local decision making, Japan recognized a provisional Indian government headed by Subhas Chandra Bose on October 23, and at the end of October Tokyo announced a new alliance treaty with the Nanking government. All seemed to be on track for the climactic event, the Greater East Asia Conference, except that Phibun refused to play his assigned role.

The Japanese had been trying without success to get Phibun to Tokyo for nearly a decade, but he had declined all invitations. When they had stepped up their efforts in the spring of 1943 he initially cited a troubled domestic situation, then later complained of poor health. By late June Ambassador Tsubokami had decided that Phibun simply did not wish to be in any way associated with the leaders of puppet states like Manchukuo and the Nanking regime.[76] Certainly this was one factor, but Phibun also knew that a visit to Japan would further incriminate him in Allied eyes, and with his political enemies drawing comfort from the decline in Axis fortunes, he also had reason to feel uneasy about leaving the country. Moreover, Phibun did not like to fly and, having survived several attempts on his life, had become increasingly paranoid about his personal security.

Tsubokami and Nakamura did their utmost to persuade Phibun to attend the November 1943 conference, but they could not sway him. In Tokyo, the Liaison Conference discussed the Thai premier's recalcitrant stand on October 9, but deemed coercion inadvisable. The Japanese leaders had long considered Phibun an indispensable asset, and even though they were fast losing faith in him, they saw no better alternative. They felt they could not risk provoking his resignation, so they agreed to accept a specially delegated personal representative, provided he was "an important person with dignity, able in name and fact to represent the Thai people." In the end, Prince Wan Waithayakon, a polished diplomat and adviser to the Foreign Ministry, headed the Thai delegation.[77]

---

[76] MAGIC Diplomatic Summary, July 7, 1943; and Tsubokami to Tokyo, June 11, 1943, file A600 1-27, vol. 2, JFMA.

[77] "Daitōa kaigi kaisai ni kansuru Teikoku seifu kunrei" [The Imperial Government's instructions regarding the convening of the Greater East Asia Conference], no date; "Yobi kōshō keii" [The circumstances of the preliminary negotiations], no date; and "Daitōa kaigi shōsei oyobi Daitōa kyōdo sengen an ni taisuru sanka kuni no ikyō" [The opinions of the participating countries in regard to the invitations to the Greater East Asia Conference and the Great East Asia Joint Declaration], no date, file A700 9-48, JFMA; Nakamura, Hotoke no shireikan, pp. 90–91; and Itō, Hirohashi, and Katashima, Tōjō naikaku sōridaijin kimitsu kiroku, p. 269.

As there had been little sign of magnanimity when the Japanese had been advancing on all fronts, the calculating, pragmatic Phibun understood very well that a growing anxiety about the war situation had inspired the change in the Japanese attitude. With the seizure of the initiative by the Allies casting a dark shadow on his political future, Phibun's top priority already had become distancing himself from the Japanese. Certainly his absence from the Greater East Asia Conference—which Military Affairs Bureau Chief Satō described as the "one stain" on the event[78]—well symbolized the fact that Japan's "New Deal" had come too late.

CONCLUSION

In speaking enthusiastically of the changes Japan had wrought in the previous months, Prime Minister Tōjō suggested to Philippine leader José P. Laurel on November 3, 1943, that the Allies had made a critical mistake in allowing Japan and the other East Asian countries two years to prepare for a long war.[79] In reality, though, the mistake had been the Japanese failure to take good advantage of the interval. Japan's leaders had not adequately recognized that a desperate struggle against materially superior enemies demanded not only a bold military strategy, but a bold political strategy as well. They failed to capitalize on the pro-Japanese "Asian mood"[80] that their stunning early victories had created. Instead of developing policies and implementing concrete measures that would have lent credence to their rhetoric of cooperation and coprosperity and given encouragement to Asian nationalism, the Japanese engaged in an all too transparent effort to turn the newly conquered region into an expanded empire of colonies and Manchukuo-style puppet states.

What difference might it have made if the Japanese had actively embraced an Asian liberation agenda from the beginning of the war? In hindsight we know that the key battles were fought in the Pacific, not in Asia, so it would be easy to dismiss the potential military impact of a fuller mobilization of the Asian peoples. However, as Shigemitsu had recognized, a Japanese policy change would have had maximum impact in China had it been made in early 1942, when the Allies were being

[78] Satō, *Satō Kenryō shōgen*, p. 429.

[79] Itō, Tadamitsu, and Katashima, *Tōjō naikaku sōridaijin kimitsu kiroku*, p. 299.

[80] This is the phrase of Burmese leader Ba Maw used to describe the excitement created by the early Japanese victories. He wrote in *Breakthrough in Burma*, p. 285: "Our public declarations of faith in the Japanese in the early part of the war when they were victorious everywhere did really mean that our Asian mood was genuine and we did have faith in Japan, though there were times when we nearly lost it."

swept from Southeast Asia and there was concern in the West that Chiang Kai-shek might reassess his resistance to Japan. Also, had they made a more active effort, the Japanese might have been able to stir up sufficient unrest in India to make the British position there untenable,[81] putting additional pressure on Chiang to come to terms. Had the Japanese succeeded in ending the war in China, this not only would have gone far in bridging the chasm between Japanese Pan-Asian rhetoric and the realities of their policy, but it would have fundamentally changed the balance of forces and could have modified the course of the war. There is still, of course, no guarantee that the Japanese ultimately would have prevailed, nor that any policy could have guaranteed the loyalty of an opportunist like Phibun. It is safe to say, however, that the policies the Japanese did pursue helped to ensure that they would fail, and that Phibun would defect at first opportunity.

While independent Thailand might have been embraced immediately as a model for the Asian peoples seeking escape from colonial domination, Japanese military and civilian bureaucrats instead pursued policies that diminished that nation's sovereignty, and acted in ways offensive to its people. Unreasonable military demands, unpopular financial impositions, the expansion of the Japanese cultural program, and the establishment of the Greater East Asia Ministry fed Thai anxieties about Japanese domination. And, even though Japanese soldiers generally behaved in a more restrained fashion in Thailand than elsewhere, their actions were still sufficiently high-handed to generate much ill will.

Thailand's ultimate passage from anomaly to role model in the Japanese perception of its role within the Co-Prosperity Sphere does illustrate a very significant shift in Japanese policy by 1943. But because the Japanese changed course only after the Allies had gained the upper hand in the war, their new policies neither rallied Asian support to the extent envisioned by the army,[82] nor did they pave the way to a negotiated settlement as Shigemitsu had hoped. Nonetheless, they did provide a cloak of idealism that postwar revisionists have not hesitated to use in disguising purely selfish Japanese war aims. Also, the new policies ultimately did offer important new scope and encouragement for nationalist activities, even in the regions where the Japanese had not initially envisioned the emergence of independent states. This was particularly true in the case of Java, but there was also an impact in Malaya, and in Indochina, after the French were overthrown in March 1945. In this

---

[81] On the missed opportunities in this regard, see Milan Hauner, *India in Axis Strategy* (Stuttgart: Klett-Cotta, 1981), pp. 411–61.

[82] Butow notes in *Tōjō and the Coming of the War*, p. 534, that in the last days before his execution, Tōjō acknowledged that Japan's failure to rally the support of the Asian peoples had been a "basic cause of her defeat."

way Japan's "New Deal" did contribute significantly to making the full restoration of the prewar colonial order impossible.

But while there is no question that the Japanese interregnum in Southeast Asia did fatally undermine Western colonialism and facilitate the emergence of independent states in the postwar period, it must be emphasized the ultimate result bore scant resemblance to the vision of expanded empire that inspired Japan's conquest. Clearly, revisionist efforts to equate outcome with intentions in this instance are based less on historical evidence than on an understandable desire for national self-justification.

CHAPTER 9

Cooperation, Submission, and Resistance of Indigenous Elites of Southeast Asia in the Wartime Empire

Ken'ichi Gotō

It was in 1936 that Japan, the only modern Asian colonial power, first exhibited a serious interest in a "southward advance" policy. In that year, an advance into Southeast Asia appeared as one pillar of Japan's foreign policy in a document, "The Bases of Our National Policies," prepared under the Hirota Kiki cabinet.

The "southward advance" became one of Japan's major policies, on a par with the "northward advance" policy, which was directed toward forging a "close relationship between the three countries of Japan, Manchukuo, and China to repulse any Soviet threat from the north and to counter any Anglo-American offensive," as "The Bases of Our National Policies" described it.[1]

For several years, the Sino-Japanese War that began in July 1937 and the Nomonhan defeat in Manchuria concentrated Japanese attention on its northern front. But ironically, as the Sino-Japanese War became a quagmire, Japan's leaders turned their attention southward, a shift further accelerated by the outbreak of World War II.[2] The defeat of the Netherlands and France by Japan's ally, Germany, seemed to afford Japan new opportunities in Southeast Asia, a region of great importance to Japan because of the rich natural resources of the Netherlands East Indies and the possibility of interdicting Allied aid flowing to Chiang Kai-Shek through French Indochina.[3] The Japanese leadership also

---

[1] Gaimusho Gaiko-shiryokan, *Nippon gaiko jiten* [Encyclopedia of Japanese diplomatic history] (Tokyo: Gaimusho Gaikō Shiryōkan, 1979), p. 150.

[2] Japan's predicament brings to mind Peter Duus's judgment that "since their presence in China was less secure or stable than it was in the colonial empire, the Japanese came to regard China as a 'problem,' the resolution of which brought the temptation to further expansion." Introduction to *The Japanese Informal Empire in China, 1895–1937*, ed. Peter Duus, Ramon H. Myers, and Mark R. Peattie (Princeton, N.J: Princeton University Press, 1984), p. xii.

[3] There were four main routes for the Allies to aid China: through Hong Kong, the Soviet Union, French Indochina, and Burma. According to an estimate of the Japanese

feared the possibility of a victorious Germany extending its influence into the region. All these considerations focused attention on Southeast Asia in Japanese political, economic, and military circles.

The Japanese wartime empire, created from Japan's base in East Asia, was not the product of careful preplanning as many early postwar historical works suggested. Japan's southern occupation policies were never thoughtfully planned or firmly carried out. As Akira Iriye has pointed out, "it was a haphazard plan" and "a piling up of established facts rather than execution of a minutely planned scheme."[4] And as Christopher Thorne has argued, "There was no explicit understanding among the people concerned of the basic character of the regimes to be established in the various countries under Japan's control."[5]

As a matter of fact, only nine months prior to the actual outbreak of the war did the General Staff of the Imperial Japanese Army draft a concrete outline for the occupation. This fact underscores Yamamoto Moichirō's testimony that the "occupation administration of Java was conducted at a stroke with insufficient preparation and knowledge by an army that was traditionally oriented towards the north."[6]

On the basis of this draft, the General Staff finally produced the definitive "Essentials for Carrying Out the Administration of Occupied Southern Regions," dated November 20, 1941. The latter document stressed that the predominant "goal of the southern operation" is to "secure resources," and argues that it is appropriate when governing the area to "utilize . . . the existing structure of government" because the populace are "of low cultural standards without much hostility toward us."

This same document proposed the establishment of a military administration that would adopt a nonconciliatory stance toward the nationalist movement in the area, because making "rash pledges" to them might incur "unnecessary frictions" and might restrain Japan from "se-

---

Army General Staff, the amount of supplies entering China through these four respective routes in June 1940 was as follows: 6,000, 500, 15,000, and 10,000 tons. Bōeichō Senshishitsu, *Daihon'ei Rikugunbu* [Imperial General Headquarters, Army Section], 10 vols. (Tokyo: Asagumo Shimbunsha, 1967–75), 2:43–44.

[4] Iriye Akira, *Nichibei sensō* [The war between Japan and the U.S.] (Tokyo: Chuokoron-sha, 1978), p. 87.

[5] Christopher Thorne, *Taiheiyōsensō to wa nandatta no ka* [What was the Pacific War?], Japanese trans. of *The Issue of War: States, Societies, and the Far Eastern Conflict of 1941–1945*, trans. Ichikawa Yoichi (Tokyo: Soshisya, 1989), p. 180.

[6] Yamamoto Moichirō, *Watakushi no Indonesia dai 16 gun jidai no kaiso* [My Indonesia: A memoir of the Sixteenth Army period] (Tokyo: Nippon-Indonesia Kyokai, 1979), p. 26. Major-General Yamamoto was the last *gunseikan* (superintendent) of the Japanese military government in Java.

lecting the best possible policies in the future." Finally, it concluded that a conciliatory attitude brings "only harm and no good."[7]

In addition, the "Draft Plan for Military Government of the Southern Forces" drawn up by the General Headquarters of the Southern Forces one month before the outbreak of the war, stated that, "for the time being, the independence movements of the natives in the occupied areas are not to be conducted." The Japanese authorities were inclined to be wary of, or regard as dangerous, the indigenous independence movements. Early in the war, therefore, the Japanese had little intention of inducing indigenous nationalists to cooperate in the pursuit of Japanese war objectives.

Yet, after Japanese forces succeeded in conquering nearly all of the "Southern Regions" in approximately one hundred days, they were obliged to seek such indigenous cooperation, making concessions in certain cases, to the nationalist movements in certain areas. They did this in order to govern the occupied region (roughly thirteen times the size and three times the population of Japan) while waging war against the Allies.

Japan had embarked on this war under the slogan of "liberating the Asian peoples from the yoke of Western rule," while hiding its real intention of acquiring resources. Some Japanese had urged that the most effective way to conduct the occupation would be to utilize those national leaders who had been imprisoned or purged under Western colonial rule. But this conciliatory attitude soon became part of a thorough policy of oppressing hostile nationalists by using a network of Japanese military police (*Kempeitai*).

For their part, nationalist leaders in Southeast Asia, recognizing that Japan had destroyed the entire colonial system of the great powers in a remarkably short period of time, were not about to undertake any military resistance against it. As a result, most nationalist leaders chose a pragmatic course of action whereby they peacefully and gradually prepared themselves for independence by cooperating with the Japanese.

Generally speaking , when a country is occupied by another country, cooperation with the invader is regarded as treason. The typical example is Norway's Vidkun Quisling, who cooperated with the Nazis. In the Southeast Asian countries that had been under Western colonial rule, the situation was different.

In one sense, cooperation with Japan meant liberation from Western

---

[7] Sambō Hombu Daiichibu Kenkyūhan, "Nanpōsakusen ni okeru senryōchi tochi yokoan" [Draft outline of the administration of the occupied areas in the Southern Operation], March 1941 (Nansei Zenpan no. 17, property of War Division, Self-Defense Agency).

rule. For the Southeast Asian elite, an enemy of Japan was not necessarily a friend. As J. Boyle suggested, if cooperation with the "enemy" was compatible with—or could be made to appear compatible with—nationalism, "puppet" status, collaborationism in the extreme, suffered little discredit and in some cases, was highly esteemed.[8]

Southeast Asian political leaders who cooperated with Japan did not consider themselves traitors to the national cause; on the contrary they tended to boast of their "strategic" collaboration with Japan because that approach was regarded as an useful means to prepare for national independence. The wartime cooperation between Japan and the Southeast Asian nations should therefore be interpreted as a complex relationship in which the two parties were "in the same bed with different dreams," as an old Japanese saying goes.

For analytical purposes, I postulate the following patterns of Japanese rule in Southeast Asia during World War II: (1) joint rule with a former colonial state, as in the case of French Indochina up to the coup d'état by Japanese forces on March 9, 1945; (2) an "allied" relationship with an independent state, as in Thailand; and (3) direct military government established by Japanese forces for all other Southeast Asian areas.

Of the areas under the third classification, Burma and the Philippines were accorded nominal independence during the war and were able to conclude treaties of alliance with Japan. Indonesia and Malaya were designated as "Imperial territories" ("Outline of Guidance for the Greater East Asian Political Strategy," May 31, 1943) and were governed by Japanese military administrations until the defeat of Japan on August 15, 1945. In the case of Indonesia, independence in the "near future" was promised in Premier Koiso's statement of September 7, 1944, but Japan's defeat preceded the realization of the promise. It is toward cooperation between Japan and the leaders of those Southeast Asian countries awarded or promised independence in this third category that I should now like to turn.

JAPAN AND THE WARTIME NATIONALIST LEADERS

The basic policy in the initial stage of Japanese military administration was to strictly suppress any political activities of nationalist leaders. When it came to executing that policy opinions differed between the Imperial Headquarters in Tokyo and local military officers on the spot.

Those who took a hard line pointed out that using the native nation-

[8] John H. Boyle, *China and Japan at War, 1937–45: The Politics of Collaboration* (Stanford, Calif.: Stanford University Press, 1972), p. 6.

alist movements might create a dangerous situation. Their policy was to keep these movements dependent on Japanese authority but ignorant of Japanese plans. The more moderate Japanese military administrators argued that it would be better to take the risk of having "both the military government and the nationalist movement succeed" through mobilizing the masses and having the nationalist leaders "confide in and cooperate with" the Japanese.[9]

The Japanese central military command in Tokyo and the headquarters of the southern forces, initially established in Saigon, wanted to impose a strict military government as had been previously decided, and they took a negative view of what they saw as the appeasement policies of the moderates. But in areas where the nationalist movement was popular and where there was very little anti-Japanese feeling and even some pro-Japanese sentiment, such as in Java in the early stage of occupation under the Sixteenth Army commander General Imamura Hitoshi, predominant Japanese military opinion favored using indigenous nationalist movements.

Initial reactions of the Southern Headquarters to the views of the 16th Army were caustic. Criticizing the more moderate administrators of Imamura's command as "playing with fire," the Saigon headquarters stated, "The Sixteenth Army will eventually repent after burning its fingers in dealing with the nationalists."[10] This disagreement between the Saigon headquarters and regional commands continued whenever the issue of national independence was brought up. Yet, for all commands, the ultimate purpose of using any nationalist movement was the supreme goal of the Japanese military administration in Southeast Asia: the achievement of Japan's war objectives. As a means to this end, they tried to win the hearts of the nationalist leaders by offering them the promise of independence.

Diverse cases can be considered when looking for the reasons that and circumstances in which most nationalist leaders (even including many who had been anti-Japanese before the war) cooperated with the Japanese. Consider the following.

First, there was the fact of the overwhelming victory of the Japanese forces against the colonial powers of the West. All indigenous nationalist movements had failed to overthrow colonial rule in their countries, and only Japan had succeeded in ousting the colonial powers from

---

[9] Saitō Shizuo, *Watakushi no gunseiki* [My records of the military administration (in Java)] (Tokyo: Nippon-Indonesia Kyōkai, 1977), pp. 50–51. Stern measures were taken against Indonesians who were not cooperative. Notification No. 1 of the Sixteenth Army commander stated that those who had dangerous thoughts such as communism or anarchism, and who were engaged in anti-Japanese activities, would be excluded from the amnesty on the emperor's birthday.

[10] Yamamoto, *Watakushi no Indonesia*, p. 28.

Southeast Asia. Given the rapidity with which Japan had done so, these leaders must have concluded that it was beyond their power to fight or resist Japan's overwhelming might. Some leaders may have had opportunistic motives to decide to cooperate with the new conquerors, but they must have concluded that to win their cherished goal of independence, they could risk the danger of being labeled collaborators. As a Japanese saying goes, "If you want to take the baby tiger you must dare to go into the tiger's den."

Second, some leaders decided to cooperate with Japan in response to Japan's slogan, "Liberation from Western Control," as this was exactly what they wanted. Some nationalist leaders in this category soon recognized the difference between their ideals and the realities of the Japanese military administration and quickly became disillusioned. This was the case with Artemio Ricarte, a Philippine anti-American nationalist before the war, who had sought political asylum in Japan.[11] In general, these leaders received cold treatment from the Japanese authorities because of their candid criticism of Japanese policies, and by and large the outstanding leaders of the various nationalist movements did not emerge from this group.

A third group, exemplified by the Philippine case, wanted to preserve the continuity of the existing setup in the country, and therefore these leaders acted in accordance with the instructions given to them by the Commonwealth elites.

Let us examine in more detail "cooperation with Japan" in Indonesia, the Philippines, and Burma.

INDONESIA

In view of its natural resources, it was inevitable that Indonesia would become the most important area in the southern quadrant of Japan's "Greater East Asia Co-Prosperity Sphere." Its strategic location made that country Japan's southern lifeline. The Japanese military administration had an unexpectedly smooth start in Indonesia, and that experience greatly influenced the military government's basic policy in the early stages of rule. There was scarcely any meaningful resistance to the Japanese from the nationalist movement in Indonesia. Support was especially strong in the heartland of Java.

One of the key figures in the military government, Saitō Shizuo,

[11] Artemio Ricarte (1863–1945) came to Japan in 1915. He was one of the best-known political refugees from Southeast Asia in prewar Japan. In 1942, he was sent back to the Philippines by the Japanese army to carry out propaganda activities. He died in Ifgao in July 1945 during the debacle of the Japanese forces led by General Yamashita Tomoyuki. See Grant K. Goodman, "General Artemio Ricarte and Japan," *Journal of Southeast Asian History* 7, no. 21 (September 1966): 48–60.

stated, "Our major objective in the war was to acquire the natural resources of the land, and this was impossible to achieve without the cooperation of the natives. Accordingly, we thought that cooperation with the people was compatible with our war aims. We felt we could get them to cooperate with us by encouraging their national consciousness."[12]

The most urgent problem for the Japanese military government in Java was to determine how to treat Sukarno and Hatta, the two top leaders of the Indonesian nationalist movement, incarcerated for eight years under the Dutch East Indies regime. Despite the Southern headquarters' warning that the attempt to "utilize their cooperation" would be "playing with fire," the military leaders in Java early decided to obtain their "cooperation" soon after the start of the military administration.

An investigation report of the Navy Ministry four months before the outbreak of the war proposed the "early release of the nationalists of the Netherlands Indies, who are maltreated by the Dutch government, so they can help acquire popular support for us."[13] Ironically, while the army authorities in Java established a military administration along the lines proposed by the Japanese navy, the occupation authorities under naval control in other areas, including Sulawesi and Kalimantan, were reluctant to use the nationalist movement until the final stages of the war.

In the late 1920s Sukarno had predicted a Pacific War. He had stated that Japan's expansionism was bound to collide with the "two imperialist states of Britain and the United States" in the Asia-Pacific region, and that Indonesia's destiny would be influenced by the rivalry of those great powers. In Sukarno's well-known court statement in 1930, referred to as the "Indictment of Indonesia," he had described Japan as the "only modern imperialist state in Asia" and clearly pointed out the fallacy of the Japanese assertion that Japan was the "standard-bearer of the oppressed Asian peoples."[14]

In spite of these past statements, Sukarno quickly shifted from noncooperation with the Dutch rulers to cooperating with Japan. What was behind his thinking? One major consideration was that he saw an op-

[12] Saitō Shizuo. "Jawagunsei ni sankakushite," in Nippon-Seryōk: Indonesia Shiryo Forum, *Shogenshū: Nippongun-senryōka no Indonesia* [A gathering of evidence: Indonesia under Japanese military occupation] (Tokyo: Ryukei Shosha, 1991), p. 191.

[13] Kaigun-chōsaka, "Ranin-taisaku no kenkyū" [A study of policy toward the Netherlands East Indies], August 15, 1941, p. 10 (property of Kishi Collection of the Institute of Developing Economies, Tokyo).

[14] See Gotō Ken'ichi, *Shōwaki-Nippon to Indonesia* [Japan and Indonesia in the Showa period] (Tokyo: Keiso shobō, 1986), pp. 345–50.

portunity to win independence for Indonesia while the great powers struggled with one another. Considering his analysis of the international situation, he must have realized he had the perfect opportunity to overthrow Dutch colonial rule. In his view, the Netherlands was the archenemy, and Japan, advocating the "liberation of Asia," could be outmaneuvered while busy at war.

Roeslan Abdulgani, a postwar Indonesian foreign minister and Sukarno's top adviser in external affairs, said that Sukarno was interested in both Sun Yat-sen's Pan-Asian doctrine and Japan's modernization. At the same time he was vehemently antifascist. According to Roeslan, Sukarno once said, "If you ask me which I would prefer, democracy or militarism, my choice would undoubtedly be democracy. But if the question concerns a choice between Dutch democracy and Japanese militarism, I would prefer Japanese militarism."[15] Sukarno's statement reveals his thinking at that time. As John D. Legge has correctly pointed out, Sukarno had no obligation to be loyal to the Netherlands or to resist Japanese occupation and aggression. Any means to achieve the goal of independence were morally justifiable.[16]

After independence, Sukarno proudly stated that 75 percent of his public speeches during the occupation were genuinely nationalist.[17] According to Sukarno's political opponents, noncooperationists Sutan Sjahrir and Tan Malaca, Sukarno's cooperation with Japan went deeper than sheer expediency. That Sukarno did not sever his relations with Japan even after it became apparent that it was losing the war led some Japanese authorities to declare that the "Indonesian people rendered hearty cooperation to our military administration."[18]

One interesting indication of Sukarno's stand on cooperation with the Japanese can be seen in his attitude toward the question of independence—his ultimate objective. He was deeply hurt by the Japanese when they promised Burma and the Philippines independence. His pride was wounded because he was certain that the nationalist leaders in Java had given more cooperation to Japan than did the leaders in other areas of Southeast Asia.

Of course Sukarno had no way of knowing that Japanese higher echelons had decided to "keep the East Indies and Malaya eternally in Japanese hands; but this decision would not be announced for the time being," as stated in the "Outline of Guidance for the Greater East Asian Political Strategy."

[15] Author's interview with Roeslan Abdulgani in Jakarta, October 5, 1977.
[16] John D. Legge, *Sukarno: A Political Biography* (Sydney: Allen and Unwin), 1972, pp. 156–57.
[17] Ibid., p. 174.
[18] Yamamoto *Watakushi no Indonesia*, p. 14.

Thus, Sukarno could not understand why neither he, nor any other Indonesian leader, had been invited to the Greater East Asia Conference (November 1943) in Tokyo. Japanese premier Tōjō Hideki had convened this conference for the top leaders of the "independent states" of Asia. Sukarno could not understand why Indonesia, which willingly cooperated with Japan, could not send a delegation to the conference and why the Indonesians were only invited to visit Japan ten days after the conference was over.

To be sure, Sukarno was gratified when Japan's leaders announced their intention to grant "independence to the East Indies" in September 1944, although some time in the "near future." But Sukarno failed to see that this announcement only reflected the Japanese view that "under the current war situation the attitudes toward Japan of these countries and peoples are not to be counted on with optimism."[19] Yet Sukarno proudly stated, "Our decision to cooperate with Japan, made in 1942, proved to be correct."[20]

But as the war turned against Japan, Sukarno never tried to achieve independence for his country outside the framework of Japan's promise of independence, despite repeated urgings from more radical nationalists who continually pressed for an immediate declaration of Indonesian independence. Some of his contemporaries argued for that action.

For example, at the end of the war Tan Malaka, a former Indonesian Communist party chairman who had worked under a pseudonym as a clerk in the Bajah mines of West Java, criticized Sukarno's remarks during his inspection tour of the mine. According to Malaka, Sukarno said, "The sweat of the rōmusha (forced laborers) is poison for the Allies," and he urged the workers to work harder and produce more coal for Japan. Malaka also reproached Sukarno for answering a question posed by Malaka: "The first thing to do is to show them how great is our contribution to them [Japan]. If our contribution is great, *Dai-Nippon* [Great Japan] will surely give us independence eventually." Then Sukarno added, "If *Dai-Nippon* were to give me independence right now, I would not accept it." Probably he thought the time was not ripe yet. Tan Malaka, however, attacked Sukarno's comment by saying it had "serious implications not to be overlooked."[21]

Even in the summer of 1945 when Japan's defeat seemed imminent, Sukarno's loyalty to Japan did not waver. When the form of postinde-

---

[19] Kajima-Heiwa Kenkyūjo, *Nippon-gaikōshi*, vol. 24, *Daitōa-sensō senji saikō* [History of Japanese diplomacy, vol. 24, The Greater East Asia War and wartime diplomacy] (Tokyo: Kajimakenkyūjo shuppankai, 1973), p. 385.

[20] *Asia Raya*, September 8, 1944.

[21] Tan Malaka, *Rōgoku kara rōgoku e* [From prison to prison], trans. Oshikawa Noriaki (Tokyo: Rokusai-sha, 1981), pp. 341, 346.

pendence government was discussed at a meeting of the Investigation Committee for the Preparation of Indonesian Independence, Sukarno warned, "We are ordered by Tokyo not to discuss any form of government." This remark angered young nationalist leaders such as Wikana and Sukarni, who abruptly left the meeting room in protest against Sukarno.[22]

On August 15, 1945, when rumors spread among the Indonesian leaders that Japan had been defeated, Sukarno admonished young nationalists like Sukarni who urged an immediate declaration of independence. According to the testimonies of Iwa Kusuma Sumantri, social affairs minister in the first Sukarno cabinet after independence, Sukarno had said that "such important matters should be consulted in advance with the Japanese military."[23] Sukarno's cooperation with the Japanese induced younger nationalists to take action. They abducted Sukarno and Hatta—the so-called Rengasdengklok Incident—and demanded a declaration of immediate independence irrespective of Japan's response.

If Sukarno's attitude was one of positive cooperation with the Japanese military administration, the attitude of Hatta, another top leader, can be described as one of passive cooperation. Hatta had visited Japan in April 1933, immediately after Japan's withdrawal from the League of Nations. An influential Japanese newspaper eulogized Hatta on his visit, saying, "A Gandhi of the Netherlands East Indies is about to set foot in the land of Japan; a new leader of Asia, to inspect our country's economy."[24] From that time onward, Hatta was better known than Sukarno among those in official and unofficial Japanese circles interested in Southeast Asian affairs.

Japan mistakenly interpreted Hatta's visit, thinking it was because he agreed with Japan's "Return to Asia" theory. They continued to regard him as a pro-Japanese Indonesian: an official Foreign Ministry paper written three months before the war identified him as favorable to Japan's southward advance and claimed that his eight-year exile was a result of his trip to Japan in 1933.[25] It was not until the outbreak of the war, in fact, that the Japanese realized that Hatta really understood their true aims.

---

[22] S. K. Trimurti, "Aku didalam kancah" [My troubled period] (mimeo) (Jakarta, 1985), p. 34.

[23] Iwa Kusuma Sumantri, *Indonesia minzokushugi no genryū* [The source of Indonesian nationalism], trans. Gotō Ken'ichi (Tokyo: Waseda Daigaku shuppanbu, 1975), pp. 120–21.

[24] *Ōsaka mainichi*, April 15, 1933.

[25] Gaimushō Nankyoku, *Tōindo minzoku-undō no genjō* [The present situation of the East Indies nationalist movements] (September 1941), p. 56 (property of Diplomatic Records Office).

But Hatta was cool-headed enough to understand Japan's real objectives. He stated immediately following his trip to Japan that "the so-called Pan-Asianism of Japan is likely to be smeared by Japanese fascist elements who dream of becoming the leader of Asia. . . . [This move] will probably give Japan a new desire for colonies of its own in Asia." He also understood international relations in Asia during the 1930s in terms of the intensification of the struggle between "fascism and democracy."[26]

In late December 1941, Hatta published a paper entitled "Pacific War and the Indonesian People," in which he analyzed the war as a natural consequence of Japan's expansionist foreign policy since the 1930s. Hatta argued that there was no other course for the Indonesians but to join the "democratic camp of the West" to "confront Japanese imperialism," and he concluded that "it is better to die for one's ideals than to live on in shame."[27]

Although Hatta's stance was one of militant democracy immediately after the war began, he changed his tactics once a Japanese military administration was installed. This change of attitude must have been humiliating in the light of his former statements, but he was forced to take a realistic approach and "live on in shame" under the shadow of Japan's overwhelming military power, which had destroyed the centuries-old myth of white supremacy. His mental agonies are partially revealed in a conversation with his younger comrade, Wangsa Widjaya, whom he met for the first time in eight years after returning from exile. He said, "All we can do is watch and see how things develop from now on. What is clear is that Japan is not a democratic country but a militaristic, fascist country. You yourself must be fully aware of what such a government is like. For the time being, we must do anything we can to help the people."[28]

Thus, Hatta became a realist who pursued his ideals by cooperating with Japan, which in his mind was the peaceful line of national resistance. But his cooperation was passive when compared to Sukarno's. Japanese military administrators recognized Hatta's participation in the

[26] Concerning Hatta's visit to Japan, see Gotō, *Shōwaki-Nippon to Indonesia*, chap. 8. Likewise, the Japanese government cordially welcomed Pridi Phanomyong, one of the most influential Thai economic planners of the day, in the hope of strengthening economic relations between Japan and Siam if he became finance minister. See Edward T. Flood, "Japan's Relations with Thailand, 1928–41" (Ph.D. dissertation, University of Washington, 1967), pp. 130–40.

[27] Mohammad Hatta, *Kumpulan Karangan* [A collection of essays] (Jakarta: Penerbitan Balai Buku Indonesia, 1953), p. 145.

[28] Wangsa Widjaya, *Mengenang Bung Hatta* [In memory of Mr. Hatta] (Jakarta: C. V. Masaagung, 1988), p. 9.

"ranks of cooperators" as a benefit and "refrained from forcing further positive cooperation" on Hatta.[29]

The Japanese expected that Hatta would transmit their war and occupation objectives to the masses through speeches at rallies and radio broadcasts in order to gain "cooperation behind the battlefront." A collection of Hatta's lectures includes fourteen public speeches given under the Japanese military administration. Although his remarks contained enough praise of Japan to seem like a pledge of cooperation, the main themes running through these speeches were those of encouraging the people and stressing their self-sacrifice and spiritual endurance until the ultimate goal of independence was achieved.

For example, at a mass rally held on the first anniversary of the war, Hatta stated that "the people of Indonesia are not satisfied only with expressing gratitude to Japan for giving them great benefits. They wish to participate in the war for achieving the ideals of Greater Asia, which has been the goal also of the nationalist movement of Indonesia." In other words, he equated the Japanese advocacy of Pan-Asianism with the Indonesian nationalist goal while calling for the Indonesian people to exercise their willpower and join the fight to achieve their own objectives. He further stated: "Indonesia was liberated by Japan from the yoke of Dutch imperialism. We never want to be ruled by a foreign power again. All the people, both young and old, are strongly resolved on that. The Indonesian people would rather be buried at the bottom of the ocean than to live under foreign colonial rule." This last sentence echoed a speech he made directly before the war, in which he said that the people must "not live on in shame."[30]

Likewise, in a speech on Asia Development Day (December 8) Hatta declared: "The Indonesian people are ready to fight with their strong spiritual power in this war afflicting Greater Asia until the day comes when their ideals are achieved." He added that their ideals are those of "Asia for Asian peoples, Asia where coprosperity and mutual assistance are manifested, and Greater Indonesia in the Greater Asian Sphere." Speaking in the context of the "Greater Asia" advocated by Japan, Hatta dared to use the term "Greater Indonesia"—the title of the nationalist movement's anthem, which made the Japanese very wary.[31]

If Sukarno and Hatta represent examples of cooperation with Japan, what of noncooperation cases?

[29] Saitō, *Watakusi no gunseiki*, p. 99.

[30] Quotations are from Mohammed Hatta. *Kumpulan Pidato 1942–49* [A collection of speeches] (Jakarta: Yayasan Idayu, 1981), pp. 14–15.

[31] Hamka, a famous Sumatran Islamic leader, Japanese as saying that "there was only one great Asia now, and no Great Indonesia." Hamka, *Kenangkenan Hidup* [My recollections] (Kuala Lumpur: Penerbitan Pustaka Antara, 1982), p. 205.

THE PHILIPPINES

The Philippines contrasted sharply with Indonesia. While Indonesia welcomed the Japanese troops as their liberators when the war started and on August 15, 1945, denounced the Netherlands as an aggressor trying to reclaim Indonesia, the Philippines labeled the invading Japanese as the aggressors and the victorious U.S. forces, on their return, as their liberators.

As indicated by this contrast, the Philippines' view of Japan in the prewar years was different from that of Indonesia and other Southeast Asian nations. Dutch historian Jan Pluvier points out that no nation in Asia had so many factors hindering cooperation with Japan as did the Philippines. The Philippines was the most Westernized country in the region, and the nationalist goal of independence was about to be realized. The Filipinos were not frustrated with U.S. policy, and there was no reason they would want to side with the enemy of the United States.[32]

This situation influenced the Japanese perception of the Philippines. The Japanese southern forces established the following policies for the Philippines: "The natives here are dissolute and lazy and continue to look up to the United States with awe and admiration while making light of the Japanese. Public peace and order are unstable. We must not flatter the natives, and we must exhibit our dignity and strength with a solemn military presence so that they will cast aside their admiration of the United States and cooperate with us with all their hearts."[33]

Manuel Quezon, president of the Philippine Commonwealth, became a symbol of Filipino elite who enjoyed peace in the arms of "Mother America."[34] So America-centered was his view of the world that his statements at times evoked the "Yellow Peril" theory. In his radio speech on August 19, 1941, four months before the outbreak of war in the Pacific, Quezon stated: "We owe loyalty to America, and we are bound to her by bonds of everlasting gratitude. Should the United States enter the war, the Philippines will follow her and fight by her side, placing at her disposal all our manpower and material resources to help her achieve victory, and for this reason America's fight is our own

[32] Jan Pluvier, *Tonanajia gendaishi* [Modern history of Southeast Asia], trans. Nagai Shinichi (Tokyo: Toyokeizei Shinpo-sha, 1977, p. 275.

[33] Nampōgun Sōshireibu, "Nampō gun jōkyō hōkoku" [Report on the present condition of the Southern Army], June 29, 1942 [Ishii Shiryō (material), no. 16, property of the War History Division].

[34] Theodore Friend, *The Blue-Eyed Enemy: Japan Against the West in Java and Luzon* (Princeton, N.J.: Princeton University Press, 1988), p. 243.

fight."[35] At his last cabinet meeting on Christmas Eve, 1941, he appealed to the pro-American Filipino elite to be loyal to the United States "Whatever happens, believe in the U.S. The U.S. will never betray you."[36]

Quezon sought exile in Australia along with General MacArthur, but he ordered the political elite in the Philippines to cooperate with the Japanese only on the condition that they never forsake their loyalty to the United States. His aim in doing so was to ensure that existing political and social institutions in the Philippines would remain intact.

One member of the political elite who followed Quezon's instructions and cooperated with the Japanese, thus winning "independence" in October 1943, was José P. Laurel, president of the Republic of the Philippines. Laurel visited Japan three times during the war, the first in early October 1943, with the objective of being granted "independence." At his meeting with Prime Minister Tōjō, Laurel learned that Japan would "not demand his nation's participation in the war" and that "independence will be granted, if feasible, as soon as possible."[37] While Prime Minister Tōjō demanded Burmese participation in the war as a condition of that nation's independence, he did not ask this in the case of the Philippines, probably in consideration of Filipino sentiments toward the United States.

In drawing up the draft for the Japan–Philippines Alliance Pact, Laurel did his best to persuade the Japanese side to adopt his own wording. The pact was to be signed at the same time as the declaration of "independence" on October 14, 1943. Japan wanted to include the phrases "In order to carry out the Greater East Asia War" and "regarding the defense of the Philippines," but Laurel appealed to the Japanese side to desist, saying, "Of course, I do not intend to reject signing the pact if the Japanese army insists, but it would impede our policies to lead the people into a war which they abhor and would endanger the position of the new government with possibilities of internal rifts."

In the end, not all of his requests were granted, but the Philippines successfully postponed making any declaration of war against the United States and Britain for nearly a year after the declaration of its "independence." Even then, the wording of the war announcement on July 23, 1944, was also altered to read: "It is proclaimed that the Philippines now enters a state of war with the United States and United King-

[35] Teodoro Agoncillo, A. The Fateful Years: Japan's Adventure in the Philippines, 1941–45, 2 vols. (Quezon City: R. P. Garcia, 1965), 2:60.

[36] Manuel L. Quezon, The Good Fight (New York: AMS Press, 1974), p. 184.

[37] Itō Takashi et al., eds., Tōjō Sōridaijin kimitsu kiroku [Premier Tōjō's secret records] (Tokyo: Tokyo Daigaku shuppankai, 1990), p. 261.

dom," thus avoiding the term "declaration of war."[38] Some, Filipino historians have suggested that Laurel and others used this wording as a clever tactic to avoid catering to Japanese demands.[39]

Laurel made his second trip to Japan in early November 1943 to attend the Greater East Asia Conference. The representatives of six "independent" states of "Greater East Asia," along with Subhas Chandra Bose (as an observer), who was the head of the Provisional Government of Free India, were invited. At the conference, these Asian delegates were pressured to cooperate with Japan's war efforts. The conference produced the "Greater East Asia Charter," which extolled the ideals of having a new order of coexistence and coprosperity, mutual respect of autonomy and independence, and the abolition of racial discrimination, and was proclaimed as a counterblast to the Atlantic Charter.[40]

Each delegate at the conference was asked to make a major address, but Laurel specifically declared that he had had no time to prepare a speech and, moreover, he had been ill.[41] Suzuki Shizuo notes in his study of this conference that when Laurel was asked by the Japanese to submit a draft in advance, he explained that this would be a form of censorship, an action that a leader of an independent state could not agree to. Suzuki cites this episode as proof that even in the mind of the main leader of the "pro-Japanese" faction in the Philippines, great distrust of Japan prevailed.[42]

Laurel was the only Asian leader who expressed solidarity with Indonesia, a territory not represented at the conference. Laurel had not used the term "Indonesia" because it had been banned by the Japanese authorities. He proposed instead that "the peoples of Java, Borneo, and Sumatra share common interests with the peoples of Burma, Thailand, Manchukuo and China, and should be called on to consolidate into one strong, effective organization connected with Japan." Laurel's speech was enthusiastically acclaimed by Ba Maw of Burma as an "emotionally

[38] *Daitōa-Sensō senji saikō*, pp. 444–50.

[39] Renato and Letizia Constantino, *Filippin minshu no rekishi* [The Philippines: The continuing past], trans. Tsurumi Yoshiyuki et al., 4 vols. (Tokyo: Keiso shobō, 1978–80), 3:741.

[40] On the Greater East Asia Conference, see Gotō Ken'ichi, "Daitoa senso no imi" [The meaning of the Greater East Asia War], in *Tōnan Ajia to Nippon* [Southeast Asia and Japan], ed. Yano Toro (Tokyo: Kobundo, 1991), pp. 171–76.

[41] Laurel, José P. *J. P. Laurel hakase sensō kaisōroku* [War memoirs of Dr. José P. Laurel], trans. Yamazaki Shikgetake (Tokyo: Nippon kyōiku shinbunsha, 1987), p. 84.

[42] Suzuki Shizuo, "Konichi no ketsui" [Characterization of the anti-Japanese movement], in *Shinsei kokka Nippon to Ajia* [The sacred state of Japan and Asia], ed. Suzuki Shizuo and Yokoyama Michiyoshi (Tokyo: Keiso shobō, 1984), p. 307.

moving speech, which expresses the fury of the Asians and the spirit of resistance of all who have been in bondage for so many centuries."[43] Ba Maw also observed that Laurel was very moved by this, the dramatic first meeting in history of Asian leaders.[44]

Laurel met with Premier Tōjō before the conference and stated that "should Japan be defeated, we know that we in East Asia will become slaves. If the Oriental people become aware of this fact, they will naturally cooperate with Japan in her task of liberating her East Asian brothers. They must be informed that Japan's victory is absolutely necessary for their own sake."[45] Laurel stressed the close connection between Asian national self-interest and a Japanese victory.

Laurel's tone, however, was a little different when he said goodbye to Tōjō after the Great East Asia Conference. Regarding Japan's offer to send 220 advisers to the Philippines, Laurel said "We do need the help of Japanese specialists in the technical field of agriculture, industry and finance, but as we have self-confidence in the political field, the guidance of Japanese advisors is not required." He further added, expressing some discontent, that "if such a large group of Japanese are to stay in our country, we are afraid it would give the impression that the Philippine government is a puppet regime."[46] It turned out later that his remarks represented a misunderstanding, but they still give us a glimpse of how he mistrusted Japan. In the end, Tōjō stated, "As for Japan, we cannot afford to dispatch such a group of many advisers, and we have no intention of imposing them on the Philippines."[47]

At the same meeting with Tōjō, Laurel did make an apology: "I am very much ashamed of the Philippines' attitude toward Japan in the past." Tōjō replied: "There is no need for such reserve between brothers. Please be free and frank."[48] This episode seems to indicate that Laurel realized the need to balance criticism with praise lest the Japanese become too upset with the complex Philippine attitude toward them.

In Laurel's postwar memoirs, all of his acts of cooperation with Japan are justified as wartime decisions. His memoir was written in Sugamo Prison, where he was detained as a war crimes suspect, and the tone is almost militant. He said that cooperation with Japan was elicited from him against his will and that he had only followed the instructions

---

[43] Ba Maw, *Biruma no yoake* [The dawn of Burma], trans. Yokobori Yoichi (Tokyo: Taiyo Shuppan, 1974), p. 351.

[44] Ibid., p. 275.

[45] Itō et al., *Tōjō Sōridaijin kimitsu kiroku*, p. 275.

[46] Ibid., p. 351.

[47] Ibid., p. 352.

[48] Ibid., pp. 352–53.

given by Quezon. Moreover, his primary principle for action was to "try to secure the survival of the nation."[49]

Laurel also stated, "I did not willingly give help to Japan in her war against the United States. . . . My actions may be construed as being against U.S. interests, but they were done under coercion and pressure. . . . In brief, I became one of the victims of U.S. unpreparedness in the Pacific, and that was my ill luck."[50] He cited the United States as politically and morally responsible for the events of the occupation, without questioning the political and moral responsibility of himself and the Filipino elite toward the Filipino people. On the conrary, he exemplified the belief of the Philippine elite who chose to cooperate with Japan claiming that "forced collaboration is not collaboration. Voluntary collaboration as a means of national survival and to tide over our people to better times is not punishable."[51] As David Steinberg points out, the "elites' self-justification of their cooperation in the guise of loyalty to the nation has been observed throughout the periods under Spanish and American rule." Steinberg asserts that this question of cooperation is, for these Filipinos, like a cancer, "secretly feared but consciously ignored in the hope that it might vanish by itself."[52] Steinberg also notes that all such leaders have tried to forget their cooperation with Japan and have avoided thorough discussion of the matter. According to Steinberg, such a discussion would very likely arouse a public demand for a sweeping inspection of the social makeup of the Philippines and reexamination of the conduct of the elite during the war.[53]

BURMA

Although Burma is the furthest Southeast Asian country from Japan by sea, the Japanese military attached great strategic importance to it for two reasons. First, Burma offered a back door to China while being a front door to India. Second, Burma was a good source for petroleum and rice.[54]

The Burmese, on the other hand, admired Japan for its successful

---

[49] Laurel, *J. P. Laurel Hakase senső kaisouroku*, p. 160.

[50] Ibid., pp. 165–68.

[51] David J. Steinberg, *Philippine Collaboration in World War II* (Manila: Solidaridad Publishing House, 1967), p. 168.

[52] Ibid., pp. 164–65. For a similar analysis, see Grant K. Goodman, "The Japanese Occupation of the Philippines: Commonwealth Sustained," *Philippine Studies* 36 (1988): 98–104.

[53] Steinberg, *Philippine Collaboration*, p. 175.

[54] Sakuma Hirayoshi, *Biruma gendai eiji* [Modern political history of Burma] (Tokyo: Keiso shobō, 1984), p. 4.

twentieth-century modernization. As for Japan's foreign policy, the Burmese nonchalantly believed that as the nationalist Ba Maw put it, "what Japan has gained poses no ethical problem."[55] Furthermore, the Thakin party under the leadership of Burma's young elite hoped for Japan's military assistance in their struggle to be free of Britain. Their aspirations led to an unusual relationship between the nationalist Thakin party and the Japanese Minami Group, directly controlled by the Japanese Army.[56]

The military authorities, for their part, observed that the Burmese "had the desire to cast off British oppression with the help of Japan's power even before the war . . . and their feelings toward Japan are very good."[57] When the Japanese established their system of governance, they found the nationalist Ba Maw a very useful leader—more so than his younger brother Aung Sang, a leading figure in the Thakin party who valued independence more than anything else and became increasingly critical of Japan.

Ba Maw had studied in England and returned with strong anti-British sentiments. He declared that "British imperialism is the real, decisive enemy for Burma" and "we must use other devils to drive away the vampire that is imposing itself on us."[58] He perceived the current Pacific conflict as the "fourth Burmese-British war."[59] As Ba Maw saw it, Japan was beneficial to the Burmese nationalist movement, just as Burma was beneficial to Japan. His pragmatism is clearly reflected in his statement that "we will take from them the same amount as they have taken from us, leaving an equal balance of payments."[60]

The Japanese side was pleased by his willingness to cooperate, and in January 1943 Japan's leaders informed Burma's elite that they would grant the country "independence"—earlier than to any other nation under Japanese occupation. The Japanese justified this step as a result of the "thoroughgoing [Burmese] support given to the Imperial Forces and in consideration of their burning aspirations for independence." But the truth of the matter was that the Japanese feared that popular disappointment might produce an "intensification of enemy maneuvers . . . leading to uneasiness in the Greater East Asia Sphere." More important, the Japanese hoped that Burmese independence would encourage the

---

[55] Ba Maw, *Biruma no yoake*, p. 66.

[56] See Bo Min Gaung, *Aungsan-Shōgun to 30 nin no shishi* [General Aung San and the thirty patriots], trans. Tanabe Hisao (Tokyo: Chūō Kōron-sha, 1990).

[57] Nampōgun Sōshireibu, "Nampōgun jōkyō hōkoku."

[58] Ba Maw. *Biruma no yoake*, p. 40.

[59] Ibid., p. 397.

[60] Ibid., p. 285.

Indian people, in turn, to launch an anti-British movement for independence.[61]

How, then, did the Japanese view Ba Maw's cooperation? Ba Maw met the Japanese top leadership five times during the short period of March 1943 to August 15, 1945. (He even met with Tōjō once in Singapore.) No other leaders in the "Southern Co-Prosperity Sphere" had such close contact with the Japanese leaders. Even in his postwar memoirs Ba Maw did not conceal his personal friendship with Tōjō Hideki. It is interesting to read Ba Maw's saying that "Tōjō not only gave wonderful impressions to C. Bose and me, but all other Southeast Asian leaders who met him were likewise deeply impressed."[62]

The Shōwa emperor (Hirohito) has attested to this statement of Ba Maw's. According to the "The Eight-Hour Monologue of the Shōwa Emperor" (March 18, 1946), one of the reasons that he did not consent to the reshuffling of the Tōjō Cabinet was that "as Tōjō has been in contact with people in various parts of the Greater East Asia, a reshuffling that disregarded those ties might make it difficult to retain public goodwill in Greater East Asia."[63] Premier Ba Maw attended the Greater East Asia Conference in November 1943, only three months after the Burmese declaration of independence and the forging of a new alliance with Japan, immediately followed by a declaration of war against Britain and the United States. While Premier Phibun Songkhram of Thailand prudently refrained from following the Burmese example, pleading illness, Ba Maw accepted an invitation to the Greater East Asia Conference through Ambassador Sawada Renzo promptly and with pleasure. Of course, we should realize that Phibun and Ba Maw were in different positions; Phibun had much more leverage to resist Japan than Ba Maw because of Thailand's prewar independent status. Had Ba Maw refused to go, he would undoubtedly have been promptly dismissed.

On the other hand, Ba Maw showed great pride in heading an independent state when he stated publicly that it would be disagreeable both to himself and the Burmese nation if the seating at the conference was arranged in Japanese alphabetical order. If this happened, Burma would be placed after the Philippines, even though Burma had won its independence first.[64] But Ba Maw's request had no effect, and the Japanese

---

[61] Sambohonbuhen, *Sugiyama memo* [Documents of General Sugiyama], 2 vols. (Tokyo: Hara shobō, 1967), 2:351.

[62] Ba Maw, *Biruma no yoake*, p. 323.

[63] "Shōwa Tenno no Dokuhaku 8 jikan" [The Eight-Hour Monologue of the Shōwa Emperor), *Bungei Shunjū*, December 1990, p. 127.

[64] "Daitōa-sensō kankei ikken: Daitōa kaigi kankei" [A file related to the Great East Asia War: Concerning the Greater East Asia Conference] (property of the Diplomatic

alphabetical order was used. (The Thai made a similar complaint and were also turned down.)

What of the attitudes of Thai leaders to this conference? Many studies have been published lately concerning Premier Phibun's wartime diplomacy with Japan (see the chapter by E. Bruce Reynolds in this volume). It is almost an established theory that his cooperation was not founded on his loyalty to Japan but on his deep concern for Thailand's national interests, that is to say, his "survival calculations."[65] One of the reasons for this conclusion is Phibun's refusal to attend the Greater East Asia Conference.

Japanese historical documents stress this same point. Japan's strong displeasure with Premier Phibun, who did not indicate his intention to attend the conference even one month before its commencement, is clear in the following passage from a contemporary diplomatic report: "Should Phibun refuse to accept our invitation when all the representatives of other nations have agreed to attend, the significance of convening the conference would be greatly reduced. Furthermore, it would create an impression, not only in the two countries concerned, but also in the world at large, that relations between Japan and Thailand are not good, and this would create unfavorable political consequences."[66]

But Phibun was adamant in his wish to boycott the conference, and Japan was able to save face only when Thailand agreed to send Prince Wanwaithayakon to represent that country. Observing Phibun's behavior as he skillfully distanced his country from Japan in accordance with his judgment of the war situation, Tōjō declared at the end of July 1943: "The country that most requires our attention regarding the unity of Greater East Asia is Thailand."[67]

Even at the war's outset, Japan had misgivings about Thailand's attitude. The military authorities of the Southern Forces stated on the one

---

Records Office, L2-2-2). Ba Maw complained to Ambassador Sawada in Rangoon about the relative scarcity of decorations given to the Burmese compared to the Filipinos. Sawada asked the Foreign Ministry to do something about it, and, as a result, Vice Premier Thakin Mya and other important leaders were decorated. Thakin Mya stated at the award ceremony, "We are very much moved by the gracious consideration of his Imperial Majesty. With the sixteen million people of Burma, we will do our utmost to strengthen Japan-Burma ties of cooperation in pursuing the war to the end. We are determined to surmount all the difficulties and fight to the last in order to respond to the kind consideration of His Imperial Majesty." Telegram from Acting Ambassador Kitazawa to Minister Shigemitsu of the Greater East Asia Affairs Ministry, August 24, 1944 (property of the Diplomatic Records Office, L2-2-2).

[65] E. Bruce Reynolds. "Aftermath of Alliance: The Wartime Legacy in Thai-Japanese Relations," *Journal of Southeast Asian Studies* 21, no. 1 (March 1990): 85.

[66] "Daitōa sensō kankei ikken."

[67] Itō et al., *Tōjō Sōridaijin kimitsu kicoku*, p. 208.

hand, "Premier Phibun and the rest of the Thai leadership trust Japan and want to receive Japan's guidance," and "Japan-Thailand relations are good enough as long as the Phibun regime continues. . . ." On the other hand, those authorities said "we must be careful in giving the Thais any guidance, as they seem to stress the integrity of national sovereignty and the extension of state power to win popular support for themselves." Therefore, "we must pay profound attention to the domestic situation in Thailand."[68]

Unlike Phibun, who declined to visit Japan, Ba Maw addressed the Greater East Asia conference, stressing that "the stronger Asia becomes, the stronger are we Burmese." He then added, "We must be aware of the fact that we who are born in Asia have a dual nationality, that is, we are nationals of our own country and at the same time we are nationals of Greater East Asia."[69] This rhetoric pleased Japanese ears, as it sounded very much like the Japanese view: "Without the construction of a Greater East Asia, there would be no completion of national independence," meaning, "independence can only be completed when independence is transcended."[70]

As far as Ba Maw's public statements are concerned, they give the impression that he was a puppet of the Japanese militarists, but as his insistence about the seating order at the Greater East Asia conference reveals, he possessed strong national pride, and the historical record shows that he was not a man who liked to be manipulated by the Japanese.

At his meeting with Tōjō immediately after the Greater East Asia conference, he told Tōjō that the major reason for the drastic drop in Burma's rice production was the Japanese army's exploitation of the agricultural labor force and the requisitioning of cattle by the troops. He also related to Tōjō how a minister of his cabinet was suspected by the *Kempeitai* of being a political offender and had been arrested without Ba Maw being first informed. Furthermore, a low-ranking *Kempeitai* officer had dared to "question Ba Maw's policy" to his face, which was "acting beyond his position" and "a grave offense." Ba Maw told Tōjō frankly, "As the head of state, I have no obligation to deal directly with this officer. . . . I want the Japanese side to trust me as the head of state. It is very embarrassing for me to have the Japanese deal with such matters without any prior consultation with me."[71]

Tōjō's record of the Tōjō-Ba Maw talks at Singapore four months

---

[68] Nampōgun Sōshireibu, "Nampōgun jōkyō hōkoku."
[69] Itō et al., *Tōjō Sōridaijin kimitsu kiroku*, p. 208.
[70] Gotō, "Daitōa sensō no imi," p. cit., p. 179.
[71] Itō et al., *Tōjō Sōridaijin kimitsu kiroku*, p. 349.

before the above episode show that Tōjō was somewhat ill at ease with such a strong personality as the Burmese leader. Tōjō commented that "Ba Maw has the confidence of the man who carries Burma on his shoulders. He sometimes makes audacious demands that are somewhat irritating." But, Tōjō added, to "hold Burma in our arms he and other Burmese like him should be given full free play so we can unite them all later."[72]

These remarks vividly indicate the Japanese intention to give "internal guidance" to the Burmese even though they were to be given "independence." When Councillor Ishii Kikujirō expressed misgivings about an "independent" Burma at a Privy Council meeting five months after Burmese independence, Tōjō replied: "Please keep in mind that Burma's coveted independence was given only because of the presence of the Imperial Army." Tōjō also replied to a query from Councillor Minami Hiroshi that "the treaty is purposely phrased so as to make both parties appear equal; therefore, Burma can save face. But as stated before, as long as we grasp the broad fundamentals, the problems that might arise in the future will be resolved with our power."[73]

While Ba Maw stuck to his fundamental line of cooperation with the Japanese (which eventually resulted in his being considered a war criminal by the Allies after the war), Burmese resistance against Japan was secretly planned by the Anti-Fascist Organization (AFO, later the Anti-fascist People's Freedom League). Organized mainly by the Burmese army leaders of the former Thakin Party and some Communists, this group wanted independence for Burma, and led a nationwide revolt on March 27, 1945. Tanabe Hisao asserts that the aim was simply to have an anti-Japanese uprising before the return of the British, so as to use this event to negotiate with the British for independence.[74]

But Ba Maw denounced the uprising as a "treacherous about-face, without any guilty feelings" on the part of the Thakin party, who predicted the return of the British after the war. Ba Maw harshly accused them of lying: "Their pronouncement of trust in Japan in the early stage of the war was a falsehood to conceal the truth."[75]

[72] Ibid., p. 509.

[73] Ibid., p. 512.

[74] Comment by Tanabe in Bo Min Gaung, *Aungsan-Shōgun to 30 nin to shishi*, p. 156.

[75] Ba Maw, *Biruma no yoake*, p. 296. After the end of the war, Ba Maw defected to Japan. However, on January 14, 1946, he received a letter from the vice minister for foreign affairs stating that, "great changes have taken place in our country since our government accepted the Potsdam Declaration, and we are sorry to say that our government is not able to meet your desire satisfactorily. Under these circumstances, I am directed to suggest you that you will surrender to the authorities of the GHQ. We earnestly hope that you will understand our position." (property of the Diplomatic Record Office, Ba Maw file 3-(3)).

The Thakin party's denunciation of Ba Maw when it came to power after the war stemmed from his public condemnation of the Thakin party rather than his close relationship with Japan. Ba Maw censured the Thakin party's behavior and attacked that party for being "obsessed to the point of paranoia with prewar Japanese militarism."[76]

COMPARING THE FOUR LEADERS

For Japan's leaders, Southeast Asia was an area where the theory of "dōbun, dōshū" (common culture, common race) could not be applied. Traditionally, that area had been regarded as a "culturally different and less civilized region," unlike Taiwan and Korea, which Japan controlled. Therefore, the Japanese considered Southeast Asia as a "lifeline in the south" that yielded various kinds of resources vital to the Japanese war effort. It was a matter of great strategic necessity that Japan adopt a forceful exploitation system to achieve its goal of acquiring human and material resources.

Yet the Japanese were also aware that coopting the national elite to achieve their war objectives could obtain maximum results at minimum cost. It became extremely difficult for those nationalist leaders in the various countries of Southeast Asia who had been committed to acquiring or maintaining their nations' independence to resist Japan and its formidable military power. Therefore, they generally tried to achieve their national goals by making use of Japan's claim to liberate Southeast Asia. Sukarno, Hatta, Laurel, and Ba Maw are typical cases of men who tried to reconcile cooperation with Japan and working for their national goals under Japanese occupation. Their complex relationships with Japan can be seen in table 9.1.

PATTERNS OF ANTI-JAPANESE MOVEMENTS

Our picture of nationalist leaders in Southeast Asia and their cooperation with Japan would not be complete without mentioning the leaders who were either noncooperative with or positively opposed to Japanese rule. The "positive noncooperation stance" taken by the anti-Japanese resistance movements in various occupied areas reflected the pattern of Japanese rule, the relations with the former colonial power or with Japan before the war, and the countries' general socioeconomic conditions. We classify these resistance movements into the following categories to emphasize the role played by certain leaders. They held different

---

[76] Ba Maw, *Biruma no yoake*, p. 281.

TABLE 9.1
Relationships of Four Southeast Asian Leaders with Japan

	Sukarno (1901–70)	Hatta (1900–80)	Laurel (1891–1959)	Ba Maw (1893–1977)
Educational background	Bandung Institute of Technology	Rotterdam Commerce College	Yale University	Cambridge University
Positions held in five years before WWII	In exile	In exile	Judge of the Supreme Court	Premier; imprisoned
Political stance	Antifascist Anti-Dutch	Antifascist Pro–Western democracy	Pro–American elite	Anti-British
Status during the war	Chairman, Central Advisory Council	Vice chairman, Central Advisory Council	President of the "independent" state	Premier of the "independent" state
Number of meetings with Japanese premiers (visits to Japan)	2 (1)	2 (1)	4 (3)	5 (4)
Participation in the Greater East Asian Conference	Not invited	Not invited	Attended	Attended
Evaluation by the Japanese authorities	Cooperative	Cooperative (although once condemned as a Communist)	Useful	Cooperative (but caused slight irritation)
Postwar position	Labeled as a "running dog" of Japan; president of Republic of Indonesia	Vice president	Sugamo prison; senator	Sugamo prison; expelled by the political enemies

ideologies, but during the war they all opposed Japan and portrayed Japan as a fascist, militarist state.

First, there were resistance movements organized through existing relationships with former colonial states or with the Allied forces. These include the anti-Japanese guerrilla activities of the Philippines under the command of the United States Forces in the Far East (USAFFE), the 136th Corps of Malaya, and the Free Thailand Movement. In Indonesia, there was no equivalent. One exceptional case was the Marxist-oriented Amir Sjarifuddin, who received twenty-five thousand guilders from the Dutch authorities in order to organize an anti-Japanese movement. But his connection with the Dutch was known by the Japanese, and he was captured and sentenced to death. Because Sukarno appealed to the Japanese, Amir finally received amnesty.

Second, there were anti-Japanese resistance movements led by the Communists, who formed a united front with peasant movements, including the Hukubalahap movement of the Philippines and the Viet Minh movement of Vietnam. The Viet Minh, led by Ho Chi Minh, had strong mass support in the rural areas. They were anti-French as well as anti-Japanese and played the most significant role in achieving independence. The Hukubalahap under the leadership of Louis Taruc cooperated with the USAFE in their fight against their common enemy, the Japanese. After MacArthur returned to the Philippines, he observed the increasing danger from the Hukubalahap in rural Luzon and suppressed them. Although their connections to the peasant movement were weak and their influence was limited to the Chinese community, the Malayan People's Anti-Japanese Army—an extension of the prewar anti-Japanese group led by local Chinese—should be included in this group.

Finally, there were "new elite" groups that the Japanese military administration nurtured and which "betrayed the parent that gave them birth." As these groups began to exert military power, they rose up to resist Japanese military rule. A good example is the February 1945 Blitar uprising by the PETA (Army for the Defense of the Fatherland)[77] in Indonesia and the anti-Japanese revolt of the Burmese army in March of the same year. The latter revolt was conducted with help from the British army, which had regained its strength and reentered Burma.[78] The revolt of the Burmese army had similar characteristics with the examples in the first category. It is interesting to note that in both Indonesia and Burma today, the military still dominates and in both cases

[77] See Nugroho Notosusanto, *The PETA Army During the Japanese Occupation in Indonesia* (Tokyo: Waseda University Press, 1979), chap. 5.

[78] Nemoto Kei. "Birma no minzoku-undō to Nippon" [Burmese nationalist movements and Japan], in *Kindai Nippon to Shokuminchi*, vol. 6 [Modern Japan and Her Colonies], ed. Ōe Shinobu et al. (Tokyo: Iwanami shoten, 1993), pp. 107–17.

the military attributes its legitimacy to the role it played in these two uprisings against Japanese fascism.

It should be noted, however, that there is one major difference concerning leadership in the two cases. In Burma, Aung Sang, the defense minister of "independent" Burma, took the initiative in the revolt and led the movement to victory. After the war, he played an outstanding role in achieving independence from Britain before his assassination in July 1947. In Indonesia, Surprijadi, a leader of the Blitar revolt, was an insignificant PETA officer from a local town. Although Surprijadi was missing (and was never found) after the suppression of the revolt, it is widely believed that he was captured and tortured to death by the Japanese. Despite his absence, Surprijadi was designated as the first army commander after the proclamation of Indonesian independence in August 1947.

There were still other resistance movements, including some that could be categorized as genuine popular uprisings against the severe economic exploitation associated with Japanese rule. There was also the Pontianak Incident in West Kalimantun, Indonesia, in 1943–44, reportedly involving an anti-Japanese resistance movement but actually a delusion on the part of overly nervous Japanese trying to crush certain anti-Japanese movements in Pontianak before they became mass movements.[79] These types of resistance occurred frequently in Southeast Asia toward the end of the war.

Between cooperation and positive noncooperation with Japan, there were also many cases of passive noncooperation in various occupied areas of Southeast Asia.

Roeslan Abdulgani has explained this passive noncooperation. In his memoir of the war period, he classified those persons involved in this type of passive resistance:

1. People who never took any specific action, were always passive, and hoped only for Japan's defeat;
2. People who listened to Allied broadcasts and transmitted information from them to a specific group of comrades;
3. People who made efforts to strengthen their negotiating position in order to gain independence, anticipating the return of the Allied Forces after Japan's defeat;

[79] Gotō Ken'ichi, *Nippon senryōki Indonesia kenkyū* [A study of Indonesia during the Japanese occupation] (Tokyo: Ryūkei Shosha, 1989), chap. 3. This tragic incident, in which many intellectuals, members of the sultan's family, and Chinese notables were arrested and executed without judicial procedure, occurred between October 1943 and August 1944. The Japanese side regarded them as opponents who were secretly working for the Allies. A Japanese source records that 2,130 people were killed, but the Indonesian side insists that more than 20,000 were killed.

4. People who were organized by the former Netherlands East Indies authorities to conduct sabotage.[80]

While acknowledging the existence of such illegal movements, Roeslan pointed out that the illegal anti-Japanese movements in Indonesia (including those in the second category, to which he belonged) were helpless in achieving Indonesian independence. Interestingly enough, the Japanese military authorities were not seriously concerned about the noncooperation groups in Indonesia. Saitō Shizuo, for example, stated that "unlike the so-called underground movement, they did not resort to direct struggles through sabotage, espionage, coup d'état and so forth, and their criticisms or dissatisfactions were directed not against Japan per se, but against the Indonesian political leaders who cooperated with Japan."[81]

Accordingly, despite the general tendency to overemphasize its importance on the part of those closely involved in illegal activity, the noncooperation movement in Indonesia was essentially not a political force that posed any real threat to Japan. Rather, as Benedict Anderson has pointed out, it was more a "frame of mind"[82] among those who led the movement.

Roeslan Abdulgani also evaluated the cooperation of Sukarno, Hatta and the other nationalist leaders with Japan as the "most effective and productive method possible" under the circumstances of those times. Armed resistance against superior Japanese force was inconceivable, and he hints that Sukarno's intent was to work for national independence through cooperation with Japan. Roeslan asserts that this strategy of Sukarno's was by no means a "humiliating cooperation," but rather a display of "political maturity" by the Indonesian leadership, and that it was indeed fortunate that Indonesia had such capable leaders when it finally won its independence.[83]

Conclusion

Various noncooperation groups played different roles in different countries in Southeast Asia. Cooperation with the Japanese was, for the top-level national leaders, the only "rational" alternative to submission. Cooperation won time and avoided the worst so that these leaders could

---

[80] Gotō Ken'ichi, "Indonesia chishikijin to Nippon gunsei" [Indonesian intellectuals and the Japanese military occupation], *Shakai Kagaku Tokyu*, no. 73 (May 1980): 111.

[81] Saitō, *Watakushi no gunseiki*, p. 105.

[82] Benedict R. o'G. Anderson, *Java in a Time of Revolution: Occupation and Resistance, 1944–1946*. (Ithaca, N.Y.: Cornell University Press, 1972), p. 49.

[83] Gotō, "Indonesia chishikijin to Nippon gunsei," p. 109.

seek more favorable conditions for national independence by their short-lived friendship with Japan.

For this reason, the question of wartime responsibility for cooperation with Japan was set aside in those countries after the war. Sukarno, who was most closely involved with Japan, was president for twenty years without ever being tenaciously questioned about his cooperation with Japan. If we compare the tragic demise of Premier Zhang Jinghui of Manchukuo and chief of state Wang Ching-wei of the Republic of China with the postwar careers of Laurel, Ba Maw, or Prince Wan-waithayakon, we have a better understanding of the special features of Southeast Asia's cooperation with Japan.[84]

Cooperation with Japan had varying implications for each country of Southeast Asia. Thailand had its independence to protect and could lose it, whereas Indonesia had no independence to lose. Premier Phibun of independent Thailand, immediately after the conclusion of a treaty of alliance with Japan at the end of December 1941, depicted the dilemma of those wartime leaders of Southeast Asia: "If we don't sign, it means we will all be destroyed. If we join with them and Japan is destroyed, we will be destroyed too. Or if Japan comes out OK, we still could be ruined. Or, if Japan does OK, we could do OK too. Or if Japan wins, we could end up like Manchukuo. So what should we do?"[85]

---

[84] The general image of Wang Ching-wei in the postwar period was that he was "blinded by self-esteem and goaded by political frustration. . . . He brought his misfortunes to the Japanese." However, John Boyle has queried the truth of the idea that Wang was merely a puppet. Boyle, *China and Japan at War*, p. 5.

[85] Quoted from Reynolds, *Aftermath of Alliance*, p. 85.

PART IV

Japan's Wartime Empire in Other Perspectives

CHAPTER 10

The "Comfort Women"

George Hicks

EMERGENCE OF THE ISSUE AND JAPANESE GOVERNMENT REACTIONS

The emergence of Japan's wartime "comfort women" as a public issue has been one of the more remarkable by-products of the end of the Cold War, which has seen a widespread revival of concern with World War II questions, either from historical interest or from a sense of unfinished business. The impact of such concerns is particularly acute in Japan's case, as Japan's abrupt postwar change of role from long-standing rival in the Pacific to anticommunist bulwark long made it expedient for both the Japanese and their anticommunist allies to write off past contentions. South Korea, which was under ironfisted authoritarian rule until 1988, was not willing to antagonize the Japanese on a human rights, let alone a women's issue.

The comfort women question, however, was not one of those issues that might have been dealt with earlier, but for the Cold War. Not only did former comfort women shrink from revealing their past "defilement"—others also regarded it as a kindness to remain silent on the matter. Nor was there yet a vocal women's movement in Japan, Korea, or elsewhere to support them and take aggressive action both domestically and on the international scene.

The "comfort system" was by no means unrecognized among Allied forces, who often encountered comfort women in the course of repatriating Japanese troops and nationals, but the system tended to be equated with the "regimental brothel" or *bordel militaire de campagne* known in some other armies, or else the women were supposed to be the "camp follower" type well known around military bases anywhere. Although United States intelligence compiled detailed information on the working of the Japanese system, including the role of force in the recruitment process,[1] it was not regarded as a live issue and long remained buried in the archives.

The only sources publicly available before systematic documentary

---

[1] Allied Translator and Interpreter Section, Supreme Commander for the Allied Powers, *Research Report: Amenities in the Japanese Armed Forces* (Tokyo, 1945).

research from the early 1990s were the wartime reminiscences that appeared in Japan in some quantity from the 1960s. The first Japanese to become concerned with this aspect was a journalist, Senda Kako, who in 1962 was doing research for the *Mainichi* newspaper on the war, which involved examining twenty-five thousand photographs banned by wartime censorship. Among them was one of two women wading in a river with a soldier grinning at them. To his query as to its significance, a former war correspondent explained that they were Korean comfort women—the first that Senda had heard of the matter.[2] He began systematic investigations, leading to numerous publications over the following years based on interviews with ex-servicemen and civilian operators involved in the system.

Material from Senda and all other available sources were compiled in Japanese in 1976 by a Korean activist, Kim Il-myon, in his major publication *The Emperor's Forces and Korean Comfort Women*.[3] It is accompanied by a sociopolitical commentary bitterly critical of Japanese colonialism but with a realistic grasp of soldiers' psychology under combat stress and savage discipline. The next major source was produced in the early 1980s by Yoshida Seiji,[4] a former administrator of the National Labor Service Association, responsible in the later phases of the war for forced drafts of laborers and comfort women in southern Korea. He remains the only member of the administration to testify on recruitment methods, regarding which nothing seems to have survived the systematic destruction at the end of the war of all documents likely to cause later embarrassment. Documents on other aspects of the comfort system, while qualitatively revealing, remain very fragmentary in terms of the whole picture.

An early move toward politicization of related issues was the initation in 1972 of Korean Forced Draft Investigation Groups in Japan and South Korea. These groups pushed the claims of conscript laborers. The only comfort women to be publicly identified before 1991 were Pae Ponggi, who figured in a film on the subject made in Okinawa in 1979, Yuyuta (No Su-bok) who was discovered living in Thailand in the early 1980s, and Shirota Suzuko, a Japanese who had broadcast her story in 1986.

Early in 1988, with the progress of democratization underway in South Korea and women's organizations beginning to form, the South

---

[2] Senda Kako, *Jūgun ianfu to tennō* [Military comfort women and the emperor] (Kyoto: Kamogawa Shuppan, 1992), pp. 2–4.

[3] Kim Il-myon, *Tennō no guntai to Chōsenjin ianfu* [The emperor's forces and Korean comfort women] (Tokyo: San'ichi shobō, 1976).

[4] Yoshida Seiji, *Watakushi no sensō hanzai: Chōsenjin kyōsei renkō* [My war crimes: The forced draft of Koreans] (Tokyo: San'ichi shobō, 1983).

Korean Church Women's Alliance established a Committee for the Study of the Voluntary Service Corps—which was the wartime term covering both female labor draftees and comfort women. This group became the main center for action on the issue, in close collaboration with women's and antiwar groups in Japan. For many years a leading concern of women's groups in both countries had been sex tourism and prostitution around United States bases. The view now came to be adopted that the comfort women issue could be used to inflame feeling against such practices as both types of sexual exploitation were shocking from the standpoints of morality, feminism, pacifism, and Korean patriotism.

In May 1990, when South Korean President Roh Tae-wu made a state visit to Japan, his Foreign Ministry demanded Japan's disclosure of all records of Korean draftees, and the government began investigations that ultimately produced some data. In response to these disclosures the comfort women issue was raised in the Diet's House of Councillors by a Social Democrat member, Motooka Shoji, who asked whether comfort women had been included under the draft. The director general of the Employment Security Office, where some of the relevant records were kept, replied that no such action had been taken under the Wartime National General Mobilization Law, which governed conscript labor. "They were just taken around the military forces by private entrepreneurs, so investigation of them was not possible."[5]

When the Korean women's groups later learnt of this reply, an open letter was drawn up, dated October 17, 1990, addressed to the Japanese prime minister and signed in the name of thirty-seven bodies that were subsequently coordinated by the Korean Comfort Women's Problem Resolution Council (its English title varies). The letter centered on six demands, the key points being the admission of forced draft, apology, compensation, and inclusion of the truth in historical education.[6]

In April 1991 the Japanese Embassy delivered an entirely negative reply, denying any evidence of the forced drafting of comfort women and asserting that all compensation claims of any sort had been settled by the Japan–South Korea Basic Treaty of 1965, a stand which the South Korean Government also accepted. Textbooks would "continue" to reflect Japan's regret for aggression against Asia. This, however, spurred the women's groups to intensified agitation which reached a turning point in August when Kim Hak-sun announced her willingness

---

[5] Suzuki Yūko, *Jūgun ianfu. Naisen kekkon* (Military comfort women. Japanese-Korean marriages] (Tokyo: Miraisha, 1992), p. 135.

[6] Suzuki Yūko, *Chōsenjin jūgun ianfu* [Korean military comfort women] (Tokyo: Iwanami Shoten, 1991), pp. 52–53.

to testify publicly about her experiences as a comfort woman. Her decision was spurred by anger at the Japanese government's denial of responsibility, as well as facilitated by the lack of any immediate family who might suffer embarrassment.

Other comfort women gradually emerged to follow her example (some under pseudonyms) and combined with other categories of claimants to launch a lawsuit at the Tokyo District Court on December 6, 1991. Besides three former comfort women, later increased to nine, compensation claims were lodged for eleven former conscript soldiers (five by the bereaved families) and for twenty-one former paramilitary (eleven by the bereaved families).

The side effects proved more decisive than the inevitably protracted court proceedings. Early in January 1991, Professor Yoshimi Yoshiaki of Chuo University, having heard of the lawsuit, recalled original wartime documents relating to comfort women that he had noticed in the library of the National Institute for Defense Studies which is attached to the Defense Agency. He promptly retrieved five of these and the next day, January 11, the *Asahi* newspaper published key extracts from these. The afternoon edition carried a variety of reactions, including a government admission that "the deep involvement of the armed forces of the time cannot be denied. . . . The truth of the matter is rapidly being revealed by the efforts of scholars and citizen groups. The facts will continue to be investigated through both official and private channels."[7] Yoshimi's smoking gun had forced the Japanese government to admit that it had been lying about the involvement of the military, but the government was still not prepared to admit the use of coercion in the recruitment process.

On a state visit to South Korea a few days later, Prime Minister Miyazawa uttered profound apologies, and although maintaining that Japan's legal obligations for compensation remained settled by the 1965 treaty, he accepted the right of the litigants to individual legal recourse. The possibility of some relief measure "in lieu of compensation" would be considered after receiving the reports of fact-finding committees being set up in Japan and South Korea. The North Korean authorities pointed out that the issue affected them as well, and the Japanese repeated an apology to them in the course of normalization talks.

During the next few months scores of similar documents were produced and a wealth of oral testimony was obtained through hot lines set up by women's and pacifist organisations in both countries. The hot line in Tokyo received 240 significant calls, that in Urawa 24, and those in Kyoto and Osaka 91 and 61 respectively. Similar results were ob-

---

[7] *Asahi Shimbun*, Yūkan, 11 January 1992, p. 14.

tained by official and unofficial lines in South Korea. In South Korea more comfort women continued to emerge, though litigants were limited to nine for the purposes of a class action. Material from all these sources were continually published both in periodical and book form, while the press maintained good coverage on related activities and debate.

The Japanese fact-finding committee's report, which appeared on July 6, 1992, included 127 documents and demonstrated official involvement in operating the comfort system so amply that the government was compelled to concede this point in the course of the lawsuit. Foreign Ministry documents proved much wider involvement than that of the armed forces alone. They fall into two main categories: the issue of identity cards, travel permits, and passports relating to the comfort system and reports from consular and diplomatic authorities, mainly in China, on the comfort system in their jurisdictions.[8]

The government report, however, included no evidence on the recruitment process itself, having excluded oral testimony such as was available from Yoshida Seiji or the comfort women—in the latter case ostensibly from concern for their privacy. The report was widely criticized on these grounds, as well as its exclusion of the now available United States records and data obtained from the hot lines. The authorities promised to continue investigations with a view to some form of redress.

As the report contained material relating to Taiwan, Indonesia, and the Philippines, interest was generated in those countries. In the months following Japan's July report, the Philippine women's organaizations were aggressively active, researching the history of local comfort women, whipping up public opinion, and putting pressure on their own foot-dragging government, culminating in a lawsuit filed by 18 Filipina comfort women in April 1993. The South Korean and North Korean governments' reports followed soon after Japan's but they added nothing of interest, except a number of new case histories.

The most effective subsequent moves arose out of approaches to the United Nations Commission on Human Rights. In February 1992 the Problem Resolution Council had applied to the commission for hearings on the subject and been strongly supported by the International Education Development, Inc., a nongovernment organization. In May the Working Group on Contemporary Forms of Slavery submitted to the Subcommission on the Prevention of Discrimination a recommendation that the Special Rapporteur on Human Rights be furnished with

---

[8] Yoshimi Yoshiaki, *Jūgun ianfu shiryōshū* [Reference material for military comfort women] (Tokyo: Otsuki Shoten, 1992), pp. 89–132.

information on forced prostitution in wartime for use in his report to the subcommission on "compensation for victims of gross violations of human rights," which was due in August 1993.

In December 1992 a public hearing was arranged in Tokyo at which the Special Rapporteur, Professor Theo Van Boven, with representatives of NGOs, was able to receive testimony from a widely representative range of victims of the comfort and forced labor systems, as well as documented research reports. The Japanese government's efforts were thenceforth directed toward some conclusive action to anticipate the August 1993 session of the subcommission. Its investigation was broadened to include interviews with comfort women, arranged after initial difficulties in late July, as well as previously excluded sources from the United States and the Problem Resolution Council.

Proceedings were complicated by the fall of the Liberal Democratic party cabinet, but on its last day, August 4, it issued a supplementary report admitting deception, coercion, and official involvement in the recruitment of comfort women: "There were numerous cases of agents using deceptive enticement or recruiting in a manner contary to the will of those concerned by such means as intimidation, while cases are also found where public officials directly participated in this."[9] This was accompanied by an apology and a promise that means of compensation would be studied and the lessons of history squarely faced.

Overview of the Comfort Women System

The objectives of the system relate to problems universally encountered among armed forces, particularly modern conscript forces. The stress of combat and the tensions of a rigidly regimented life incline troops to seek sexual outlets, which in turn involve serious problems of disorder and venereal disease, so that most armed forces have adopted measures to control such behavior or safeguard health. The Japanese armed forces adopted a distinctively pragmatic and thoroughgoing approach, well expressed in a War Ministry directive: "The psychological influence received from sexual comfort stations is most direct and profound and it must be realised how greatly their appropriate direction and supervision affect the raising of morale, the maintenance of discipline, and the prevention of crime and venereal disease."[10]

Despite the randomly preserved or anecdotal nature of the sources, a remarkable picture emerges of a vast and dense network of sexual ser-

---

[9] Naikaku kambō, naikaku gaisei shingishitsu [Office of the cabinet councillor for external affairs] release, August 4, 1993.

[10] Yoshimi, *Jūgun ianfu*, p. 168.

vices pervading virtually all Japanese-occupied areas from the Siberian frontier in the north, to the Solomon Islands in the southeast, and Burma in the southwest. There were even comfort stations in remote ares as Chichijima in the Bonin Islands and Ishigaki in the Ryukyus. The comfort system was an integral part of the logistics system and subject to the overall supervision of the *Kempeitai* or of the Naval Police, though routine operations were controlled by local units.

The Japanese hot lines provided the widest range of references to specific areas. Among the Tokyo callers, 79 referred to comfort stations in China, 56 to Manchuria, 36 to Southeast Asia, 22 to the Western Pacific, 23 to Japan and 6 to Korea.[11] In Kyoto, 65 referred to China, here combined with Manchuria, 4 to Korea, 2 to New Guinea (specifically Rabaul), 4 to the Netherlands Indies, 8 to the Philippines, 3 to Burma, and 2 each to Malaya, Thailand, French Indochina, Japan, and Taiwan.[12] In this Kyoto survey, approximate figures for women in particular places were given in over 60 cases. The most frequent total, often of mixed national origin, is about 15, with occasional figures under 10 and one case each of 40, 50, and 80 women.

Sound data for estimating the overall total of comfort women is most unlikely to exist, but these and some other samples have been used to make generalizations on the basis of ratios of women to troop numbers. The Tokyo survey obtained a series of ratios for different areas in China in which each year from 1937 to 1945 was reppresented. In four cases the ratio was 50 to 1, in others the ratios ranged from 35 to 1 to 100 to 1, with an average overall of a little over 50 to 1.[13] An official document referring to health reports from Canton showed 1,004 women for the Twenty-First Army, which would have numbered 40,000 to 50,000.[14] A United States report on a comfort station in northern Burma indicated that the 22 women there, all Korean, serviced about 100 men per day between them.[15]

The only indication of an official target ratio comes from a good authority interviewed by Senda. This officer, Hara Zenshiro, who was in command of the Logistics Division of the Kwantung Army in Manchuria, was sent to Seoul in mid-1941 to demand that the Government-General provide twenty thousand comfort women within twenty days. The basis of this figure was that, in the light of experience in the war in China and calculating in terms of troops' pay rates, fees, and frequency

---

[11] Jūgun ianfu 110-ban henshū iinkai, *Jūgun ianfu 110-ban* [Military Comfort Women Hot line] (Tokyo: Akashi Shoten, 1992), p. 96.

[12] Unpublished analysis, privately supplied.

[13] *Jūgun ianfu 110-ban*, p. 141.

[14] Yoshimi, *Jūgun ianfu*, pp. 215–16.

[15] *Amenities in the Japanese Armed Forces*, p. 18.

of demand, one comfort woman was needed for every thirty-five to forty-five men.[16] On this basis and on the light of his other research, Senda estimated the overall total of comfort women to be of the order of one hundred thousand, of whom 80 percent were Korean and the others either Japanese, generally of prostitute background, or women recruited locally in occupied areas. A figure much in excess of this would have resulted in a much lighter workload than the daily figures for clients commonly reported, which tend to be about thirty.

Regarding national origins, the Tokyo survey again presents the largest sample. Koreans were mentioned by 175 callers, out of which 78 had encounted only Koreans, while 86 mentioned only Japanese, who tended to be reserved for officers in base areas. Smaller numbers mentioned Taiwanese, both ethnic Chinese and aborigenes, "Manchus" (meaning non-Chinese ethnic groups in that region), Chinese, Indonesians, who were also found in Rabaul, Dutch, Burmese, Malays, and White Russians (in Manchuria).[17] In Kyoto, 68 mentioned Koreans, 40 Japanese, 29 Chinese, and 5 Filipinas, 2 each mentioned White Russians, Taiwanese, and Vietnamese, while 1 each mentioned Dutch, Malays, Eurasians, Indonesians, Thais, and Burmese.[18]

There is naturally less specific knowledge of the women's social status, but from case histories and other incidental references it appears, not surprisingly, that in Korea at least the daughters of the gentry and local official class were normally spared either labor or comfort women service because the Japanese authorities relied on these groups to control the populace and only made exceptions when members of this class showed signs of fomenting resistance movements.

A study of the first thirteen detailed case histories to emerge shows that six of the women had been enticed away from home by civilian agents, sometimes Korean, by the promise of well-paid work—implying a background of poverty. Five were forcibly seized—two from home and two in the street, implying a powerless class background. The other, Kim Hak-sun, was seized in China, where she had been taken by her employer and foster-father, who had trained her as a *kisaeng* or traditional geisha-type entertainer. The other two cases were of more privileged background but in both of these there was a clear punitive aspect associated with anti-Japanese tendencies.[19] The women whose seizure on Cheju Island is graphically described by Yoshida Seiji

---

[16] Senda, *Jūgun ianfu*, p. 24.

[17] *Jūgan ianfu 110-ban*, pp. 96–97.

[18] Unpublished analysis.

[19] Nihon no sengo sekinin o hakkiri-saseru kai [Association for the clarification of Japan's postwar responsibility], *Hakkiri tsūshin* (Clarification Reports), no. 3 (June 1992), pp. 15–39.

were of humble rural background of the fishing, farming, or small workshop type.[20] In the wartime occupied areas the Japanese always found a class of collaborators who were spared ill-treatment in return for acting as their agents. Cases are mentioned where in China the village chief was given the role of obtaining local comfort women and was paid a fee for the service.[21] Local operators are mentioned in many accounts.

Yoshida and the oral case histories are also the only sources bearing directly on recruitment methods, but it needs to be noted that these belong to later phases of the war when increasing demand led to more draconian methods than were necessary in the early phases. In the penetration of Manchuria and North China through the 1930s there was little official initiative in providing sexual services, which at first formed a natural outgrowth of the established prostitution system in Japan and its colonies. This took the form of a contract system, whereby women were employed by licensed brothels on the basis of a loan, usually to their families, to be repaid from their earnings. This formed the basis of much of the military prostitution system, though later supplemented by more arbitrary methods.

The swarm of fortune hunters "following the flag" included many licenced brothel keepers and their staffs. To many of the latter, a move to the continent seemed preferable to the stagnant scene at home under depression conditions. Indeed business was so much better that debts normally needing years to pay off could be cleared in months, allowing the women to start their own businesses. It even became necessary to draw lots for permission to move to the continent.[22] The system of permits developed by the authorities was mainly concerned with issues of public order.[23]

The earliest evidence of a regular official policy of establishing and controlling comfort stations dates from late 1937 in the Shanghai area. The Rape of Nanking had raised problems of order and discipline in the starkest form and had also attracted international criticism. The local authorities therefore decided to establish an army-operated comfort station, which opened in early 1938 with about one hundred women, of whom twenty were Japanese of prostitute background and eighty were young, nonprofessional Korean women from the Korean community in northern Kyushu. These seemed to have been enticed by the promise of good pay. The report by the medical officer who examined them, a

[20] Yoshida, *Watakushi no sensō hanzai*, pp. 100–151.
[21] *Jūgan ianfu 110-ban*, pp. 38–39.
[22] Ibid., pp. 87–88.
[23] Yoshimi, *Jūgan ianfu*, pp. 123–29.

gynecologist Dr. Aso Tetsuo, indicates that the unspoilt Koreans were much better health risks than the Japanese professionals who, as he put it, were "really dubious as gifts to the Imperial Forces."[24] This became the prototype of much expanded operations in later years.

A couple of documents from early 1938, one from the War Ministry and one from the Home Ministry, hint at the growth of arbitrary methods of recruitment. The former states: "As a result of those engaging in recruitment not being suitably selected, there have been cases of recruitment methods amounting to abduction, which have resulted in charges and investigation by police authorities."[25] According to the latter, "if proper control is lacking in such recruitment of women, this will not only injure the dignity of the Empire and the honor of the Imperial Forces but will have an undesirable effect on the home front, particularly the families of soldiers on active service."[26]

By 1943, however, the situation had reached the stage illustrated by an official order recorded in a diary entry preserved by Yoshida Seiji. In this example, the Western Army Headquarters orders the procurement by 30 May of two hundred women from Korea, to be aged eighteen to twenty-nine ("married permissible, except pregnant") and free from venereal disease. Their term was to be one year (as prescribed in the labor draft laws but voluntarily renewable). They were to receive an advance payment of twenty yen and a monthly wage of thirty yen (twice a private soldier's pay).[27]

In the occupied areas all of these varied methods applied in different circumstances. Sometimes existing brothels or professional women were utilized, subject to health checks and general supervision. Sometimes women tried military prostitution as an alternative to existing hardships, as in internment camps. A record of internment life in Java, while noting cases of forcible or deceptive recruitment, adds: "There were others who went voluntarily because they couldn't stand the restrictions of camp life anymore."[28]

The most detailed testimony, however, relates to cases of forcible recruitment. One is the case of an anonymous Malaysian Chinese woman seized and raped at home before confinement in a comfort station.[29] The Filipina cases are all of this type with variations in detail.[30]

---

[24] Suzuki, *Chōsenjin*, p. 26.

[25] Yoshimi, *Jūgun ianfu*, p. 105.

[26] Ibid., p 103.

[27] Yoshida, *Watakushi no sensō hanzai*, p. 101.

[28] Shirley Fenton Huie, *The Forgotten Ones* (Sydney: Collins Angus and Robertson, 1992), p. 91.

[29] Interview with G. L. Hicks, Kuala Lumpur, 1993.

[30] Japanese People's Movement 90s, *Nihon seifu wa tadachi ni sengo hoshō o okonae* [The Japanese government must pay war compensation immediately] (Osaka, 1992).

The best documented cases of this type relate to the forced prostitution of a number of Dutch internees in comfort stations in Semarang, Java, which led to the only war crimes trials relating to this type of offence.[31]

Women who were not either prepared for their role or at least fatalistic about it were inevitably broken in by rape, either in the form of intimidation or outright violence, and any reluctance at a latter stage was treated similarly. The case histories virtually all contain an element of this, as do many of the war reminiscences, although some of the latter were perhaps influenced by the motive of pornographic interest. The most detailed and circumstantial account of such experiences comes from Jeanne O'Herne, one of the Semarang victims.[32]

Once in comfort stations, the women's lives were subject to close supervision, although conditions varied greatly. Women in their own country with some prospect of help would be more likely to abscond than those in alien settings. At the least they were subject to the same kind of restrictions as all military personnel—one plaintiff described the military type of leave pass issued to her in Burma on her monthly day off, a frequently mentioned concession. In her case the pass was issued for perscribed hours to a group whose names were listed.[33] The usual military rule of collective responsibility applied to comfort women.

Sometimes they might be included in social amusements in the company of troops. A typical case of this kind occurs in a United States report: "While in Burma they amused themselves by participating in sports events with both officers and men; and attended picnics, entertainments and social dinners. They had a phonograph; and in the towns were allowed to go shopping."[34] Sometimes, however, confinement was much closer. An official document relating to comfort stations in Iloilo in the Philipppines contains a map, indicating where the Filipina comfort women were allowed to walk from 8 A.M. to 10 A.M. each morning, any other movement requiring permission from the local military administration.[35] Some callers to the Tokyo survey report having seen comfort women in barbed-wire enclosures under twenty-four-hour guard, being locked in at night.[36]

Many of the comfort stations were mobile, being forced to accom-

---

[31] Bart Van Poelgeest, "Tewerkgesteld in de Japanse bordelen van Nederlands-Indie" [Forced to work in the Japanese brothels of the Netherlands Indies], *NRC Handelsblad, Zaterdags Bijvoegsel*, August 8, 1992.

[32] International Public Hearing Executive Committee, *War Victimisation and Japan* (Tokyo, 1993), pp. 60–67.

[33] *Hakkiri tsūshin*, no. 3, p. 28.

[34] United States Office of War Information Japanese Prisoner of War Interrogation Report no. 49, Ledo Stockade, October 1944, p. 2.

[35] Yoshimi, *Jūgan ianfu*, p. 326.

[36] *Jūgan ianfu 110-ban*, pp. 111–12.

pany troop movements even into combat zones. Rail-borne comfort stations are mentioned in Manchuria and on the notorious Burma railway. The most obviously dangerous situations reported were the "death-defying expeditions" on the Communist front in North China. These were visits to the advanced posts known as pillboxes, designed to monitor or counter guerrilla movements. A couple of women would accompany a supply run, being issued with a pistol each to use against guerrilla attack and in the last resort for suicide.[37]

Adequate evidence on the distribution system as a whole is unlikely ever to be established. The otherwise meticulous records of military operations convey little in this area. In transport records, comfort women were sometimes merely recorded as "units of war supplies," for lack of any appropriate prescribed category.[38] In some records found in Taiwan comfort women are indistinguishable from nurses, who were also recruited in some numbers there. It is clear that there was some high-level organization of distribution, as well as considerable local initiative. An example of the former comes from a magazine article dated 1955 by former Commander Shigemura Minoru under the title "The Units called Special Personnel." It reproduces a directive dated May 30, 1942, from the Navy Ministry to the Chief of Staff, Southwest Fleet, concerning a "Second Despatch of Special Personnel." It contains a table listing destinations as Ambon, Makassar, Balikpapan, Surabaya, Penang, and Shonan (Singapore), with the numbers of personnel for each listed in two columns headed "Restaurants" and "Simple Special Personnel," the latter offering sexual services only.[39]

A couple of War Ministry documents suggest something comparable for the army. One, dated March 12, 1942, is a message from the Taiwan command requesting the ministry's approval of travel permits for three operators, one Korean, who had been selected by the local *Kempeitai* in accordance with a request from the Southern Army GHQ, Saigon, for the despatch of "native" comfort women to Borneo. It is not clear whether "native" refers to indigenes or local ethnic Chinese. A later message dated June 13, 1942 requests arrangements for twenty more comfort women.[40] These messages indicate coordination by the Southern Army, with ministry approval, over a vast area in Southeast Asia of a comfort woman network under *Kempeitai* supervision. Other documentary sources indicate that coordination in and around Shanghai conurbation was handled by a liaison conference of army, navy, and consular authorities.[41]

[37] Kim, *Tennō no guntai*, pp. 114–16.
[38] Senda, *Jūgun ianfu*, p. 18.
[39] Kim, *Tennō no guntai*, pp. 172–73.
[40] Yoshimi, *Jūgun ianfu*, pp. 144–46.
[41] Ibid., pp 177–80.

The officially prescribed guidelines for the operation of comfort stations are well documented by several sets of meticulous regulations, drawn up by local units though having general features in common. Oral evidence indicates that conditions in practice were often worse than the standards laid down. The regulations for the pioneer official station in Shanghai, which were recorded in a photograph by Dr. Aso, formed a prototype. They set out hours of opening, fee, and time allowed—two yen for thirty minutes—and procedural details such as the banning of intercourse without a condom which was issued at the time of payment. The financial basis was the contract system, the army advancing one thousand yen to be worked off. Army rations were supplied to the comfort women.[42]

Direct operation by the army, however, did not remain the usual model except in forward areas. In most areas the establishments of private operators—sometimes retired officers—were available, and did their best to to satisfy official standards and provide an attractive service. Besides, international observers would be contemptuous of an army that ran prostitution services. So the prevailing pattern was one where the actual management of comfort stations was left to private operators—often with paramilitary status—while the forces maintained supervision, with support in logistics, transport, and health services.

Under these conditions regulations became much elaborated. The most comprehensive set in the original Japanese are the "serviceman's club regulations" issued by a unit code-named YAMA3475 in Okinawa and dated December 1944. The rules clearly reflect long experience in the handling of such matters. One rule forbids violence arising from dissatisfaction with the women's service. The women were to be regarded as a "common possession, not to be appropriated," presumably to guard against disorder arising from emotional complications or jealousy. The women could not leave the enclosure without special permission.

A diagram illustrates the form and dimensions of a permit to visit the club. Fees were three yen for officers, two-and-a half yen for noncommissioned officers, and two yen for privates. All ranks were allowed a maximum of forty minutes. Hours were 12 noon to 5 P.M. for privates, 5 P.M. to 8 P.M. for NCOs, and 8 P.M. to midnight for officers. The club was closed on the eighth of each month. Service was tax-exempt. Medical examinations were held three times a month, and a form is set out for reporting the results. Treatment was by local doctors, and operators were to meet the costs. The operators were forbidden to engage in undue profiteering or to abet a breach of discipline. They had to guard

---

[42] Kim, *Tennō no guntai*, pp. 47–48.

against espionage—an additional reason sometimes advanced for the
control of troops' social contacts by the comfort system. Accounts had
to be kept and made available for inspection. The club would be closed
if the rules were infringed.[43]

A still more elaborate set of regulations, prescribed for the Manila
area, is preserved in translation in United States material. They contain
extremely detailed forms and procedures for an application to establish
a comfort station; women could apply to be released or could be dismissed if unsatisfactory; they received half the takings; were forbidden
to work while menstruating and could not be kissed; fees for Filipinas
were less than for Japanese nationals (here including Koreans and Taiwanese)—a racial distinction often occurring in other regulations.[44] In
Ch'angchou, China, fees were two yen for Japanese, one-and-a-half yen
for Koreans, and one yen for Chinese, officers being charged double
these rates.[45] Fee structures reflected the dual Japanese hierarchies of race
and rank.

In a few reported cases women seem to have been paid a regular
wage without charge to the clients, but most of the litigants claim not
to have been paid at all, receiving only the most basic necessities. However, the weight of evidence indicates that these cases were exceptional
and therefore the testimony of the Korean and Filipina comfort women
is suspect on this point. Given that the privates' pay was only fifteen
yen per month and an average civilian wage only several times this, the
comfort women's earnings were fairly high for the time, but overall
they derived little benefit from this. Under wartime conditions, goods
available for purchase were limited except in a few favored areas, and in
more remote or primitive areas nothing might be available. The comfort station operators sometimes arranged for goods to be procured
through the military transport network but sold these to the women at
exorbitant rates. The women are often described as hoping to benefit
from their savings for a better life after the war but, as they were often
paid in military scrip, such hopes were ruled out when this currency
lost all value on Japan's defeat.

Sometimes the women were paid in valid currencies but in the case of
women being repatriated to other countries after the war such currencies would not usually have been convertible. One of the litigants
avoided both these hazards by depositing a considerable sum in tips
(totalling over ¥26,000) through the field post office in an account kept

---

[43] Nishino Rumiko, *Jūgun ianfu* [Military comfort women] (Tokyo: Akashi Shoten,
1992), pp. 232–38.

[44] *Amenities in the Japanese Armed Forces*, pp. 9–12, 30.

[45] Yoshimi, *Jūgun ianfu*, p. 207.

in Japan. However, when she attempted to claim this many years later, she found she had lost all entitlement to it as a result of the Korea-Japan Basic Treaty of 1965. Under this, all claims on Japan by South Korean citizens were regarded as discharged by a global grant to South Korea, even though very little of this was ever distributed to claimants.

Many of the comfort women failed to live long enough to experience such disappointments. Although no statistics whatever are available, in contrast to the accurate figures kept for servicemen, it is clear that the women shared exactly the same hazards as troops and would have suffered comparable losses from enemy action, as in bombardment or the sinking of ships. Health hazards are also inseparable from military life, with large concentrations of men brought together under often impoverished living conditions. The comfort women faced the added health risk imposed by their occupation. As communications broke down during the latter part of the war, medical supplies grew scarce and were likely to be reserved for personnel on combat duty. The messages from the South requesting reinforcements of comfort women are an ominous index of death or incapacitation.

For venereal disease, prophylaxis was the first line of defence. Great efforts were made to maintain adequate supplies of condoms. Hygiene reports for the Malaya military administration record the distribution of condoms for certain months in 1943: in July, 1,000 for Negri Sembilan, 10,000 for Perak; in August, 5,000 for Malacca, 10,000 for Selangor and 30,000 for Penang; in September, 5,000 for administrative staff and 1,500 for civilian businesses.[46] But stocks of condoms were often inadequate and the washing and reuse of them became an unpleasant necessity as supplies of almost everything dwindled.

As a further defense, containers of permanganic acid solution were commonly installed in women's rooms, with a rubber tube for the men to wash their genitals after intercourse. The women were also expected to douche after each contact and were often injected with salvarsan or teramycin, either as a prophylactic or as treatment. This practice is blamed to some extent for the sterility that affected many comfort women later, though damage to the reproductive system was also a factor. Lectures on hygiene were given to the women.

In practice the troops sometimes broke the rules prescribing the use of condoms and prohibiting sexual activity outside the comfort stations. Infection in the women would be detected in the periodical medical examinations, when they would be named as infected at evening roll call or in daily routine orders and become statistics in hygiene reports.

[46] Kaihō shuppansha henshūbu, *Kimu Hakusun-san no shōgen* (Kim Hak-sun's testimony) (Osaka, 1993), pp. 241–42.

An example of these occurs in the report on comfort stations for the Twenty-First Army in Canton in 1939 where the following percentages of women were infected in various units: 28 percent among 159, 1 percent among 223, 10 percent among 192, 4 percent among 122, 2 percent among 41, and nil among 180.[47]

Treatment of the women seems to have been the normal policy in stable areas. Conditions varied among military hospitals, civilian hospitals, North China Railway hospitals, and free clinics for all types of prostitutes in Manchuria. The Manila regulations indicate that medical officers could diagnose whether illness was due to overwork, in which case the proprietor had to bear the cost of treatment. When the women had to pay for treatment, this could consume much of their earnings or be added to the amount of the loan to be repaid. There are also references to women being allowed to die untreated, abandoned, or even killed.

At the end of the war most of the comfort women remaining in areas not affected by intensive combat were repatriated with other elements of the Japanese forces while some, like Yuyuta in Thailand, preferred to stay where they were. But a grim fate had overtaken many who were caught up in hotly contested areas. Apart from deaths due directly to enemy action, some died in the mass suicides that were the alternative to surrender. There are vivid accounts of such tragedies from the Chinese sector of the North Burma front and from Micronesia where no possibility of retreat remained. In the former area, seven Korean women are reported as having been dispatched by hand grenade in their dugout in T'engyueh, while in nearby Lameng the Japanese comfort women took their own lives by potassium cyanide, though the Koreans here were allowed to escape and were found by Allied forces.[48]

At Truk, the major naval base in Micronesia, seventy comfort women are reported to have been massacred in their dugout by automatic fire on the eve of the expected final American assault.[49] On Saipan, comfort women joined practically the whole female population in drowning themselves rather than fall into enemy hands. On Luzon in the Philippines similar tragedies occurred, though there was apparently no deliberate killing of comfort women except for the Filipinas caught up in the aimless massacres accompanying the fall of Manila. Japanese and Korean comfort women faced months of extreme hardship in jungles where a terrible toll in lives was exacted—the Japanese forces resorting to cannibalism in extreme cases.

[47] Yoshimi, *Jūgun ianfu*, pp. 215–16.
[48] Kim, *Tennō no guntai*, pp. 237–38.
[49] Ibid., pp. 246–47.

Among those who reached their homelands, many were unable to resume normal lives as a result of their traumatic experiences, and the sense of "defilement" that prevented any prospect of marriage even among those who could still bear the sight of men. Many remained in prostitution, some with the occupation forces, as with Pae Ponggi in Okinawa. Even those who married carried a heavy burden of fear and shame: decades of enforced silence and fear of exposure.

THE HISTORICAL PERSPECTIVE

The North Korean report, describing the comfort women system as "exceeding anything that the Nazis committed," asserts that "whether in ancient or recent times, whether in East or West, there has never been a case in the history of any war when women have been carried around the battlefield as sex slaves."[50] After making due allowance for North Korean hyperbole, the question remains: do they have a point? The sex life of soldiers throughout history is a subject ignored by most military historians; references to camp followers appear only marginally in accounts which are concerned mainly with national glory or military science.

A South Korean activist is on safe ground when he declares that "it is often said that military comfort women are unique to the Japanese forces, but this should be taken in the sense that at this stage no other such example is known."[51] Professor Yoshimi notes that current investigations in Korea and Japan are stimulating similar research elsewhere and may make an international contribution to exposing the realities of "war and sex."[52] A Japanese feminist activist, on inquiring during a conference in London whether such a phenomenon as comfort women had occurred in Western history, was told that the crusaders had been accompanied by prostitutes on their campaigns, which seems to have suggested to her that nothing of the sort had happened since.[53]

Actually, of course, passing references to such practices both earlier and later are not uncommon. There was, however, a major transformation between premodern wars, fought in a leisurely manner by elite military castes or professional mercenaries, and the mass conscript armies of later times. The latter presented much greater problems of

---

[50] Kaihō shuppansha, *Kimu Hakusun*, pp. 139, 143.

[51] Kim Yong-dal, "Kaisetsu" [Commentary] in Yun Chung-mo, *Haha: Jūgun ianfu* [My mother: A military comfort woman], trans. Kashima Setsuko (Kobe: Gakusei Seinen Senta, 1992), p. 141.

[52] Yoshimi, *Jūgun ianfu*, p. 61.

[53] Tomiyama Taeko, *Kaeranu onnatachi* [Women who do not return] (Tokyo: Iwanami Shoten, 1991), p. 30.

discipline, disease control and desertion, which in large measure involved the problem of military-related prostitution. Measures to control it and their degree of openness varied with attitudes to prostitution in different societies, and in the absence of formal records, information tends to come from informal war reminiscences, as was the case with the earlier sources in Japan. There is rarely any indication of the origins of the women involved, as to how far they may have been voluntary, or how far obtained by "white slave" practices.

One exceptionally well-documented case derives from a House of Commons inquiry into prostitution in the British Army in India in the later nineteenth century and is summarized in F. Henriques's classic *Prostitution and Society*. The findings anticipate many of the later Japanese practices. Each cantonment or base area had an attached "bazaar" or service settlement, which included an enclosed prostitutes' quarter, staffed mainly by Indians with occasional foreign women. The minimum age was fourteen, most being a few years older. A register of prostitutes was maintained, together with a system of compulsory medical examinations. The regiment paid each woman one rupee per month for soap and a towel. The women often followed the regiment on its movements and witnesses mentioned that their presence was needed to avert offenses against the local population. As with the comfort women half a century later, the Indian women were frequent victims of violence. Henriques comments in general that "Venus has been in constant attendance upon Mars wherever the British soldier has served in our once far-flung Empire."

Yoshimi summarizes information on the German army's prostitution facilities in the Second World War from F. Seidler's *Prostitution, Homosexuality, Self-Mutilation: Problems of German Public Hygiene Control 1939–1945*. Military brothels were established in all logistical zones in occupied areas under orders from the central command, local commanders being responsible for equipment, supervision, and supply. Health inspections were conducted by local doctors under supervision by medical officers. In Western Europe, existing brothels were reserved for German army use, while in Eastern Europe women were given the choice of compulsory labor or prostitution. Examples of detailed regulations are given.[54]

But whatever the limitations of our knowledge of other examples, it seems quite unlikely that the Japanese case would find any complete parallel, comparably systematic, pervasive, and arbitrary. The logistics alone, covering such a vast area of difficult land and sea routes, bear witness to an intense drive and conformism that seem distinctively Jap-

[54] Yoshimi, *Jūgun ianfu,* pp. 60–61.

anese, particularly at that period. Some factors in the cultural background also suggest themselves, such as an often-remarked situational
pragmatism that tackles perceived problems purely with a view to direct results, uninhibited by broader principles or any considerations of
morality. Yoshida Seiji recalls a War Ministry directive quoting a
maxim that "a higher loyalty overrides personal morality" (*taigi shin o
messu*) in the cause of the sacred war.[55] The attitude to other races falling
under Japanese occupation also suggests a projection onto world society
of traditions of hierarchy in Japanese society, with a corollary of a
"transfer of oppression" passing down the social scale. None of these
features are unique in themselves but, as in other fields, the Japanese
contribution is distinctive.

The circumstances of the system's exposure are also historically noteworthy in that this could hardly have occurred without a strong emergence of feminist and pacifist idealism of a kind unknown in Japanese
and Korean society in the past. The comfort women in their youth
were the victims of man's inhumanity to woman. In old age, they are
symbols of the Asian woman's determination to right past wrongs, to
speak out and be accepted as human beings. This, too, is something
new.

[55] Yoshida, *Watakushi no sensō hanzai*, p. 100.

CHAPTER 11

The Postwar Economic Legacy of Japan's Wartime Empire

Hideo Kobayashi

The goal of Japan's wartime Greater East Asia Co-Prosperity Sphere was to create a regional economic structure that would allow Japan to mobilize wealth and resources in its colonies and newly occupied regions to support the war effort. During the 1930s and 1940s Japanese planners and officials drafted plans for developing and integrating the other economies of East Asia with Japan's metropolitan economy, and government agencies, semigovernment corporations, and private firms invested capital to finance the development of Taiwan, Korea, Manchuria, and north China. Did these wartime changes have any influence on the postwar economic development of the countries of East Asia?

The historical record suggests that the wartime legacy varied considerably in different parts of East Asia. One of the most striking features of the postwar period has been the rapid industrialization of South Korea and Taiwan, the two largest of the "four little dragons," that began in the late 1970s and early 1980s. Both countries grew at rates equaling that of Japan during its period of rapid economic growth, and their roles as major producers of textiles, electronic goods, merchant ships, steel, and the like have increased steadily. On the other hand, neither North Korea nor Northeast China (the former state of Manchukuo), where the Japanese made heavy investments in infrastructure and industrial plant, flourished economically in the postwar period. In Northeast China, for example, until the late 1980s economic change was not significant; productivity in the industrial sector remained low; and technological innovation remained limited despite the enormous Japanese effort to build the economy during the 1930s and 1940s.

No doubt one reason why South Korea and Taiwan followed a different economic path is political. The division of the Korean peninsula at the Thirty-Eighth Parallel in 1945 and the triumph of the Chinese Communist forces in 1949 brought North Korea and Manchuria under the control of Soviet-style regimes. By contrast, by 1949 both South Korea and Taiwan, along with Japan, had been incorporated into America's sphere of influence in East Asia. As a result, these societies developed under rather different political economies: centrally directed command economies in North Korea and Manchuria versus bureaucratically guided market systems in Taiwan and South Korea. The failure of central planners to allocate resources as efficiently as market mechanisms may be the major reason why postwar economic performance in Northeast China and North Korea was so much less impressive than that of Taiwan and South Korea. Whatever the economic legacy of the wartime empire, the shape of the postwar political economic structure was probably more significant in explaining postwar economic development.

It is nevertheless useful to speculate on the ways in which the experience of Japanese colonial domination, before and during the war, may have contributed to the rapid industrialization of Taiwan and South Korea in ways that were obvious and ways that were less self-evident. To be sure, the experience of these two societies under Japanese control and afterward was quite different. Nevertheless, one can identify several common elements that may have contributed to the postwar industrialization of these two economies: human and institutional resources; the supply of productive factors; and the reduction of transaction costs in marketplaces. But, as I will stress in the concluding section, it was the intrusion of American influence in the region that allowed the early postwar regimes in South Korea and Taiwan to make effective use of these legacies of the Japanese colonial period.

HUMAN AND INSTITUTIONAL RESOURCES

Perhaps the most immediate postwar legacy of the Japanese colonial era was the existence of the hundreds of thousands of educated South Koreans and Taiwanese who became the core of the postwar political and economic elites. Most were products of the public-school systems that the Japanese had developed in Korea and Taiwan to train literate manpower and inculcate the local populations with Japanese cultural and social values. By 1940, about 38 percent of school-age children attended elementary school in Korea, and about 58 percent of school-age Taiwanese children did so.[1] During the 1930s some children of elite families in both societies began to take the road of higher education, while many others attended technical schools that aimed at producing skilled workers, technicians, and low-echelon managers. The result was the emergence of a small but important class of well-educated white-collar

[1] Hirotani Takio and Hirokawa Shukuko, "Nihon tōchika no Taiwan/Chōsen ni okeru shokuminchi kyōiku seisaku no hikakushiteki kenkyū" [A comparative investigation of the Japanese colonial federation policy toward Korea and Taiwan], *Kyōiku gakubu kiyō* 22 (1973): 56, 62.

and technical workers who appreciated the need for technical knowledge and who possessed skills required to run a modern industrial economy. After 1945, new regimes in both countries adopted this dual-track educational system based on the Meiji educational model that had so effectively served the needs of Japanese economic development.

The most important members of this educated class were probably those in the lower and middle echelons of the Japanese colonial bureaucracy. By the end of the war, for example, 56 percent of all officials in the Taiwan colonial government were Taiwanese; of the top six ranks only 35 percent were Taiwanese, but in the lowest two ranks three out of four were indigenes.[2] The situation in Korea was similar. These officials could all read and speak Japanese, and they were accustomed to relying on Japanese newspapers and journals as sources of news and information. As Chou Wan-you's research indicates (see chapter 2 in this volume), many of these persons even adopted Japanese surnames during the wartime period. Although none of these indigenous officials ever became department heads, many acted as assistants to section chiefs, had access to official documents in Japanese, and became familiar with the techniques the Japanese used to mobilize the wartime economy and society. After 1945 they were able to deploy the skills and knowledge acquired under the supervision of Japanese superiors to develop the postwar society and economy.

First of all, they were familiar with Japanese techniques for mobilizing the mass of the populace behind a collective effort. As already mentioned, postwar regimes in both countries adopted Japanese-style educational systems, including the inculcation of certain values, such as social harmony and loyalty to superiors, that had been at the core of the Japanese "morals education" curriculum. The bureaucratic elite in South Korea and Taiwan were familiar with the Japanese wartime social mobilization structure as well. In March 1938, the Japanese Diet passed a National Mobilization Law, which was emulated in wartime Taiwan and Korea. In October 1940, the Japanese set up the Korean League for National Mobilization (*Kokumin Sōryoku Chōsen Renmei*), a Korean version of the Imperial Rule Assistance Association, headed by the governor-general. From top levels to "patriot units" (similar to the Japanese *tonarigumi*, or neighborhood associations) at the bottom, Korean society was integrated with the official administration. Similarly, in Taiwan the Imperial Subjects' Service Society (*Kōmin Hōkōkai*) was organized in April 1941. Its smallest unit, the "service unit," functioned like the

---

[2] Lai Tse-han, Ma Joh-meng, and Wei O, *Pei-chü hsing ti k'ai-tuan: T'ai-wan erh-erh-pa shih-pien* [A tragic beginning: The Taiwan uprising of February 28, 1947] (Taipei: Shih-pao wen-hua, 1993), p. 119.

neighborhood association in Japan, monitoring citizen behavior, mobilizing public campaigns at the behest of the administration, and eliciting voluntary contributions of labor and materials for the war effort. Other preexisting organizations, such as the irrigation and credit association in Korea and agricultural associations in Taiwan, were also integrated into this mobilization structure through connections with the Korean League for National Mobilization and the Imperial Subjects' Service Society.

Second, the local bureaucratic elites in South Korea and Taiwan also came to appreciate the importance of central planning for industrial development. Beginning in 1936 with the promulgation of a Five-Year Plan for the development of Manchukuo, the central Japanese bureaucracy had constructed overall "material mobilization plans" to expand munitions and military-related production, such as steelmaking, artificial petroleum, light metals, and the like. In the late 1930s the colonial territories of Taiwan and Korea were included in these plans as well.[3] By 1945, lower-echelon officials in Korea and Taiwan had a good understanding of how the Japanese bureaucracy carried out these plans: assigned committees gathered, reviewed, evaluated, and reported information to their superiors; on the basis of this information officials convened conferences and drafted recommendations; then superiors revised these recommendations and requested further changes from below. As part of the process, Japanese bureaucrats worked with managers and owners of private enterprises, melding state power with business resources to expand physical infrastructure such as roads, railways, and telephone and telegraph systems, and to build a modern manufacturing base. Under this system of cooperation between state planners and private enterprise during the 1930s and 1940s, the colonial regimes in both Taiwan and Korea promoted the establishment of oil refineries, chemical factories, cement plants, machine-tool facilities, and hydroelectric stations.[4]

As a result of their experience with wartime economic mobilization and planning, the postwar bureaucratic and business elites in both Taiwan and Korea learned the importance of public institutions and central planning in large-scale endeavors to promote industrialization. They

[3] Kobayashi Hideo, *Dai Tōa-a kyōeiken no keisei to hōkai* [Development and collapse of the Greater East Asia Co-Prosperity Sphere] (Tokyo Ochanomizu shobō, 1975), p. 304; Kasuya Ken'ichi, "Seiji keizai to Chōsen ni okeru Nichitsu zaibatsu no tenkai" [Evolution of the Nichitsu financial clique in the Korean polity and environment], *Chōsen shi kenkyūkai ronbunshū* 12, no. 3 (1975): 175–209.

[4] See, for example, see the descriptions of industrial enterprises built on Taiwan in National Resources Commission: *Industrial Enterprises of National Resources Commission in Taiwan* (Taipei: National Resources Commission, 1951).

were knowledgeable about the ways in which the Japanese bureaucracy established production targets, financial and labor inputs, price-control machinery, and rules to enforce law and contracts. They were also familiar with the idea that economic development need not be left entirely to market forces and that bureaucratic guidance through indicative planning and economic regulation could accelerate economic growth. It is no surprise, then, that when General Park Chung-hee, who had received Japanese military training and who appreciated the achievements of Meiji Japan, came to power in 1961, he initiated South Korea's first Five-Year Plan, mobilizing large business organizations to cooperate with the state in stimulating rapid industrialization.

Finally, the postwar bureaucratic and business elites inherited from their pre-1945 experience with Japanese policymaking a hostility toward labor unions and labor activism. In the wartime colonies as well as in the metropolitan economy, the Japanese bureaucracy had banned independent labor organizations and had promoted the view that workers and employers should cooperate. Workers were discouraged from challenging the authority of employers with demands for higher wages and better working conditions and were encouraged to work with employers in the pursuit of national goals. During the postwar period, antiunion views prevailed among officials and business leaders in Taiwan and South Korea, giving business enterprises free rein to set wages and earn profits as they pleased in the hopes of encouraging the rapid expansion of business earnings and savings for reinvestment in plant and technology.

By 1945, then, as a result of their experience with Japanese efforts to put their colonies on a wartime footing, educated elites in both Taiwan and South Korea had acquired an appreciation and understanding of the power of bureaucratically guided and managed public institutions and organizations and the value of rational bureaucratic management. I have enumerated various examples of the institutions created by the Japanese colonial authorities in Korea and Taiwan: public and higher education mixed with a system of technical training and worker manual schools; irrigation and credit associations to promote a "green revolution" in agriculture; patriotic neighborhood organizations to mobilize the citizenry to support the war effort; and various new economic organizations in finance, labor, agriculture, and, above all, manufacturing to build industries necessary to supply resources such as chemicals and electrical power for the production of weapons, vehicles, and various machines. This large machinery of rational organizational planning was managed by the Japanese bureaucracy and assisted by indigenous elites. The experiences and values that the Korean and Taiwanese elites obtained from that period served them well in the 1950s and 1960s, when they played important roles in managing economic policy or private business enterprises.

THE SUPPLY OF PRODUCTIVE FACTORS

In contrast to Manchukuo, North China, and other parts of the wartime empire, the Japanese presence in the colonies of Korea and Taiwan lasted for a long time—fifty years in Taiwan and thirty-five in Korea. Even before the wartime period, the Japanese colonial administrations had worked to increase the supply of basic productive factors such as land, labor, and capital, and to increase their productivity as well. At first these efforts were directed at the agricultural sector, but by the late 1920s colonial officials were paying attention to the modern manufacturing sector as well (see the chapter by Carter J. Eckert in this volume). In contrast to the other areas under Japan's wartime domination, neither Korea nor Taiwan was the scene of battle, nor did economic infrastructure and industrial plant in either country sustain the same degree of bomb damage as did the Japanese metropolitan economy. When new regimes came to power in both countries after 1945, they had at their disposal a larger and more productive supply of land, labor, and physical capital than other societies that had been under Japan's wartime control. To be sure, the Korean economy suffered from heavy physical destruction during the Korean War. Nevertheless, the long-term promotion of economic growth under Japanese rule may have given Korea and Taiwan a major economic advantage in rehabilitating their postwar economies and initiating rapid industrialization.

Under Japanese colonial rule, not only had the area of land under cultivation expanded in both societies, but its productivity had been increased by the introduction of such techniques as multiple cropping, large-scale irrigation systems, and increased inputs of chemical and other fertilizers. In both colonies, the Japanese organized farmers' associations, irrigation and fertilizer associations, and agricultural research stations to transmit superior agricultural technology, such as better seed varieties, new crops such as cotton, better tools, and new fertilizers, of the same kind that had transformed Japanese agriculture in the Meiji period. Farmers in both societies at first often resisted the sometimes heavy-handed efforts of colonial officials to promote agricultural change. Gradually, however, they began to reallocate their land and labor inputs to take advantage of new opportunities created by the development of modern road and rail systems that gave them access to distant urban and external markets. By the end of the war, both colonies had experienced "green revolutions" characterized by higher production, greater crop diversity, and increased levels of agricultural specialization and exchange. During the 1950s and after, the prewar agrotechnical infrastructure merely had to be restored to revive the prewar high agricultural output growth rate that had more than kept pace with growth of population. Redistributing property rights during the 1950s also provided new incentives for farmers to better manage their land, invest, and market their surplus, making agriculture far more efficient than it had been in prewar times, when there had been far greater inequality in property rights ownership.

Under colonial rule, especially during the period of wartime industrialization, urbanization also accelerated, and a modern work force began to emerge in both societies. At the turn of the century, nine out of ten Taiwanese had lived in communities smaller than two thousand persons, but by 1937 only two-thirds of them did so; a similar process occurred in Korea to a slightly lesser degree. More important, modern work forces, comprising between four-hundred thousand and eight hundred thousand persons, had come into being in both colonies, and in both societies women were very much part of the work force as well. Most workers were educated, with a functional ability to understand and read Japanese, and possessed a wide range of skills needed by a modern industrial economy. For example, after Japanese technicians and managers departed from Korea in 1945, indigenous workers were able to keep the railway system operating and to man the factories which rapidly resumed production.[5]

Since the colonial educational system had encouraged the inculcation of values such as social harmony and loyalty, and since the colonial bureaucracy had discouraged union activity, these work forces were docile, diligent, and disciplined, accustomed to doing what managers and owners told them to do. In neither country did workers show much enthusiasm for labor unions in the postwar period. To be sure, Korea experienced a wave of strikes between 1945 and 1949, but these had more to do with political disputes than demands about wages or working conditions. It was only with the emergence of political parties pressing for greater democratization in the 1980s that unions became

---

[5] An Byong-jig, "1930 nendai ni okeru Chōsenjin rōdōsha kaikyū no tukushitsu" [The characteristics of the Korean working class in the 1930s], in Chōsen kindai no rekishizō [Modern historical materials on Korea] (Tokyo: Nihon hyōronsha, 1988), pp. 120–47; An Byong-jig, "Shokuminchi Chōsen no kōyō kōzō ni kansuru kenkyū" [Research on the Korean employment structure under Japanese colonial rule], in Chōsen kindai no keizai kōzō, ed. Nakumura Satoru [Modern economic structure of Korea) (Tokyo: Nihon hyōronsha, 1990), pp. 303–39; Jeong Jae-Jeong, "Chōsen sōtokufu tetsudō kyoku no kōyō kōzō" [Employment structure of the Railway Bureau of the Korean Government-General), ibid., pp. 341–74.

important or influential in either country, especially in Korea. During most of the postwar period, then, private enterprises, unchallenged by militant worker demands, were able to keep wages down, enabling them to plow profits back into investment for expanding plant and enterprise facilities.

Although their functions changed to some degree, financial institutions created under the colonial regimes continued to play a significant role in both colonies. During the colonial period, except for indigenous pawnbrokers and moneylenders, the Japanese owned and operated the financial institutions that mobilized savings, issued loans, and made investments. These institutions remained intact at war's end and became the key players under the new regimes. In Korea, the prewar Bank of Chōsen became the Bank of Korea; the Chōsen Industrial Bank which had helped to finance the prewar industrialization became the Korea Industrial Bank. Elements of the prewar Oriental Development Company and various credit associations merged after the war to become the Agricultural Bank and the Credit Branch of the Agricultural Cooperatives. The story was the same in Taiwan. The prewar Bank of Taiwan, the Taiwan Savings Bank, and the Taiwan Sanwa Bank became the components making up the Bank of Taiwan. The Japan Industrial Bank became the Taiwan Land Bank; the Taiwan Commercial and Industrial Bank became the First Taiwan Commercial Bank; the Hua-nan Bank became the Hua-nan Commercial Bank, and the Chang-hua Bank became the Chang-hua Commercial bank. Although the owners of these institutions changed, their clerical and managerial personnel continued at their jobs, making for a smooth transition in operations.

Just how postwar business enterprises were shaped by the prewar experiences is more difficult to evaluate. It is clear that many of the major postwar business firms in both Taiwan and Korea were created by entrepreneurs who had already gained business experience in the prewar period, often in small- and medium-scale enterprises. For example, Taiwan Plastic, which ultimately became the largest financial conglomerate in Taiwan, specializing in plastic, plywood, chemical fibers, and petrochemicals, was founded by Wang Yu-ch'ing, who began his career in the prewar period as a rice trader. And Jeong Ju-yung, the founder of the Hyundai conglomerate, came from an equally humble background. But the postwar impact of the Japanese enterprise model seems to have been rather different in both economies. The four *chaebol* that dominated the Korean economy during its spurt of rapid growth during the 1960s and 1970s—Samsung, Daewoo, Hyundai, and Lucky-Sunstar—were deliberately created on the model of the Japanese *zaibatsu* and enjoyed insider connections with high government officials. In Taiwan, on the other hand, most large enterprises seem to have grown out of small- and medium-scale enterprises, without the same degree of official backing that the *chaebol* enjoyed.

Reduced Transaction Costs

In postwar South Korea and Taiwan rapid industrialization was facilitated by the ability of business enterprises to reduce transaction costs by obtaining access to valuable information and monitoring the activities of government. As Ronald A. Coase has pointed out, firms that reduce their transaction costs by developing new organizational forms can grow in size and complexity.[6] Firms that earn profit through such innovations and cost-reduction strategies usually are successful in maintaining or reducing their transaction costs per unit if they have relevant information, enforce contracts, and maintain quality control over output and services. Often firms can benefit from contacts with outside organizations, either public or private, to reduce their market transaction costs. In the case of postwar business firms in Korea and Taiwan, two aspects of the prewar experience are relevant in this connection.

First, the postwar official and business elites in both economies benefited from pre-1945 contacts and interactions with the Japanese elites. Personal networks and personal friendships, usually between officials and/or business persons, served as pipelines for the flow of valuable market, financial, and technical information between both sides. For this reason, it is not surprising that Japanese investment in South Korea and Taiwan resumed after the Korean War, although more smoothly in Taiwan than in Korea. Between 1952 and 1970, Japanese investment in Taiwan amounted to US$89 million, just behind overseas Chinese and American investments; in South Korea the total came to US$140 million, making Japan the second largest investor behind the United States.[7] Information exchanged between the Korean or Taiwan elites and their Japanese counterparts helped Japanese business enterprises to target projects believed appropriate to forge new links with South Korea and Taiwan for increasing their investment there.

Second, members of the postwar elite in both former colonies had the experience of serving on local government councils (city, county, and township), selected by appointment and limited elections.[8] These

[6] R. H. Coase, *The Firm, the Market, and the Law* (Chicago: University of Chicago Press, 1988), chap. 2.

[7] Data obtained from Chi Shive, "Japanese Investment in Taiwan," in *The Effect of Japanese Investment on the World Economy: A Six-Country Study, 1970–1991*, ed. Leon Hollerman and Ramon H. Myers (Stanford: Hoover Institution Press, 1996), table 4.

[8] Edward I-ti Chen, "Japanese Colonialism in Korea and Formosa: A Comparison of

councils, which began around 1937 and continued in the Pacific War years, gave local colonial elites valuable experience in discussing affairs related to local interest groups, taxation, and spending, with Japanese officials. In the process, they learned how these councils might serve as effective watchdogs of the public if their power were expanded. Such local councils could demand some accountability for local and central government performance, thereby facilitating the deployment of more resources to local government—a process that invariably helped local business firms to reduce their market transaction costs.

THE AMERICAN ROLE IN FACILITATING CONTINUITY WITH THE PAST

As I have already suggested, without a suitable political or international context to nurture them, the legacies of Japanese colonial and wartime control might have had little effect on the postwar economies of Taiwan and South Korea. With the outbreak of the Korean War in 1950, however, the United States government had come to see both societies as crucial to building a fire wall against communism in East Asia. Dispensing massive amounts of economic aid and providing arms and military training assistance, the Truman and Eisenhower administrations hoped to shore up both countries politically. This new American commitment worked to produce a stable environment in Taiwan by the mid-1950s in which the revitalized ruling party, the Kuomintang, initiated reforms and the policies that set the stage for rapid industrialization. In South Korea, reform only occurred later, when, after nearly a decade of inflation, corruption, and political indecision under Syngman Rhee, General Park Chung-hee and his colleagues seized political power through a military coup in 1961.

The powerful American defense umbrella to thwart military expansion by Communist China and North Korea, and the supplies of crucial military and economic aid it provided South Korea and Taiwan, enabled both countries to divert more resources to domestic reform and industrialization. During the 1960s both governments pursued foreign policies aimed at better integration with the expanding world market. At the same time, domestic policies helped to integrate their internal markets and increase mass consumption, thereby stimulating greater local demand for the goods and services produced by the small and medium enterprises that sprang up in those years. These processes interacted in a beneficial circle to accelerate industrialization: rising exports and domestic market integration made possible the greater imports nec-

the Systems of Political Control," *Harvard Journal of Asiatic Studies* 3 (1970): 150–55, for a discussion of these councils.

essary for both investment and consumption; increased trade encouraged greater specialization by firms, making it possible for them to expand in scale and production, adopt new technology, and increase productivity; similarly, these steps were associated with the gradual
reduction of enterprises' long-run average unit costs and the growth of
scale and complexity of the firm. While underemployment had been a
serious problem in both South Korea and Taiwan in the immediate
postwar years, by the 1960s, as manufacturing expanded and exports
increased, labor began to stream from provincial villages and towns to
the factories, shops, and offices of medium and large cities. Rapid and
sustained industrial growth was well on its way in both countries by
the end of the decade.

Thus, while the legacy of the colonial and wartime periods may have
contributed to this growth, we must draw attention to many new factors as well: the nature of the postwar political regimes, the intervention of the United States, and the growth of the "free world" market.
In other words, the discontinuities in the historical process were probably as important as, and perhaps more important than historical conti-
nuities in explaining the "economic miracles" in postwar South Korea
and Taiwan.

CHAPTER 12

Reflections on the Japanese and German Empires of World War II

L. H. Gann

Germany and Japan—what countries could be more unlike? Germany is a continental state, Japan a group of islands; Germany a land of rye, Japan of rice; Germany's society shaped historically by Christianity, Japan's by Buddhism and the ways of Shinto; Germans a Caucasian and Japanese an Oriental people. Germany and Japan took opposing sides in World War I. In World War II, they failed to cooperate, their anticommunist rhetoric notwithstanding. (Had they done so, and had Japan joined Germany in assaulting the Soviet Union in 1941 instead of going to war with the Western powers, the Soviet Union would probably have collapsed fifty years earlier.) Countless cultural misunderstandings continue to divide Germany from Japan—sketched with humor and understanding by Hisako Matsubara, a journalist as proficient in German as in her native Japanese.[1]

Nevertheless there are a number of striking parallels between these two countries which are ethnically and geographically so far apart. These are evident even to a generalist such as myself, a historian interested in the comparative aspects of empire, but unable to read Japanese. Both Germany and Japan came late in joining the great powers; both did so as the result of victorious wars whose glory lost nothing in the telling. (Germany was unified under Prince Otto von Bismarck in 1871 after the allied German states had crushingly defeated France in the war of 1870–71; Japan was internationally accepted as a great power after it crushed Czarist Russia in the war of 1904–05. Not surprisingly, Bismarck was the most admired foreigner in Japan at the beginning of the present century.)

[1] Hisako Matsubara, *Blick aus Mandelaugen: Ost-westliche Miniaturen* (Hamburg: Albrecht Knaus Verlag, 1980). For a scholarly discussion, see Kentaro Hayashi, "Japan and Germany," in *Dilemmas of Growth in Pre-War Japan*, ed. James Morley (Princeton, N.J.: Princeton University Press, 1971), pp. 189–215. Josef Schusslburner, "Japan: Erfolg eines preussischen Entwicklungsweges," *Criticon*, March–April 1992, pp. 65–70.

EXISTENTIAL PARALLELS

Germans and Japanese thereafter had a favorable image of one another—unclouded by excessive familiarity. (It was only from the 1960s that growing prosperity in Japan created a massive tourist industry that permitted numerous Japanese to visit Europe.) Early contacts touched only the elites. German experts such as General Klemens Meckel played an important part in modernizing the Japanese army before World War I; thereafter Japanese military organization remained much indebted to the pattern provided by the Kaiser's armed forces. The Japanese constitution of 1889 was specifically based on the Prussian constitution of 1850. (Indeed two German jurists, Hermann Roesler and Albert Mosse, played a major part in drafting the Japanese document.) The Japanese owed an equally substantial debt to German scholarship. In particular, Ranke's doctrines had a great appeal to the Japanese—his belief in the importance of the state in historical development, also his view of the *Primat der Aussenpolitik* (primacy of foreign policy), namely that the dictates of foreign policy determine domestic policy. Prussia also provided an economic model for Japan. In Prussia, a reformist, hardworking, frugal bureaucracy had traditionally played a major part in guiding economic development for the sake of augmenting the power of the state. The Japanese followed a similarly *étatiste* course. The Japanese prized Germany efficiency, hard work, and discipline; indeed the Japanese fully lived up to their German mentors' exacting demands. German scholars wrote favorably about Japan; so did German lexicographers; all were suitably impressed in particular by the Japanese soldiers. "Their discipline is excellent," wrote the encyclopedic dictionary *Der Grosse Brockhaus* after World War I, "they are distinguished by their zeal, learning ability, courage and skillful use of terrain"[2]—high praise indeed in a country not wont to pay unnecessary compliments to former enemies of World War I.

There were many other parallels between Germany and Japan. Both Japanese and German nationalists regarded their respective peoples as "proletarian nations," supposed victims in an international class struggle that pitted "rich" against "poor" countries. Both Japan and Germany were relative latecomers to the industrial revolution, though both countries later came to excel in industrial pursuits. Similarly, Germany and Japan appeared late on the stage of history, by which time the places in the sun had supposedly been taken by undeserving Britons, Frenchmen, Russians, and Americans. Nationalists both in Japan and Germany thereafter widely suffered from what might be called a na-

[2] *Der Grosse Brockhaus* (Leipzig, 1931), 9:368.

tional inferiority complex, a sense of being ridiculed by insolent foreigners. Hermann Löns's artless song "Denn wir fahren gegen Engelland" ("We Sail against England") actually justified German sacrifice on the grounds that Englishmen sniggered at the German flag. And injured pride went with a mood of national anxiety.

Evidently, such generalizations are hard to sustain statistically—especially at a time when the technique of eliciting public opinion through polls had not as yet been well developed, and in any case could not have been impartially applied in either Nazi Germany or Imperial Japan. The great majority of Germans and Japanese at all times cared more for the immediate needs of their families and friends than for grand national destinies, as elaborated by party bosses, journalists, college professors, and such like. The aims of policymakers and opinion leaders can, however, be studied with some objectivity, and they did affect ordinary people—if only by dint of skilful presentation and steady repetition.

The sense of national anxiety had many springs. Japanese in the past had feared hunger and foreign predators. (Japan had actually been opened to Western enterprise by the threat of armed force.) Germany in the past had seen numerous foreign invasions. Germany, like Japan, regarded itself as a *Volk ohne Raum*, a people without living space for its emigrants, inadequately supplied with national resources. Ill placed these fears might have been, but they were real enough, and were accentuated by the Depression and its aftermath.

This mixture of offended dignity and ill-focused fear found expression in many different ways. For instance, German and Japanese nationalists alike felt that their respective countries had been cheated of well-merited victory in World War I. German nationalists (and not only nationalists) talked themselves into believing that the German army had never been defeated on the field of battle (*im Felde unbesiegt*). Instead, Germany had succumbed only to the trickery of Communists, Freemasons, Jews, and other assorted miscreants. The crushing military defeats inflicted on Germany by the Allies, especially by the British, in 1918, were relegated to oblivion. The Japanese contribution to Allied victory in World War I had been small; nevertheless Japanese nationalists maintained that the territorial gains secured to Japan by the peace settlement had been beggarly. This sense of outrage was heightened by the unwillingness of U.S. and British negotiators in subsequent disarmament conferences to concede full equality in naval armaments to Japan, by U.S. restrictions on Japanese immigration, and other grievances. Militant Japanese officers, willing to use terrorist methods against their domestic opponents, in many respects resembled young German *Freikorps* volunteers in their glorification of violence for the pursuit of a "conservative revolution."

Japanese and Germans, on the other hand, did not criticize one another. Japanese philippics concerning obnoxious Western ways did not extend to supposedly manly Germans. Even the Nazis—whose references to "Mongols" were distinctly unflattering in the normal course of events—accepted the Japanese as "honorary Aryans," subject to reservations. (Hitler, in *Mein Kampf*, had good things to say about the Japanese, especially their navy. But despite their maritime achievements, the Japanese—in the Führer's opinion—would sink back into a cultural sleep, once the original creative Aryan spark was removed.)[3]

The Japanese and the Nazi empires were both expansionist. When Karl Haushofer, foremost theoretician of *Geopolitik*, published his great study *Dai Nihon: Betrachtungen über Gross-Japans Wehrkraft, Weltstellung und Zunkunft* (1913), he not only praised Japan, but also deliberately emphasized the analogy between Greater German and Greater Japanese traditions. Similar analogies were drawn by other German experts who contributed to historical studies in Japan, to science, and even the organization of archives.

Both the Japanese and the Germans formulated grandiose plans for conquest, but both were equally deficient in the long-term execution of these designs. The Japanese and Germans alike produced brilliant commanders of armies and army groups—but they were equally faulty in grand strategy. Both made the identical mistake of failing to concentrate on one enemy at a time, and attacking a second opponent while the first remained unconquered. (Hitler invaded the Soviet Union in 1941 without having settled with Britain. The Japanese, unable to subdue China, assaulted the United States and Britain in the same year.) Japan's designs were enormous—China, the Dutch East Indies, French Indo-China, Thailand, Burma, for a start.

The German war aims were, if anything, even more unbounded than the Japanese. They had already been thus in World War I. The Reich then wished for a German sphere of influence stretching all the way from Belgium and northern France to the Ukraine, with a German *Mittelafrika* whose future shape was still being discussed by officials in their Colonial Office at a time when the German colonies had been overrun, and the Reich confronted by imminent defeat.[4] But the German war aims of World War I were almost modest compared with Hitler's in World War II. The Führer sought to subjugate the whole of Europe, including Russia to the Urals, if not further. Ultimately, the new Greater Germanic Empire would build a giant navy and smash the

---

[3] Adolf Hitler, *Mein Kampf* (Munich, Franz Eher Verlag, 1944), pp. 300, 318.

[4] L. H. Gann and Peter Duignan, *The Rulers of German Africa, 1884–1914* (Stanford, Calif.: Stanford University Press, 1977), p. 230.

United States. There was indeed to Nazi foreign policy a truly manic element—best expressed in a Nazi marching song once familiar to every member of the Hitler Youth and every member of the Wehrmacht (in my translation):

The tired, the old are shaking
In terror of coming strife
The old, the cowards are quaking
In dread of the glorious new life.

But we march, and march on through shambles,
Our Swastika banner unfurl'd
Today we are masters in Germany
Tomorrow we master the world.[5]

The Germans and Japanese alike in World War II dreamt of what the Nazis called *Grossraumwirtschaft*—economic planning on a continental scale. Imperial planners in Berlin and Tokyo alike looked to a partnership among selected state agencies, the armed forces, and favored corporations. As a part of *Grossraumwirtschaft* the metropolitan countries would supply the major industries; the conquered territories would supply an assured source of raw materials, protected markets, and cheap labor. (Neither the Nazis nor the Japanese considered their conquered subjects as potential mass consumers who would buy an endless variety of manufactured articles from the "mother country." Instead of relying on market incentives, German and Japanese occupiers alike imposed delivery quotas on peasants in conquered lands—a self-defeating practice familiar already during World War I to the Kaiser's government.) The Japanese and German empires of World War II were alike poorly organized, poorly administered, and of brief duration. Hence they were equally unsuited for systematic governance or systematic development. In their respective home countries both the Japanese and the Nazis tried to appeal, not only to their own middle class, but also to the working class who would form an aristocracy of labor among the conquered. (Marxists never got round to interpreting Japanese and German imperial dreams as a foreman's ideology, though Marxists would have been partially justified in such speculations.) Both the German and Japanese planners moreover looked to the empire for providing farms to landless farmers. The Japanese did settle a substantial number of Japa-

---

[5] Hans Baumann's song was reprinted in a slightly expurgated version in *Morgen marschieren wir: Liederbuch der deutschen Soldaten* (Potsdam: Ludwig Voggenreiter Verlag, 1939), p. 197. For reference to its true text, as actually sung, see Christian Graf von Krockow, *Die Deutschen in ihrem Jahrhundert 1890–1990* (Hamburg: Rowohlt Verlag, 1990), p. 427, n. 20.

nese overseas; the Japanese thereby created Japanese enclaves in which the military, the settlers, and corporate enterprise would cooperate. The Nazis had grandiose plans for settling German peasants in the distant Ukraine and elsewhere. But these schemes all came to nought; few German farmers would have wanted to make their home in these distant lands. For all practical purposes the Nazis simply relied on existing ethnic German minorities in Eastern Europe. All of them would experience disaster when the empires broke asunder.

By contrast, neither German nor Japanese designs for expansion can be explained in terms of the motivation that Lenin had ascribed to modern imperialism—a superfluity of capital at home requiring profitable investment in imperial conquests abroad. There was some surplus German capital, much of which had traditionally been invested in the United States, but the overwhelming proportion of German capital was invested at home. In Japan's case, the Leninist interpretation makes even less sense: in 1938 Japan's foreign investments were less in value than those of a secondary power such as Canada.[6] However, the Nazi and Japanese warlords alike did not look so much for investment opportunities but for an illusory security. For the Germans this entailed a gigantic continental empire; the Japanese desired to control both China as well as Southeast Asia, providing the homeland with a gigantic chain of bastions safeguarding it from every possible assault. This program was enormous in extent, thereby contributing to Japanese insecurity rather than to the island nation's safety. Bismarck used to joke that the Italians, in looking for new territorial acquisitions, had a vast appetite but poor teeth. He would surely have included both the Japanese and his own countrymen, had he lived to see their apocalyptic designs of the twentieth century.

The German and Japanese wartime empires shared a common hostility toward the Anglo-Saxon powers; both professed also a common hatred of the Soviet Union. But for all their ringing declarations of mutual friendship, the Germans and Japanese did not coordinate their efforts. There was indeed considerable ambivalence in Nazi-Japanese relations. During the 1930s, Germany provided China with massive arms deliveries and military instructors. German arms exports to China even continued for a time after they had been nominally terminated in 1937. Thereafter Hitler's nonaggression pact with the Soviet Union in 1939 came as a stunning surprise to Japan; indeed the Japanese defeat in Manchuria at Soviet hands was facilitated by the Nazi-Soviet pact

---

[6] Foreign investments abroad in 1938 stood as follows (in $ million): Canada: 1,855. Japan: 1,230. See Richard Morris and Graham W. Irwin, eds., *Harper Encyclopedia of the Modern World* (New York: Harper and Row, 1970), p. 279.

which left the Soviet Union free to deal with the Japanese. The Germans and the Japanese did collaborate on a technical level: for instance, the Japanese handed to the Germans technical data about Japanese aerial torpedoes, and transferred blueprints.[7] But there was no coordination on decisive strategic issues such as Germany's invasion of the Soviet Union.

IMPERIAL ADMINISTRATION

Hastily constructed, the German and Japanese wartime empires possessed no cohesion. Both derived from rapid, ill-consolidated conquests. Neither the Japanese nor the German wartime empires could compare to the Japanese and German colonial empires as they had respectively existed before World War I, both set on well-defined legal foundations, and resting on international recognition. The wartime empires, by contrast, were rapidly improvised, and rapidly disintegrated in defeat. Neither the Japanese or the German wartime empires possessed anything corresponding to elite British administrative services such as the ICS (Indian Civil Service, the most select body in the empire) or the British Colonial Service. The German and Japanese empires were run by a collection of feuding chieftains. In Japan itself there was a reasonably efficient civilian administration, but in the empire pride of place went with the fighting services. These in turn were divided between army and navy. (Fortunately for the consistency of Japanese military policy, there was no independent air force, as there was in Germany.) Each fighting service had its own ideas concerning foreign policy. The army traditionally looked for expansion on the Asian mainland, particularly China. Within the land forces, the Kwantung Army was especially powerful, having previously done its own empire building almost independent of the civilian administration. In this respect there was no parallel between the Japanese fighting services and the *Wehrmacht* which remained firmly under the Führer's control. But there was an analogy, however, faint, between the Kwantung Army and the French *Armée d'Afrique* which, during the late nineteenth century, had also done its own empire building without taking too much account of the despised politicians in Paris. And like the French colonial army, the Kwantung army developed its own version of a *mission civilisatrice* meant by its makers to provide social justice in uniform.

The Japanese army in turn both cooperated and competed with the navy which traditionally had favored a southward advance. (Japan's de-

---

[7] John W. Chapman, *The Price of Admiralty: The War Diary of the German Naval Attaché in Japan 1939–1943*, 3 vols. (Lewes, East Sussex: Saltire Press, 1982), 2:37.

cision to go on the attack alike in China, Southeast Asia, and the Pacific represented a compromise between the two.) Occupied Southeast Asia was territorially partitioned between the army and the navy, as between rival powers, but this agreement did not prevent ongoing rivalry for strategic resources and territory. This crazy quilt was replicated in the new empire's legal structure. The Japanese had made little preparation for the governance of the immense territories they had seized. The "old empire" (Taiwan and Korea) continued to be governed as integral parts of Japan under their respective governors-general. Manchukuo was run by the Japanese army as a dependency, comparable, as Peter Duus puts it in the introduction to this volume to a Soviet satellite. In China proper, the Japanese army attempted to rule through local Chinese collaborators assisted by self-proclaimed Japanese experts. (The Kwantung Army was unwilling to set up autonomous regions bypassing both the Kuomintang government at Nanking and the Japanese Foreign Ministry.) Indochina was controlled by cooperation with France, the former colonial power, until a coup d'état by the Japanese forces in March 1945, as Ken'ichi Gotō points out. Thailand was a dependent ally to Japan (as were Hungary, Rumania, and Bulgaria to Germany). The military lorded it over the remainder—but not necessarily on the same lines. Burma and the Philippines were accorded nominal independence during the war, whereas Indonesia and Malaya remained under direct military authority.

Japan's imperial administration was a model of rational efficiency compared with Nazi Germany's. Hitler's guiding principle was to rule over competing military, civilian, and Nazi party fiefs; the very rivalry would assure the Führer's unlimited power. German military and governmental agencies were engaged in a war of all against all; senior Japanese administrators might be brutal, but they were not generally corrupt. The Third Reich, by contrast, was run by rival bosses, men such as Hermann Gvring, Reich marshall, commander in chief of the air force, commissioner general of the Four-Year Plan, grand master of the German Hunt. Each of these magnates presided over great clientage networks; each of them tried to expand their hold on designated sectors of the economy; between them they carried to its limit the art of personal corruption.[8] Divided power likewise characterized the armed forces whose command structure was of incredible complexity. (There was a dual command structure, with the OKH *(Oberkommando des Heeres)* directing the Eastern Front, and the OKW *(Oberkommando der*

---

[8] See for instance the chapter on "Corruption" in Richard Grunberger, *The Twelve-Year Reich: A Social History of Nazi Germany, 1933–1945* (New York: Holt, Rhinehart, and Winston, 1971), pp. 90–107.

Wehrmacht) responsible for the other theaters of war; in addition there were Göring's OKL *(Oberkommando der Luftwaffe)*, complete with its own infantry divisions, the OKM *(Oberkommando der Marine)*, the SS formations under Heinrich Himmler, the *Organisation Todt* (the labor service, under Albert Speer, the *Reichsminister* for Arms and Ammunition), and the *Volkssturm* (subordinate to the Nazi party).

Within the civilian administration of the Nazi empire, there again was no common pattern, only a tangle of conflicting jurisdictions. Some conquered territories were directly annexed to the Reich, for instance Alsace-Lorraine, Luxembourg, and the former Polish Corridor. Norway and the Netherlands (regarded as racially "Nordic") were ruled by civilian *Reichskommissare*. Denmark (likewise considered to be akin to Germany) was permitted, until 1943, to function under its existing government. Belgium and northern France (later the whole of France) were placed under military governance. Rumania, Hungary, and Bulgaria were nominally allies but increasingly came under direct Nazi sway. They shared this fate with Italy which was gradually reduced in status from a would-be great power to an annex of the Reich. Germany's only truly independent ally in Europe was Finland, until it deserted the German cause and turned on its former associate, as did Rumania in the last stage of the war. Terror ruled in Czechoslovakia, a Reich Protectorate. Terror was even more savage in what remained of Poland, a Government-General, and in the conquered Soviet territories. All of them became fiefs for high-ranking Nazi functionaries whose cruelty rivaled their incompetence. The administrative chaos was such that a lengthy disquisition would be required for the elaboration of Germany's administrative structure in the conquered East. Suffice it to say that Hitler planned to create four *Reichskommisariate* in the conquered Soviet Union—*Ukraine, Ostland, Moskowien,* and *Kaukasien*. Only the first two actually came into existence;[9] neither lasted long.

These ramshackle empires held together in part because both the Japanese and the Germans managed to attract a substantial number of collaborators. Not all of them were time servers. Moreover, just by following their ordinary avocations, ordinary people might contribute to the continuance of imperial rule. For instance, in occupied territories, mail carriers continued to do their duty, as did police detectives, engine drivers, and chemical engineers. All their respective skills were of use to the occupying power; hence the border between collaboration and resistance is hard to draw. But there was also an army of overt sympa-

---

[9] Wolfgang Michalka, "Das Dritte Reich: Besatzungspolitik und Wirtschaft im Kriege, in *Deutsche Geschichte*, ed. Martin Vogt (Stuttgart: Metzlersche Verlagsbuchhandlung, 1991), pp. 707–713.

thizers—from cabinet ministers to janitors. Not that the conquerors managed to attract top-flight leaders of great personal quality: Pierre Laval was a political crook; Subhas Chandra Bose, the Indian nationalist, was even worse, an Anglophobe fanatic who deceived himself as much as others.[10] Bose lived in Nazi Germany from 1941 to 1943. During this period he neither noticed nor cared that the Nazis were engaged in murdering several hundred thousand Indians known as Gypsies. The point also escaped other Indian nationalists such as Mohandas Karamchand Gandhi, named the Mahatma by his admirers.)

Military Predominance

What held the German and Japanese empires together? The answer is clear—in large measure the military. As I have pointed out elsewhere[11] the structure of the military profoundly affected the very nature of colonial rule under whatever flag. The British Empire depended on a minimum of armed force. Thus after World War I, the British ran the entire Indian subcontinent with an army of 206,000 men, of whom only one-third were British. In Africa, Northern Rhodesia (now Zambia) was policed in peacetime with just one African battalion—800 men commanded by 30 British officers and NCOs—who ensured peace in a colony larger than France, the Netherlands, and Switzerland together. Promotion therefore came to British governors who knew how to govern with a small military force. By contrast, a Japanese or a German official always knew that he could rely on strong military support, unstintingly given without criticism from legislators, journalists, missionaries, professors, or other inconvenient kibitzers.

Whatever the deficiencies of German and Japanese imperial domination, both countries had superbly good armies. According to both Nazi and Japanese ideologues, it was indeed the superior fighting prowess of their respective armies that legitimized German and Japanese imperial ambitions—as against those of supposedly effete Chinese and decadent Westerners. Not that the might of these armies went unchallenged by their subjects; there was extensive guerrilla warfare behind the enemy lines alike in the Soviet Union and in China. In parts of the former Yugoslavia, partisans managed to set up their own administration; there

---

[10] For a biography sympathetic to Bose see Leonard A. Gordon, *Brothers against the Raj: A Biography of Indian Nationalists Sarat and Subhas Chandra Bose* (New York: Columbia University Press, 1990).

[11] L. H. Gann, "Western and Japanese Colonialism: Some Preliminary Comparisons," in *The Japanese Colonial Empire, 1895–1914*, ed. Ramon H. Myers and Mark R. Peattie (Princeton, N.J.: Princeton University Press, 1983), pp. 497–524.

was extensive resistance in France and Holland. But overall, the conquerors prevailed without excessive difficulties.

Armies, and their auxiliary organizations, also shaped the empire in more intangible ways. Imagine a young German born in 1919, just after World War I. When the Nazis took power in 1933, he would have reached the highly impressionable age of fourteen, just old enough to join the Hitler Youth (four years). Thereafter he would have done a year's service in the Labor Service (*Reichsarbeitsdienst*). Assuming that he survived the war, he would, by 1945, have worn uniform for twelve years altogether. A Japanese contemporary, inducted into the army in 1935, two years before the China Incident, would have done ten years' service. Assuming that both escaped unscathed, they would have emerged as tough and highly trained regulars. They would also have been exposed to unending propaganda. The Germans would have mastered a huge repertoire of marching and campfire songs which unendingly rhymed *Mut* with *Blut*, and *Not* with *Tod* (courage and blood, distress and death), where flaming light ceaselessly burst through the darkness. The Japanese soldier's song would have been more restrained—but still redolent of death and sacrifice.

> How long will this muddy trail last?
> For three days and two nights without food
> Rain pours down on the helmet.
>
> My horse fell and whines no more;
> Cutting off his mane as memento
> I bid farewell to his remains.
>
> Gone already are cigarettes,
> The matches I counted on are wet,
> How cold is the night when hunger stalks.
>
> If it must be, so be it—
> I am a fighting man of the land of the rising sun:
> I have little regret to have my corpse decay in the grass.[12]

How far was this propaganda effective? The question is hard to answer. How far does even an unbeliever remain affected by hymns learned in childhood and endlessly repeated through his youth? One thing, however, may be asserted with complete certitude. The songs sung by, say, a British soldier during World War II were utterly different; the British soldier whistled more than he sang; when he did sing,

---

[12] "Marching in Pursuit of Bandits," which became a hit in 1932, the year after Manchuria had been seized, when antiguerilla campaigns were in full swing. Kindly translated for me by my colleague Tetsuya Kataoka.

he drew on traditional music hall numbers, the latest hits from the United States, and on a vast supply of popular ditties for which the military imagination had supplied naively pornographic words. It was an army in which German and Japanese war songs would have been met with incomprehension or ribald laughter. The British army, like the British empire, was a civil institution; their German and Japanese equivalents, by contrast, were military to the core.

Left-wing interpretations of history notwithstanding, the German military had met with widespread approval among workers as well as middle-class people, Jews as well as gentiles. Whatever theoreticians might say, the German Social Democratic workers in Wilhelminian Germany made the most loyal and punctilious soldiers, the most conscientuous NCOs. In 1918 the Wilhelminian empire collapsed. The subsequent revolution was the child—not the parent—of defeat. The same generalization applied with even greater force to the *Wehrmacht*. For all the ink spilled about "antifascist" resistance in Nazi Germany, not a single battalion mutinied in Nazi Germany, not one warship, not one air squadron. Leftist tales concerning Germany's "betrayed revolution" belong to the same realm of political folklore as does the stab-in-the back legend elaborated by the Germans right after World War I. The most revolutionary force in modern Germany history were those Allied armies that first broke the Kaiser's governance, and later Hitler's and Tōjō's. What was true of Germany was truer still of Japan. The Japanese fought on grimly, whether confident in victory, or without a glimmer of hope. Antimilitarism of course had existed long before in both Germany and Japan. But antimilitarism only became a popular force in the wake of the shattering defeats suffered in World War II— other interpretations read history backwards.

Whence the strength of German and Japanese militarism? Unlike the Western democracies, both Nazi Germany and Imperial Japan were ready to risk war; hence the latter initially enjoyed diplomatic superiority in their dealings with peaceful countries. Both Germany and Japan took the lead in building up massive armaments. German and Japanese generals acquired experience in handling large bodies of troops well before their opposite numbers in Britain and the United States. Both the Japanese and the German armies drew on the nobilitarian prestige respectively of junkers and samurai. Within the German army, the Christian and aristocratic ethos remained strong enough to inspire some genuine military resistance against Hitler—resistance of a kind found neither within the Red Army under Stalin nor within the Japanese army under Tōjō. The nobilitarian ethos, however, failed to prevail. On the contrary, both the Japanese and German armies acted as avenues of social advancement for "new men." In Japan numerous soldiers of lower middle-class origin made their way as officers. The same applied to Hitler's armies, especially the SS, where plebeians such as Sepp Dietrich (a one-time chauffeur) rose to be general officers, whereas in the olden days he would have been confined to the sergeants' mess. The same applied to the civilian administration of empire where *arriviste* party bosses made Germany's name hated all over Europe.

Imperial militarism, unfortunately, enjoyed a great deal of popular respect—in part because the Japanese and German armies were well led at the company and the platoon level; conscripts in general thought well of the noncoms and junior officers who commanded the men in combat. Progressive German literature was apt to misrepresent reality in this respect, being full of characters such as Sergeant Himmelstoss (an NCO in Erich Maria Remarque's *All Quiet on the Western Front* who rejoiced in making his men miserable). Such men existed in the German as well as in all other armies. But the real-life sergeants who actually drilled squads on the barrack square did not necessarily resemble Himmelstoss; on the contrary they were relatively well educated (just as were foremen in German industry, and supervisers in German business). A *Feldwebel* (sergeant major) traditionally enjoyed respect among his civilian friends and neighbors drawn from the lower middle and the upper working classes. The *Reichswehr* under the Weimar Republic, the *Wehrmacht* under Hitler managed to preserved the relatively high standards that distinguished the German noncoms, a much-neglected group in military history. The same consideration applied to the German reserve officers, who commanded the bulk of the small units engaged in actual fighting. The reserve officers in two world wars led from the front (as witnessed by their high casualty rate); they were reasonably well educated; they took pride in their commissions, not because they wished to ape East Elbian junkers, but because they regarded military leadership as a form of civic service.

Both the Japanese and the German armies therefore possessed considerable assimilative powers, as shown by their ability to attract outsiders and foreigners. A common experience of hardship, the bonds of camaraderie and those of discipline, have commonly welded together disparate ethnic elements in organizations as varied as the old British-Indian army and the Austro-Hungarian. Germany and Japan were no exceptions. German Jews had once served with enthusiasm in the Imperial German Army, and some thereafter took pride in their combat record even during the initial years of Nazi tyranny.[13]

---

[13] For German-Jewish military service see Rolf Vogel, *Ein Stück von uns: Deutsche Juden in den deutschen Armeen, 1813–1976: Eine Dokumentation* (Mainz: von Hase und Koehler, 1977). In the initial years of the Nazi era, when a Jewish community was still permitted to

For all the Führer's racial fantasies, the *Wehrmacht*, even more so the *Waffen SS*, continued to make copious use of foreigners in World War II—provided they were not Jewish. The Germans recruited vast numbers of Russians, Ukrainians, Bosnians, and other men of dubious racial antecedents from the Nazi standpoint. These men did not necessarily fight badly. "Can we really expect Russians to fight in France for Germans against Americans?" doubtfully exclaimed General von Schlieben when commenting on the conduct of Russians who had been press-ganged into or volunteered for the *Wehrmacht*.[14] The fact remains that large numbers faithfully served in the *Wehrmacht*. So did a large number of Western Europeans whose volunteer status did not admit doubt. They numbered approximately 120,000 men—three times as many soldiers as had joined the International Brigades during the Spanish Civil War. More Dutchmen fought and died wearing German field grey than the Allies' khaki. French soldiers from the Charlemagne divisions were among the last defenders holding out in Berlin.[15]

As Way-yao Chou and Carter J. Eckert indicate in their chapters in this volume, the Japanese managed to persuade many of their subjects to put on Japanese uniforms. Two hundred thousand Koreans served in the Japanese army, and another twenty thousand in the Japanese navy—an astonishing number, given the harshness of Japanese rule in Korea. Admittedly, certain reservations are in order. The Japanese never trusted the Koreans enough to let them fight in independent indigenous units. In this respect there were no parallels between the Japanese Imperial units on the one hand, and the British Gurkha or King's Africa Rifles battalions, or the Scandinavian-manned SS Viking Division on the other. Nevertheless, a substantial number of Koreans and Taiwanese, an even a handful of White Russians, were willing to die for the emperor.

I do not wish to be misunderstood. Both the Imperial Japanese Army and the *Wehrmacht* were involved in wartime atrocities—far more so than any Western army. During World War II this record was obscured by a massive propaganda campaign in which the military enthusiastically cooperated. It was a time of *la carrière ouverte au mensonge* (ca-

---

exist in Germany, the principal mass organization was the *Reichsbund Jüdischer Frontsoldaten*, a Jewish veterans' league for men who had been in combat. In 1935 its membership astonishingly stood at thirty thousand, out of a total Jewish population of six hundred thousand. See under that heading in *Philo Lexikon: Handbuch jüdischen Wissens* (Berlin: Philo Verlag, 1935).

[14] Cited in Samuel W. Mitcham, Jr., *Rommel's Last Battle: The Desert Fox and the Normandy Campaign* (New York: Jove Books, 1991), p. 81.

[15] John Keegan, *Waffen SS: The Asphalt Soldiers*, New York, Ballantyne Books, 1970, passim.

reers open to lying). Wartime misconceptions have been perpetuated by more recent apologias. (These include, for example, a pen portrait of Sept Dietrich by Franz Kurowski in *Hitler's Generals* [1989], edited by Corelli Barnett, a military historian, critic of the British Establishment, and hammer of the British generals who defeated the Nazis in World War II. Kurowski describes Dietrich, commander of Hitler's own dreaded *Leibstandarte* [bodyguard battalions], as a jolly good fellow who led a chosen band of comrades. In the words of Field Marshal Sir William Robertson—like Dietrich a promoted ranker—"I've 'eard different!'") Nevertheless, the Japanese and German armies alike did create a remarkable esprit de corps which in turned helped to cement their respective wartime empires.

For all their skill and courage, both the *Wehrmacht* and the Japanese armies suffered decisive defeat. World War II turned into a disaster for Japan, a country hitherto accustomed to victory. Despite the Nazis' strident propaganda, the *Wehrmacht* in World War II was in no wise as effective as the *Kaiserheer*, led in World War I by those military aristocrats whom Hitler despised. By 1917 the Kaiser's armies had overthrown Russia, a feat that the *Wehrmacht* never achieved. Germany could then still have negotiated a compromise peace, had it been willing to surrender its conquests on the Western Front, its African colonies, and the *Reichsland* (imperial territory) Alsace-Lorraine, in exchange for supremacy in East-Central Europe. Hitler, by contrast, was already beaten in 1944, and no Allied power by that time would have contemplated negotiations with him. Germany, in World War I, had been the world's first in science and technology—until 1933 Germany led in the number of Nobel prizes gained in the sciences. Under Hitler's domination, Germany dropped behind in the race, and after 1933, the U.S. maintained a consistent lead. In World War II the Germans still led in rocketry and the design of jet engines. But most other breakthroughs, including radar, sonar, the proximity fuse, the Norden bombsight, the first rudimentary computers, and ultimately, the atomic bomb, derived from the West. As Germany fell behind in military production and technological accomplishments, the Führer and his minions increasingly believed that Hitler's providential leadership and steely willpower would make up for material deficiencies. Hitler thus insisted that the army should make no withdrawals and accept limitless casualties—a disastrous prescription. German losses in World War II turned out to be even heavier than those suffered in World War I.

Notwithstanding Germany's reputation for efficiency, long-range planning was ill conceived, and strategic intelligence inadequate—faults that equally beset the Japanese military. The Japanese at least did not underestimate the Soviet Union, having been taught a grim lesson during Russo-Japanese fighting in Manchuria in 1939. The Germans, by contrast, had no occasion to revise their mistaken estimates before invading the Soviet Union in 1941. Both the Germans and the Japanese fatally underestimated the United States. Worse still was the German generals' inability to preserve their professional independence from Hitler's usurpation. There was a pervasive lack of moral courage within the military leadership. Many a subordinate German officer thus translated the acronym OKW (*Oberkommando der Wehrmacht*) as *oben kein Wiederstand*—no backbone at the top. By the end of the war, much of the *Wehrmacht* had turned into a crazy quilt of disparate organizations with an excessive administrative tail, many of them hastily raised and ill-equipped. They would still fight—but fight without hope.[16]

The Japanese army faced even greater difficulties than the *Wehrmacht*. Japan, during the 1930s, was much less highly industrialized than Germany. Japanese military leaders were therefore even more inclined than Hitler to exaggerate the importance of spiritual qualities in war as against military technology. (This error transcended political ideology. Old-fashioned cavalry generals in the Soviet Union, men such as Marshal Voroshilov who had made his name in the Civil War, mistakenly believed that blood and guts would beat superior firepower; noble-born Polish cavalry commanders at the time would share the same faith in superior élan.) Even before Japan went to war against the Western powers, the Japanese army had already displayed serious weaknesses in its encounter against Soviet forces in Manchuria in 1939—as explained by Alvin D. Coox in his magisterial study *Nomonhan*.[17] The Kwantung Army's original sense of idealism soon evaporated as jingoes, carpet baggers, and shady characters flocked to Manchuria. Old-fashioned and honorable gentlemen such as Lieutenant General Hishikari Tadashi (commander of the Kwantung Army 1933–34) were hounded from office. The South Manchuria Railway burgeoned into a huge, corrupt, and inefficient conglomerate, run by a vast and parasitical bureaucracy whose main function consisted apparently in recklessly spending money on nonproductive enterprises connected with domestic politics. Manchukuo remained a shadow state under a Japanese raj: as Coox explains, the Japanese proconsul was always the Kwantung army's commander as well as nominal ambassador to a client state solely dependent on Japanese bayonets.

Not that the Japanese army was uninventive. In its initial campaign

---

[16] Peter Duignan and L. H. Gann, *The Rebirth of the West: The Americanization of the Democratic World, 1945–1958* (Oxford: Basil Blackwell, 1991), pp. 9–14.

[17] Alvin D. Coox, *Nomonhan: Japan Against Russia, 1939*, 2 vols. (Stanford, Calif.: Stanford University Press, 1985), especially the chapter "Afterthoughts," 2:1075–94.

against the British in Malaya and Burma, the Japanese worked out jungle-fighting tactics that at first totally outfoxed the British. But the Japanese, far more than the Germans, were rigid in tactics once proven successful; Japnese leadership was apt to be inflexible; the bravery and fighting skills of Japanese soldiers were wasted all too often in heroic but useless frontal assaults, and also by a tendency to commit forces in a piecemeal and disjointed fashion. (*Klotzen, nicht kleckern*—"hammer blows, not pin pricks"—the German armored forces' tactical motto—had no Japanese equivalent.) Japanese training manuals stressed the virtues of the offensive; the tactical and strategic role of the defensive were equally underplayed in Japanese military thought; logistics were held in low esteem—this with disastrous results in ventures such as the Imphal-Kohima campaign in which they tried to break out from Burma into India. Japan suffered from what Coox calls "disjointed command relationships and lack of central planning"—a vice that also beset the *Wehrmacht*. On an even deeper level, the Japanese army experienced profound misperceptions of reality. "The Japanese army did not ignore intelligence; it tended to twist reality to fit its preconceptions and could not or would not accept evidence to the contrary."[18] Coox's generalization stands as a fitting epitaph both for the German and Japanese armies of World War II, and for the empires that these respectively sustained.

Economic and Cultural Aspects

What did the empires achieve? The argument concerning empire is as ancient as the empires themselves. How splendid are the works of the Romans, pleaded Rabbi Judah two millennia ago. They have made roads; they have constructed bridges; they have built baths; they have created markets. And so they have replied Rabbi Simeon bar-Yohai; but all the Romans wrought they did for themselves. They have built roads for their soldiers, bridges to levy tolls, baths for their delight, and markets to set up their whores.[19] In the case of the Japanese and German wartime empires, I side with Rabbi Simeon. It is, moreover, far from clear how far these empires paid in economic sense. Individual corporations made great profits (balanced often by huge losses entailed through wartime destruction, or postwar confiscation of assets by the victors). Germany remained well fed until nearly the end of World War II—in part because the Nazis exploited the food resources in the conquered territories. Much wealth was looted: there was ruthless use of forced

[18] Ibid., 2:1086.

[19] Cited from the Babylonian Talmud by Bruce Fetter, *Colonial Rule and Regional Power in Central Africa* (Boulder, Colo.: Westview Press, 1983), p. 336.

labor. *Grossraumwirtschaft* did not create the promised prosperity. Both Germany and Japan were infinitely better off after they recovered from World War II than they had been during the heyday of empire.

Grossraumwirtschaft and its Japanese equivalent did not so much derive from economic considerations alone as from deep-seated national anxiety feelings. Both German and Japanese policymakers feared an uncertain future in which their respective countries would be cut off from markets, raw materials, and opportunities for emigration. These anxieties derived in part from the Depression, and—in Germany's case—from the experience of World War I. Hitler, during the 1920s already, made plans for a *Grossraum* economy that elaborated World War I designs for a German-ruled *Mitteleuropa*. In Hitler's version of this design, Germany would form the industrial center of a great empire in which Germany would exploit with the utmost ruthlessness the natural and human resources of Eastern Europe and the Soviet Union; at the same time German peasants would find new land in the boundless east, and thereby end the misery of the German people, the *Volk ohne Raum*. Japanese imperial planners likewise feared that Japan could only safeguard its future access to raw materials and opportunities for emigrants by seizing a huge empire.

Such fantasies in fact bore little relation to reality. Germany did not need to conquer Eastern Europe or the Soviet Union for the purpose of carrying on a profitable trade with them. Even Stalin was glad enough to deal with Germany during the era of the Nazi-Soviet Nonaggression Pact. In any case Nazi theorists and their nationalist predecessors overestimated the economic role of *Mitteleuropa*. During the 1920s, for instance, when Hitler dreamed up his design for occupying Eastern Europe, German exports to the three small countries now comprised within Benelux nearly equaled the combined German exports to the huge *Grossraum* comprised by Bulgaria, Czechoslovakia, Estonia, Hungary, Latvia, Lithuania, Poland, Rumania, and Yugoslavia.[20] German emigration abroad by that time had largely come to an end. German farmers migrated to the cities, not to foreign fields. The German economy as a whole could have developed perfectly well without an empire, and the enormous interruption of existing ties, as well as the physical and human damage that the construction of a great land empire was bound to entail.

Similar considerations applied to the Japanese wartime empire. The Japanese justified their conquests by reference to a Greater Asian Co-Prosperity Sphere. Japan would function as the industrialized center; the

---

[20] The respective percentages of total German exports in 1927 were 14.5 and 15.4. See "Deutsches Reich" in *Der Grosse Brockhaus* (Leipzig, 1929), 4:633.

periphery would supply raw materials, markets, and industrial enterprises of a subsidiary nature. Japan would therefore attain economic as well as military security; the state and private corporations would cooperate in a profitable partnership. Japanese, like German theoreticians, however, were quite incapable of understanding the economic losses entailed in empire building. Armed conquest would create economic disruption. An enormous amount of trade would be lost. As Mark R. Peattie has pointed out to me, between 1932 and 1941, the value of Japanese commerce with North America alone was ten times that of Japanese trade with Southeast Asia—that reputed treasurehouse whose conquest supposedly would make Japan rich. Even the value of Japan's China trade, though considerable, was less than the value of Japan's trade with Europe and North America combined. Moreover, it simply was not true that Japanese business had been excluded from the British or Dutch colonies in peacetime: for example, the British positively encouraged Japanese iron mining in Malaya. From a pure profit-and-loss standpoint, the Japanese would have done better to cooperate with the existing colonial empires, leaving the Western nations with the expense of administration, while relying on Japan's natural advantages at the time—lower labor costs, lower transport costs, and superior marketing skills.

As several contributors have shown, the Japanese, for all their faults, promoted economic development on a considerable scale in Korea and Taiwan. New factories and workshops opened their doors, though the Japanese ability to develop the colonies naturally declined as the war ground on, and as the Japanese could no longer supply the requisite skills and capital. A parallel is offered by Germany's development of Austria. Postwar Austrian mythologies to the contrary notwithstanding, Austria did benefit in certain respects from its incorporation into the Third Reich. The Germans massively developed the iron and steel industry, heavy chemicals, aluminum, machinery, and new hydroelectric power plants.[21] All were designed to enhance war production; nevertheless this industrial development had the unintended effect of facilitating Austria's future as an independent nation. But even Dr. Goebbels would not have had much to say about German economic development in occupied Poland or Russia, lands supposedly inhabited by *Untermenschen* destined to serve Germany as serfs. (Hitler and his coadjutors were quite incapable of seeing such people as "economic men" willing to respond to economic incentives.)

---

[21] Eduard März and Maria Szecsi, "Austria's Economic Development, 1945–1978," in *Modern Austria*, ed. Kurt Steiner (Palo Alto, Calif.: Society for the Promotion of Science and Scholarship, 1981), pp. 123–40.

The Japanese were an immensely proud people who believed themselves superior to everybody else. The Japanese ruled their empire with a rod of iron—no nonsense in their case about trusteeship, about a "dual mandate," or *Eingeborenenfürsorge, moralisation, política de atracção* (looking after the natives, moral uplift, assimilation policy) whereby British, German, Belgian, and Portuguese colonizers in Africa respectively had tried to justify colonial rule from the start of the present century. Racism was rife in Japan (as in China). It is an agreeable superstition to believe that only Westerners despise people of different physical appearance, or that only Westerners consider disagreeable aliens to be endowed with excessive sexual capacities.[22]

The Japanese army was a mass organization, and—like all such bodies—also contained the worst. When aroused, it was capable of unbelievable cruelty as in the Rape of Nanking (1937). In many instances Japanese soldiers simply went berserk, suddenly freed abroad from those tight restrictions that prevailed at home. The army entered the narcotics business, especially in China. Army laboratories engaged in biological warfare research that used human beings as guinea pigs. The Japanese did not much care either for the sufferings of Japanese civilians. A great many military men were willing to fight on when the war was obviously lost—no matter how many civilians would die of hunger, disease, and high explosives. In this respect the Japanese senior military cadres did not so much resemble a professional elite, as represented by the olden-day German army instructors at work in Japan, but the ideological fanatics who made up the Nazi leadership. (Hitler was likewise willing to soldier on, even if the German people were destroyed—an attitude resisted for once by Albert Speer, the Führer's architect, and a professional man.)

The Japanese, like the German army was increasingly barbarized during World War II. In World War I, Russian soldiers had no special fear of falling into German hands; during World War II, a Soviet soldier taken prisoner by the Germans could consider himself a doomed man. The treatment received by German soldiers captured by the Japanese during the siege of Tsingtao (1914) was exemplary; the fate of Allied prisoners in World War II, by contrast, was deplorable.

Nevertheless, there was a fundamental difference between the Japanese and German wartime empires—the ideological dimension. The Japanese did not engage in ethnic mass extermination for the sake of cre-

---

[22] For a discussion of racism in China, see Frank Dikotter, *The Discourse of Race in Modern China* (London: Hurst, 1991). For a detailed critique of the Japanese army see Merion Harries and Susie Harries, *Soldiers of the Sun: The Rise and Fall of the Imperial Japanese Army* (New York: Random House, 1992).

ating a better world. There is nothing in the Japanese record corresponding to the Nazi campaign designed to liquidate the Polish intelligentsia. Neither did the Japanese desire to destroy any particular people, as the Nazis vowed to kill the Jews.

Nazism, by contrast, was a millennial creed that sought to establish a millennial empire—ruled by the Aryan race, the noblest of human stocks. In Nazi estimation, only the "Nordic" people among the conquered deserved to be treated more or less as equals—Dutch, Flemings, Danes, and Norwegians. The Japanese, by contrast, were obliged by their own Pan-Asian, anti-Western, and anticolonial propaganda to regard subject Asians in a somewhat more favorable light than that in which the Germans looked upon conquered Slavs. In practice, the Japanese might treat Chinese and Filipinos with brutality. The wartime drive for "the imperialization of subject peoples" rested on the assumption of Japanese superiority."[23] But no Japanese theoretician regarded fellow Asians simply as subhumans, fit only to work for the victor or starve.

Hitler was a man of many hates—but the worst of his wrath was reserved for the Jews. To Hitler and his henchmen, the Jews formed a subhuman counterrace, predestined by their biological heritage to do evil. In Hitler's view, the Jews were the mortal enemies of mankind; they sought world domination; once established, their rule would lead to humanity's extinction. The struggle between Jews and Aryans was a battle between darkness and light; the battle could end only with the annihilation of one side or the other. This was a Gnostic doctrine incomprehensible to most Westerners. It was initially shrugged off as hot air, or subjected to reductionist explanations of a Marxist kind, pure or vulgarized. For instance, in Charlie Chaplin's dark comedy *The Great Dictator,* persecution of Jews under the "Double Cross" is temporarily called off while the great Leader seeks a loan from a banker named Epstein. Klaus Mann, in his otherwise perceptive novel *Mephisto,* dating from the same period, describes with equal lack of realism, a splendid Nazi party to which His Excellency the Nazi minister president nevertheless has also invited a handful of super-rich Jewish businessmen. In fact there was nothing pragmatic about the Nazi creed. Hitler's hatred was unyielding and deadly.

The greatest, and also the most metaphysical purpose of the Nazi empire was to kill Jews. No other considerations mattered. (Indeed a good cause can be made for the assumption that Hitler engaged in such unprofitable military actions as the last-ditch defense of Hungary

---

[23] Mark R. Peattie, "Japanese Attitudes toward Colonialism, 1995–1945," in Myers and Peattie, *The Japanese Colonial Empire,* pp. 80–127.

merely for the purpose of liquidating one of the few remaining Jewish communities in Europe.) But Hitler also hated Slavs—especially Poles and Russians. Afflicted with their racialist superstitions, the Nazis never even attempted to wage political warfare against the Stalin regime, even though initially, advanced *Wehrmacht* units were greeted as liberators in the Ukraine and the Baltic states. Hitler meant to raze Moscow and Leningrad, enslave the people, and rob the country of its food supplies, even at the cost of famines; the remnant population would be ruled through socialist ministates. It was a program that made even Stalin's tyranny seem benign. Yet to privatize the Soviet economy would have been infinitely easier in 1941 than fifty years later; the Nazis could certainly have promised to return the land to the peasants. Instead they disgraced the name of Germany. In a certain sense Neville Chamberlain turned out to be right after all—Hitler missed the bus.

In Japanese thought there was nothing to correspond to such lethal fantasies. The Japanese did not persecute those (mainly German) Jewish refugees whom they encountered in the Shanghai International Settlement: they were treated no worse than any other residents.[24] Many high-ranking Japanese civilian and military bureaucrats had the most exaggerated notions of the influence exerted by Jews on U.S. foreign and domestic policies. Future peace negotiations with Washington would therefore be served by leaving the Jews alone. The Japanese moreover lacked inherited antipathies towards the Jews; Japanese culture had never associated Jews with hucksters or with Christ-killers. Jews were just another lot of foreigners. As a German-Jewish lady, a temporary resident in Hong Kong during World War II, assured me many years ago, "Japanese officers were simply as arrogant as our own." Indeed among Japanese military and politicians there was also an ambivalent admiration for the Jews, a people clannish but influential from whom much might be learned. A number of German-Jewish refugee scholars obtained appointments at Japanese universities. During World War II a number of Jews from Poland were allowed to take refuge in Japan, thanks to such humanitarians as Sugihara Sempo, then Japanese consul in Kaunas.

Nazism represented a cultural revolution against all that great Germans such as Goethe, Schiller, and Lessing had held dear. Japanese imperialism never represented such a shattering break from tradition.

---

[24] The Japanese permitted Jews to come to Shanghai after the takeover in 1937. About eighteen thousand German-speaking Jews temporarily settled in Shanghai as a city of transit until the Japanese ended immigration with the outbreak of war in Europe. See Suzanne D. Rutland, "Waiting Room Shanghai," in *Leo Baeck Institute Yearbook*, 1987, pp. 407–436. For a general work see Ben-Ami Shilloney, *The Jews and the Japanese: The Successful Outsiders* (Rutland, Vt.: Charles E. Tuttle, 1992).

Moreover, there was in Japan, and even in a colony such as Taiwan, nothing like the thought control that characterized both Hitler's Germany and Stalin's Soviet Union. German expansion carried the Nazis' nihilist revolt to formerly stable countries such as France, Poland, and Norway (but also into the Soviet Union, a tyranny of almost equal destructiveness). The Japanese were ill advised in their attempt to conquer China; they did at least have the excuse that China at the time was a war-torn land, and that the Taiwanese then preferred Japanese to Chinese domination. As far as Japanese expansion into Southeast Asia was concerned, the Japanese could plead that they merely replaced one form of foreign colonial domination by another. The Nazis had no such excuse.

The Japanese and German empires differed in another fundamental sense. Germany was a *Führerstaat*. Until late in the war, Hitler represented to the majority of his people both a legitimate monarch and a revolutionary leader—king and *sans-culotte* all at once. Hitler might jest that he had to command a Royal Prussian army, an Imperial German navy, and a National Socialist air force, but in fact his authority was undisputed. There were nothing like the political quarrels between army and navy, or even between different segments of the army, that troubled Japan. More than that, Hitler considered himself, and was considered by a substantial minority of his countrymen, as an earthly redeemer. Hitler's ideas, dismissed as mumbo jumbo by his opponents, formed a coherent ideology, Gnostic in kind, that pitted eternal goodness against eternal evil. His party became almost like a church, with its martyrs, feast days, processions, hymns, and mass rallies. In doing so, Hitler and his associates combined the ceremonial paraphernalia of the German military with that of the German youth movement with its campfire ritual and songs, replete with allusions to sacred flames and light breaking through darkness.

During the last years of Hitler's rule, this propaganda began to lose some of its former appeal; like all totalitarian propaganda it became boring by dint of repetition. But its initial appeal was extraordinary, helping Hitler to consolidate his position as an absolute autocrat. "Essentially it all depends me, on my existence because of my political talents," Hitler told his assembled generals just before the outbreak of the war. "Furthermore, probably no one will ever have the confidence of the whole German people as I have." Hence this was the time to strike, while he, the Führer was still in the prime of life. This was Germany's great hour; he could only hope that no *Schweinehund* would turn up at the last moment to propose mediation.[25] This was not the

[25] Anthony Read and David Fisher, *The Deadly Embrace: Hitler, Stalin, and the Nazi-Soviet Pact 1939–1941* (New York: Norton, 1988), pp. 236–45.

language of an ordinary autocrat. Hitler was indeed the country's supreme leader, at the same time his party's Marx, Lenin, and Stalin. Hitler had the political gangster's eye for human weakness. He was also a military strategist of no mean ability; he had more combat experience than most of his generals. He had flashes of insight. Postwar attempts on the part of German professional soldiers to shoulder Hitler with every German defeat and credit his generals with every victory are feats of self-serving publicity. But Hitler was more than that, the supreme propagandist of the twentieth century, the supreme cult leader, the supreme terrorist. The Third Reich was not, as Marxists mistakenly assumed, the creation of monopoly capitalism; neither did it reflect the political ambitions and fears of the German petty bourgeoisie. Hitler drew on a widespread coalition, the Third Reich was Hitler's Empire par excellence. Not surprisingly, those Germans who did resist often thought that they were battling the Antichrist.

Japan's case was very different. Japan is not a Christian country. Japan therefore lacked Western beliefs in a Messianic kingdom or a Second Coming. The monarchy survived in Japan (as in Italy), a potential counterweight against purely military rule. Power in Japan was not centralized in the hands of a great leader; it was dispersed through interlocking cabals that linked the military, the civilian administration, and big business in an anonymous structure where no one took responsibility, where power was anonymous. The German elite glorified in the pomp of power. The Japanese, by contrast, gave enormous scope to anonymous military officers, to anonymous "staff politics." As Sir Ian Hamilton, a British observer, had already put it during the Russo-Japanese War in 1904, "the Japanese mind seems readily to lend itself to a system of one supporting all the weight, pomp, and responsibility of position, whilst another man works free and untrammeled in the shadow afforded by that latent power."[26] The Allies after World War II hanged Tōjō Hideki, the Japanese prime minister. But no one imagined that Tōjō had been another Hitler. Indeed in 1944 Tojo Hideki had already quietly and voluntarily stepped down as prime minister. The Führer, by contrast, was truly sui generis.

END OF EMPIRE

The Napoleonic empire ended in a splendid legend, created in part by Napoleon himself. Heinrich Heine's famous poem "The Two Grenadiers" idealizes the captured emperor in retrospect. Neither the Third Reich nor the Japanese Empire inherited such a legacy of glory. On the

---

[26] Coox, *Nomonhan,* 2:1076.

contrary, even right-wing German politicians distance themselves from Adolf Hitler; even the German skinheads today do not want to be storm troopers. These street-corner thugs may rail at foreigners; but no German skinhead now wants to put on a uniform, drill on the barrack square, or dive for cover into some Ukrainian ditch. Young Japanese feel the same about their own country's wartime empire. Peacetime democracy has worked well. By contrast, wartime defeat was too patent, too destructive, to be psychologically shunted aside.

Why did the empires fail? Their end was not predestined. It was only from 1942 onward that the tide of battle began to turn with the battles of Midway, El Alamein, and Stalingrad. In the end, however, both empires succumbed to hubris, to overweening pride displayed alike in the military and ideological spheres. There was surely an element of the irrational when the *Wehrmacht* attacked the Soviet Union without adequate intelligence, without adequate maps, without winter equipment, and without much knowledge concerning the location and capacity of Soviet industry, or of the extent of Soviet reserves. The much-derided British army of the Crimean War had done considerably better; at least the British had not unduly extended their lines of communication, and in the end they had won. The *Wehrmacht's* failings were all the more remarkable in an army that had shatteringly defeated Russia just over twenty years earlier, and which had collaborated in secret rearmament with the Red Army thereafter. The complacency, ignorance, and arrogance displayed by the Japanese army on the eve of its war with China in 1937 matched the *Wehrmacht*'s with regard to Russia before the German invasion of the Soviet Union had begun.[27]

Equally foolish was the contempt felt by Japanese and Germans alike for the Americans. According to Hitler, the United States was a mongrel society perverted by Negroes and Jews. In the United States "the scum naturally floated to the top."[28] Professional military and naval opinion was hardly better informed. A top-secret analysis produced by the German naval command thus argued that Germany would benefit from U.S. entry into the war by being able to attack U.S. shipping without restraint; U.S. arms production capacity would be limited to what the United States itself required, and probably bring about a reduction of the war materiel supplied to Britain[29]—a fantastic underestimation of U.S. productive capabilities, shared by Japan before it

---

[27] See Mark R. Peattie, *Ishiwara Kanji: The Japanese Confrontation with the West* (Princeton, N.J.: Princeton University Press, 1975).

[28] Cited by Gerhard L. Weinberg, *The Policy of Hitler's Germany: Diplomatic Revolution in Europe, 1933–1936* (Chicago: Chicago University Press, 1970), pp. 21–22.

[29] Memo by the Naval High Command (*Seekriegsleitung*) for the Armed Forces Command 14 January 1991, reprinted in Chapman, *The Price of Admiralty:* 3:514–19.

went to war. Both the Germans and the Japanese placed tremendously high value on military morale, a quality in which they held the United States deficient—an estimate not borne out by even a cursory study of U.S. military history. The Japanese were equally mistaken about the British. The British conformed to their traditional pattern of initial disasters, followed by an amazing recovery. The British victory at Imphal-Kohima in Burma in 1944, though thereafter forgotten in a mood of imperial abnegation, was the greatest single defeat ever sustained up to then by Japanese forces on land.

In the end, both the Nazi and the Japanese empires proved counterproductive in terms of their own professed aims. Nazi racism and Nazi atrocities aroused Russian patriotism, and thereby strengthened, and perhaps prolonged Stalin's tyranny. The Japanese invasion of China weakened Chiang Kai-Shek's rule, and thereby boosted the Communist opposition. Not that there were no honest and competent Japanese officials: Japanese, like Prussian, civil servants were notable for their financial integrity, a major asset in the process of industrialization. There were young and idealistic officers within the Kwantung Army whose social concern for the "natives" rivalled a similar philosophy developed by young French officers within the *Armée d'Afrique*. In Taiwan especially, Japanese culture left an imprint that would have deepened had the Japanese stayed. For instance, President Lee Teng-hui of Taiwan grew up when the island was a Japanese colony, and his Japanese is said to be better than his Mandarin. Not all German officials and officers in occupied Europe were conscienceless brutes. Far from it. To this day therefore German continues to be widely spoken in countries such as Czechoslovakia and Hungary, once under the Nazi heel.

Nevertheless, both the Japanese and German empires ended in total disrepute. The British Empire was transformed into the Commonwealth whose members take pride in their former associations and those honors that the British queen still bestows on the deserving. The English language remains a lingua franca in every country where the Union Jack has flown. Even bitter critics of the British imperial record such scholars such as the Nigerian historian J. U. J. Asiegbu, still give credit to the former British rulers' "patriotism and probity . . . self discipline and other remarkable ideals of public duty and responsibility as now remain, unfortunately, yet to be learned and emulated by the succeeding generations of indigenous African leaders."[30] No Korean will ever write like that about Korea's erstwhile Japanese overlords; no Pole will pen a similar tribute to the thugs who once ran the *Generalgouverne-*

[30] J. U. J. Asiegbu, *Nigeria and Its British Invaders* (New York: Nok Publishers International, 1984), p. xxlx.

ment. Even the Manchukuo experiment, apparently the most successful, turned out, in Peter Duus's words, "a millstone around Japan's neck." The Japanese legacy was widely admired in Taiwan. But overall, as Mark Peattie concludes, the Japanese bequeathed no legacy of cultural deference—only envy for Japanese diligence and efficiency.

The Nazi imperial legacy was even worse. By proclaiming the Slav and "Mongols" as *Untermenschen*, the Nazis gave up all hopes of waging political warfare against the Soviet Union's Communist rulers. Equally counterproductive, even from a purely imperial standpoint, was Nazi policy toward the Jews. By persecuting the German Jews, the Nazis inflicted great damage on the German economy, and a greater loss still on German science, including such sciences valuable in war as medicine and nuclear physics. By murdering the Yiddish-speaking Jews of Eastern Europe, the Nazis destroyed one of the most Germanophile of ethnic minorities. (Yiddish had derived from medieval German; Yiddish speakers could easily learn High German, and had been wont to regard German as the homeland of progress and technical efficiency.) Thereafter millions of ethnic Germans were expelled from Poland, Czechoslovakia, and other countries. An even greater number were driven from the former East German territories ceded to Poland and the Soviet Union. It was a German disaster of immeasurable proportions. The Führer, however, would surely have grieved even more had he known that the Jews, after nearly two thousand years, would regain their own state in the Promised Land.

The German and Japanese empires moreover fell foul even in terms of their makers' own professed values. The Nazis had extolled heroism. Nothing was more unheroic than the conduct shown by most Nazi officials at the end of the war and thereafter. Siegfried hid his sword in the attic and sued for his pension rights! Nazism as an ideology could never survive this mass display of moral cowardice. Japanese disillusionment with empire took somewhat different forms, but was just as real. As Alvin D. Coox points out, the Japanese Kwantung Army disgraced itself in Japanese eyes by retreating helter-skelter at the end of the war, leaving Japanese civilians in the lurch.[31] Japanese civilians residing in Japanese-occupied islands were systematically murdered by Japanese soldiers, lest these civilians should fall under U.S. domination. Such incidents could not be consigned to permanent oblivion. Finally there was the psychological impact of defeat on the armed forces itself. Whereas older men in German and Japanese uniforms had experienced

---

[31] Alvin D. Coox, "The Kwantung Army Dimension," in *The Japanese Informal Empire in China, 1895–1937*, ed. Peter Duus, Ramon H. Myers, and Mark R. Peattie (Princeton, N.J.: Princeton University Press, 1989), pp. 394–428.

great initial victories, the younger age cohorts had known only disaster. Thus, a German or Japanese born in 1925 who had joined the army at the age of eighteen, in 1943, would only have witnessed defeats. It was this experience rather than Allied reeducation that laid the foundations of postwar democracy alike in Japan and Germany.

The tale of the defunct empires was therefore one

> Of carnal, bloody, and unnatural acts;
> Of accidental judgments, casual slaughters;
> Of deaths put on by cunning and forc'd cause;
> And, in this upshot, purposes mistook
> Fall'n on the inventors' heads.[32]

Compared to modern Japan and modern Germany, the Japanese and German wartime empires seem light years away. The *Bundesrepublik* is not the Third Reich, the *Bundeswehr* is not the *Wehrmacht*. Present-day parliamentarians in Japan may have their faults; but they have nothing in common with the imperial fascists who had once lorded it in Tokyo. In spite of all fashionable complaints concerning modernity, mankind has indeed been fortunate.

[32] William Shakespeare, *Hamlet, A Prince of Denmark*, 5.3, 380–84.

Contributors

Wan-yao Chou is Assistant Research Fellow of the Institute of Taiwan History, Academia Sinica, Taipei. She received both her bachelor's and master's degrees from National Taiwan University and is the holder of a doctorate from Yale University. Before returning to Taiwan, she taught at the University of British Columbia from 1991 to 1993. Her research focuses on colonial Taiwan and the cultural history of Ch'ing China.

Peter Duus is William H. Bonsall Professor of History at Stanford University. He has taught at several other institutions, including Washington University, Harvard University, and Claremont Graduate School. He is the author of *Party Rivalry and Political Change in Taishō Japan*, *Feudalism in Japan*, and *The Rise of Modern Japan*, and the editor of volume 6 of the *Cambridge History of Japan*. He is currently at work on a book about the Japanese takeover of Korea during the Meiji period.

Carter J. Eckert is Professor of Korean History at Harvard University and the director of the Harvard Korea Institute. He is the author of *Offspring of Empire: The Koch'ang Kims and the Colonial Origins of Korean Capitalism, 1876–1945*, and winner of the American Historical Association's John K. Fairbank Prize in East Asian History and the John Whitney Hall Book Prize of the Association for Asian Studies. He is also the coauthor of a popular university textbook on Korean history, *Korea, Old and New*.

L. H. Gann is a Senior Fellow at the Hoover Institution, Stanford University, and also Curator of the Western European Collection. He holds his doctorate from the University of Oxford and is author, co-author, or co-editor of some forty published works dealing with European colonialism in Africa, comparative colonialism, and Atlantic community. He is a Fellow of the Royal Historical Society and holds the German Federal Republic's Order of Merit.

Ken'ichi Gotō is Professor of Modern Southeast Asian History at Waseda University. He is the author of *Prewar Shōwa-Period Japan and Indonesia* and *Modern Japan and Southeast Asia*. He is also a member of the compilation committee for the eight-volume handbook *Modern Japan and Her Colonies* published by Iwanami Shoten.

George Hicks is an economist and writer who divides his time between Singapore and Australia. He is the author of *The Comfort Women* and various studies of the Chinese in Southeast Asia and is currently completing a book on the Korean minority in Japan.

Hideo Kobayashi attended Tōkyō Toritsu University, specializing in Asian economics and Japanese history with an emphasis on the study of fascism. His doctoral dissertation dealt with "Activities of Japanese Enterprises in Asia Before and After World War II." His most recent publications include *The Greater East Asian Co-Prosperity Sphere* and *Japanese Enterprises in South-East Asia*. He is currently professor of economics at Komazawa University in Tokyo.

Y. Tak Matsusaka is Assistant Professor of History at Wellesley College. He received graduate training in Japanese history at Harvard University. Currently he is at work on a book on Japanese imperialism and the South Manchuria Railway Company, 1904–1937.

Ramon H. Myers is Senior Fellow and Curator-Scholar of the East Asian Collection of the Hoover Institution on War, Revolution, and Peace at Stanford, California. He is also the author of *The Chinese Peasant Economy* and *The Chinese Economy, Past and Present*. He was formerly associate editor of the *Journal of Asian Studies* and editor of *Ch'ing-shih wen-t'i* (*Ch'ing Studies*). With Mark R. Peattie he co-edited *The Japanese Colonial Empire, 1895–1945*.

Takafusa Nakamura is Professor Emeritus of the University of Tokyo. One of Japan's leading economic scholars, he served as director general of the Economic Research Institute in Japan's Planning Agency from 1977 to 1979. Professor Nakamura, who has taught at Ochanomizu University and is currently Professor at Toyo Eiwa Women's University, has published thirteen book-length studies of the modern Japanese economy during his career. Works translated into English include *The Postwar Japanese Economy: Its Development and Structure* and *Economic Growth in Prewar Japan*. Professor Nakamura was awarded the Osaragi Jiro Prize for his two-volume *Shōwashi* (*The History of Shōwa*).

Mark R. Peattie is Senior Research Fellow at the Hoover Institution on War, Revolution, and Peace at Stanford University. He served for nine years with the United States Information Agency in Japan before obtaining a doctorate from Princeton University in modern Japanese history. Subsequently, he taught at the Pennsylvania State University, the University of California at Los Angeles, and the University of Massachusetts at Boston. He is the author of *Ishiwara Kanji and Japan's Confrontation with the West* and *Nany'ō: The Rise and Fall of the Japanese in Micronesia, 1885–1945*. He has been co-editor with Ramon H. Myers of *The Japanese Colonial Empire, 1895–1945*, and, with Myers and Peter Duus, co-editor of *The Japanese Informal Empire in China, 1895–1937*. With David Evans, he is currently completing a major study on the Japanese navy.

E. Bruce Reynolds is Associate Professor and Chair of the History Department at San Jose State University in California, and author of *Thailand and Japan's Southern Advance, 1940–1945*. He is currently conducting research on the Thailand operations of the American Office of Strategic Services (OSS).

Louise Young is Assistant Professor of Japanese History at New York University. She is the author of *Total Empire: Japan and Manchukuo* (forthcoming), and is currently working on a study of urban modernism in interwar Japan.

Index

About the Editors

PETER DUUS is William H. Bonsall Professor of History at Stanford University; RAMON H. MYERS is Senior Fellow and Scholar-Curator of the East Asian Collection at the Hoover Institution; and MARK R. PEATTIE is Senior Research Fellow at the Hoover Institution.